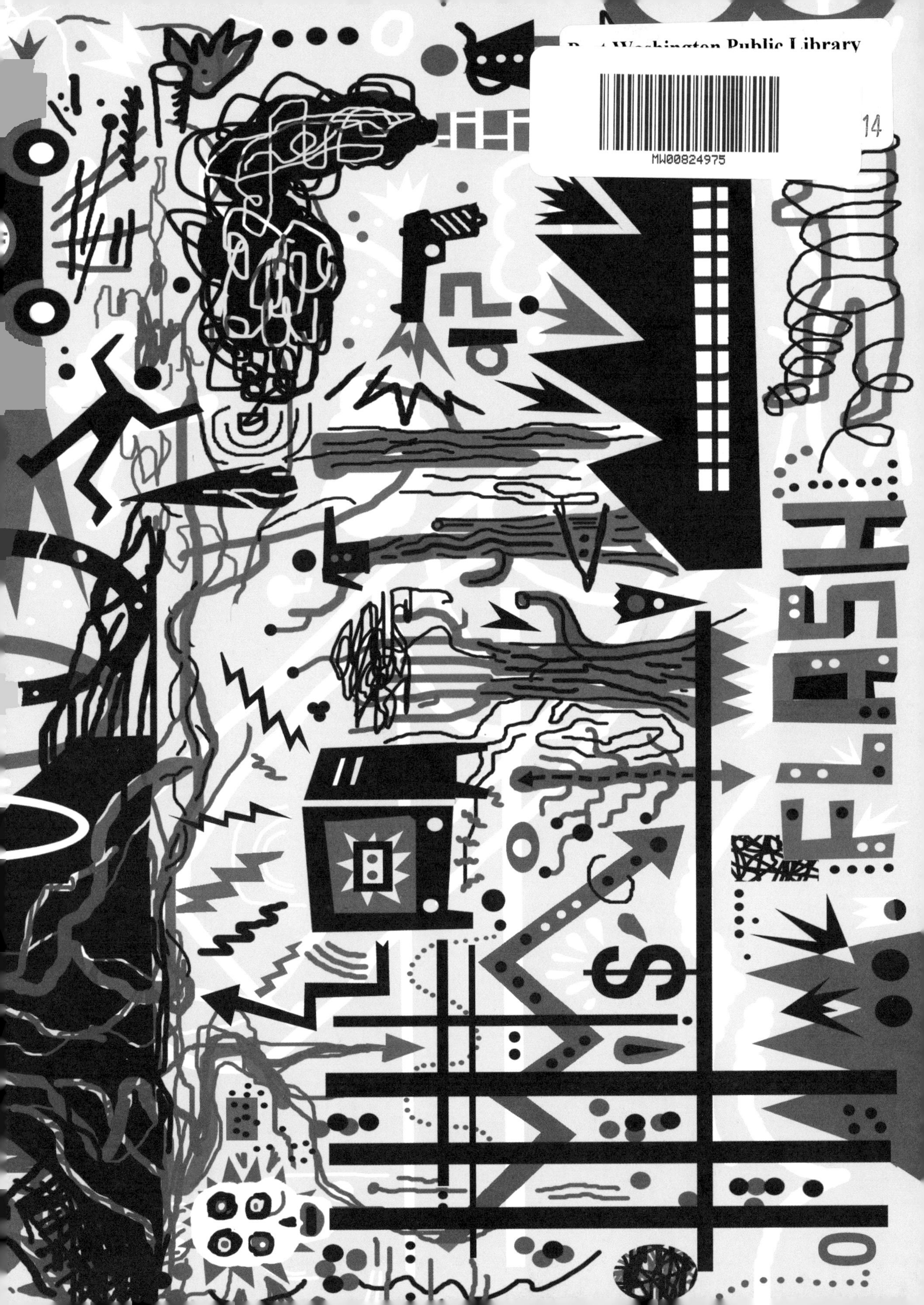
FLASH

feggo

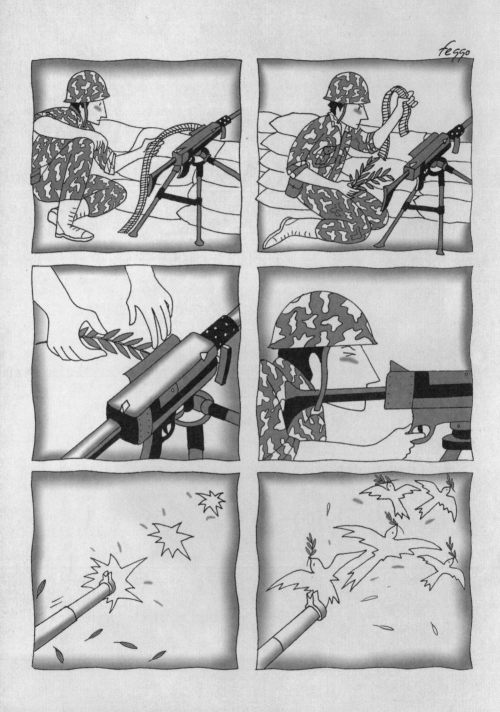

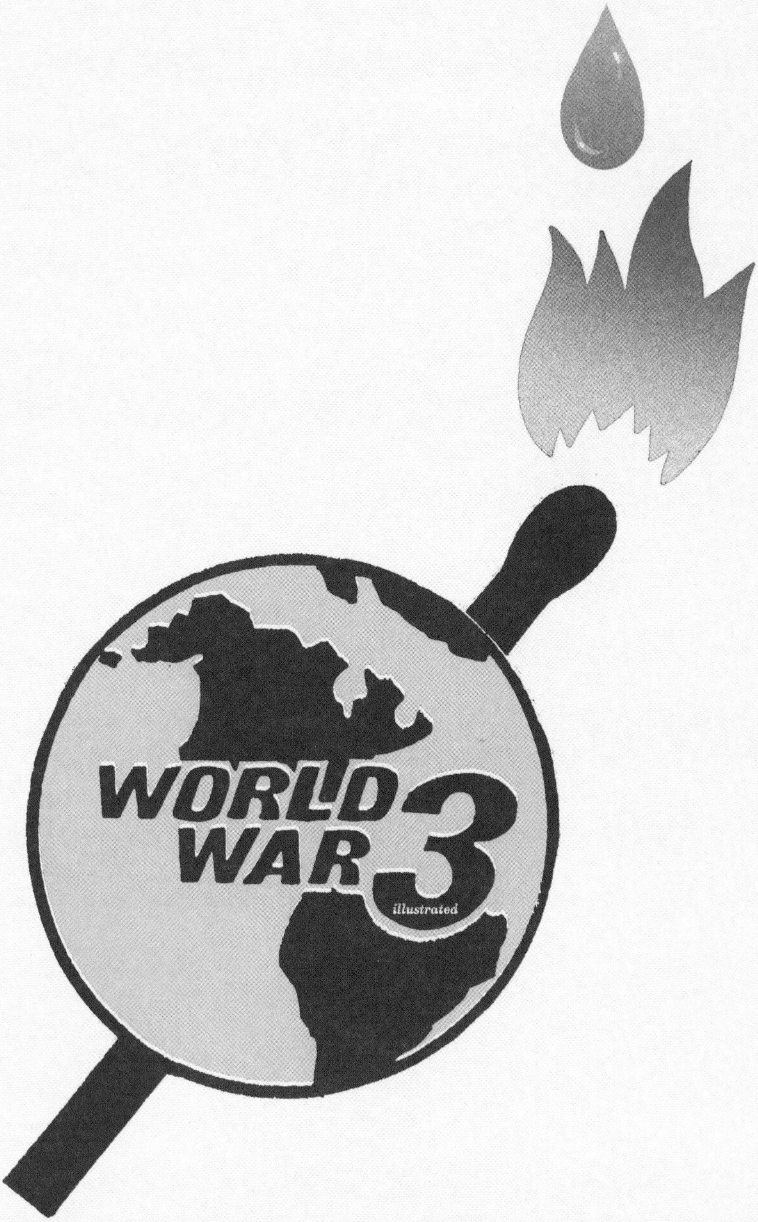
WORLD
WAR 3
illustrated

WORLD WAR 3 ILLUSTRATED 1979–2014

Edited by Peter Kuper and Seth Tobocman
© 2014 World War 3 Illustrated Inc.
All art, photos, and text © 2014 to the individual artists
All rights reserved.
No part may be reproduced without
written permission from the individual
artists except for small excerpts
for review purposes.
www.worldwar3illustrated.org
Introduction © 2014 Bill Ayers
Book design by Peter Kuper
Production assistance by
Hilary Allison, Minah Kim,
Jonathan Rowland, and Kat Fajardo
Cover by Eric Drooker
Endpapers by MATS!?
Photo credits: All walls by Hilary Allison, except page 248 wall in Egypt by
Tamara Tornado, pages 224–225 wall in Palestine by Danielle Sarah Frank,
page 249 wall in Mexico and pages 290–291 Zuccotti Park by Peter Kuper.

First edition, April 2014
ISBN: 978-1-60486-958-3
Library of Congress
Control Number:
2013956917
Printed in Singapore

THANKS

To Nicole Schulman for her initial help in the selection process and to Hilary, Minah,
Jonathan, and Kat for assisting in the daunting task of assembling and adjusting
every page. To Bill Ayers for being in cahoots and Joe Sacco for his kind words.
To everyone at PM who brought this book to light and above all, a deep gratitude to
the other editors, designers, writers, and artists who have kept
World War 3 Illustrated alive and kicking over the last 35 years.

Published by
PM Press
PO Box 23912
Oakland, CA 94623
510-658-3906
info@pmpress.org

ABOUT PM PRESS

PM Press was founded at the end of 2007 by a small collection of folks
with decades of publishing, media, and organizing experience. PM Press
co-conspirators have published and distributed hundreds of books,
pamphlets, CDs, and DVDs. Members of PM have founded enduring book fairs,
spearheaded victorious tenant organizing campaigns, and worked closely with
bookstores, academic conferences, and even rock bands to deliver political and
challenging ideas to all walks of life. We're old enough to know what we're doing
and young enough to know what's at stake.
For more information please visit us at www.pmpress.org

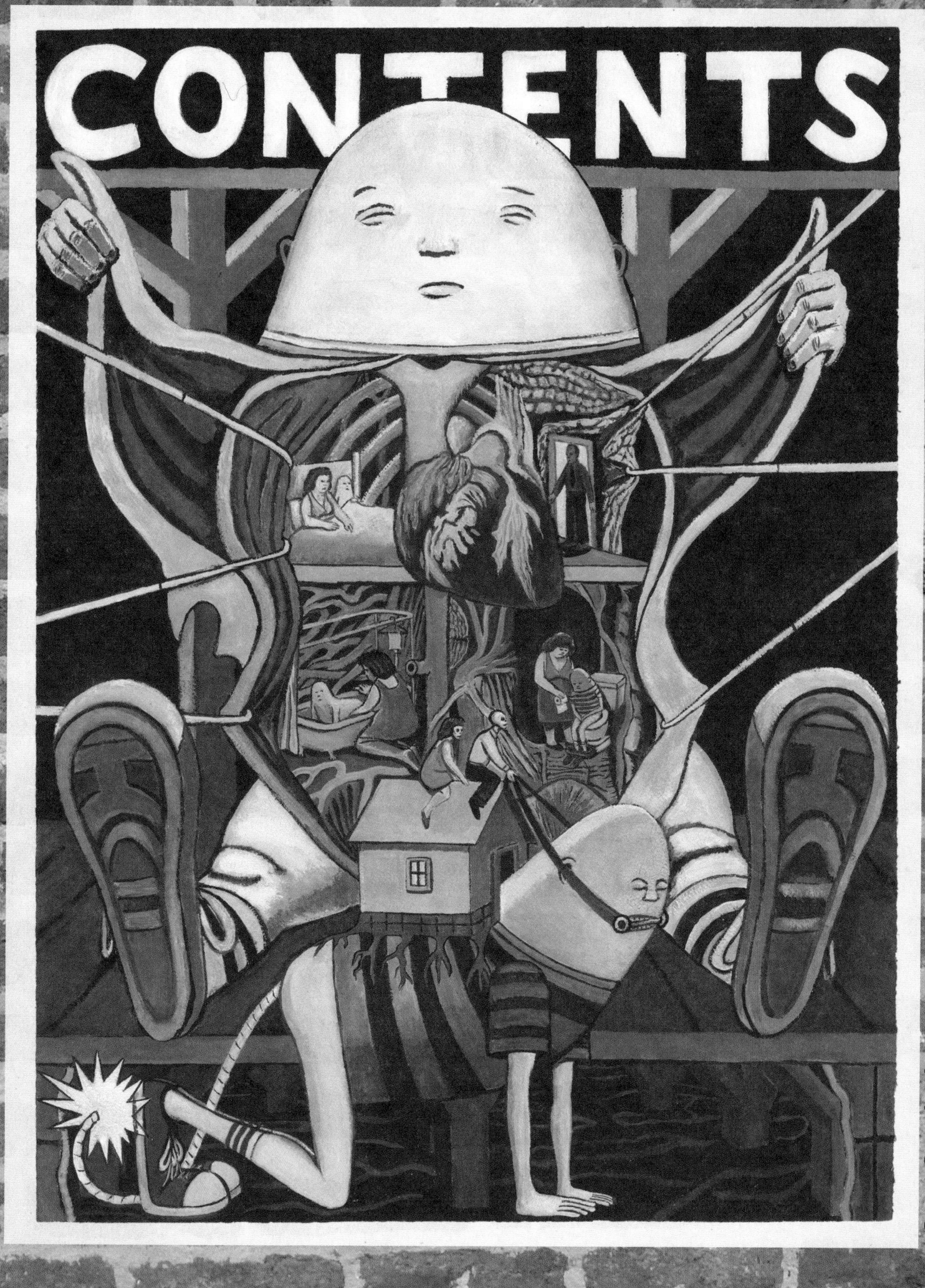
CONTENTS

Scott Cunningham

INTRODUCTION
IN CAHOOTS!

This book needs a warning label: DANGER! CONTENTS UNDER PRESSURE: OPEN AT YOUR OWN RISK! For some of us, that's an enticing summons, and we discover that *World War 3 Illustrated* is essential nourishment for these troubled times, the perfect companion to cram into the backpack between a toothbrush and a bottle of water, and as necessary to daily survival as either of these. It's a punch in the gut and a kick in the ass, an incitement to pay attention and to be astonished, and then to get up and act out. *World War 3* is an invitation to a revolution.

Open any page, rub your eyes hard, blink twice and look again: here is a world in flames, its hot breath scorching and painful, the everyday agony and unnecessary suffering everywhere we turn. There's a wondrous vision binding this extraordinary community of artists together: a shared belief in the creation of a society without coercion or domination.

This is no scholarly manifesto, no emotional massage, neither an instruction manual nor an easy point of arrival—rather it's an opening and a provocation. My pulse quickens—without a second thought I'm down the stairs and into the streets, up and at it, making art and making love, howling at the moon, linking arms, fighting back.

The artists of *World War 3* draw a vibrant and terrifyingly accurate map of the known universe: appalling poverty and unprecedented wealth, acts of war and words of peace, liveliness and chronic social depression, oppression and resistance. Reality TV, and then reality itself. There's much more here, of course, and this is in no way the whole story. America has its counter-story; we subsist on contradiction. It's a land of wild diversity, extremes and opposites, conflict and contestation, and it's a time that demands the arts as antidote and guide.

Chicagoan Gwendolyn Brooks, winner of the Pulitzer Prize for poetry in the early 1950s, asked in her "Dedication to Picasso," "Does man love art?" Her answer: "Man visits art but cringes. Art hurts. Art urges voyages." Picasso had something similar in mind when he said, "Art is not chaste. Those ill-prepared should be allowed no contact with art. Art is dangerous. If it is chaste it is not art."

My oldest son is a playwright, and he tells me I waste a lot of time reading newspapers and listening to what he calls National Pentagon Radio. "Artists have always been the real purveyors of the news," he argues, "and imagination is a better guide to what's happening in the world than the *New York Times*, which is little more than a self-important, dressed-up, and heavily perfumed toxic waste dump."

WW3 often begins in pain and horror, but it embraces the entire territory of the imaginable. Here we find life struggles hard against democracy's dreams. Next to the world as such, the given or the received world, stands a world that should be, or a world that could be but is not yet. So those who believe that the world is perfect and in need of no improvement—or that the world is none of our business, or that we are at the end of history and that this is as good as it gets and that no repair is possible—banish the arts, cuff and gag the artists. If, on the other hand, we see ourselves as works-in-progress, catapulting through a vibrant history-in-the-making, and if we feel a responsibility to engage and participate, then the arts are our strongest ally.

All human beings are entitled to expect decent standards of behavior concerning freedom and justice, and all violations of these standards must be opposed consistently and courageously. This is the work of *WW3*—exuberant, passionate, driven by authentic interest and concern and commitment and a deep sense of delight, waving a colorful flag gesturing toward a future in balance. These are willful and engaged outsiders, gratified if discomforted disrupters of the status quo, advocates, critics of orthodoxy and dogma, stereotype and received wisdom of every kind, all the reductive categories that limit human thought and communication.

The artists of *World War 3* have forged a space by turns harsh and exciting, honest and rowdy, boisterous and straight-forward, always powered by the wild and unruly harmonies of love. It's a space where hope and history rhyme, where joy and justice meet. Their voices provoke and soothe and energize.

I want to hear more. I want to play back-up.

I'm in cahoots.

—Bill Ayers

William Ayers is an activist, education reformer, and author. He is known as a leader of the radical 1960s student movement opposing U.S. involvement in Vietnam and a co-founder of the Weather Underground. He is a former Distinguished Professor of Education and Senior University Scholar at the University of Illinois at Chicago. His books include *Fugitive Days*, *Public Enemy: Confessions of an American Dissident*, *Teaching Toward Freedom*, and, with Ryan Alexander-Tanner, *To Teach: The Journey, in Comics*.

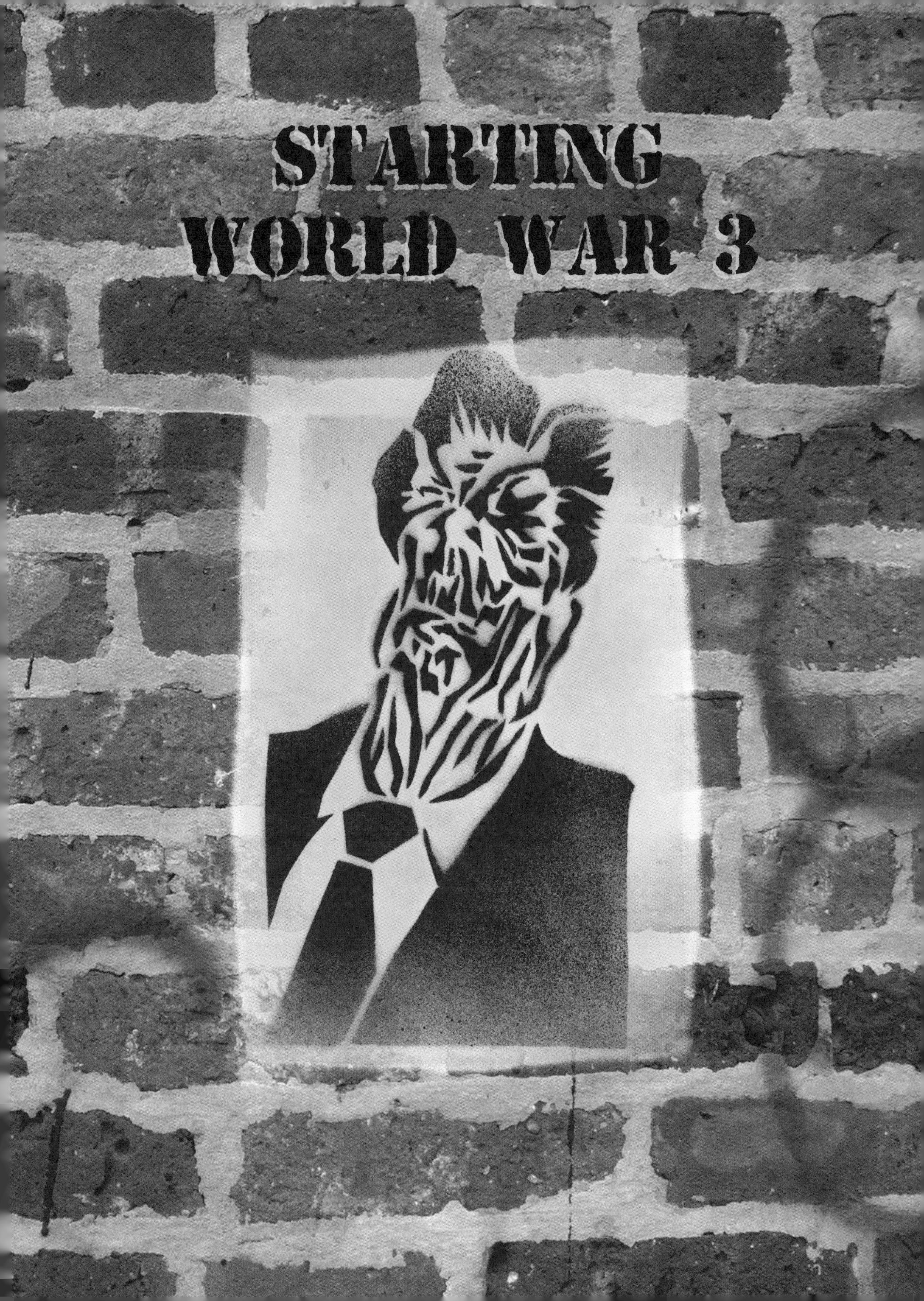
STARTING
WORLD WAR 3

In 1979 Ronald Reagan was heading toward the Oval Office with an itchy trigger-finger. We were art college students in New York, itching to express some form of rebellion against the direction our country was taking.

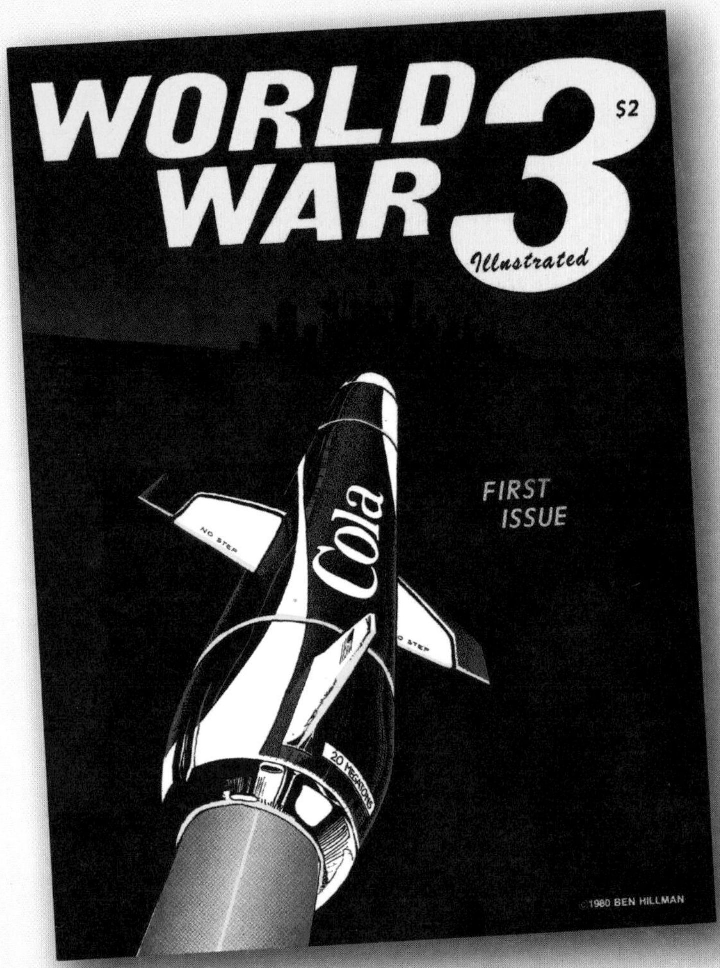
WORLD WAR 3
$2
Illustrated
Cola
NO STEP
NO STEP
20 MEGATONS
FIRST ISSUE
©1980 BEN HILLMAN

The underground comix movement had faded and there were few outlets for non-superhero comics to be found. Fortunately, we'd done fanzines as kids growing up in Cleveland, so the idea of self-publishing wasn't far-fetched.

We didn't begin *WW3* with a formal manifesto; we just wanted to create a home for political comics and the artful commentary we saw on lampposts and walls around New York City. It was work that shared our sense of outrage against the status quo and we wanted to preserve it. Because the 1980s in the United States was such a conservative period, publishing this magazine was like raising a flag. All sorts of people were drawn to that banner: punks, painters, graffiti writers, anarchists, photojournalists, feminists, squatters, political prisoners, and people with AIDS. All of these people interacted and educated one another, expanding the art and politics of *WW3*. If we had written a manifesto, it might have said: "If you want to bring people together to make the world a better place, publishing your own magazine is a decent starting point."

In many ways *WW3* represents a microcosm of the type of society we'd like to see—a place where

MANIFESTO BY SETH AND PETER

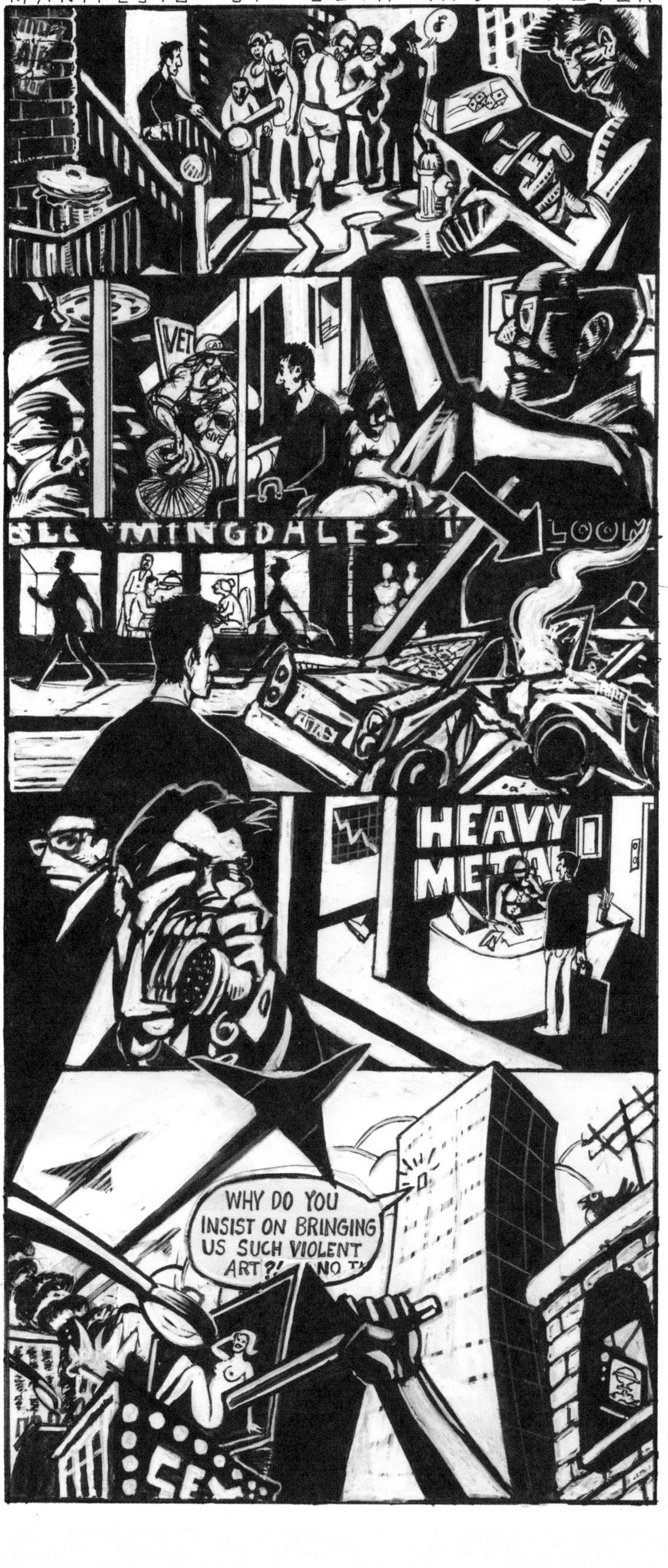
HEAVY
WHY DO YOU INSIST ON BRINGING US SUCH VIOLENT ART?!

people of various backgrounds, sexual orientations, and abilities pull together to create something that benefits the whole. It fulfills that intent with each new issue as more and more artists of all stripes have joined the magazine and whole new generations are given a voice in its pages.

From the beginning, *WW3* has served as a forum for artists to document an often untold history, but it was during crisis periods that it found its greatest purpose—from New York's Tompkins Square riots of the 1980s, to the build-up to the war in the Persian Gulf and the rebuilding of New Orleans after Hurricane Katrina, up to the Arab Spring and the Occupy movement. In the aftermath of September 11th, when major media outlets were unwilling to publish opinions that did not support a rush to war, *WW3* was one of the few venues that enabled artists to tell their stories and speak their minds.

For 35 years, *WW3* has walked in the giant footsteps of artists like Francisco de Goya, Honoré Daumier, Thomas Nast, George Grosz, Käthe Kollwitz, and John Heartfield, and publications like *The Masses* and *Simplicissimus*. It is our hope that we honor their intent—by continuing to use art to expose, inform, connect, and catalogue a history that may otherwise be rendered invisible. We dedicate this anthology to legions of artist, as yet unborn, who will carry that banner into the future.

—The Editors

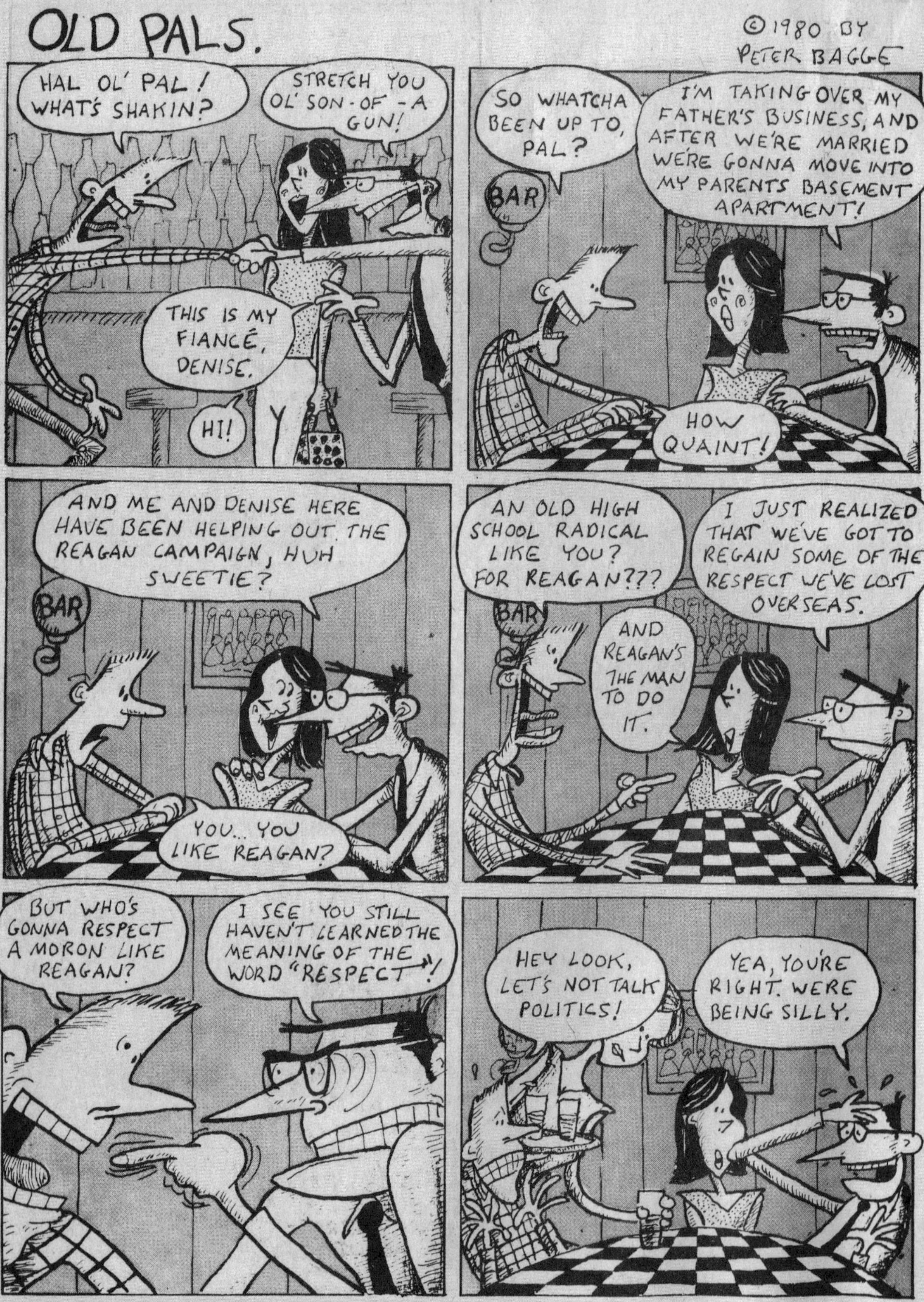
OLD PALS.
©1980 BY PETER BAGGE
HAL OL' PAL! WHAT'S SHAKIN?
STRETCH YOU OL' SON-OF-A GUN!
THIS IS MY FIANCÉ, DENISE.
HI!
SO WHATCHA BEEN UP TO, PAL?
I'M TAKING OVER MY FATHER'S BUSINESS, AND AFTER WE'RE MARRIED WE'RE GONNA MOVE INTO MY PARENTS BASEMENT APARTMENT!
BAR
HOW QUAINT!
AND ME AND DENISE HERE HAVE BEEN HELPING OUT THE REAGAN CAMPAIGN, HUH SWEETIE?
BAR
YOU... YOU LIKE REAGAN?
AN OLD HIGH SCHOOL RADICAL LIKE YOU? FOR REAGAN???
I JUST REALIZED THAT WE'VE GOT TO REGAIN SOME OF THE RESPECT WE'VE LOST OVERSEAS.
BAR
AND REAGAN'S THE MAN TO DO IT.
BUT WHO'S GONNA RESPECT A MORON LIKE REAGAN?
I SEE YOU STILL HAVEN'T LEARNED THE MEANING OF THE WORD "RESPECT"!
HEY LOOK, LET'S NOT TALK POLITICS!
YEA, YOU'RE RIGHT. WE'RE BEING SILLY.

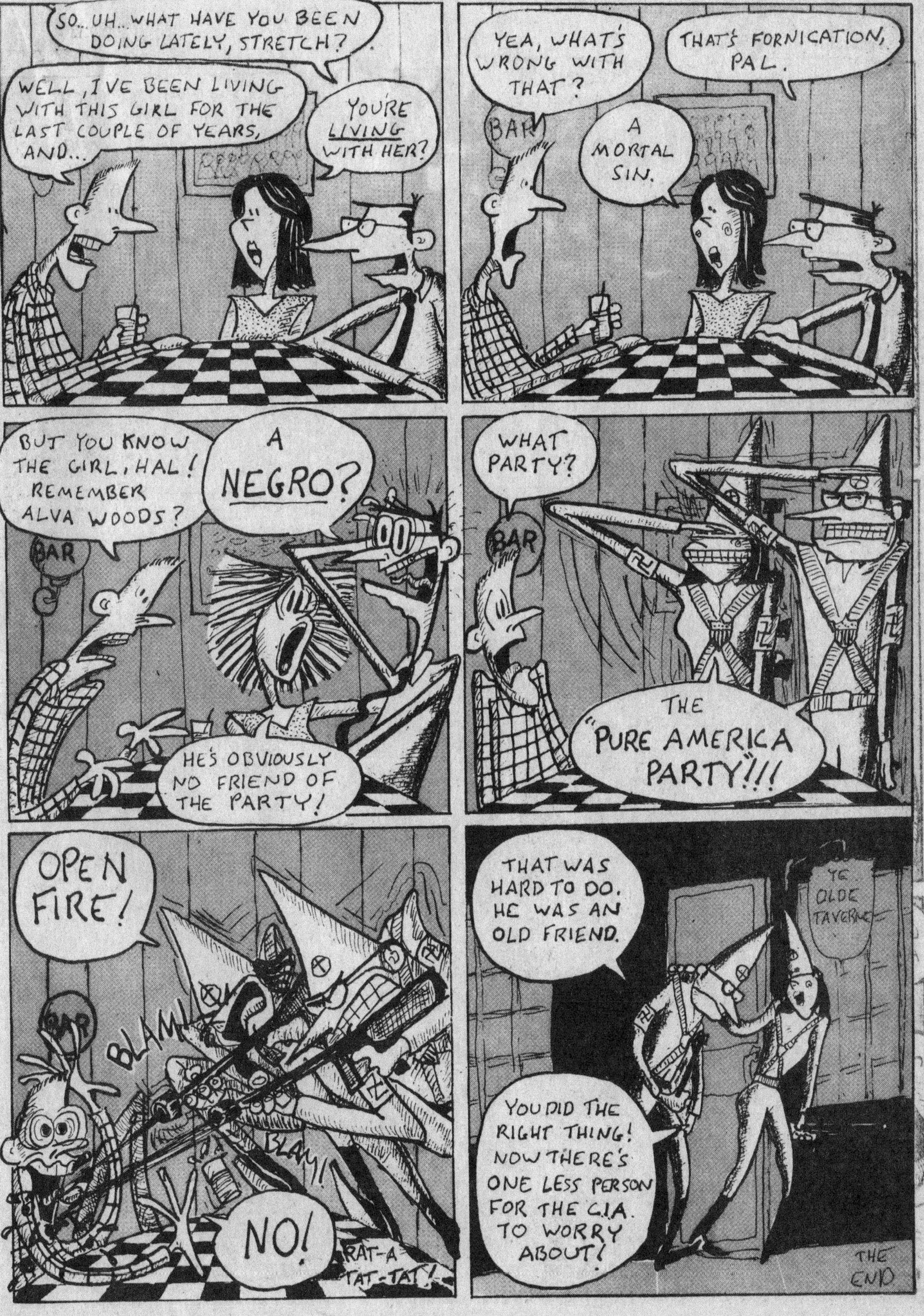
SO... UH... WHAT HAVE YOU BEEN DOING LATELY, STRETCH?
WELL, I'VE BEEN LIVING WITH THIS GIRL FOR THE LAST COUPLE OF YEARS, AND...
YOU'RE LIVING WITH HER?
YEA, WHAT'S WRONG WITH THAT?
THAT'S FORNICATION, PAL.
A MORTAL SIN.
BAR
BUT YOU KNOW THE GIRL, HAL! REMEMBER ALVA WOODS?
A NEGRO?
HE'S OBVIOUSLY NO FRIEND OF THE PARTY!
WHAT PARTY?
THE "PURE AMERICA PARTY"!!!
OPEN FIRE!
BLAM!
BLAM!
NO!
RAT-A-TAT-TAT!
THAT WAS HARD TO DO. HE WAS AN OLD FRIEND.
YE OLDE TAVERNE
YOU DID THE RIGHT THING! NOW THERE'S ONE LESS PERSON FOR THE C.I.A. TO WORRY ABOUT!
THE END

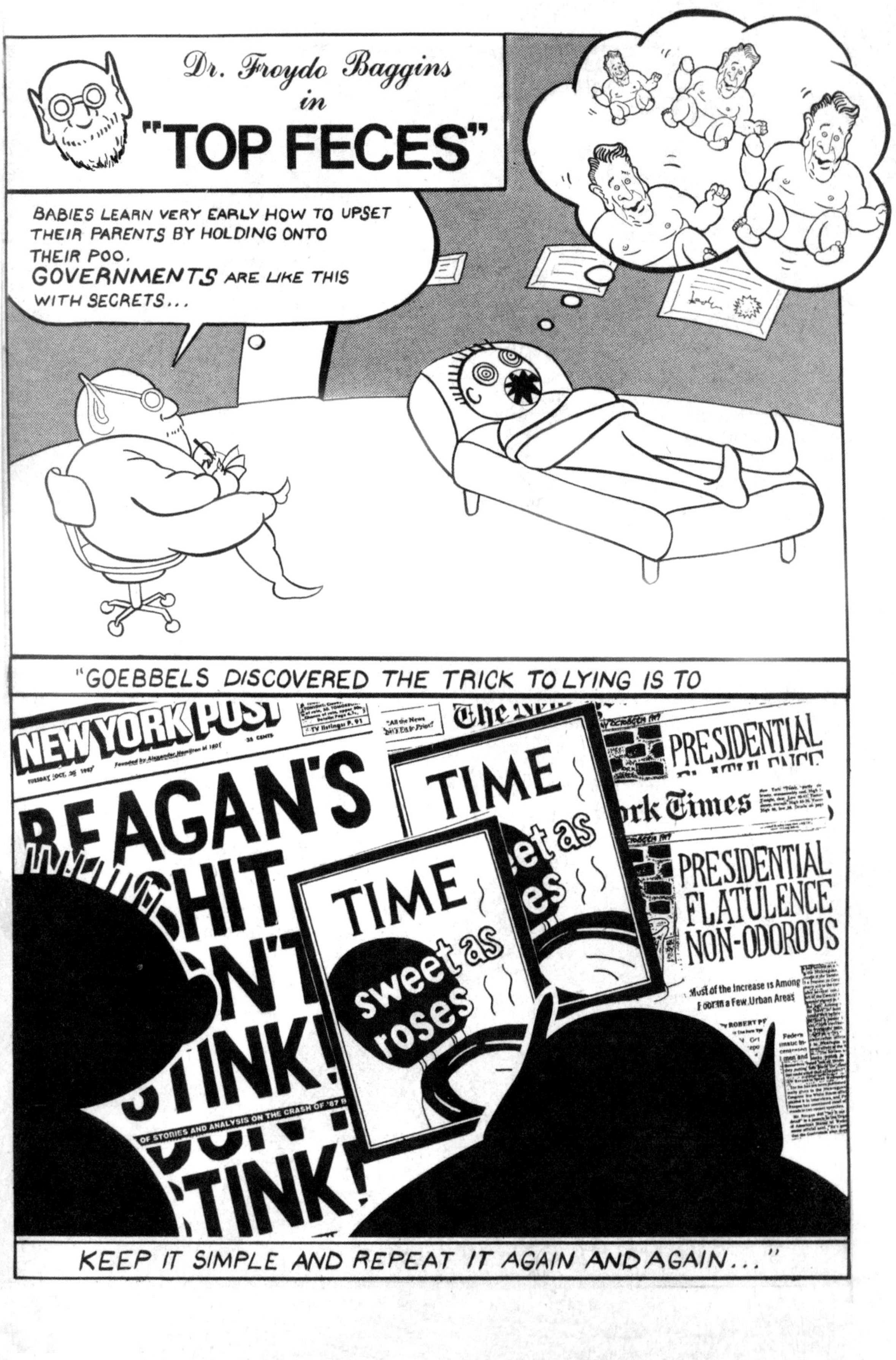
Dr. Froydo Baggins
in
"TOP FECES"
BABIES LEARN VERY EARLY HOW TO UPSET THEIR PARENTS BY HOLDING ONTO THEIR POO. GOVERNMENTS ARE LIKE THIS WITH SECRETS...
"GOEBBELS DISCOVERED THE TRICK TO LYING IS TO
NEW YORK POST
REAGAN'S SHIT DON'T STINK!
TIME
sweet as roses
TIME
sweet as roses
PRESIDENTIAL FLATULENCE NON-ODOROUS
York Times
Most of the Increase is Among Four in a Few Urban Areas
KEEP IT SIMPLE AND REPEAT IT AGAIN AND AGAIN..."

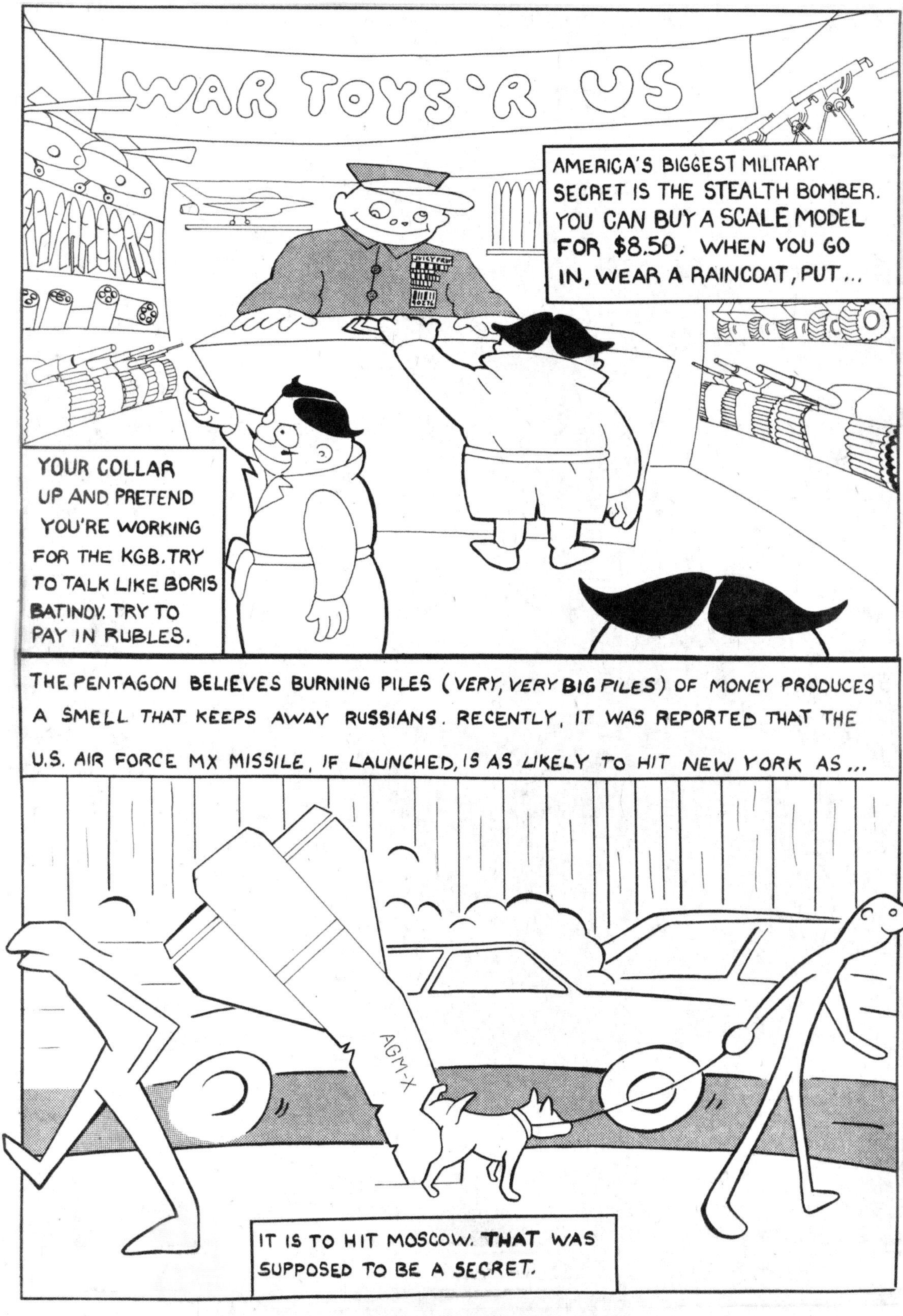
WAR TOYS 'R US
AMERICA'S BIGGEST MILITARY SECRET IS THE STEALTH BOMBER. YOU CAN BUY A SCALE MODEL FOR $8.50. WHEN YOU GO IN, WEAR A RAINCOAT, PUT...
YOUR COLLAR UP AND PRETEND YOU'RE WORKING FOR THE KGB. TRY TO TALK LIKE BORIS BATINOV. TRY TO PAY IN RUBLES.
THE PENTAGON BELIEVES BURNING PILES (VERY, VERY BIG PILES) OF MONEY PRODUCES A SMELL THAT KEEPS AWAY RUSSIANS. RECENTLY, IT WAS REPORTED THAT THE U.S. AIR FORCE MX MISSILE, IF LAUNCHED, IS AS LIKELY TO HIT NEW YORK AS...
AGM-X
IT IS TO HIT MOSCOW. THAT WAS SUPPOSED TO BE A SECRET.

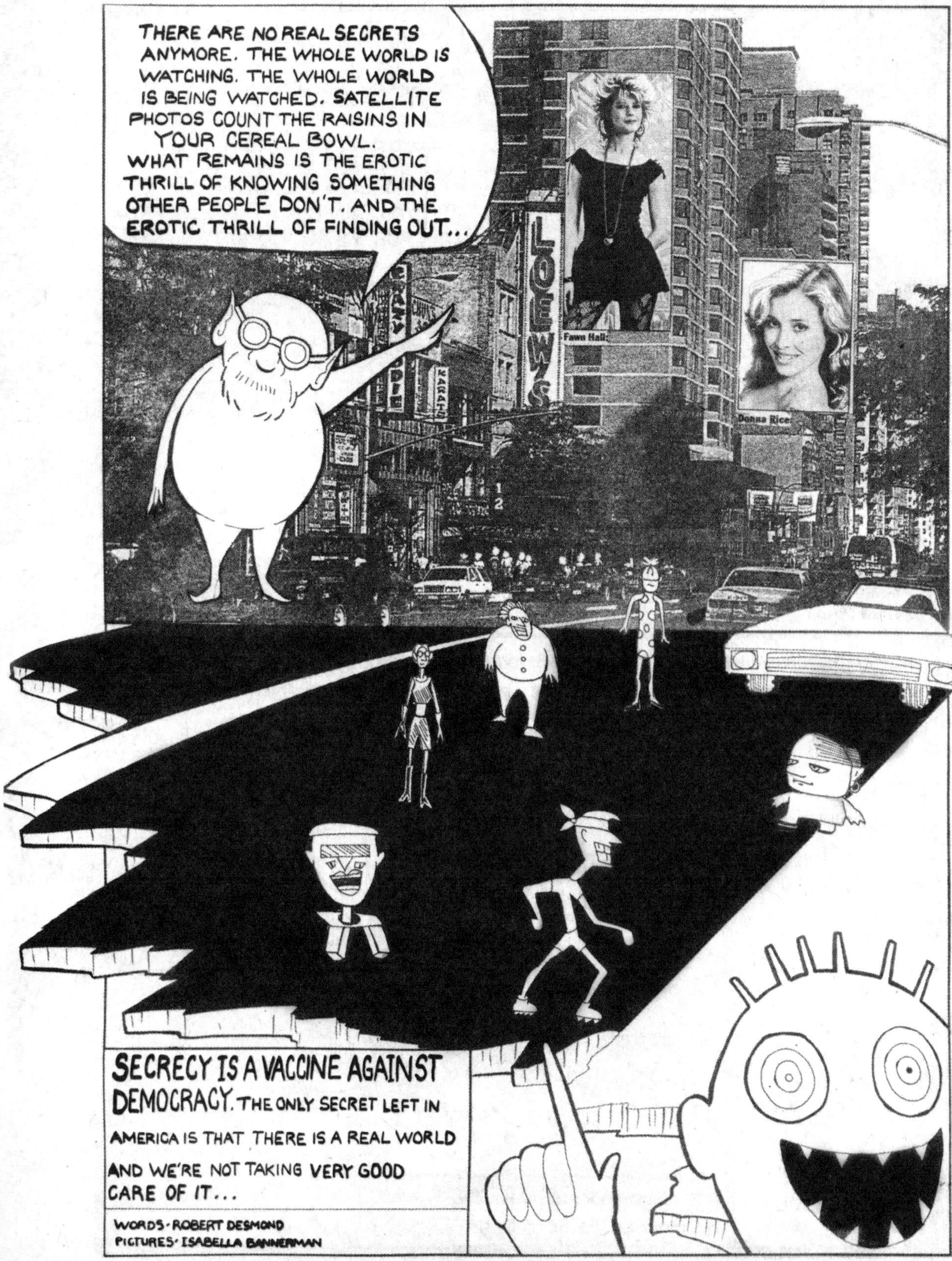

THERE ARE NO REAL SECRETS ANYMORE. THE WHOLE WORLD IS WATCHING. THE WHOLE WORLD IS BEING WATCHED. SATELLITE PHOTOS COUNT THE RAISINS IN YOUR CEREAL BOWL. WHAT REMAINS IS THE EROTIC THRILL OF KNOWING SOMETHING OTHER PEOPLE DON'T. AND THE EROTIC THRILL OF FINDING OUT...
LOEWS
Fawn Hall
Donna Rice
SECRECY IS A VACCINE AGAINST DEMOCRACY. THE ONLY SECRET LEFT IN AMERICA IS THAT THERE IS A REAL WORLD AND WE'RE NOT TAKING VERY GOOD CARE OF IT...
WORDS - ROBERT DESMOND
PICTURES - ISABELLA BANNERMAN

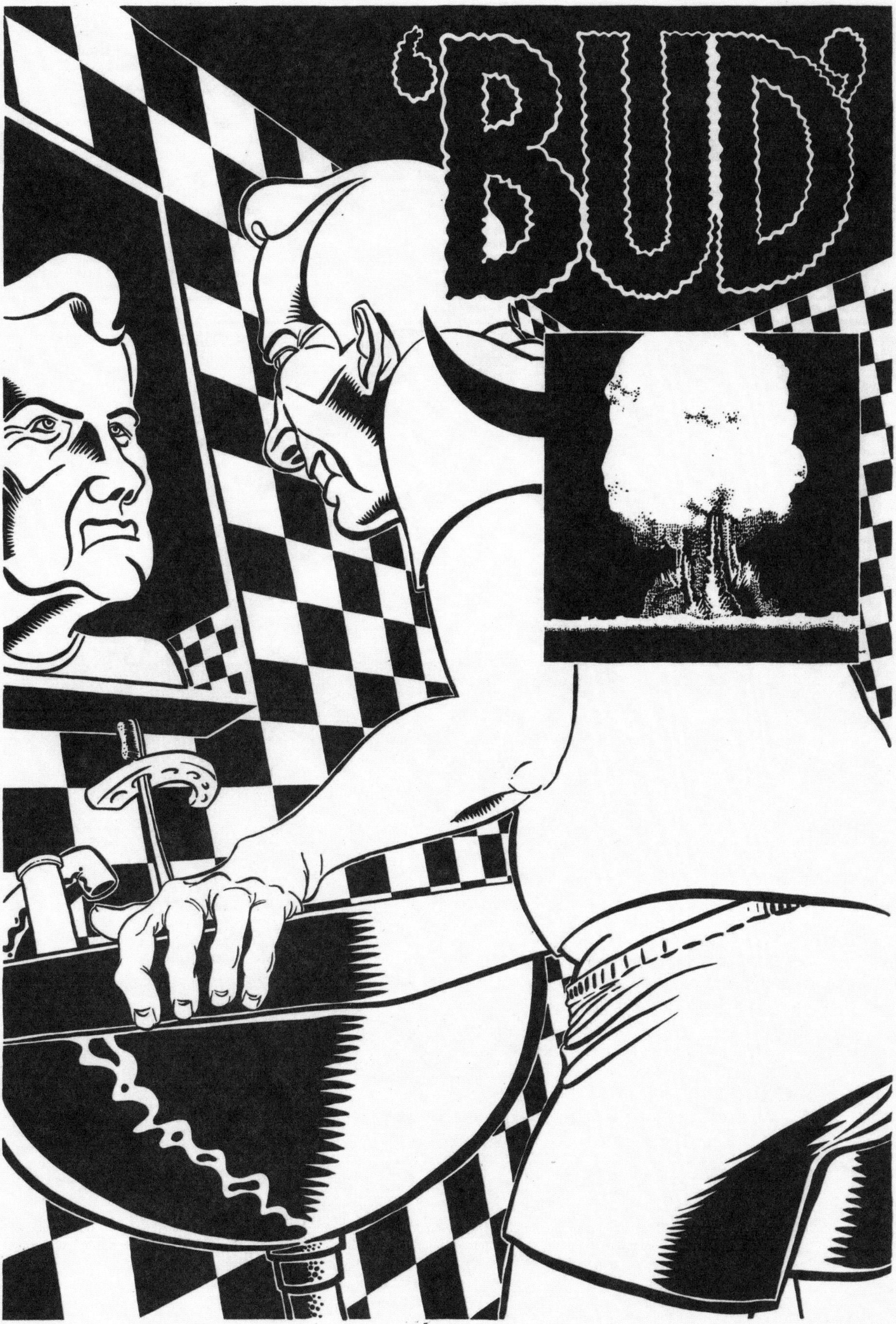

'BUD'

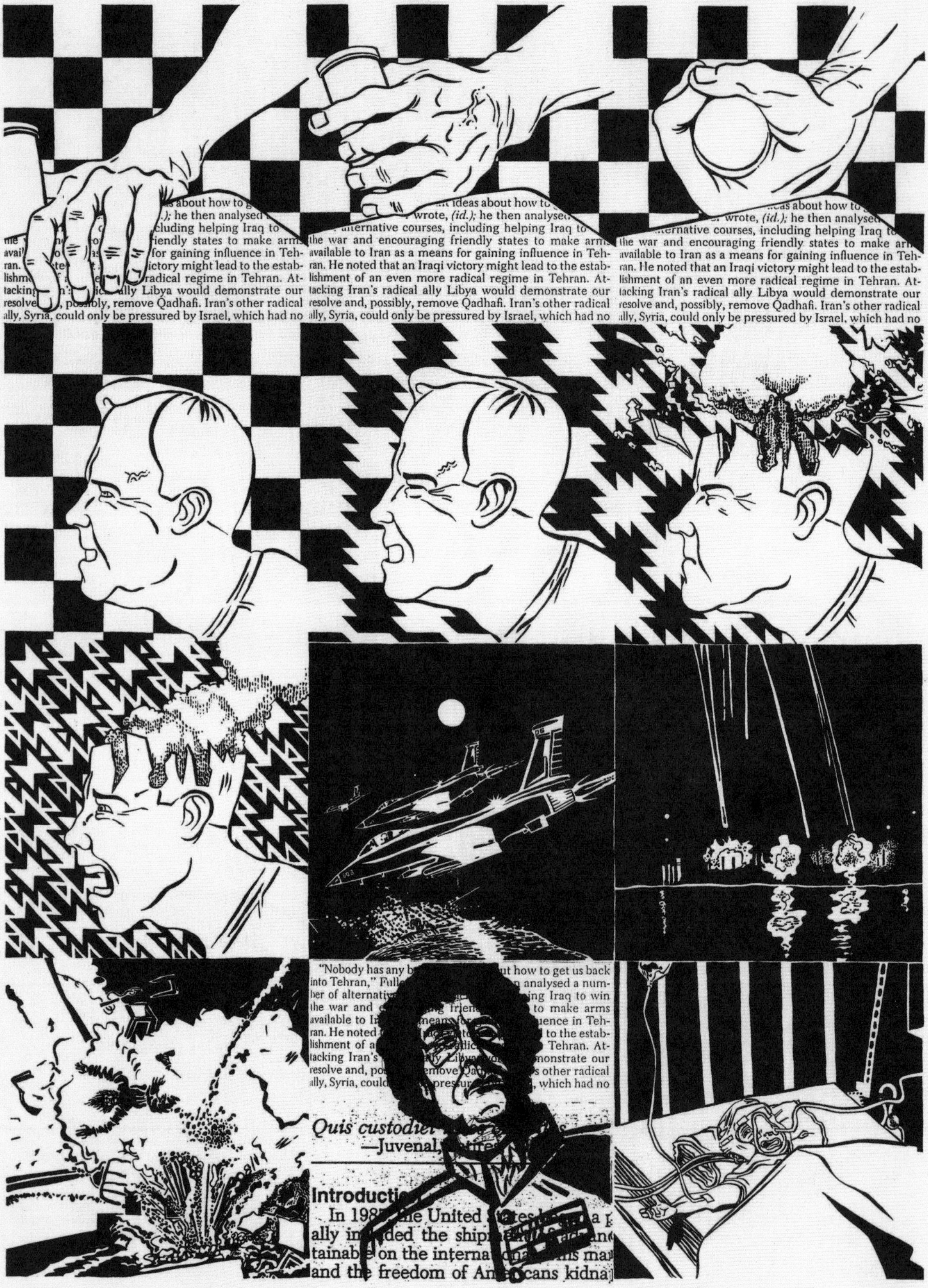
.); he then analysed
cluding helping Iraq to
friendly states to make arms
for gaining influence in Teh-
ictory might lead to the estab-
radical regime in Tehran. At-
ally Libya would demonstrate our
possibly, remove Qadhafi. Iran's other radical
ally, Syria, could only be pressured by Israel, which had no
ideas about how to
wrote, (id.); he then analysed
alternative courses, including helping Iraq to
the war and encouraging friendly states to make arms
available to Iran as a means for gaining influence in Tehran. He noted that an Iraqi victory might lead to the estab-
lishment of an even more radical regime in Tehran. Attacking Iran's radical ally Libya would demonstrate our
resolve and, possibly, remove Qadhafi. Iran's other radical
ally, Syria, could only be pressured by Israel, which had no
eas about how to
wrote, (id.); he then analysed
alternative courses, including helping Iraq to
the war and encouraging friendly states to make arm
available to Iran as a means for gaining influence in Tehran. He noted that an Iraqi victory might lead to the estab-
lishment of an even more radical regime in Tehran. Attacking Iran's radical ally Libya would demonstrate our
resolve and, possibly, remove Qadhafi. Iran's other radical
ally, Syria, could only be pressured by Israel, which had no
"Nobody has any b
ut how to get us back
into Tehran," Fulle
g analysed a num-
ber of alternativ
Iraq to win
the war and
to make arms
available to Ir
uence in Teh-
ran. He noted
lishment of a
Tehran. At-
tacking Iran's
monstrate our
resolve and, pos
s other radical
ally, Syria, could
which had no
Quis custodiet
—Juvenal,
Introducti
In 198
the United
ally in
ded the ship
tainable on the interna
and the freedom of Am
cans kidna

the Great Satan In the course of the 4 hour meeting it became evident that the three Iranian leaders are each traumatized by the recollection

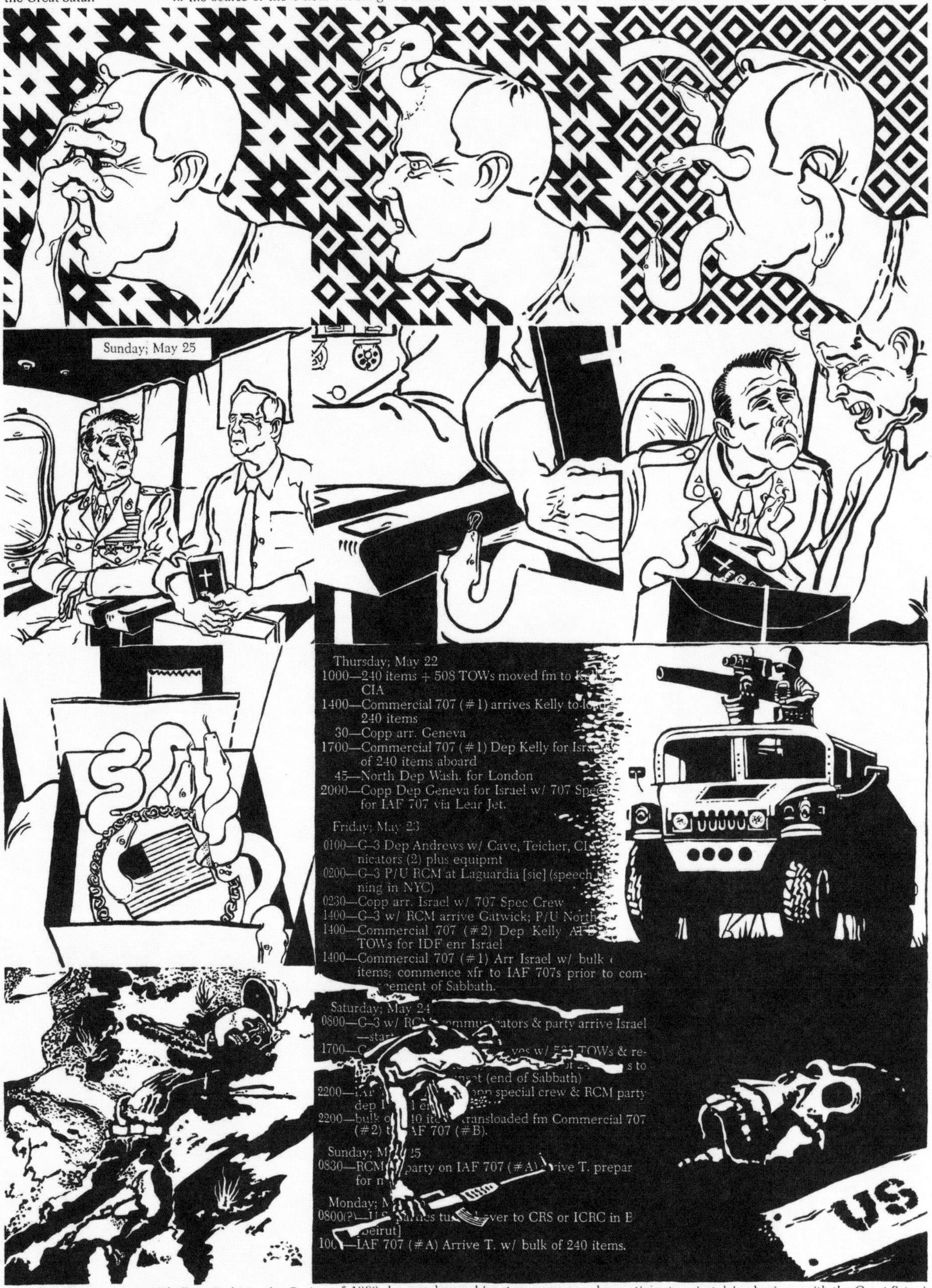

Sunday; May 25
Thursday; May 22
1000—240 items + 508 TOWs moved fm to
CIA
1400—Commercial 707 (#1) arrives Kelly to
240 items
30—Copp arr. Geneva
1700—Commercial 707 (#1) Dep Kelly for
of 240 items aboard
45—North Dep Wash. for London
2000—Copp Dep Geneva for Israel w/ 707
for IAF 707 via Lear Jet.
Friday; May 23
0100—G-3 Dep Andrews w/ Cave, Teicher,
nicators (2) plus equipmt
0200—G-3 P/U RCM at Laguardia [sic] (speech
ning in NYC)
0230—Copp arr. Israel w/ 707 Spec Crew
1400—G-3 w/ RCM arrive Gatwick; P/U North
1400—Commercial 707 (#2) Dep Kelly
TOWs for IDF enr Israel
1400—Commercial 707 (#1) Arr Israel w/ bulk
items; commence xfr to IAF 707s prior to com-
ement of Sabbath.
Saturday; May 24
0800—G-3 w/ ators & party arrive Israel
1700— TOWs & re-
s to
(end of Sabbath)
2200— special crew & RCM party
2200— transloaded fm Commercial 707
AF 707 (#B).
Sunday;
0830— party on IAF 707 (#A) rive T. prepar
Monday;
ver to CRS or ICRC in B
eirut]
IAF 707 (#A) Arrive T. w/ bulk of 240 items.
US

that after Bazargan met with Brzezinski in the Spring of 1980, he was deposed (so strong was popular sentiment against doing business with the Great Satan).

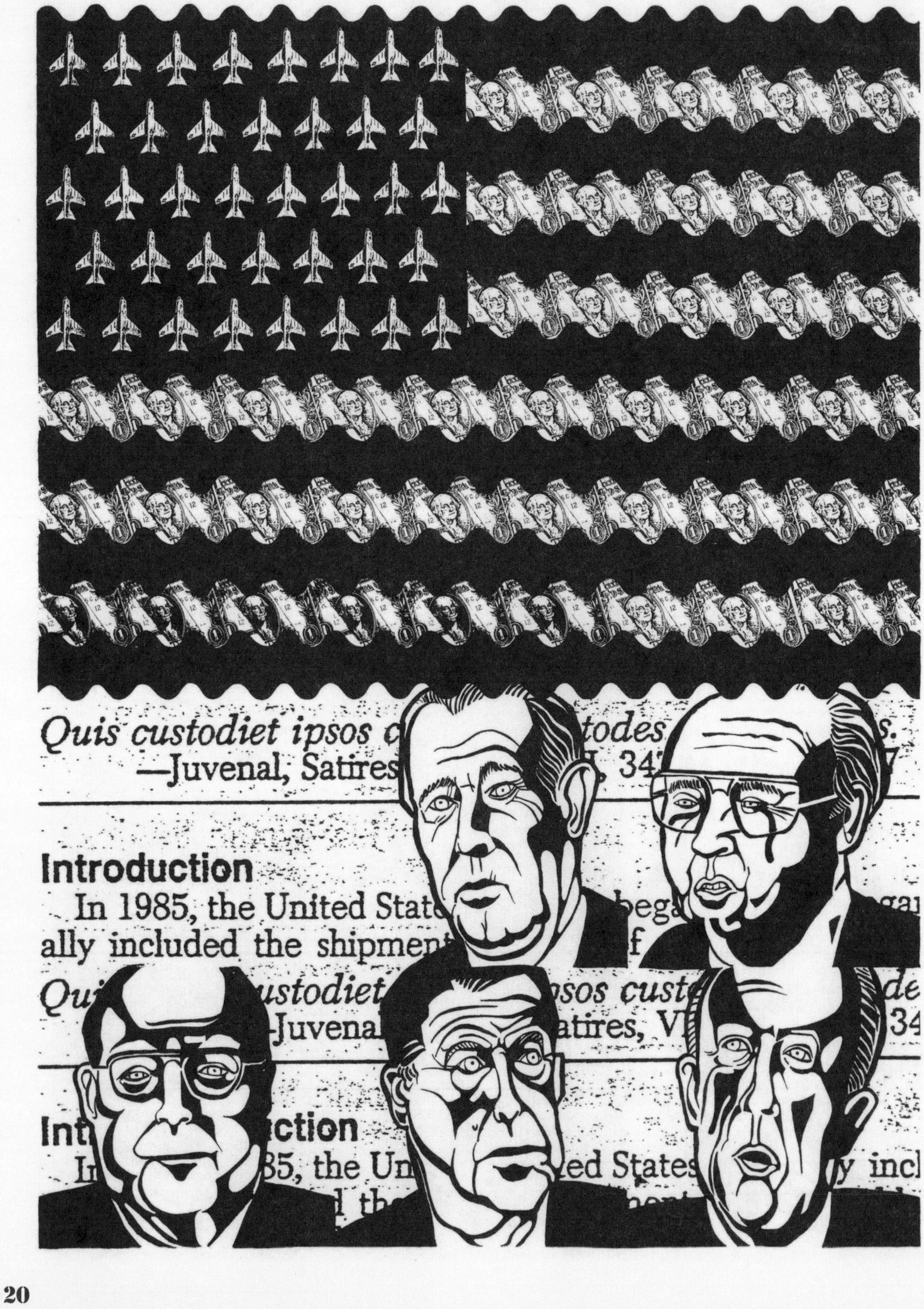

Quis custodiet ipsos c
todes
—Juvenal, Satires
Introduction
In 1985, the United State
bega
ally included the shipmen
ustodiet
osos custo
-Juvena
atires, V
ction
85, the Un
ed States

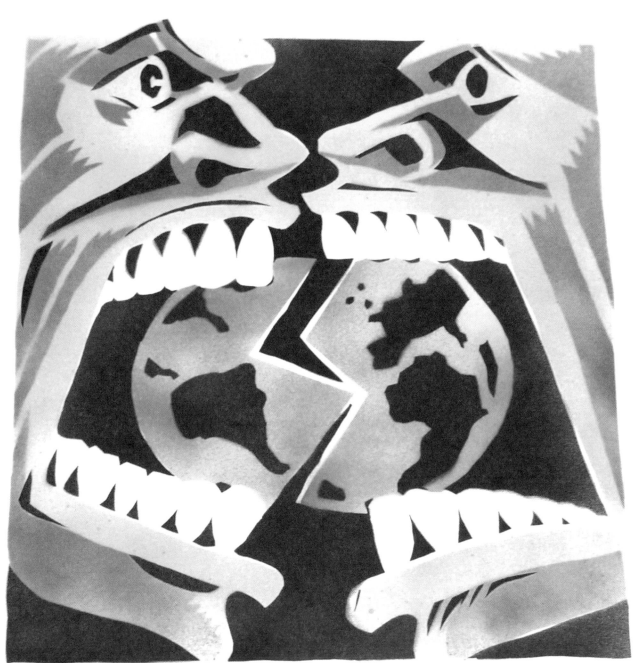

THE WORLD IS
BEING RIPPED

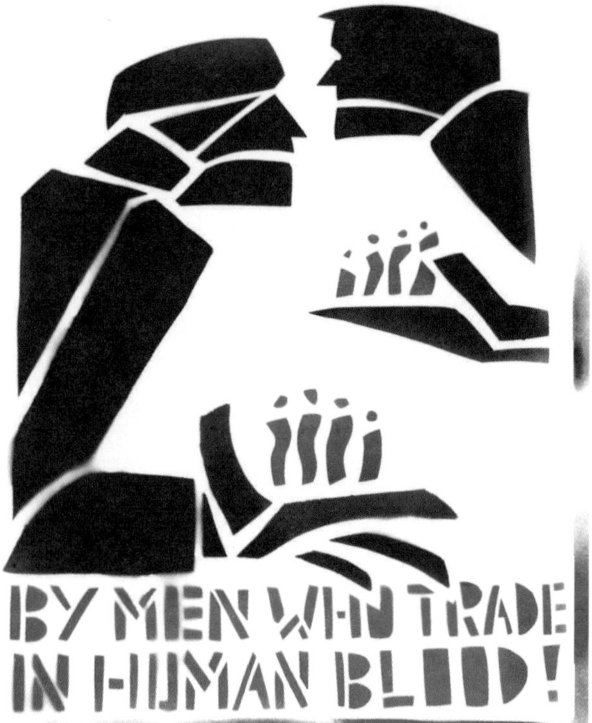
BY MEN WHO TRADE
IN HUMAN BLOOD!

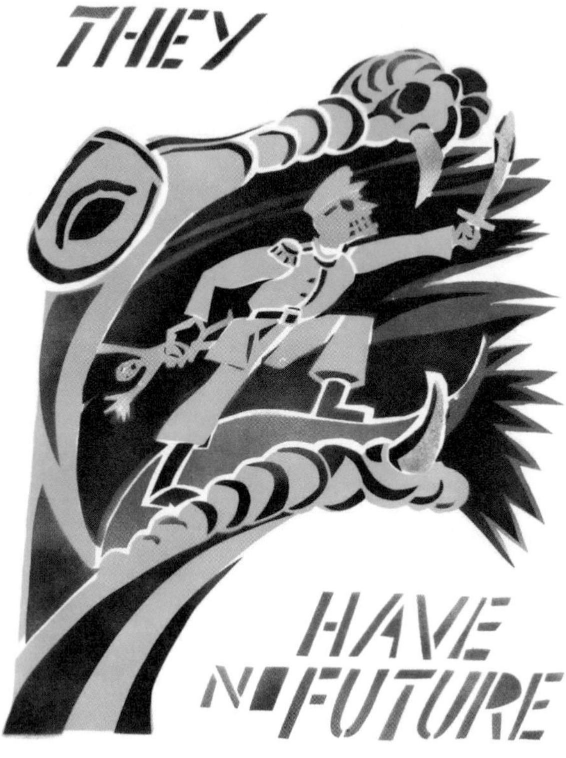
THEY
HAVE
NO FUTURE

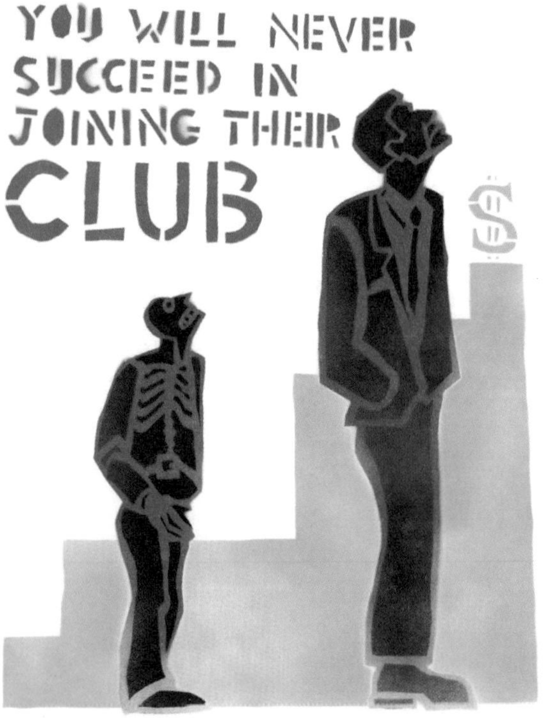
YOU WILL NEVER
SUCCEED IN
JOINING THEIR
CLUB
$

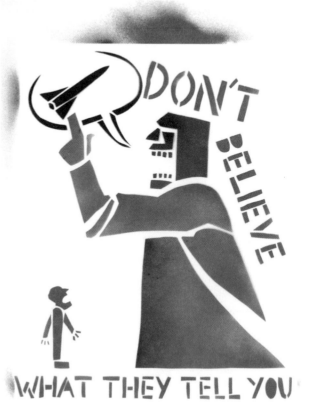

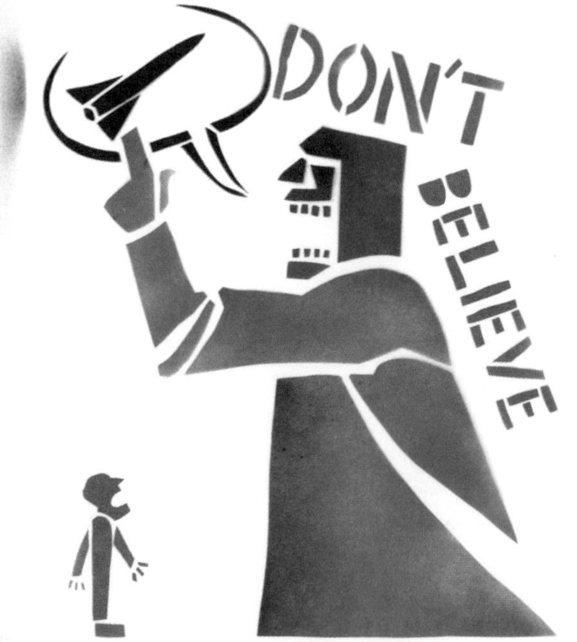
DON'T
BELIEVE
WHAT THEY TELL YOU

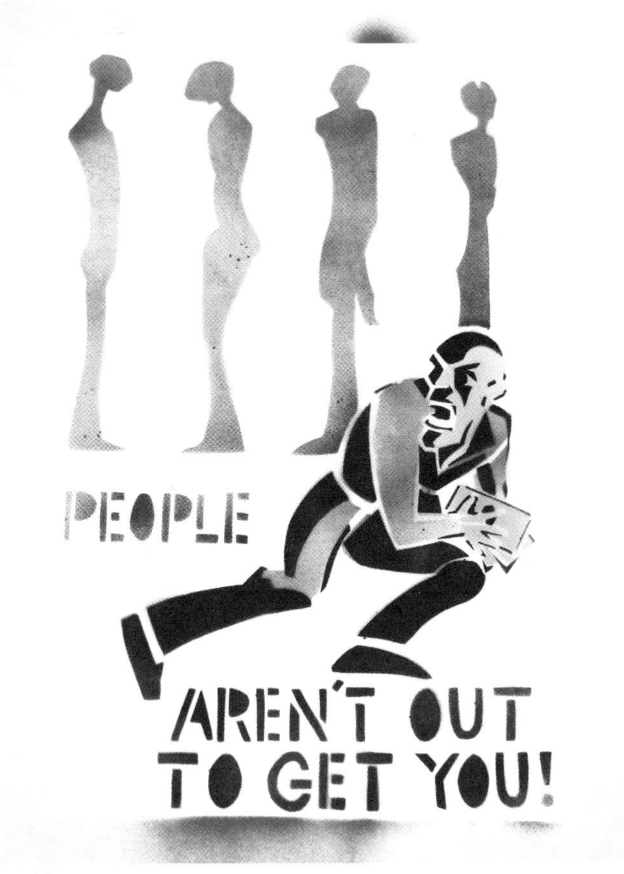
PEOPLE
AREN'T OUT
TO GET YOU!

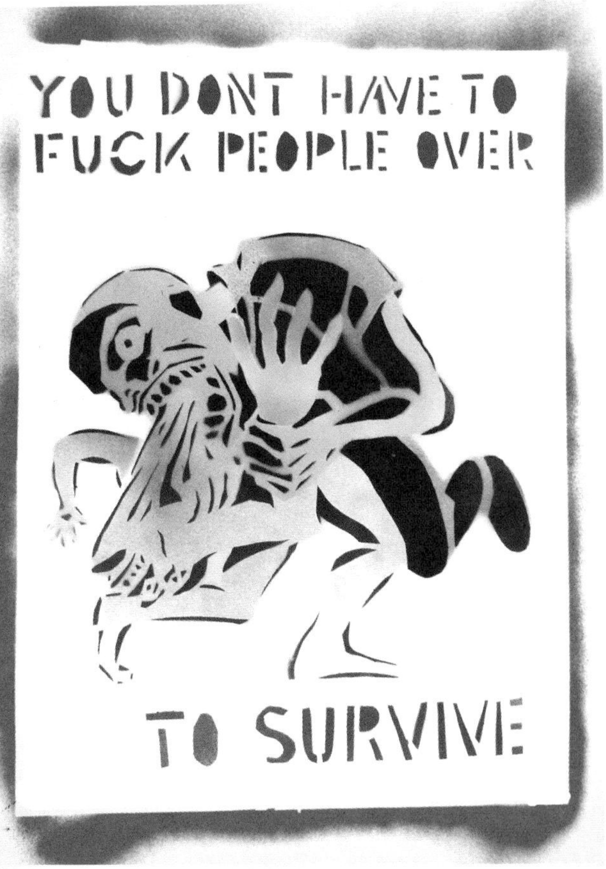
YOU DONT HAVE TO
FUCK PEOPLE OVER
TO SURVIVE

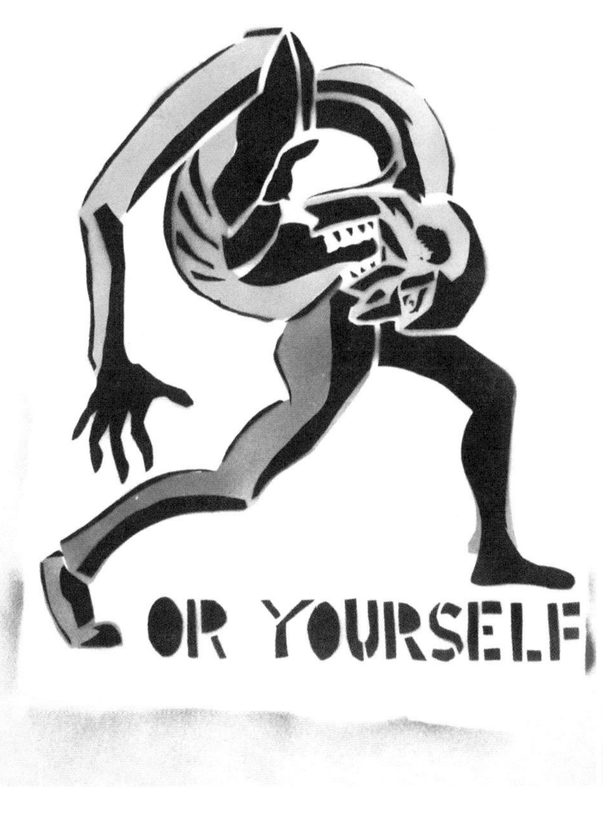
OR YOURSELF

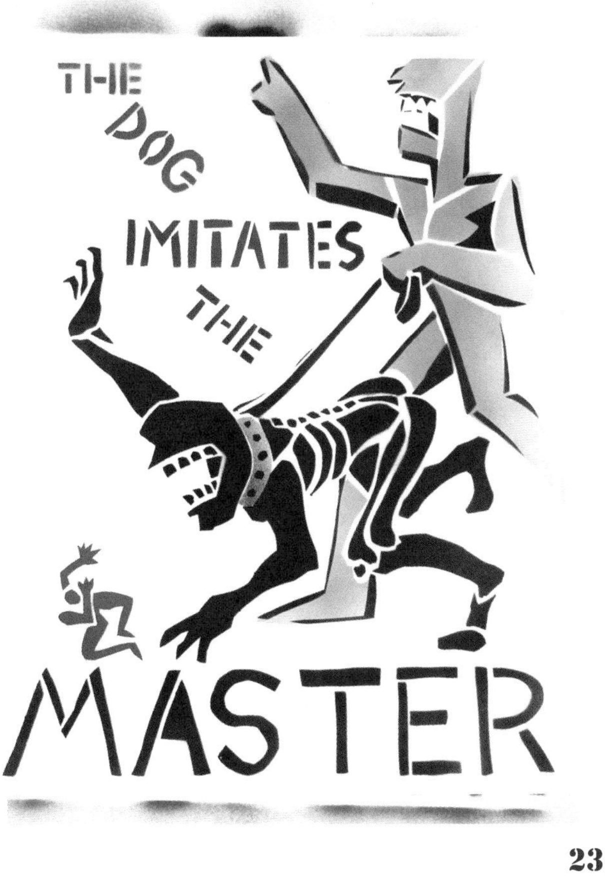
THE
DOG
IMITATES
THE
MASTER

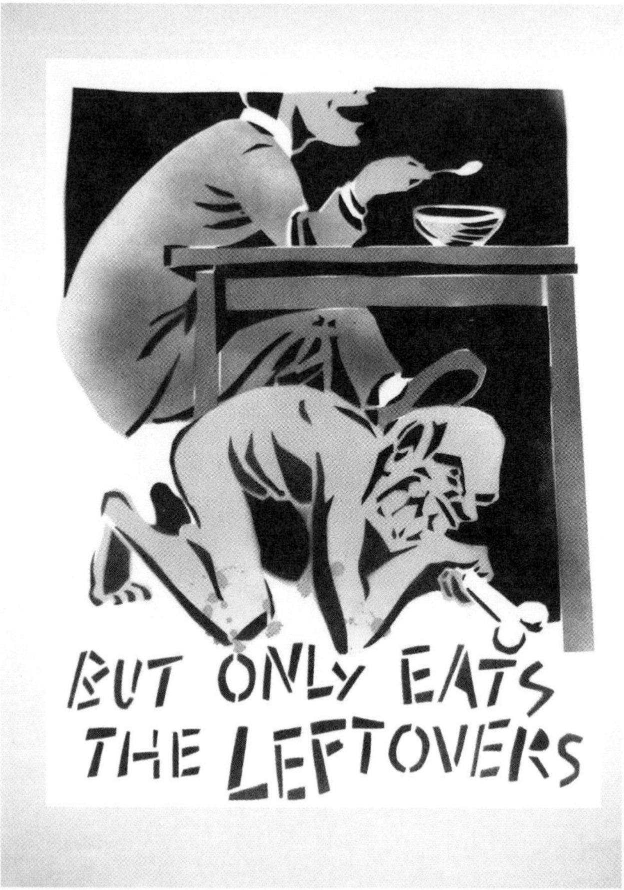
BUT ONLY EATS
THE LEFTOVERS

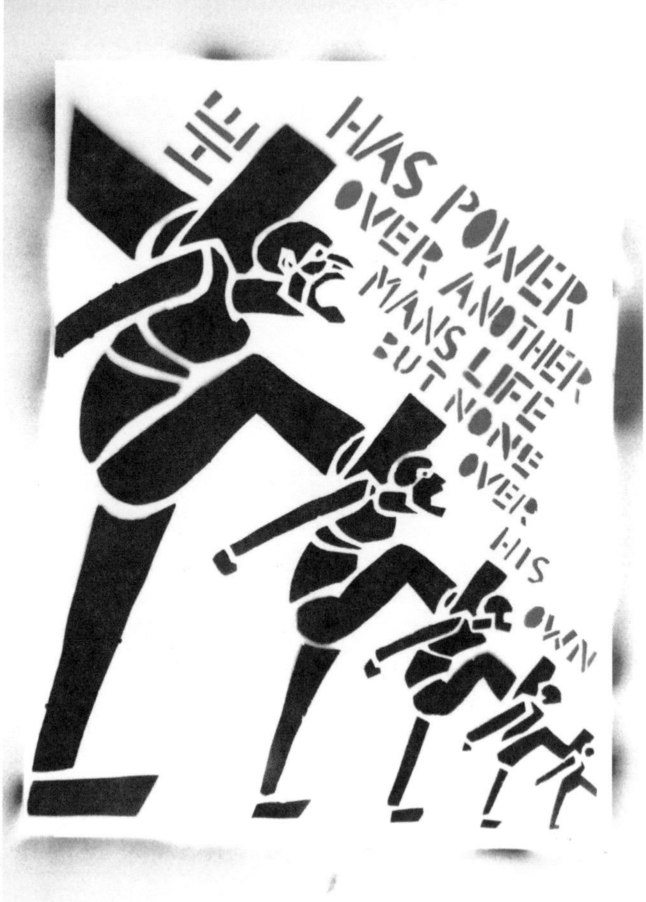
HE
HAS POWER
OVER ANOTHER
MANS LIFE
BUT NONE
OVER
HIS
OWN

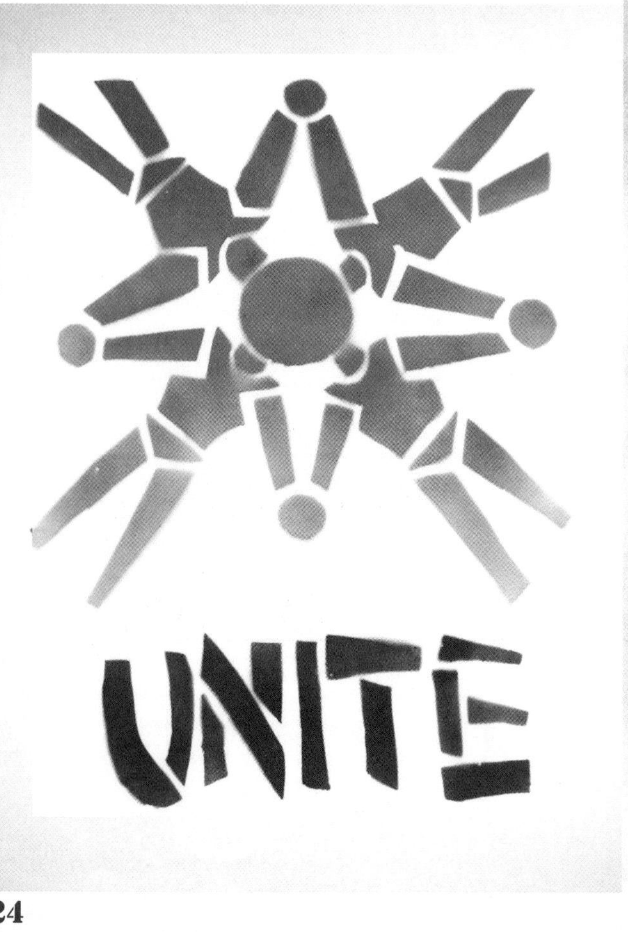
UNITE

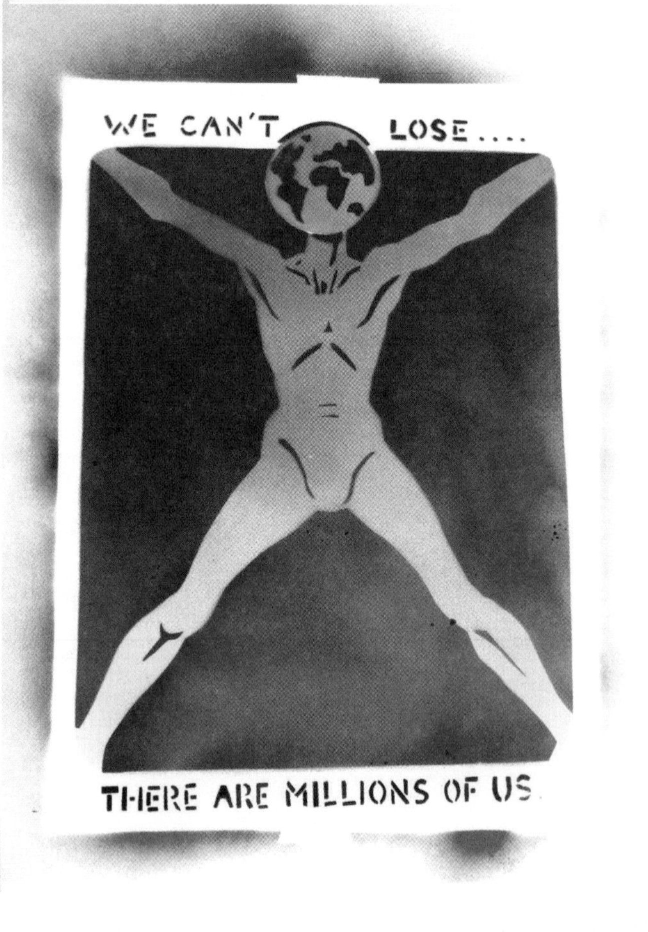
WE CAN'T LOSE....
THERE ARE MILLIONS OF US.

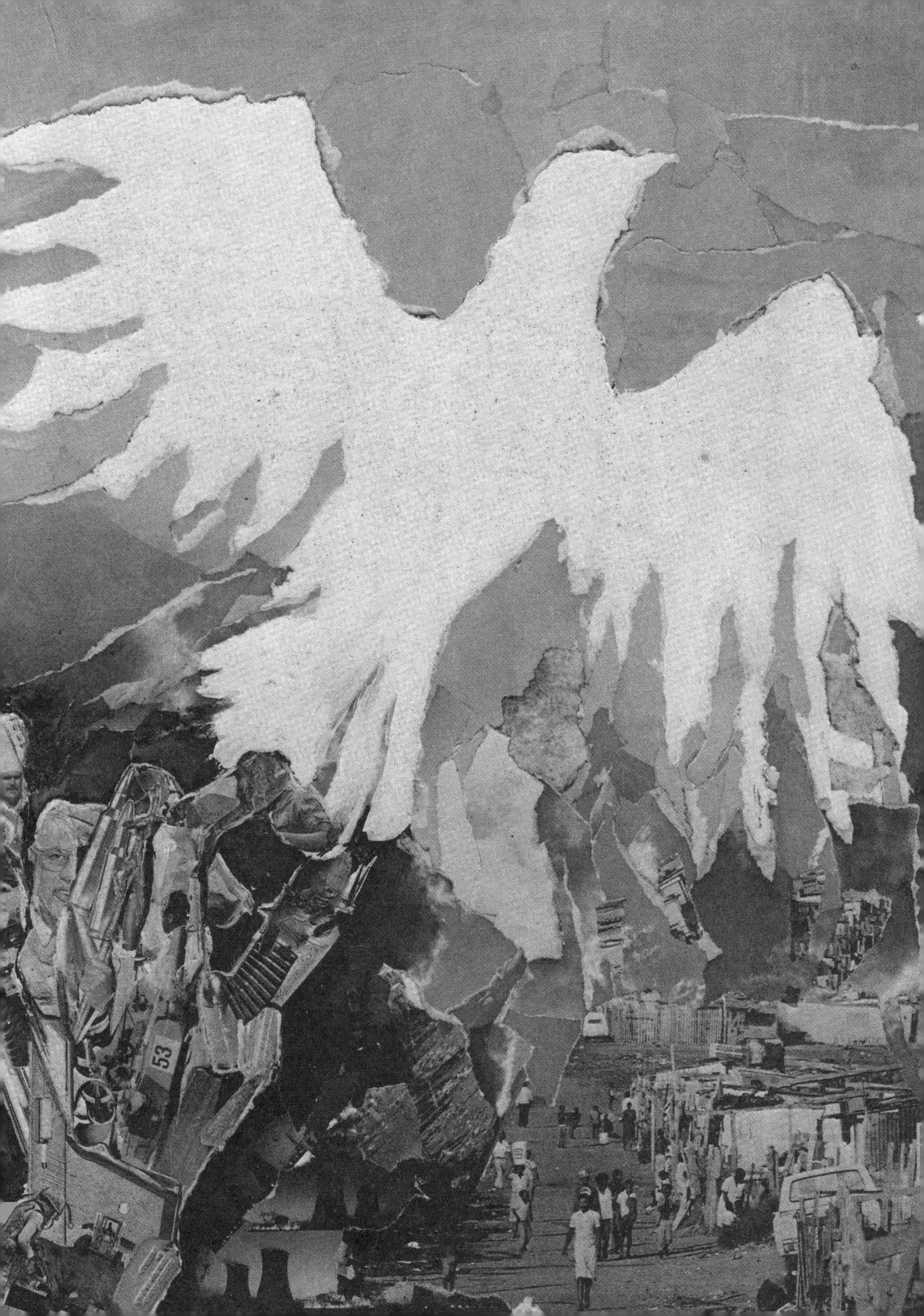
53

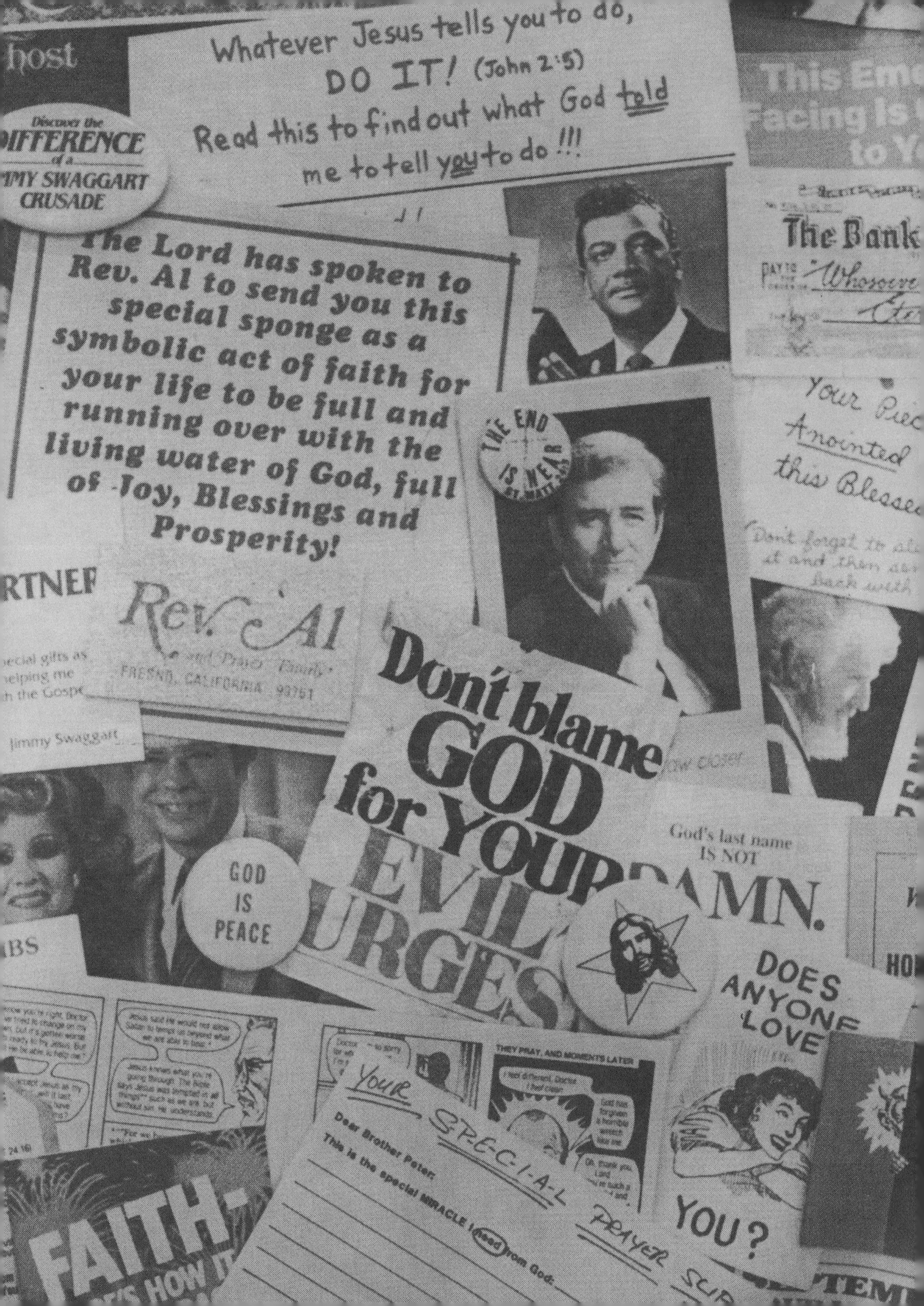
Whatever Jesus tells you to do,
DO IT! (John 2:5)
Read this to find out what God told me to tell you to do !!!
Discover the
SWAGGART
CRUSADE
The Lord has spoken to Rev. Al to send you this special sponge as a symbolic act of faith for your life to be full and running over with the living water of God, full of Joy, Blessings and Prosperity!
Rev. Al
FRESNO, CALIFORNIA
Jimmy Swaggart
THE END IS NEAR
The Bank
Anointed
this Blessed
Don't blame GOD for YOUR EVIL URGES
GOD IS PEACE
God's last name IS NOT DAMN.
DOES ANYONE LOVE YOU?
THEY PRAY, AND MOMENTS LATER
YOUR S-P-E-C-I-A-L PRAYER
Dear Brother Peter:
This is the special MIRACLE I need from God:
FAITH-

IN GOD WE TRUST?

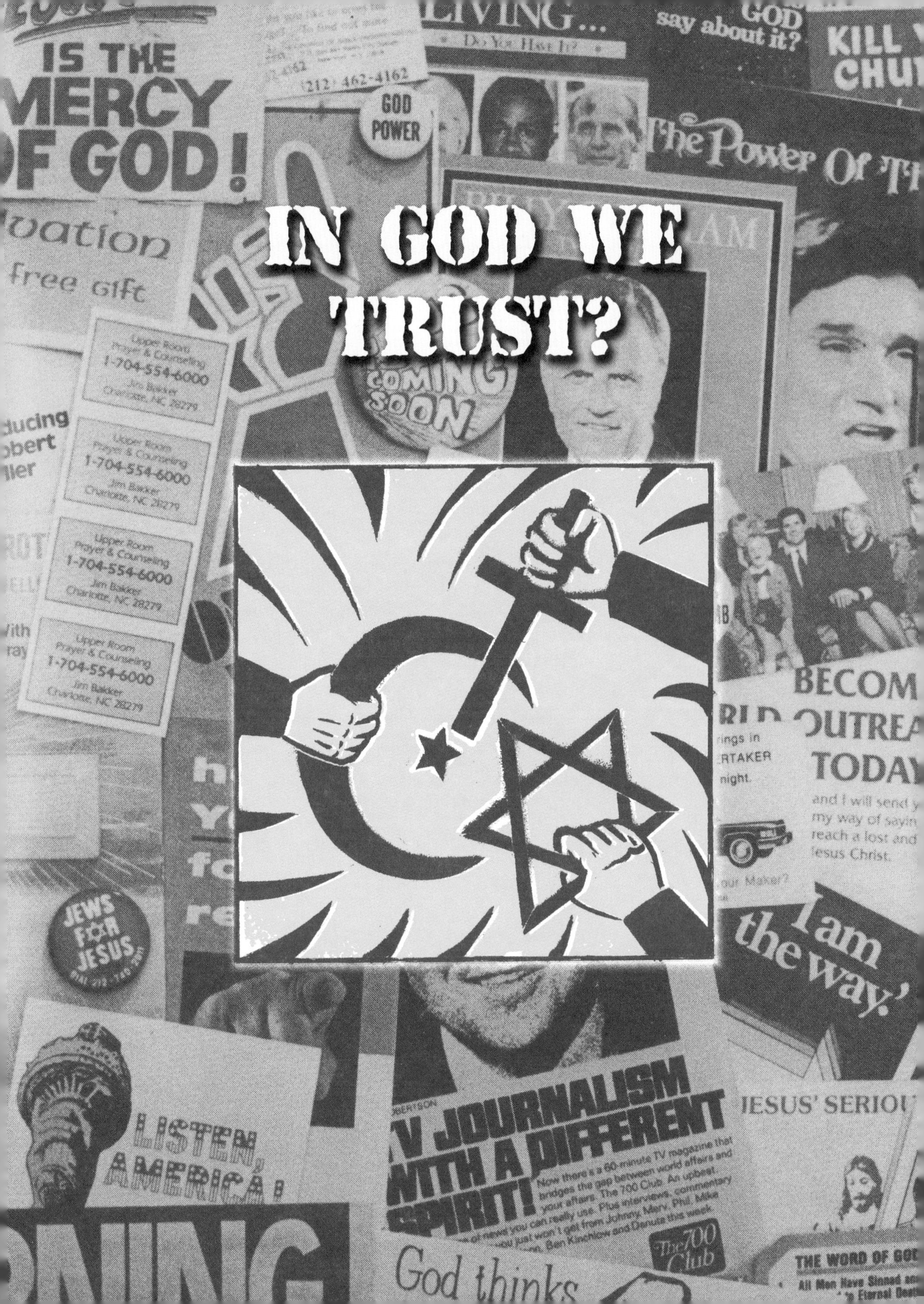
IS THE MERCY OF GOD!
LIVING...
DO YOU HAVE IT?
GOD say about it?
KILL
(212) 462-4162
GOD POWER
The Power Of
vation
free gift
Upper Room
Prayer & Counseling
1-704-554-6000
Jim Bakker
Charlotte, NC 28279
COMING SOON
BECOM
OUTREA
TODAY
and I will send y
my way of sayin
reach a lost and
Jesus Christ.
JEWS FOR JESUS
I am the way.'
JESUS' SERIOU
LISTEN, AMERICA!
TV JOURNALISM WITH A DIFFERENT SPIRIT!
Now there's a 60-minute TV magazine that bridges the gap between world affairs and your affairs. The 700 Club. An upbeat
The 700 Club
God thinks
THE WORD OF GOD

WHAT FOLLOWS IS A VERBATIM TRANSCRIPT OF A RADIO SERMON BY REVEREND JERRY FALWELL...

RAPTURE

"YOU'LL BE RIDING ALONG IN AN AUTOMOBILE..."

"YOU'LL BE THE DRIVER PERHAPS, YOU'RE A CHRISTIAN."

"THERE'LL BE SEVERAL PEOPLE IN THE AUTOMOBILE WITH YOU, MAYBE SOMEONE WHO IS NOT A CHRISTIAN!"

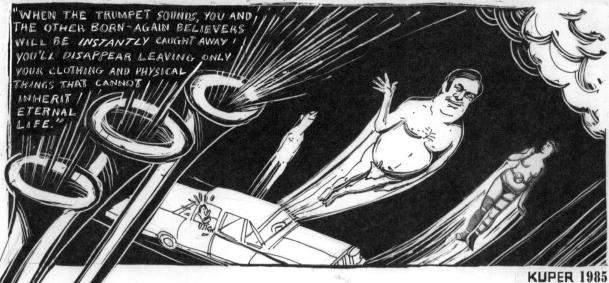

"WHEN THE TRUMPET SOUNDS, YOU AND THE OTHER BORN-AGAIN BELIEVERS WILL BE INSTANTLY CAUGHT AWAY! YOU'LL DISAPPEAR LEAVING ONLY YOUR CLOTHING AND PHYSICAL THINGS THAT CANNOT INHERIT ETERNAL LIFE."

KUPER 1985

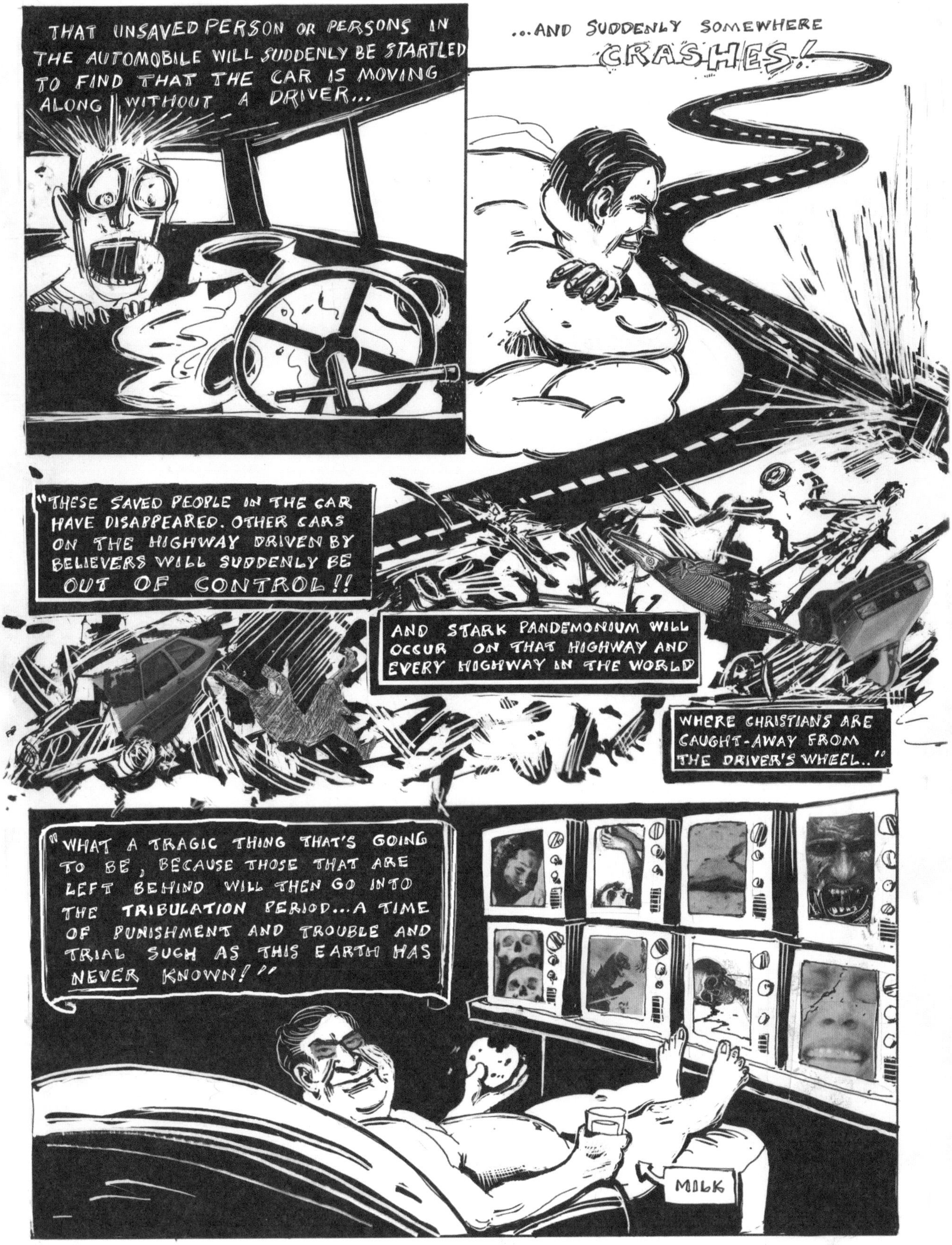

THAT UNSAVED PERSON OR PERSONS IN THE AUTOMOBILE WILL SUDDENLY BE STARTLED TO FIND THAT THE CAR IS MOVING ALONG WITHOUT A DRIVER...
...AND SUDDENLY SOMEWHERE
CRASHES!
"THESE SAVED PEOPLE IN THE CAR HAVE DISAPPEARED. OTHER CARS ON THE HIGHWAY DRIVEN BY BELIEVERS WILL SUDDENLY BE OUT OF CONTROL!!
AND STARK PANDEMONIUM WILL OCCUR ON THAT HIGHWAY AND EVERY HIGHWAY IN THE WORLD
WHERE CHRISTIANS ARE CAUGHT-AWAY FROM THE DRIVER'S WHEEL.."
"WHAT A TRAGIC THING THAT'S GOING TO BE, BECAUSE THOSE THAT ARE LEFT BEHIND WILL THEN GO INTO THE TRIBULATION PERIOD...A TIME OF PUNISHMENT AND TROUBLE AND TRIAL SUCH AS THIS EARTH HAS NEVER KNOWN!"
MILK

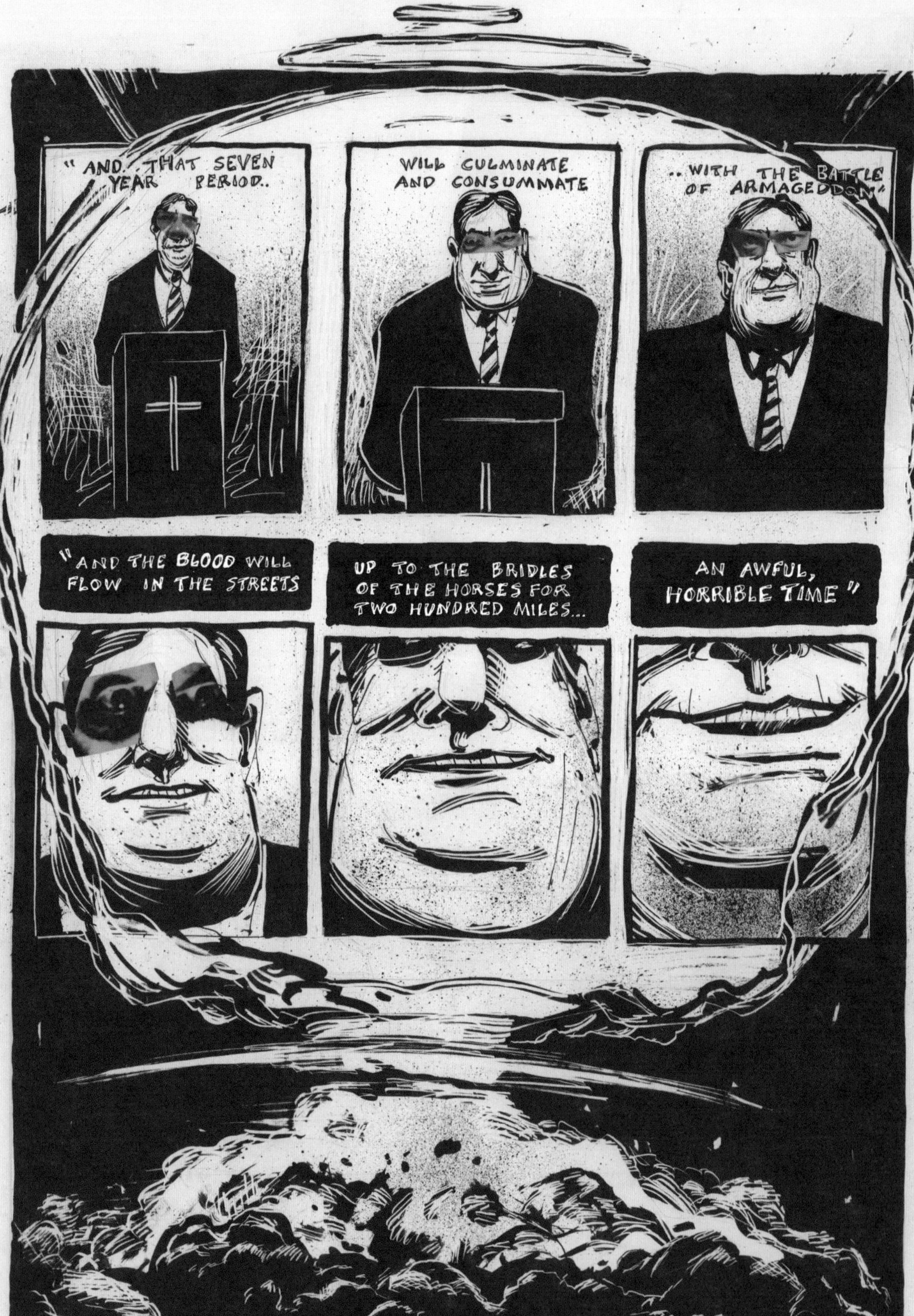
"AND THAT SEVEN YEAR PERIOD..
WILL CULMINATE AND CONSUMMATE
..WITH THE BATTLE OF ARMAGEDDON"
"AND THE BLOOD WILL FLOW IN THE STREETS
UP TO THE BRIDLES OF THE HORSES FOR TWO HUNDRED MILES...
AN AWFUL, HORRIBLE TIME"

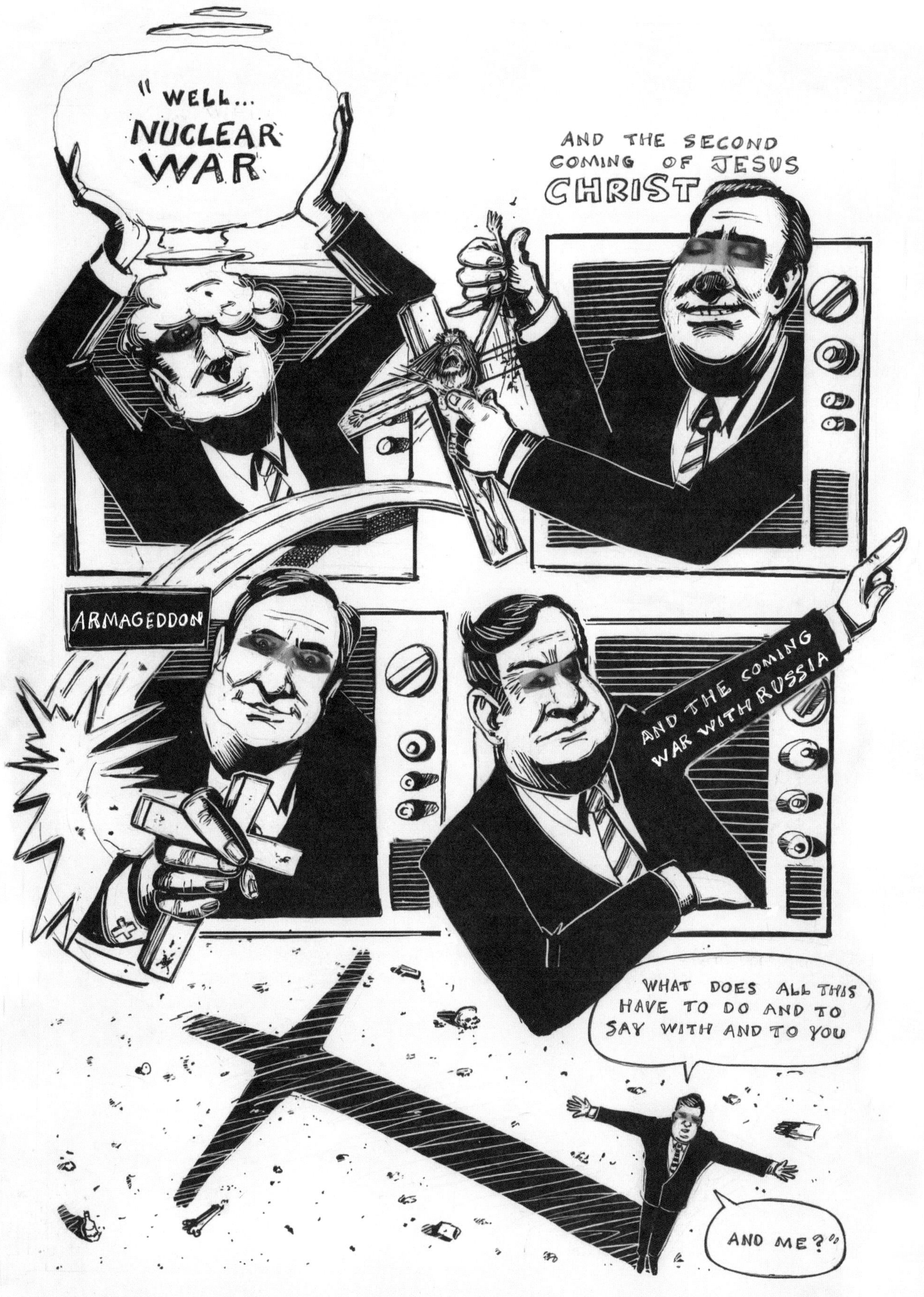
"WELL...
NUCLEAR WAR
AND THE SECOND COMING OF JESUS CHRIST
ARMAGEDDON
AND THE COMING WAR WITH RUSSIA
WHAT DOES ALL THIS HAVE TO DO AND TO SAY WITH AND TO YOU
AND ME?"

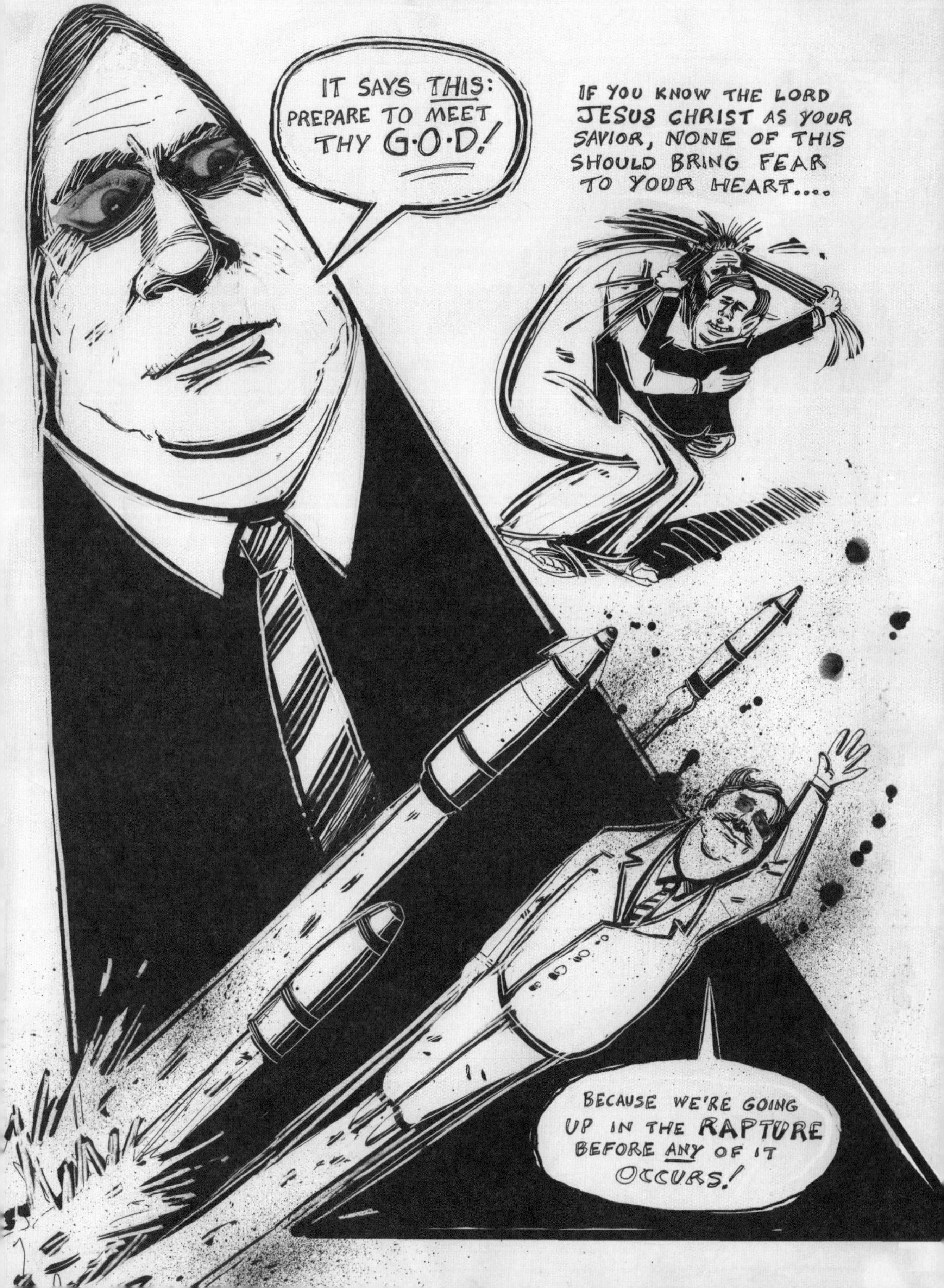
IT SAYS THIS: PREPARE TO MEET THY G·O·D!
IF YOU KNOW THE LORD JESUS CHRIST AS YOUR SAVIOR, NONE OF THIS SHOULD BRING FEAR TO YOUR HEART....
BECAUSE WE'RE GOING UP IN THE RAPTURE BEFORE ANY OF IT OCCURS!

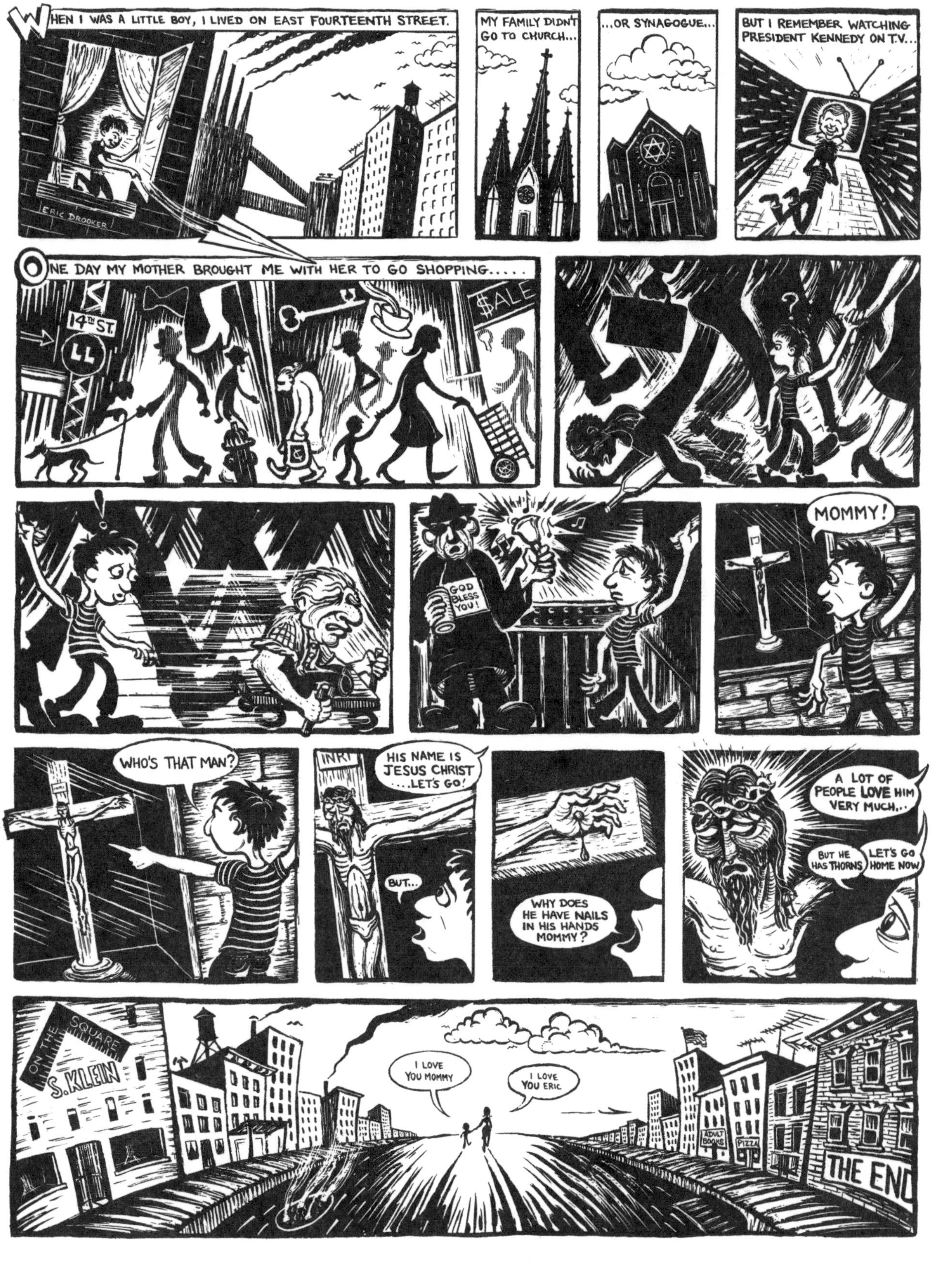
When I was a little boy, I lived on East Fourteenth Street.
Eric Drooker
My family didn't go to church...
...or synagogue...
But I remember watching President Kennedy on T.V...
One day my mother brought me with her to go shopping.....
14th St.
LL
$ale
?
God bless you!
Mommy!
Who's that man?
INRI
His name is Jesus Christ ....Let's go!
But...
Why does he have nails in his hands Mommy?
A lot of people love him very much...
But he has thorns
Let's go home now
On the square
S. Klein
I love you Mommy
I love you Eric.
Adult books
Pizza
The End

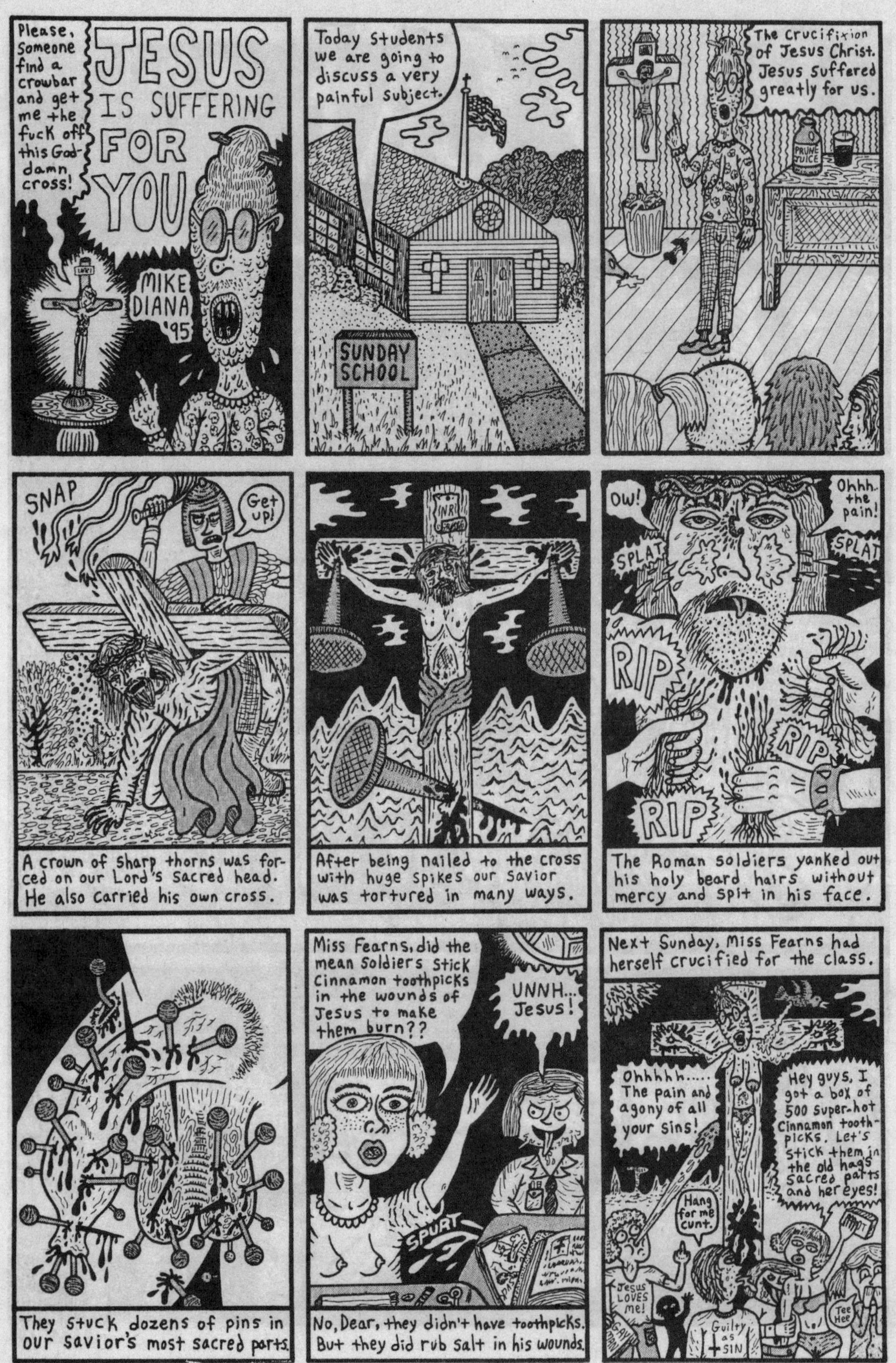
Please, someone find a crowbar and get me the fuck off this God-damn cross!
JESUS IS SUFFERING FOR YOU
MIKE DIANA '95
Today students we are going to discuss a very painful subject.
SUNDAY SCHOOL
The crucifixion of Jesus Christ. Jesus suffered greatly for us.
PRUNE JUICE
SNAP
Get up!
A crown of sharp thorns was forced on our Lord's sacred head. He also carried his own cross.
INRI
After being nailed to the cross with huge spikes our savior was tortured in many ways.
OW!
Ohhh.. the pain!
SPLAT
SPLAT
RIP
RIP
RIP
The Roman soldiers yanked out his holy beard hairs without mercy and spit in his face.
They stuck dozens of pins in our savior's most sacred parts.
Miss Fearns, did the mean soldiers stick cinnamon toothpicks in the wounds of Jesus to make them burn??
UNNH... Jesus!
SPURT
No, Dear, they didn't have toothpicks. But they did rub salt in his wounds.
Next Sunday, Miss Fearns had herself crucified for the class.
Ohhhhh..... The pain and agony of all your sins!
Hey guys, I got a box of 500 super-hot cinnamon toothpicks. Let's stick them in the old hag's sacred parts and her eyes!
Hang for me cunt.
Jesus LOVES me!
Guilty as SIN
Tee Hee

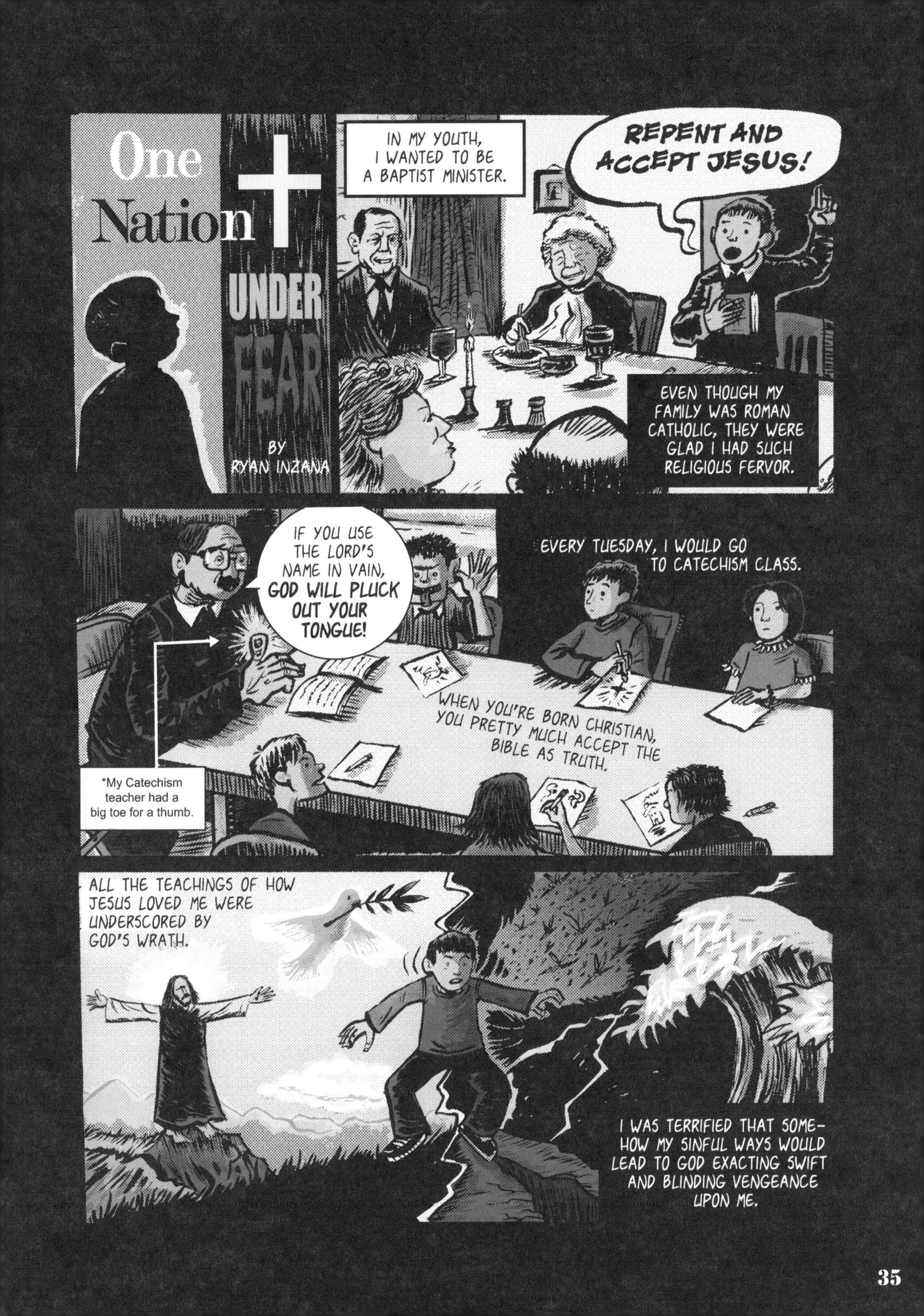
One Nation Under Fear
BY RYAN INZANA
IN MY YOUTH, I WANTED TO BE A BAPTIST MINISTER.
REPENT AND ACCEPT JESUS!
EVEN THOUGH MY FAMILY WAS ROMAN CATHOLIC, THEY WERE GLAD I HAD SUCH RELIGIOUS FERVOR.
IF YOU USE THE LORD'S NAME IN VAIN, GOD WILL PLUCK OUT YOUR TONGUE!
EVERY TUESDAY, I WOULD GO TO CATECHISM CLASS.
WHEN YOU'RE BORN CHRISTIAN, YOU PRETTY MUCH ACCEPT THE BIBLE AS TRUTH.
*My Catechism teacher had a big toe for a thumb.
ALL THE TEACHINGS OF HOW JESUS LOVED ME WERE UNDERSCORED BY GOD'S WRATH.
I WAS TERRIFIED THAT SOME-HOW MY SINFUL WAYS WOULD LEAD TO GOD EXACTING SWIFT AND BLINDING VENGEANCE UPON ME.

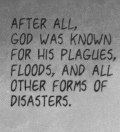

AFTER ALL, GOD WAS KNOWN FOR HIS PLAGUES, FLOODS, AND ALL OTHER FORMS OF DISASTERS.

I DIDN'T KNOW WHAT SCIENTIFIC FORCES IN NATURE CAUSED AN EARTHQUAKE...

WHAT! HOW DARE RYAN INZANA USE MY NAME IN VAIN! I WILL SHOW THAT LITTLE BRAT A THING OR TWO!

...I FIGURED GOD MUST BE PISSED OFF AT SOMETHING OR OTHER.

AROUND THIS TIME, MY MOTHER WAS STARTING A GROUP HOME FOR MOTHERS AND BABIES WITH AIDS IN TRENTON, NJ.

WE DON'T WANT **AIDS** IN THIS NEIGHBORHOOD!

GOD HATES AIDS

LOCAL RELIGIOUS ORGANIZATIONS PROTESTED THE GROUP HOME.

THEY SAID THAT GOD WAS PUNISHING THE AIDS VICTIMS FOR THEIR WICKED WAYS.

I WONDERED WHY GOD WOULD WANT TO PUNISH SICK WOMEN AND CHILDREN...

...MY PUZZLEMENT QUICKLY TURNED TO ANGER.

IF GOD HAS SO MUCH LOVE, WHY WOULD HE WANNA KILL WOMEN AND KIDS?

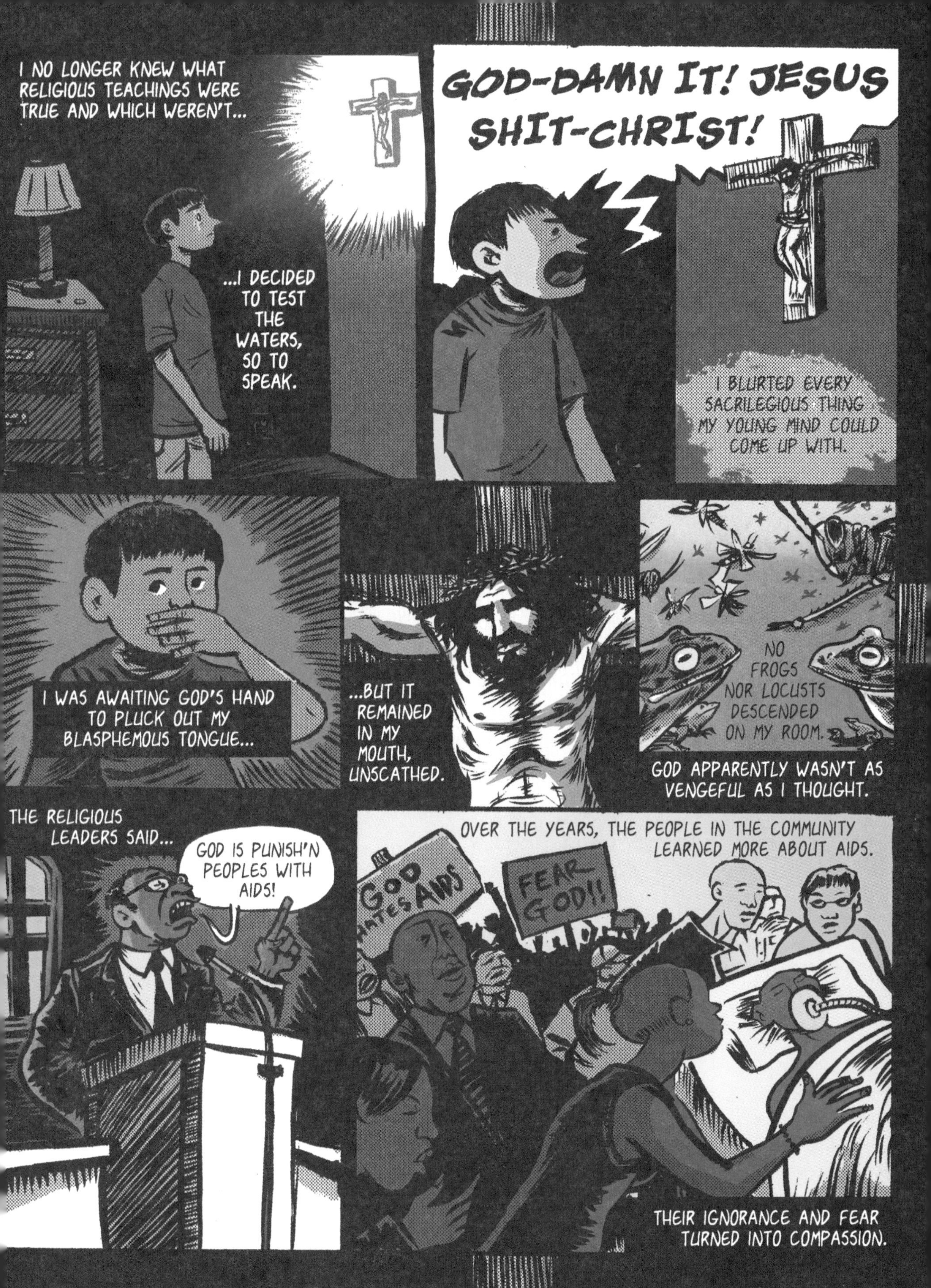

I NO LONGER KNEW WHAT RELIGIOUS TEACHINGS WERE TRUE AND WHICH WEREN'T...
...I DECIDED TO TEST THE WATERS, SO TO SPEAK.
GOD-DAMN IT! JESUS SHIT-CHRIST!
I BLURTED EVERY SACRILEGIOUS THING MY YOUNG MIND COULD COME UP WITH.
I WAS AWAITING GOD'S HAND TO PLUCK OUT MY BLASPHEMOUS TONGUE...
...BUT IT REMAINED IN MY MOUTH, UNSCATHED.
NO FROGS NOR LOCUSTS DESCENDED ON MY ROOM.
GOD APPARENTLY WASN'T AS VENGEFUL AS I THOUGHT.
THE RELIGIOUS LEADERS SAID...
GOD IS PUNISH'N PEOPLES WITH AIDS!
OVER THE YEARS, THE PEOPLE IN THE COMMUNITY LEARNED MORE ABOUT AIDS.
GOD HATES AIDS
FEAR GOD!!
THEIR IGNORANCE AND FEAR TURNED INTO COMPASSION.

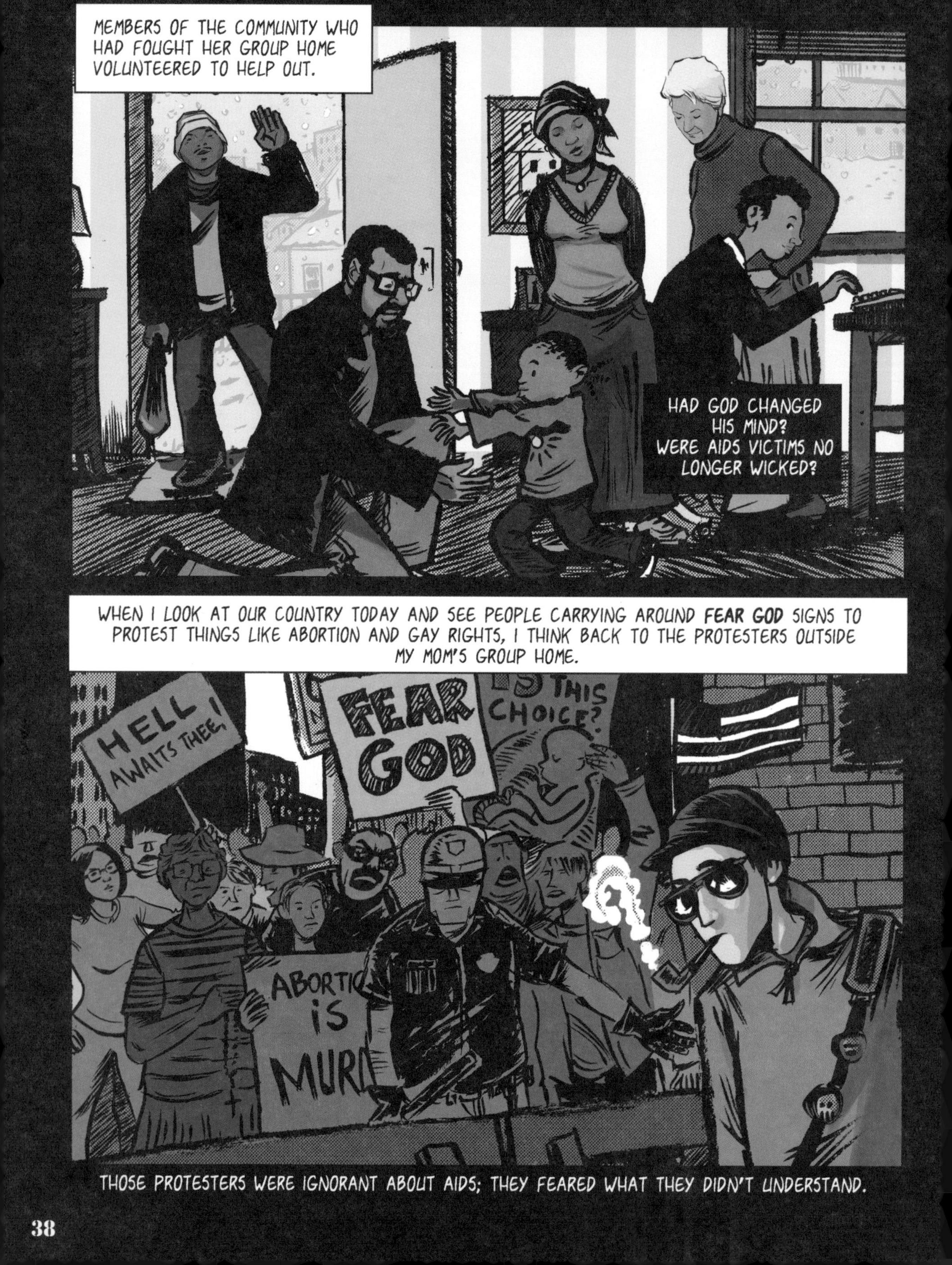
MEMBERS OF THE COMMUNITY WHO HAD FOUGHT HER GROUP HOME VOLUNTEERED TO HELP OUT.
HAD GOD CHANGED HIS MIND? WERE AIDS VICTIMS NO LONGER WICKED?
WHEN I LOOK AT OUR COUNTRY TODAY AND SEE PEOPLE CARRYING AROUND **FEAR GOD** SIGNS TO PROTEST THINGS LIKE ABORTION AND GAY RIGHTS, I THINK BACK TO THE PROTESTERS OUTSIDE MY MOM'S GROUP HOME.
HELL AWAITS THEE!
FEAR GOD
IS THIS CHOICE?
ABORTIO IS MUR
THOSE PROTESTERS WERE IGNORANT ABOUT AIDS; THEY FEARED WHAT THEY DIDN'T UNDERSTAND.

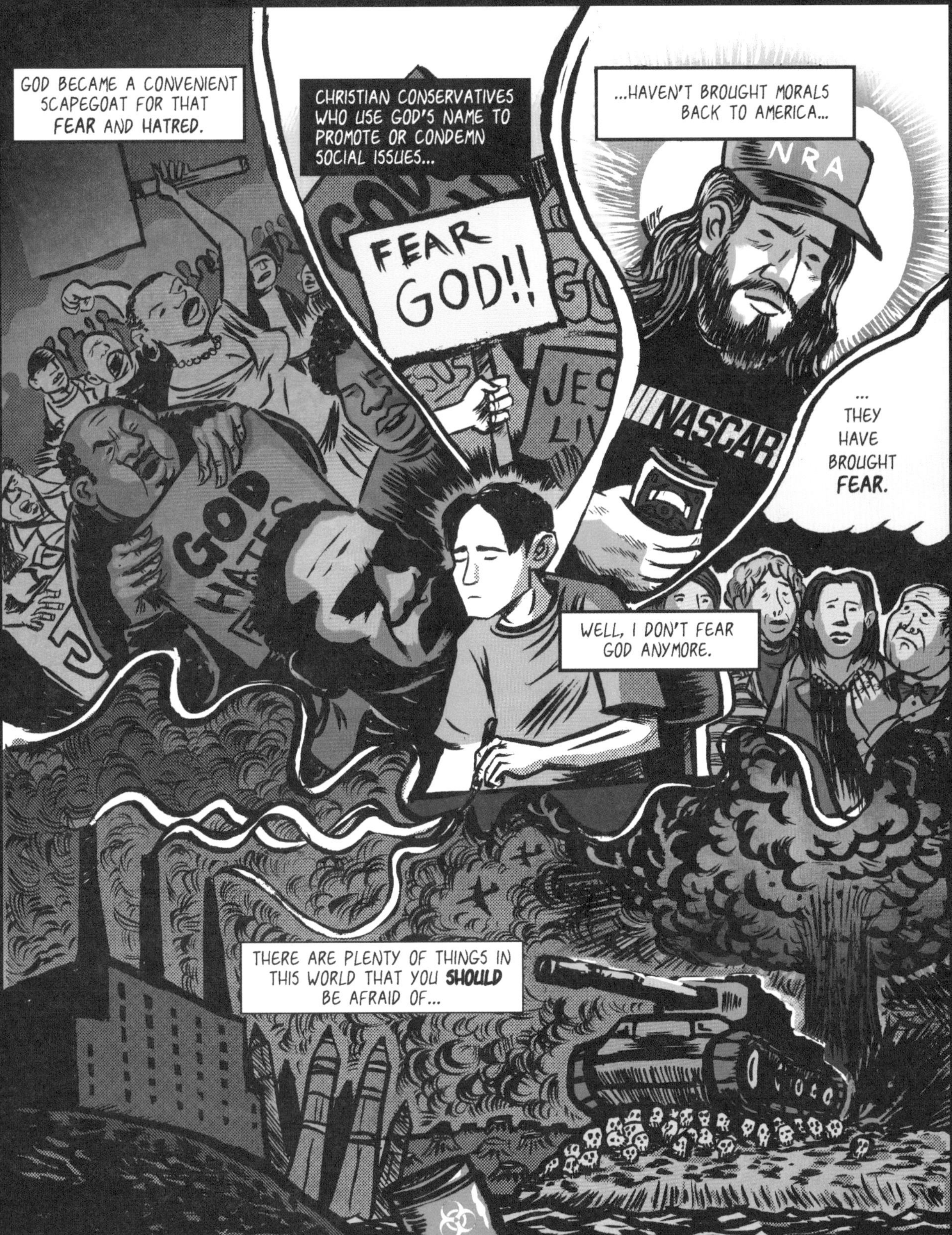

GOD BECAME A CONVENIENT SCAPEGOAT FOR THAT FEAR AND HATRED.
CHRISTIAN CONSERVATIVES WHO USE GOD'S NAME TO PROMOTE OR CONDEMN SOCIAL ISSUES...
FEAR GOD!!
...HAVEN'T BROUGHT MORALS BACK TO AMERICA...
NRA
NASCAR
GOD HATES
... THEY HAVE BROUGHT FEAR.
WELL, I DON'T FEAR GOD ANYMORE.
THERE ARE PLENTY OF THINGS IN THIS WORLD THAT YOU SHOULD BE AFRAID OF...

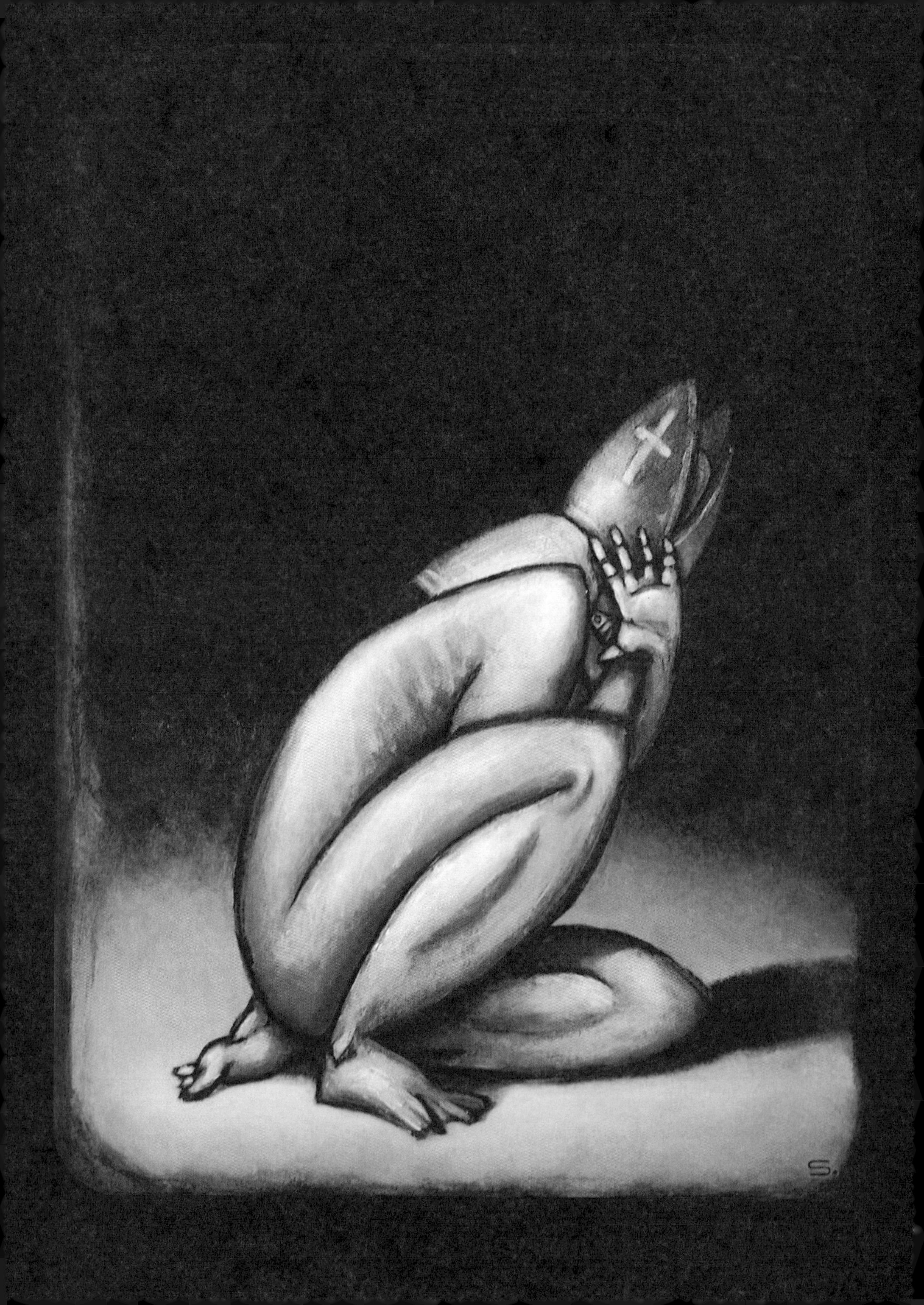

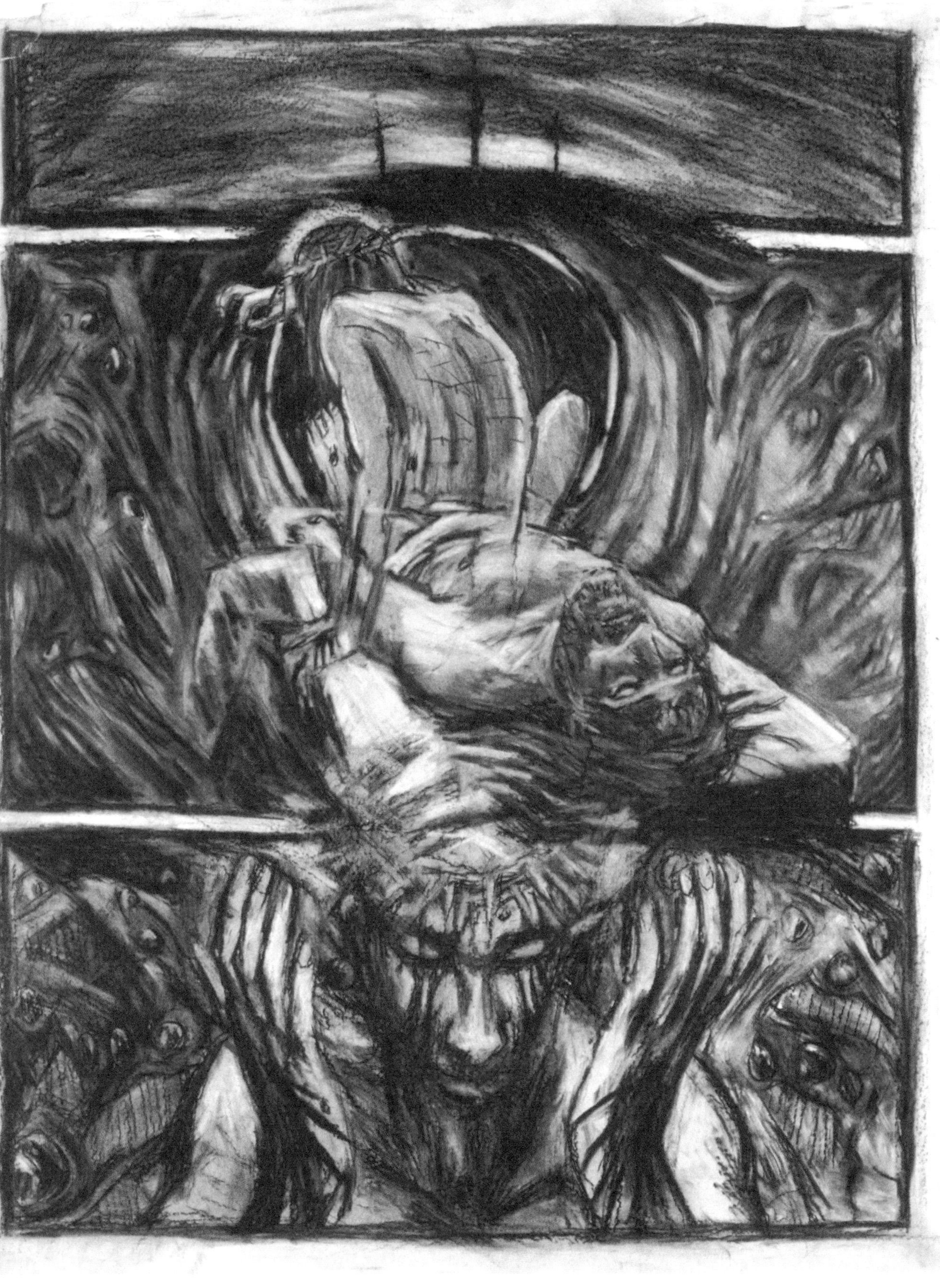

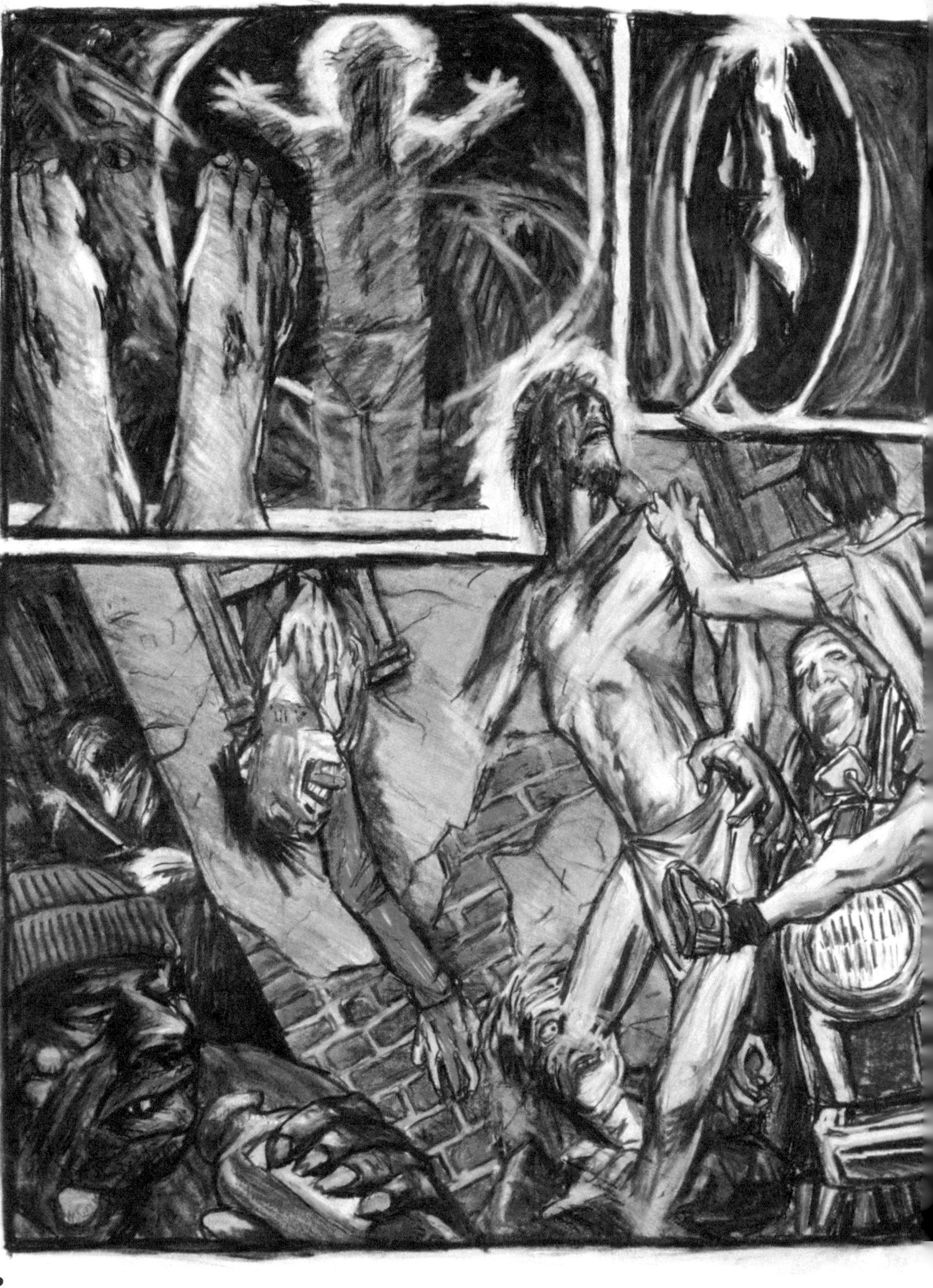

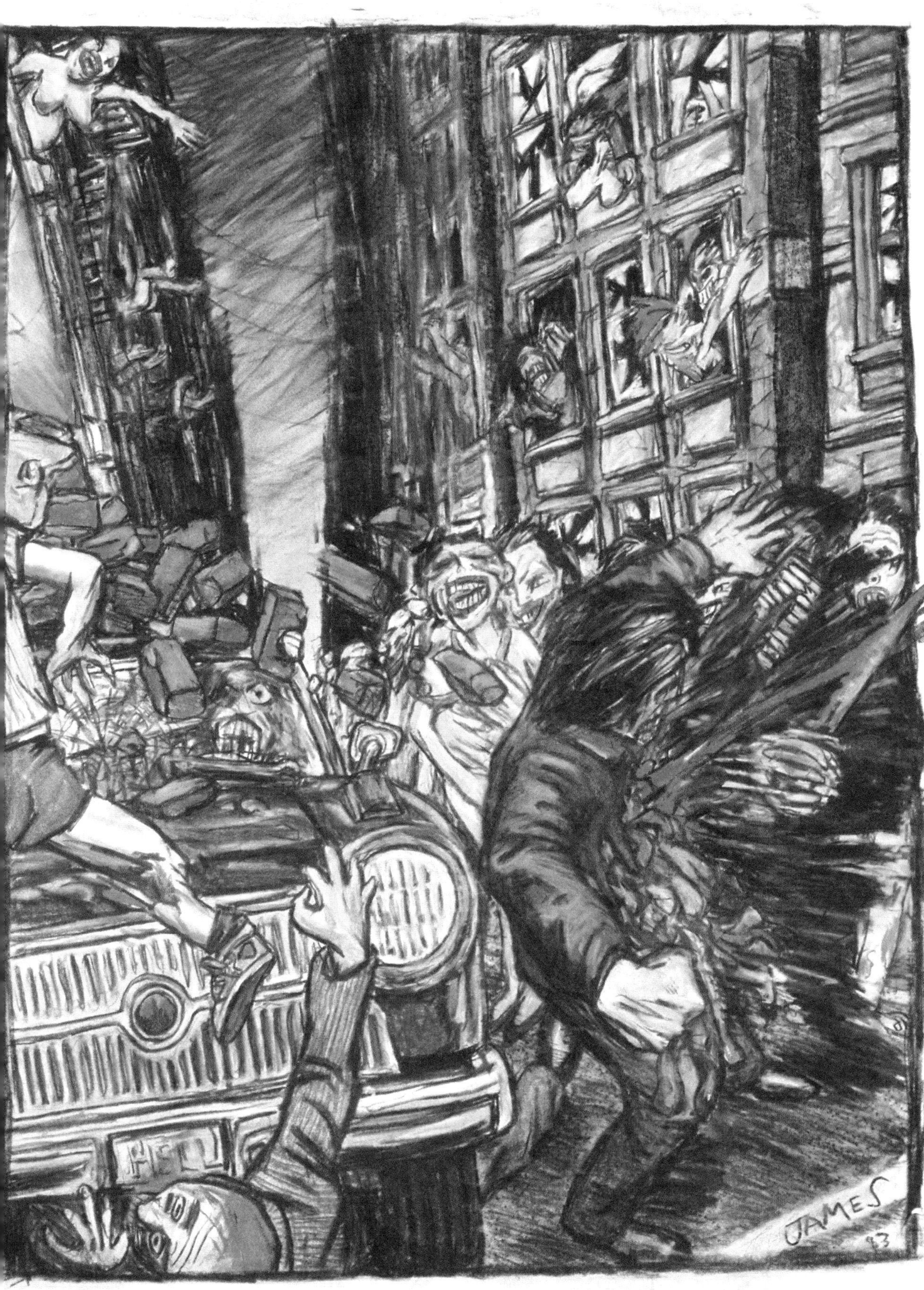
JAMES
93

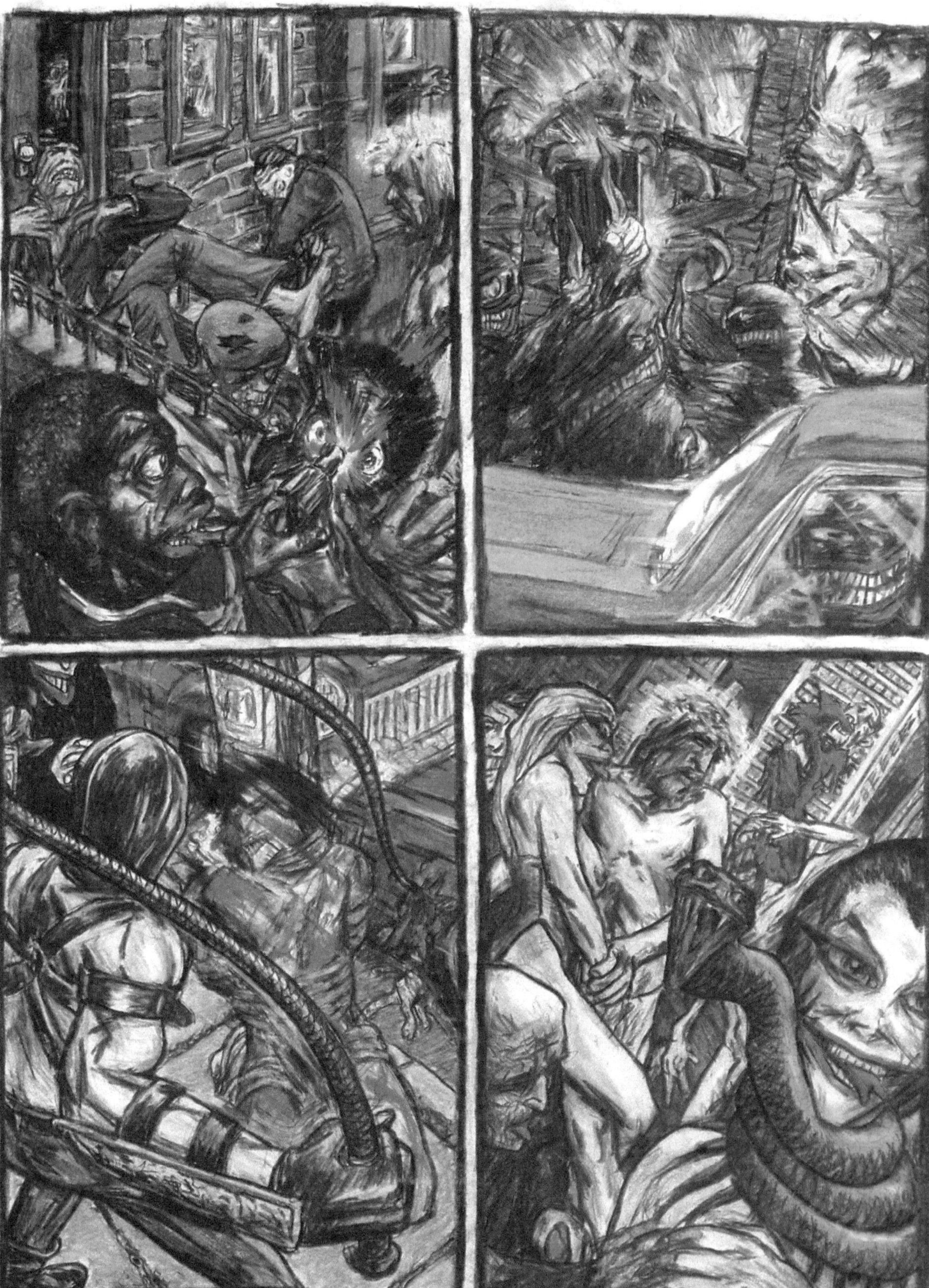

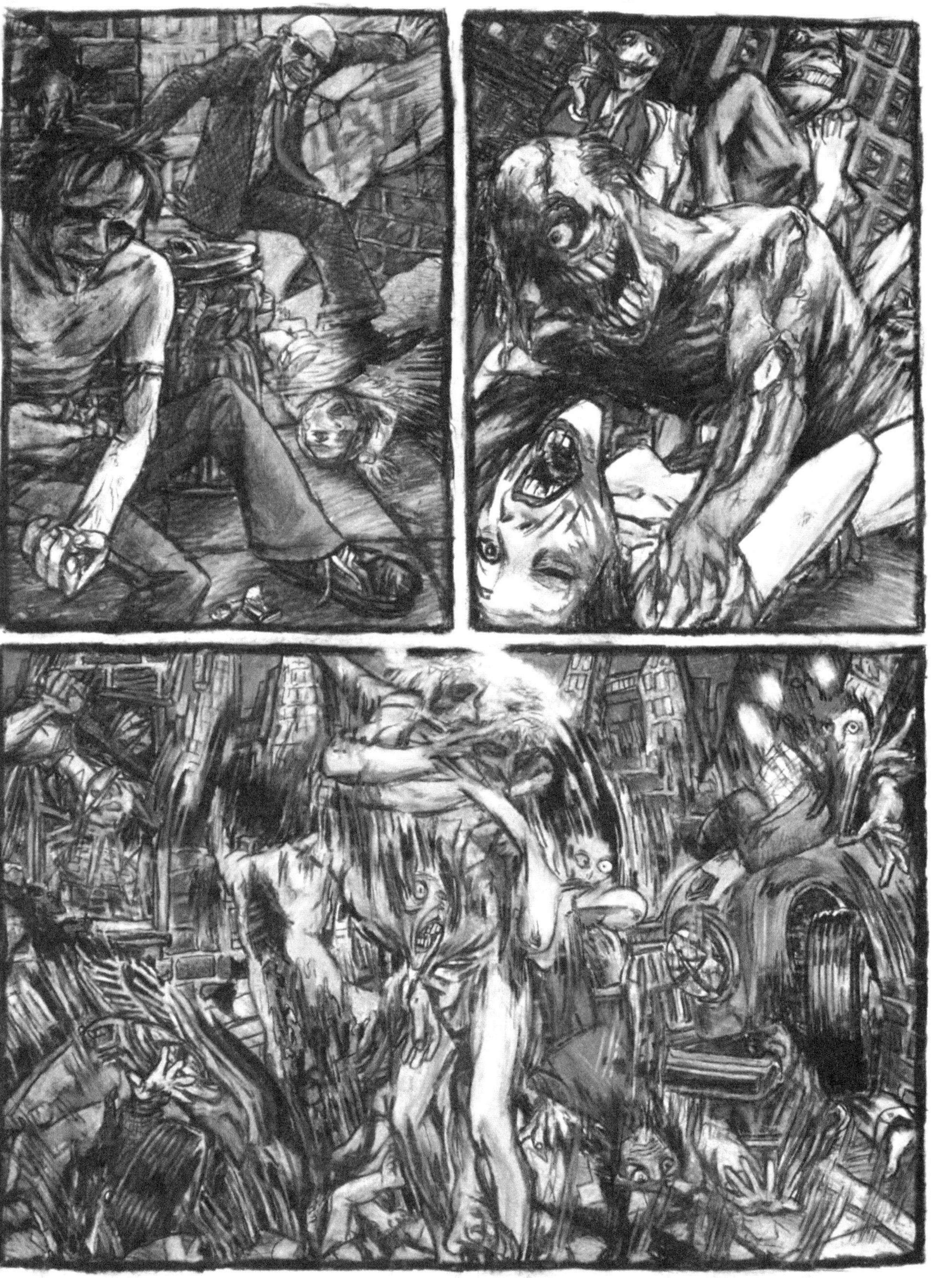

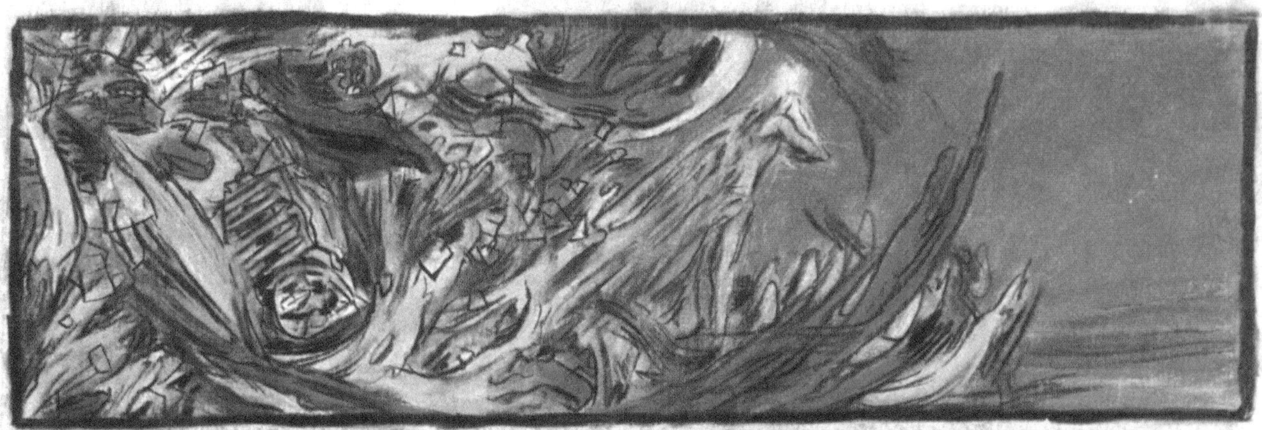

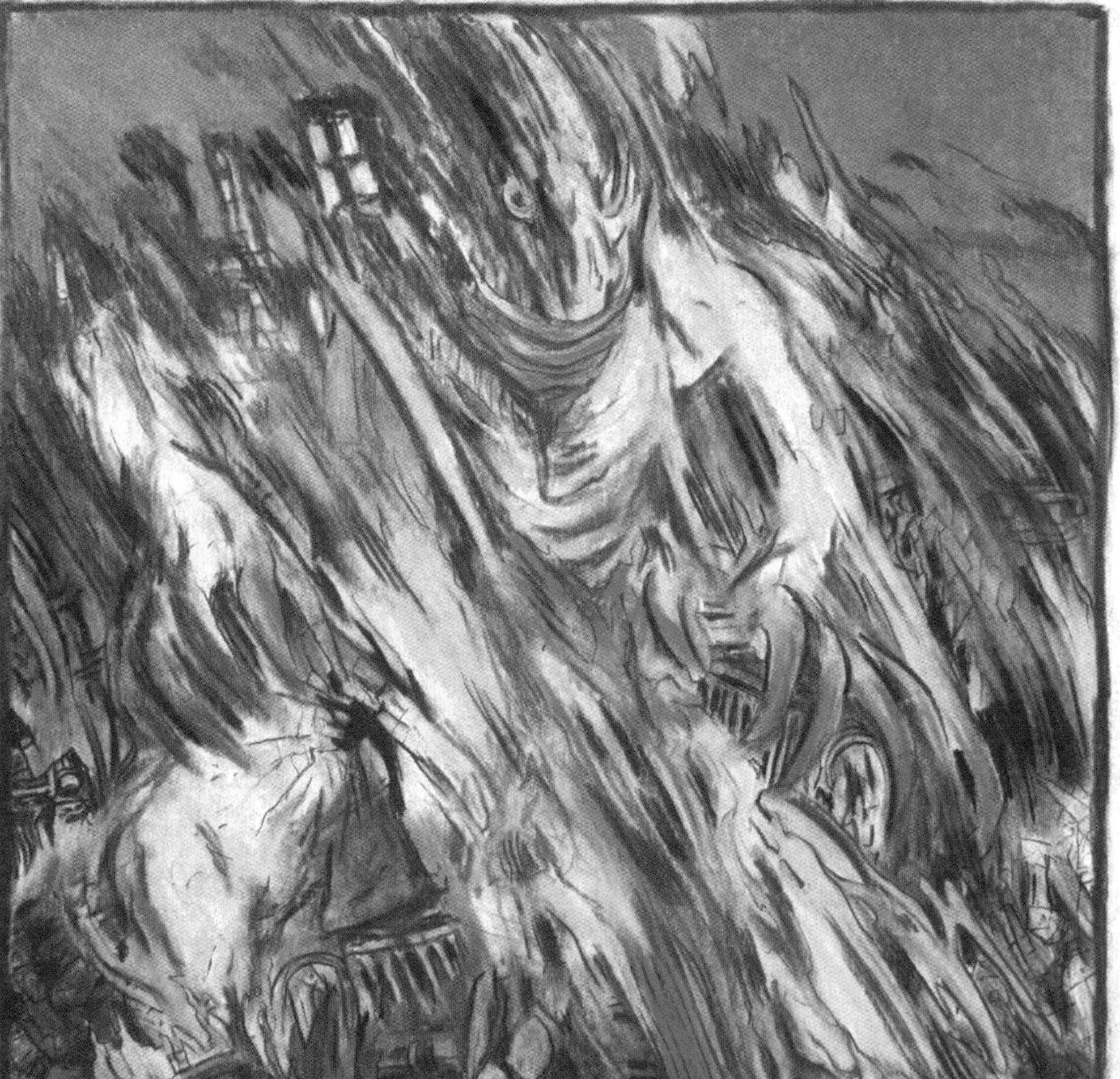

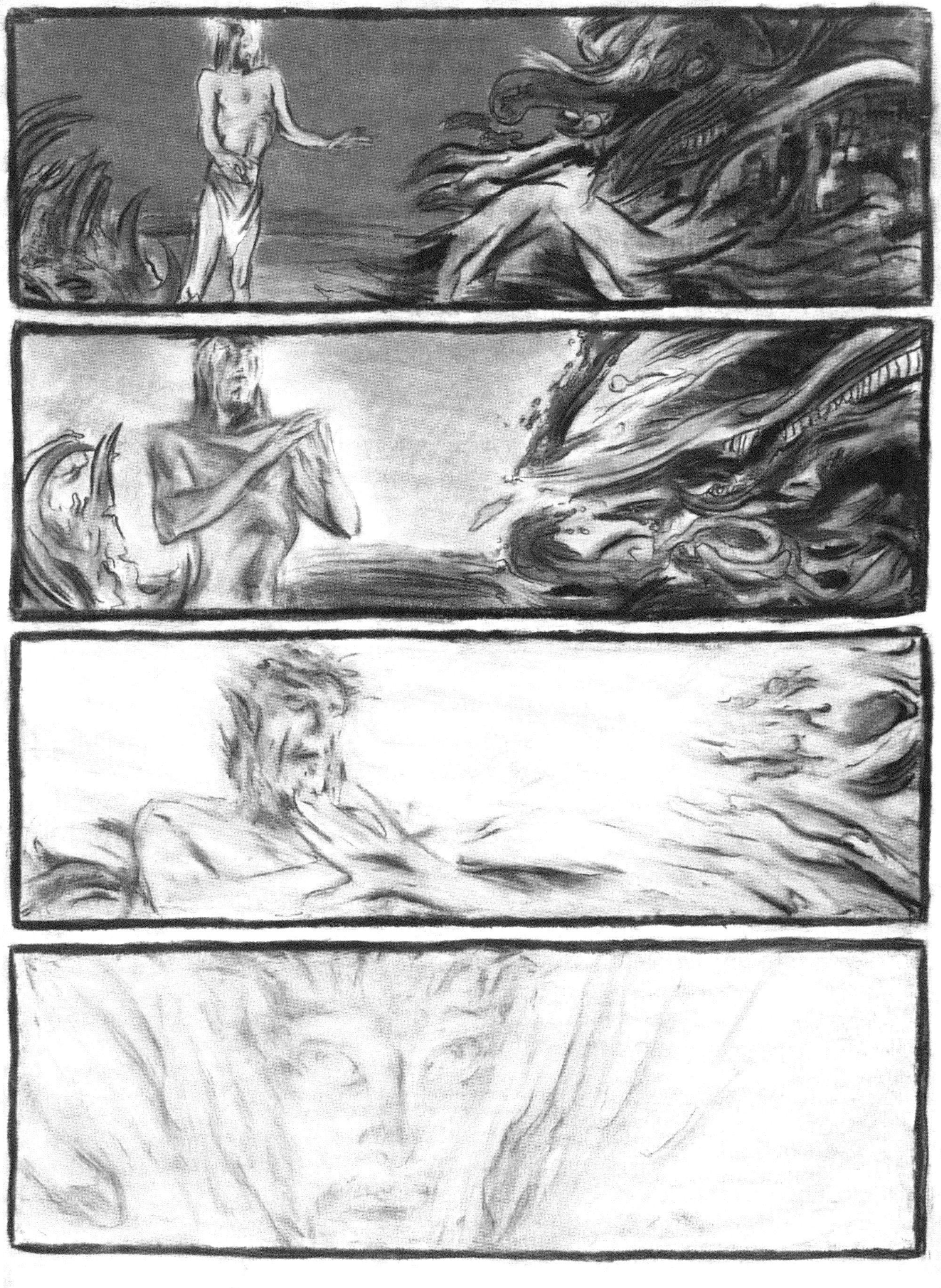

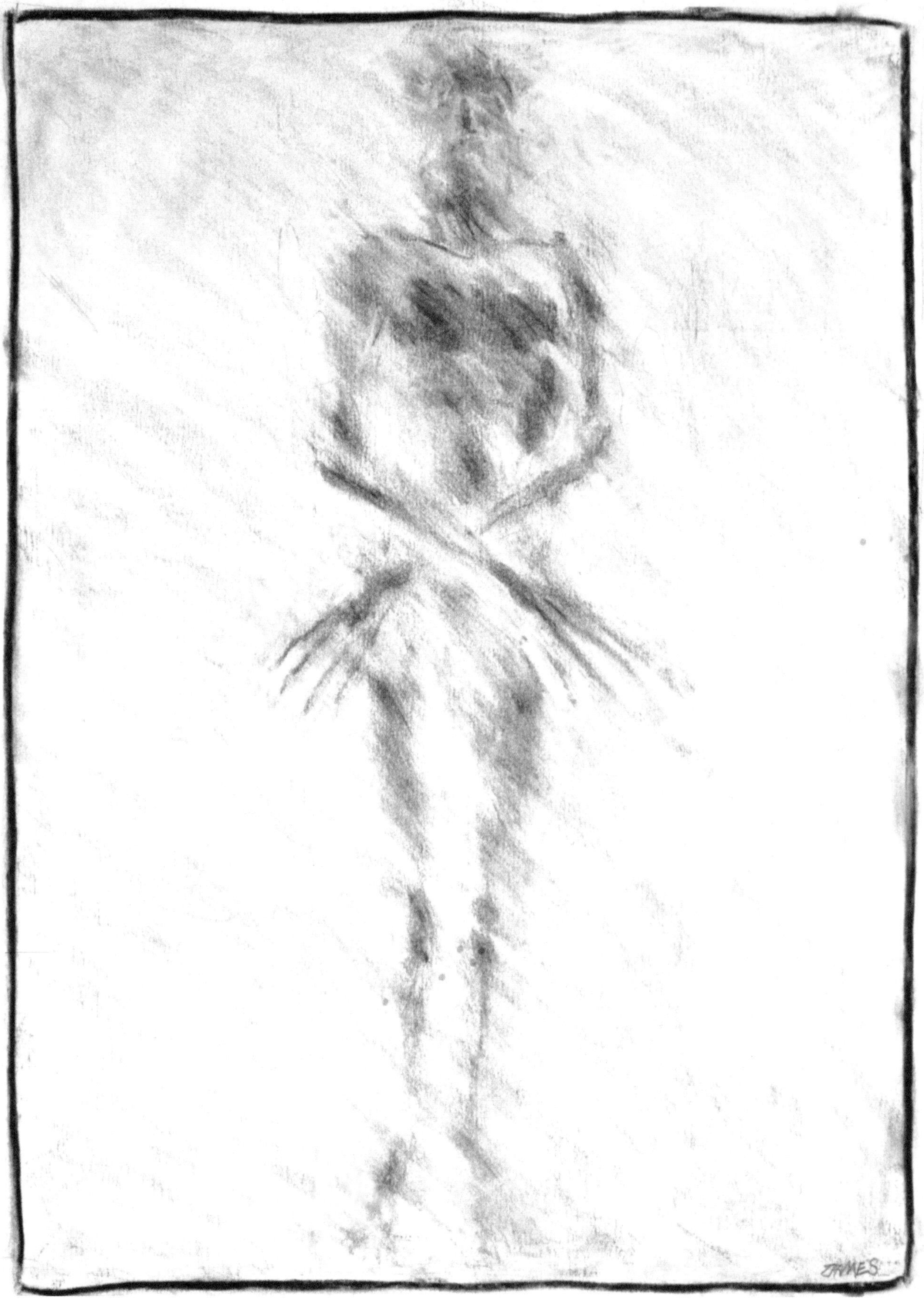
JAMES

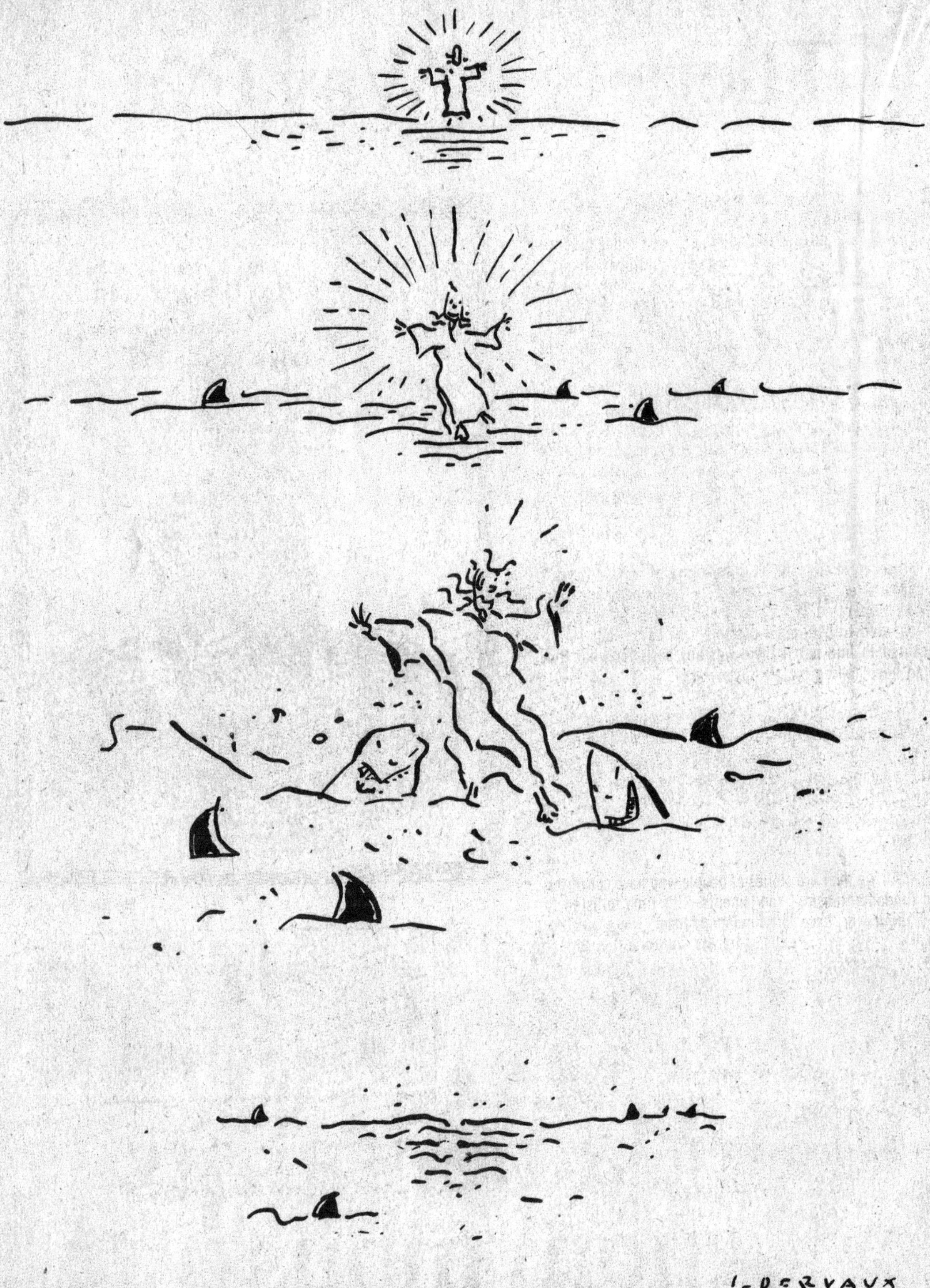

I. DERVAUX

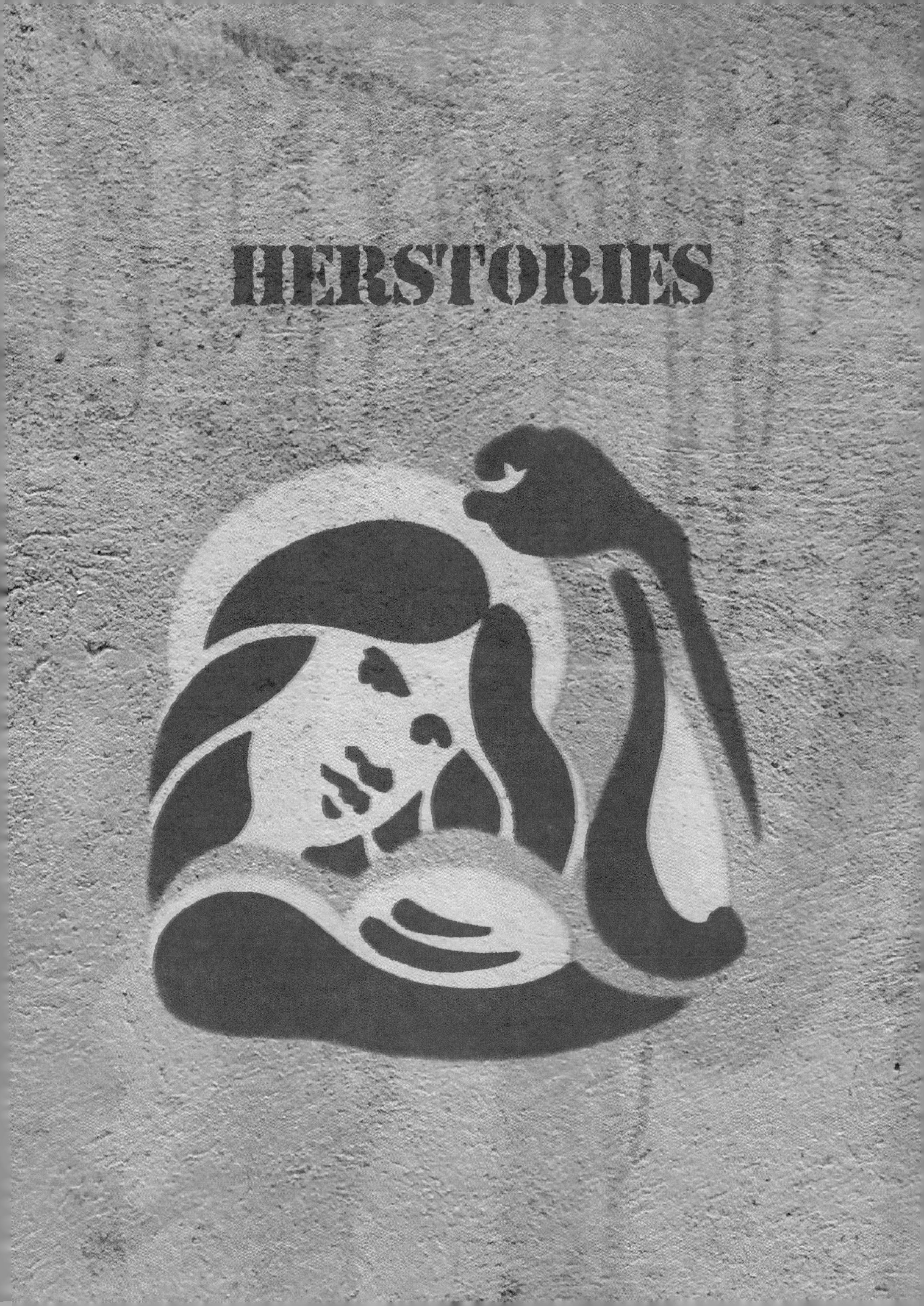
HERSTORIES

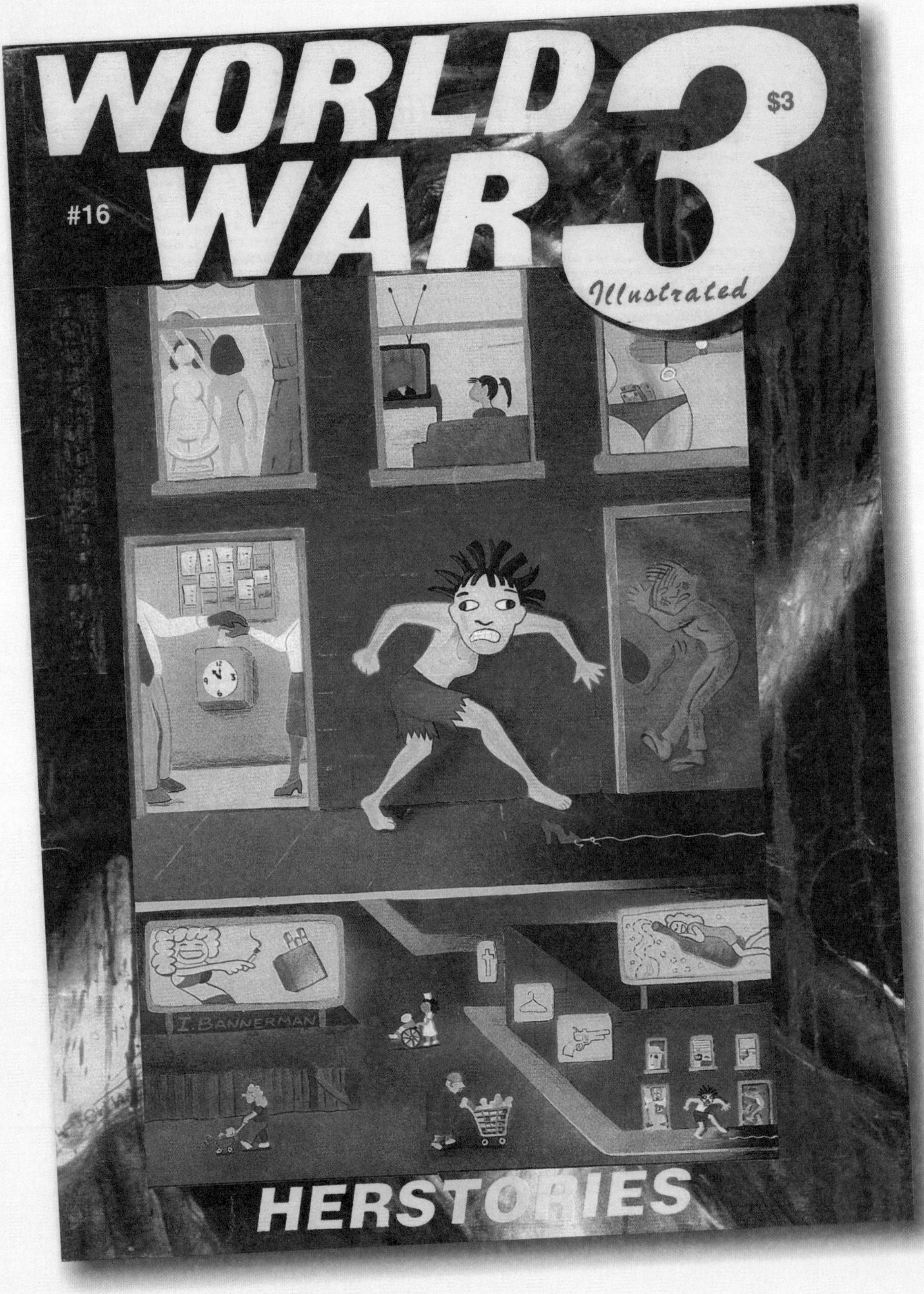
WORLD WAR 3
Illustrated
$3
#16
I. BANNERMAN
HERSTORIES

SINGLE WOMEN WITH CHILDREN, THE ELDERLY, THE INFIRM, THE DISABLED, THE UNEMPLOYED..............CAPITALISM OFFERS NO SYSTEMATIC SUPPORT TO THESE PEOPLE SO THAT DEVICES OUTSIDE THE CAPITALIST DISTRIBUTION SYSTEM BECOME NECESSARY:...WELFARE PUBLIC HOUSING, SOCIALIZED MEDICINE...EXIST TO SUPPORT PEOPLE OF LOW PRODUCTIVITY BUT THEY ALL CONFLICT WITH THE BASIC PRINCIPLES OF CAPITALISM AND THEREFORE TEND TO BE POORLY-RUN, HUMILIATING, AND SHORT-LIVED..............REFORM OR REVOLUTION?

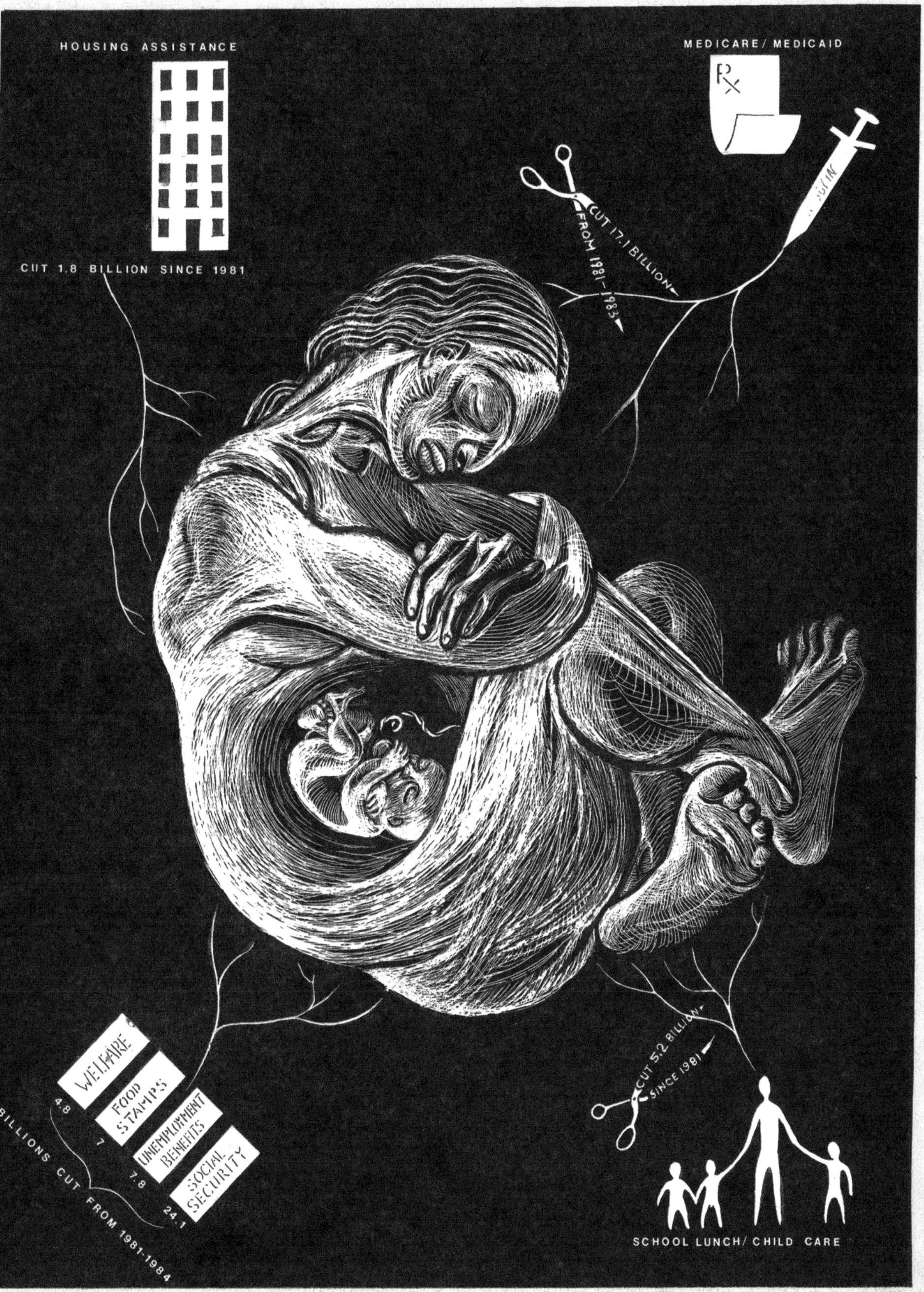
HOUSING ASSISTANCE
CUT 1.8 BILLION SINCE 1981
MEDICARE/ MEDICAID
Rx
CUT 17.1 BILLION FROM 1981-1983
WELFARE
FOOD STAMPS
UNEMPLOYMENT BENEFITS
SOCIAL SECURITY
4.8
7
7.8
24.1
BILLIONS CUT FROM 1981-1984
CUT 5.2 BILLION SINCE 1981
SCHOOL LUNCH/ CHILD CARE

source of statistics: Congressional Budget Office, Washington.

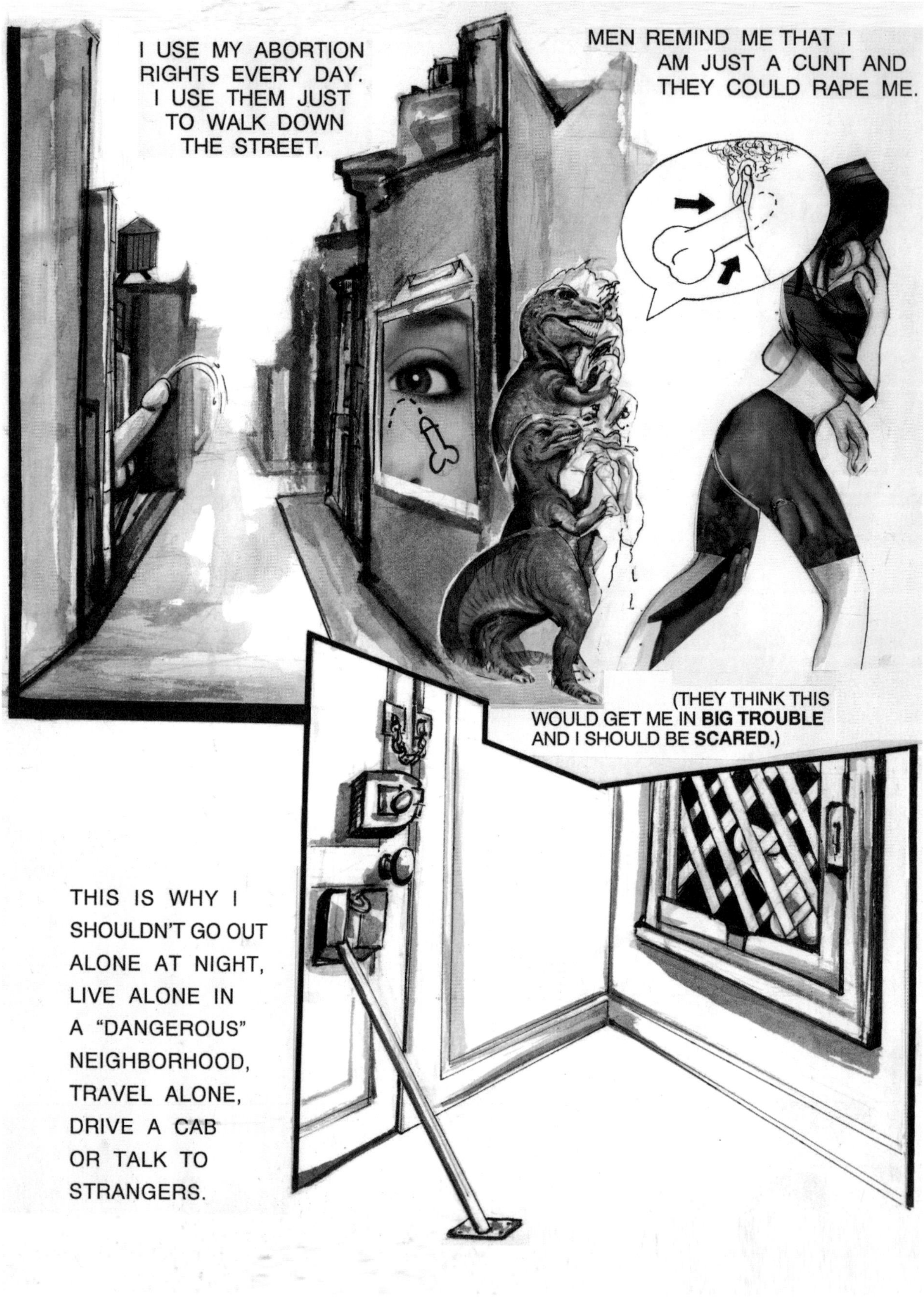
I USE MY ABORTION RIGHTS EVERY DAY. I USE THEM JUST TO WALK DOWN THE STREET.
MEN REMIND ME THAT I AM JUST A CUNT AND THEY COULD RAPE ME.
(THEY THINK THIS WOULD GET ME IN **BIG TROUBLE** AND I SHOULD BE **SCARED.**)
THIS IS WHY I SHOULDN'T GO OUT ALONE AT NIGHT, LIVE ALONE IN A "DANGEROUS" NEIGHBORHOOD, TRAVEL ALONE, DRIVE A CAB OR TALK TO STRANGERS.

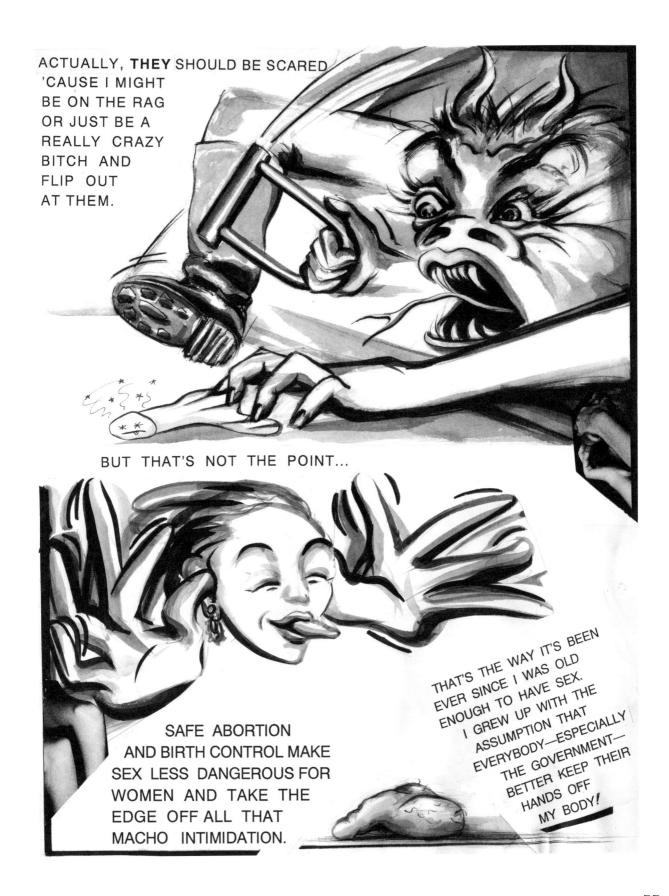

ACTUALLY, **THEY** SHOULD BE SCARED 'CAUSE I MIGHT BE ON THE RAG OR JUST BE A REALLY CRAZY BITCH AND FLIP OUT AT THEM.

BUT THAT'S NOT THE POINT...

SAFE ABORTION AND BIRTH CONTROL MAKE SEX LESS DANGEROUS FOR WOMEN AND TAKE THE EDGE OFF ALL THAT MACHO INTIMIDATION.

THAT'S THE WAY IT'S BEEN EVER SINCE I WAS OLD ENOUGH TO HAVE SEX. I GREW UP WITH THE ASSUMPTION THAT EVERYBODY—ESPECIALLY THE GOVERNMENT—BETTER KEEP THEIR HANDS OFF MY BODY!

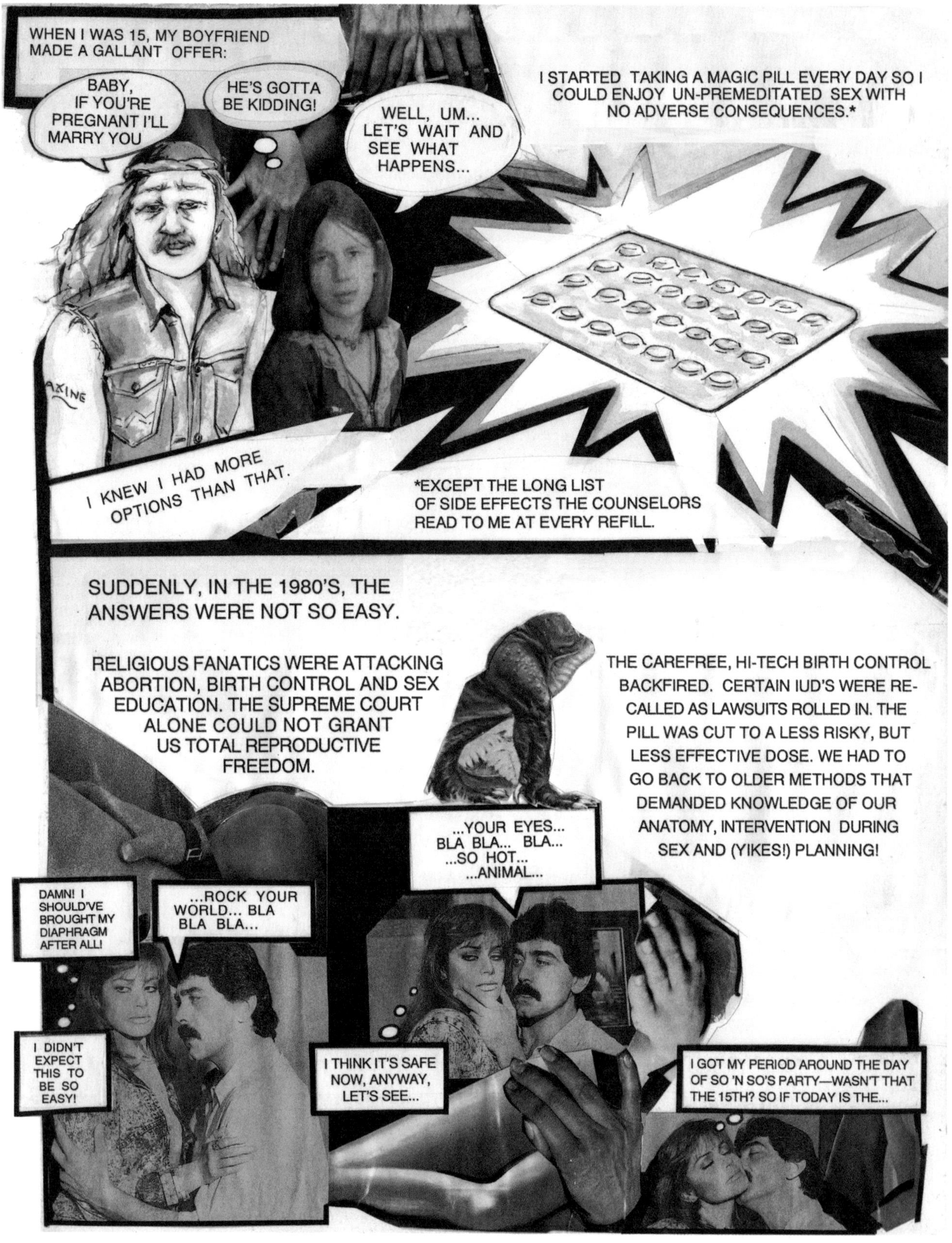
WHEN I WAS 15, MY BOYFRIEND MADE A GALLANT OFFER:
BABY, IF YOU'RE PREGNANT I'LL MARRY YOU
HE'S GOTTA BE KIDDING!
WELL, UM... LET'S WAIT AND SEE WHAT HAPPENS...
I STARTED TAKING A MAGIC PILL EVERY DAY SO I COULD ENJOY UN-PREMEDITATED SEX WITH NO ADVERSE CONSEQUENCES.*
I KNEW I HAD MORE OPTIONS THAN THAT.
*EXCEPT THE LONG LIST OF SIDE EFFECTS THE COUNSELORS READ TO ME AT EVERY REFILL.
SUDDENLY, IN THE 1980'S, THE ANSWERS WERE NOT SO EASY.
RELIGIOUS FANATICS WERE ATTACKING ABORTION, BIRTH CONTROL AND SEX EDUCATION. THE SUPREME COURT ALONE COULD NOT GRANT US TOTAL REPRODUCTIVE FREEDOM.
THE CAREFREE, HI-TECH BIRTH CONTROL BACKFIRED. CERTAIN IUD'S WERE RE-CALLED AS LAWSUITS ROLLED IN. THE PILL WAS CUT TO A LESS RISKY, BUT LESS EFFECTIVE DOSE. WE HAD TO GO BACK TO OLDER METHODS THAT DEMANDED KNOWLEDGE OF OUR ANATOMY, INTERVENTION DURING SEX AND (YIKES!) PLANNING!
DAMN! I SHOULD'VE BROUGHT MY DIAPHRAGM AFTER ALL!
...ROCK YOUR WORLD... BLA BLA BLA...
I DIDN'T EXPECT THIS TO BE SO EASY!
...YOUR EYES... BLA BLA... BLA... ...SO HOT... ...ANIMAL...
I THINK IT'S SAFE NOW, ANYWAY, LET'S SEE...
I GOT MY PERIOD AROUND THE DAY OF SO 'N SO'S PARTY—WASN'T THAT THE 15TH? SO IF TODAY IS THE...

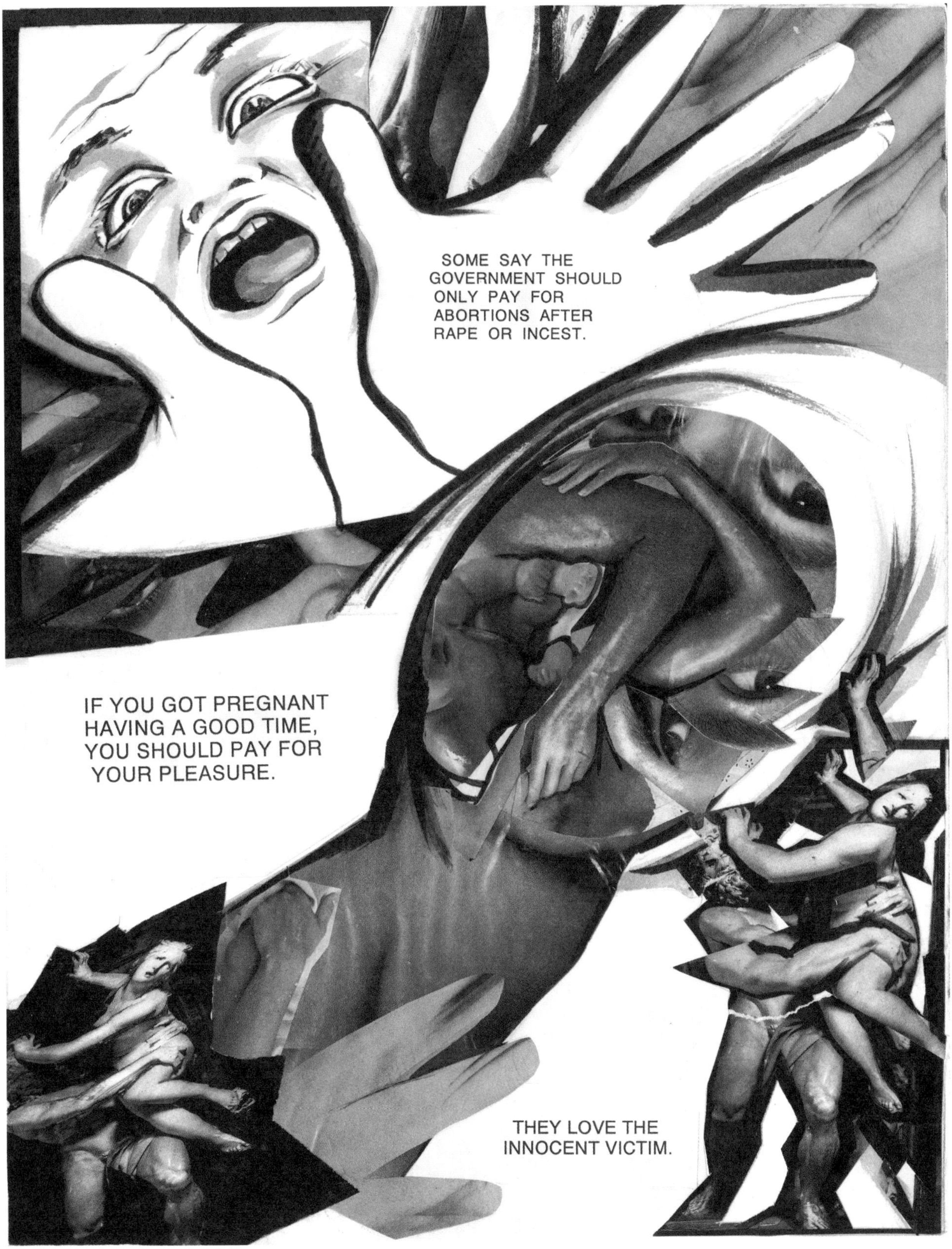
SOME SAY THE GOVERNMENT SHOULD ONLY PAY FOR ABORTIONS AFTER RAPE OR INCEST.
IF YOU GOT PREGNANT HAVING A GOOD TIME, YOU SHOULD PAY FOR YOUR PLEASURE.
THEY LOVE THE INNOCENT VICTIM.

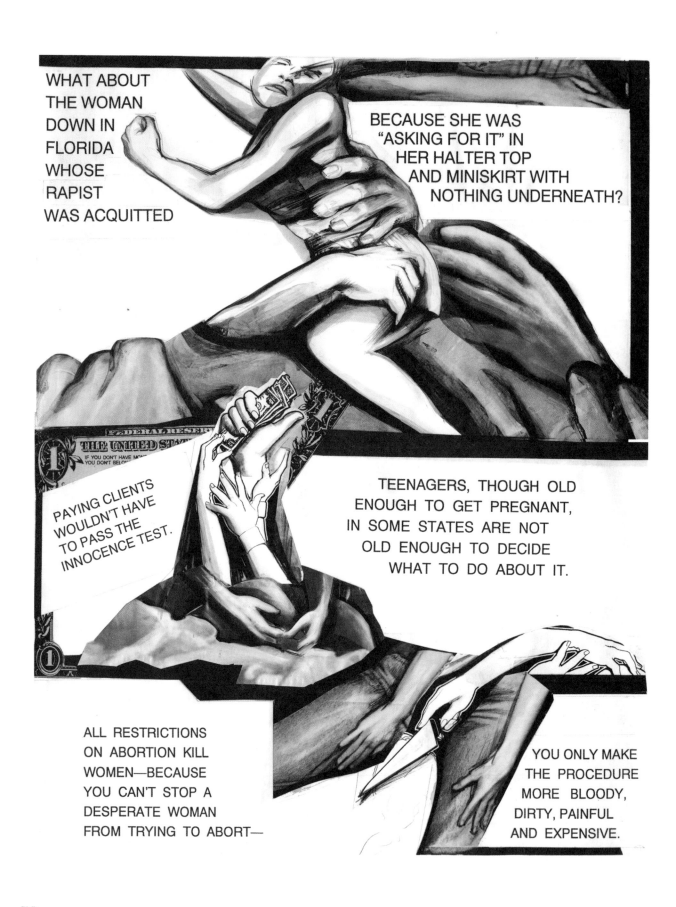

WHAT ABOUT THE WOMAN DOWN IN FLORIDA WHOSE RAPIST WAS ACQUITTED

BECAUSE SHE WAS "ASKING FOR IT" IN HER HALTER TOP AND MINISKIRT WITH NOTHING UNDERNEATH?

PAYING CLIENTS WOULDN'T HAVE TO PASS THE INNOCENCE TEST.

TEENAGERS, THOUGH OLD ENOUGH TO GET PREGNANT, IN SOME STATES ARE NOT OLD ENOUGH TO DECIDE WHAT TO DO ABOUT IT.

ALL RESTRICTIONS ON ABORTION KILL WOMEN—BECAUSE YOU CAN'T STOP A DESPERATE WOMAN FROM TRYING TO ABORT—

YOU ONLY MAKE THE PROCEDURE MORE BLOODY, DIRTY, PAINFUL AND EXPENSIVE.

I DON'T LIVE IN FLORIDA AND I'M NOT A TEEN-AGER ANYMORE, BUT WHERE'S THE CHOICE IF I CAN'T EARN ENOUGH TO SUPPORT MORE THAN MYSELF?

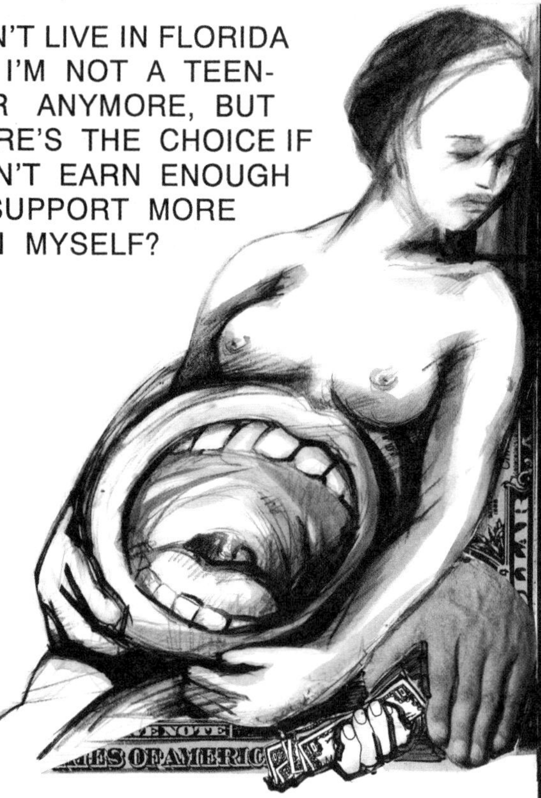

IT'S NOT ONLY THE CHOICE **NOT** TO HAVE KIDS, BUT **HOW.**

UNTIL WE EARN AS MUCH AS MEN DO, THE PRESSURE WILL BE ON US TO GIVE UP OUR JOBS

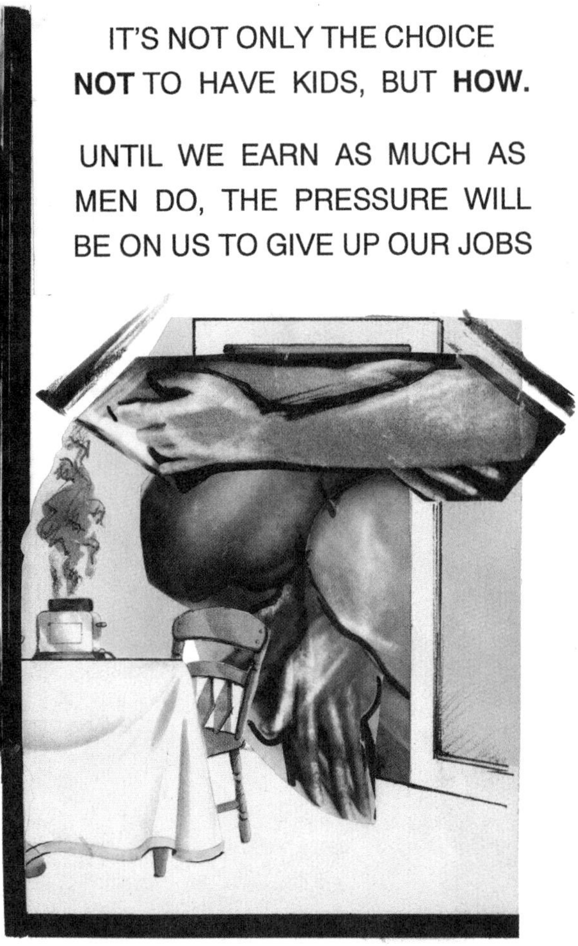

MEN DON'T HAVE TO CHOOSE BETWEEN THEIR WORK AND FAMILY—

SO WHY SHOULD WE?

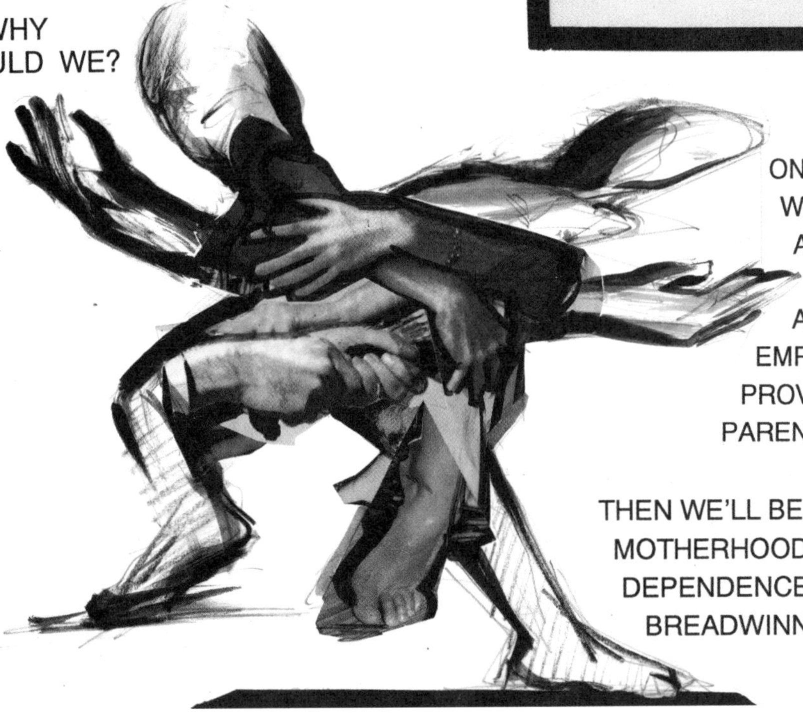

CHOICE WILL ONLY BE A REALITY WHEN MEN WORRY ABOUT CHILDCARE AS MUCH AS WE DO AND WHEN OUR EMPLOYERS ROUTINELY PROVIDE DAYCARE AND PARENTAL LEAVE FOR ALL.

THEN WE'LL BE ABLE TO CHOOSE MOTHERHOOD WITHOUT CHOOSING DEPENDENCE—EITHER ON A BREADWINNER OR WELFARE.

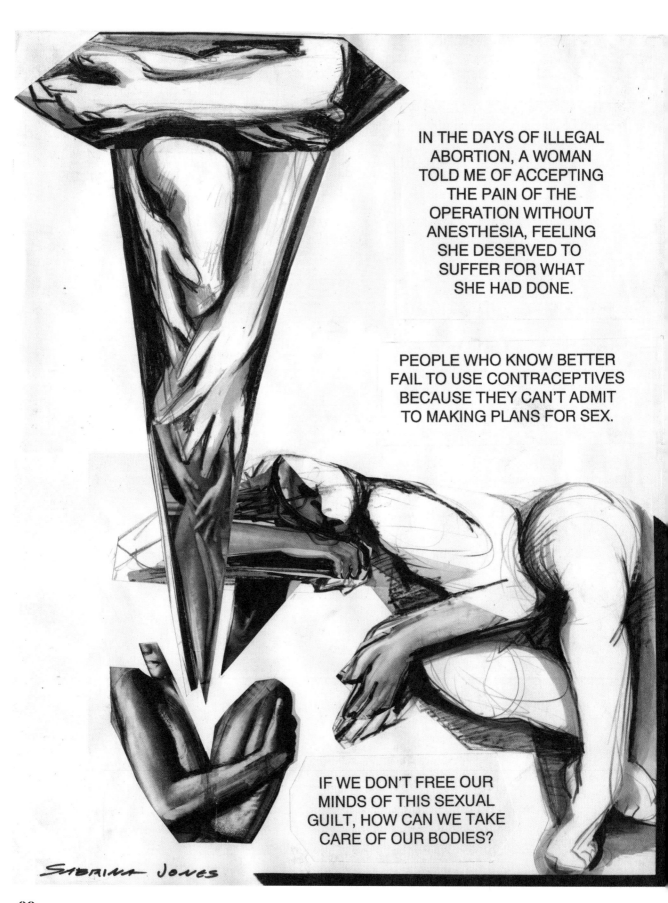

IN THE DAYS OF ILLEGAL ABORTION, A WOMAN TOLD ME OF ACCEPTING THE PAIN OF THE OPERATION WITHOUT ANESTHESIA, FEELING SHE DESERVED TO SUFFER FOR WHAT SHE HAD DONE.

PEOPLE WHO KNOW BETTER FAIL TO USE CONTRACEPTIVES BECAUSE THEY CAN'T ADMIT TO MAKING PLANS FOR SEX.

IF WE DON'T FREE OUR MINDS OF THIS SEXUAL GUILT, HOW CAN WE TAKE CARE OF OUR BODIES?

SABRINA JONES

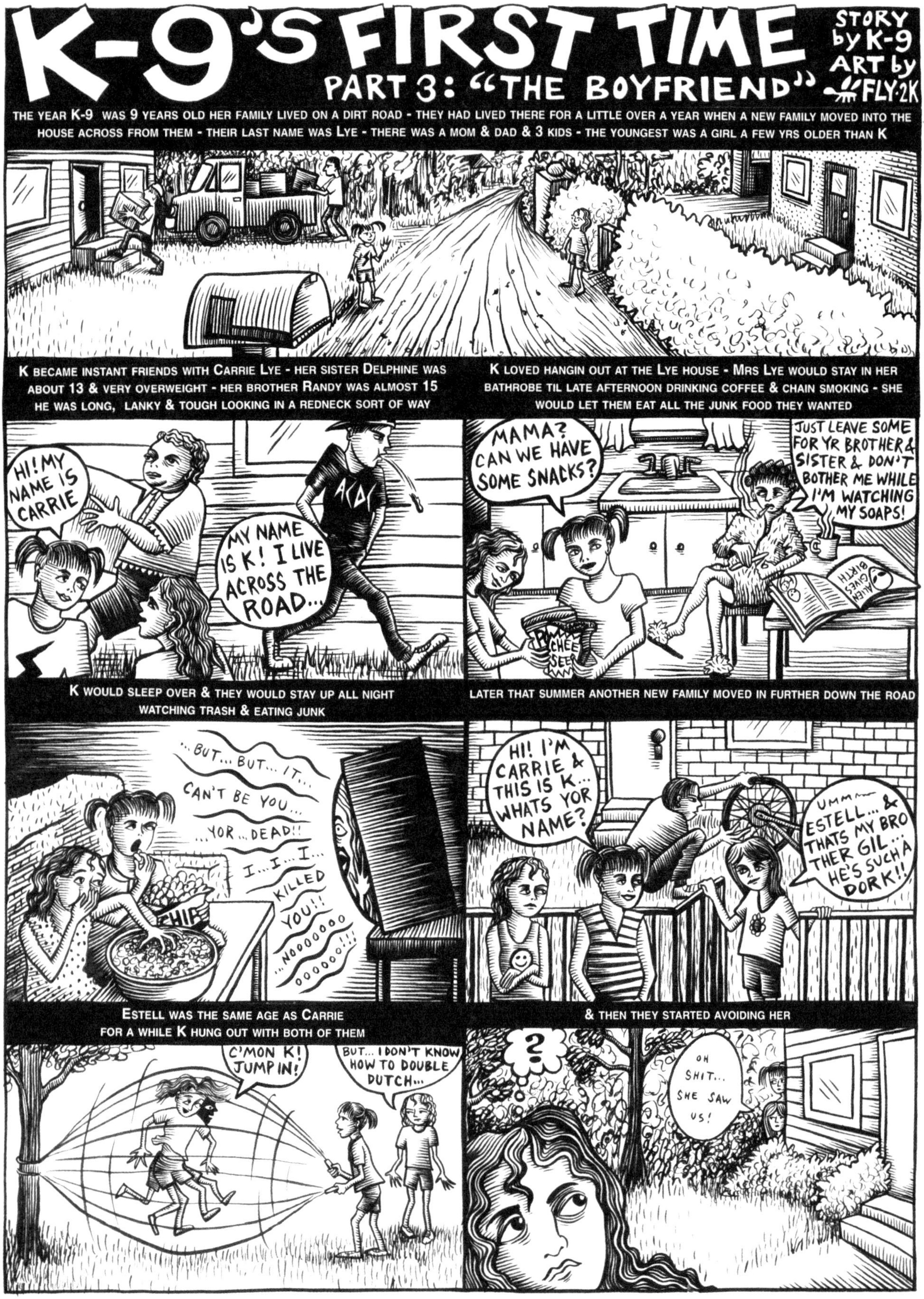

K-9'S FIRST TIME
PART 3: "THE BOYFRIEND"
STORY by K-9
ART by FLY·2K
THE YEAR K-9 WAS 9 YEARS OLD HER FAMILY LIVED ON A DIRT ROAD - THEY HAD LIVED THERE FOR A LITTLE OVER A YEAR WHEN A NEW FAMILY MOVED INTO THE HOUSE ACROSS FROM THEM - THEIR LAST NAME WAS LYE - THERE WAS A MOM & DAD & 3 KIDS - THE YOUNGEST WAS A GIRL A FEW YRS OLDER THAN K
K BECAME INSTANT FRIENDS WITH CARRIE LYE - HER SISTER DELPHINE WAS ABOUT 13 & VERY OVERWEIGHT - HER BROTHER RANDY WAS ALMOST 15 HE WAS LONG, LANKY & TOUGH LOOKING IN A REDNECK SORT OF WAY
HI! MY NAME IS CARRIE
MY NAME IS K! I LIVE ACROSS THE ROAD...
AC/DC
K LOVED HANGIN OUT AT THE LYE HOUSE - MRS LYE WOULD STAY IN HER BATHROBE TIL LATE AFTERNOON DRINKING COFFEE & CHAIN SMOKING - SHE WOULD LET THEM EAT ALL THE JUNK FOOD THEY WANTED
MAMA? CAN WE HAVE SOME SNACKS?
JUST LEAVE SOME FOR YR BROTHER & SISTER & DON'T BOTHER ME WHILE I'M WATCHING MY SOAPS!
ALIEN GIVES BIRTH
CHEE SEE
K WOULD SLEEP OVER & THEY WOULD STAY UP ALL NIGHT WATCHING TRASH & EATING JUNK
...BUT...BUT...IT... CAN'T BE YOU... ...YOR...DEAD!! I...I...I... KILLED YOU!! ...NOOOOOOOOOOOOOO!!!
CHIP
LATER THAT SUMMER ANOTHER NEW FAMILY MOVED IN FURTHER DOWN THE ROAD
HI! I'M CARRIE & THIS IS K... WHATS YOR NAME?
UMM... ESTELL... & THATS MY BRO THER GIL... HE'S SUCH A DORK!!
ESTELL WAS THE SAME AGE AS CARRIE FOR A WHILE K HUNG OUT WITH BOTH OF THEM
C'MON K! JUMP IN!
BUT... I DON'T KNOW HOW TO DOUBLE DUTCH...
& THEN THEY STARTED AVOIDING HER
?
OH SHIT... SHE SAW US!

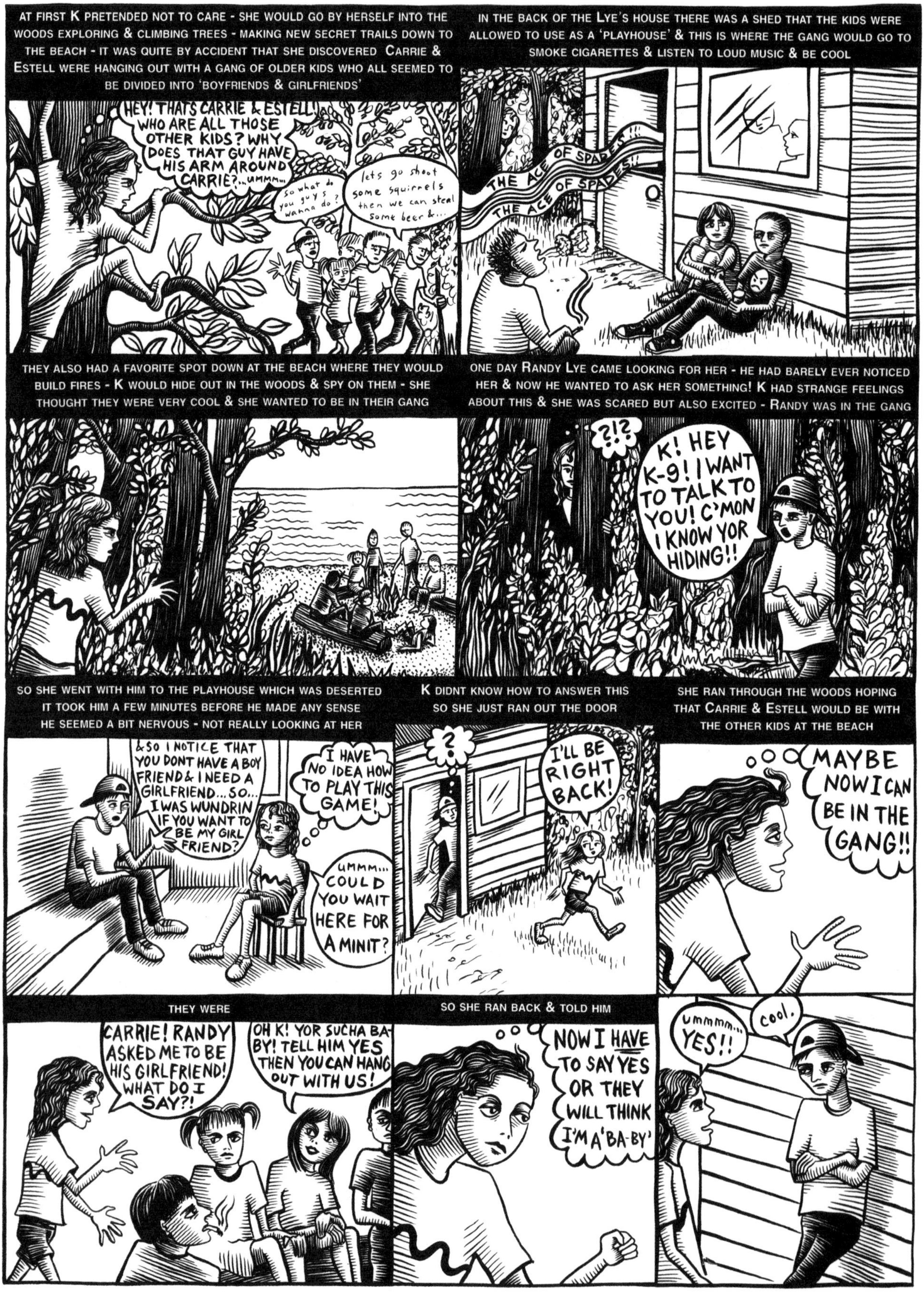
AT FIRST K PRETENDED NOT TO CARE - SHE WOULD GO BY HERSELF INTO THE WOODS EXPLORING & CLIMBING TREES - MAKING NEW SECRET TRAILS DOWN TO THE BEACH - IT WAS QUITE BY ACCIDENT THAT SHE DISCOVERED CARRIE & ESTELL WERE HANGING OUT WITH A GANG OF OLDER KIDS WHO ALL SEEMED TO BE DIVIDED INTO 'BOYFRIENDS & GIRLFRIENDS'
HEY! THATS CARRIE & ESTELL! WHO ARE ALL THOSE OTHER KIDS? WHY DOES THAT GUY HAVE HIS ARM AROUND CARRIE?...UMMM...
so what do you guy's wanna do?
lets go shoot some squirrels then we can steal some beer &...
IN THE BACK OF THE LYE'S HOUSE THERE WAS A SHED THAT THE KIDS WERE ALLOWED TO USE AS A 'PLAYHOUSE' & THIS IS WHERE THE GANG WOULD GO TO SMOKE CIGARETTES & LISTEN TO LOUD MUSIC & BE COOL
THE ACE OF SPADES!!
THE ACE OF SPADES!!
THEY ALSO HAD A FAVORITE SPOT DOWN AT THE BEACH WHERE THEY WOULD BUILD FIRES - K WOULD HIDE OUT IN THE WOODS & SPY ON THEM - SHE THOUGHT THEY WERE VERY COOL & SHE WANTED TO BE IN THEIR GANG
ONE DAY RANDY LYE CAME LOOKING FOR HER - HE HAD BARELY EVER NOTICED HER & NOW HE WANTED TO ASK HER SOMETHING! K HAD STRANGE FEELINGS ABOUT THIS & SHE WAS SCARED BUT ALSO EXCITED - RANDY WAS IN THE GANG
?!?
K! HEY K-9! I WANT TO TALK TO YOU! C'MON I KNOW YOR HIDING!!
SO SHE WENT WITH HIM TO THE PLAYHOUSE WHICH WAS DESERTED IT TOOK HIM A FEW MINUTES BEFORE HE MADE ANY SENSE HE SEEMED A BIT NERVOUS - NOT REALLY LOOKING AT HER
&SO I NOTICE THAT YOU DONT HAVE A BOY FRIEND & I NEED A GIRLFRIEND... SO... I WAS WUNDRIN IF YOU WANT TO BE MY GIRL FRIEND?
I HAVE NO IDEA HOW TO PLAY THIS GAME!
UMMM... COULD YOU WAIT HERE FOR A MINIT?
K DIDNT KNOW HOW TO ANSWER THIS SO SHE JUST RAN OUT THE DOOR
?
I'LL BE RIGHT BACK!
SHE RAN THROUGH THE WOODS HOPING THAT CARRIE & ESTELL WOULD BE WITH THE OTHER KIDS AT THE BEACH
MAYBE NOW I CAN BE IN THE GANG!!
THEY WERE
CARRIE! RANDY ASKED ME TO BE HIS GIRLFRIEND! WHAT DO I SAY?!
OH K! YOR SUCHA BA-BY! TELL HIM YES THEN YOU CAN HANG OUT WITH US!
SO SHE RAN BACK & TOLD HIM
NOW I HAVE TO SAY YES OR THEY WILL THINK I'M A 'BA-BY'
UMMMM... YES!!
cool.

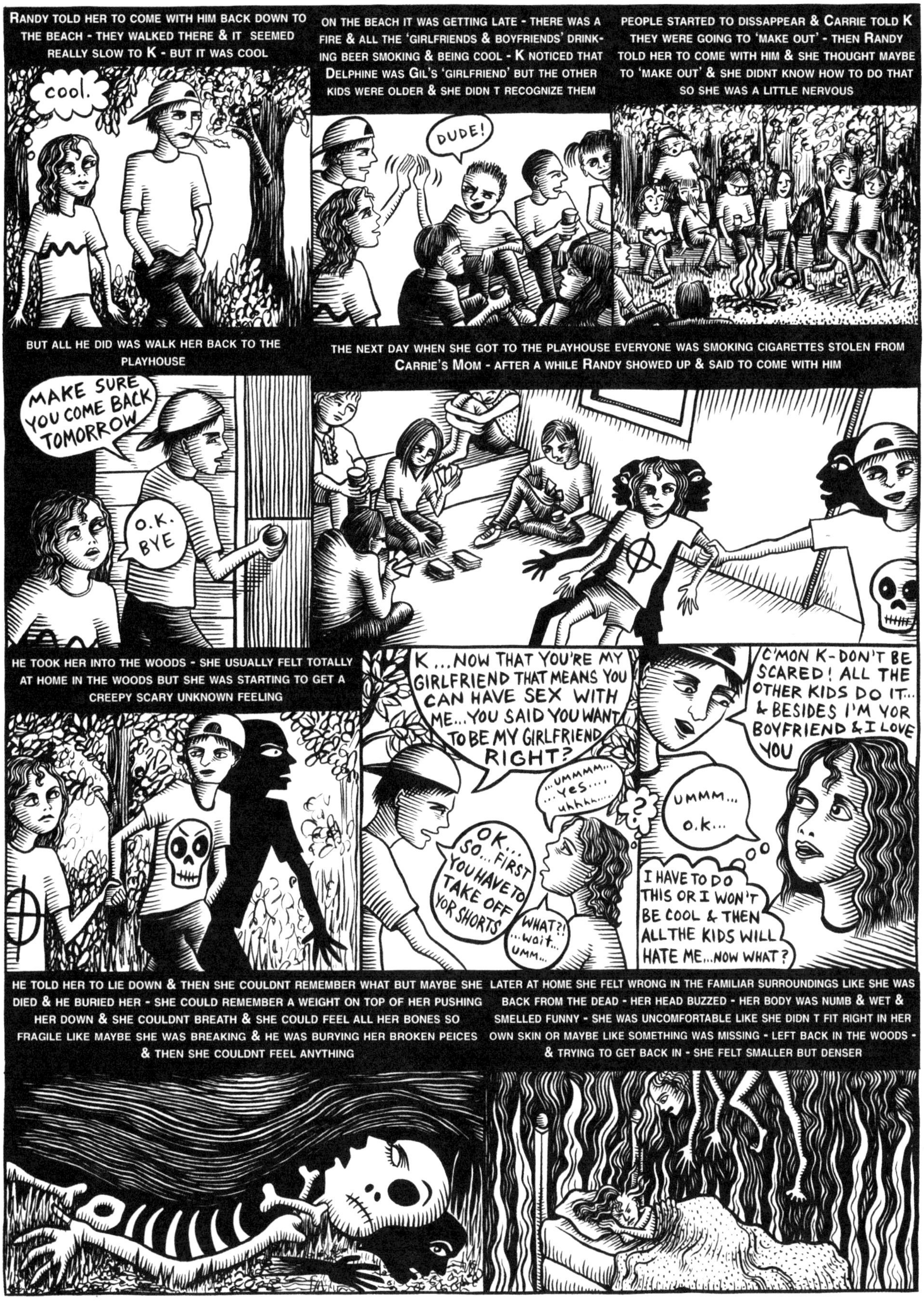

RANDY TOLD HER TO COME WITH HIM BACK DOWN TO THE BEACH - THEY WALKED THERE & IT SEEMED REALLY SLOW TO K - BUT IT WAS COOL
COOL.
ON THE BEACH IT WAS GETTING LATE - THERE WAS A FIRE & ALL THE 'GIRLFRIENDS & BOYFRIENDS' DRINK-ING BEER SMOKING & BEING COOL - K NOTICED THAT DELPHINE WAS GIL'S 'GIRLFRIEND' BUT THE OTHER KIDS WERE OLDER & SHE DIDN T RECOGNIZE THEM
DUDE!
PEOPLE STARTED TO DISSAPPEAR & CARRIE TOLD K THEY WERE GOING TO 'MAKE OUT' - THEN RANDY TOLD HER TO COME WITH HIM & SHE THOUGHT MAYBE TO 'MAKE OUT' & SHE DIDNT KNOW HOW TO DO THAT SO SHE WAS A LITTLE NERVOUS
BUT ALL HE DID WAS WALK HER BACK TO THE PLAYHOUSE
MAKE SURE YOU COME BACK TOMORROW
O.K. BYE
THE NEXT DAY WHEN SHE GOT TO THE PLAYHOUSE EVERYONE WAS SMOKING CIGARETTES STOLEN FROM CARRIE'S MOM - AFTER A WHILE RANDY SHOWED UP & SAID TO COME WITH HIM
HE TOOK HER INTO THE WOODS - SHE USUALLY FELT TOTALLY AT HOME IN THE WOODS BUT SHE WAS STARTING TO GET A CREEPY SCARY UNKNOWN FEELING
K ... NOW THAT YOU'RE MY GIRLFRIEND THAT MEANS YOU CAN HAVE SEX WITH ME... YOU SAID YOU WANT TO BE MY GIRLFRIEND RIGHT?
...UMMMM... ...YES... ...UHHHH...
?
OK... SO... FIRST YOU HAVE TO TAKE OFF YOR SHORTS
WHAT?! ...WAIT... UMM...
C'MON K - DON'T BE SCARED! ALL THE OTHER KIDS DO IT... & BESIDES I'M YOR BOYFRIEND & I LOVE YOU
UMMM... O.K...
I HAVE TO DO THIS OR I WON'T BE COOL & THEN ALL THE KIDS WILL HATE ME...NOW WHAT?
HE TOLD HER TO LIE DOWN & THEN SHE COULDNT REMEMBER WHAT BUT MAYBE SHE DIED & HE BURIED HER - SHE COULD REMEMBER A WEIGHT ON TOP OF HER PUSHING HER DOWN & SHE COULDNT BREATH & SHE COULD FEEL ALL HER BONES SO FRAGILE LIKE MAYBE SHE WAS BREAKING & HE WAS BURYING HER BROKEN PEICES & THEN SHE COULDNT FEEL ANYTHING
LATER AT HOME SHE FELT WRONG IN THE FAMILIAR SURROUNDINGS LIKE SHE WAS BACK FROM THE DEAD - HER HEAD BUZZED - HER BODY WAS NUMB & WET & SMELLED FUNNY - SHE WAS UNCOMFORTABLE LIKE SHE DIDN T FIT RIGHT IN HER OWN SKIN OR MAYBE LIKE SOMETHING WAS MISSING - LEFT BACK IN THE WOODS - & TRYING TO GET BACK IN - SHE FELT SMALLER BUT DENSER

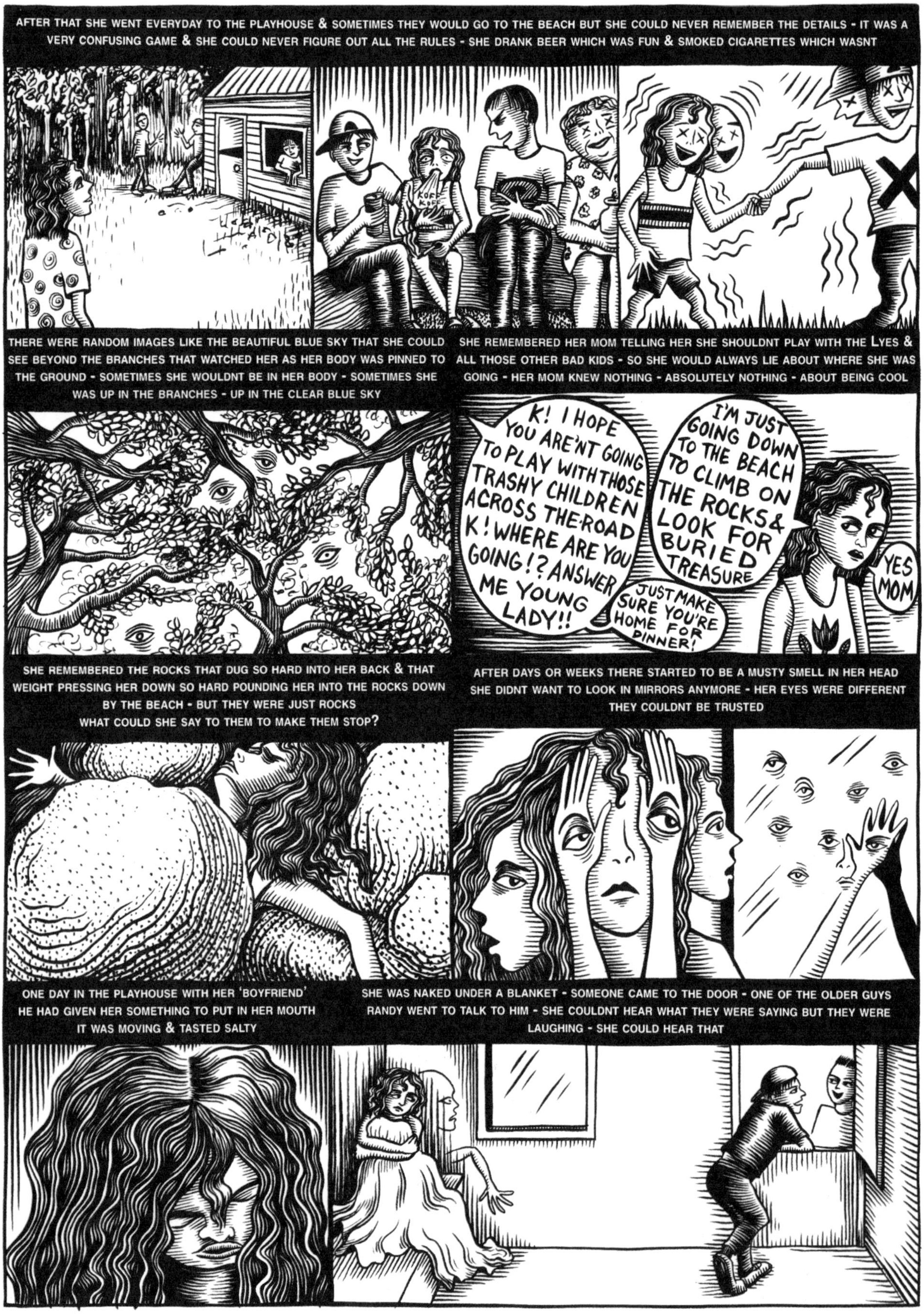
AFTER THAT SHE WENT EVERYDAY TO THE PLAYHOUSE & SOMETIMES THEY WOULD GO TO THE BEACH BUT SHE COULD NEVER REMEMBER THE DETAILS - IT WAS A VERY CONFUSING GAME & SHE COULD NEVER FIGURE OUT ALL THE RULES - SHE DRANK BEER WHICH WAS FUN & SMOKED CIGARETTES WHICH WASNT
KOFF KOFF
THERE WERE RANDOM IMAGES LIKE THE BEAUTIFUL BLUE SKY THAT SHE COULD SEE BEYOND THE BRANCHES THAT WATCHED HER AS HER BODY WAS PINNED TO THE GROUND - SOMETIMES SHE WOULDNT BE IN HER BODY - SOMETIMES SHE WAS UP IN THE BRANCHES - UP IN THE CLEAR BLUE SKY
SHE REMEMBERED HER MOM TELLING HER SHE SHOULDNT PLAY WITH THE LYES & ALL THOSE OTHER BAD KIDS - SO SHE WOULD ALWAYS LIE ABOUT WHERE SHE WAS GOING - HER MOM KNEW NOTHING - ABSOLUTELY NOTHING - ABOUT BEING COOL
K! I HOPE YOU ARE'NT GOING TO PLAY WITH THOSE TRASHY CHILDREN ACROSS THE ROAD K! WHERE ARE YOU GOING!? ANSWER ME YOUNG LADY!!
I'M JUST GOING DOWN TO THE BEACH TO CLIMB ON THE ROCKS & LOOK FOR BURIED TREASURE
JUST MAKE SURE YOU'RE HOME FOR DINNER!
YES MOM
SHE REMEMBERED THE ROCKS THAT DUG SO HARD INTO HER BACK & THAT WEIGHT PRESSING HER DOWN SO HARD POUNDING HER INTO THE ROCKS DOWN BY THE BEACH - BUT THEY WERE JUST ROCKS WHAT COULD SHE SAY TO THEM TO MAKE THEM STOP?
AFTER DAYS OR WEEKS THERE STARTED TO BE A MUSTY SMELL IN HER HEAD SHE DIDNT WANT TO LOOK IN MIRRORS ANYMORE - HER EYES WERE DIFFERENT THEY COULDNT BE TRUSTED
ONE DAY IN THE PLAYHOUSE WITH HER 'BOYFRIEND' HE HAD GIVEN HER SOMETHING TO PUT IN HER MOUTH IT WAS MOVING & TASTED SALTY
SHE WAS NAKED UNDER A BLANKET - SOMEONE CAME TO THE DOOR - ONE OF THE OLDER GUYS RANDY WENT TO TALK TO HIM - SHE COULDNT HEAR WHAT THEY WERE SAYING BUT THEY WERE LAUGHING - SHE COULD HEAR THAT

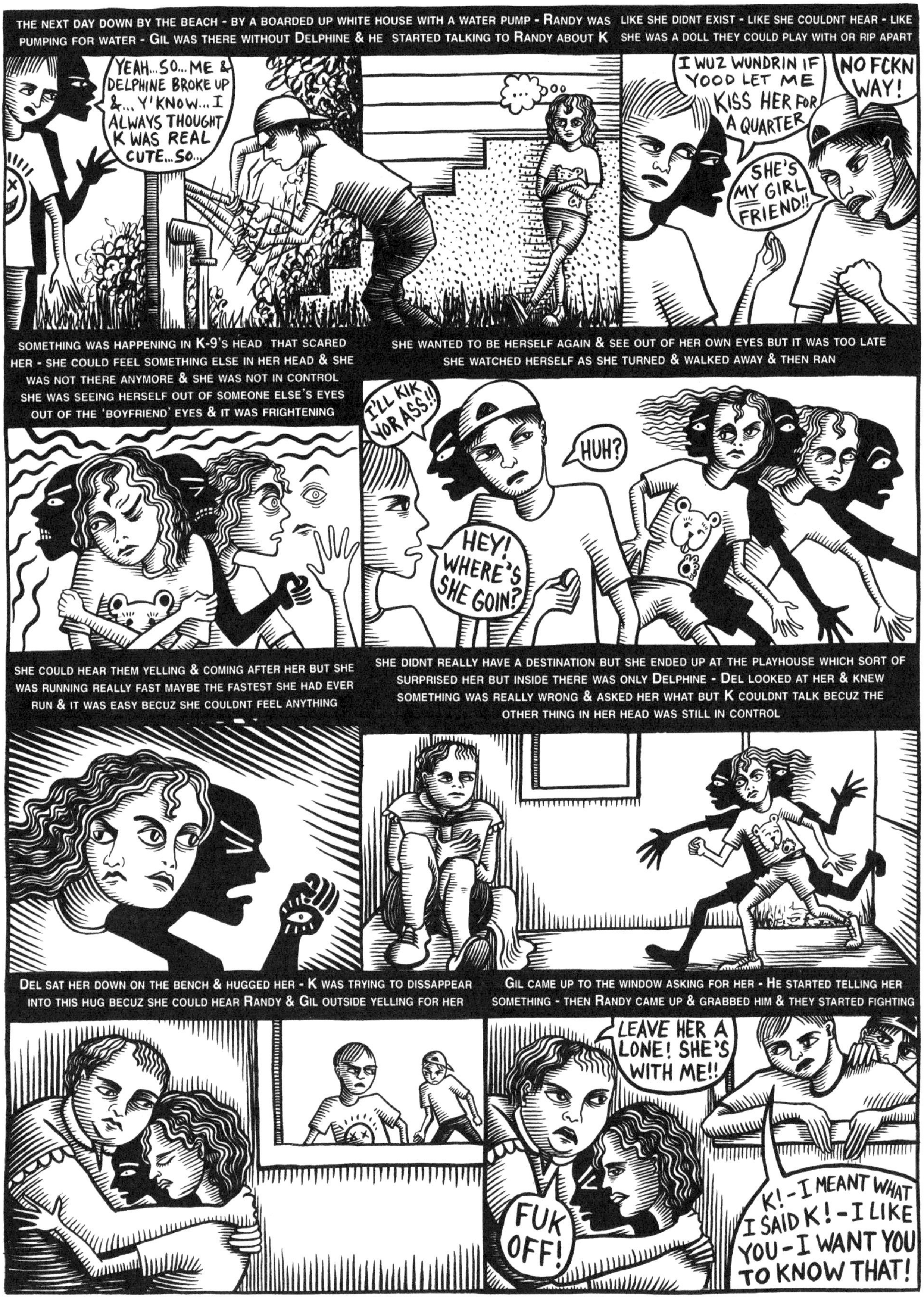
THE NEXT DAY DOWN BY THE BEACH - BY A BOARDED UP WHITE HOUSE WITH A WATER PUMP - RANDY WAS PUMPING FOR WATER - GIL WAS THERE WITHOUT DELPHINE & HE STARTED TALKING TO RANDY ABOUT K
YEAH...SO...ME & DELPHINE BROKE UP &...Y'KNOW...I ALWAYS THOUGHT K WAS REAL CUTE...SO...
LIKE SHE DIDNT EXIST - LIKE SHE COULDNT HEAR - LIKE SHE WAS A DOLL THEY COULD PLAY WITH OR RIP APART
I WUZ WUNDRIN IF YOOD LET ME KISS HER FOR A QUARTER
NO FCKN WAY!
SHE'S MY GIRL FRIEND!!
SOMETHING WAS HAPPENING IN K-9'S HEAD THAT SCARED HER - SHE COULD FEEL SOMETHING ELSE IN HER HEAD & SHE WAS NOT THERE ANYMORE & SHE WAS NOT IN CONTROL SHE WAS SEEING HERSELF OUT OF SOMEONE ELSE'S EYES OUT OF THE 'BOYFRIEND' EYES & IT WAS FRIGHTENING
SHE WANTED TO BE HERSELF AGAIN & SEE OUT OF HER OWN EYES BUT IT WAS TOO LATE SHE WATCHED HERSELF AS SHE TURNED & WALKED AWAY & THEN RAN
I'LL KIK YOR ASS!!
HUH?
HEY! WHERE'S SHE GOIN?
SHE COULD HEAR THEM YELLING & COMING AFTER HER BUT SHE WAS RUNNING REALLY FAST MAYBE THE FASTEST SHE HAD EVER RUN & IT WAS EASY BECUZ SHE COULDNT FEEL ANYTHING
SHE DIDNT REALLY HAVE A DESTINATION BUT SHE ENDED UP AT THE PLAYHOUSE WHICH SORT OF SURPRISED HER BUT INSIDE THERE WAS ONLY DELPHINE - DEL LOOKED AT HER & KNEW SOMETHING WAS REALLY WRONG & ASKED HER WHAT BUT K COULDNT TALK BECUZ THE OTHER THING IN HER HEAD WAS STILL IN CONTROL
DEL SAT HER DOWN ON THE BENCH & HUGGED HER - K WAS TRYING TO DISSAPPEAR INTO THIS HUG BECUZ SHE COULD HEAR RANDY & GIL OUTSIDE YELLING FOR HER
GIL CAME UP TO THE WINDOW ASKING FOR HER - HE STARTED TELLING HER SOMETHING - THEN RANDY CAME UP & GRABBED HIM & THEY STARTED FIGHTING
LEAVE HER A LONE! SHE'S WITH ME!!
FUK OFF!
K! - I MEANT WHAT I SAID K! - I LIKE YOU - I WANT YOU TO KNOW THAT!

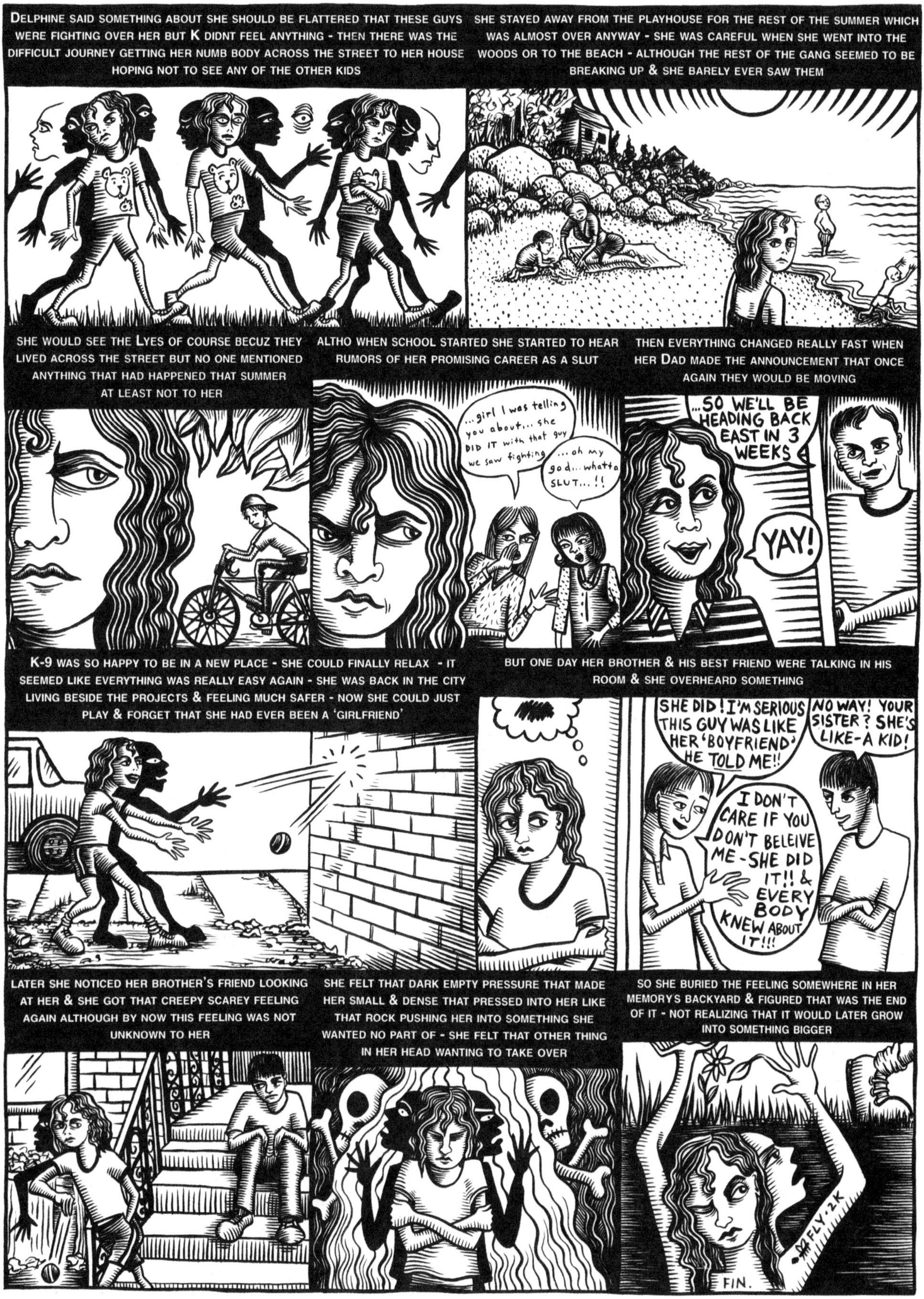
DELPHINE SAID SOMETHING ABOUT SHE SHOULD BE FLATTERED THAT THESE GUYS WERE FIGHTING OVER HER BUT K DIDNT FEEL ANYTHING - THEN THERE WAS THE DIFFICULT JOURNEY GETTING HER NUMB BODY ACROSS THE STREET TO HER HOUSE HOPING NOT TO SEE ANY OF THE OTHER KIDS
SHE STAYED AWAY FROM THE PLAYHOUSE FOR THE REST OF THE SUMMER WHICH WAS ALMOST OVER ANYWAY - SHE WAS CAREFUL WHEN SHE WENT INTO THE WOODS OR TO THE BEACH - ALTHOUGH THE REST OF THE GANG SEEMED TO BE BREAKING UP & SHE BARELY EVER SAW THEM
SHE WOULD SEE THE LYES OF COURSE BECUZ THEY LIVED ACROSS THE STREET BUT NO ONE MENTIONED ANYTHING THAT HAD HAPPENED THAT SUMMER AT LEAST NOT TO HER
ALTHO WHEN SCHOOL STARTED SHE STARTED TO HEAR RUMORS OF HER PROMISING CAREER AS A SLUT
...girl I was telling you about... she DID IT with that guy we saw fighting
...oh my god...whatta SLUT...!!
THEN EVERYTHING CHANGED REALLY FAST WHEN HER DAD MADE THE ANNOUNCEMENT THAT ONCE AGAIN THEY WOULD BE MOVING
...SO WE'LL BE HEADING BACK EAST IN 3 WEEKS
YAY!
K-9 WAS SO HAPPY TO BE IN A NEW PLACE - SHE COULD FINALLY RELAX - IT SEEMED LIKE EVERYTHING WAS REALLY EASY AGAIN - SHE WAS BACK IN THE CITY LIVING BESIDE THE PROJECTS & FEELING MUCH SAFER - NOW SHE COULD JUST PLAY & FORGET THAT SHE HAD EVER BEEN A 'GIRLFRIEND'
BUT ONE DAY HER BROTHER & HIS BEST FRIEND WERE TALKING IN HIS ROOM & SHE OVERHEARD SOMETHING
SHE DID! I'M SERIOUS THIS GUY WAS LIKE HER 'BOYFRIEND' HE TOLD ME!!
NO WAY! YOUR SISTER? SHE'S LIKE-A KID!
I DON'T CARE IF YOU DON'T BELEIVE ME - SHE DID IT!! & EVERY BODY KNEW ABOUT IT!!!
LATER SHE NOTICED HER BROTHER'S FRIEND LOOKING AT HER & SHE GOT THAT CREEPY SCAREY FEELING AGAIN ALTHOUGH BY NOW THIS FEELING WAS NOT UNKNOWN TO HER
SHE FELT THAT DARK EMPTY PRESSURE THAT MADE HER SMALL & DENSE THAT PRESSED INTO HER LIKE THAT ROCK PUSHING HER INTO SOMETHING SHE WANTED NO PART OF - SHE FELT THAT OTHER THING IN HER HEAD WANTING TO TAKE OVER
SO SHE BURIED THE FEELING SOMEWHERE IN HER MEMORY'S BACKYARD & FIGURED THAT WAS THE END OF IT - NOT REALIZING THAT IT WOULD LATER GROW INTO SOMETHING BIGGER
FLY·2K
FIN.

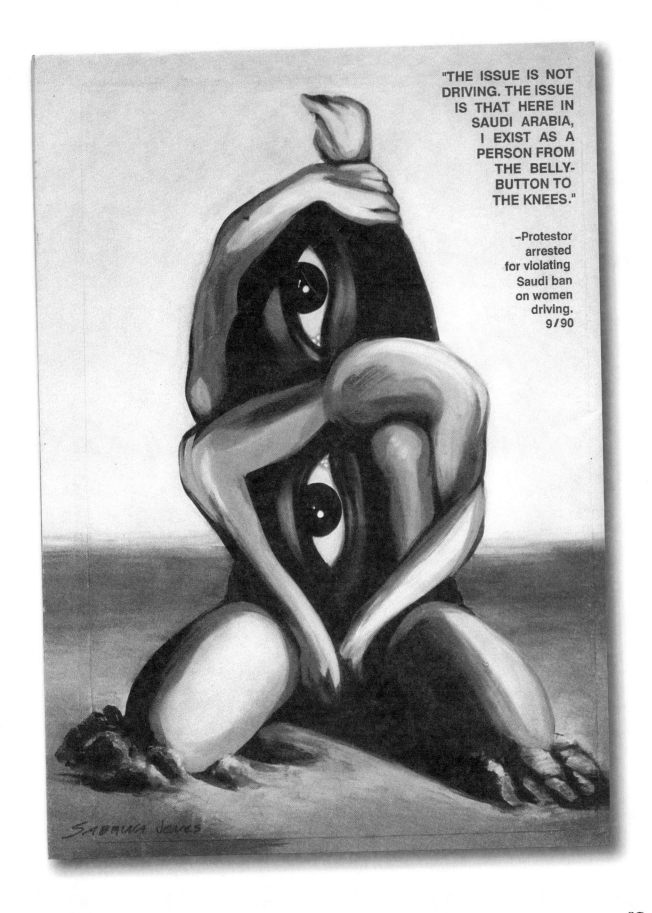

"THE ISSUE IS NOT DRIVING. THE ISSUE IS THAT HERE IN SAUDI ARABIA, I EXIST AS A PERSON FROM THE BELLY-BUTTON TO THE KNEES."

–Protestor arrested for violating Saudi ban on women driving. 9/90

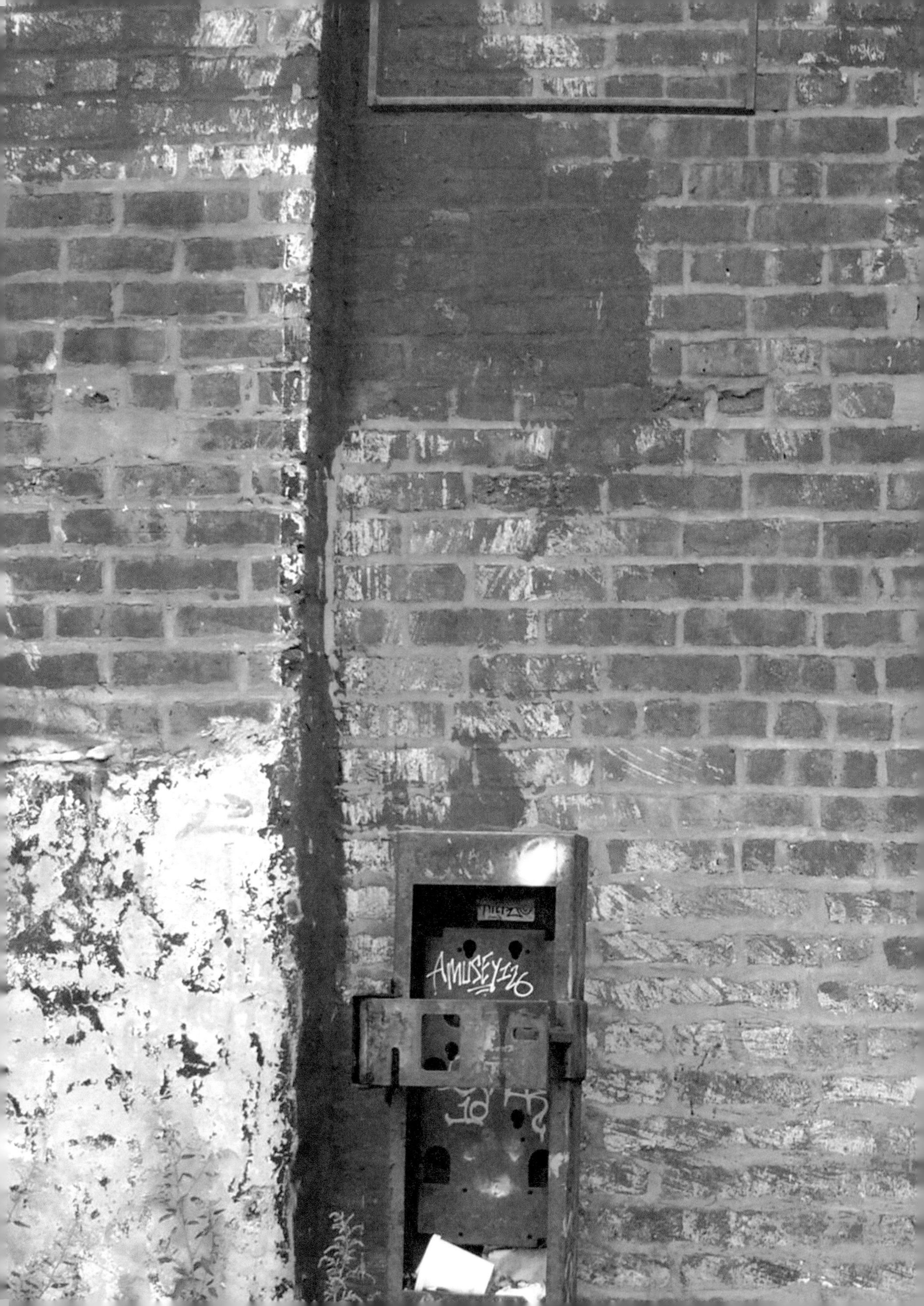
AMUSEY126

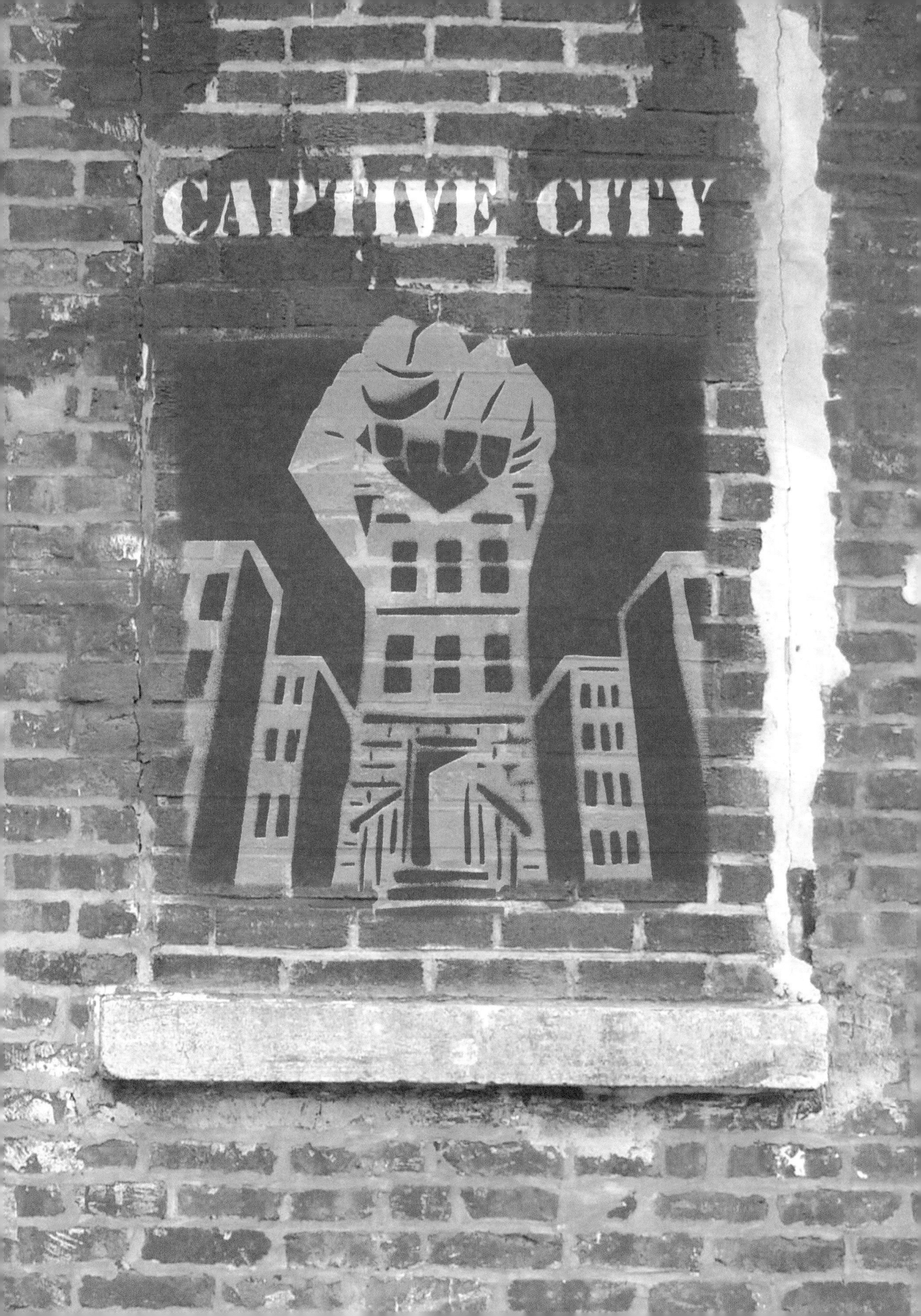
CAPTIVE CITY

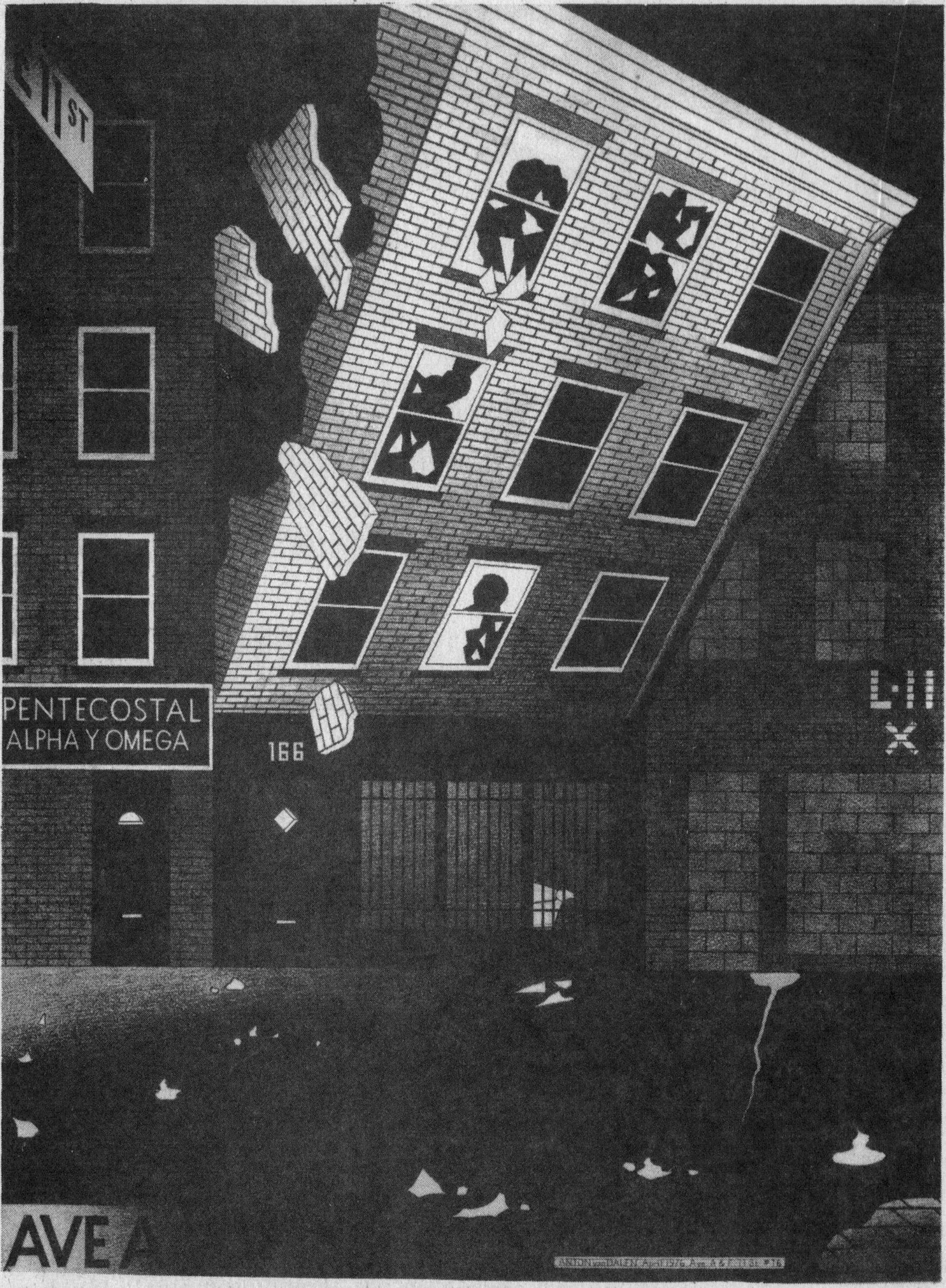
11 ST
PENTECOSTAL
ALPHA Y OMEGA
166
AVE A

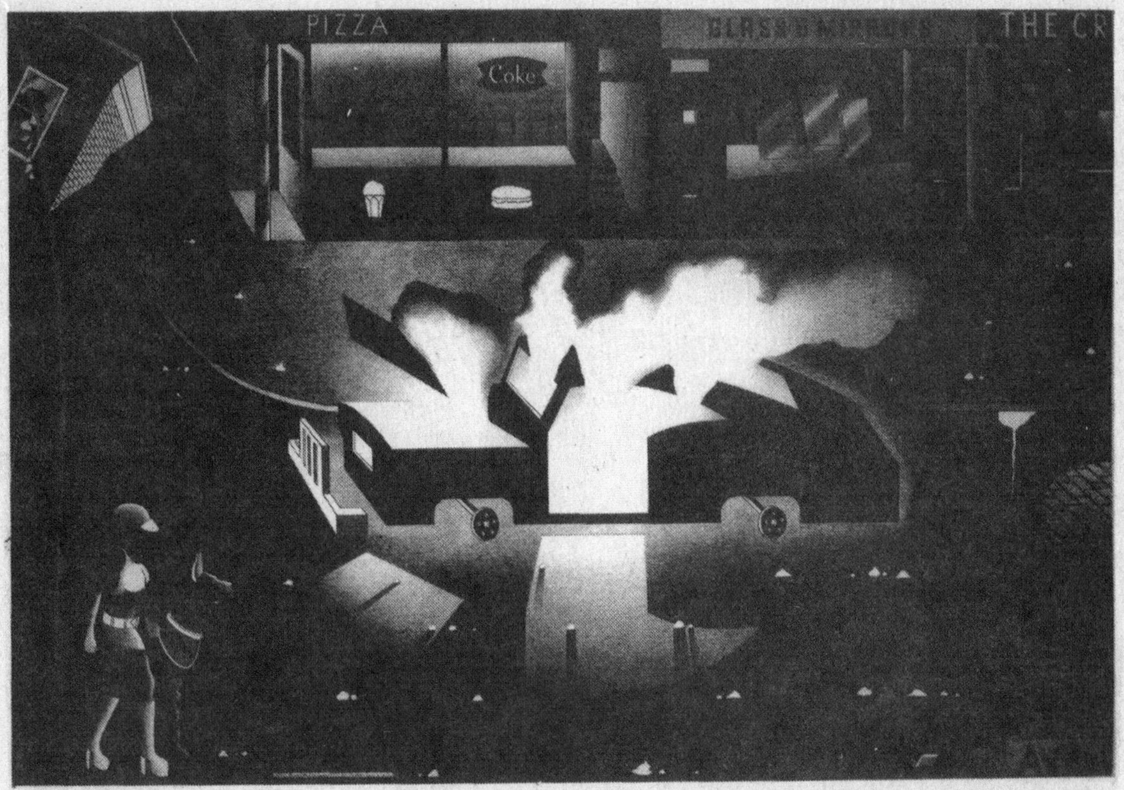
PIZZA
Coke

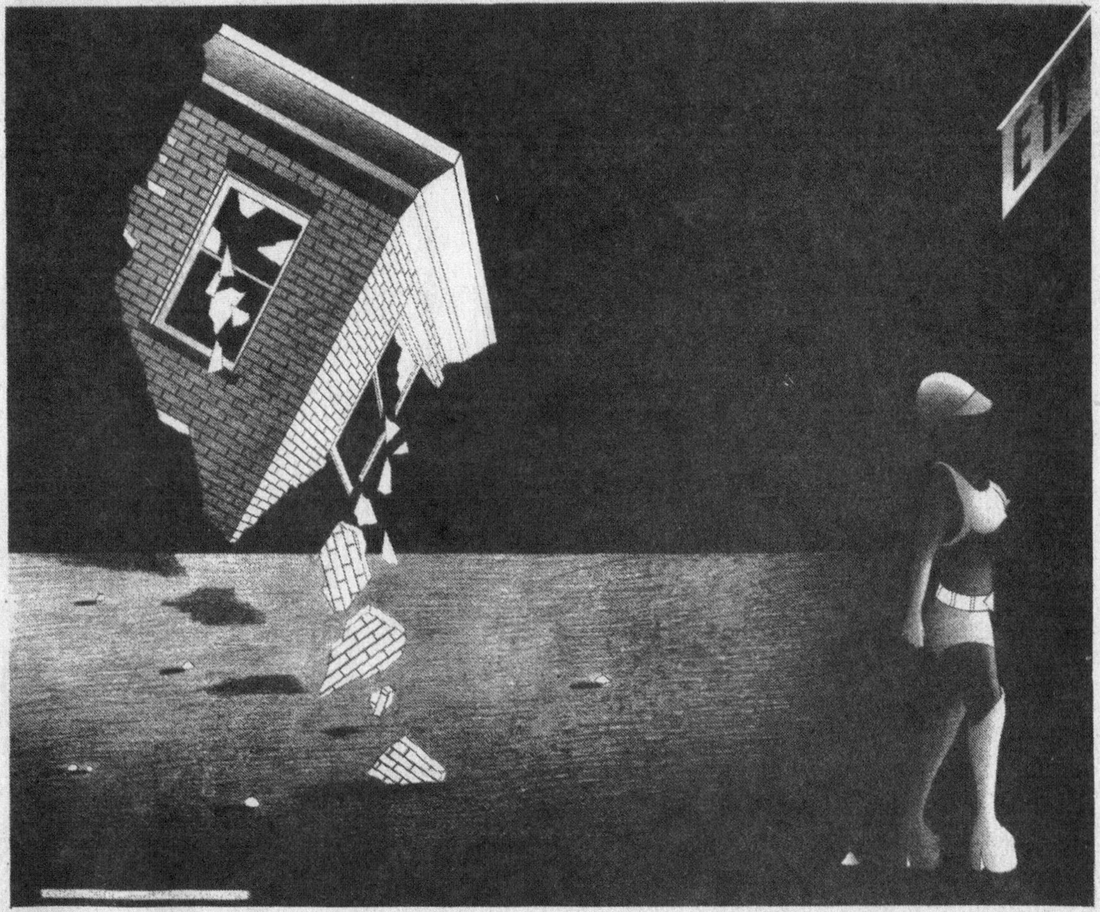

WHY ARE APARTMENTS EXPENSIVE ?

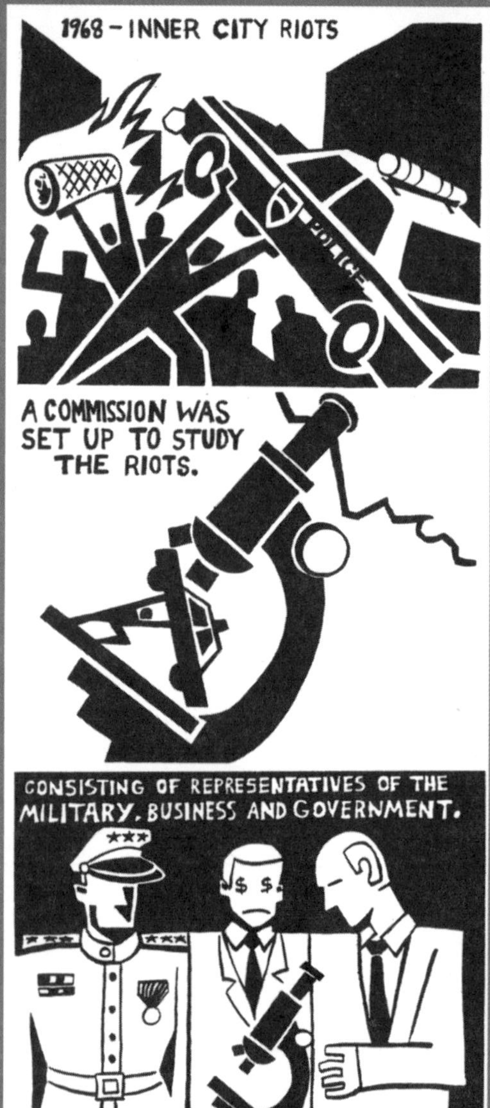
1968 – INNER CITY RIOTS
POLICE
A COMMISSION WAS SET UP TO STUDY THE RIOTS.
CONSISTING OF REPRESENTATIVES OF THE MILITARY, BUSINESS AND GOVERNMENT.

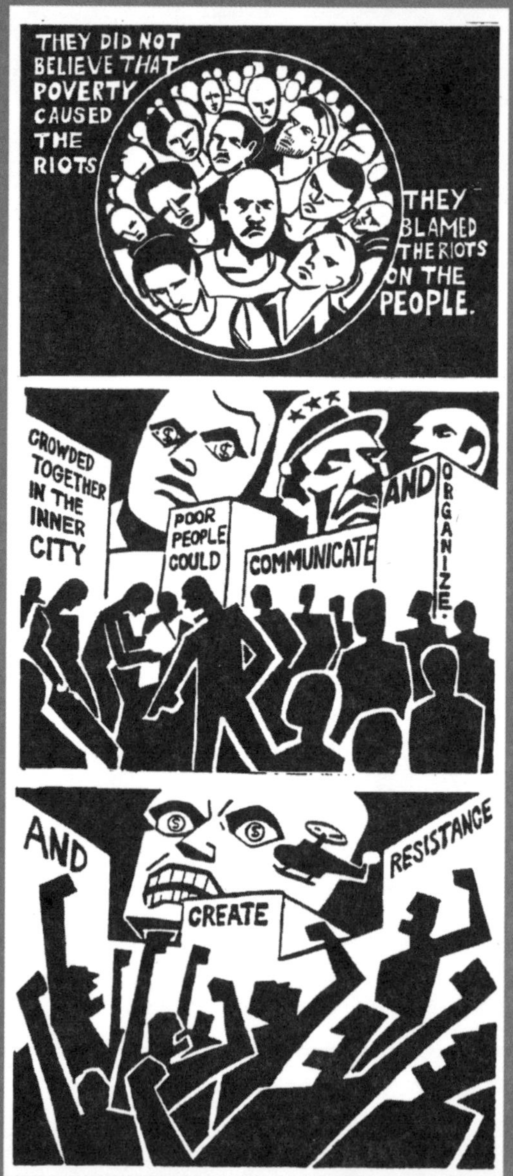
THEY DID NOT BELIEVE THAT POVERTY CAUSED THE RIOTS
THEY BLAMED THE RIOTS ON THE PEOPLE.
CROWDED TOGETHER IN THE INNER CITY
POOR PEOPLE COULD
COMMUNICATE
AND
ORGANIZE.
AND
CREATE
RESISTANCE

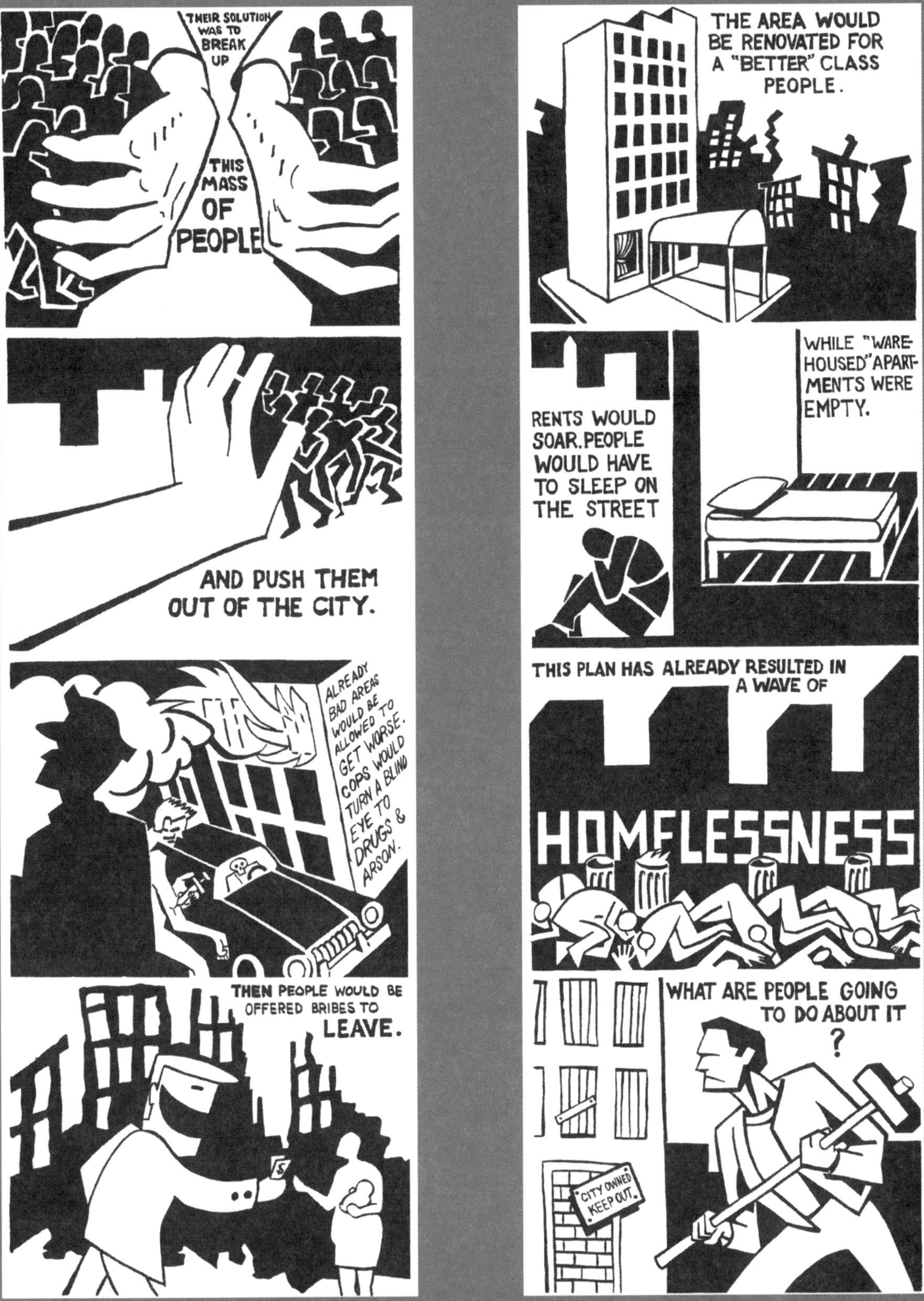
THEIR SOLUTION WAS TO BREAK UP
THIS MASS OF PEOPLE
AND PUSH THEM OUT OF THE CITY.
ALREADY BAD AREAS WOULD BE ALLOWED TO GET WORSE. COPS WOULD TURN A BLIND EYE TO DRUGS & ARSON.
THEN PEOPLE WOULD BE OFFERED BRIBES TO LEAVE.
$
THE AREA WOULD BE RENOVATED FOR A "BETTER" CLASS PEOPLE.
RENTS WOULD SOAR. PEOPLE WOULD HAVE TO SLEEP ON THE STREET
WHILE "WARE-HOUSED" APART-MENTS WERE EMPTY.
THIS PLAN HAS ALREADY RESULTED IN A WAVE OF
HOMELESSNESS
WHAT ARE PEOPLE GOING TO DO ABOUT IT ?
CITY OWNED
KEEP OUT.

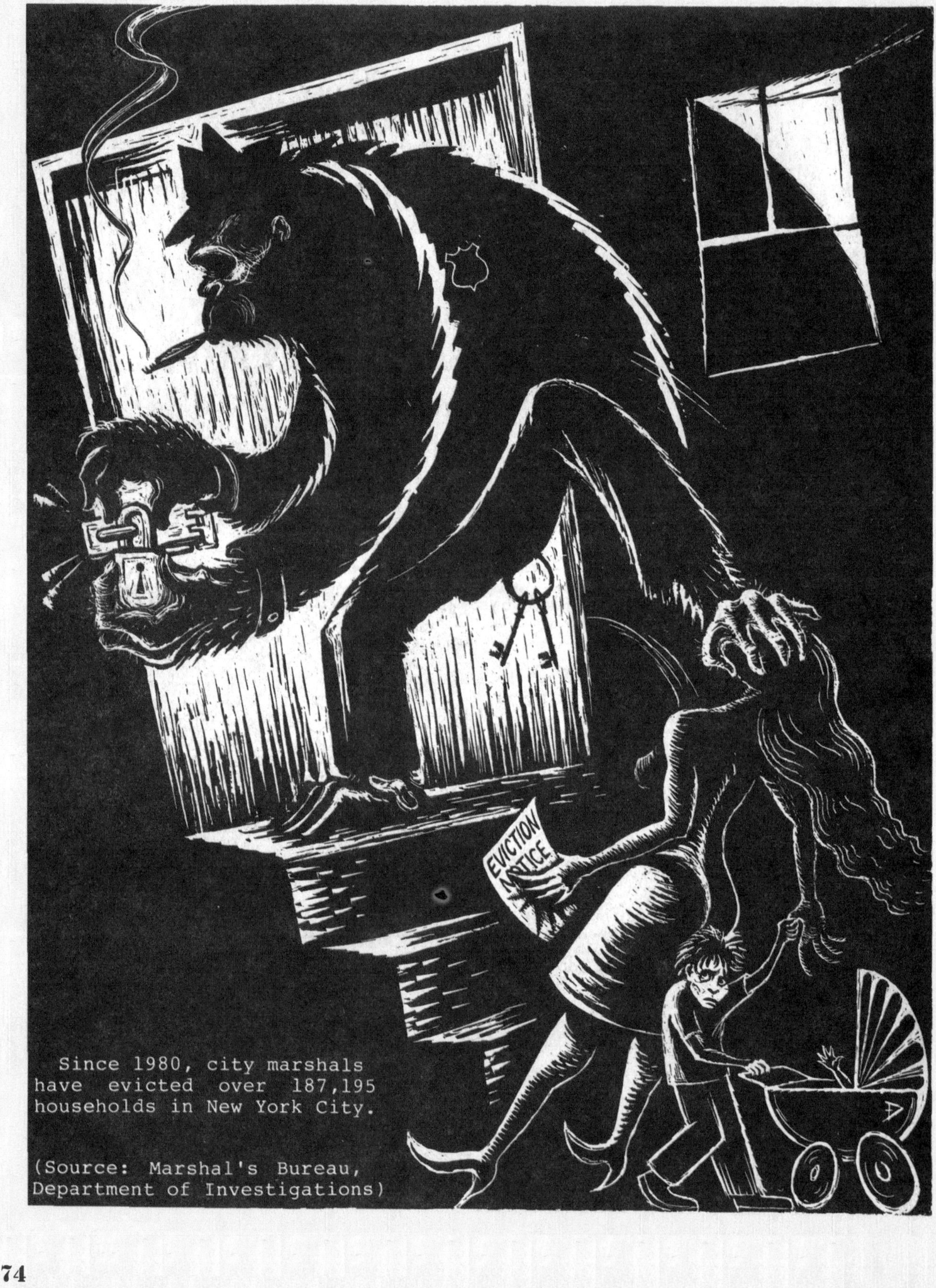
EVICTION NOTICE

Since 1980, city marshals have evicted over 187,195 households in New York City.

(Source: Marshal's Bureau, Department of Investigations)

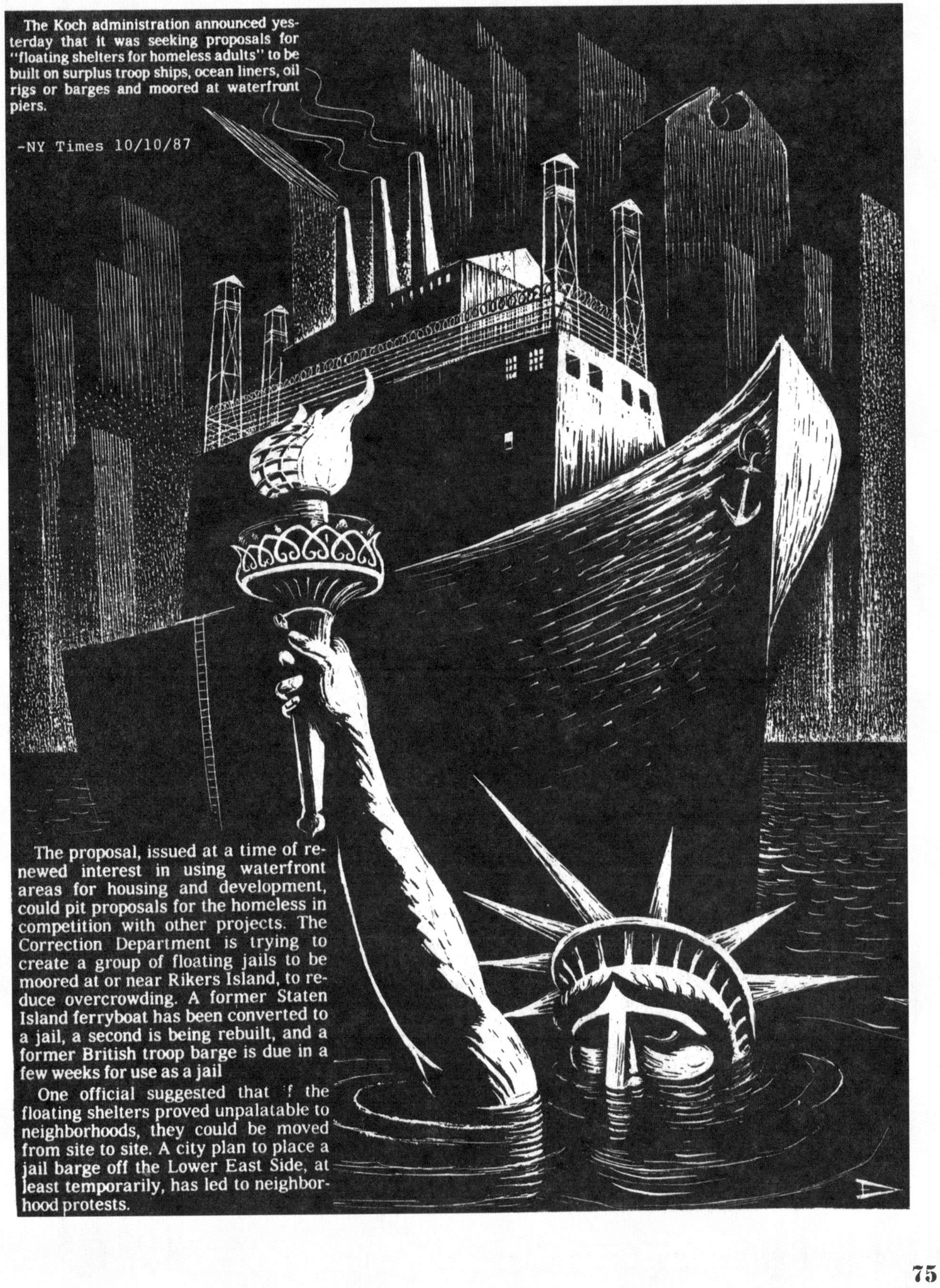

The Koch administration announced yesterday that it was seeking proposals for "floating shelters for homeless adults" to be built on surplus troop ships, ocean liners, oil rigs or barges and moored at waterfront piers.

-NY Times 10/10/87

The proposal, issued at a time of renewed interest in using waterfront areas for housing and development, could pit proposals for the homeless in competition with other projects. The Correction Department is trying to create a group of floating jails to be moored at or near Rikers Island, to reduce overcrowding. A former Staten Island ferryboat has been converted to a jail, a second is being rebuilt, and a former British troop barge is due in a few weeks for use as a jail

One official suggested that if the floating shelters proved unpalatable to neighborhoods, they could be moved from site to site. A city plan to place a jail barge off the Lower East Side, at least temporarily, has led to neighborhood protests.

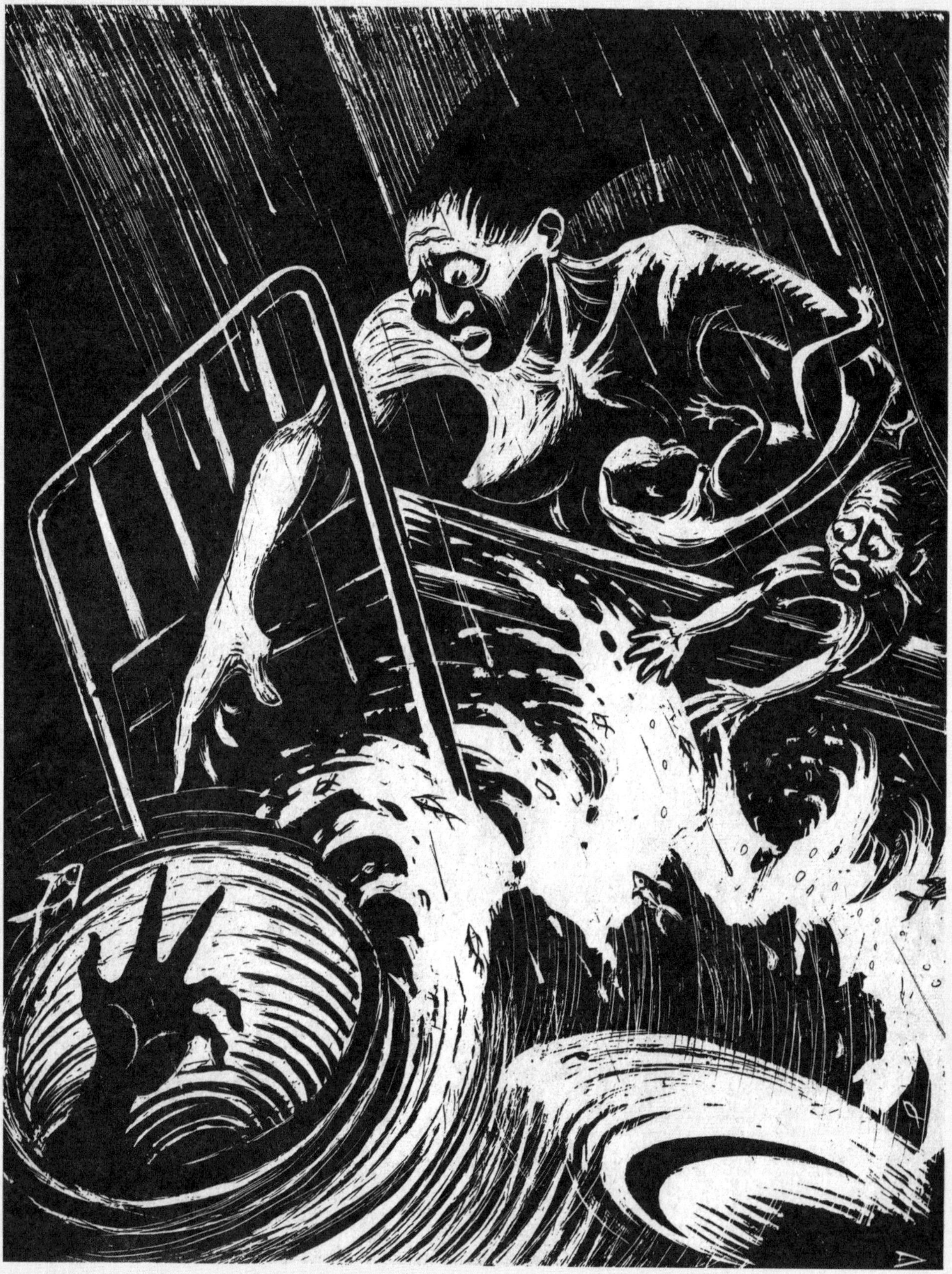

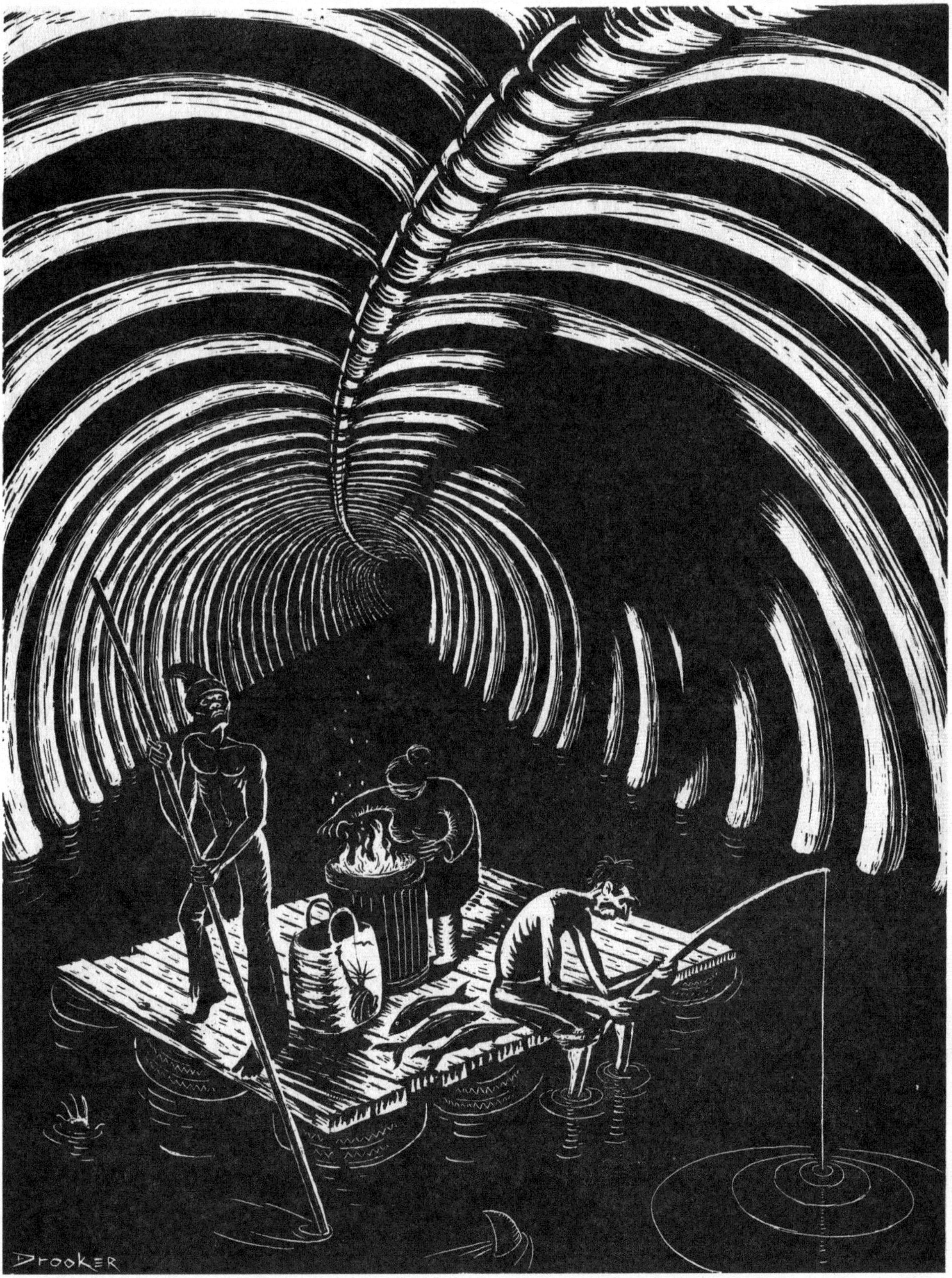
DROOKER

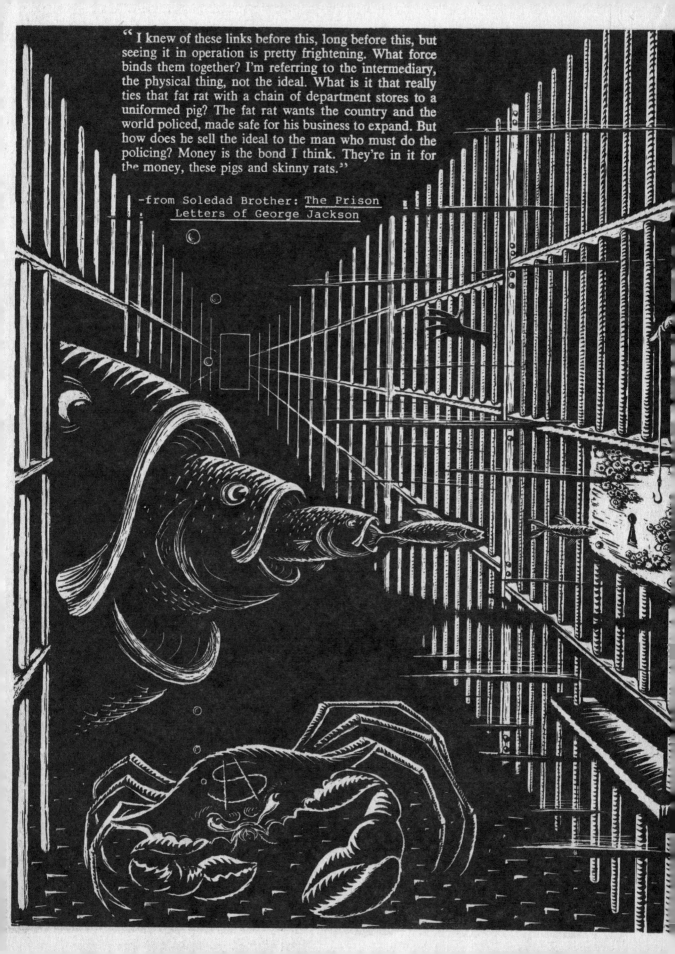

"I knew of these links before this, long before this, but seeing it in operation is pretty frightening. What force binds them together? I'm referring to the intermediary, the physical thing, not the ideal. What is it that really ties that fat rat with a chain of department stores to a uniformed pig? The fat rat wants the country and the world policed, made safe for his business to expand. But how does he sell the ideal to the man who must do the policing? Money is the bond I think. They're in it for the money, these pigs and skinny rats."

—from Soledad Brother: The Prison
Letters of George Jackson

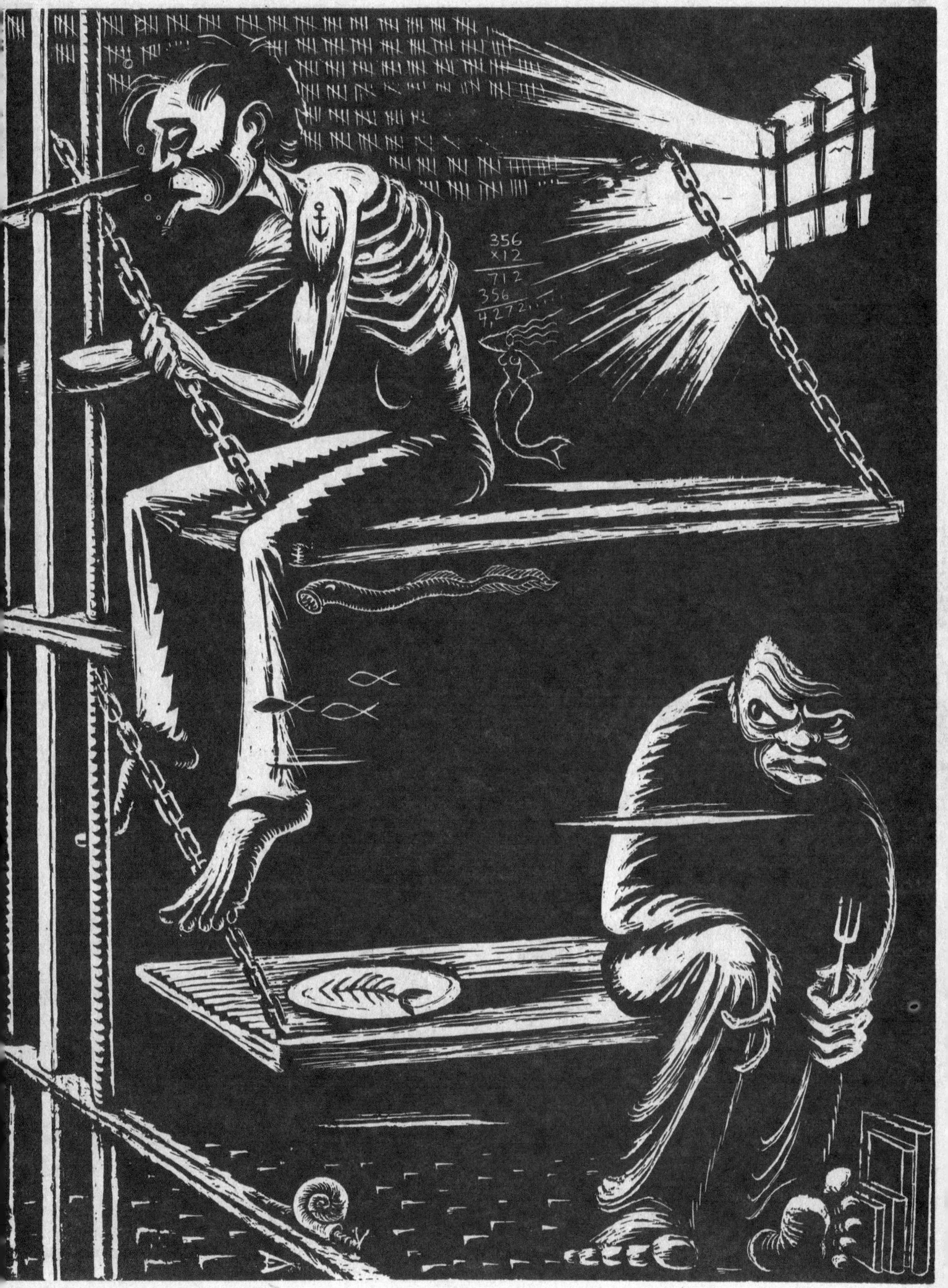
356
x12
712
356
4,272

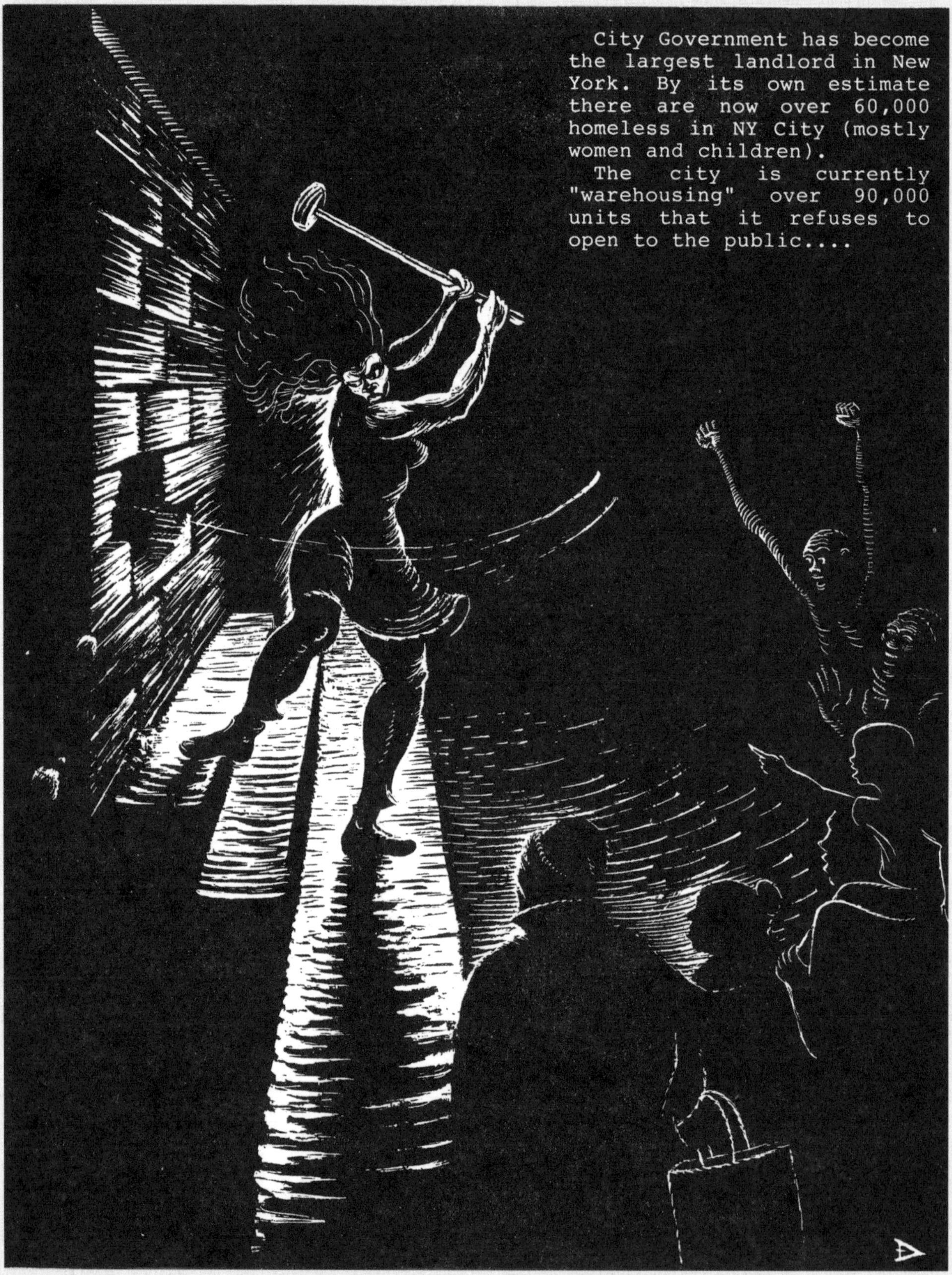
City Government has become the largest landlord in New York. By its own estimate there are now over 60,000 homeless in NY City (mostly women and children).
The city is currently "warehousing" over 90,000 units that it refuses to open to the public....

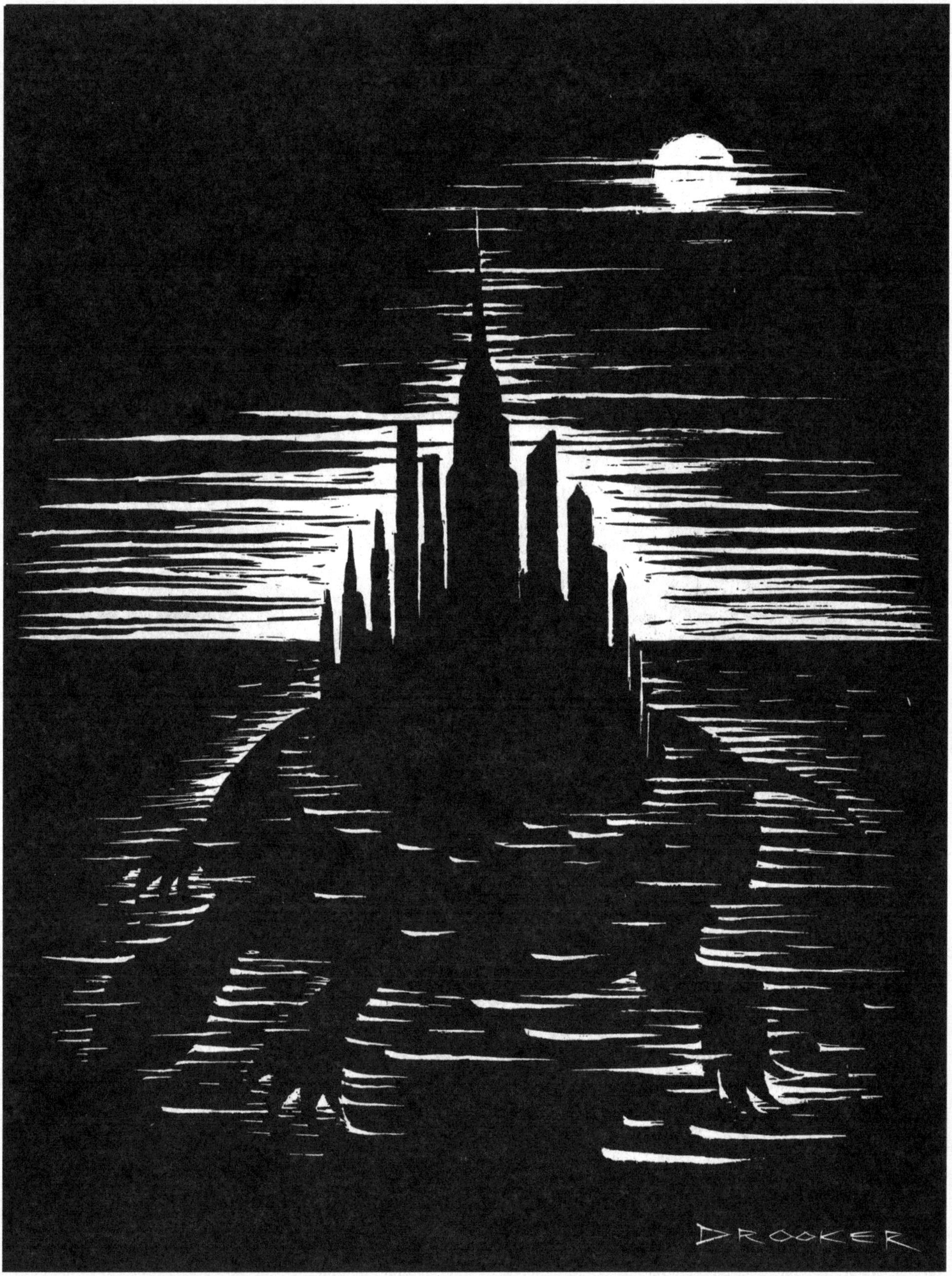
DROOKER

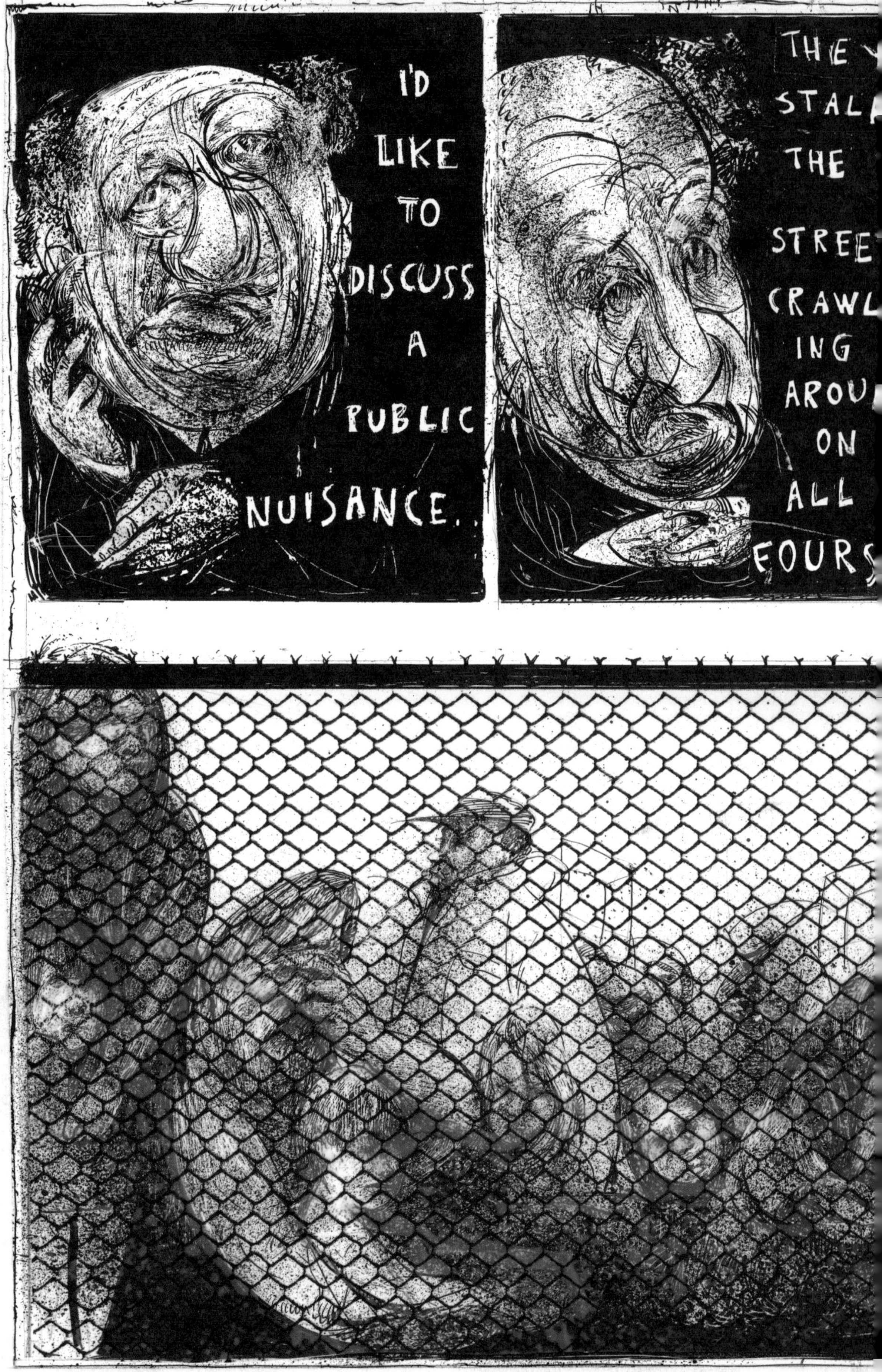
I'D LIKE TO DISCUSS A PUBLIC NUISANCE.
THE
STAL
THE
STREE
CRAWL
ING
AROU
ON
ALL
FOURS

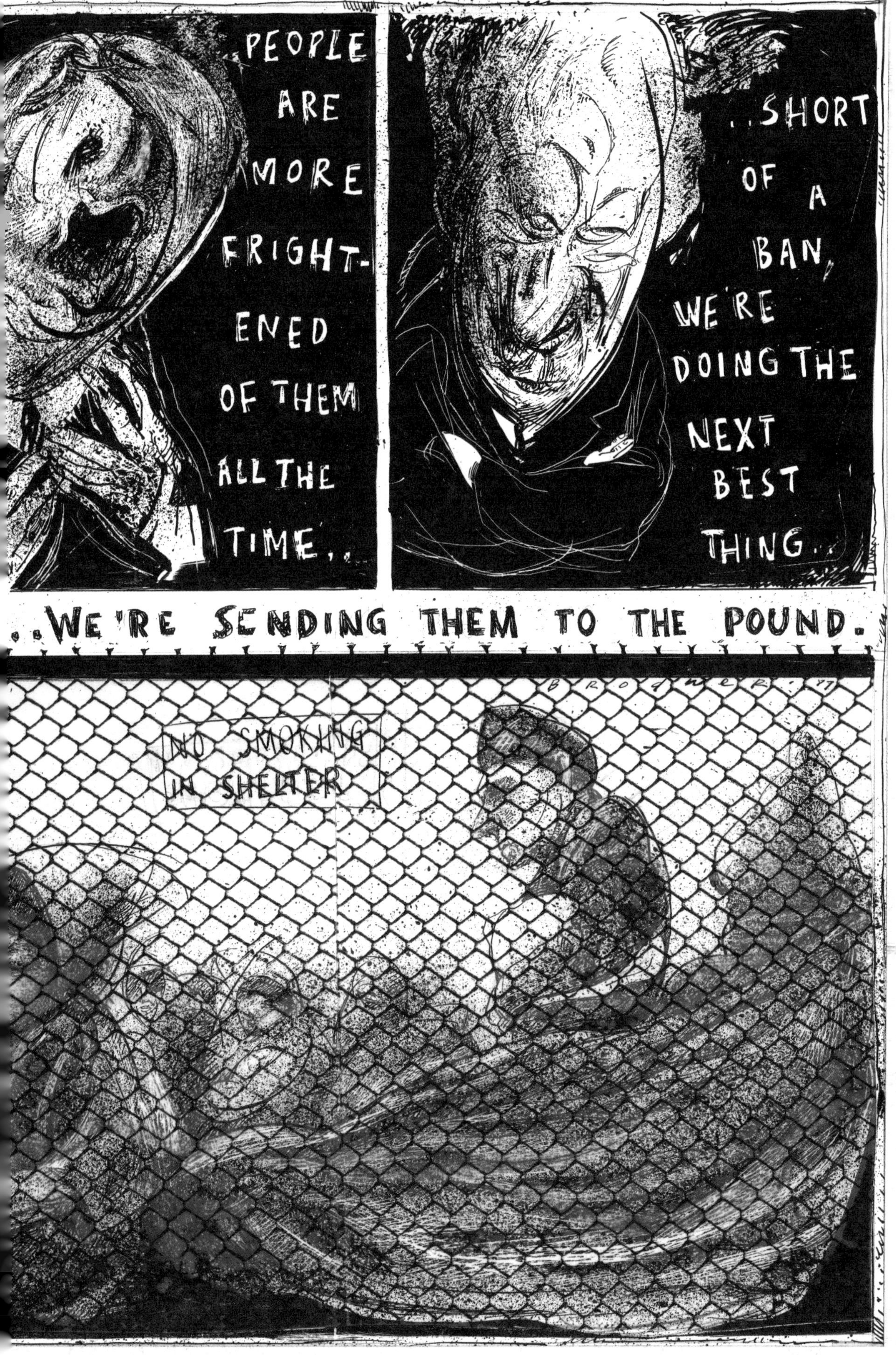
..PEOPLE ARE MORE FRIGHT-ENED OF THEM ALL THE TIME..
..SHORT OF A BAN, WE'RE DOING THE NEXT BEST THING..
..WE'RE SENDING THEM TO THE POUND.
NO SMOKING IN SHELTER
BRODNER '97

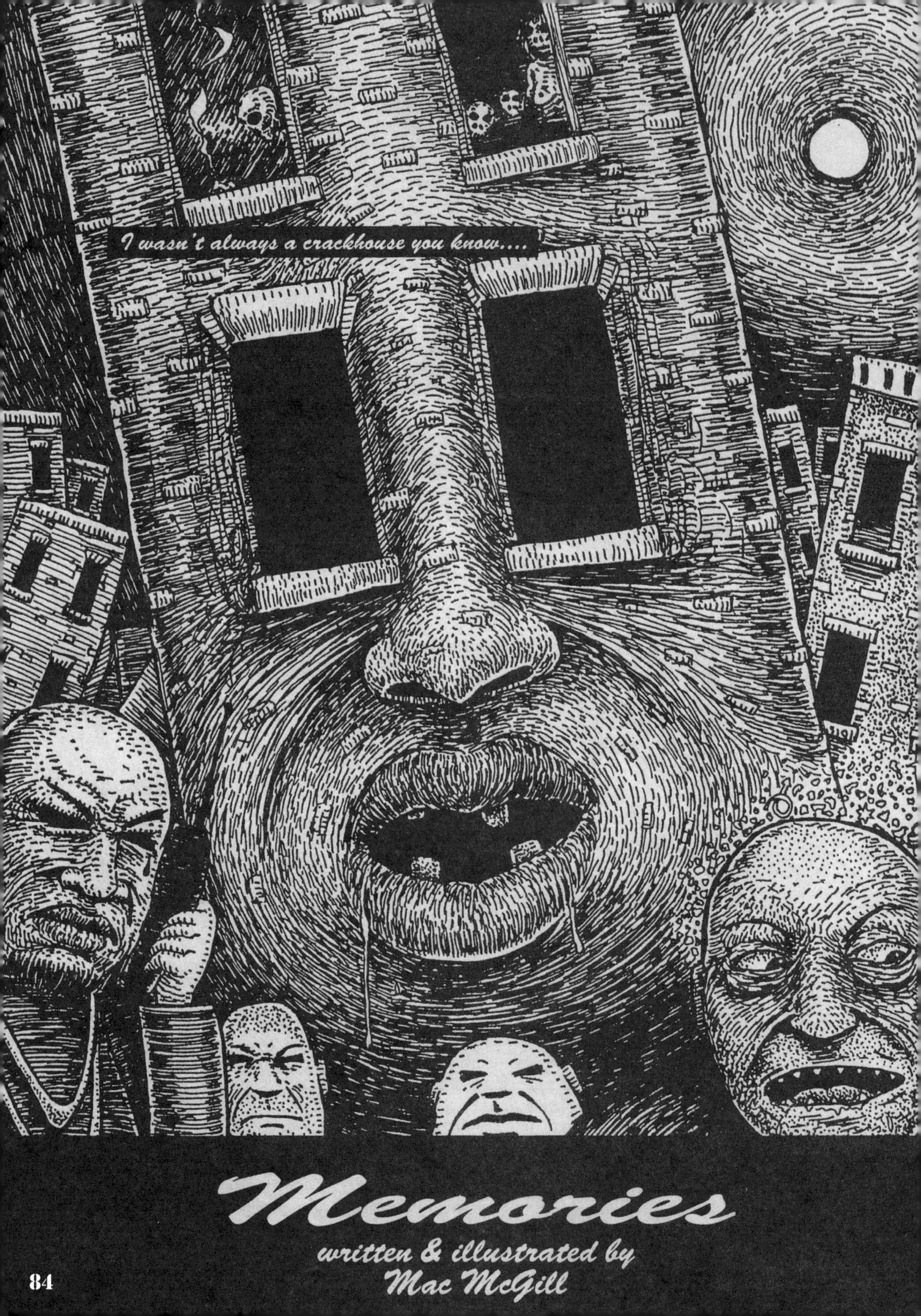
I wasn't always a crackhouse you know....

Memories

written & illustrated by
Mac McGill

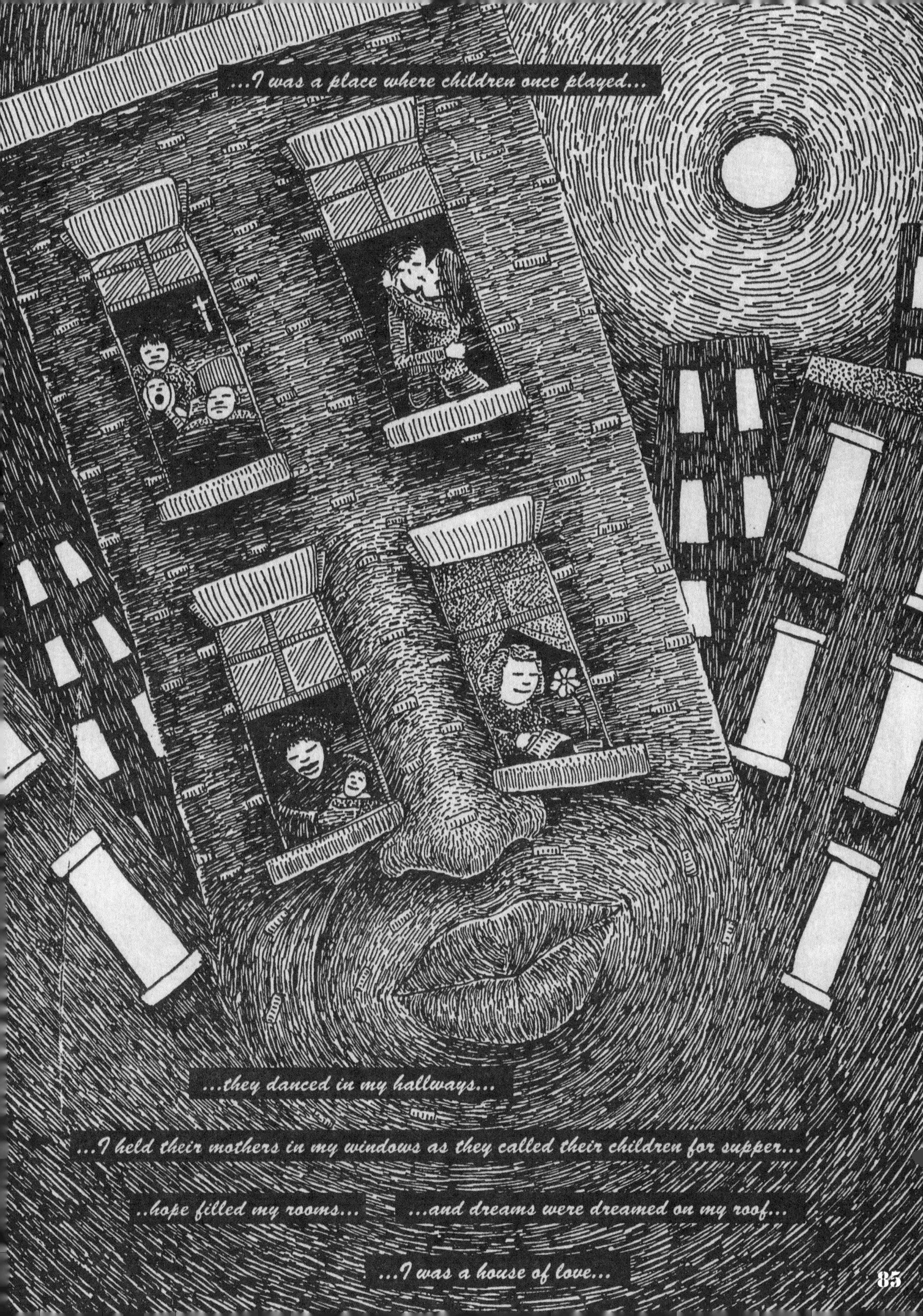
...I was a place where children once played...
...they danced in my hallways...
...I held their mothers in my windows as they called their children for supper...
..hope filled my rooms...
...and dreams were dreamed on my roof...
...I was a house of love...

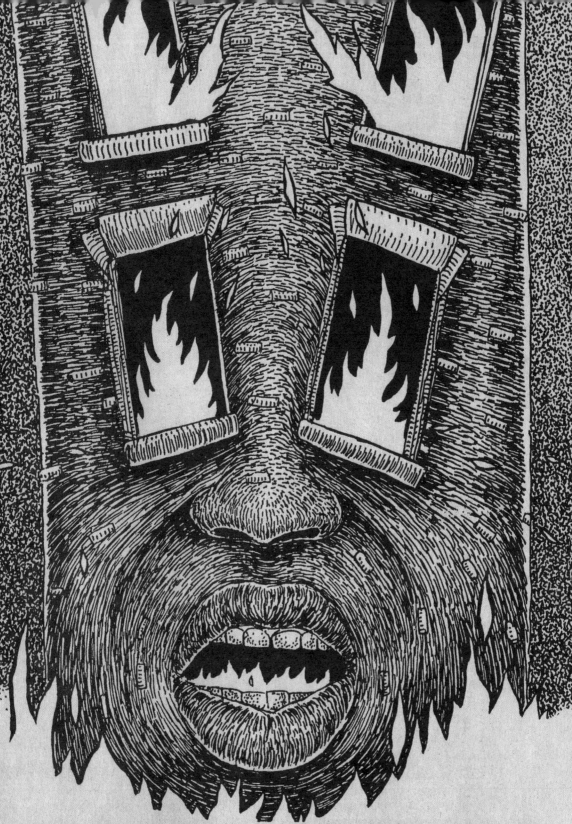

The landlord abandoned me years ago...I felt the heat inside of me as the fire raged through my body...I thought this must be the end...I see the humans with the rubber suits and red trucks...I know it must be bad...because they have come for my brothers and sisters in the same manner...I have no tears...they were stolen long ago...

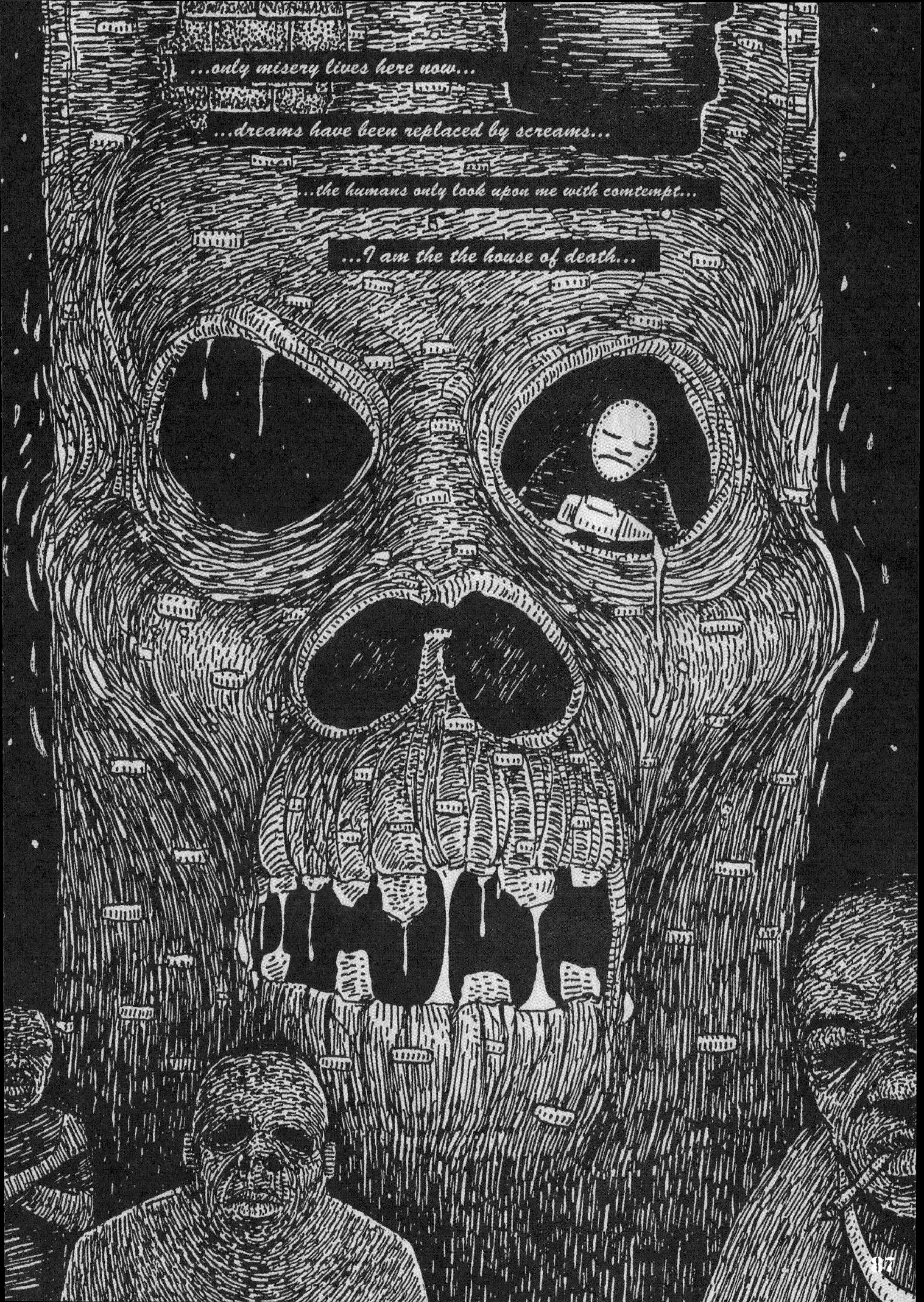
...only misery lives here now...
...dreams have been replaced by screams...
...the humans only look upon me with comtempt...
...I am the the house of death...

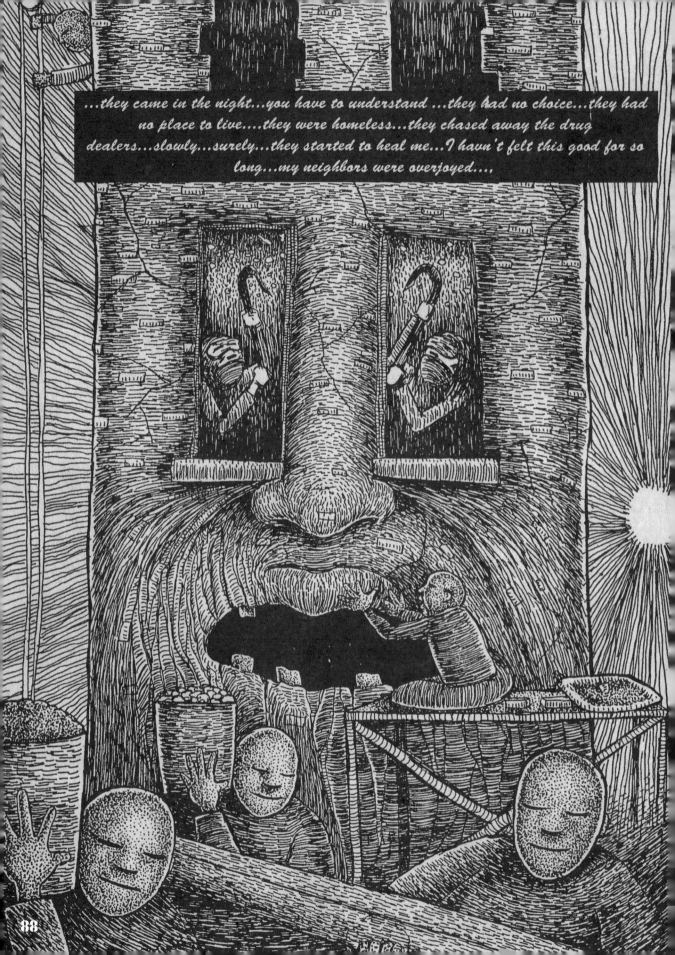

...they came in the night...you have to understand ...they had no choice...they had no place to live....they were homeless...they chased away the drug dealers...slowly...surely...they started to heal me...I havn't felt this good for so long...my neighbors were overjoyed....

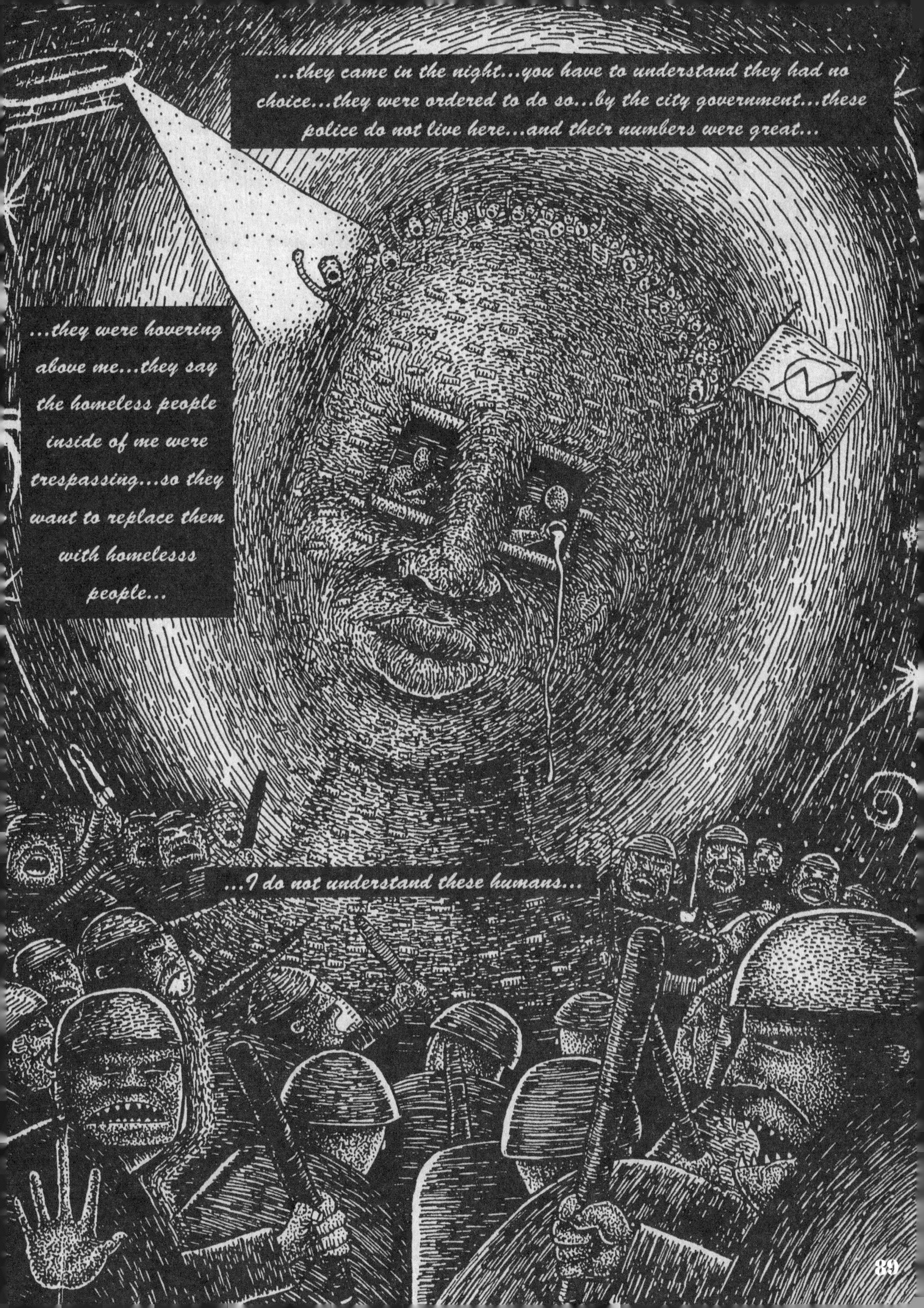
...they came in the night...you have to understand they had no choice...they were ordered to do so...by the city government...these police do not live here...and their numbers were great...
...they were hovering above me...they say the homeless people inside of me were trespassing...so they want to replace them with homelesss people...
...I do not understand these humans...

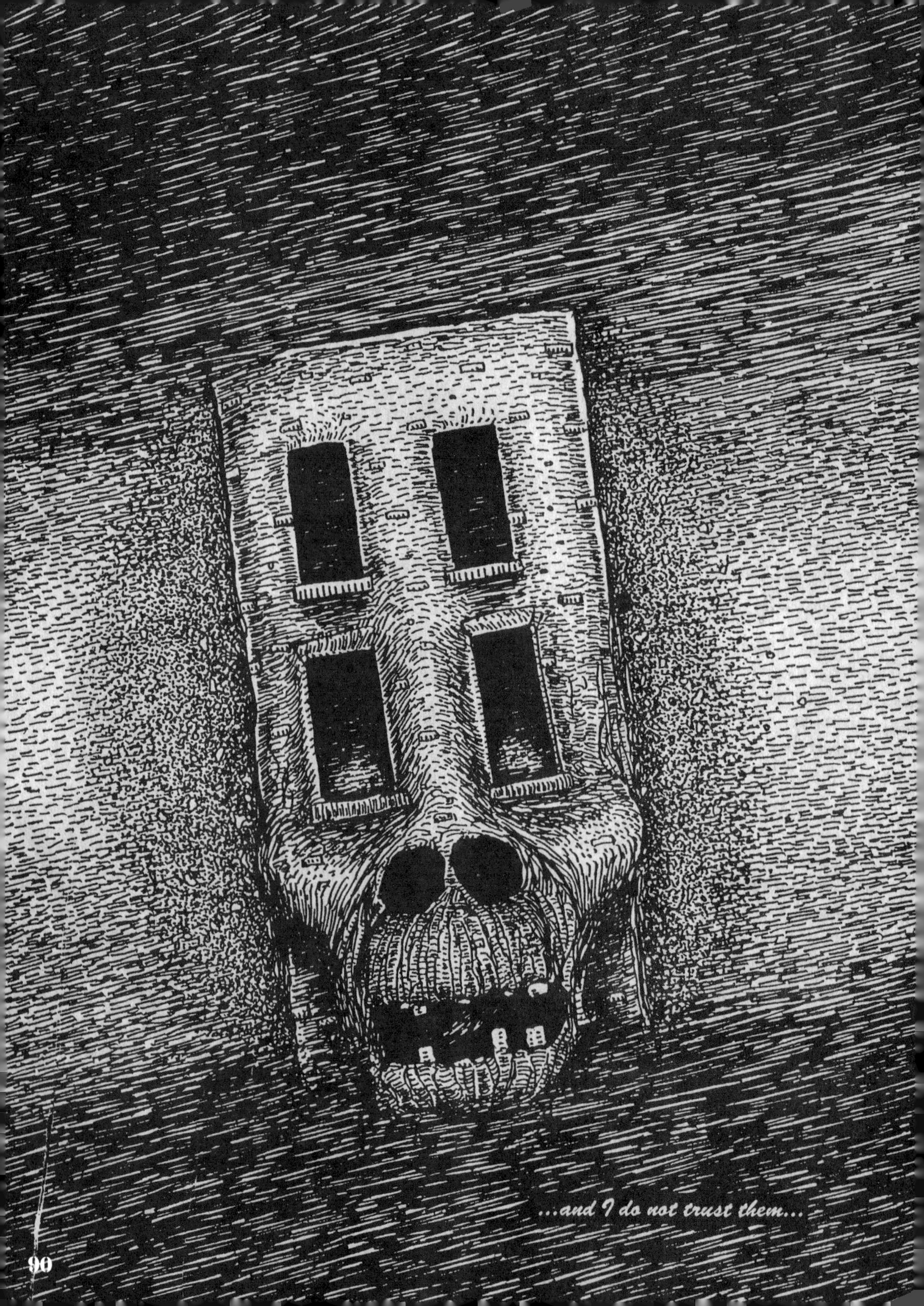

...and I do not trust them...

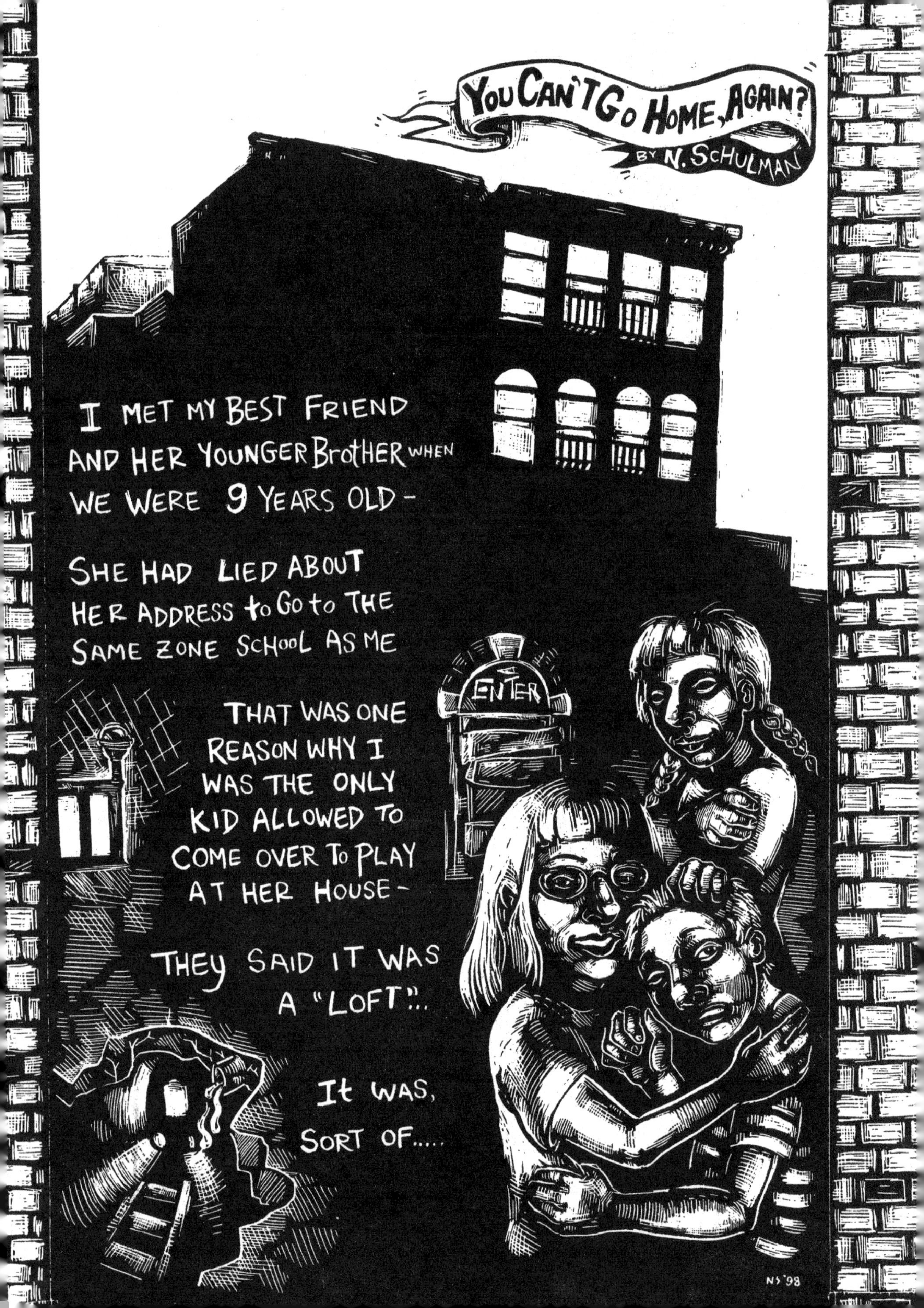
YOU CAN'T GO HOME, AGAIN?
BY N. SCHULMAN
I MET MY BEST FRIEND AND HER YOUNGER BROTHER WHEN WE WERE 9 YEARS OLD -
SHE HAD LIED ABOUT HER ADDRESS TO GO TO THE SAME ZONE SCHOOL AS ME
ENTER
THAT WAS ONE REASON WHY I WAS THE ONLY KID ALLOWED TO COME OVER TO PLAY AT HER HOUSE -
THEY SAID IT WAS A "LOFT"...
IT WAS, SORT OF....
NS '98

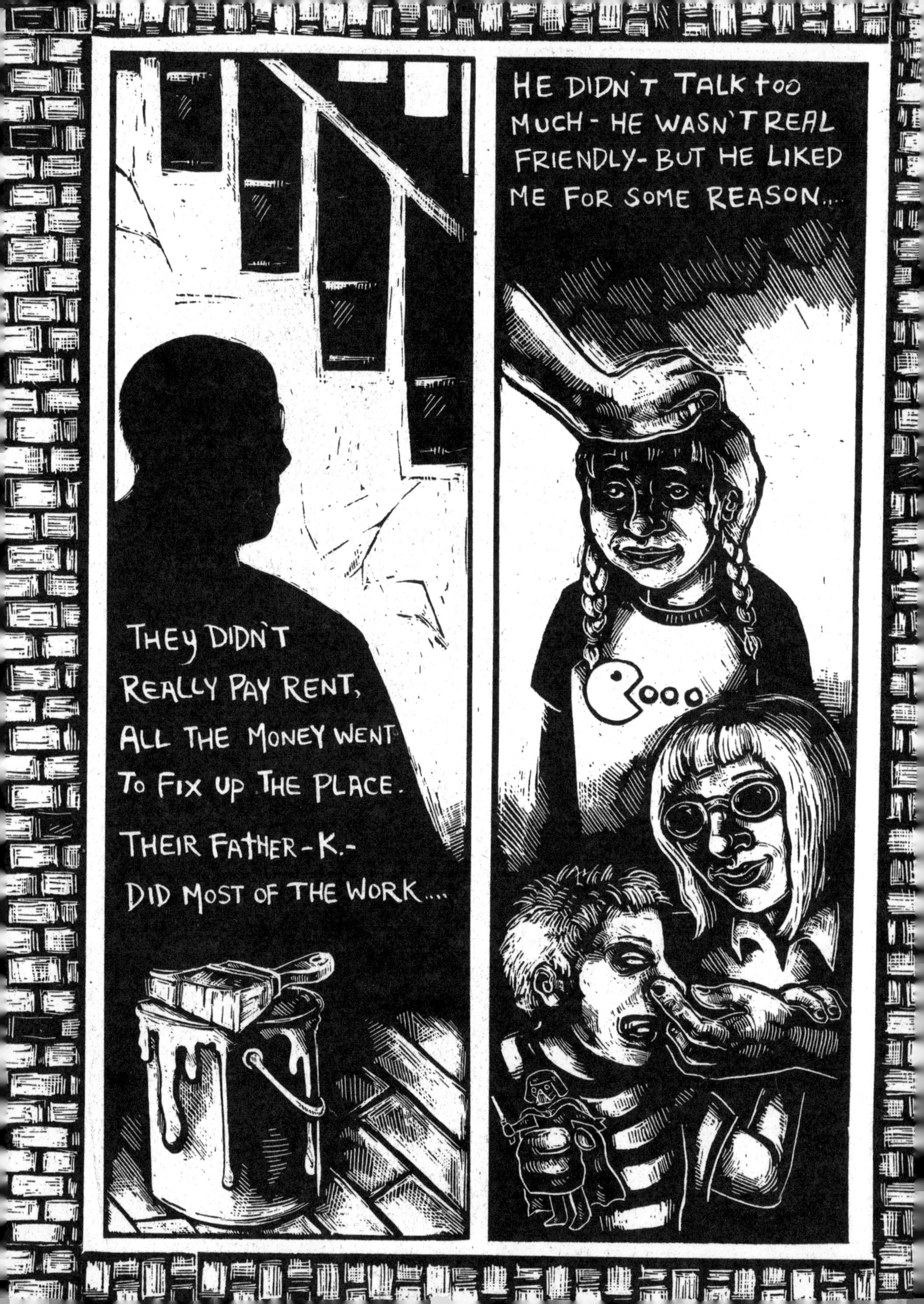
THEY DIDN'T REALLY PAY RENT, ALL THE MONEY WENT TO FIX UP THE PLACE.
THEIR FATHER - K. - DID MOST OF THE WORK....
HE DIDN'T TALK too MUCH - HE WASN'T REAL FRIENDLY - BUT HE LIKED ME FOR SOME REASON....

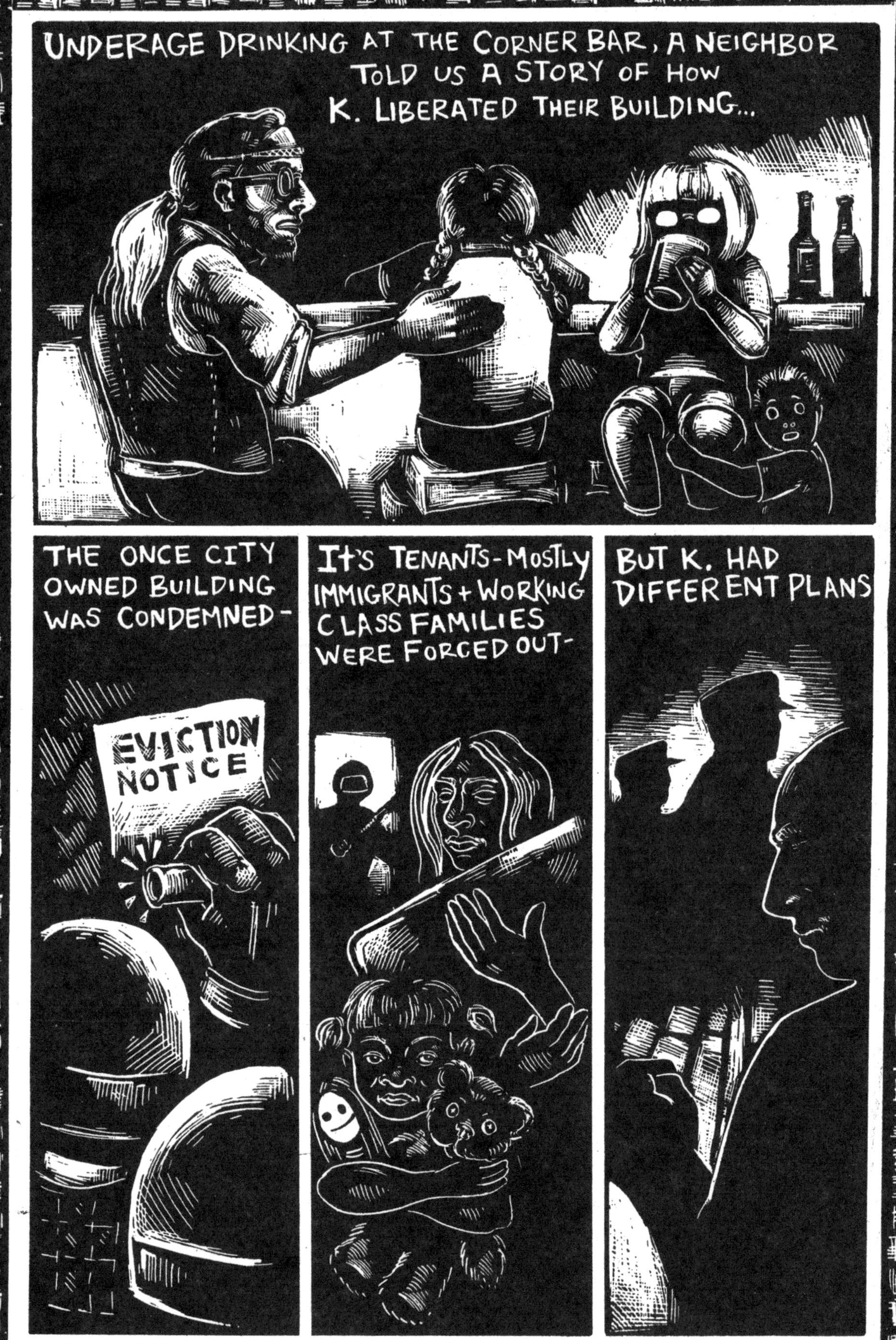
UNDERAGE DRINKING AT THE CORNER BAR, A NEIGHBOR TOLD US A STORY OF HOW K. LIBERATED THEIR BUILDING...
THE ONCE CITY OWNED BUILDING WAS CONDEMNED-
EVICTION NOTICE
IT'S TENANTS-MOSTLY IMMIGRANTS + WORKING CLASS FAMILIES WERE FORCED OUT-
BUT K. HAD DIFFERENT PLANS

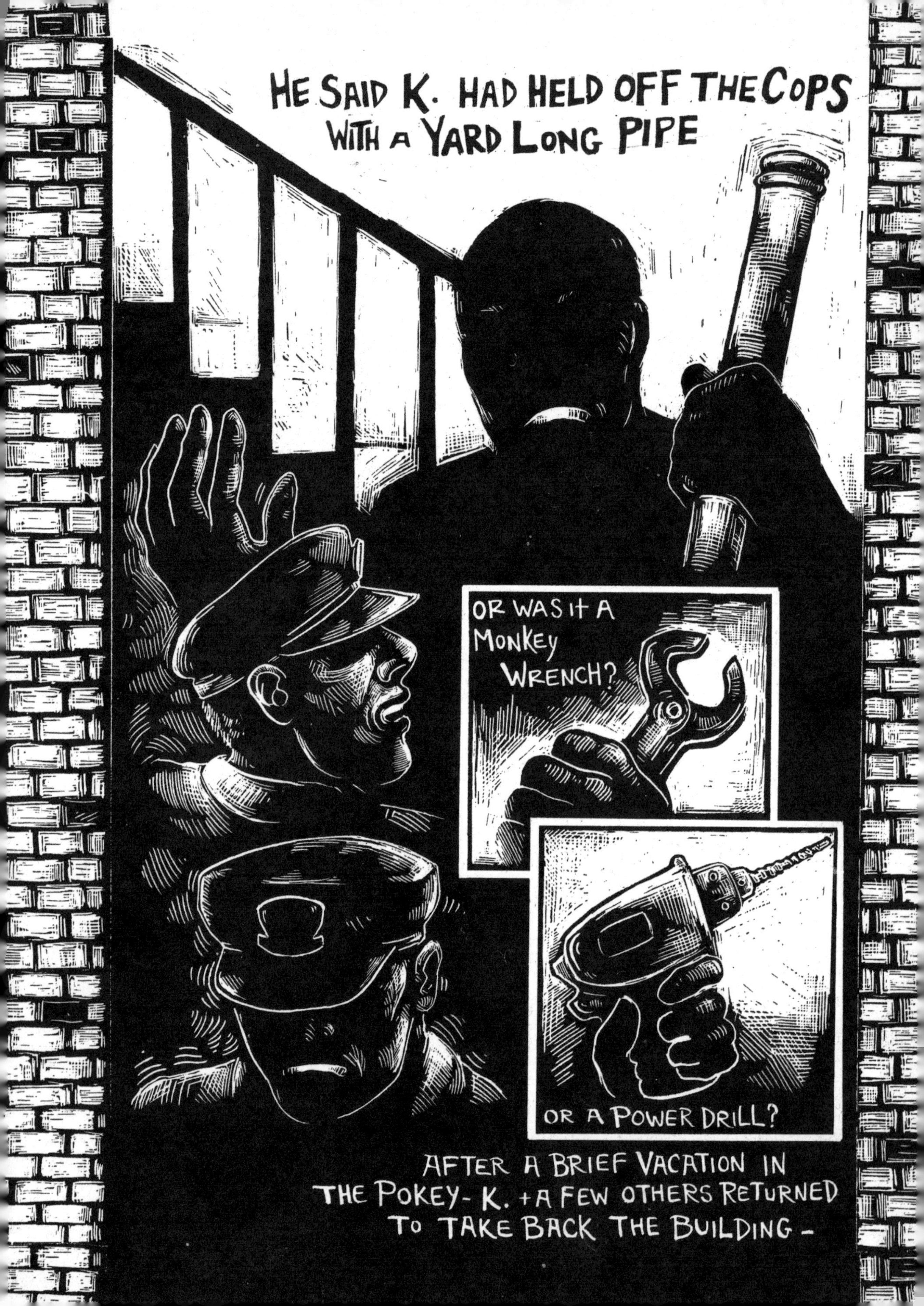
HE SAID K. HAD HELD OFF THE COPS WITH A YARD LONG PIPE
OR WAS IT A MONKEY WRENCH?
OR A POWER DRILL?
AFTER A BRIEF VACATION IN THE POKEY- K. +A FEW OTHERS RETURNED TO TAKE BACK THE BUILDING -

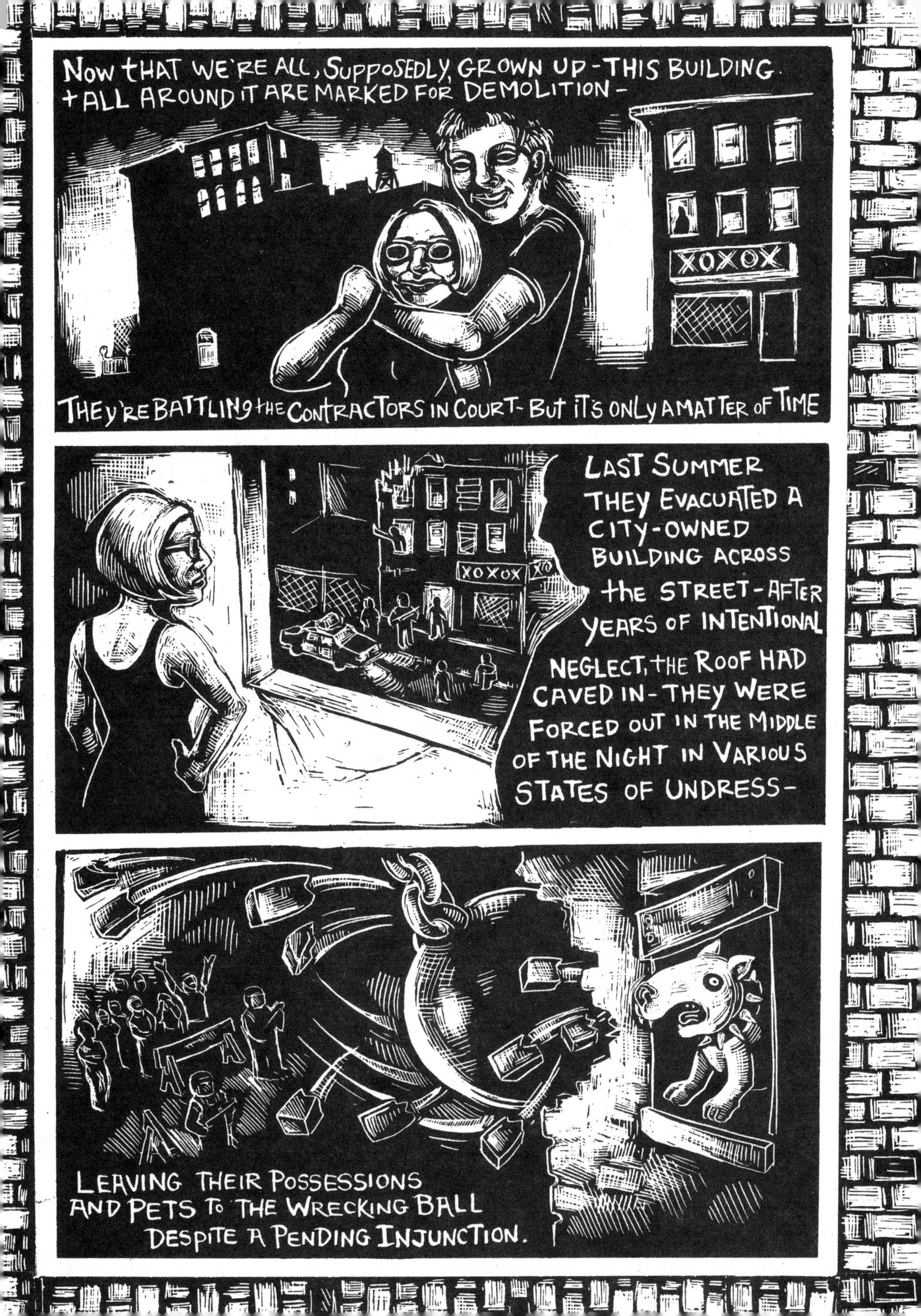

Now THAT WE'RE ALL, SUPPOSEDLY, GROWN UP - THIS BUILDING + ALL AROUND IT ARE MARKED FOR DEMOLITION -
XOXOX
THEY'RE BATTLING THE CONTRACTORS IN COURT - BUT IT'S ONLY A MATTER OF TIME
LAST SUMMER THEY EVACUATED A CITY-OWNED BUILDING ACROSS THE STREET - AFTER YEARS OF INTENTIONAL NEGLECT, THE ROOF HAD CAVED IN - THEY WERE FORCED OUT IN THE MIDDLE OF THE NIGHT IN VARIOUS STATES OF UNDRESS -
XOXOX
LEAVING THEIR POSSESSIONS AND PETS TO THE WRECKING BALL DESPITE A PENDING INJUNCTION.

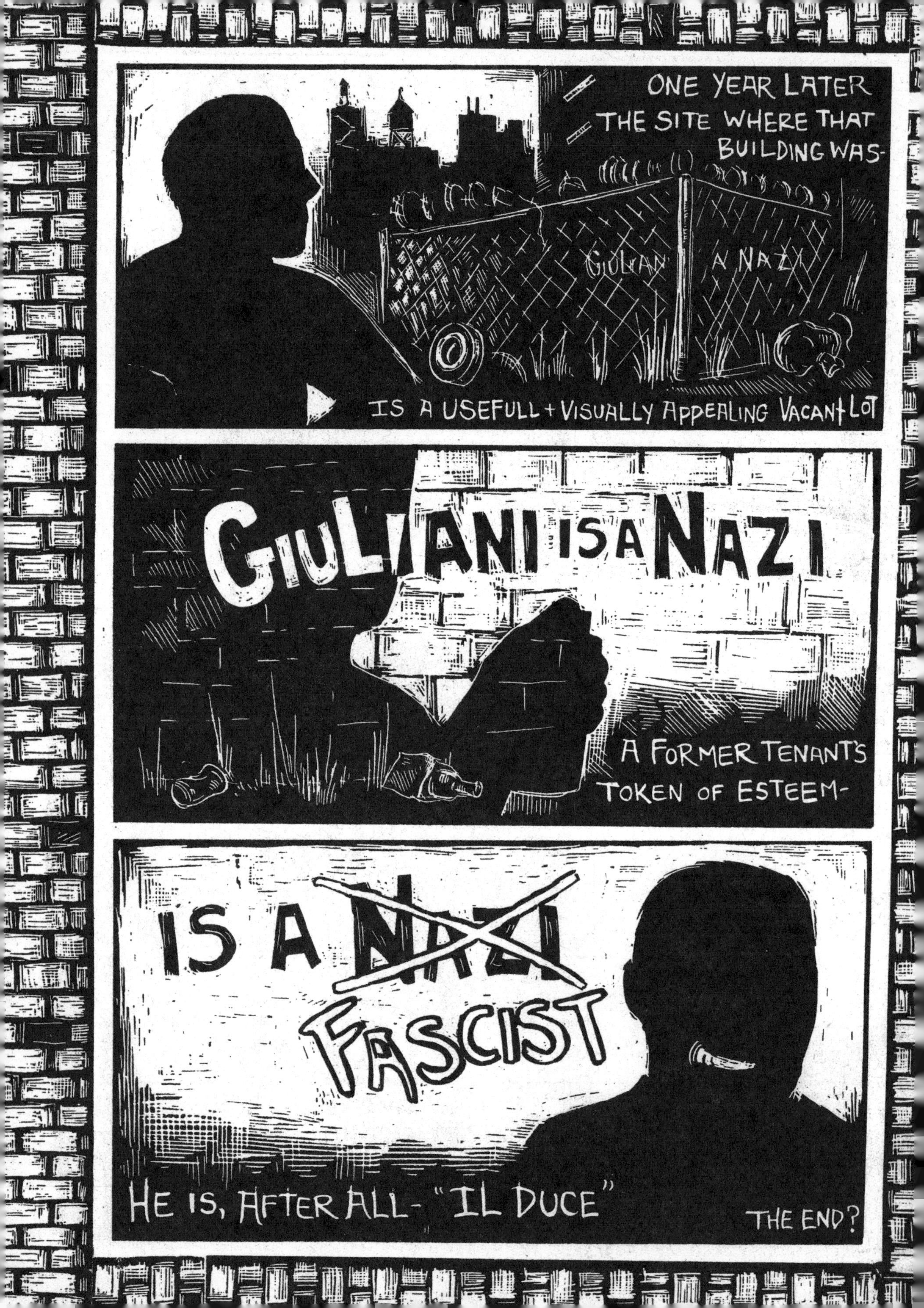

ONE YEAR LATER THE SITE WHERE THAT BUILDING WAS-
GIULIAN
A NAZI
IS A USEFULL + VISUALLY APPEALING VACANT LOT
GIULIANI IS A NAZI
A FORMER TENANT'S TOKEN OF ESTEEM-
IS A NAZI
FASCIST
HE IS, AFTER ALL- "IL DUCE"
THE END?

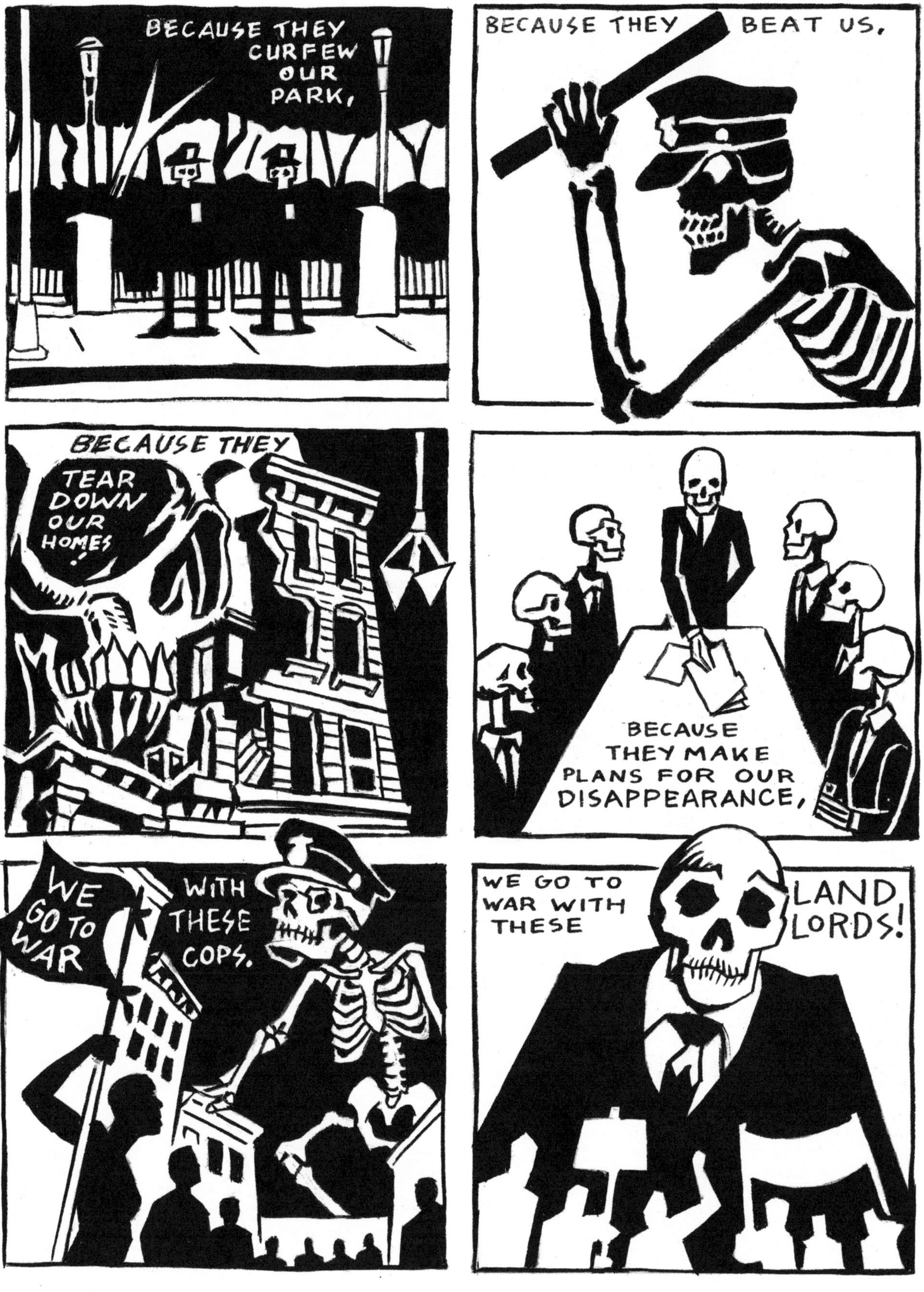
BECAUSE THEY CURFEW OUR PARK,
BECAUSE THEY BEAT US,
BECAUSE THEY
TEAR DOWN OUR HOMES!
BECAUSE THEY MAKE PLANS FOR OUR DISAPPEARANCE,
WE GO TO WAR
WITH THESE COPS.
WE GO TO WAR WITH THESE
LAND LORDS!

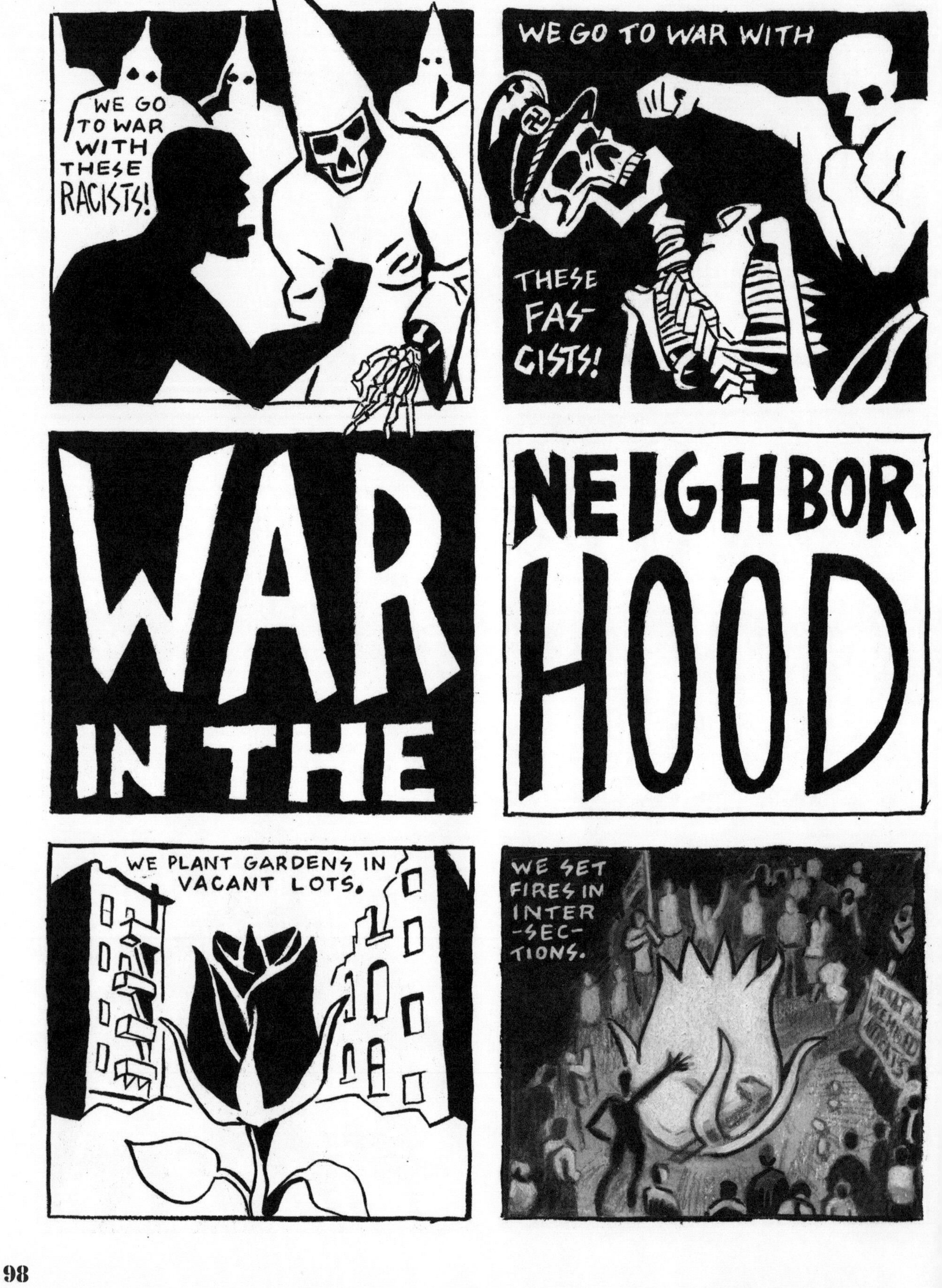
WE GO TO WAR WITH THESE RACISTS!
WE GO TO WAR WITH
THESE FAS-CISTS!
WAR IN THE
NEIGHBOR HOOD
WE PLANT GARDENS IN VACANT LOTS.
WE SET FIRES IN INTER-SEC-TIONS.

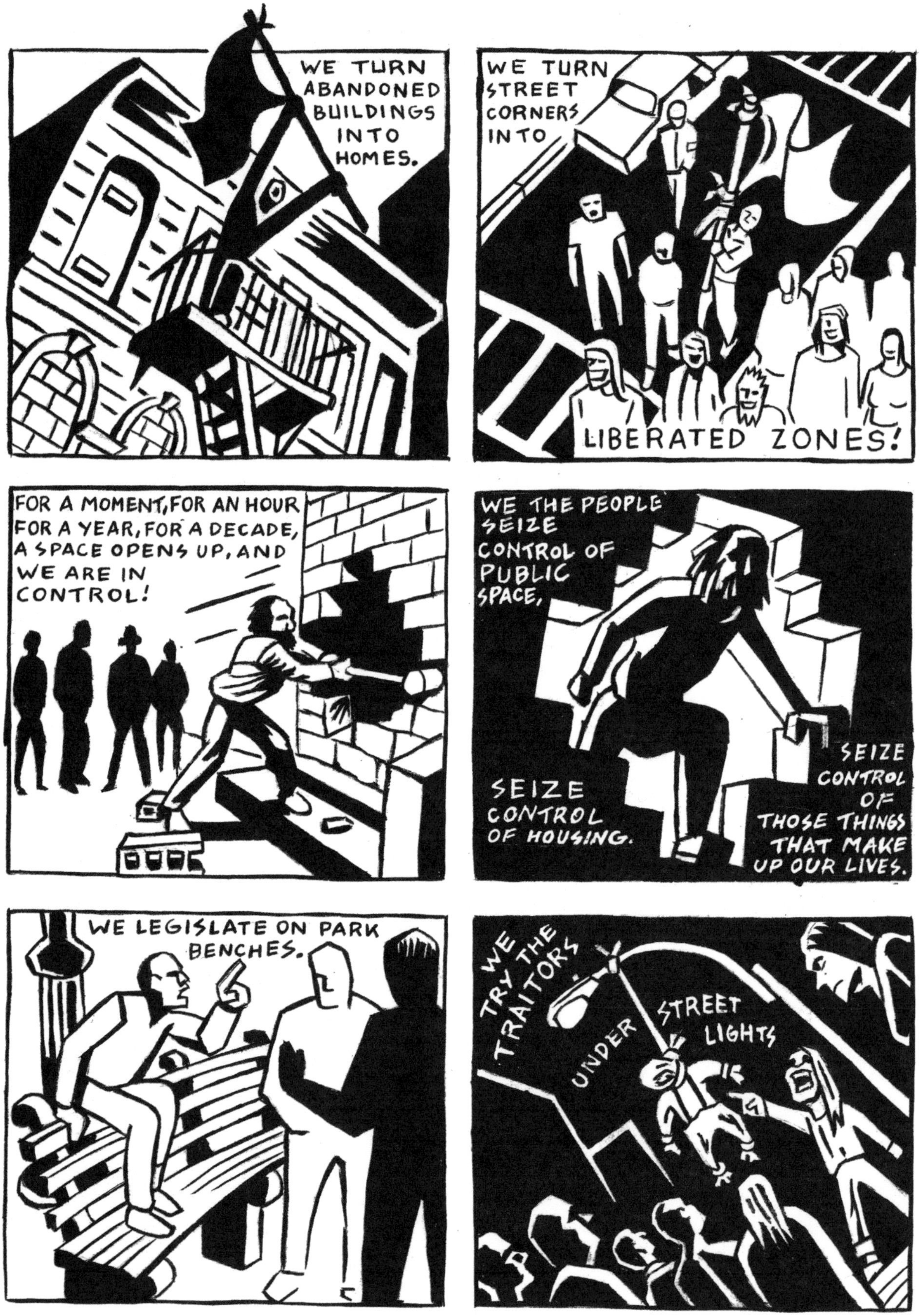

WE TURN ABANDONED BUILDINGS INTO HOMES.
WE TURN STREET CORNERS INTO
LIBERATED ZONES!
FOR A MOMENT, FOR AN HOUR FOR A YEAR, FOR A DECADE, A SPACE OPENS UP, AND WE ARE IN CONTROL!
WE THE PEOPLE SEIZE CONTROL OF PUBLIC SPACE,
SEIZE CONTROL OF HOUSING.
SEIZE CONTROL OF THOSE THINGS THAT MAKE UP OUR LIVES.
WE LEGISLATE ON PARK BENCHES.
WE TRY THE TRAITORS
UNDER STREET LIGHTS

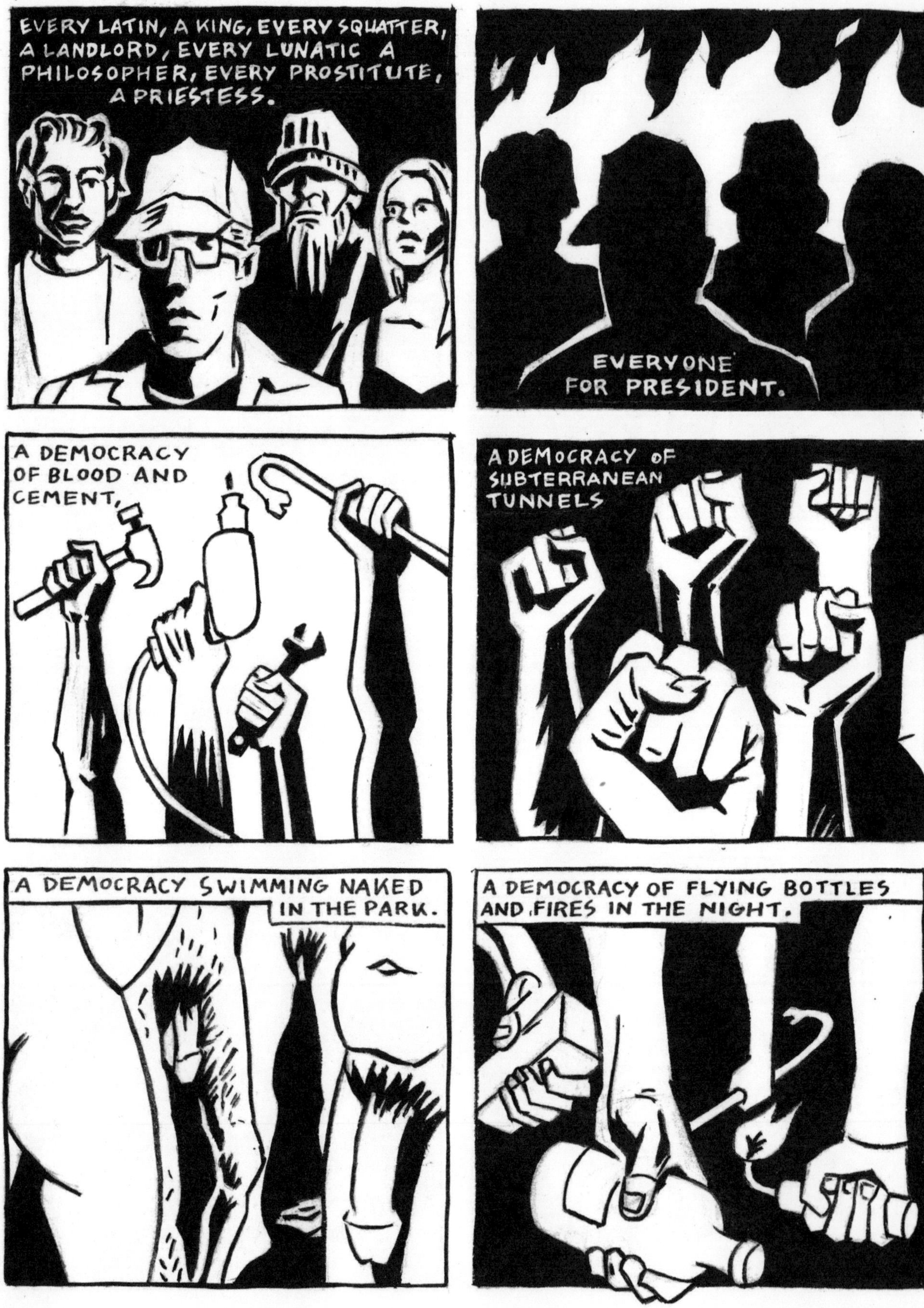
EVERY LATIN, A KING, EVERY SQUATTER, A LANDLORD, EVERY LUNATIC A PHILOSOPHER, EVERY PROSTITUTE, A PRIESTESS.
EVERYONE FOR PRESIDENT.
A DEMOCRACY OF BLOOD AND CEMENT,
A DEMOCRACY OF SUBTERRANEAN TUNNELS
A DEMOCRACY SWIMMING NAKED IN THE PARK.
A DEMOCRACY OF FLYING BOTTLES AND FIRES IN THE NIGHT.

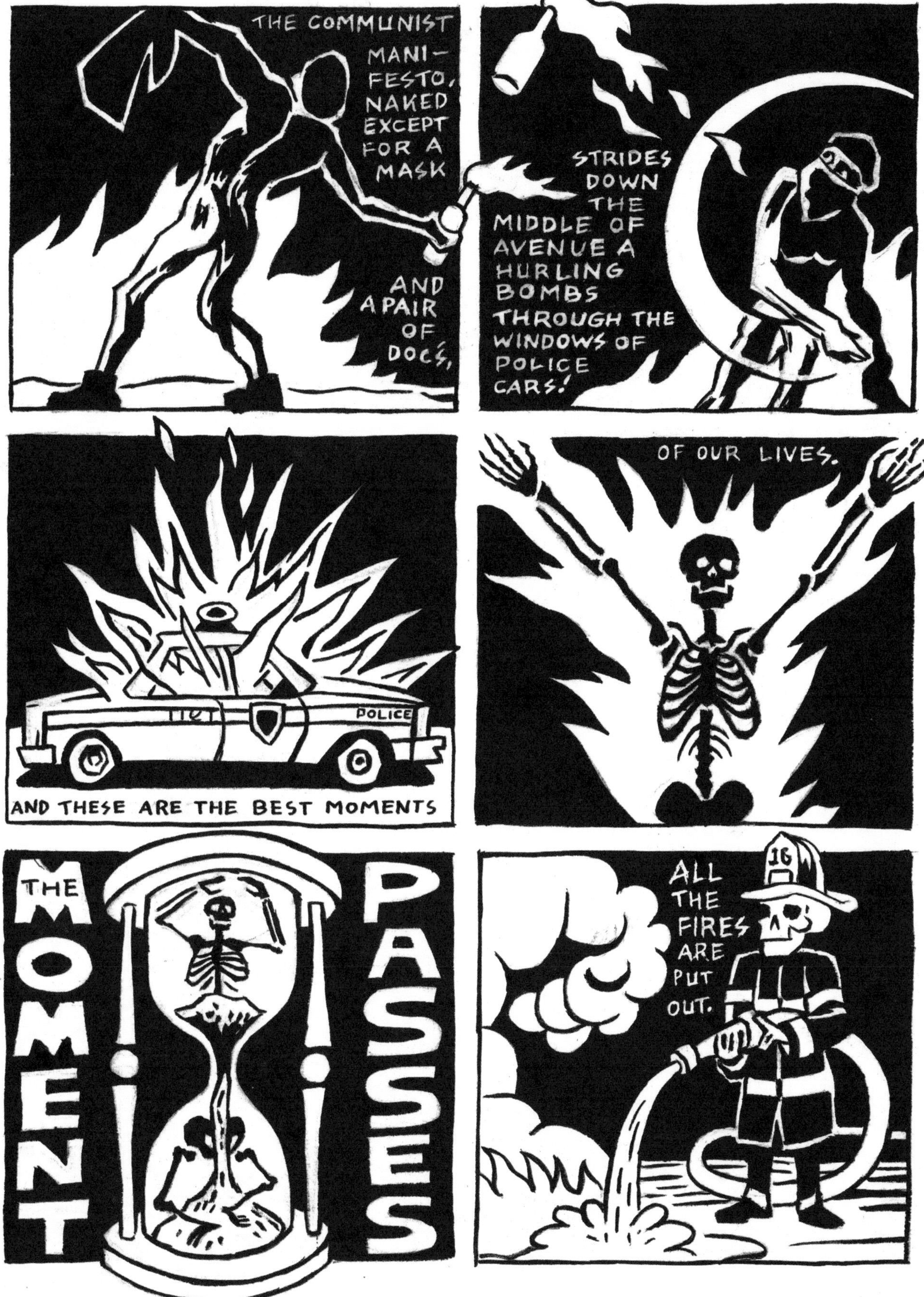
THE COMMUNIST MANIFESTO, NAKED EXCEPT FOR A MASK
AND A PAIR OF DOC'S,
STRIDES DOWN THE MIDDLE OF AVENUE A HURLING BOMBS THROUGH THE WINDOWS OF POLICE CARS!
POLICE
AND THESE ARE THE BEST MOMENTS
OF OUR LIVES.
THE MOMENT PASSES
16
ALL THE FIRES ARE PUT OUT.

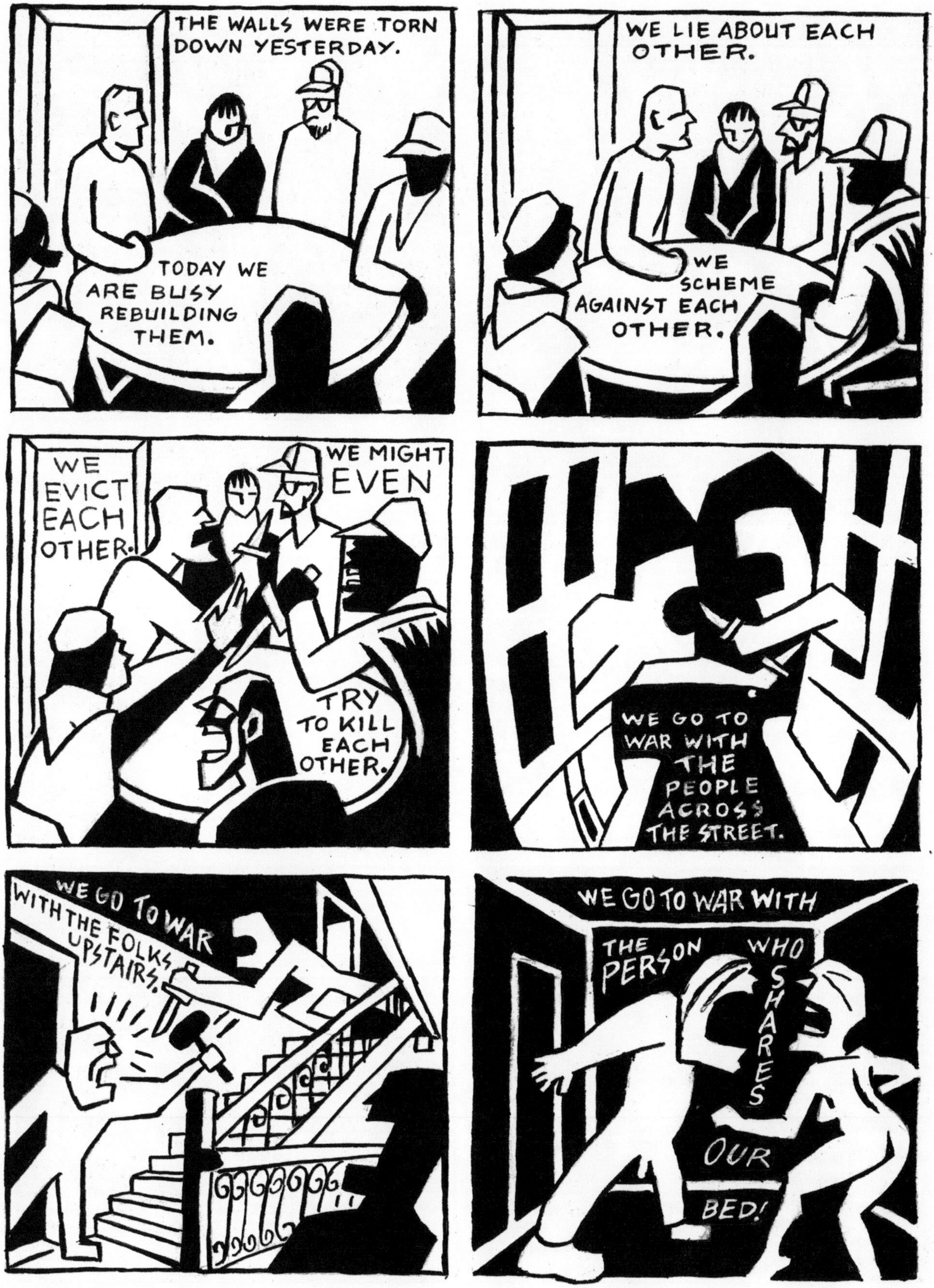
THE WALLS WERE TORN DOWN YESTERDAY.
TODAY WE ARE BUSY REBUILDING THEM.
WE LIE ABOUT EACH OTHER.
WE SCHEME AGAINST EACH OTHER.
WE EVICT EACH OTHER.
WE MIGHT EVEN
TRY TO KILL EACH OTHER.
WE GO TO WAR WITH THE PEOPLE ACROSS THE STREET.
WE GO TO WAR WITH THE FOLKS UPSTAIRS.
WE GO TO WAR WITH
THE PERSON WHO SHARES OUR BED!

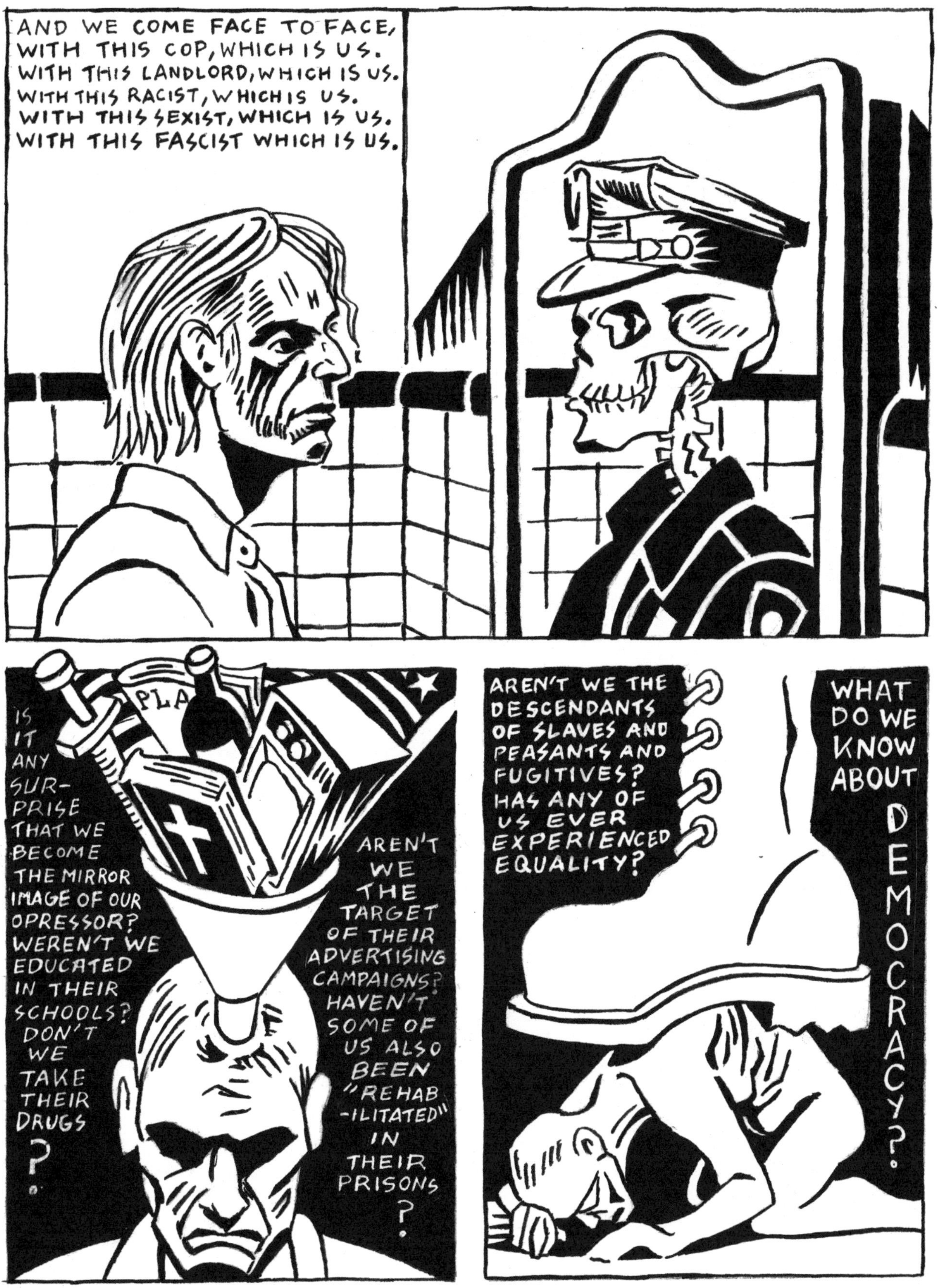
AND WE COME FACE TO FACE, WITH THIS COP, WHICH IS US. WITH THIS LANDLORD, WHICH IS US. WITH THIS RACIST, WHICH IS US. WITH THIS SEXIST, WHICH IS US. WITH THIS FASCIST WHICH IS US.
PLA
IS IT ANY SUR-PRISE THAT WE BECOME THE MIRROR IMAGE OF OUR OPRESSOR? WEREN'T WE EDUCATED IN THEIR SCHOOLS? DON'T WE TAKE THEIR DRUGS?
AREN'T WE THE TARGET OF THEIR ADVERTISING CAMPAIGNS? HAVEN'T SOME OF US ALSO BEEN "REHAB-ILITATED" IN THEIR PRISONS?
AREN'T WE THE DESCENDANTS OF SLAVES AND PEASANTS AND FUGITIVES? HAS ANY OF US EVER EXPERIENCED EQUALITY?
WHAT DO WE KNOW ABOUT DEMOCRACY?

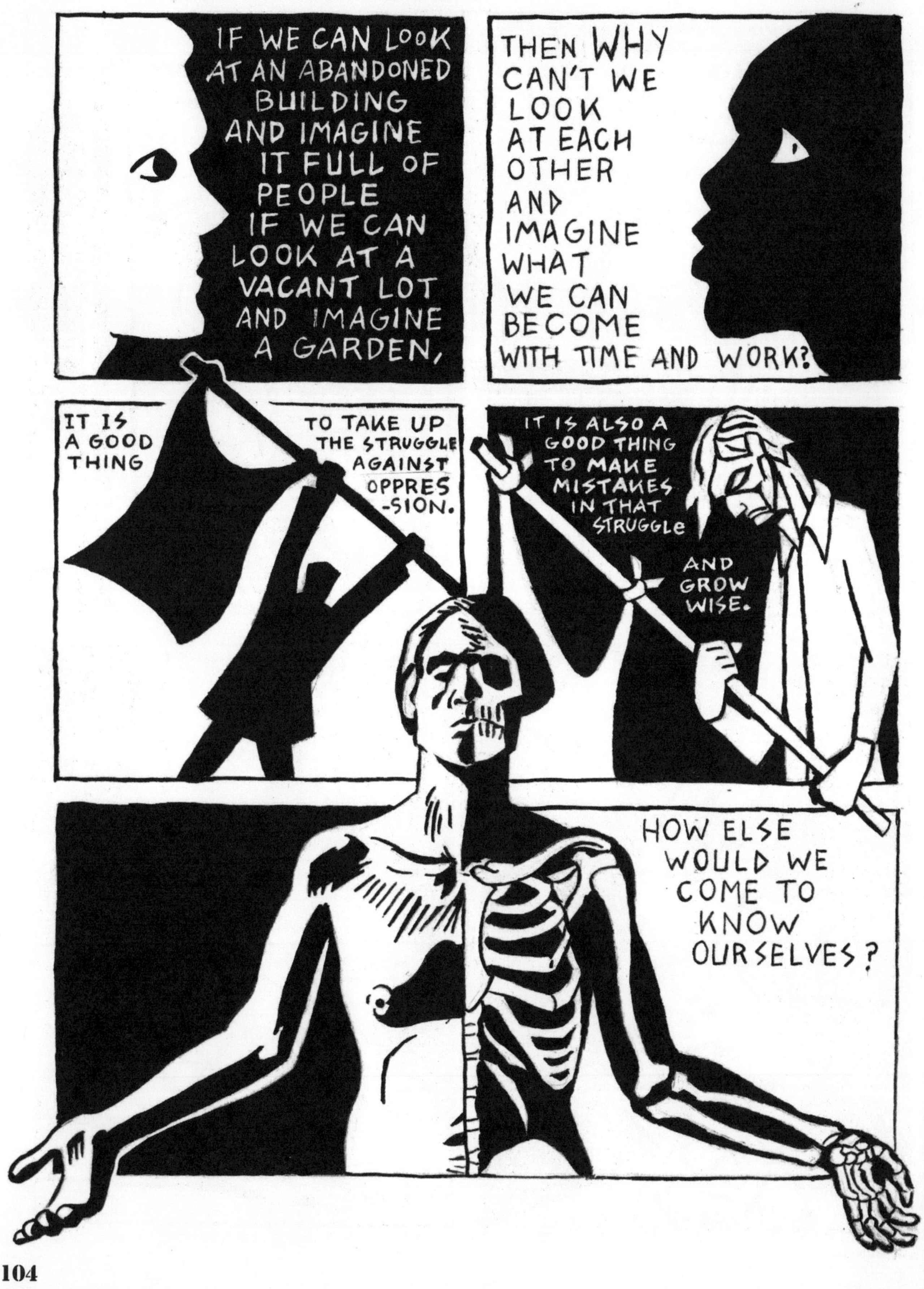
IF WE CAN LOOK AT AN ABANDONED BUILDING AND IMAGINE IT FULL OF PEOPLE IF WE CAN LOOK AT A VACANT LOT AND IMAGINE A GARDEN,
THEN WHY CAN'T WE LOOK AT EACH OTHER AND IMAGINE WHAT WE CAN BECOME WITH TIME AND WORK?
IT IS A GOOD THING
TO TAKE UP THE STRUGGLE AGAINST OPPRES -SION.
IT IS ALSO A GOOD THING TO MAKE MISTAKES IN THAT STRUGGLE
AND GROW WISE.
HOW ELSE WOULD WE COME TO KNOW OURSELVES?

"I WAS RAISED ON THE LOWER EAST SIDE"

story and art by Jeffrey Lewis

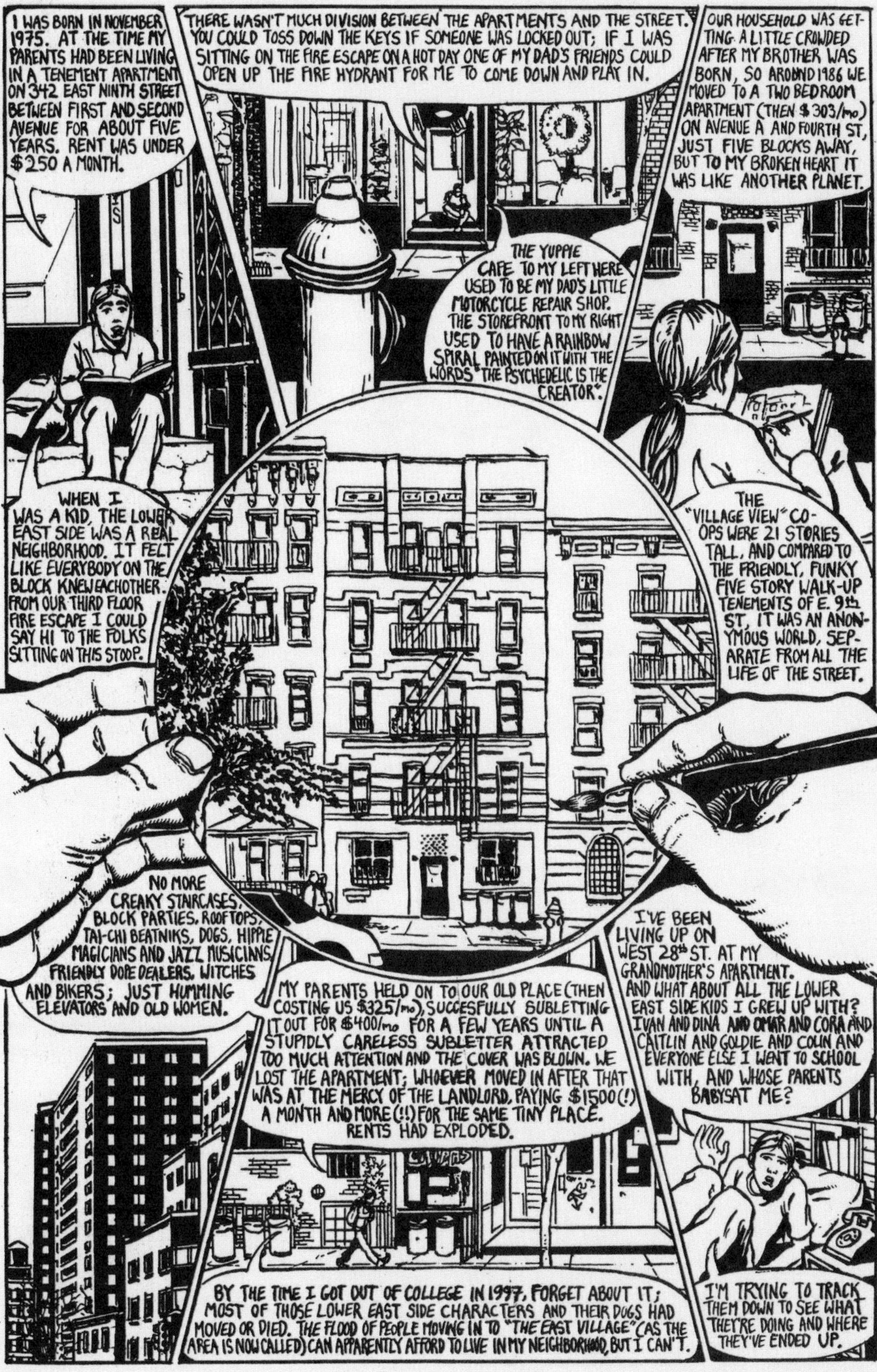

I WAS BORN IN NOVEMBER 1975. AT THE TIME MY PARENTS HAD BEEN LIVING IN A TENEMENT APARTMENT ON 342 EAST NINTH STREET BETWEEN FIRST AND SECOND AVENUE FOR ABOUT FIVE YEARS. RENT WAS UNDER $250 A MONTH.
THERE WASN'T MUCH DIVISION BETWEEN THE APARTMENTS AND THE STREET. YOU COULD TOSS DOWN THE KEYS IF SOMEONE WAS LOCKED OUT; IF I WAS SITTING ON THE FIRE ESCAPE ON A HOT DAY ONE OF MY DAD'S FRIENDS COULD OPEN UP THE FIRE HYDRANT FOR ME TO COME DOWN AND PLAY IN.
OUR HOUSEHOLD WAS GETTING A LITTLE CROWDED AFTER MY BROTHER WAS BORN, SO AROUND 1986 WE MOVED TO A TWO BEDROOM APARTMENT (THEN $303/mo) ON AVENUE A AND FOURTH ST, JUST FIVE BLOCKS AWAY, BUT TO MY BROKEN HEART IT WAS LIKE ANOTHER PLANET.
THE YUPPIE CAFE TO MY LEFT HERE USED TO BE MY DAD'S LITTLE MOTORCYCLE REPAIR SHOP. THE STOREFRONT TO MY RIGHT USED TO HAVE A RAINBOW SPIRAL PAINTED ON IT WITH THE WORDS "THE PSYCHEDELIC IS THE CREATOR".
WHEN I WAS A KID, THE LOWER EAST SIDE WAS A REAL NEIGHBORHOOD. IT FELT LIKE EVERYBODY ON THE BLOCK KNEW EACHOTHER. FROM OUR THIRD FLOOR FIRE ESCAPE I COULD SAY HI TO THE FOLKS SITTING ON THIS STOOP.
THE "VILLAGE VIEW" CO-OPS WERE 21 STORIES TALL, AND COMPARED TO THE FRIENDLY, FUNKY FIVE STORY WALK-UP TENEMENTS OF E. 9th ST, IT WAS AN ANONYMOUS WORLD, SEPARATE FROM ALL THE LIFE OF THE STREET.
NO MORE CREAKY STAIRCASES, BLOCK PARTIES, ROOFTOPS, TAI-CHI BEATNIKS, DOGS, HIPPIE MAGICIANS AND JAZZ MUSICINS, FRIENDLY DOPE DEALERS, WITCHES AND BIKERS; JUST HUMMING ELEVATORS AND OLD WOMEN.
MY PARENTS HELD ON TO OUR OLD PLACE (THEN COSTING US $325/mo), SUCCESFULLY SUBLETTING IT OUT FOR $400/mo FOR A FEW YEARS UNTIL A STUPIDLY CARELESS SUBLETTER ATTRACTED TOO MUCH ATTENTION AND THE COVER WAS BLOWN. WE LOST THE APARTMENT; WHOEVER MOVED IN AFTER THAT WAS AT THE MERCY OF THE LANDLORD, PAYING $1500(!) A MONTH AND MORE (!!) FOR THE SAME TINY PLACE. RENTS HAD EXPLODED.
I'VE BEEN LIVING UP ON WEST 28th ST. AT MY GRANDMOTHER'S APARTMENT. AND WHAT ABOUT ALL THE LOWER EAST SIDE KIDS I GREW UP WITH? IVAN AND DINA AND OMAR AND CORA AND CAITLIN AND GOLDIE AND COLIN AND EVERYONE ELSE I WENT TO SCHOOL WITH, AND WHOSE PARENTS BABYSAT ME?
BY THE TIME I GOT OUT OF COLLEGE IN 1997, FORGET ABOUT IT; MOST OF THOSE LOWER EAST SIDE CHARACTERS AND THEIR DOGS HAD MOVED OR DIED. THE FLOOD OF PEOPLE MOVING IN TO "THE EAST VILLAGE" (AS THE AREA IS NOW CALLED) CAN APPARENTLY AFFORD TO LIVE IN MY NEIGHBORHOOD, BUT I CAN'T.
I'M TRYING TO TRACK THEM DOWN TO SEE WHAT THEY'RE DOING AND WHERE THEY'VE ENDED UP.

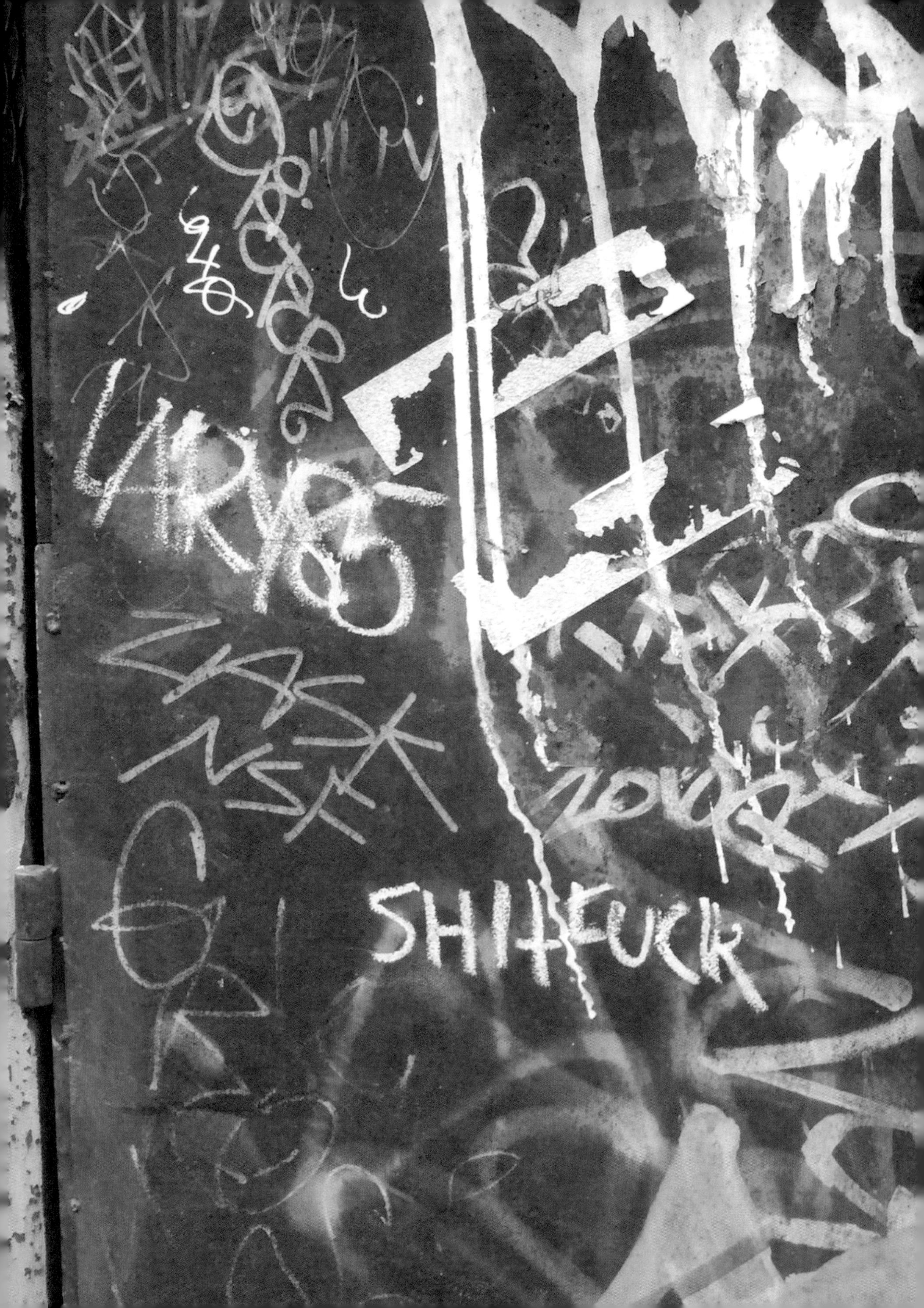
SHITFUCK

AUTOBIOLOGY

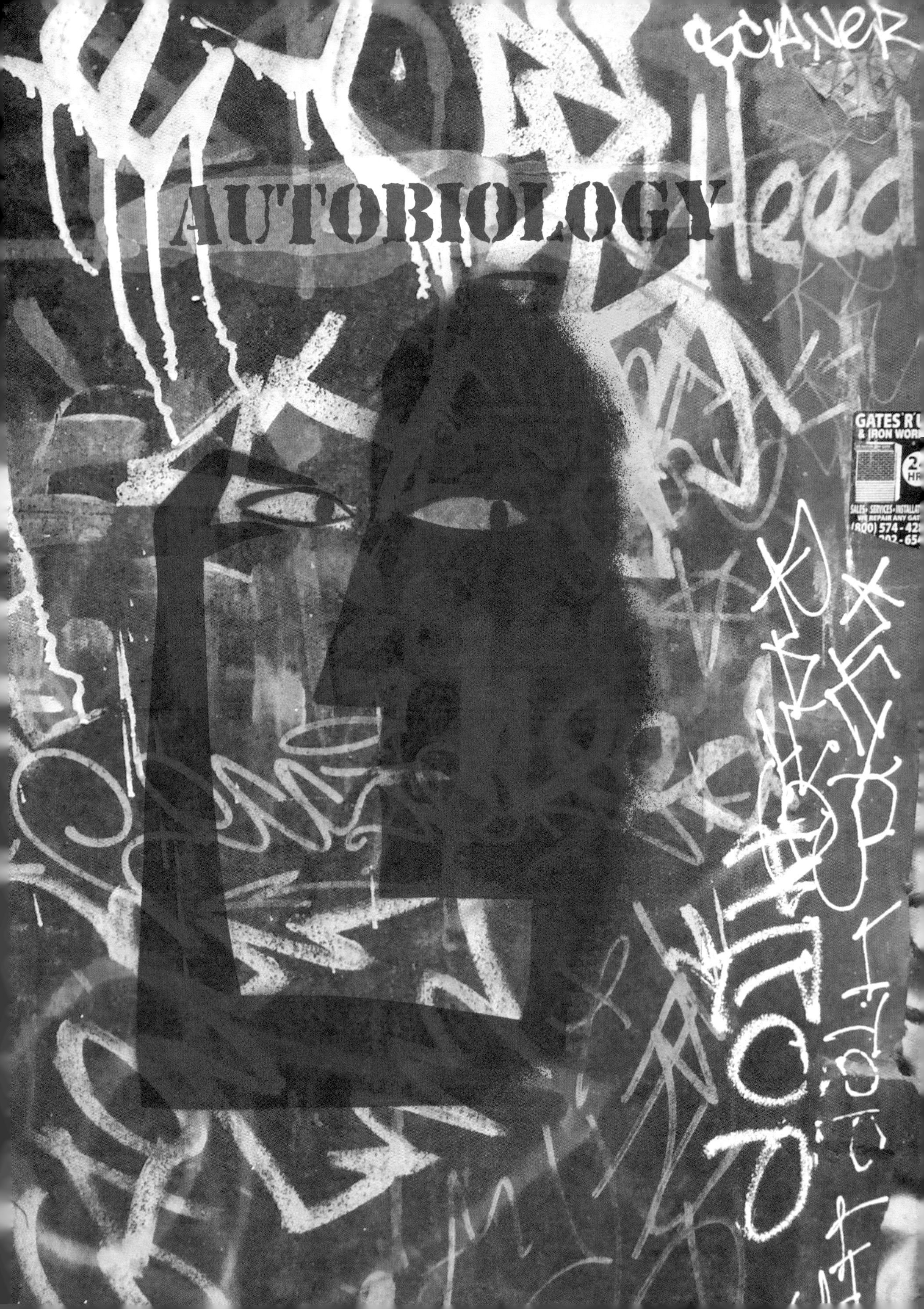

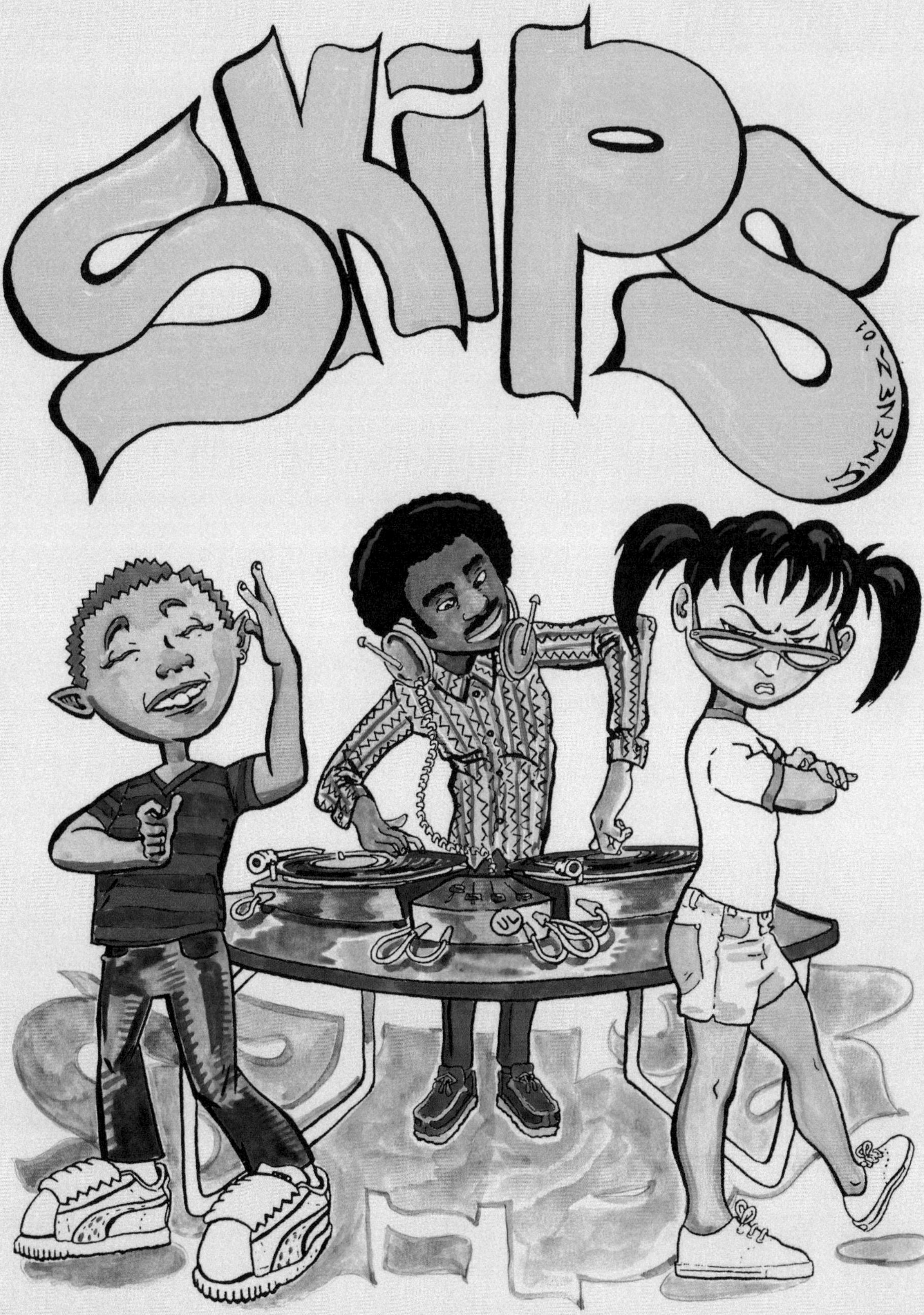
SKIPS

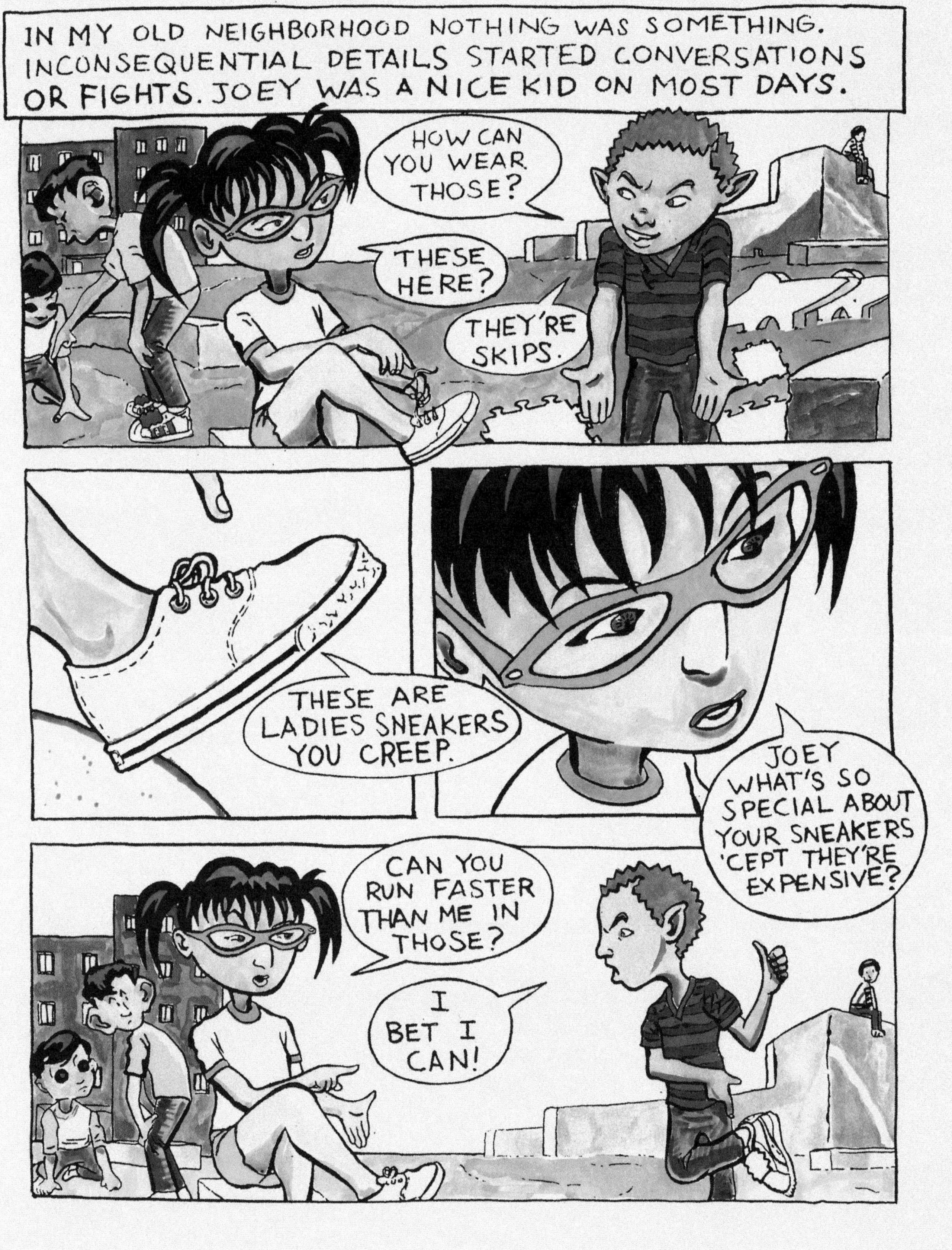
IN MY OLD NEIGHBORHOOD NOTHING WAS SOMETHING. INCONSEQUENTIAL DETAILS STARTED CONVERSATIONS OR FIGHTS. JOEY WAS A NICE KID ON MOST DAYS.
HOW CAN YOU WEAR THOSE?
THESE HERE?
THEY'RE SKIPS.
THESE ARE LADIES SNEAKERS YOU CREEP.
JOEY WHAT'S SO SPECIAL ABOUT YOUR SNEAKERS 'CEPT THEY'RE EXPENSIVE?
CAN YOU RUN FASTER THAN ME IN THOSE?
I BET I CAN!

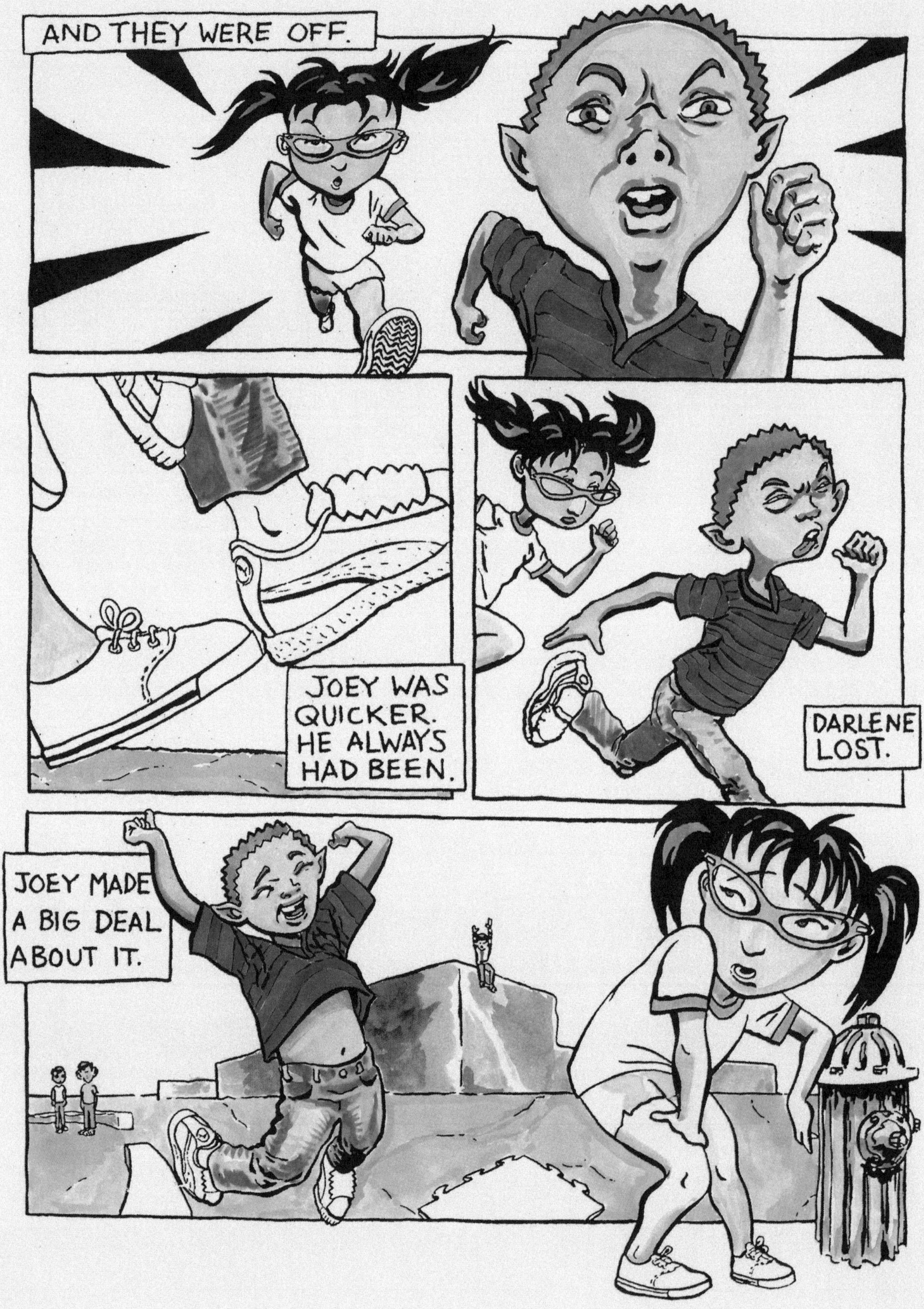
AND THEY WERE OFF.
JOEY WAS QUICKER. HE ALWAYS HAD BEEN.
DARLENE LOST.
JOEY MADE A BIG DEAL ABOUT IT.

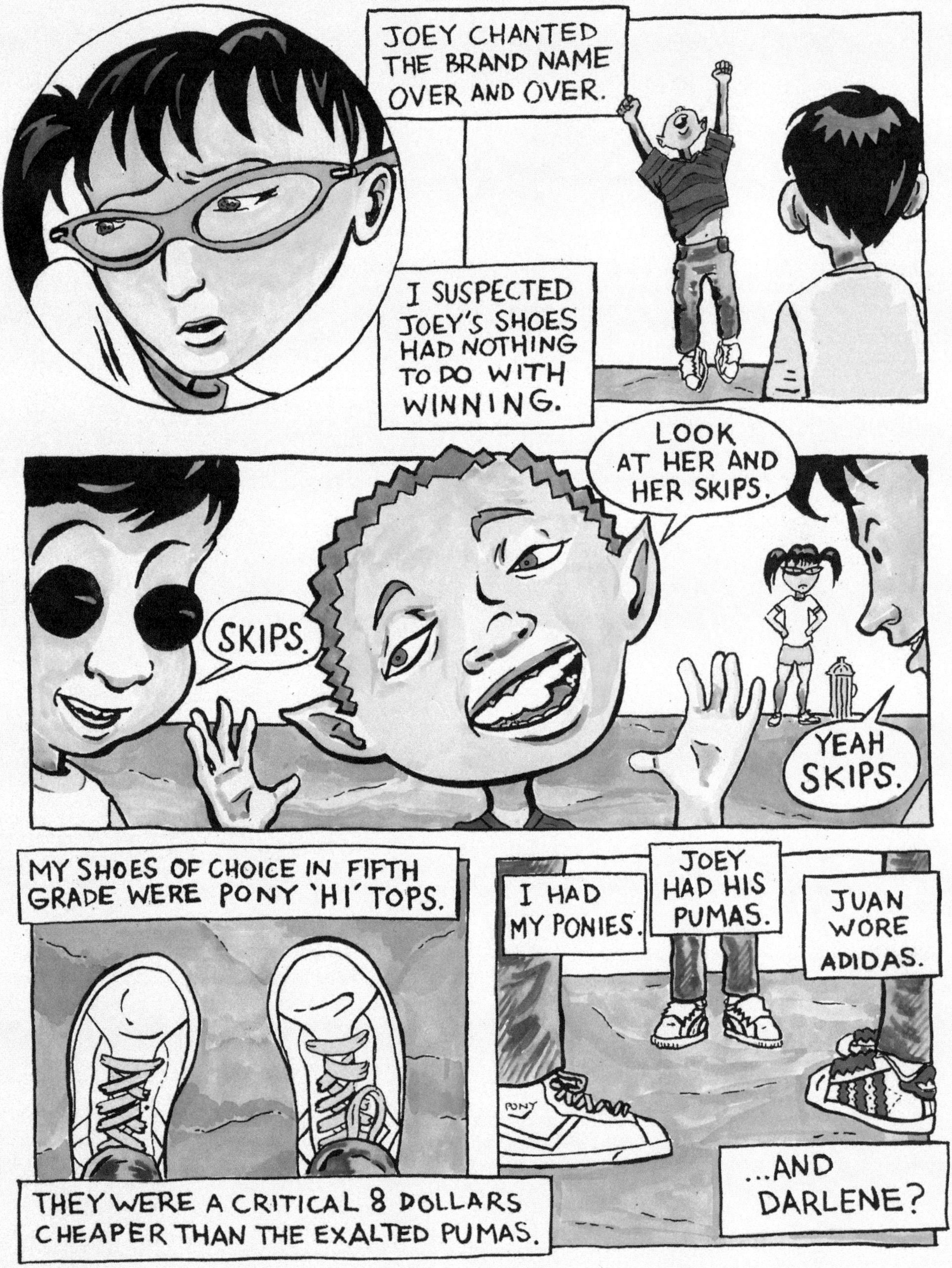
JOEY CHANTED THE BRAND NAME OVER AND OVER.
I SUSPECTED JOEY'S SHOES HAD NOTHING TO DO WITH WINNING.
LOOK AT HER AND HER SKIPS.
SKIPS.
YEAH SKIPS.
MY SHOES OF CHOICE IN FIFTH GRADE WERE PONY 'HI' TOPS.
PONY
THEY WERE A CRITICAL 8 DOLLARS CHEAPER THAN THE EXALTED PUMAS.
I HAD MY PONIES.
JOEY HAD HIS PUMAS.
JUAN WORE ADIDAS.
...AND DARLENE?

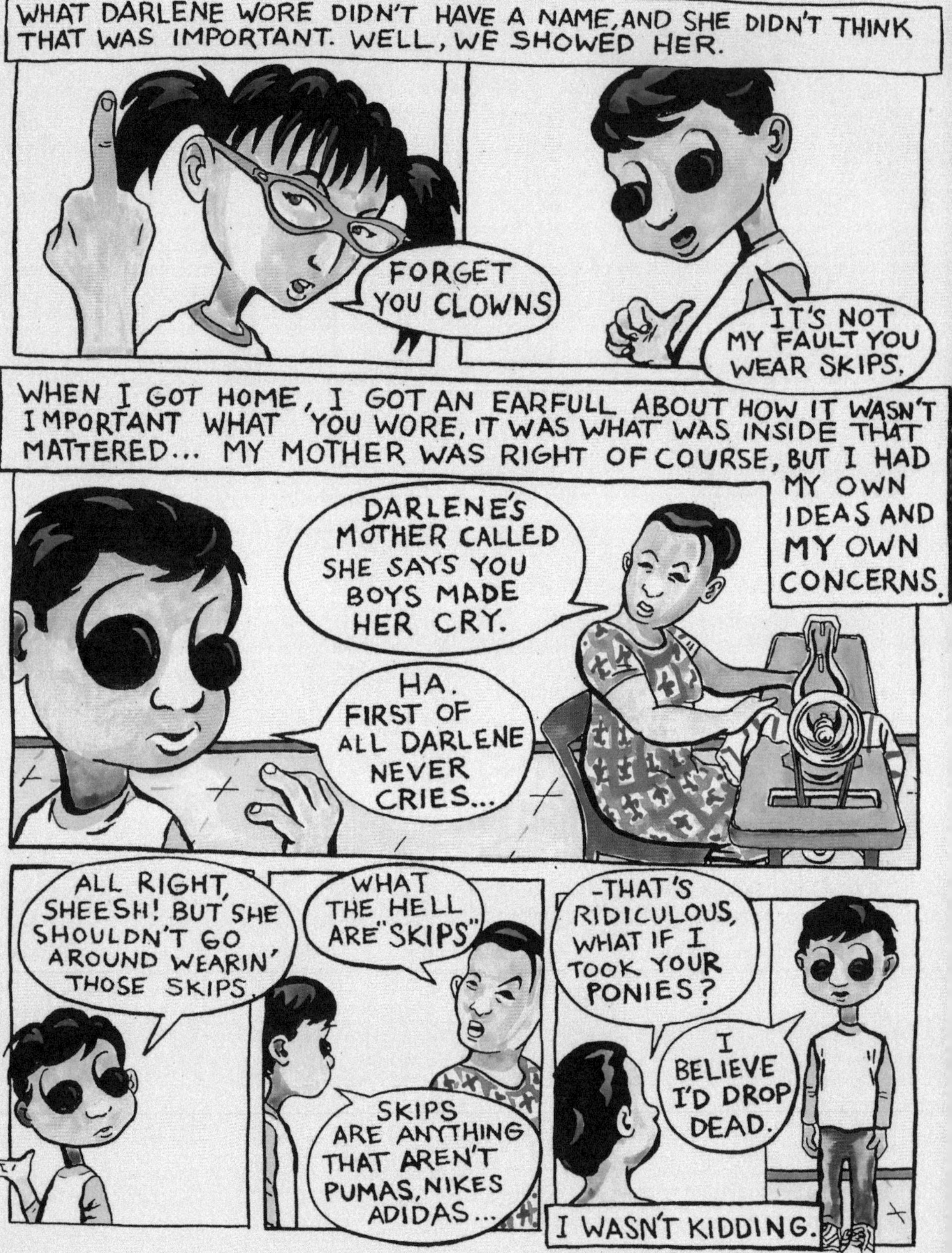
WHAT DARLENE WORE DIDN'T HAVE A NAME, AND SHE DIDN'T THINK THAT WAS IMPORTANT. WELL, WE SHOWED HER.
FORGET YOU CLOWNS
IT'S NOT MY FAULT YOU WEAR SKIPS.
WHEN I GOT HOME, I GOT AN EARFULL ABOUT HOW IT WASN'T IMPORTANT WHAT YOU WORE, IT WAS WHAT WAS INSIDE THAT MATTERED... MY MOTHER WAS RIGHT OF COURSE, BUT I HAD MY OWN IDEAS AND MY OWN CONCERNS.
DARLENE'S MOTHER CALLED SHE SAYS YOU BOYS MADE HER CRY.
HA. FIRST OF ALL DARLENE NEVER CRIES...
ALL RIGHT, SHEESH! BUT SHE SHOULDN'T GO AROUND WEARIN' THOSE SKIPS.
WHAT THE HELL ARE "SKIPS"
SKIPS ARE ANYTHING THAT AREN'T PUMAS, NIKES ADIDAS...
-THAT'S RIDICULOUS, WHAT IF I TOOK YOUR PONIES?
I BELIEVE I'D DROP DEAD.
I WASN'T KIDDING.

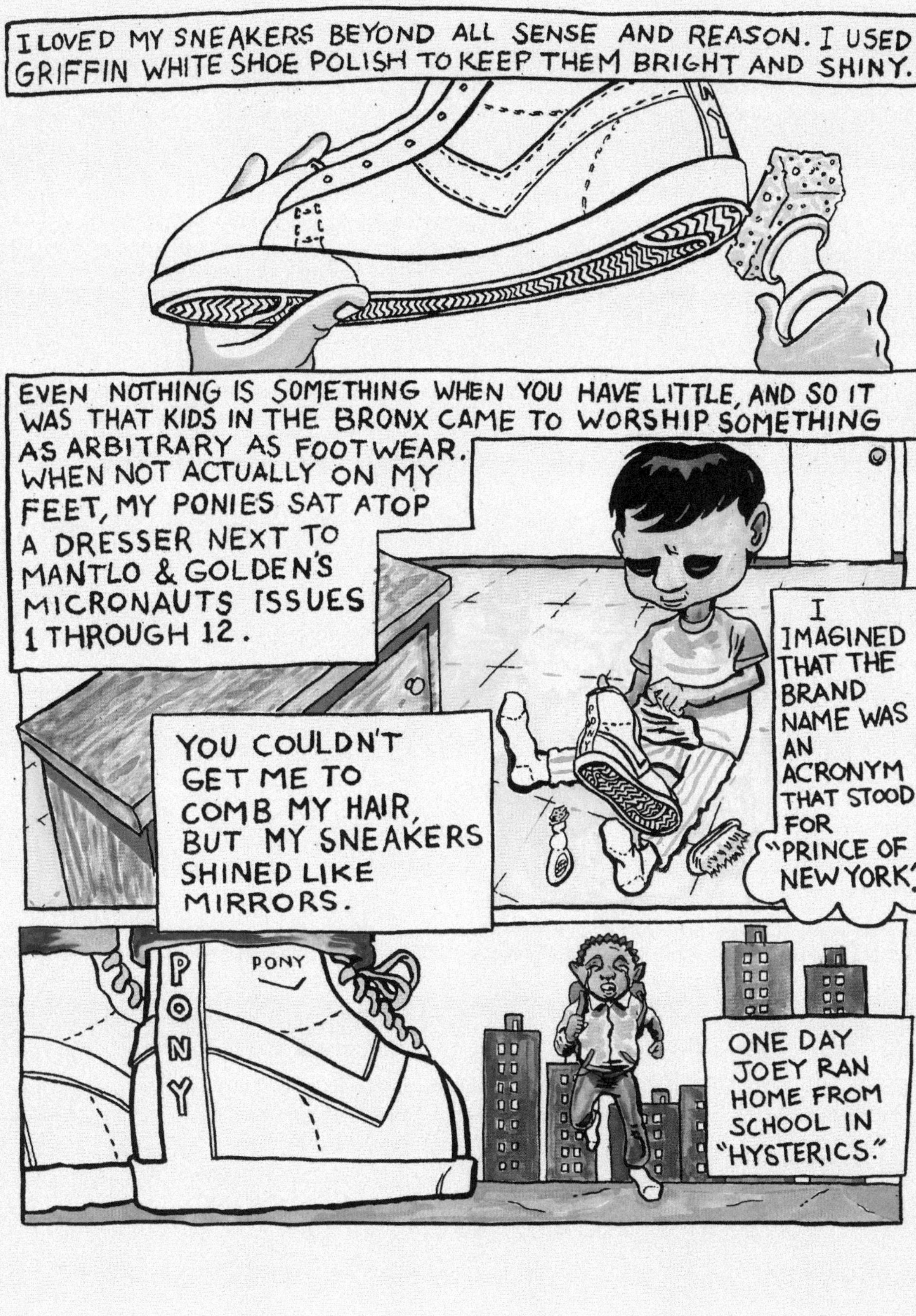

I LOVED MY SNEAKERS BEYOND ALL SENSE AND REASON. I USED GRIFFIN WHITE SHOE POLISH TO KEEP THEM BRIGHT AND SHINY.
EVEN NOTHING IS SOMETHING WHEN YOU HAVE LITTLE, AND SO IT WAS THAT KIDS IN THE BRONX CAME TO WORSHIP SOMETHING AS ARBITRARY AS FOOTWEAR. WHEN NOT ACTUALLY ON MY FEET, MY PONIES SAT ATOP A DRESSER NEXT TO MANTLO & GOLDEN'S MICRONAUTS ISSUES 1 THROUGH 12.
I IMAGINED THAT THE BRAND NAME WAS AN ACRONYM THAT STOOD FOR "PRINCE OF NEW YORK."
YOU COULDN'T GET ME TO COMB MY HAIR, BUT MY SNEAKERS SHINED LIKE MIRRORS.
PONY
PONY
ONE DAY JOEY RAN HOME FROM SCHOOL IN "HYSTERICS."

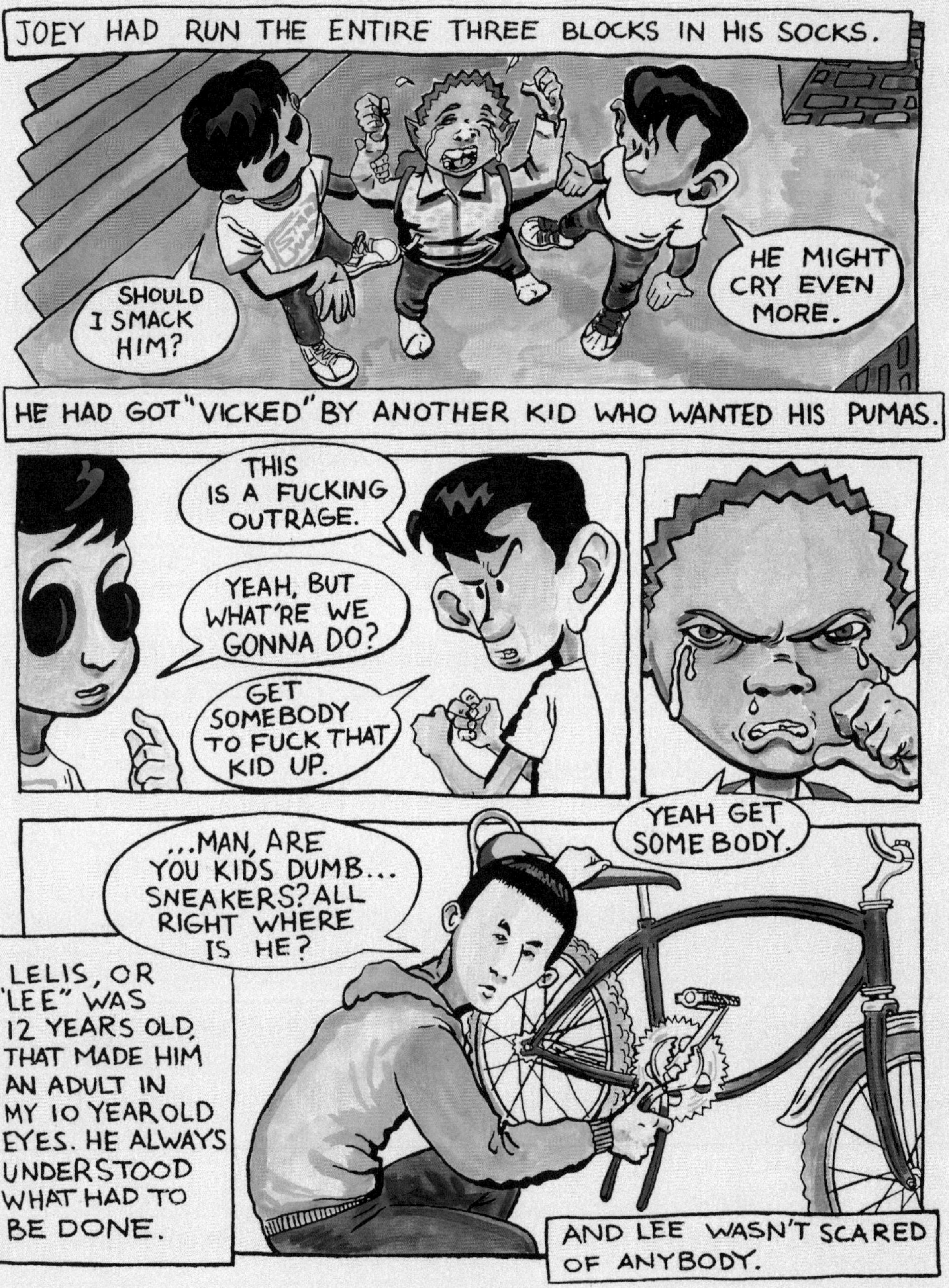
JOEY HAD RUN THE ENTIRE THREE BLOCKS IN HIS SOCKS.
SHOULD I SMACK HIM?
HE MIGHT CRY EVEN MORE.
HE HAD GOT "VICKED" BY ANOTHER KID WHO WANTED HIS PUMAS.
THIS IS A FUCKING OUTRAGE.
YEAH, BUT WHAT'RE WE GONNA DO?
GET SOMEBODY TO FUCK THAT KID UP.
YEAH GET SOMEBODY.
...MAN, ARE YOU KIDS DUMB... SNEAKERS? ALL RIGHT WHERE IS HE?
LELIS, OR "LEE" WAS 12 YEARS OLD, THAT MADE HIM AN ADULT IN MY 10 YEAR OLD EYES. HE ALWAYS UNDERSTOOD WHAT HAD TO BE DONE.
AND LEE WASN'T SCARED OF ANYBODY.

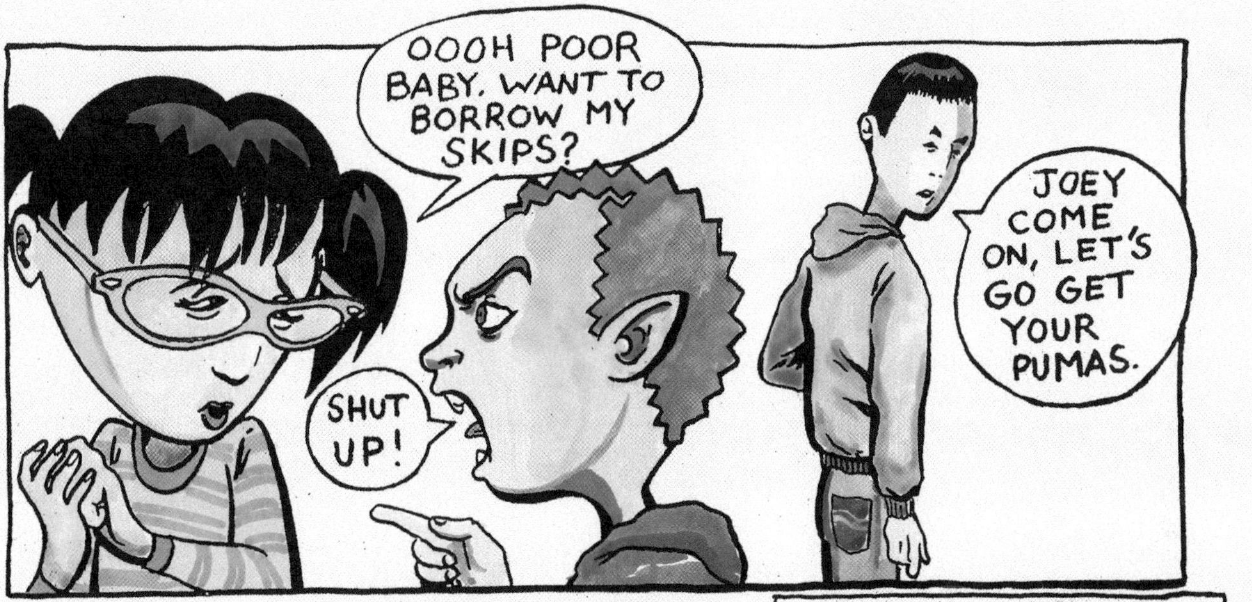
OOOH POOR BABY. WANT TO BORROW MY SKIPS?
SHUT UP!
JOEY COME ON, LET'S GO GET YOUR PUMAS.

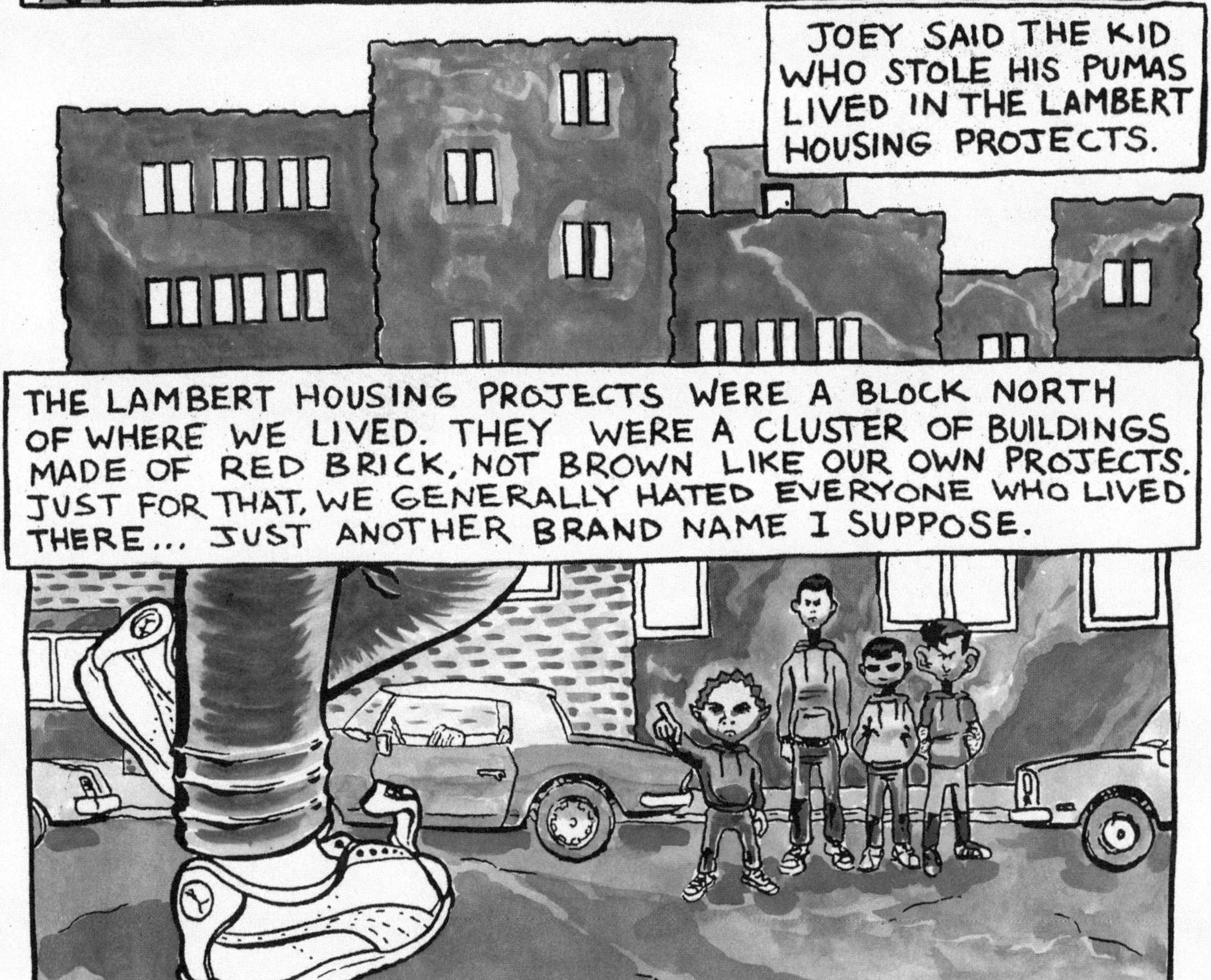
JOEY SAID THE KID WHO STOLE HIS PUMAS LIVED IN THE LAMBERT HOUSING PROJECTS.
THE LAMBERT HOUSING PROJECTS WERE A BLOCK NORTH OF WHERE WE LIVED. THEY WERE A CLUSTER OF BUILDINGS MADE OF RED BRICK, NOT BROWN LIKE OUR OWN PROJECTS. JUST FOR THAT, WE GENERALLY HATED EVERYONE WHO LIVED THERE... JUST ANOTHER BRAND NAME I SUPPOSE.

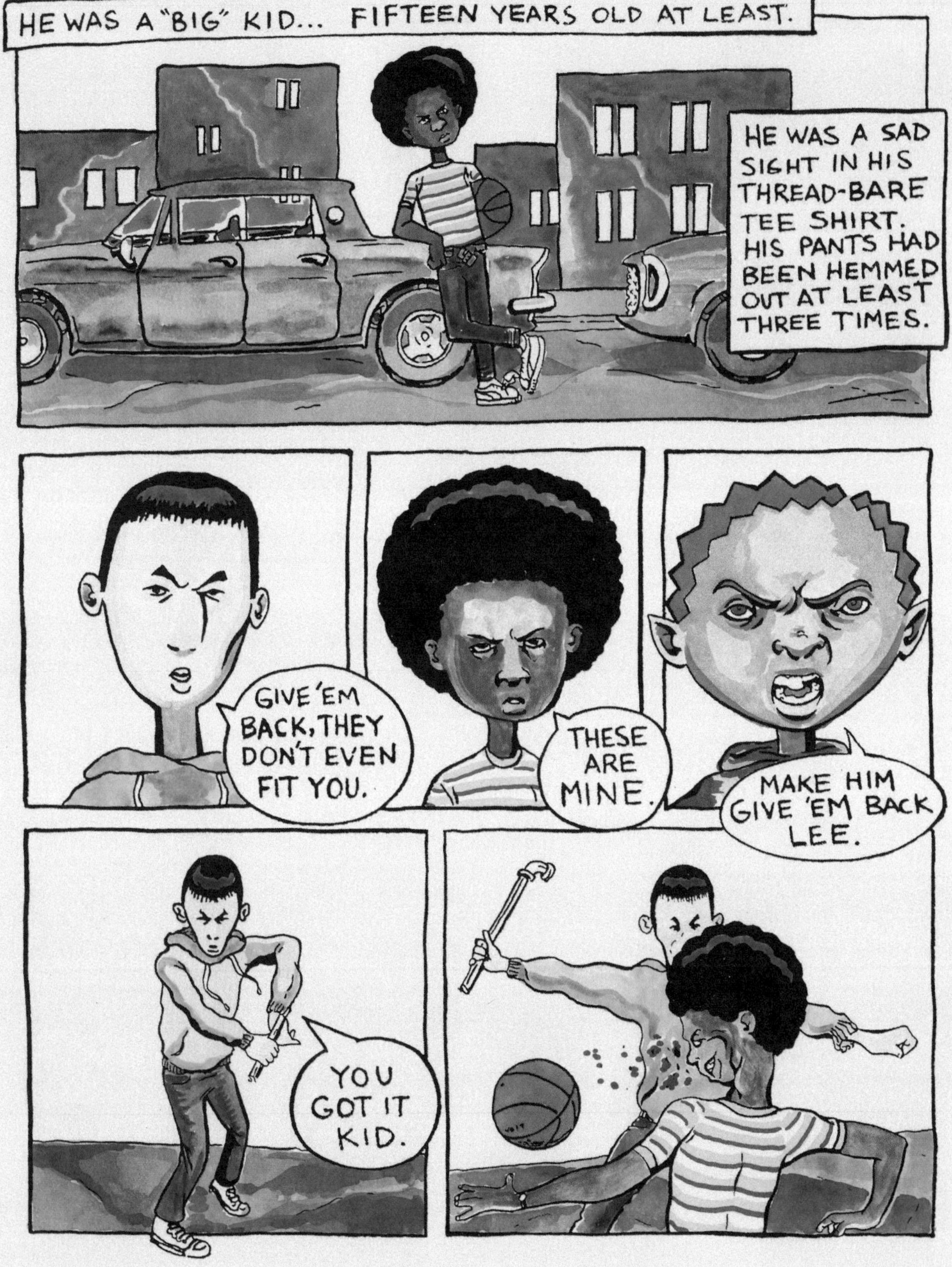

HE WAS A "BIG" KID... FIFTEEN YEARS OLD AT LEAST.
HE WAS A SAD SIGHT IN HIS THREAD-BARE TEE SHIRT. HIS PANTS HAD BEEN HEMMED OUT AT LEAST THREE TIMES.
GIVE 'EM BACK, THEY DON'T EVEN FIT YOU.
THESE ARE MINE.
MAKE HIM GIVE 'EM BACK LEE.
YOU GOT IT KID.

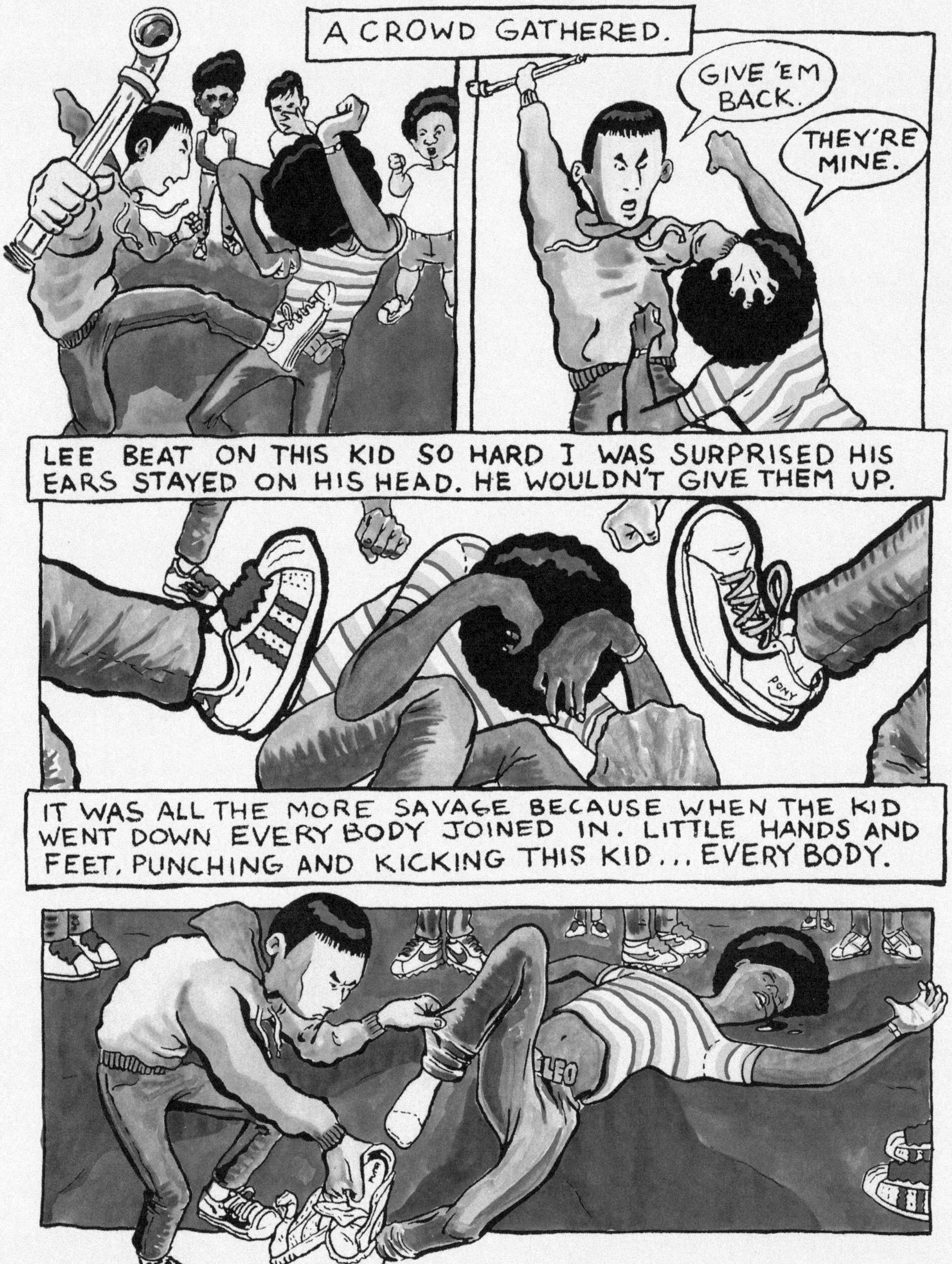
A CROWD GATHERED.
GIVE 'EM BACK.
THEY'RE MINE.
LEE BEAT ON THIS KID SO HARD I WAS SURPRISED HIS EARS STAYED ON HIS HEAD. HE WOULDN'T GIVE THEM UP.
PONY
IT WAS ALL THE MORE SAVAGE BECAUSE WHEN THE KID WENT DOWN EVERY BODY JOINED IN. LITTLE HANDS AND FEET, PUNCHING AND KICKING THIS KID... EVERY BODY.

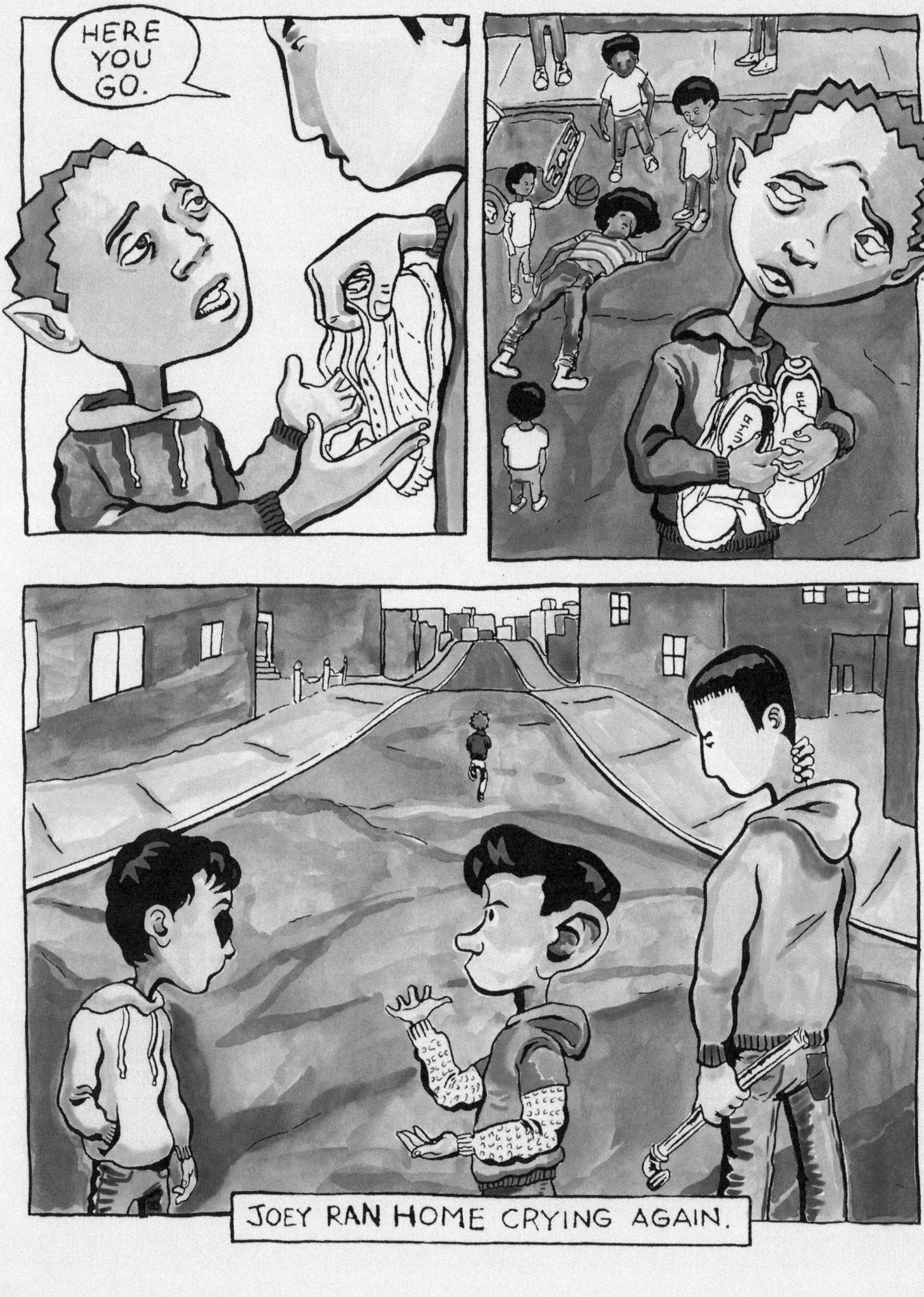

HERE YOU GO.
PUMA
JOEY RAN HOME CRYING AGAIN.

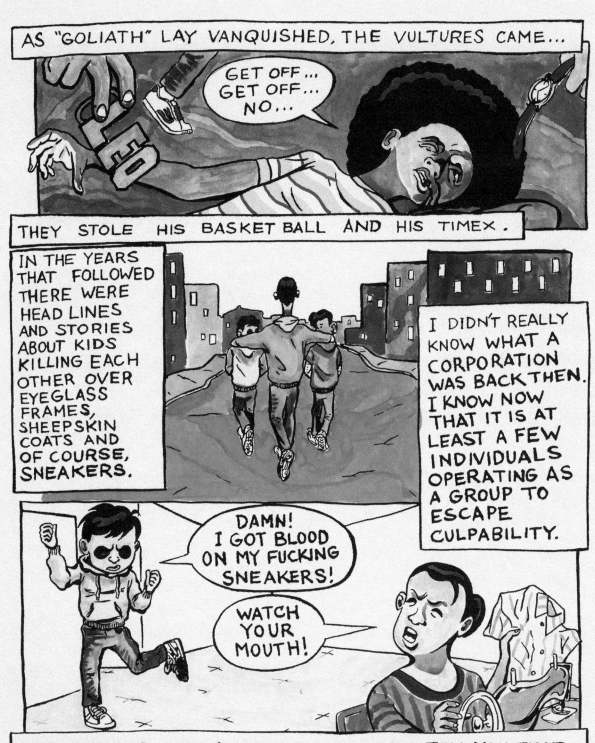

AS "GOLIATH" LAY VANQUISHED, THE VULTURES CAME...

GET OFF... GET OFF... NO...

THEY STOLE HIS BASKET BALL AND HIS TIMEX.

IN THE YEARS THAT FOLLOWED THERE WERE HEAD LINES AND STORIES ABOUT KIDS KILLING EACH OTHER OVER EYEGLASS FRAMES, SHEEPSKIN COATS AND OF COURSE, SNEAKERS.

I DIDN'T REALLY KNOW WHAT A CORPORATION WAS BACK THEN. I KNOW NOW THAT IT IS AT LEAST A FEW INDIVIDUALS OPERATING AS A GROUP TO ESCAPE CULPABILITY.

DAMN! I GOT BLOOD ON MY FUCKING SNEAKERS!

WATCH YOUR MOUTH!

CORPORATIONS AND MANUFACTURERS WILL TELL YOU THAT IT'S NOT THEIR FAULT, THAT NO ONE IS TO BLAME FOR THE TWISTED DESIRES OF ANGRY CHILDREN. I WILL TELL YOU IT IS AT LEAST THEIR FAULT, MY FAULT, AND YOURS.

— SANDY JIMENEZ   INK = 2001
                   PAINT = 2012

119

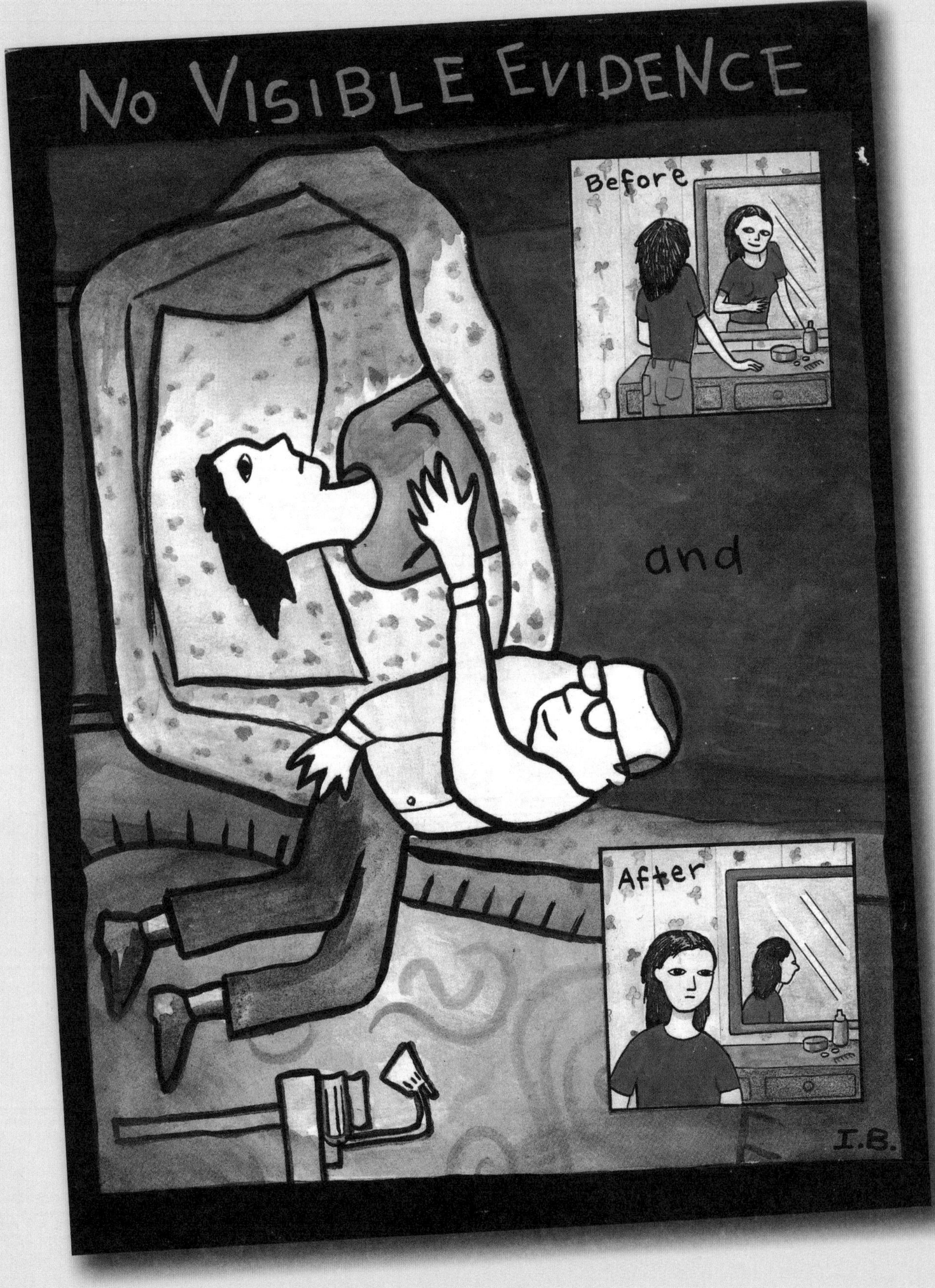

NO VISIBLE EVIDENCE
Before
and
After
I.B.

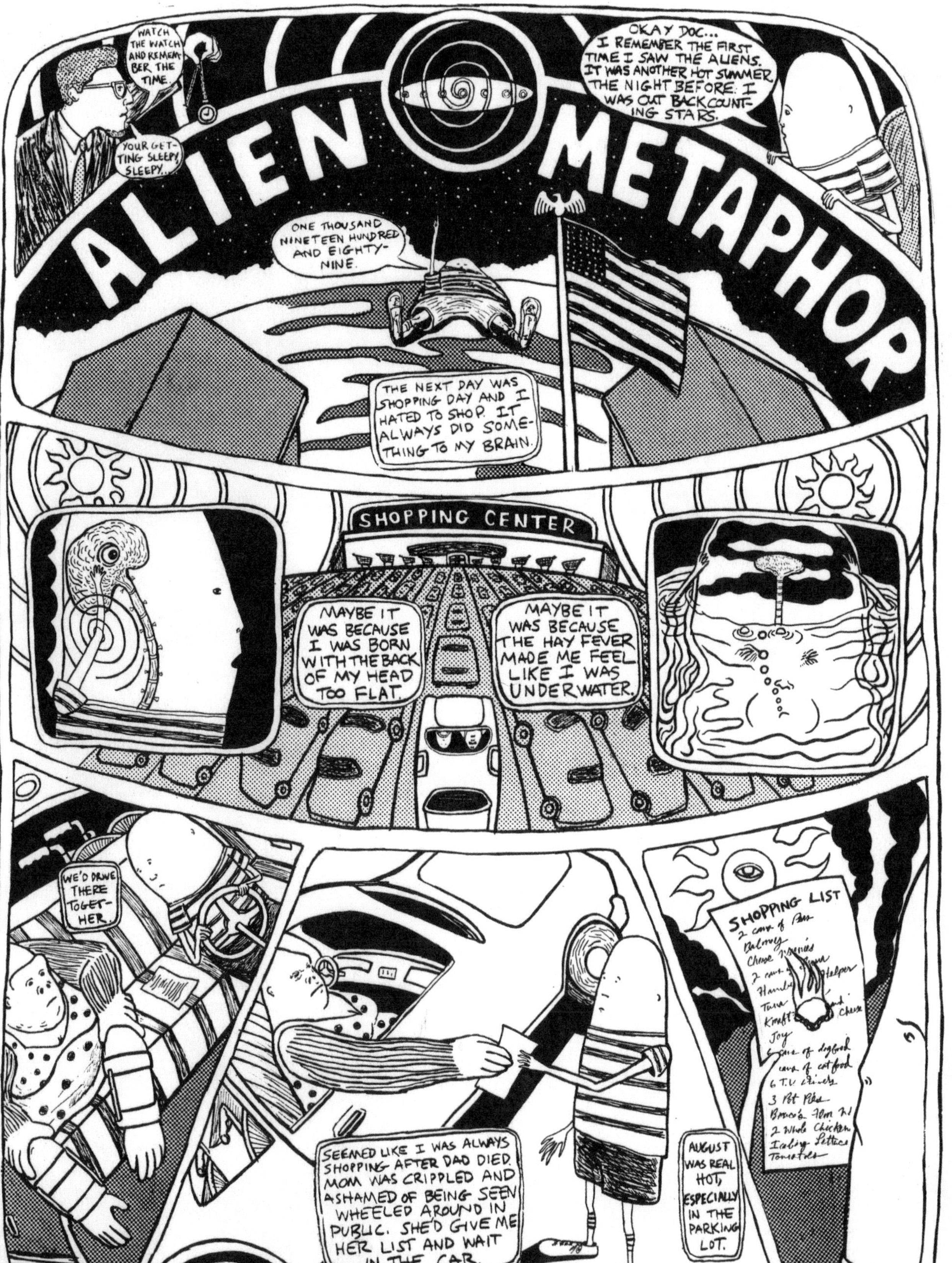

WATCH THE WATCH AND REMEMBER THE TIME.
YOUR GETTING SLEEPY, SLEEPY...
OKAY DOC... I REMEMBER THE FIRST TIME I SAW THE ALIENS. IT WAS ANOTHER HOT SUMMER THE NIGHT BEFORE. I WAS OUT BACK COUNTING STARS.
ALIEN METAPHOR
ONE THOUSAND NINETEEN HUNDRED AND EIGHTY-NINE.
THE NEXT DAY WAS SHOPPING DAY AND I HATED TO SHOP. IT ALWAYS DID SOMETHING TO MY BRAIN.
SHOPPING CENTER
MAYBE IT WAS BECAUSE I WAS BORN WITH THE BACK OF MY HEAD TOO FLAT.
MAYBE IT WAS BECAUSE THE HAY FEVER MADE ME FEEL LIKE I WAS UNDERWATER.
WE'D DRIVE THERE TOGETHER.
SEEMED LIKE I WAS ALWAYS SHOPPING AFTER DAD DIED. MOM WAS CRIPPLED AND ASHAMED OF BEING SEEN WHEELED AROUND IN PUBLIC. SHE'D GIVE ME HER LIST AND WAIT IN THE CAR.
AUGUST WAS REAL HOT, ESPECIALLY IN THE PARKING LOT.
SHOPPING LIST
Joy
3 Pot Pies
2 Whole Chicken
Iceberg Lettuce
Tomatoes

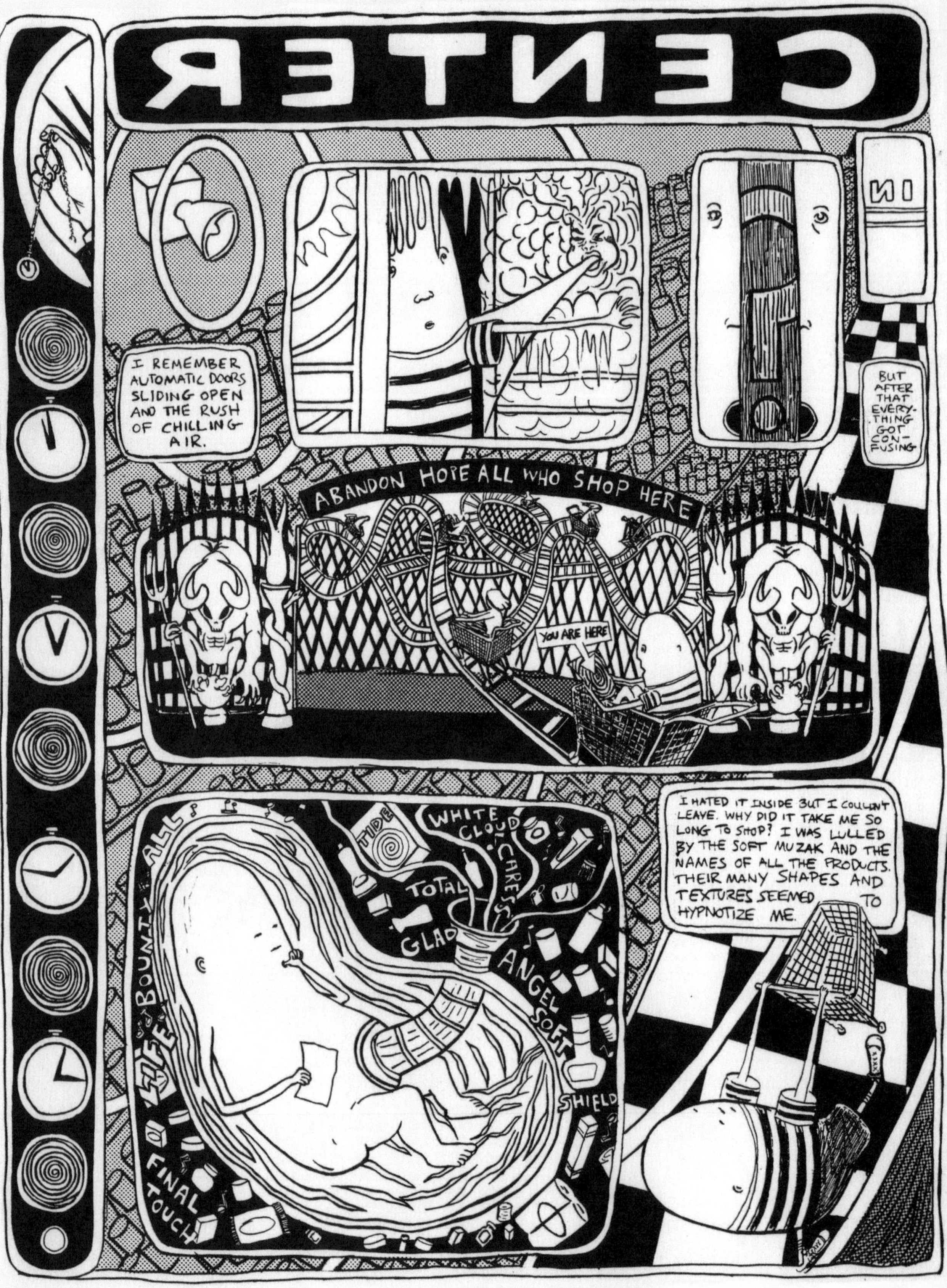

CENTER
IN
I REMEMBER AUTOMATIC DOORS SLIDING OPEN AND THE RUSH OF CHILLING AIR.
BUT AFTER THAT EVERY-THING GOT CON-FUSING
ABANDON HOPE ALL WHO SHOP HERE
YOU ARE HERE
I HATED IT INSIDE BUT I COULDN'T LEAVE. WHY DID IT TAKE ME SO LONG TO SHOP? I WAS LULLED BY THE SOFT MUZAK AND THE NAMES OF ALL THE PRODUCTS. THEIR MANY SHAPES AND TEXTURES SEEMED TO HYPNOTIZE ME.
TIDE
WHITE CLOUD
CARESS
TOTAL
GLAD
ANGEL SOFT
SHIELD
ALL
BOUNTY
FINAL TOUCH

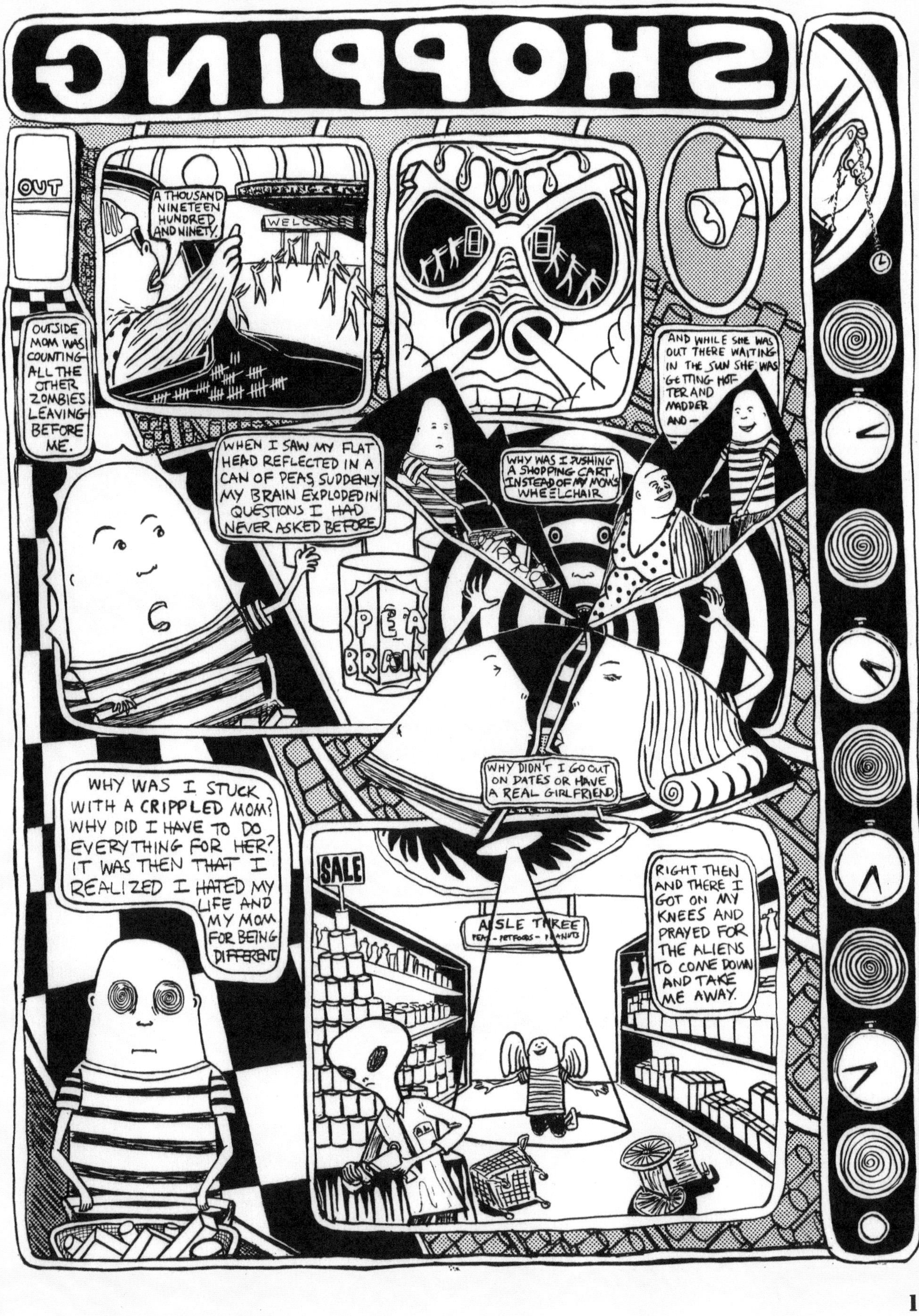
SHOPPING
OUT
A THOUSAND NINETEEN HUNDRED AND NINETY.
OUTSIDE MOM WAS COUNTING ALL THE OTHER ZOMBIES LEAVING BEFORE ME.
AND WHILE SHE WAS OUT THERE WAITING IN THE SUN SHE WAS GETTING HOT-TER AND MADDER AND—
WHEN I SAW MY FLAT HEAD REFLECTED IN A CAN OF PEAS, SUDDENLY MY BRAIN EXPLODED IN QUESTIONS I HAD NEVER ASKED BEFORE.
WHY WAS I PUSHING A SHOPPING CART INSTEAD OF MY MOM'S WHEELCHAIR
PEA BRAIN
WHY DIDN'T I GO OUT ON DATES OR HAVE A REAL GIRLFRIEND.
WHY WAS I STUCK WITH A CRIPPLED MOM? WHY DID I HAVE TO DO EVERYTHING FOR HER? IT WAS THEN THAT I REALIZED I HATED MY LIFE AND MY MOM FOR BEING DIFFERENT.
SALE
AISLE THREE
RIGHT THEN AND THERE I GOT ON MY KNEES AND PRAYED FOR THE ALIENS TO COME DOWN AND TAKE ME AWAY.

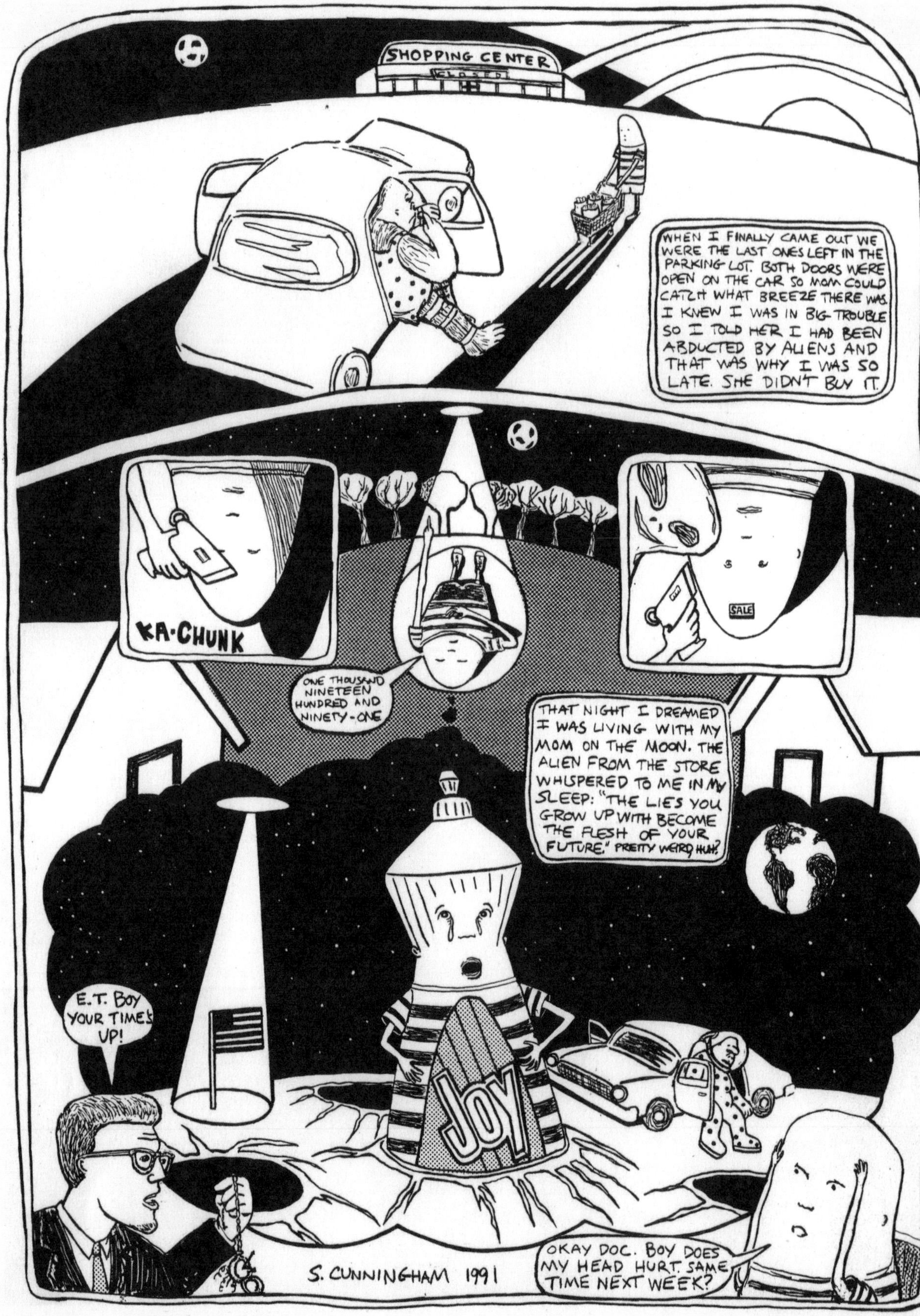

SHOPPING CENTER
CLOSED
WHEN I FINALLY CAME OUT WE WERE THE LAST ONES LEFT IN THE PARKING LOT. BOTH DOORS WERE OPEN ON THE CAR SO MOM COULD CATCH WHAT BREEZE THERE WAS. I KNEW I WAS IN BIG TROUBLE SO I TOLD HER I HAD BEEN ABDUCTED BY ALIENS AND THAT WAS WHY I WAS SO LATE. SHE DIDN'T BUY IT.
KA-CHUNK
SALE
ONE THOUSAND NINETEEN HUNDRED AND NINETY-ONE
THAT NIGHT I DREAMED I WAS LIVING WITH MY MOM ON THE MOON. THE ALIEN FROM THE STORE WHISPERED TO ME IN MY SLEEP: "THE LIES YOU GROW UP WITH BECOME THE FLESH OF YOUR FUTURE." PRETTY WEIRD, HUH?
E.T. BOY YOUR TIME'S UP!
JOY
OKAY DOC. BOY DOES MY HEAD HURT. SAME TIME NEXT WEEK?
S. CUNNINGHAM 1991

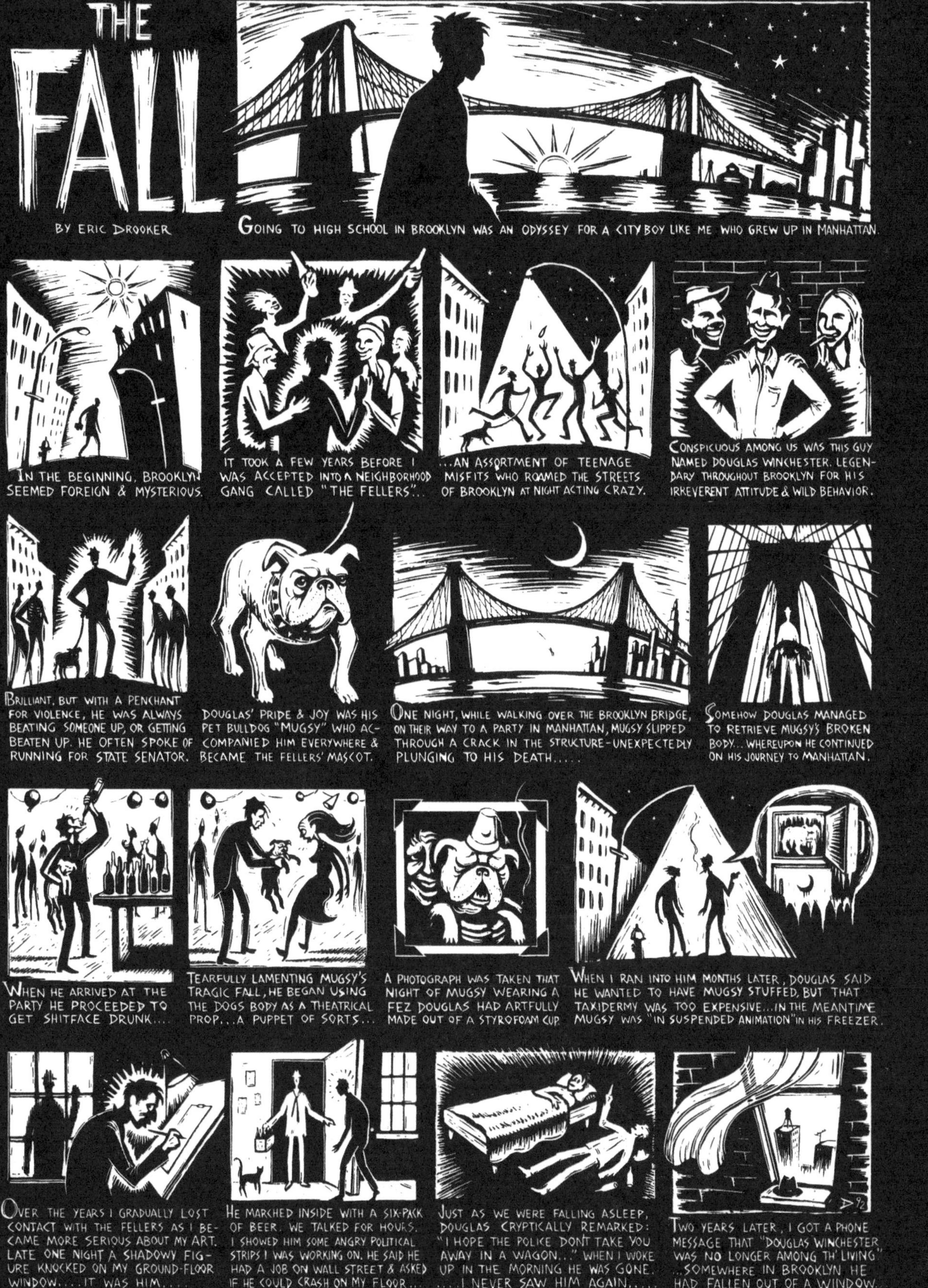
THE FALL
BY ERIC DROOKER
GOING TO HIGH SCHOOL IN BROOKLYN WAS AN ODYSSEY FOR A CITY BOY LIKE ME WHO GREW UP IN MANHATTAN.
IN THE BEGINNING, BROOKLYN SEEMED FOREIGN & MYSTERIOUS.
IT TOOK A FEW YEARS BEFORE I WAS ACCEPTED INTO A NEIGHBORHOOD GANG CALLED "THE FELLERS"...
...AN ASSORTMENT OF TEENAGE MISFITS WHO ROAMED THE STREETS OF BROOKLYN AT NIGHT ACTING CRAZY.
CONSPICUOUS AMONG US WAS THIS GUY NAMED DOUGLAS WINCHESTER. LEGENDARY THROUGHOUT BROOKLYN FOR HIS IRREVERENT ATTITUDE & WILD BEHAVIOR.
BRILLIANT, BUT WITH A PENCHANT FOR VIOLENCE, HE WAS ALWAYS BEATING SOMEONE UP, OR GETTING BEATEN UP. HE OFTEN SPOKE OF RUNNING FOR STATE SENATOR.
DOUGLAS' PRIDE & JOY WAS HIS PET BULLDOG "MUGSY" WHO ACCOMPANIED HIM EVERYWHERE & BECAME THE FELLERS' MASCOT.
ONE NIGHT, WHILE WALKING OVER THE BROOKLYN BRIDGE, ON THEIR WAY TO A PARTY IN MANHATTAN, MUGSY SLIPPED THROUGH A CRACK IN THE STRUCTURE - UNEXPECTEDLY PLUNGING TO HIS DEATH.....
SOMEHOW DOUGLAS MANAGED TO RETRIEVE MUGSY'S BROKEN BODY... WHEREUPON HE CONTINUED ON HIS JOURNEY TO MANHATTAN.
WHEN HE ARRIVED AT THE PARTY HE PROCEEDED TO GET SHITFACE DRUNK...
TEARFULLY LAMENTING MUGSY'S TRAGIC FALL, HE BEGAN USING THE DOGS BODY AS A THEATRICAL PROP... A PUPPET OF SORTS...
A PHOTOGRAPH WAS TAKEN THAT NIGHT OF MUGSY WEARING A FEZ DOUGLAS HAD ARTFULLY MADE OUT OF A STYROFOAM CUP.
WHEN I RAN INTO HIM MONTHS LATER, DOUGLAS SAID HE WANTED TO HAVE MUGSY STUFFED, BUT THAT TAXIDERMY WAS TOO EXPENSIVE... IN THE MEANTIME MUGSY WAS "IN SUSPENDED ANIMATION" IN HIS FREEZER.
OVER THE YEARS I GRADUALLY LOST CONTACT WITH THE FELLERS AS I BECAME MORE SERIOUS ABOUT MY ART. LATE ONE NIGHT A SHADOWY FIGURE KNOCKED ON MY GROUND-FLOOR WINDOW.... IT WAS HIM....
HE MARCHED INSIDE WITH A SIX-PACK OF BEER. WE TALKED FOR HOURS. I SHOWED HIM SOME ANGRY POLITICAL STRIPS I WAS WORKING ON. HE SAID HE HAD A JOB ON WALL STREET & ASKED IF HE COULD CRASH ON MY FLOOR...
JUST AS WE WERE FALLING ASLEEP, DOUGLAS CRYPTICALLY REMARKED: "I HOPE THE POLICE DON'T TAKE YOU AWAY IN A WAGON..." WHEN I WOKE UP IN THE MORNING HE WAS GONE. .....I NEVER SAW HIM AGAIN.....
D 92
TWO YEARS LATER, I GOT A PHONE MESSAGE THAT "DOUGLAS WINCHESTER WAS NO LONGER AMONG TH' LIVING" ...SOMEWHERE IN BROOKLYN HE HAD FALLEN OUT OF A WINDOW.

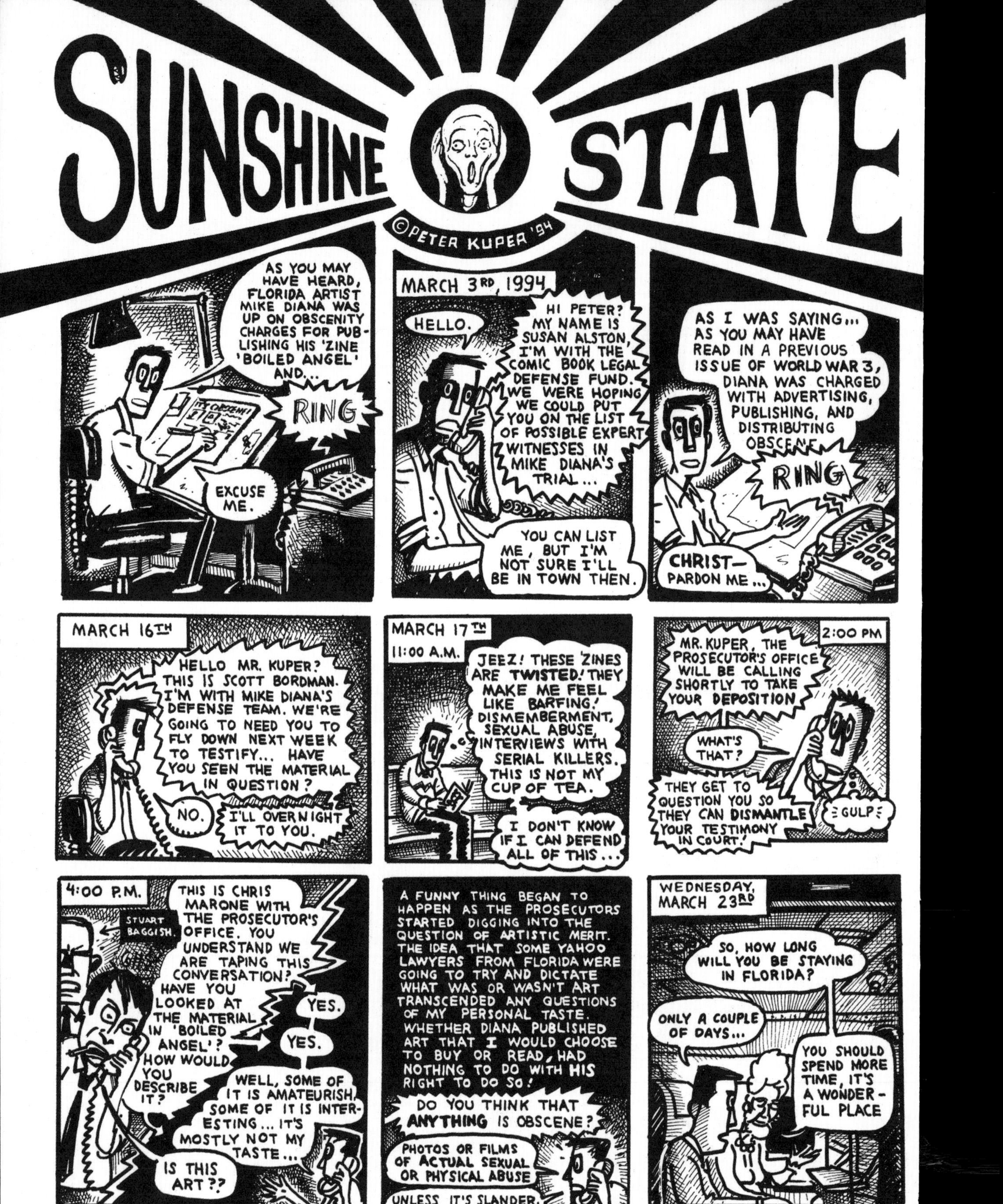
SUNSHINE STATE
©PETER KUPER '94
AS YOU MAY HAVE HEARD, FLORIDA ARTIST MIKE DIANA WAS UP ON OBSCENITY CHARGES FOR PUBLISHING HIS 'ZINE 'BOILED ANGEL' AND...
RING
EXCUSE ME.
MARCH 3RD, 1994
HELLO.
HI PETER? MY NAME IS SUSAN ALSTON, I'M WITH THE COMIC BOOK LEGAL DEFENSE FUND. WE WERE HOPING WE COULD PUT YOU ON THE LIST OF POSSIBLE EXPERT WITNESSES IN MIKE DIANA'S TRIAL...
YOU CAN LIST ME, BUT I'M NOT SURE I'LL BE IN TOWN THEN.
AS I WAS SAYING... AS YOU MAY HAVE READ IN A PREVIOUS ISSUE OF WORLD WAR 3, DIANA WAS CHARGED WITH ADVERTISING, PUBLISHING, AND DISTRIBUTING OBSCENE
RING
CHRIST— PARDON ME...
MARCH 16TH
HELLO MR. KUPER? THIS IS SCOTT BORDMAN. I'M WITH MIKE DIANA'S DEFENSE TEAM. WE'RE GOING TO NEED YOU TO FLY DOWN NEXT WEEK TO TESTIFY... HAVE YOU SEEN THE MATERIAL IN QUESTION?
NO.
I'LL OVERNIGHT IT TO YOU.
MARCH 17TH 11:00 A.M.
JEEZ! THESE 'ZINES ARE TWISTED! THEY MAKE ME FEEL LIKE BARFING! DISMEMBERMENT, SEXUAL ABUSE, INTERVIEWS WITH SERIAL KILLERS. THIS IS NOT MY CUP OF TEA.
I DON'T KNOW IF I CAN DEFEND ALL OF THIS...
2:00 PM
MR. KUPER, THE PROSECUTOR'S OFFICE WILL BE CALLING SHORTLY TO TAKE YOUR DEPOSITION
WHAT'S THAT?
THEY GET TO QUESTION YOU SO THEY CAN DISMANTLE YOUR TESTIMONY IN COURT!
GULP
4:00 P.M.
STUART BAGGISH.
THIS IS CHRIS MARONE WITH THE PROSECUTOR'S OFFICE. YOU UNDERSTAND WE ARE TAPING THIS CONVERSATION?
YES.
HAVE YOU LOOKED AT THE MATERIAL IN 'BOILED ANGEL'?
YES.
HOW WOULD YOU DESCRIBE IT?
WELL, SOME OF IT IS AMATEURISH, SOME OF IT IS INTERESTING... IT'S MOSTLY NOT MY TASTE...
IS THIS ART??
A FUNNY THING BEGAN TO HAPPEN AS THE PROSECUTORS STARTED DIGGING INTO THE QUESTION OF ARTISTIC MERIT. THE IDEA THAT SOME YAHOO LAWYERS FROM FLORIDA WERE GOING TO TRY AND DICTATE WHAT WAS OR WASN'T ART TRANSCENDED ANY QUESTIONS OF MY PERSONAL TASTE. WHETHER DIANA PUBLISHED ART THAT I WOULD CHOOSE TO BUY OR READ, HAD NOTHING TO DO WITH HIS RIGHT TO DO SO!
DO YOU THINK THAT ANYTHING IS OBSCENE?
PHOTOS OR FILMS OF ACTUAL SEXUAL OR PHYSICAL ABUSE
UNLESS IT'S SLANDER, INK ON PAPER CAN'T HURT ANYBODY.
WEDNESDAY, MARCH 23RD
SO, HOW LONG WILL YOU BE STAYING IN FLORIDA?
ONLY A COUPLE OF DAYS...
YOU SHOULD SPEND MORE TIME, IT'S A WONDERFUL PLACE
LETTERING BY GREGORY BENTON

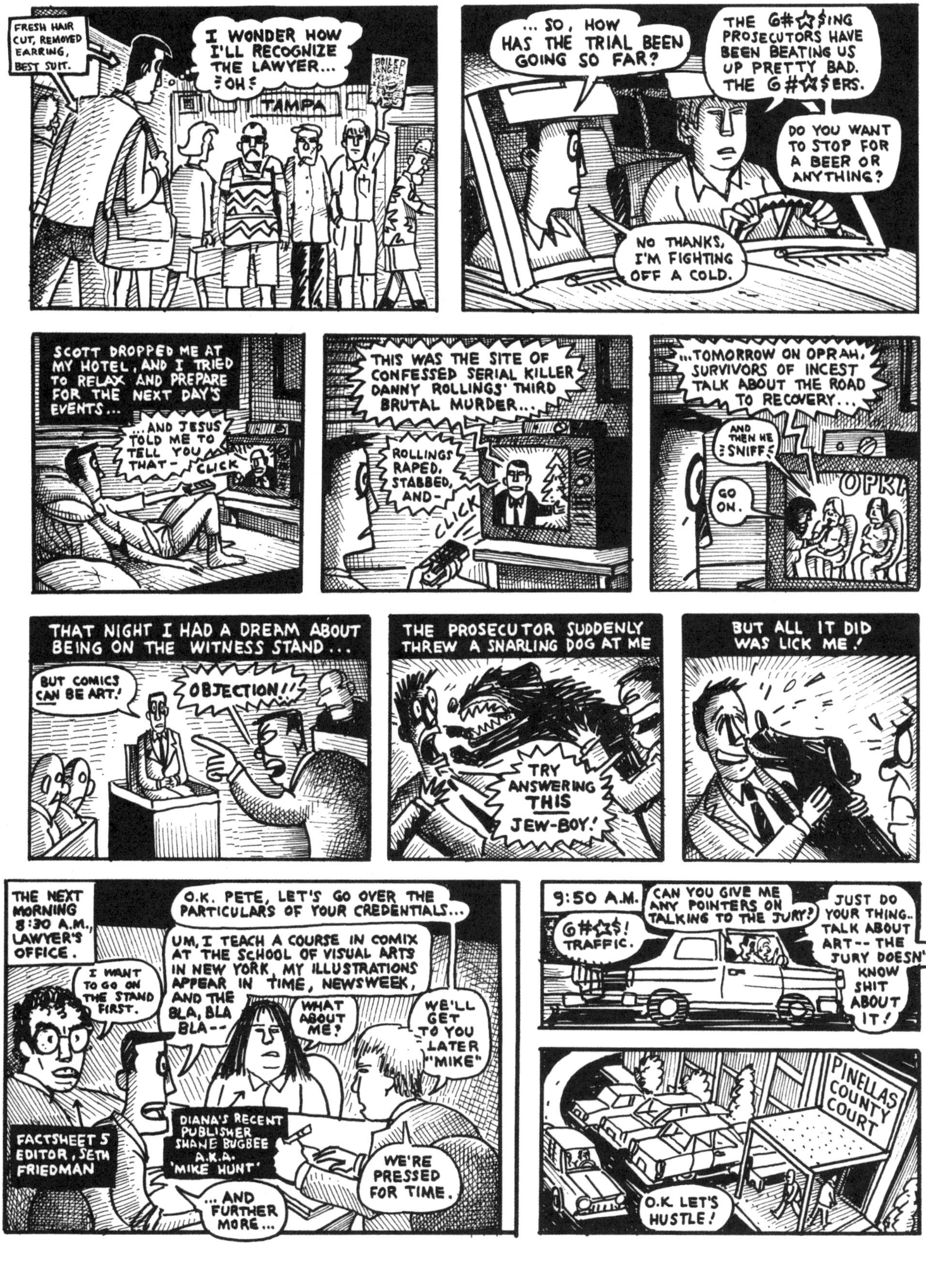
FRESH HAIR CUT, REMOVED EARRING, BEST SUIT.
I WONDER HOW I'LL RECOGNIZE THE LAWYER... OH!
TAMPA
BOILED ANGEL
... SO, HOW HAS THE TRIAL BEEN GOING SO FAR?
THE G#☆$ING PROSECUTORS HAVE BEEN BEATING US UP PRETTY BAD. THE G#☆$ERS.
DO YOU WANT TO STOP FOR A BEER OR ANYTHING?
NO THANKS, I'M FIGHTING OFF A COLD.
SCOTT DROPPED ME AT MY HOTEL, AND I TRIED TO RELAX AND PREPARE FOR THE NEXT DAY'S EVENTS...
...AND JESUS TOLD ME TO TELL YOU THAT-
CLICK
THIS WAS THE SITE OF CONFESSED SERIAL KILLER DANNY ROLLINGS' THIRD BRUTAL MURDER...
ROLLINGS RAPED, STABBED, AND-
CLICK
...TOMORROW ON OPRAH, SURVIVORS OF INCEST TALK ABOUT THE ROAD TO RECOVERY...
AND THEN HE SNIFF
GO ON.
THAT NIGHT I HAD A DREAM ABOUT BEING ON THE WITNESS STAND...
BUT COMICS CAN BE ART!
OBJECTION!!
THE PROSECUTOR SUDDENLY THREW A SNARLING DOG AT ME
TRY ANSWERING THIS JEW-BOY!
BUT ALL IT DID WAS LICK ME!
THE NEXT MORNING 8:30 A.M., LAWYER'S OFFICE.
O.K. PETE, LET'S GO OVER THE PARTICULARS OF YOUR CREDENTIALS...
UM, I TEACH A COURSE IN COMIX AT THE SCHOOL OF VISUAL ARTS IN NEW YORK, MY ILLUSTRATIONS APPEAR IN TIME, NEWSWEEK, AND THE BLA, BLA BLA--
I WANT TO GO ON THE STAND FIRST.
WHAT ABOUT ME?
WE'LL GET TO YOU LATER "MIKE"
FACTSHEET 5 EDITOR, SETH FRIEDMAN
DIANA'S RECENT PUBLISHER SHANE BUGBEE A.K.A. 'MIKE HUNT'
WE'RE PRESSED FOR TIME.
...AND FURTHER MORE...
9:50 A.M.
CAN YOU GIVE ME ANY POINTERS ON TALKING TO THE JURY?
G#☆$! TRAFFIC.
JUST DO YOUR THING.. TALK ABOUT ART-- THE JURY DOESN'T KNOW SHIT ABOUT IT!
PINELLAS COUNTY COURT
O.K. LET'S HUSTLE!

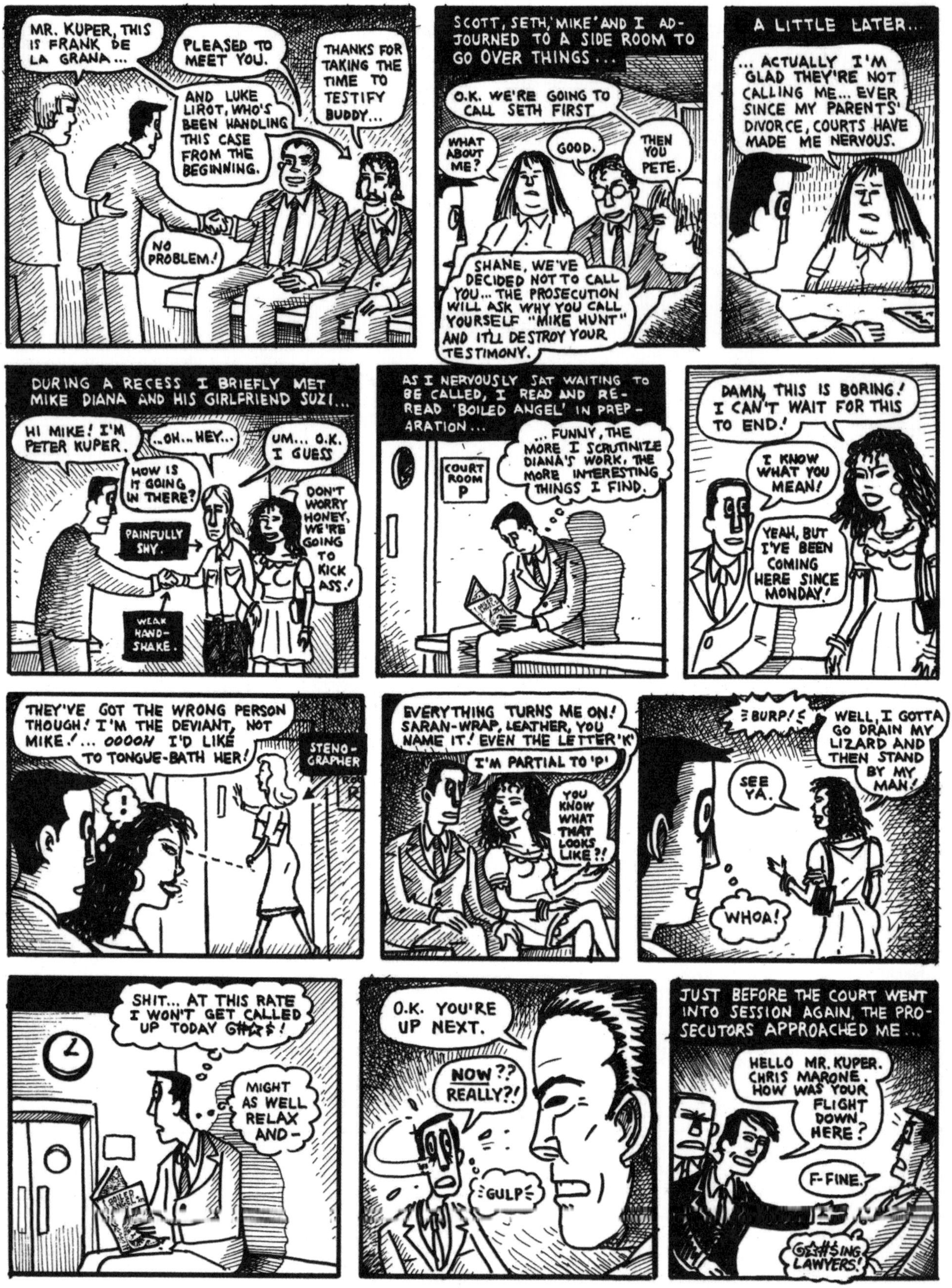
MR. KUPER, THIS IS FRANK DE LA GRANA...
PLEASED TO MEET YOU.
AND LUKE LIROT, WHO'S BEEN HANDLING THIS CASE FROM THE BEGINNING.
THANKS FOR TAKING THE TIME TO TESTIFY BUDDY...
NO PROBLEM!
SCOTT, SETH, 'MIKE' AND I ADJOURNED TO A SIDE ROOM TO GO OVER THINGS...
O.K. WE'RE GOING TO CALL SETH FIRST
GOOD.
THEN YOU PETE.
WHAT ABOUT ME?
SHANE, WE'VE DECIDED NOT TO CALL YOU... THE PROSECUTION WILL ASK WHY YOU CALL YOURSELF "MIKE HUNT" AND IT'LL DESTROY YOUR TESTIMONY.
A LITTLE LATER...
... ACTUALLY I'M GLAD THEY'RE NOT CALLING ME... EVER SINCE MY PARENTS' DIVORCE, COURTS HAVE MADE ME NERVOUS.
DURING A RECESS I BRIEFLY MET MIKE DIANA AND HIS GIRLFRIEND SUZI...
HI MIKE! I'M PETER KUPER.
..OH...HEY...
UM... O.K. I GUESS
HOW IS IT GOING IN THERE?
DON'T WORRY HONEY, WE'RE GOING TO KICK ASS!
PAINFULLY SHY.
WEAK HAND-SHAKE.
AS I NERVOUSLY SAT WAITING TO BE CALLED, I READ AND RE-READ 'BOILED ANGEL' IN PREPARATION...
... FUNNY, THE MORE I SCRUTINIZE DIANA'S WORK, THE MORE INTERESTING THINGS I FIND.
COURT ROOM P
DAMN, THIS IS BORING! I CAN'T WAIT FOR THIS TO END!
I KNOW WHAT YOU MEAN!
YEAH, BUT I'VE BEEN COMING HERE SINCE MONDAY!
THEY'VE GOT THE WRONG PERSON THOUGH! I'M THE DEVIANT, NOT MIKE!... OOOOH I'D LIKE TO TONGUE-BATH HER!
!
STENO-GRAPHER
EVERYTHING TURNS ME ON! SARAN-WRAP, LEATHER, YOU NAME IT! EVEN THE LETTER 'K'
I'M PARTIAL TO 'P'
YOU KNOW WHAT THAT LOOKS LIKE?!
BURP!
WELL, I GOTTA GO DRAIN MY LIZARD AND THEN STAND BY MY MAN!
SEE YA.
WHOA!
SHIT... AT THIS RATE I WON'T GET CALLED UP TODAY G#☆$!
MIGHT AS WELL RELAX AND-
O.K. YOU'RE UP NEXT.
NOW?? REALLY?!
GULP
JUST BEFORE THE COURT WENT INTO SESSION AGAIN, THE PROSECUTORS APPROACHED ME...
HELLO MR. KUPER. CHRIS MARONE. HOW WAS YOUR FLIGHT DOWN HERE?
F-FINE.
G☆#$ING LAWYERS!

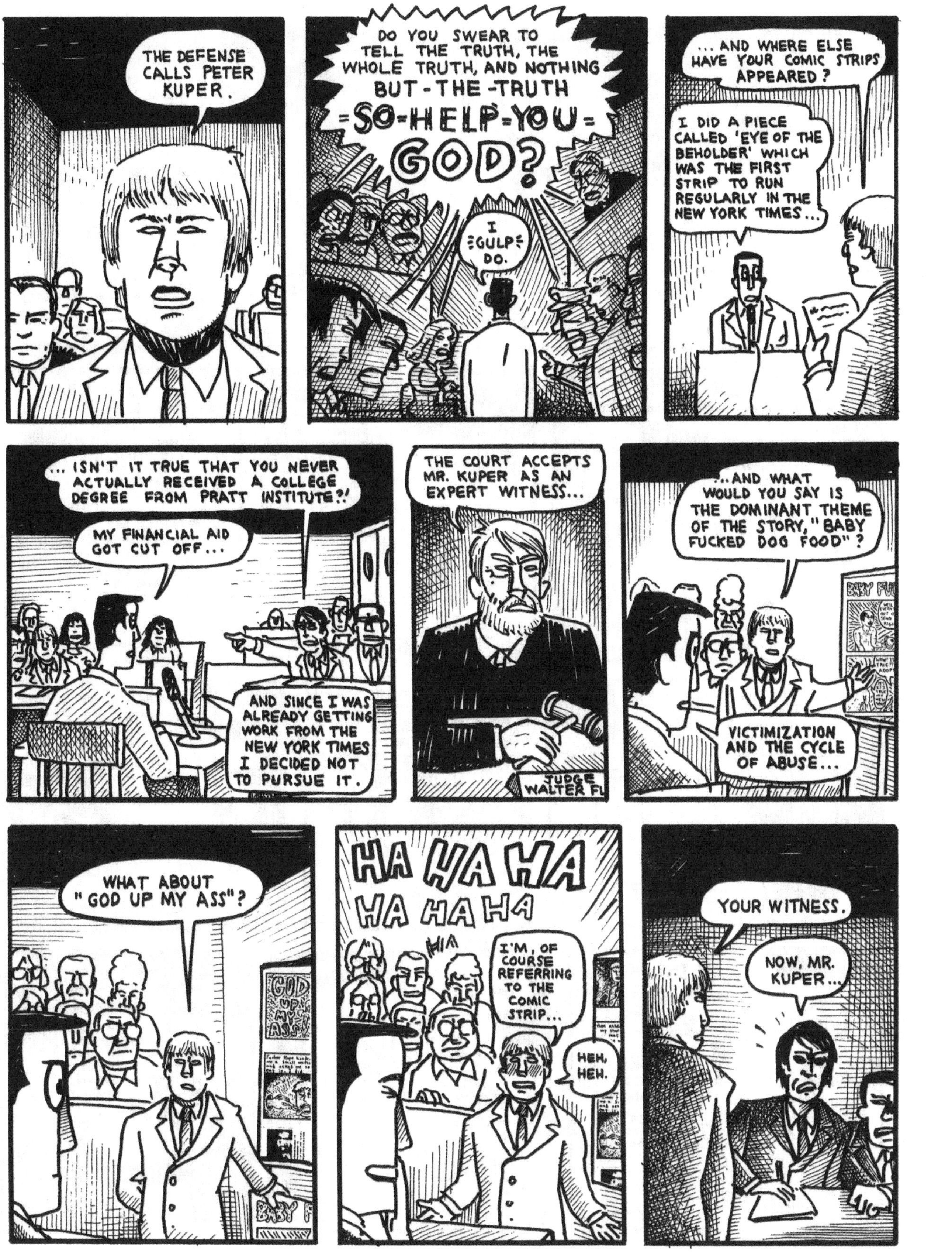
THE DEFENSE CALLS PETER KUPER.
DO YOU SWEAR TO TELL THE TRUTH, THE WHOLE TRUTH, AND NOTHING BUT-THE-TRUTH =SO-HELP-YOU= GOD?
I GULP DO.
...AND WHERE ELSE HAVE YOUR COMIC STRIPS APPEARED?
I DID A PIECE CALLED 'EYE OF THE BEHOLDER' WHICH WAS THE FIRST STRIP TO RUN REGULARLY IN THE NEW YORK TIMES...
...ISN'T IT TRUE THAT YOU NEVER ACTUALLY RECEIVED A COLLEGE DEGREE FROM PRATT INSTITUTE?!
MY FINANCIAL AID GOT CUT OFF...
AND SINCE I WAS ALREADY GETTING WORK FROM THE NEW YORK TIMES I DECIDED NOT TO PURSUE IT.
THE COURT ACCEPTS MR. KUPER AS AN EXPERT WITNESS...
JUDGE WALTER FL
...AND WHAT WOULD YOU SAY IS THE DOMINANT THEME OF THE STORY, "BABY FUCKED DOG FOOD"?
VICTIMIZATION AND THE CYCLE OF ABUSE...
WHAT ABOUT "GOD UP MY ASS"?
HA HA HA HA
HA HA HA HA
HA
I'M, OF COURSE REFERRING TO THE COMIC STRIP...
HEH, HEH.
YOUR WITNESS.
NOW, MR. KUPER...

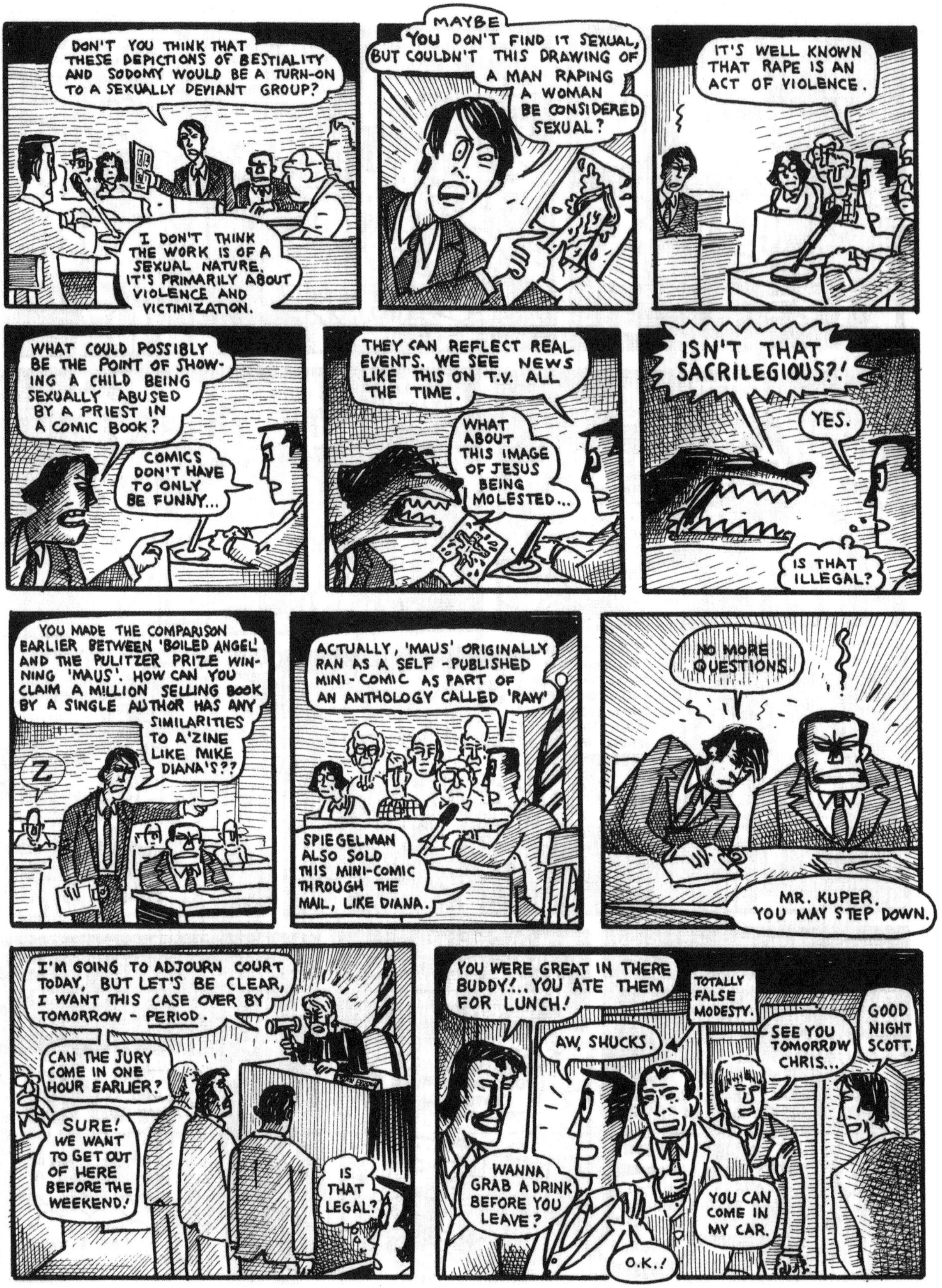

DON'T YOU THINK THAT THESE DEPICTIONS OF BESTIALITY AND SODOMY WOULD BE A TURN-ON TO A SEXUALLY DEVIANT GROUP?
I DON'T THINK THE WORK IS OF A SEXUAL NATURE. IT'S PRIMARILY ABOUT VIOLENCE AND VICTIMIZATION.
MAYBE YOU DON'T FIND IT SEXUAL, BUT COULDN'T THIS DRAWING OF A MAN RAPING A WOMAN BE CONSIDERED SEXUAL?
IT'S WELL KNOWN THAT RAPE IS AN ACT OF VIOLENCE.
WHAT COULD POSSIBLY BE THE POINT OF SHOWING A CHILD BEING SEXUALLY ABUSED BY A PRIEST IN A COMIC BOOK?
COMICS DON'T HAVE TO ONLY BE FUNNY...
THEY CAN REFLECT REAL EVENTS. WE SEE NEWS LIKE THIS ON T.V. ALL THE TIME.
WHAT ABOUT THIS IMAGE OF JESUS BEING MOLESTED...
ISN'T THAT SACRILEGIOUS?!
YES.
IS THAT ILLEGAL?
YOU MADE THE COMPARISON EARLIER BETWEEN 'BOILED ANGEL' AND THE PULITZER PRIZE WINNING 'MAUS'. HOW CAN YOU CLAIM A MILLION SELLING BOOK BY A SINGLE AUTHOR HAS ANY SIMILARITIES TO A 'ZINE LIKE MIKE DIANA'S??
Z
ACTUALLY, 'MAUS' ORIGINALLY RAN AS A SELF-PUBLISHED MINI-COMIC AS PART OF AN ANTHOLOGY CALLED 'RAW'
SPIEGELMAN ALSO SOLD THIS MINI-COMIC THROUGH THE MAIL, LIKE DIANA.
NO MORE QUESTIONS.
MR. KUPER. YOU MAY STEP DOWN.
I'M GOING TO ADJOURN COURT TODAY, BUT LET'S BE CLEAR, I WANT THIS CASE OVER BY TOMORROW - PERIOD.
CAN THE JURY COME IN ONE HOUR EARLIER?
SURE! WE WANT TO GET OUT OF HERE BEFORE THE WEEKEND!
IS THAT LEGAL?
YOU WERE GREAT IN THERE BUDDY!... YOU ATE THEM FOR LUNCH!
TOTALLY FALSE MODESTY.
AW, SHUCKS.
SEE YOU TOMORROW CHRIS...
GOOD NIGHT SCOTT.
WANNA GRAB A DRINK BEFORE YOU LEAVE?
O.K.!
YOU CAN COME IN MY CAR.

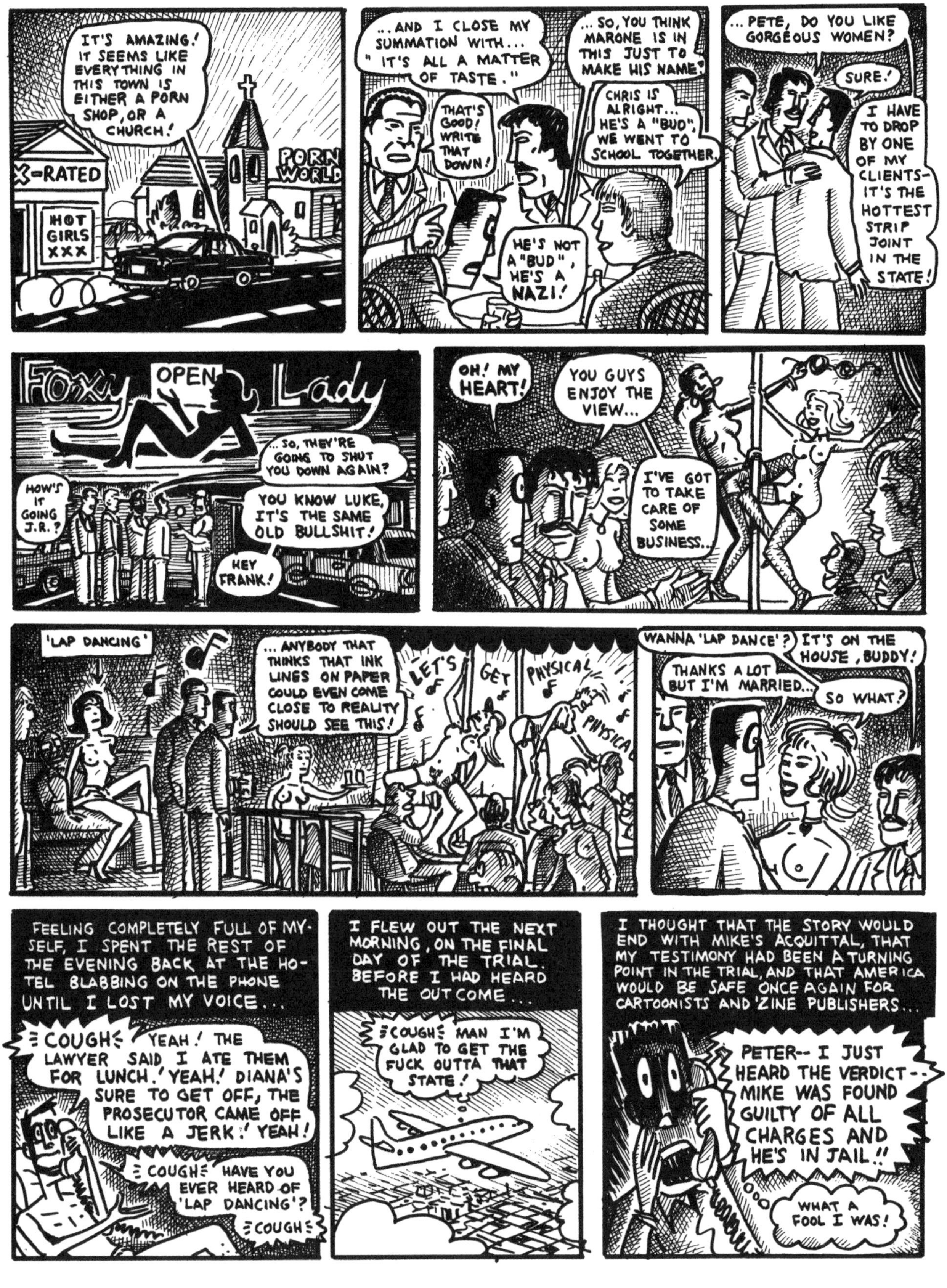
IT'S AMAZING! IT SEEMS LIKE EVERYTHING IN THIS TOWN IS EITHER A PORN SHOP, OR A CHURCH!
X-RATED
HOT GIRLS XXX
PORN WORLD
...AND I CLOSE MY SUMMATION WITH... "IT'S ALL A MATTER OF TASTE."
THAT'S GOOD! WRITE THAT DOWN!
...SO, YOU THINK MARONE IS IN THIS JUST TO MAKE HIS NAME?
CHRIS IS ALRIGHT... HE'S A "BUD", WE WENT TO SCHOOL TOGETHER.
HE'S NOT A "BUD", HE'S A NAZI!
...PETE, DO YOU LIKE GORGEOUS WOMEN?
SURE!
I HAVE TO DROP BY ONE OF MY CLIENTS-- IT'S THE HOTTEST STRIP JOINT IN THE STATE!
Foxy OPEN Lady
...SO, THEY'RE GOING TO SHUT YOU DOWN AGAIN?
HOW'S IT GOING J.R.?
YOU KNOW LUKE, IT'S THE SAME OLD BULLSHIT!
HEY FRANK!
OH! MY HEART!
YOU GUYS ENJOY THE VIEW...
I'VE GOT TO TAKE CARE OF SOME BUSINESS...
'LAP DANCING'
...ANYBODY THAT THINKS THAT INK LINES ON PAPER COULD EVEN COME CLOSE TO REALITY SHOULD SEE THIS!
LET'S GET PHYSICAL PHYSICAL
WANNA 'LAP DANCE'? IT'S ON THE HOUSE, BUDDY!
THANKS A LOT BUT I'M MARRIED...
SO WHAT?
FEELING COMPLETELY FULL OF MYSELF, I SPENT THE REST OF THE EVENING BACK AT THE HOTEL BLABBING ON THE PHONE UNTIL I LOST MY VOICE...
COUGH YEAH! THE LAWYER SAID I ATE THEM FOR LUNCH! YEAH! DIANA'S SURE TO GET OFF, THE PROSECUTOR CAME OFF LIKE A JERK! YEAH!
COUGH HAVE YOU EVER HEARD OF 'LAP DANCING'?
COUGH
I FLEW OUT THE NEXT MORNING, ON THE FINAL DAY OF THE TRIAL, BEFORE I HAD HEARD THE OUTCOME...
COUGH MAN I'M GLAD TO GET THE FUCK OUTTA THAT STATE!
I THOUGHT THAT THE STORY WOULD END WITH MIKE'S ACQUITTAL, THAT MY TESTIMONY HAD BEEN A TURNING POINT IN THE TRIAL, AND THAT AMERICA WOULD BE SAFE ONCE AGAIN FOR CARTOONISTS AND 'ZINE PUBLISHERS...
PETER-- I JUST HEARD THE VERDICT-- MIKE WAS FOUND GUILTY OF ALL CHARGES AND HE'S IN JAIL!!
WHAT A FOOL I WAS!

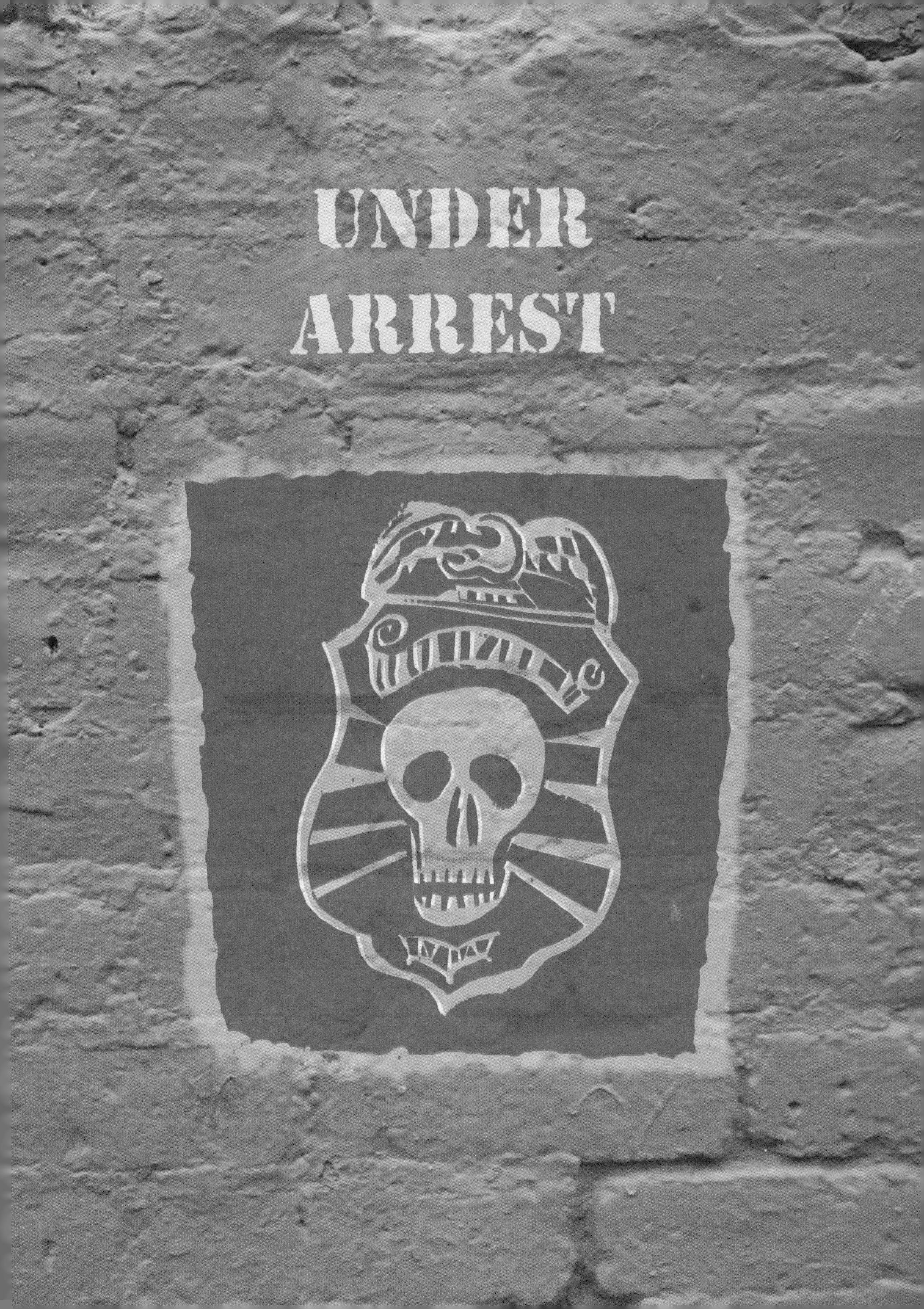
UNDER
ARREST

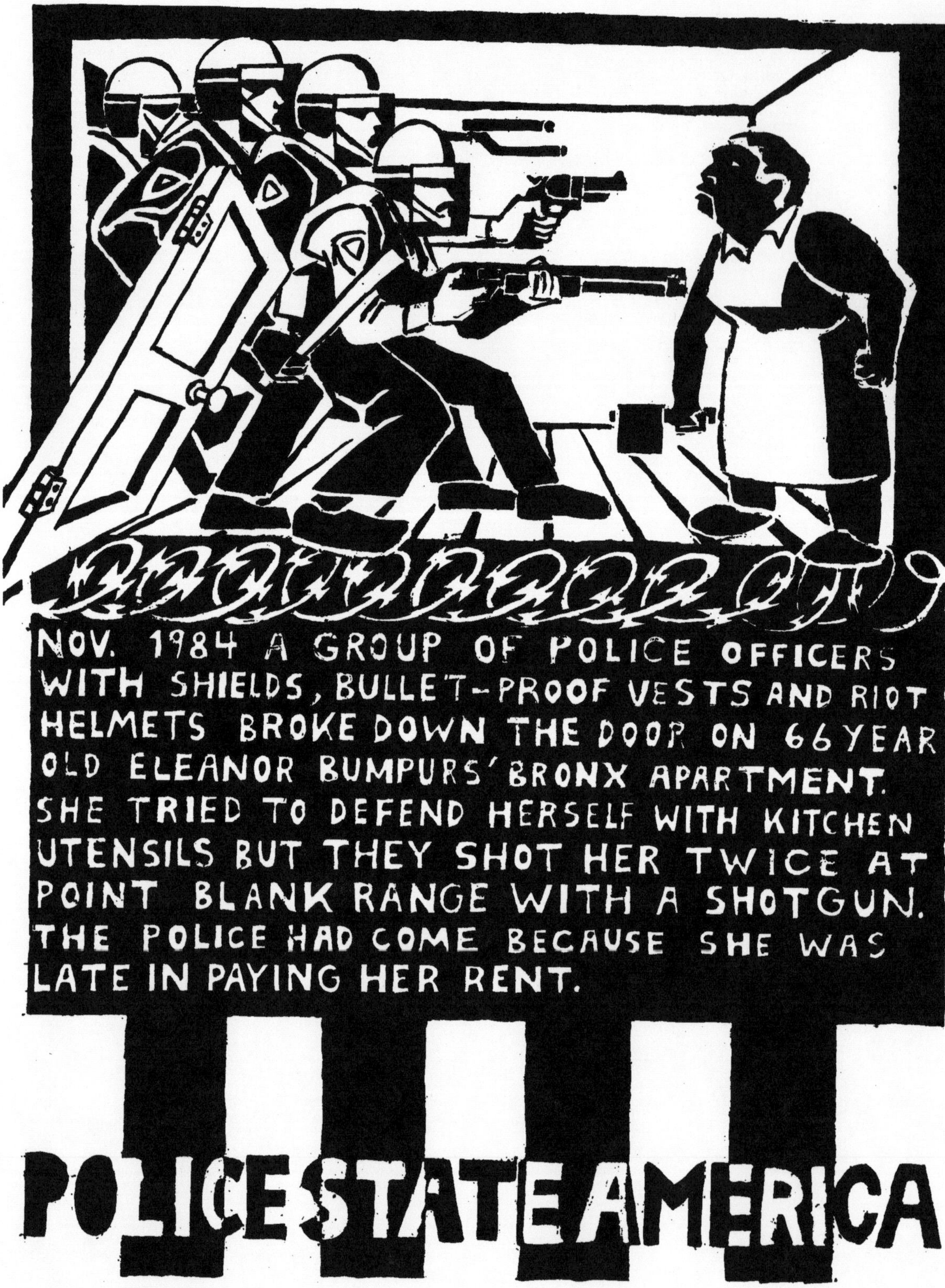
NOV. 1984 A GROUP OF POLICE OFFICERS WITH SHIELDS, BULLET-PROOF VESTS AND RIOT HELMETS BROKE DOWN THE DOOR ON 66 YEAR OLD ELEANOR BUMPURS' BRONX APARTMENT. SHE TRIED TO DEFEND HERSELF WITH KITCHEN UTENSILS BUT THEY SHOT HER TWICE AT POINT BLANK RANGE WITH A SHOTGUN. THE POLICE HAD COME BECAUSE SHE WAS LATE IN PAYING HER RENT.
POLICE STATE AMERICA

SETH TOBOCMAN

ART BY ERIC DROOKER

COUP D'ETAT OF THE SPIRIT

Smiling in Tompkins Square Park Mayday
You squeezed my hand
As saxaphone lady blew jazz from bandshell
Your thick, Black, artist hands felt so *alive*
Always busy transforming dead street junk
Into fresh fruit for the soul
That's where I first met you...*yeah-on the street*
Both of us peddlers hustling our work on the streets
     of Manhattan
Me, born on this island, you, born on Carribean
     island
Together now looking out for cops on Astor Place
As we try to make a living in Reaganomic Eighties
Damn Grady! I didn't know that was the last time
You'd squeeze my hand
Cop driving jeep had no uniform--he was off duty!
How were you to know to avoid him?!
Wish I could have been there to warn you:
"PACK IT IN-SPLIT! THE HEAT'S COMING!!"
Sorry man...this city island is mean-*moves quickly*
We're living on the back of a giant snapping turtle
A mechanical terrapin with jaws of steel always
          hungry
For passionate young souls to devour

Remember-these Manhattan streets have swallowed
     the best of them:
Malcolm X, John Lennon, Michael Stewart,
     Irving Haimes...
And my friend Grady Alexis
I reached out and touched you at your wake in
     Brooklyn
Your hands were soft and cold
Your family wants you buried in your native soil
Where Ghede Nimbo-Voodoo god of sex, death and
     the underworld
Awaits you with petro drums
And now you're flying back home to Haiti
Different from colonial way you left it
No more Papa Doc, No more Baby Doc-CIA-Duvalier
Your people are busy freeing themselves
With their hot sugar cane hands and hearts
Creating a new island in the Carribean sun
...While up here-alone, I feel my city island slowly
     sinking
Into acid waters of despair and chaos
Thank you, man, Merci merci, thank you for sharing
Your colors with me
I'm picking up the brush right where you left it...

                    —Eric D.
                    Lower East Side, NYC
                    May 23, 1991, 3AM...

135

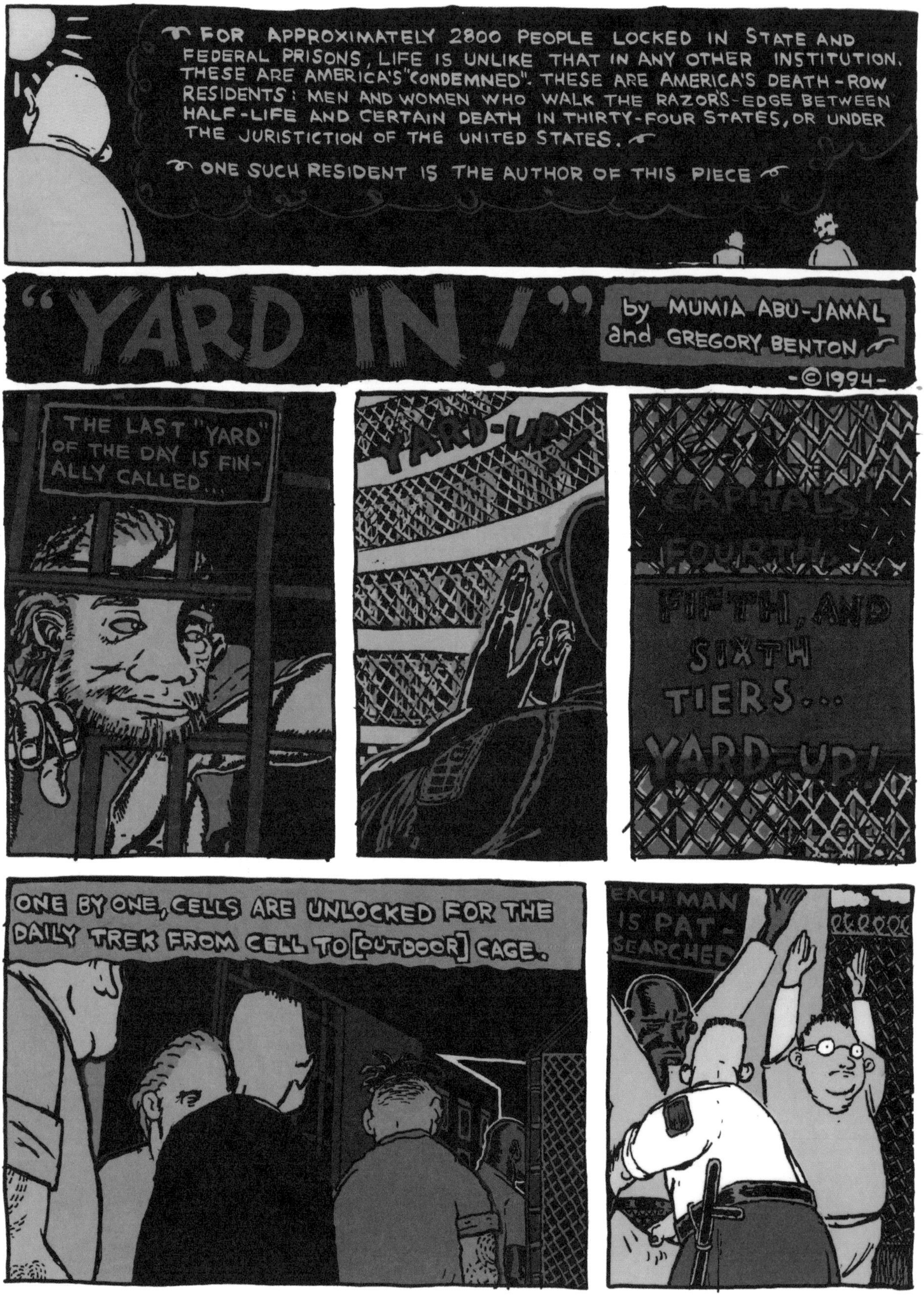
FOR APPROXIMATELY 2800 PEOPLE LOCKED IN STATE AND FEDERAL PRISONS, LIFE IS UNLIKE THAT IN ANY OTHER INSTITUTION. THESE ARE AMERICA'S "CONDEMNED". THESE ARE AMERICA'S DEATH-ROW RESIDENTS: MEN AND WOMEN WHO WALK THE RAZOR'S-EDGE BETWEEN HALF-LIFE AND CERTAIN DEATH IN THIRTY-FOUR STATES, OR UNDER THE JURISTICTION OF THE UNITED STATES.
ONE SUCH RESIDENT IS THE AUTHOR OF THIS PIECE
"YARD IN!"
by MUMIA ABU-JAMAL and GREGORY BENTON
-©1994-
THE LAST "YARD" OF THE DAY IS FINALLY CALLED...
YARD-UP!
CAPITALS! FOURTH, FIFTH, AND SIXTH TIERS... YARD-UP!
ONE BY ONE, CELLS ARE UNLOCKED FOR THE DAILY TREK FROM CELL TO [OUTDOOR] CAGE.
EACH MAN IS PAT-SEARCHED

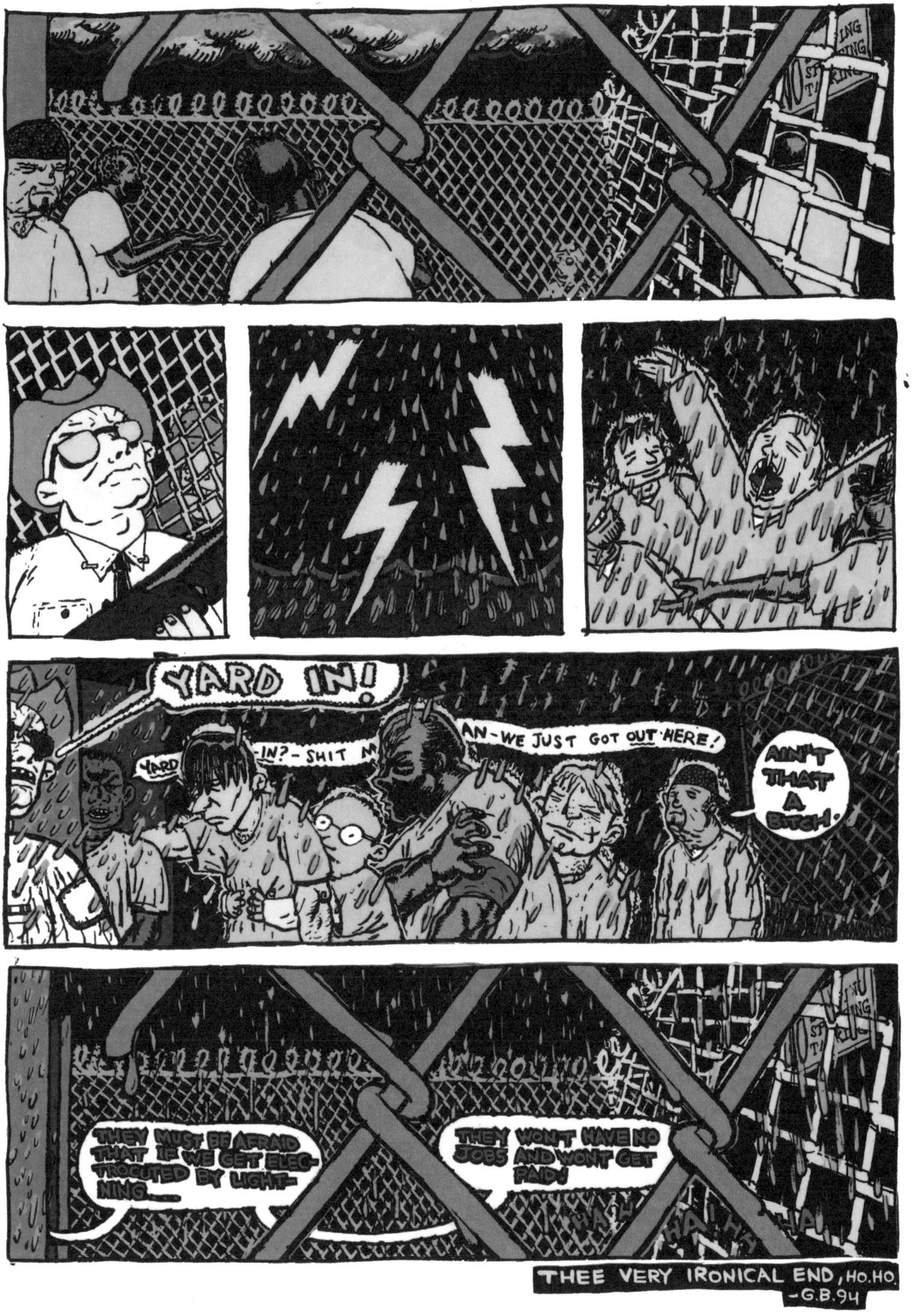
YARD IN!
YARD -IN?- SHIT MAN- WE JUST GOT OUT HERE!
AIN'T THAT A BITCH.
THEY MUST BE AFRAID THAT IF WE GET ELEC-TROCUTED BY LIGHT-NING....
THEY WON'T HAVE NO JOBS AND WON'T GET PAID!
HA HA HA
THEE VERY IRONICAL END, HO.HO.
-G.B.94

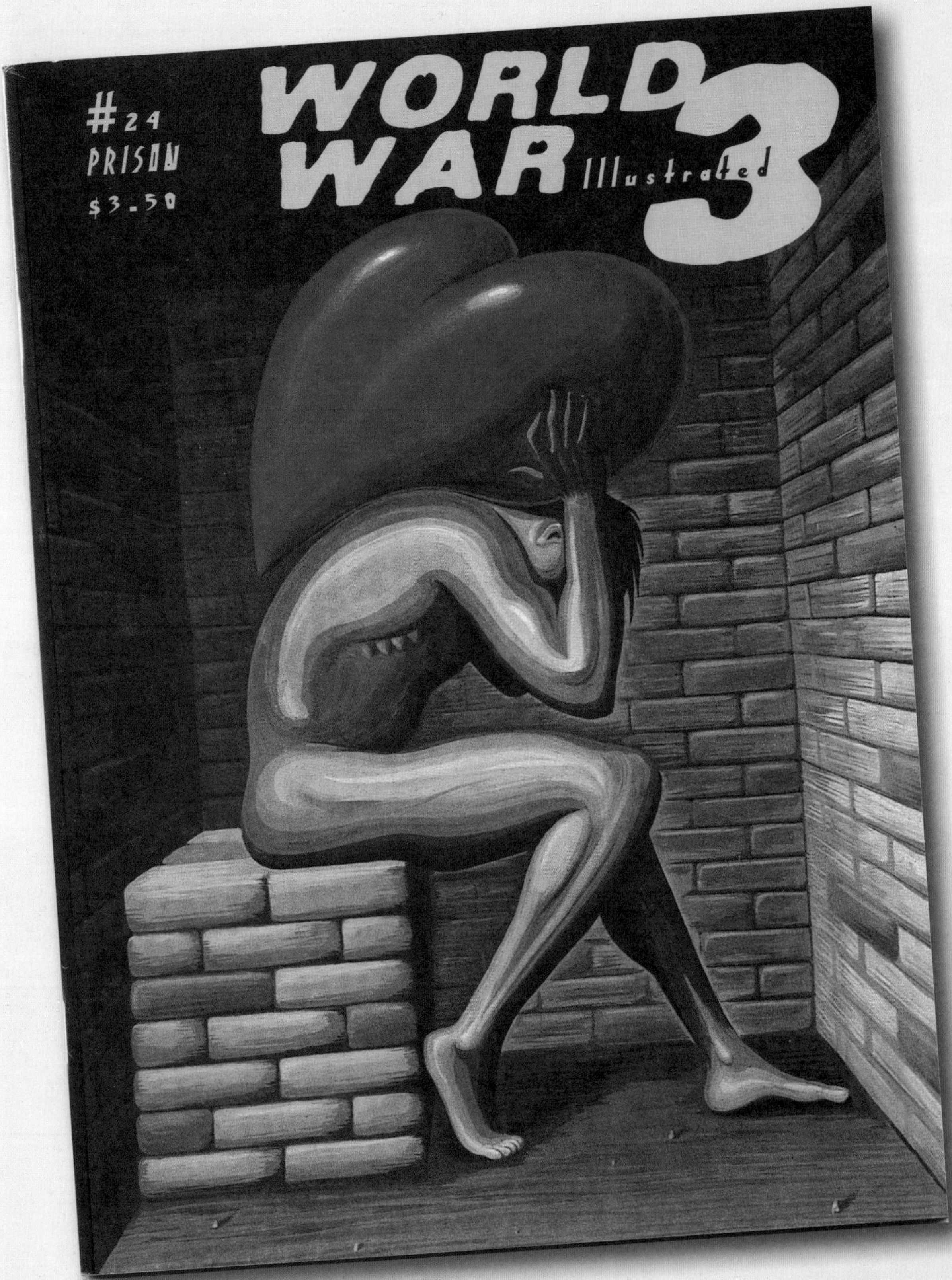

#24
PRISON
$3.50
WORLD WAR Illustrated 3

ON THE ROAD

BASED ON
PHOTOS BY
JIM BARNES

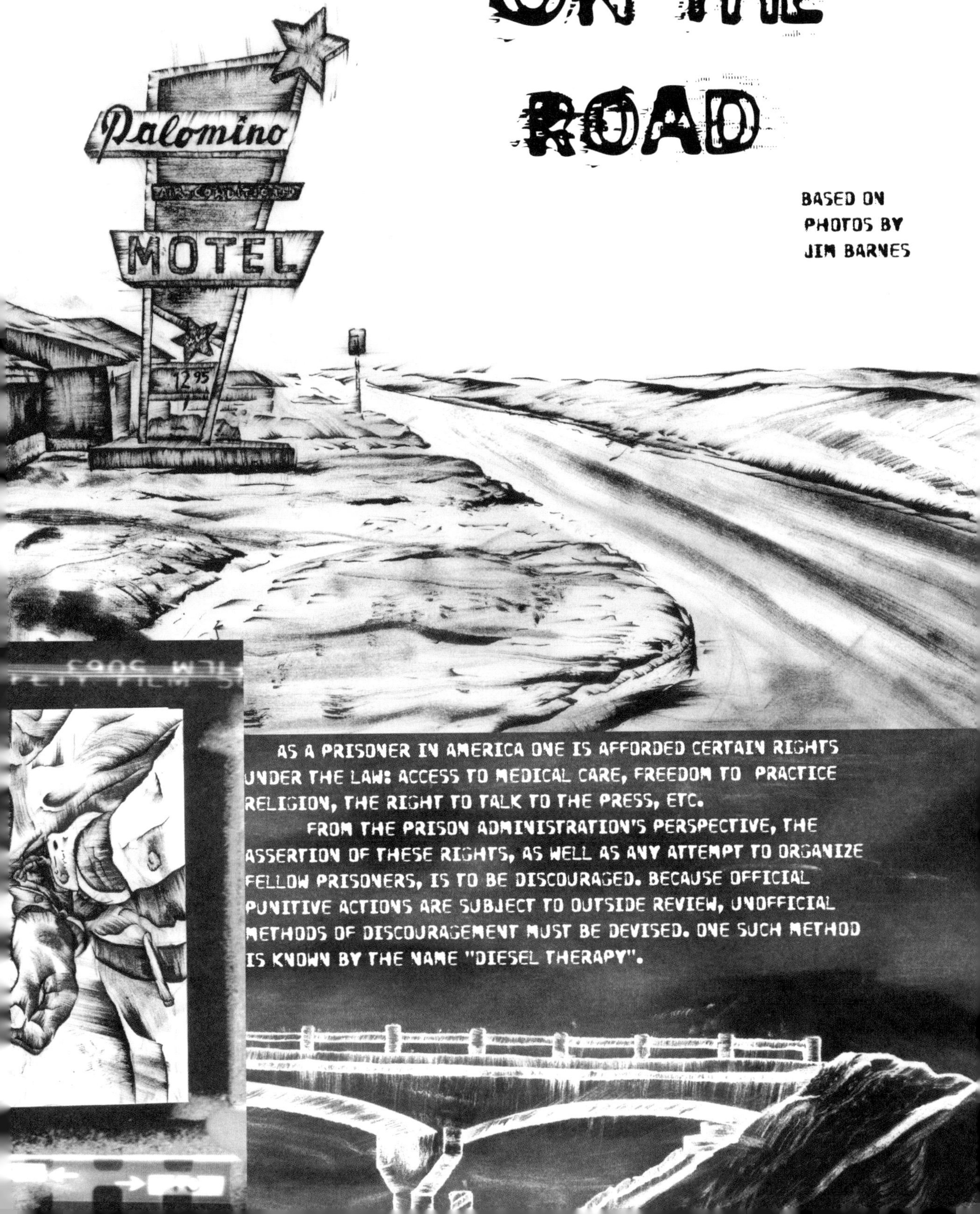

Palomino
MOTEL
12.95

AS A PRISONER IN AMERICA ONE IS AFFORDED CERTAIN RIGHTS UNDER THE LAW: ACCESS TO MEDICAL CARE, FREEDOM TO PRACTICE RELIGION, THE RIGHT TO TALK TO THE PRESS, ETC.

FROM THE PRISON ADMINISTRATION'S PERSPECTIVE, THE ASSERTION OF THESE RIGHTS, AS WELL AS ANY ATTEMPT TO ORGANIZE FELLOW PRISONERS, IS TO BE DISCOURAGED. BECAUSE OFFICIAL PUNITIVE ACTIONS ARE SUBJECT TO OUTSIDE REVIEW, UNOFFICIAL METHODS OF DISCOURAGEMENT MUST BE DEVISED. ONE SUCH METHOD IS KNOWN BY THE NAME "DIESEL THERAPY".

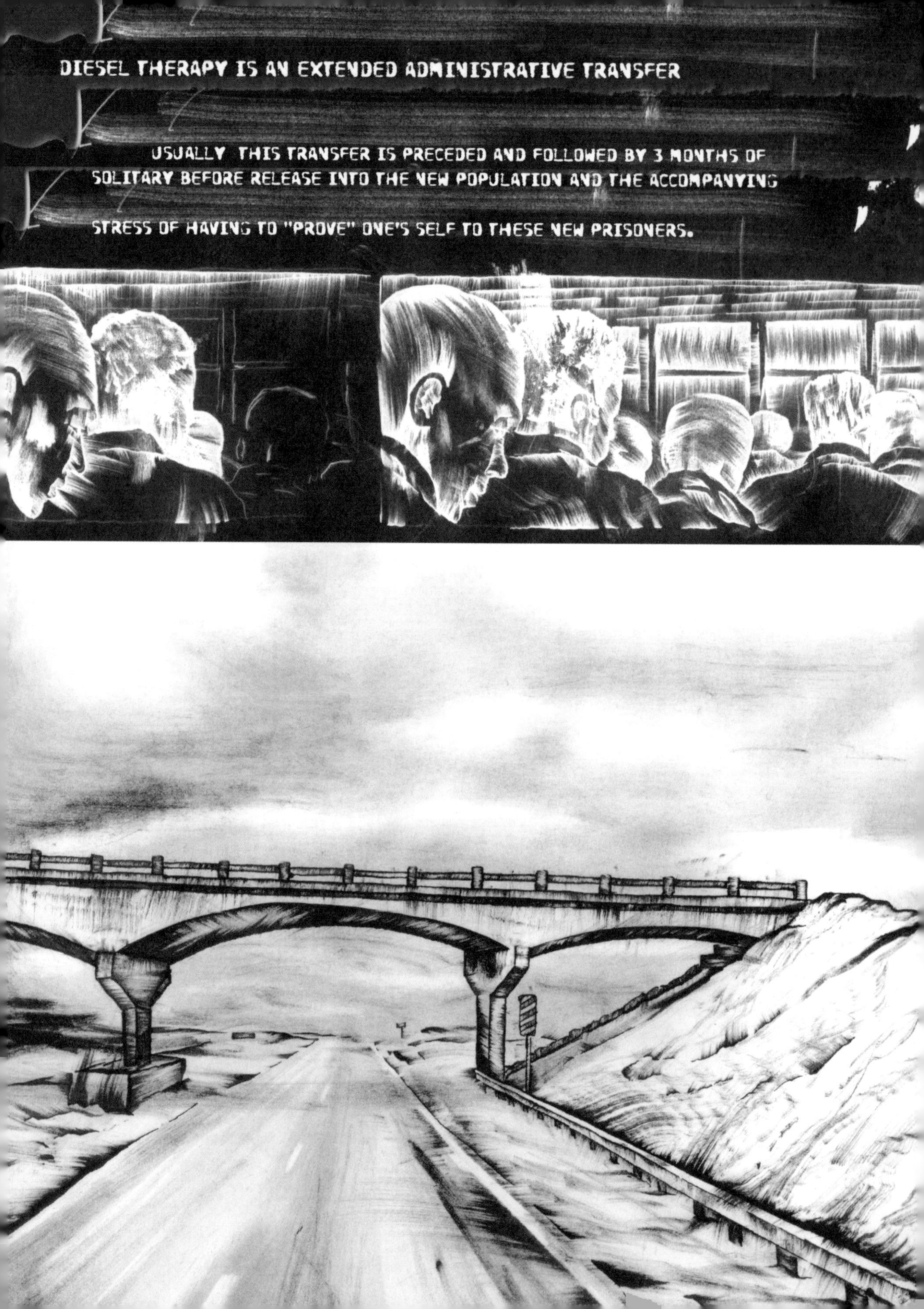
DIESEL THERAPY IS AN EXTENDED ADMINISTRATIVE TRANSFER
USUALLY THIS TRANSFER IS PRECEDED AND FOLLOWED BY 3 MONTHS OF SOLITARY BEFORE RELEASE INTO THE NEW POPULATION AND THE ACCOMPANYING STRESS OF HAVING TO "PROVE" ONE'S SELF TO THESE NEW PRISONERS.

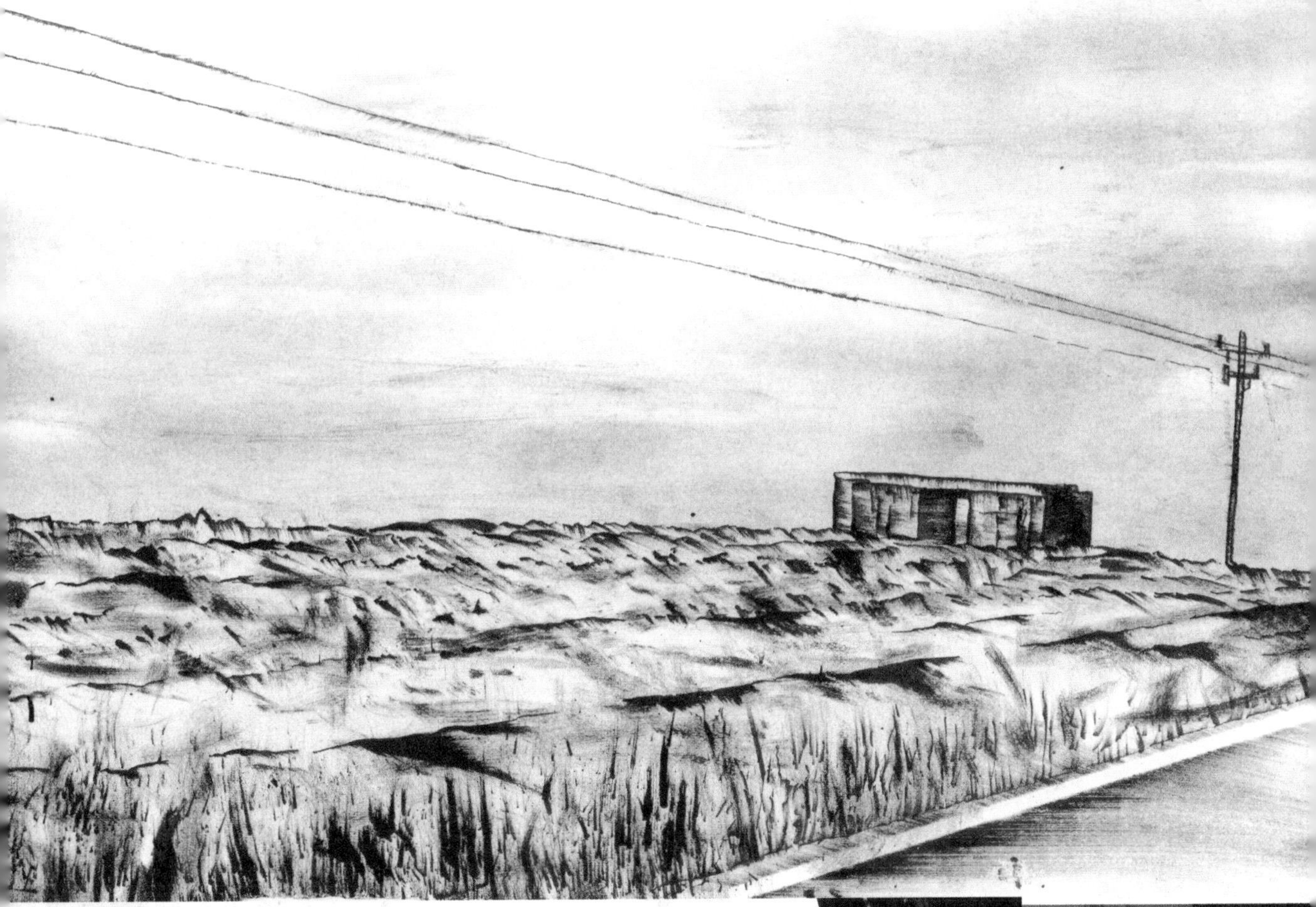

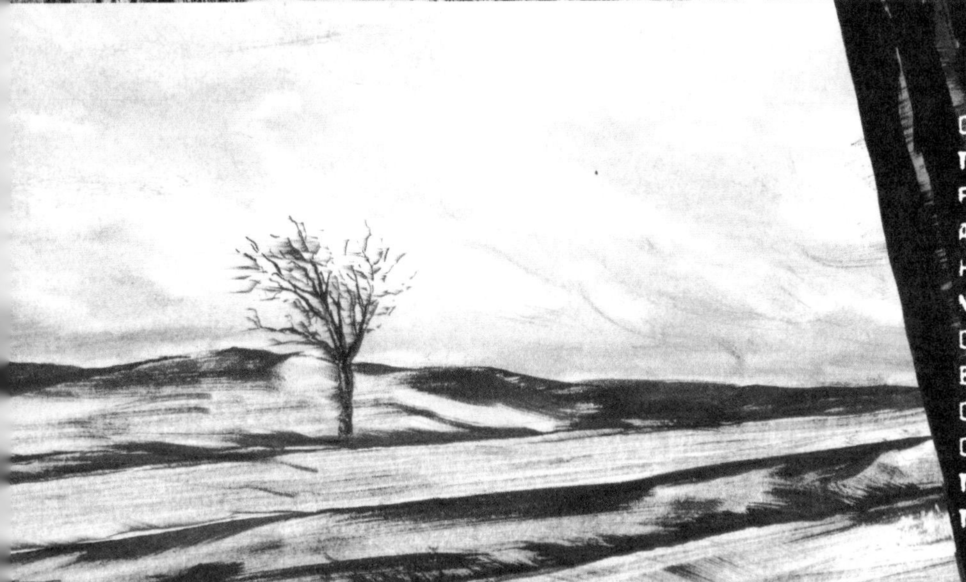

PRISONERS ARE OFTEN CHAINED WHILE IN TRANSIT, SUBJECT TO FREQUENT STRIP SEARCHS, AND ENTITLED TO ONLY ONE HOT MEAL A DAY. THEY HAVE NO CONTACT WITH FRIENDS OR FAMILY, NO ACCESS TO BOOKS OR POSSESSIONS, AND OFTEN HAVE NO KNOWLEDGE OF WHERE THEY ARE, WHERE THEY'RE GOING OR WHEN THEY'LL ARRIVE.

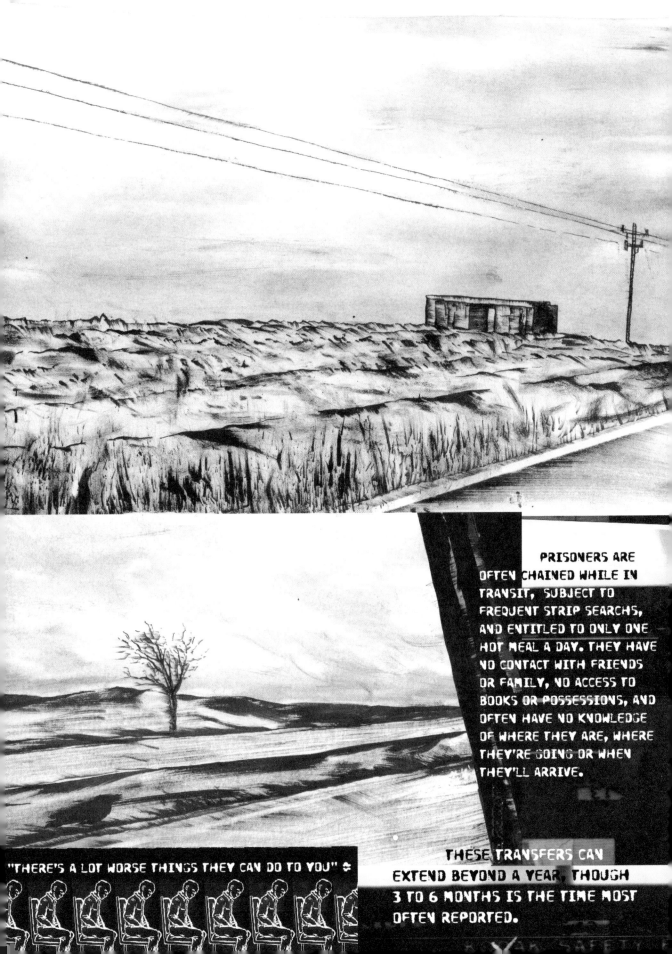

"THERE'S A LOT WORSE THINGS THEY CAN DO TO YOU" ≑

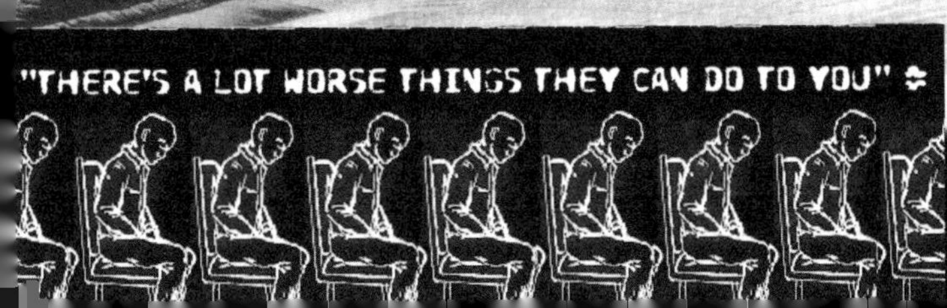

THESE TRANSFERS CAN EXTEND BEYOND A YEAR, THOUGH 3 TO 6 MONTHS IS THE TIME MOST OFTEN REPORTED.

"ONE OF THE FEW ADVANTAGES IS GETTING TO SEE SOME SCENERY" ✛

SAFETY FILM 5063

"THE NOT KNOWING WHERE YOU ARE GOING, AND FOR HOW LONG, THEIR ATTEMPTS TO KEEP YOU FROM CONTACTING YOUR FAMILY THROUGH ALL THIS, IT'S ALL MEANT TO BREAK YOU DOWN. LUCKILY I'M VERY HARD & BELLIGER-ENT AND THEY STILL HAVEN'T BROKEN ME..." ✛

✛ ALL QUOTES BY PRISONERS WHO HAVE EXPERIENCED " DIESEL THERAPY"

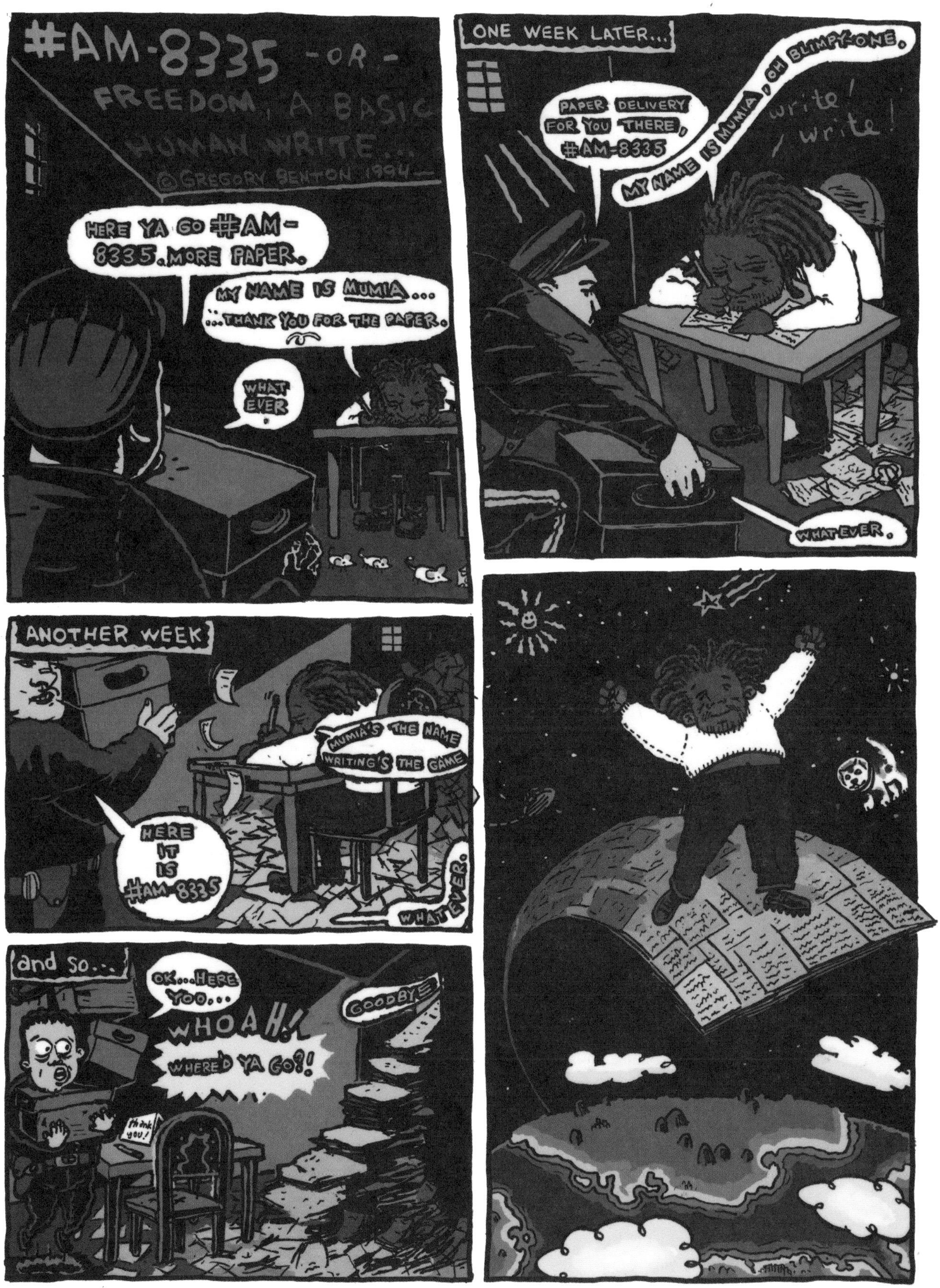
#AM-8335 -OR- FREEDOM, A BASIC HUMAN WRITE...
© GREGORY BENTON 1994
HERE YA GO #AM-8335, MORE PAPER.
MY NAME IS MUMIA... ...THANK YOU FOR THE PAPER.
WHAT EVER.
ONE WEEK LATER...
PAPER DELIVERY FOR YOU THERE, #AM-8335
MY NAME IS MUMIA, OH BLIMPY-ONE.
write! write!
WHATEVER.
ANOTHER WEEK
MUMIA'S THE NAME WRITING'S THE GAME
HERE IT IS #AM-8335
WHATEVER.
and so...
OK...HERE YOO...
GOODBYE
WHOAH!
WHERE'D YA GO?!
thank you!

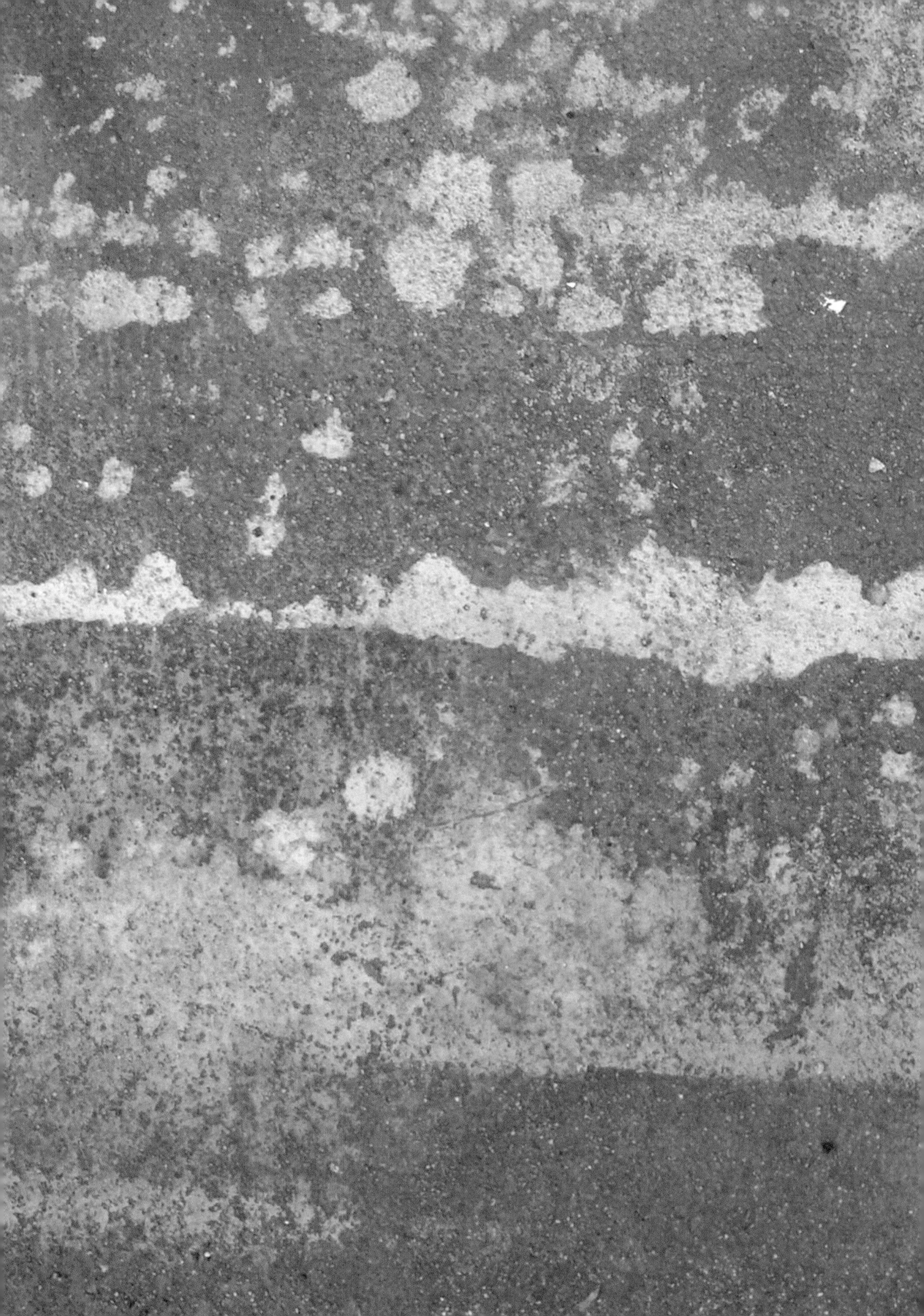

BIOHAZARD

MY MOTHER MY MOTHER

TEXT AND ART BY C. SPERRY

DAD CALLED FROM FORT LAUDERDALE. HE TOLD ME MOM HAD ANOTHER SPELL AND WAS BACK IN THE HOSPITAL. I TOLD HIM I'D FLY DOWN.

I WAS GETTING OUT BUT

IT WASN'T MY IDEA OF A VACATION.

MY MOTHER'S BRAIN TUMOR. WAS LIKE A CLOSING DOOR. I'D NEVER GET OUT OF HERE THE SAME WAY I CAME IN.

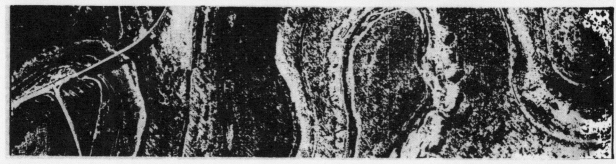

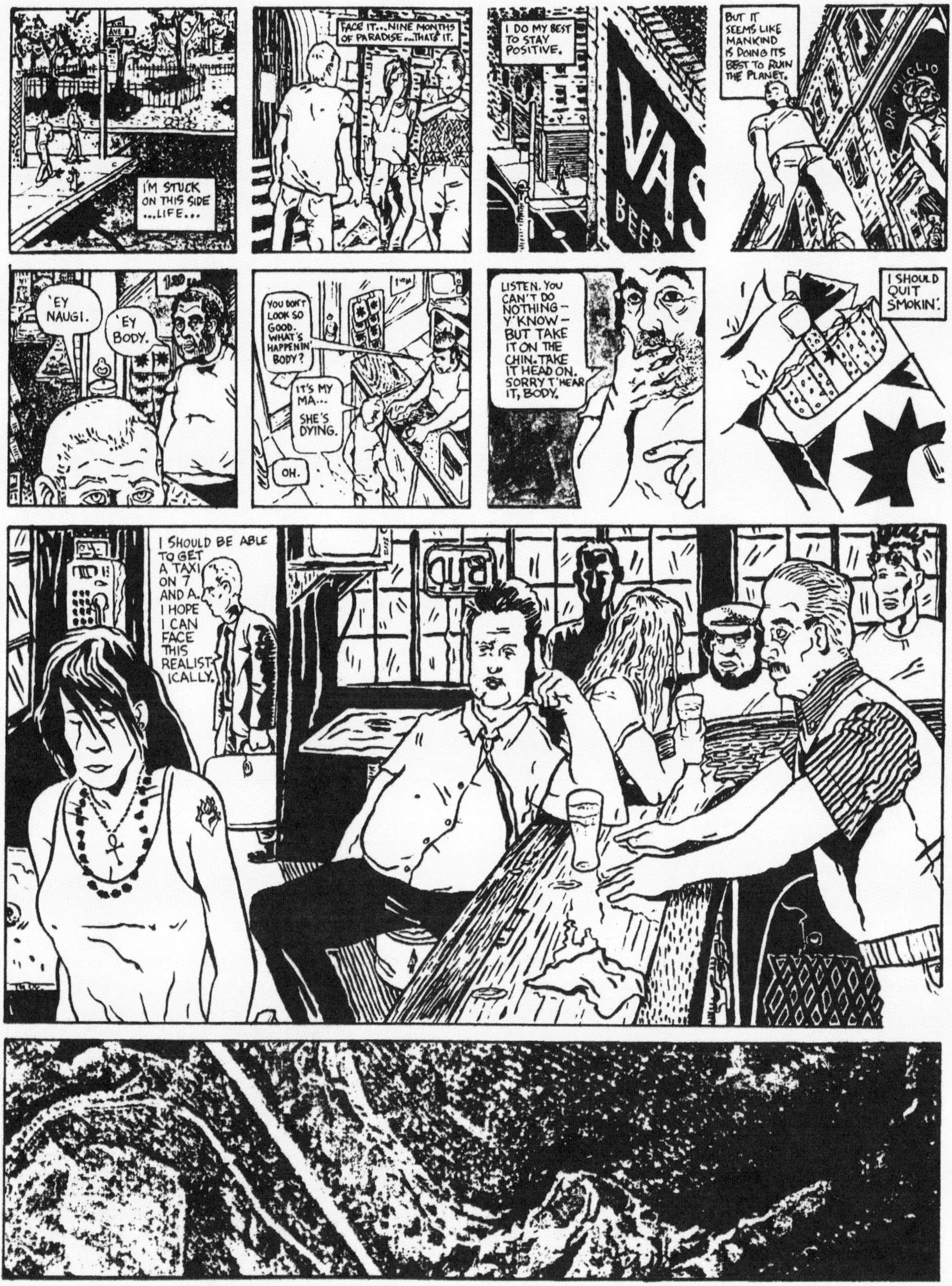

I'M STUCK ON THIS SIDE ...LIFE...
FACE IT... NINE MONTHS OF PARADISE... THAT'S IT.
I DO MY BEST TO STAY POSITIVE.
BEER
BUT IT SEEMS LIKE MANKIND IS DOING ITS BEST TO RUIN THE PLANET.
'EY NAUGI.
'EY BODY.
YOU DON'T LOOK SO GOOD. WHAT'S HAPPENIN' BODY?
IT'S MY MA... SHE'S DYING.
OH.
LISTEN. YOU CAN'T DO NOTHING - Y'KNOW - BUT TAKE IT ON THE CHIN. TAKE IT HEAD ON. SORRY T'HEAR IT, BODY.
I SHOULD QUIT SMOKIN'.
I SHOULD BE ABLE TO GET A TAXI ON 7 AND A. I HOPE I CAN FACE THIS REALISTICALLY.

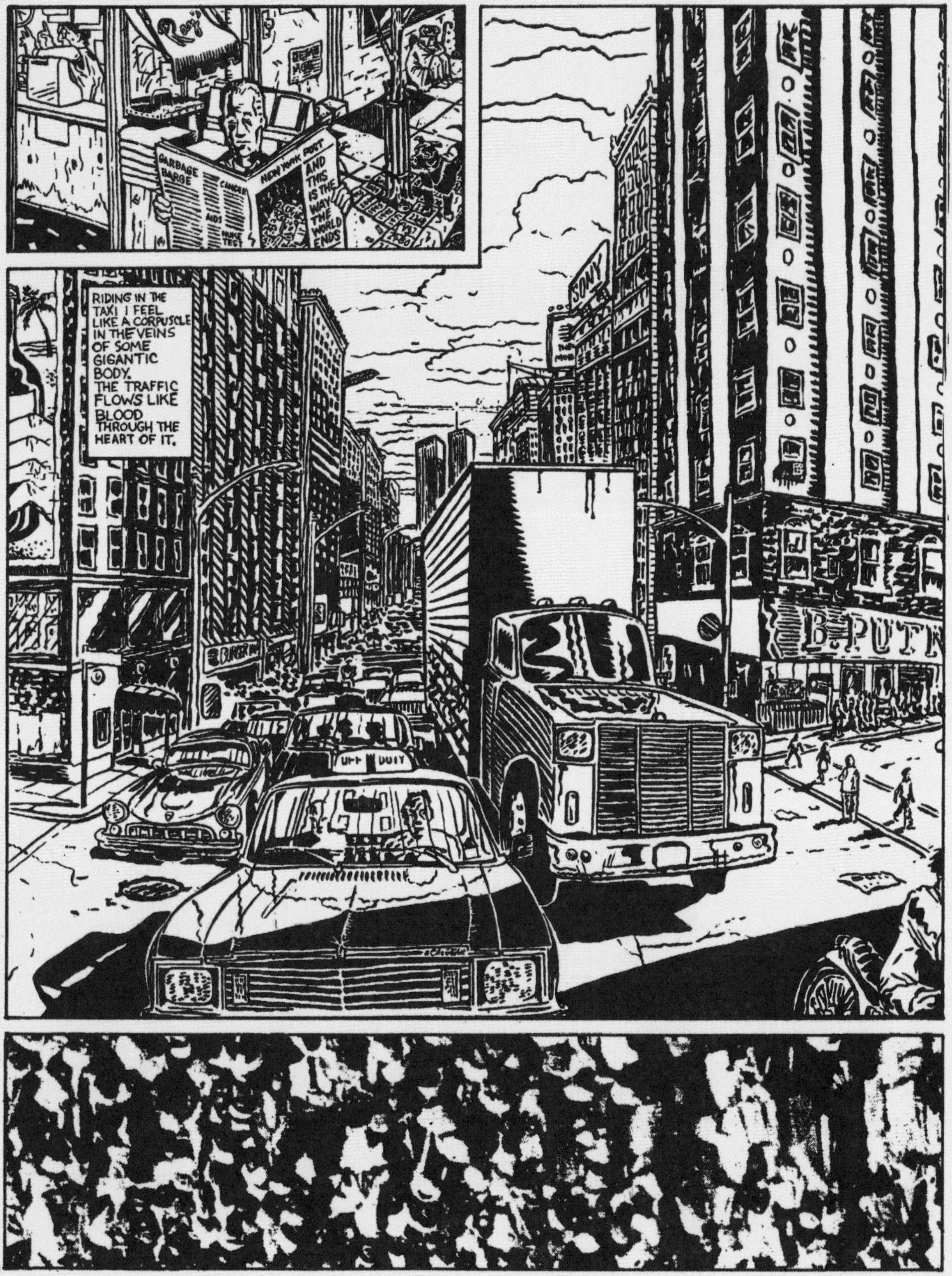
GARBAGE BARGE
CANCER
AIDS
NUKE TEST
NEW YORK POST
AND THIS IS THE WAY THE WORLD ENDS
RIDING IN THE TAXI I FEEL LIKE A CORPUSCLE IN THE VEINS OF SOME GIGANTIC BODY. THE TRAFFIC FLOWS LIKE BLOOD THROUGH THE HEART OF IT.
SONY
OFF DUTY

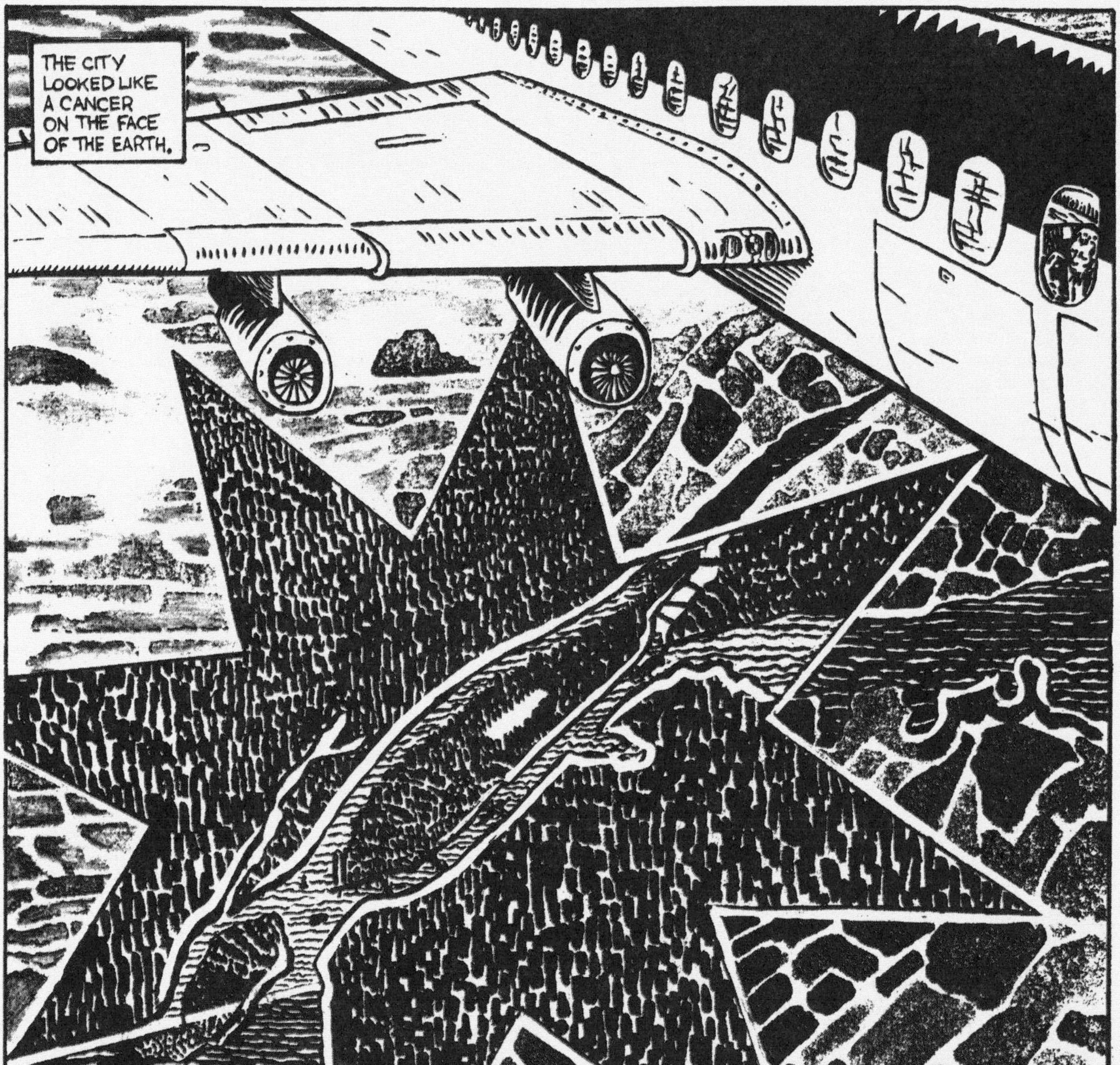
THE CITY LOOKED LIKE A CANCER ON THE FACE OF THE EARTH.
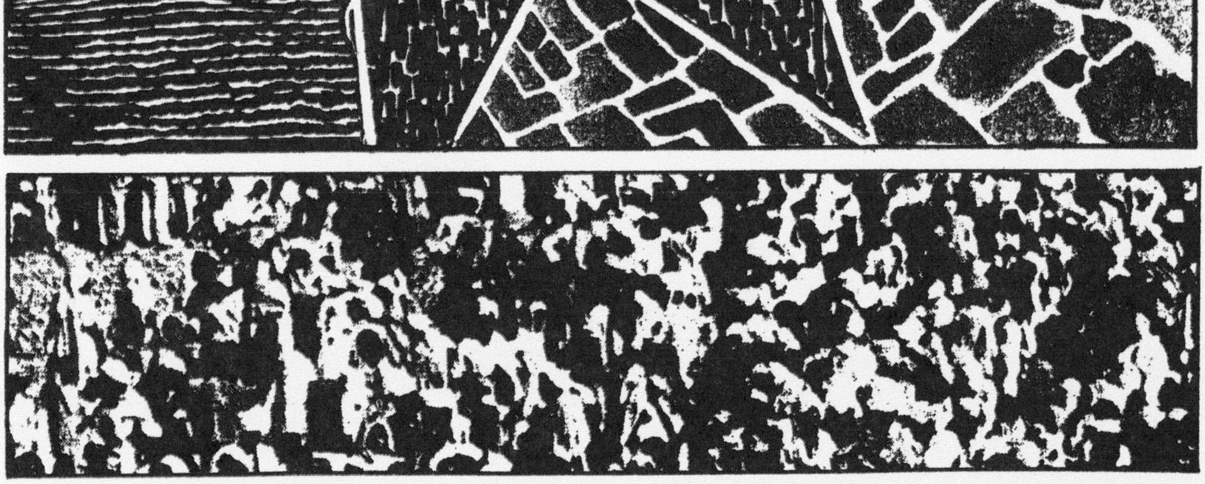

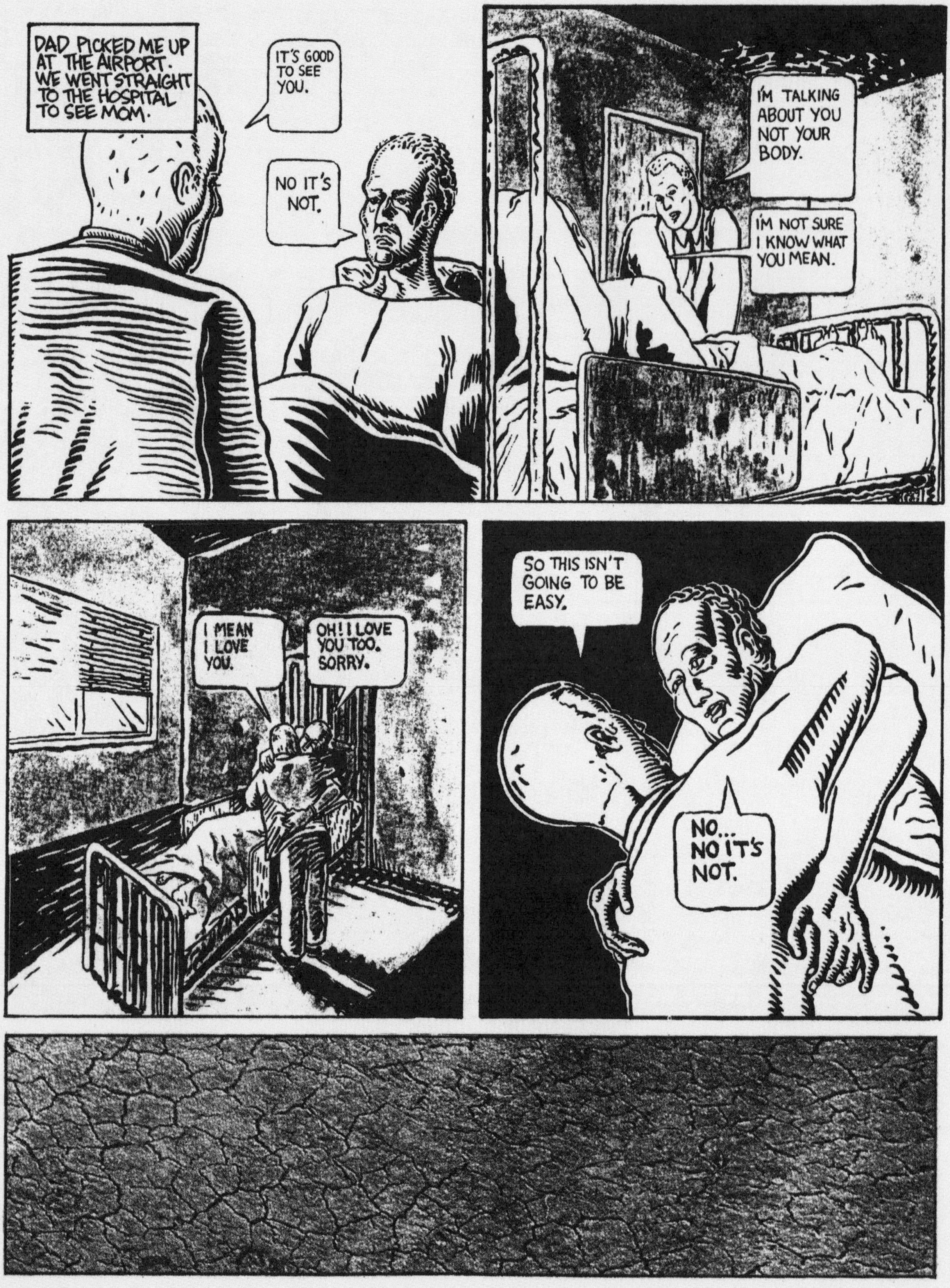
DAD PICKED ME UP AT THE AIRPORT. WE WENT STRAIGHT TO THE HOSPITAL TO SEE MOM.
IT'S GOOD TO SEE YOU.
NO IT'S NOT.
I'M TALKING ABOUT YOU NOT YOUR BODY.
I'M NOT SURE I KNOW WHAT YOU MEAN.
I MEAN I LOVE YOU.
OH! I LOVE YOU TOO. SORRY.
SO THIS ISN'T GOING TO BE EASY.
NO... NO IT'S NOT.

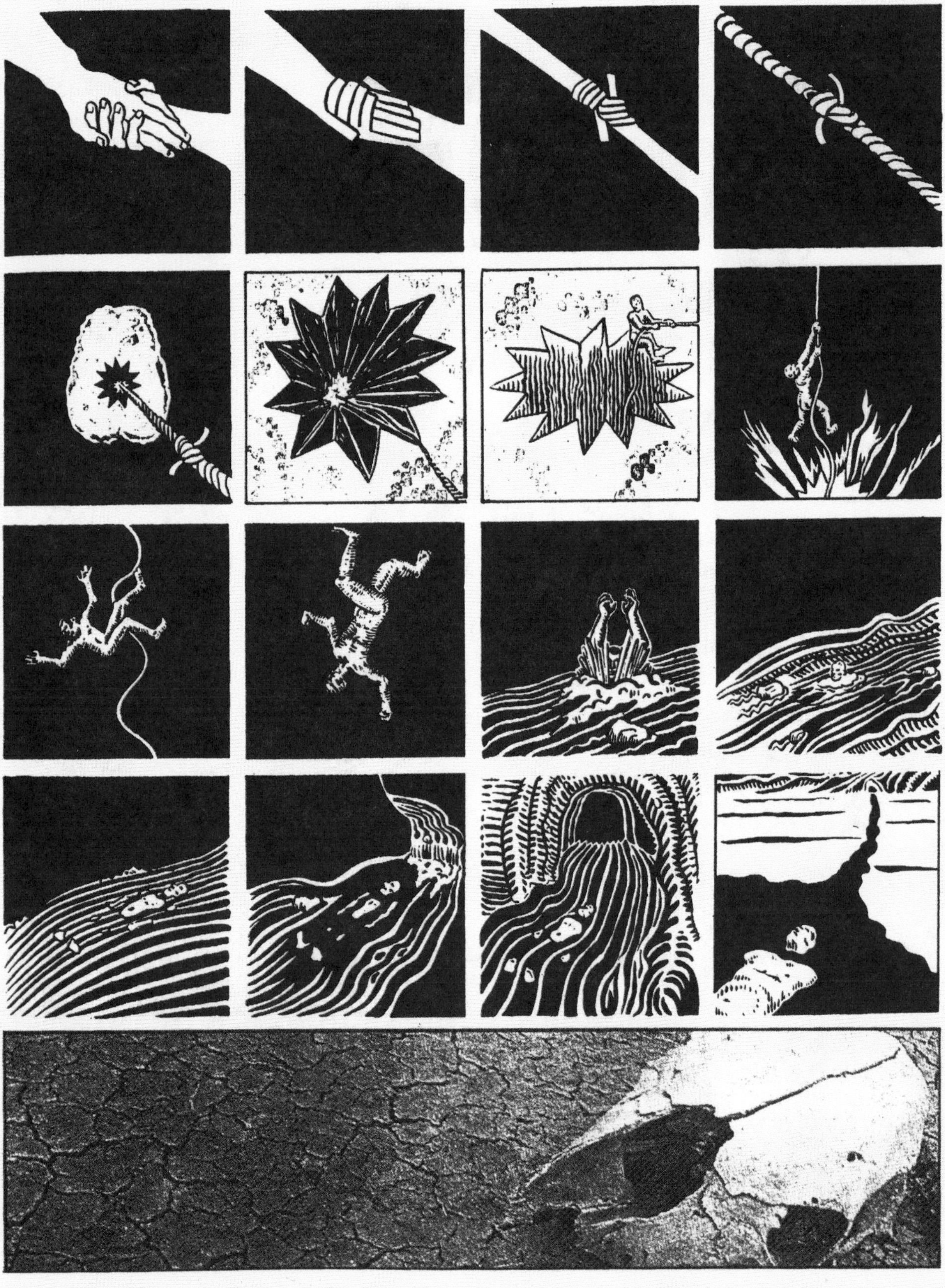

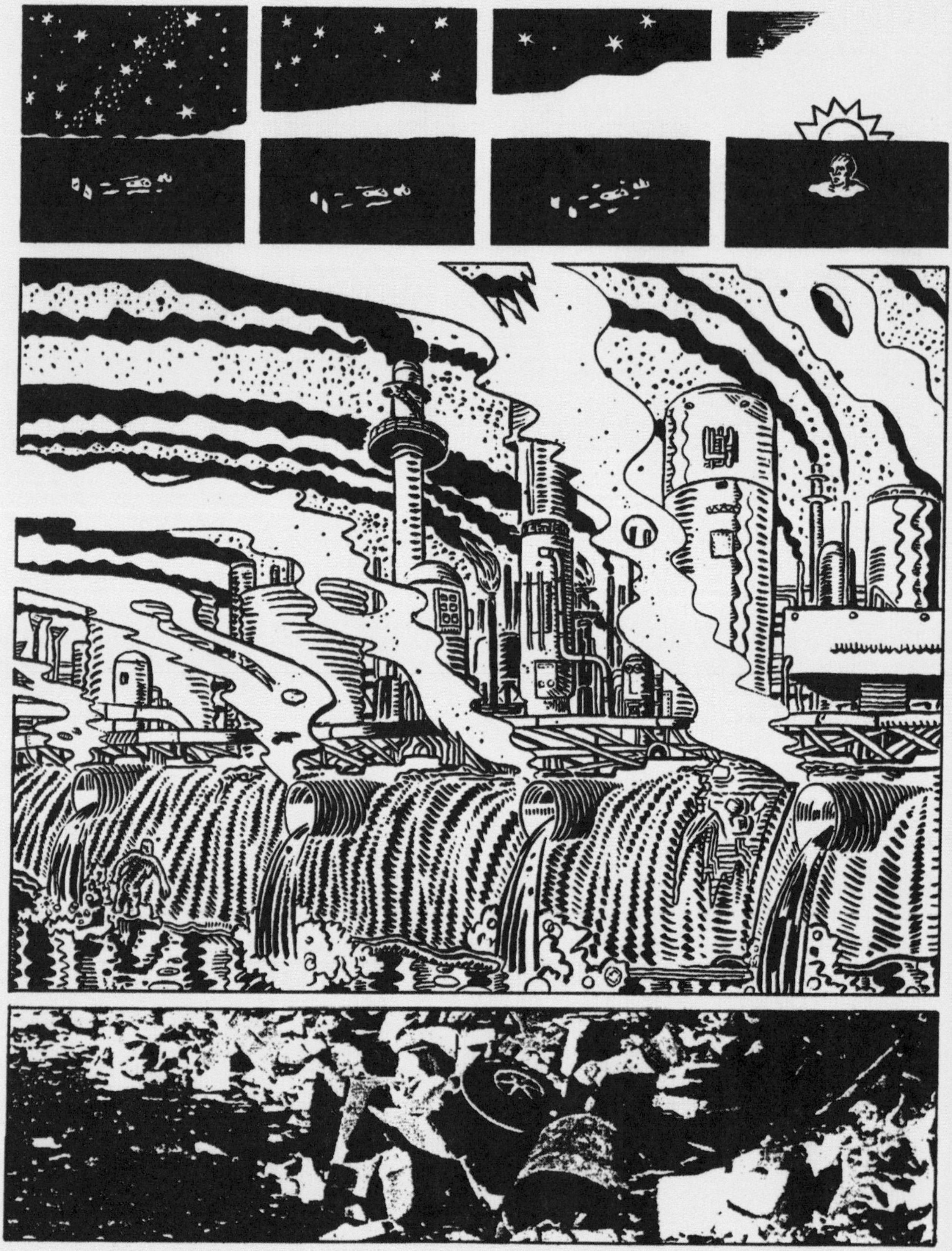

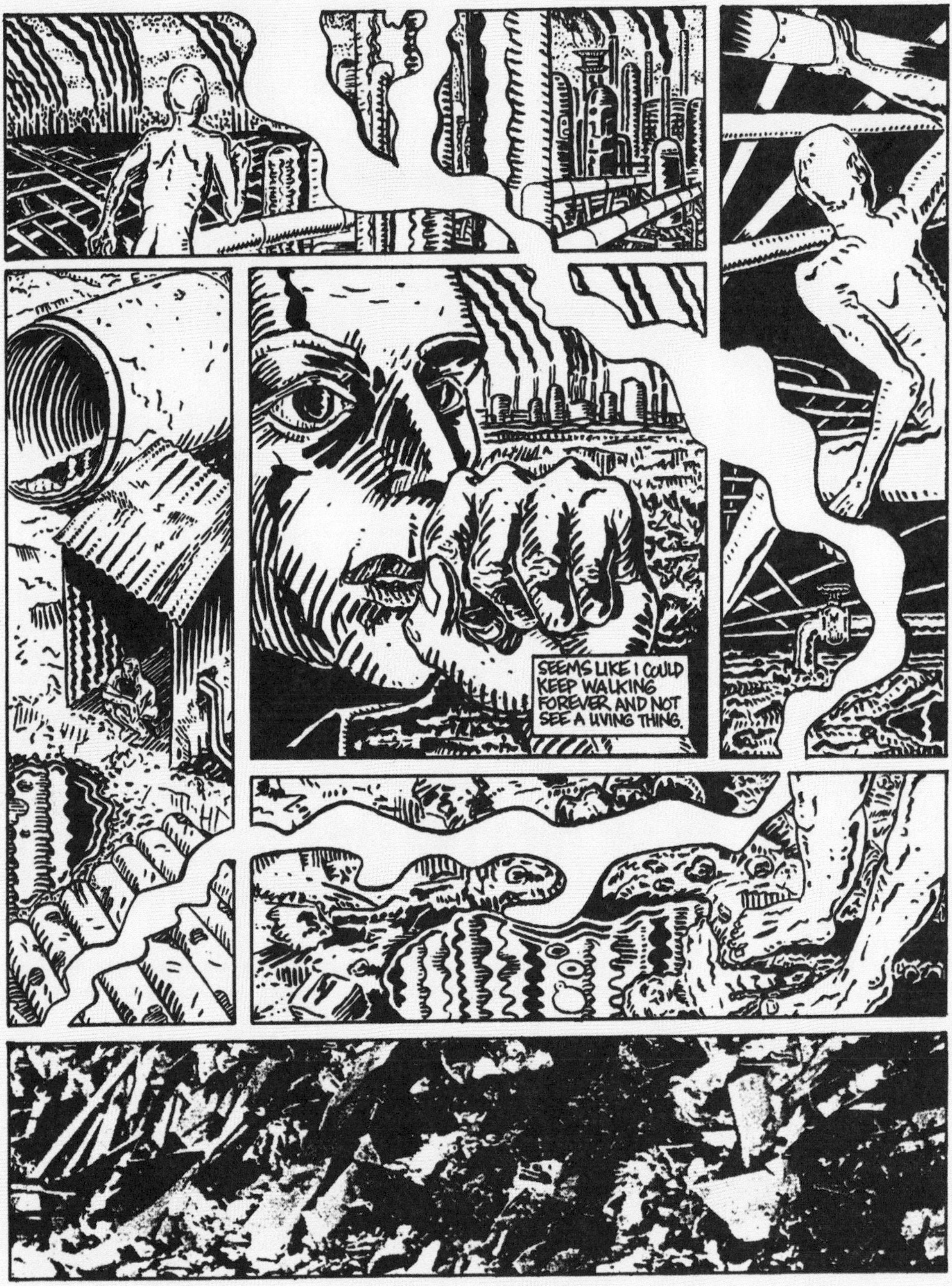
SEEMS LIKE I COULD KEEP WALKING FOREVER AND NOT SEE A LIVING THING.

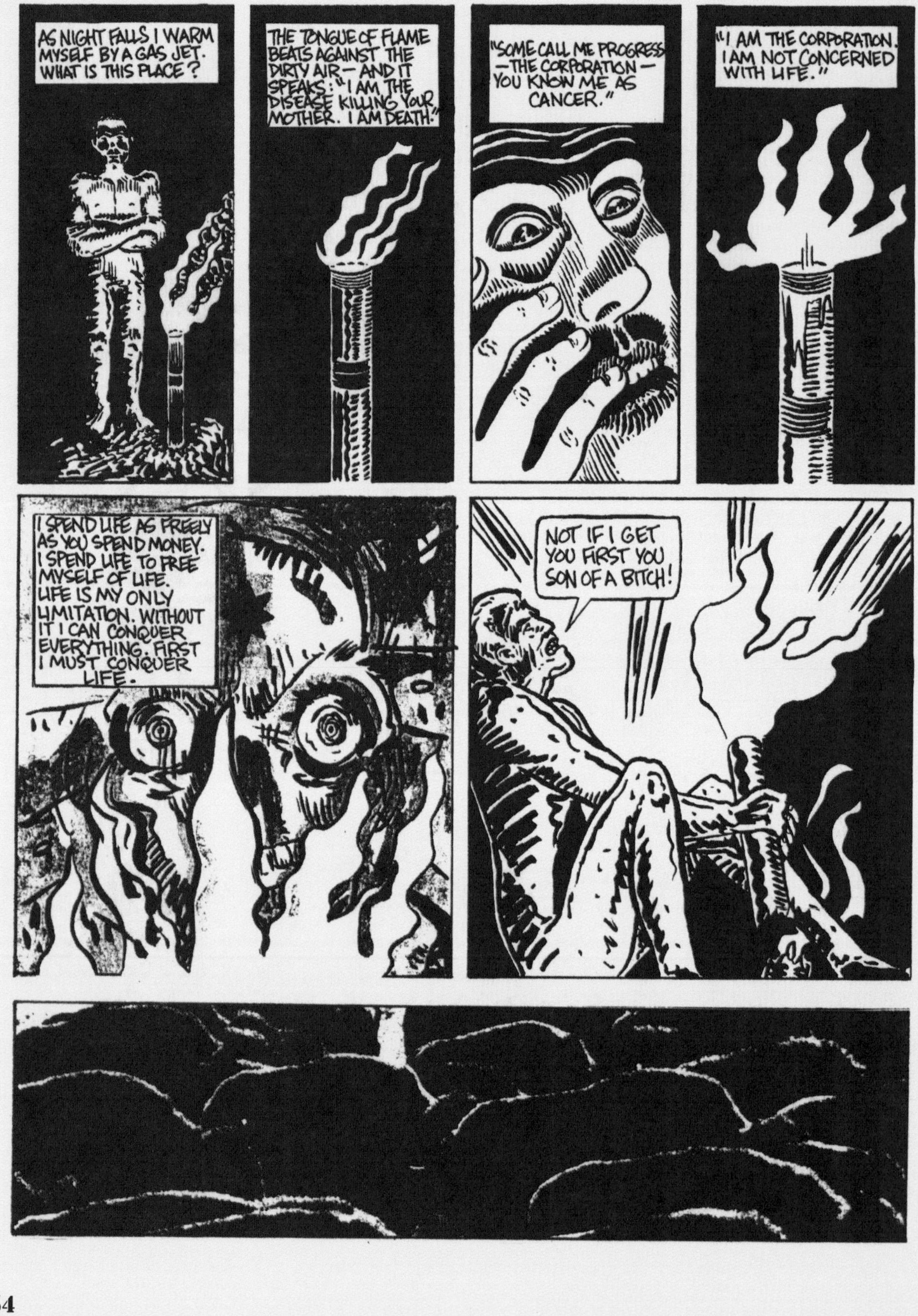
AS NIGHT FALLS I WARM MYSELF BY A GAS JET. WHAT IS THIS PLACE?
THE TONGUE OF FLAME BEATS AGAINST THE DIRTY AIR — AND IT SPEAKS: "I AM THE DISEASE KILLING YOUR MOTHER. I AM DEATH."
"SOME CALL ME PROGRESS — THE CORPORATION — YOU KNOW ME AS CANCER."
"I AM THE CORPORATION. I AM NOT CONCERNED WITH LIFE."
I SPEND LIFE AS FREELY AS YOU SPEND MONEY. I SPEND LIFE TO FREE MYSELF OF LIFE. LIFE IS MY ONLY LIMITATION. WITHOUT IT I CAN CONQUER EVERYTHING. FIRST I MUST CONQUER LIFE.
NOT IF I GET YOU FIRST YOU SON OF A BITCH!

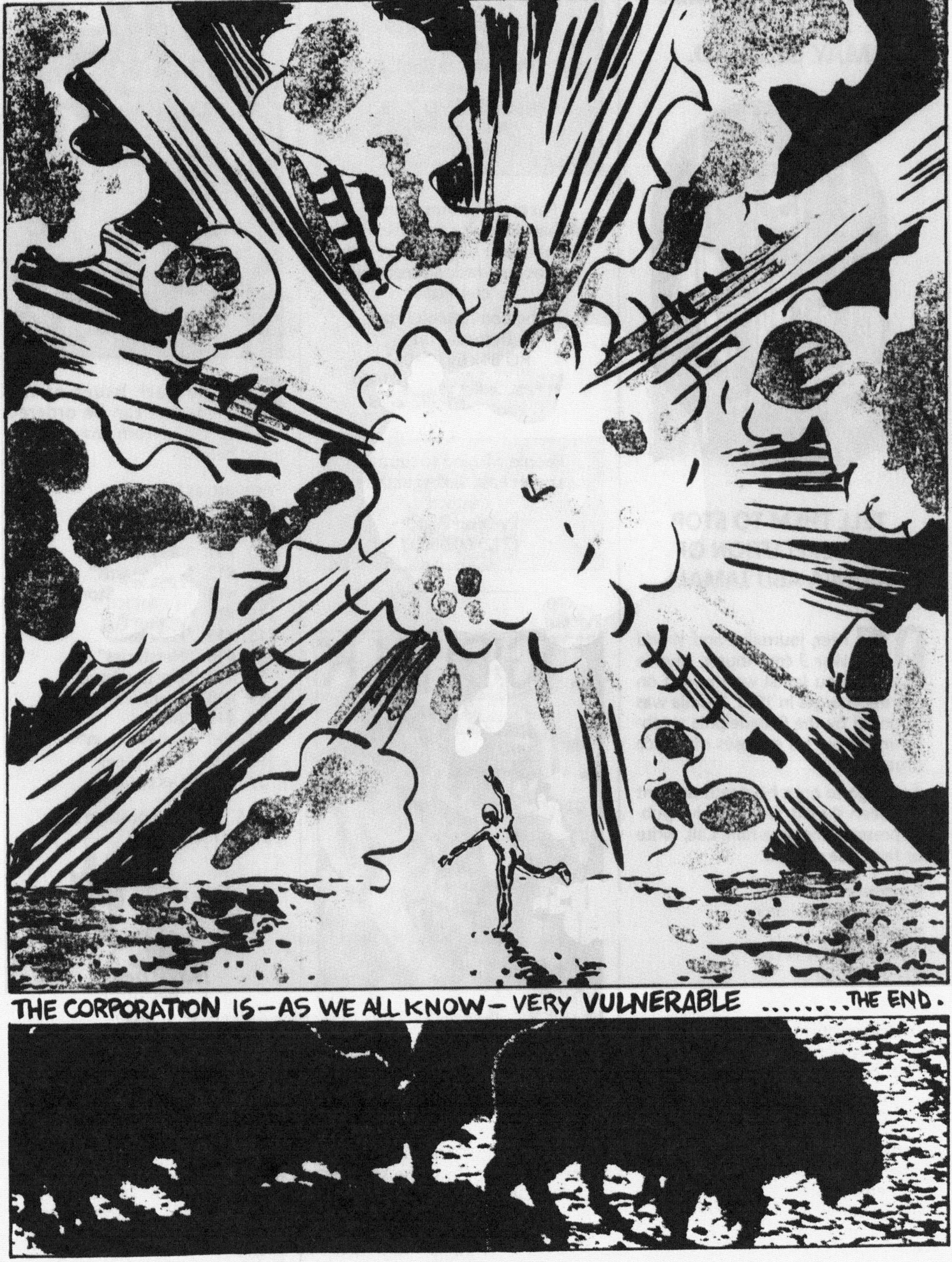
THE CORPORATION IS—AS WE ALL KNOW—VERY VULNERABLE ....THE END.

PINK MEDICINE!

by kevin c. pyle

for more info: BAD BLOOD by James H. Jones

SYPHILIS: Highly contagious disease caused by the spirochete Treponema pallidum. Disease may be acquired or congential. In acquired syphilis, T. pallidum enters the body through skin or mucous membranes, usually during sexual contact. Congenital syphilis is transmitted to the fetus from the infected mother when the spirochete penetrates the placenta.

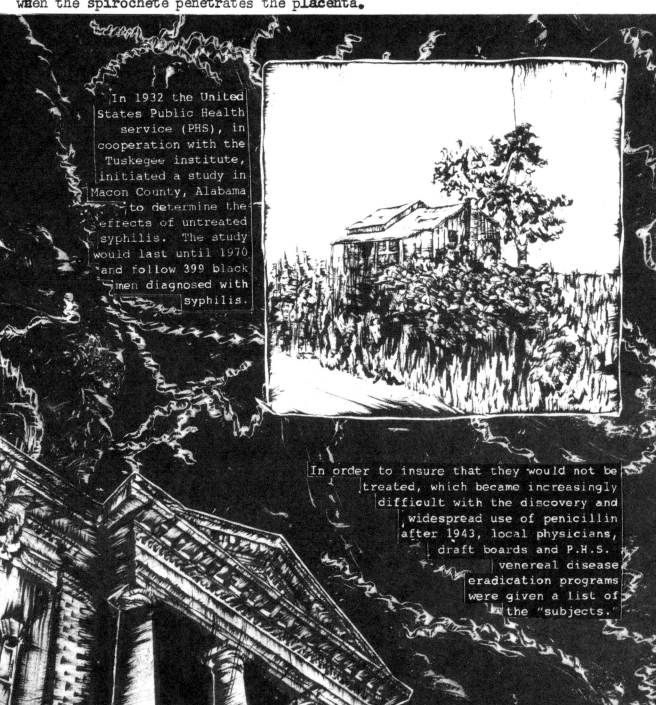

In 1932 the United States Public Health service (PHS), in cooperation with the Tuskegee institute, initiated a study in Macon County, Alabama to determine the effects of untreated syphilis. The study would last until 1970 and follow 399 black men diagnosed with syphilis.

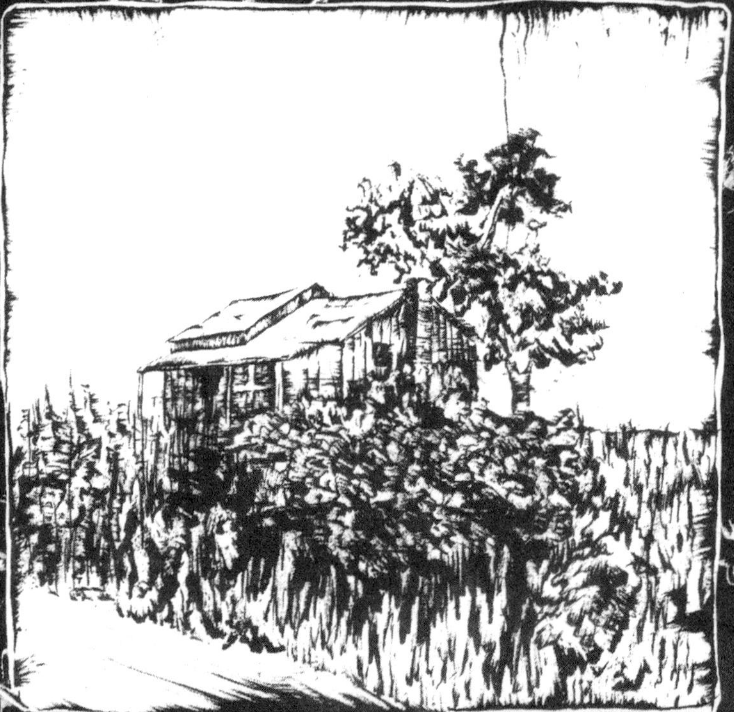

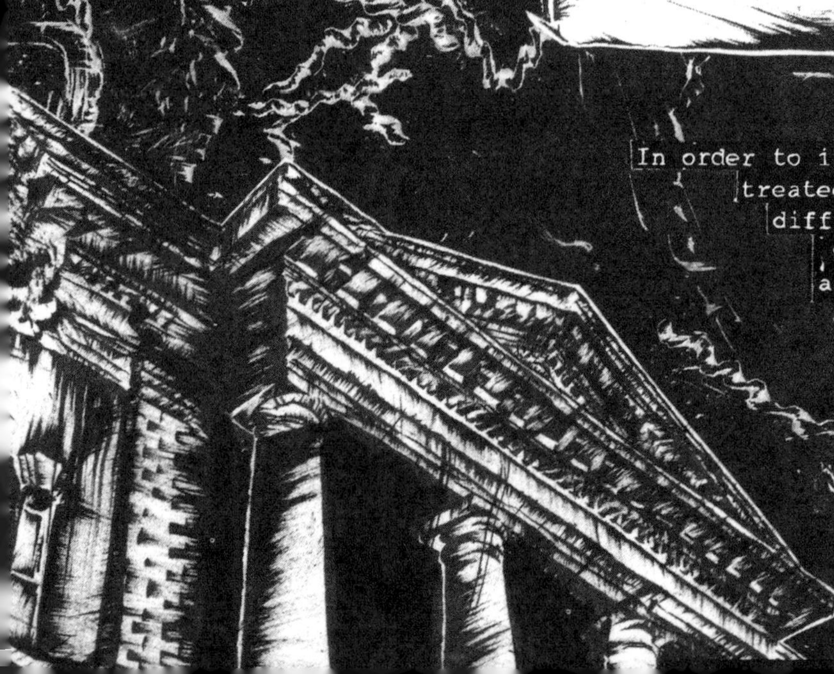

In order to insure that they would not be treated, which became increasingly difficult with the discovery and widespread use of penicillin after 1943, local physicians, draft boards and P.H.S. venereal disease eradication programs were given a list of the "subjects."

Syphilis is a systemic disease, involving tissues throughout the body. After initial penetration, the spirochetes multiply rapidly. First they enter the lymph capillaries where they are transported to the nearest lymph gland. There they multiply and are released into the blood stream. Within days the spirochetes invade every part of the body. Three stages mark the progression of the disease; primary, secondary, and tertiary.

The men, the most educated of which completed 7th grade, were told they were being treated for "bad blood," a term the white doctors claimed was a synonym for syphilis in the black community. One participant responded, "that could be true. But I have never heard no such thing."

In reality, the only treatment the men recieved was aspirin (what the doctors chose to call "pink medicine") and an iron supplement. Having previously encountered little or no health care, the partipants were delighted. "They were always glad to see us," one doctor recalled, explaining how the men showed their gratitude by giving the "government doctors" gifts. "They brought cornbread, cookies, whatever they could make and they were very, very pleased if you ate it - most pleased."

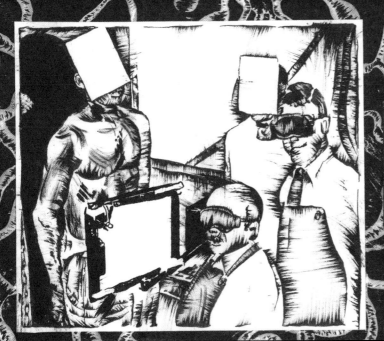

In order to chart the progression of the disease the subjects were frequently, under the guise of treatment, required to give blood samples disguised as treatment. They also were subjected to a procedure known as the "lumbar-puncture" to diagnose neural syphilis.

PRIMARY STAGE: 10 - 60 days after infection. Primary lesion usually appears at point of contact, usually genitals. Typically a painless, slightly elevated, round ulcer, the chancre may be so small as to elude detection. Barring secondary infection, chancre will heal without treatment within 30 - 60 days leaving scar that persists for several months.

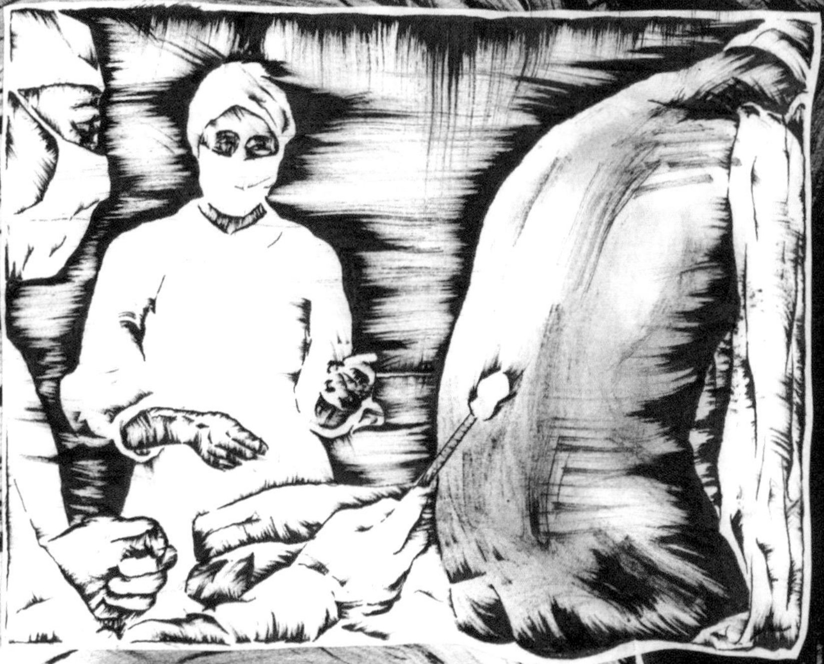

To obtain a sample of fluid, a large needle was inserted directly into the spinal canal. The procedure was painful, and patients often suffered severe headaches. In rare cases it can result in paralysis or even death.

Fearing word of "Dr. Vonderlehr's golden needle treatments," as the doctors referred to it, would discourage participation, whole regions were done at one time and letters were sent out promising / "Special Free Treatment" and warning / "Last Chance for Special Examination."

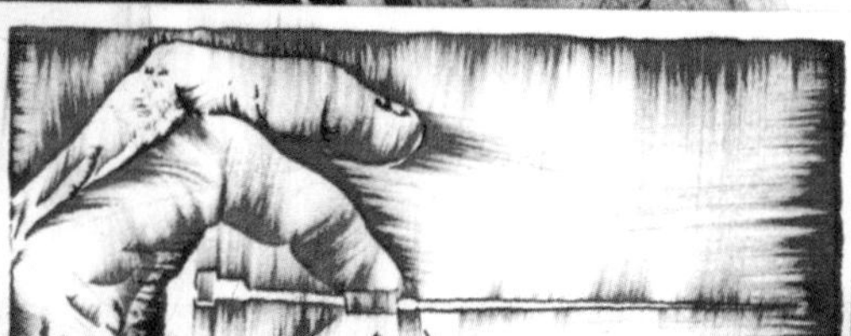

FIGURE 14-3 A spinal needle with the stylet protruding from the hub.

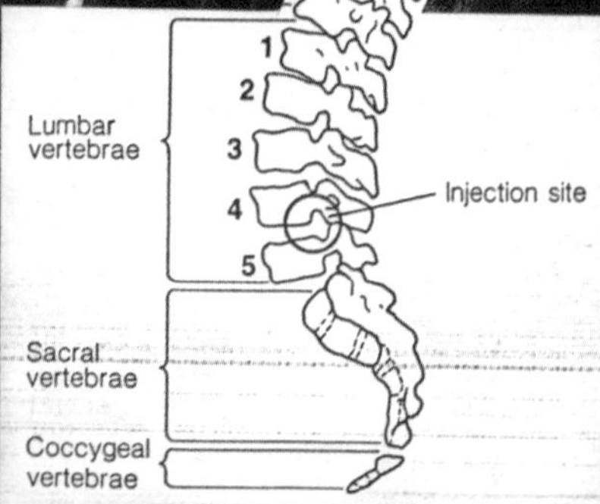
Lumbar vertebrae
1
2
3
4
5
Injection site
Sacral vertebrae
Coccygeal vertebrae

SECONDARY STAGE: 6 weeks - 6 months. Appearance of rash resembling measles, chicken pox or any number of skin eruptions. Pain in bones and joints and cardiac palpitations may develop. Fever, indigestion, headaches may accompany rash. In some cases highly infectious, spirochete-laden ulcers may appear in mouth. Scalp hair may drop out in patches, creating "moth-eaten" appearance.

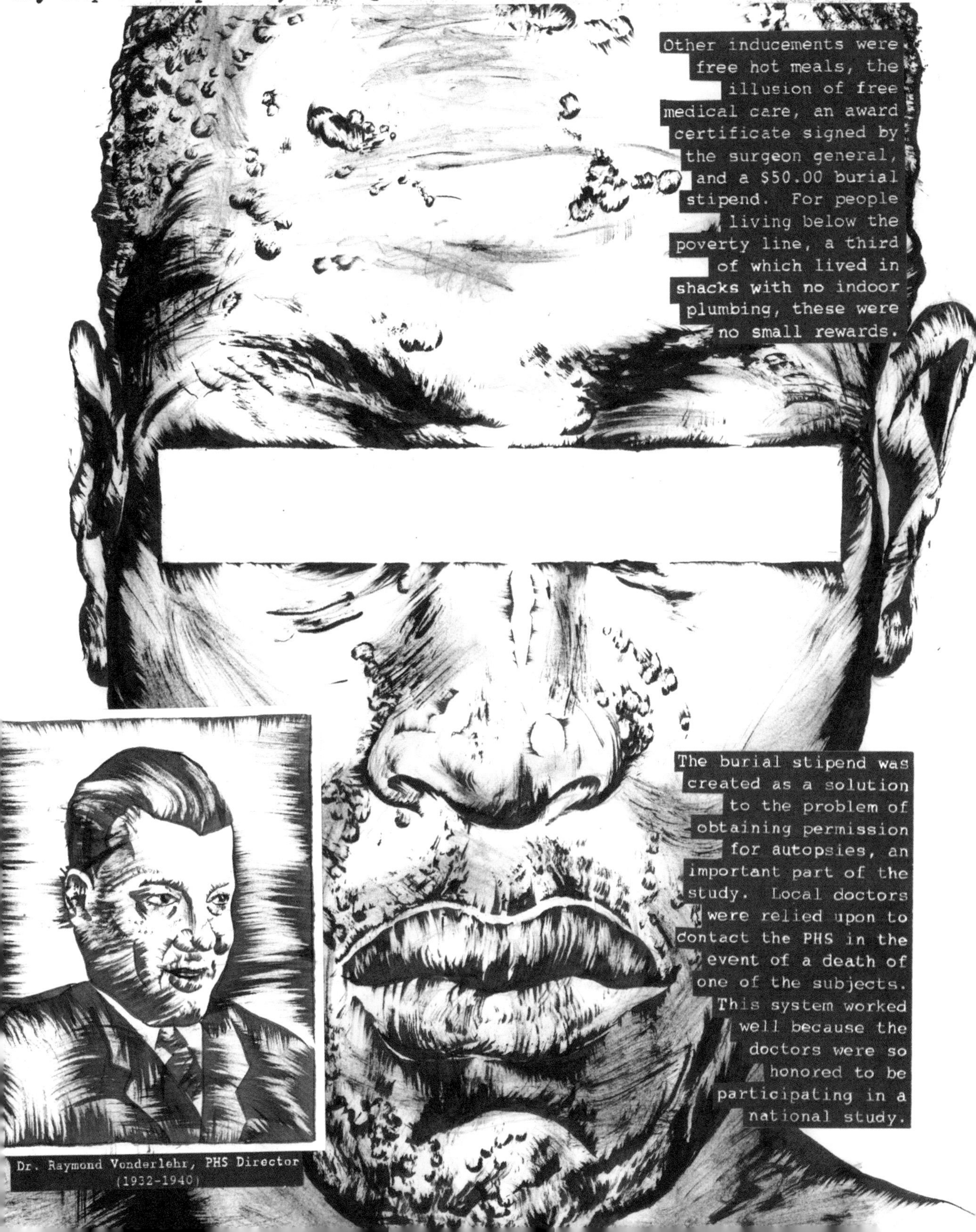
Other inducements were free hot meals, the illusion of free medical care, an award certificate signed by the surgeon general, and a $50.00 burial stipend. For people living below the poverty line, a third of which lived in shacks with no indoor plumbing, these were no small rewards.
The burial stipend was created as a solution to the problem of obtaining permission for autopsies, an important part of the study. Local doctors were relied upon to contact the PHS in the event of a death of one of the subjects. This system worked well because the doctors were so honored to be participating in a national study.

Dr. Raymond Vonderlehr, PHS Director (1932-1940)

TERTIARY STAGE: Appearance of gummy or rubbery tumors (gummas), resulting from spirochete concentration in body tissue. On the skin these often coalesce into large encrusted ulcers consisting of several layers of dry exuded matter. Tumors may be absorbed, leaving slight scarred depressions, or may cause wholesale destruction of bone resulting in mutilation when nasal and palate bones are eaten away.

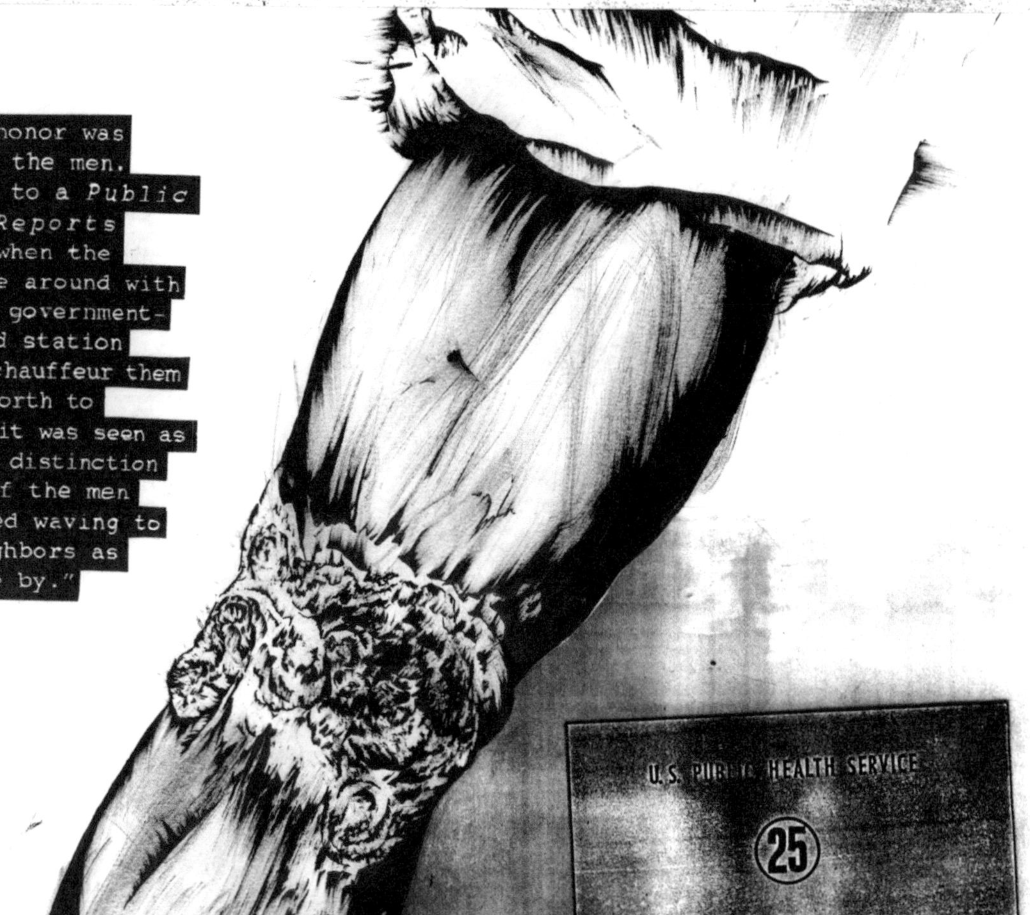

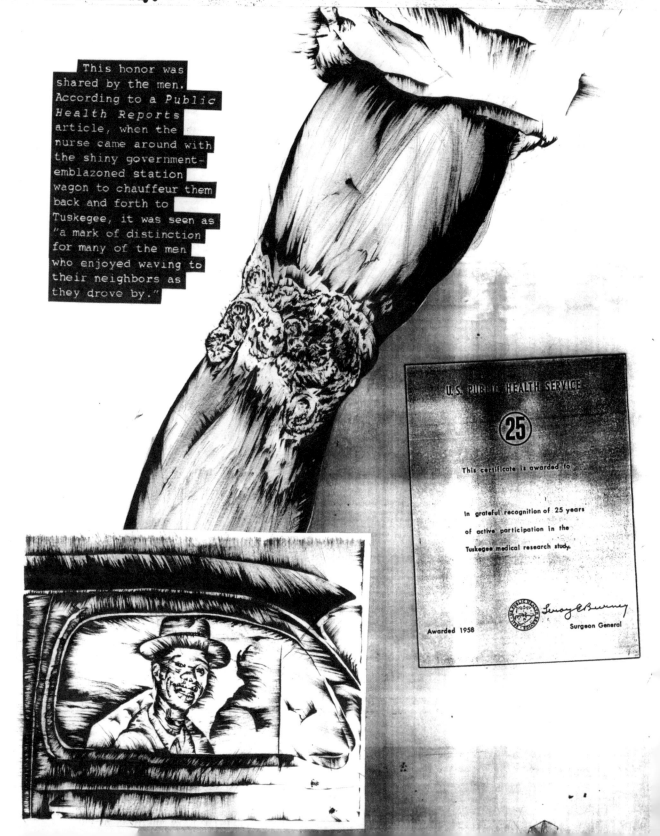

This honor was shared by the men. According to a *Public Health Reports* article, when the nurse came around with the shiny government-emblazoned station wagon to chauffeur them back and forth to Tuskegee, it was seen as "a mark of distinction for many of the men who enjoyed waving to their neighbors as they drove by."

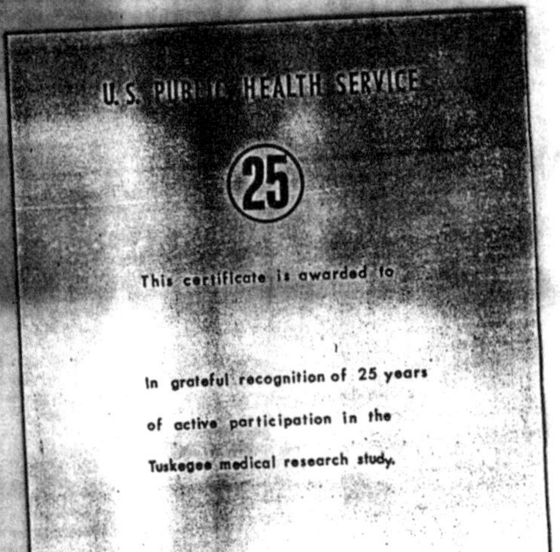

U.S. PUBLIC HEALTH SERVICE

25

This certificate is awarded to

In grateful recognition of 25 years of active participation in the Tuskegee medical research study.

Awarded 1958

Surgeon General

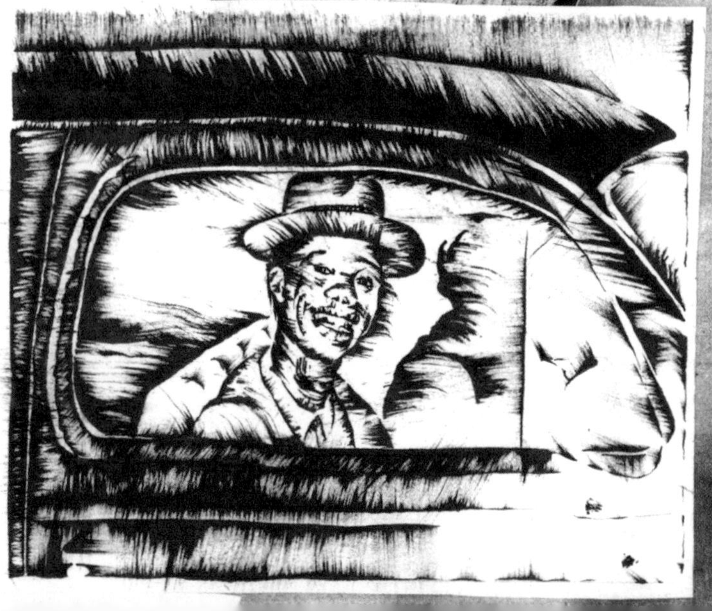

The presence of T.pallidum in cerebrospinal may cause NEUROSYPHILIS which may take several forms including a general softening of the brain resulting in paralysis and insanity, as well as Tabes dorsalis, a degeneration off the spinal cord causing a stumbling,foot-stamping gait. Can also cause irreversible blindness,or the 8th cranial nerve,inflicting permanent deafness

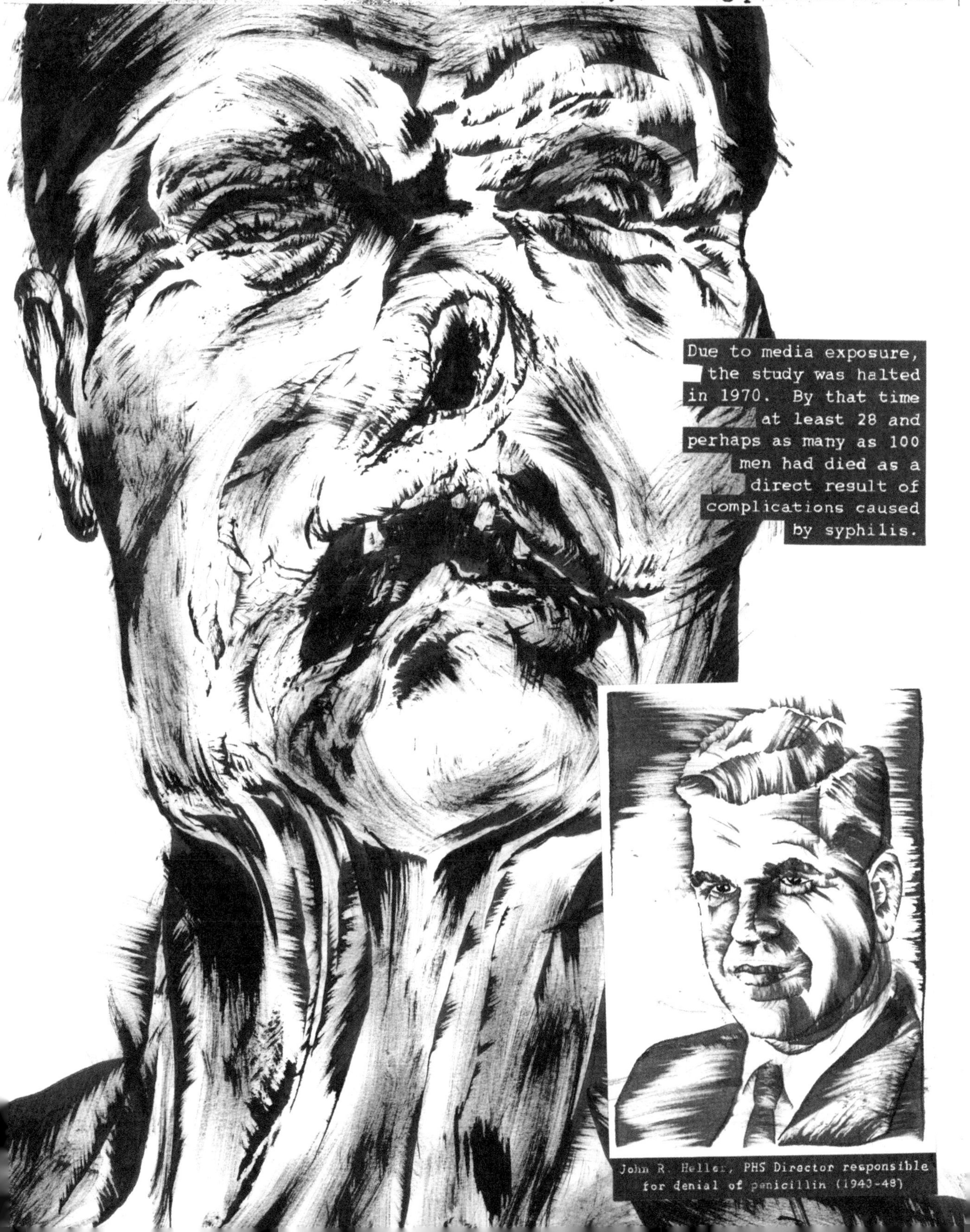
Due to media exposure, the study was halted in 1970. By that time at least 28 and perhaps as many as 100 men had died as a direct result of complications caused by syphilis.

John R. Heller, PHS Director responsible for denial of penicillin (1943-48)

Tumors may also attack and weaken the walls of heart or blood vessels. Heart valves may no longer open & close properly resulting in leakage. The stretching vessel walls may produce an aortic aneurysm, a balloonlike bulge. If the bulge bursts, as often is the case, the result is sudden death.

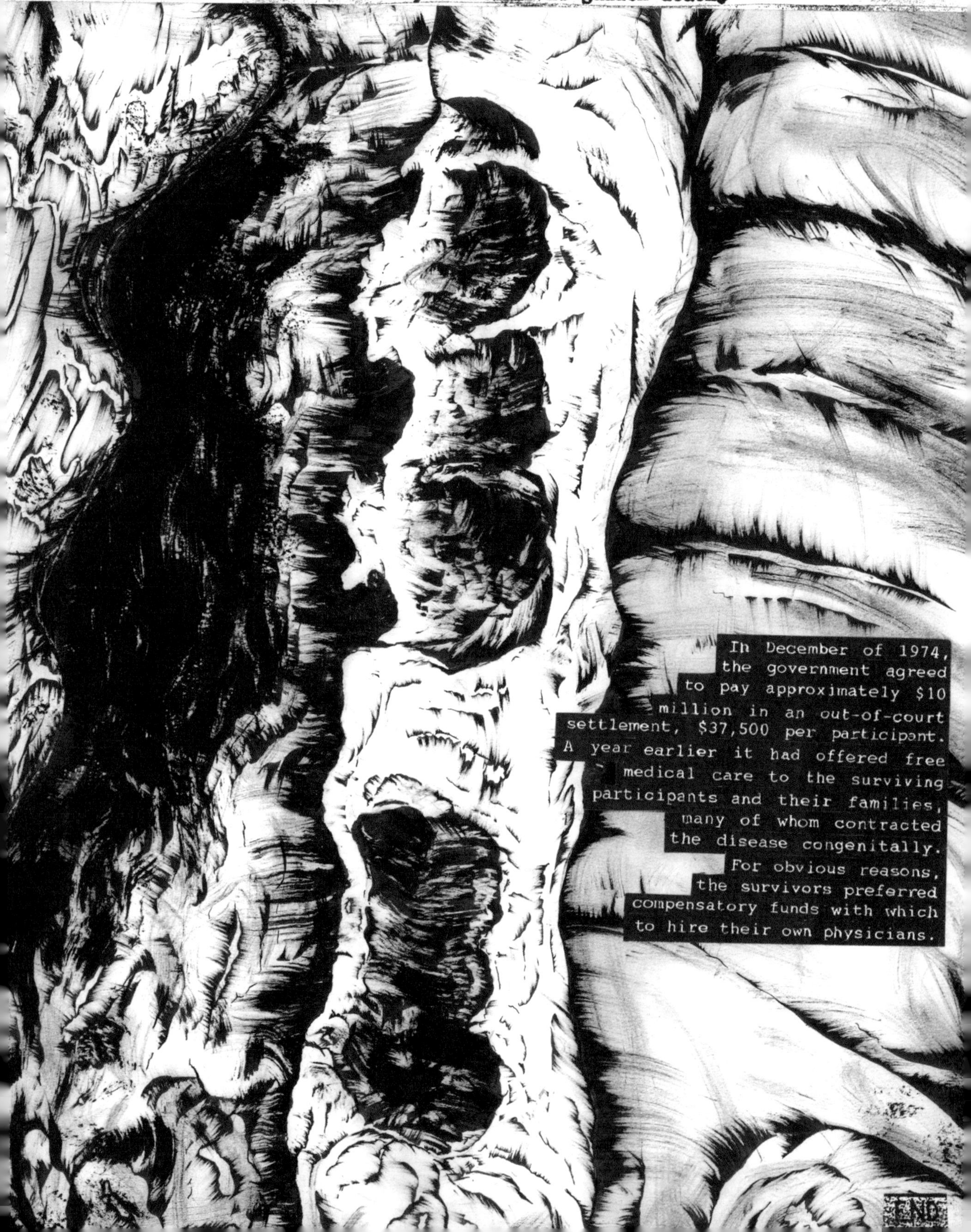

In December of 1974, the government agreed to pay approximately $10 million in an out-of-court settlement, $37,500 per participant. A year earlier it had offered free medical care to the surviving participants and their families, many of whom contracted the disease congenitally. For obvious reasons, the survivors preferred compensatory funds with which to hire their own physicians.
END

GREEN HOUSE, BLUE PLANET

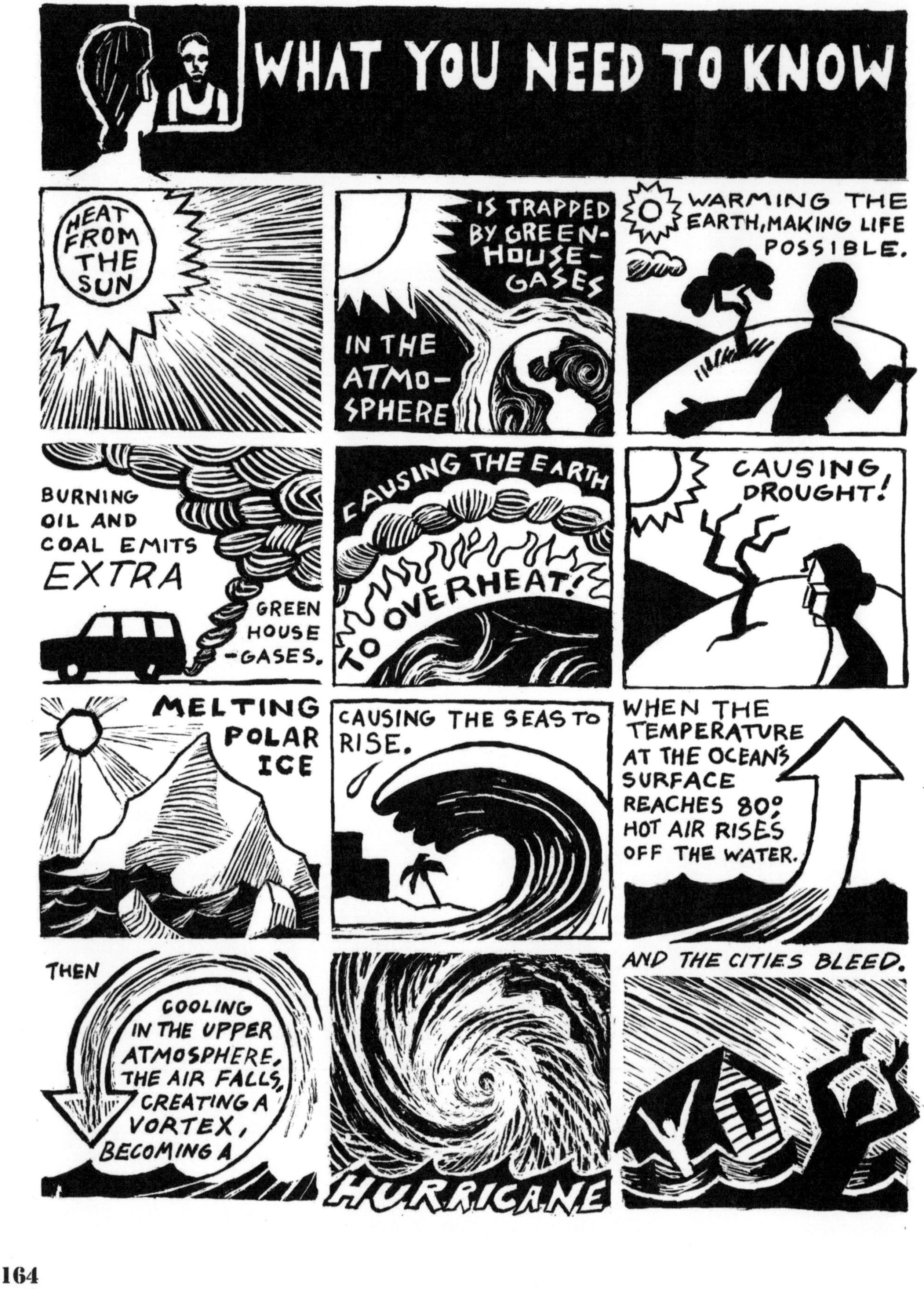

WHAT YOU NEED TO KNOW
HEAT FROM THE SUN
IS TRAPPED BY GREEN-HOUSE-GASES
IN THE ATMO-SPHERE
WARMING THE EARTH, MAKING LIFE POSSIBLE.
BURNING OIL AND COAL EMITS EXTRA
GREEN HOUSE -GASES.
CAUSING THE EARTH
TO OVERHEAT!
CAUSING DROUGHT!
MELTING POLAR ICE
CAUSING THE SEAS TO RISE.
WHEN THE TEMPERATURE AT THE OCEAN'S SURFACE REACHES 80°, HOT AIR RISES OFF THE WATER.
THEN
COOLING IN THE UPPER ATMOSPHERE, THE AIR FALLS, CREATING A VORTEX, BECOMING A
HURRICANE
AND THE CITIES BLEED.

FORESTS ABSORB GREENHOUSE GASES.

CUT-TING DOWN FOR-ESTS RE-LEASES THESE GASES.

SO IF WE STOP LOG-GING,

AND REPLACE OIL WITH

OTHER FORMS OF ENERGY,

THE EARTH CAN SLOWLY HEAL.

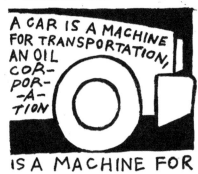

A CAR IS A MACHINE FOR TRANSPORTATION, AN OIL COR-POR-A-TION IS A MACHINE FOR

MAKING MONEY.

THEY AIN'T IN BUSINESS TO SAVE THE WORLD.

THEY WON'T STOP UNTIL WE STOP THEM.

TO FIGHT FOR SURVIVAL IS HUMAN NA-TURE

SO WE, THE PEOPLE WILL RISE UP AGAINST THE CORPORATIONS.

WHAT YOU NEED TO KNOW IS THAT YOU ARE THE SOLUTION TO GLOBAL WARMING.

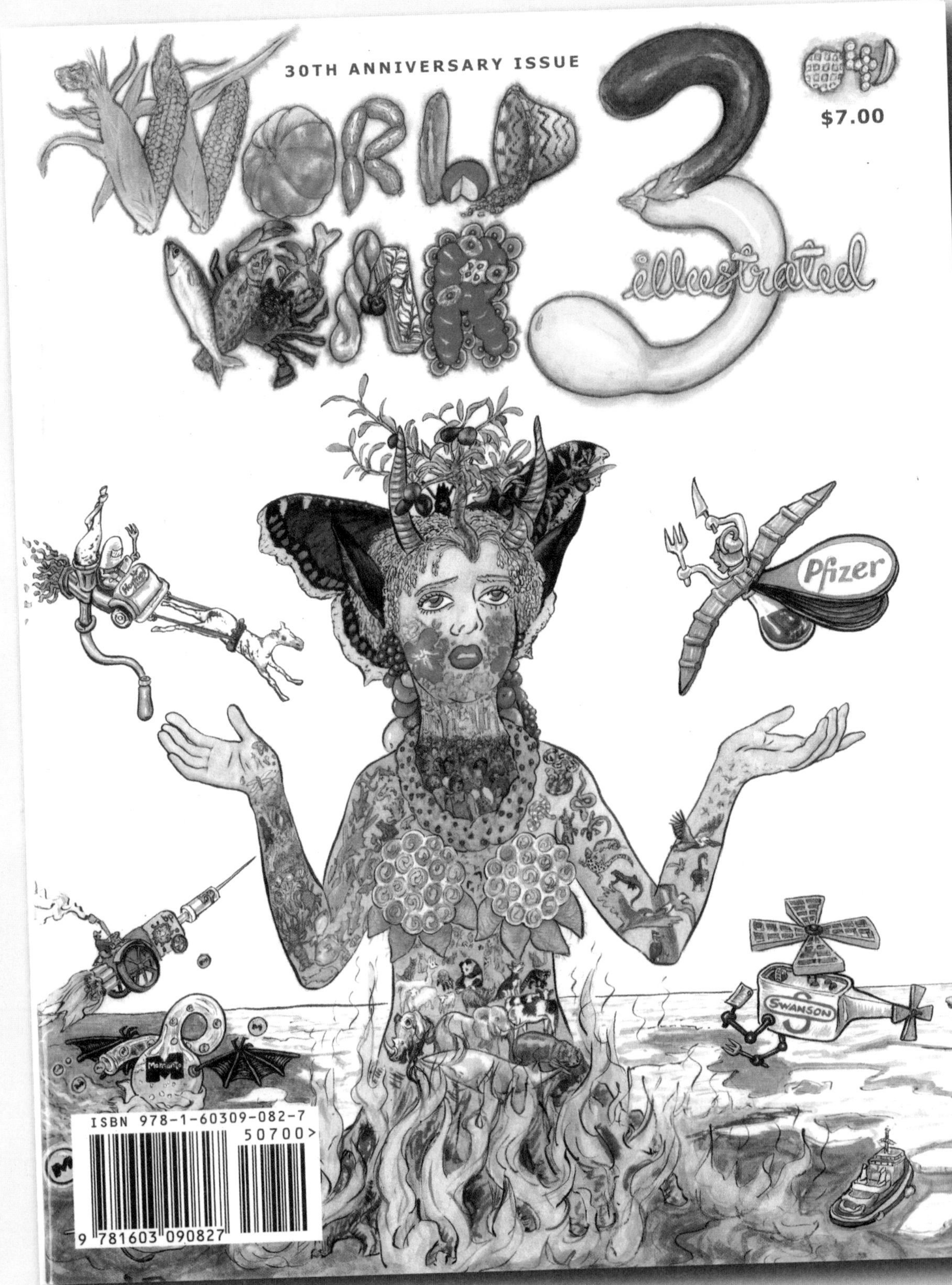
30TH ANNIVERSARY ISSUE
WORLD WAR 3
illustrated
$7.00
Pfizer
SWANSON
ISBN 978-1-60309-082-7
50700>
9 781603 090827

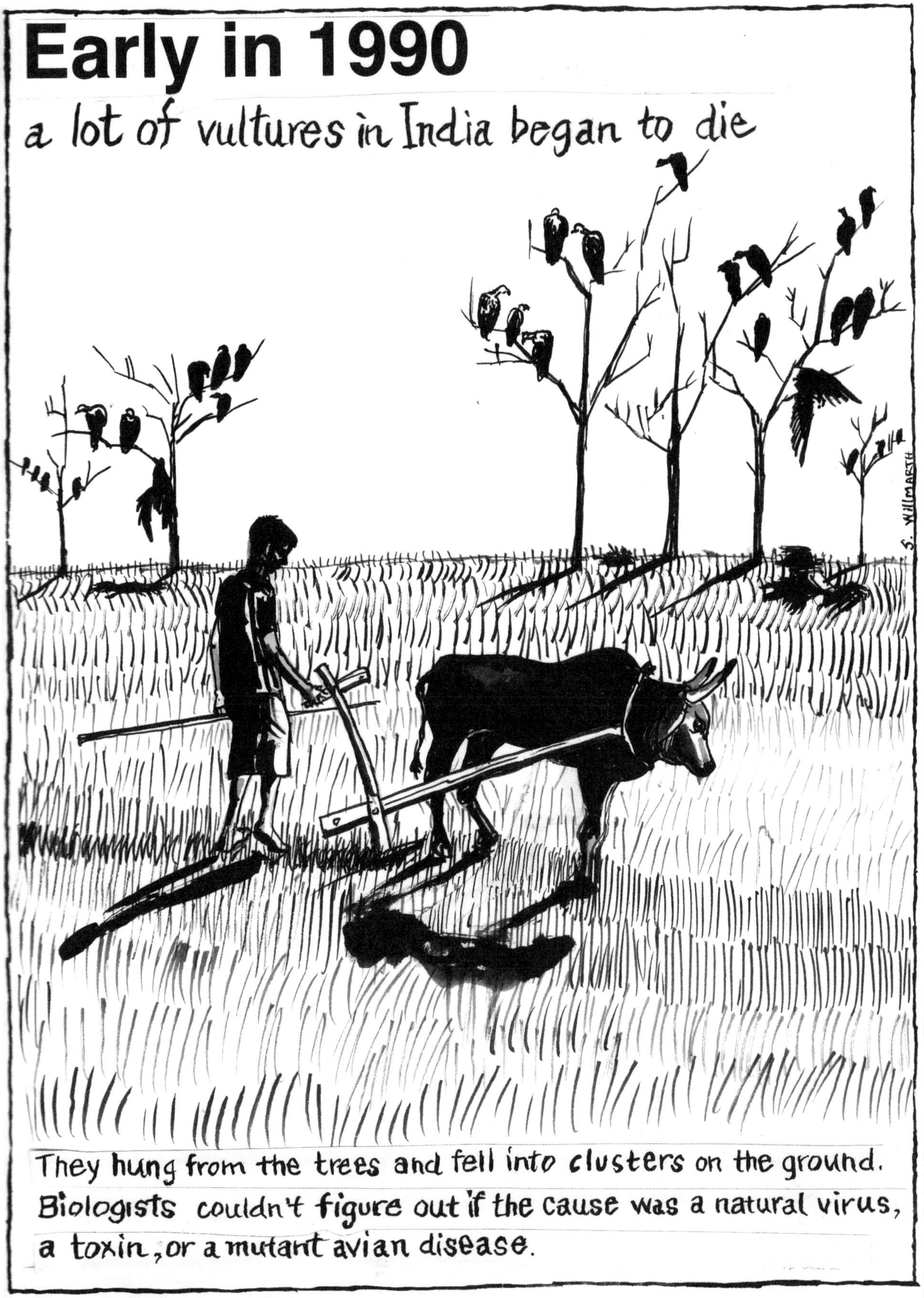
Early in 1990
a lot of vultures in India began to die
They hung from the trees and fell into clusters on the ground. Biologists couldn't figure out if the cause was a natural virus, a toxin, or a mutant avian disease.

Thirteen years later...

A group of **scientists and wildlife workers in Pakistan** proved that an anti-inflammatory painkiller called diclofenac has been causing instant kidney failure in vultures.

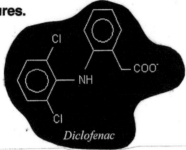

Diclofenac

Diclofenac (marketed as **Voltaren®, Voltarol®, Diclon®** and **Cataflam®**) is a non-steroidal anti-inflammatory drug (NSAID) taken to reduce inflammation, such as in arthritis or acute injury. It can also be used to reduce menstrual pain.

Diclofenac had been sold to humans for 30 years.

In 1990 it was **niche marketed** as a cheap **livestock drug**. Village farmers used it to medicate their lame or injured cows. This secondary market became very successful. 12 million doses are sold every year.

In South Asia, the main food source for vultures is dead livestock and almost all of it dosed with diclofenac.

For over a decade diclofenac use in livestock has been quietly killing off vultures all over south Asia.

Three major vulture species; the white-backed, the long-billed and slender-billed are very close to extinction.

As of 2006 over 97% of India's vultures have died off.

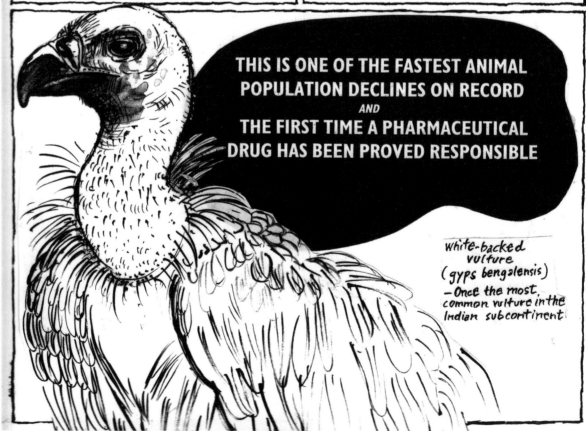

THIS IS ONE OF THE FASTEST ANIMAL POPULATION DECLINES ON RECORD
AND
THE FIRST TIME A PHARMACEUTICAL DRUG HAS BEEN PROVED RESPONSIBLE

white-backed vulture (gyps bengalensis)
- Once the most common vulture in the Indian subcontinent

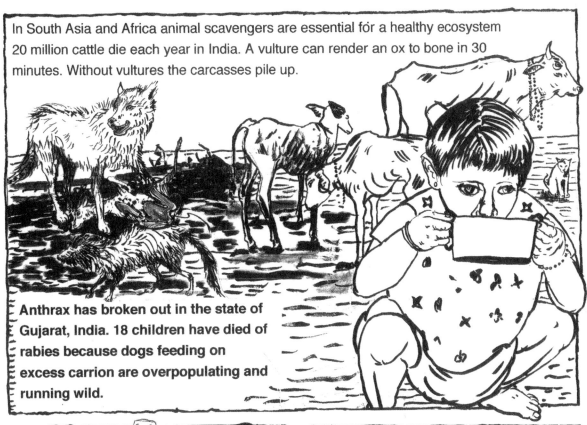

In South Asia and Africa animal scavengers are essential for a healthy ecosystem 20 million cattle die each year in India. A vulture can render an ox to bone in 30 minutes. Without vultures the carcasses pile up.

Anthrax has broken out in the state of Gujarat, India. 18 children have died of rabies because dogs feeding on excess carrion are overpopulating and running wild.

Bone harvesters used to follow the vultures and gather bones to make into fertilizer and bone meal. Now they can't do their work.

For the first time in thousands of years the Parsi can't complete their sacred burial ceremony which leave the dead outside to be disposed of by vultures.

Now, the mystery is not what is killing off the vultures but why can't it be stopped?

The Indian Prime Minister has called for a total ban on diclofenac. Unfortunately over 25 companies make the drug and 110 companies market it. It is available over the counter and on line. Trying to ban it is like trying to get the genie back in the bottle . . .

Meloxicam is an alternative painkiller that is safe for livestock and vultures. Unfortunately it costs twice as much as diclofenac.

NOVARTIS, the developer and largest company to manufacture diclofenac in India, is not interested in helping create any competitive drug which could be marketed to poor rural farmers.

Philip Rush, leader of NOVARTIS global strategic marketing says *"there are patent issues that make it difficult to produce meloxicam"* besides diclofenac *" is the most widely used painkiller in humans"* in South Asia and it *"has a very good safety and efficacy profile"*

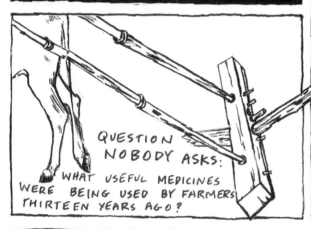

QUESTION NOBODY ASKS:
WHAT USEFUL MEDICINES WERE BEING USED BY FARMERS THIRTEEN YEARS AGO?

Safe for Who?

2006: As the U.S. and India make a deal to share nuclear technology, the vultures continue to die off and the carrion continues to pile up. International wildlife groups are busy collecting remaining vulture pairs to breed.

They hope a new generation of young birds can be released someday in the future...

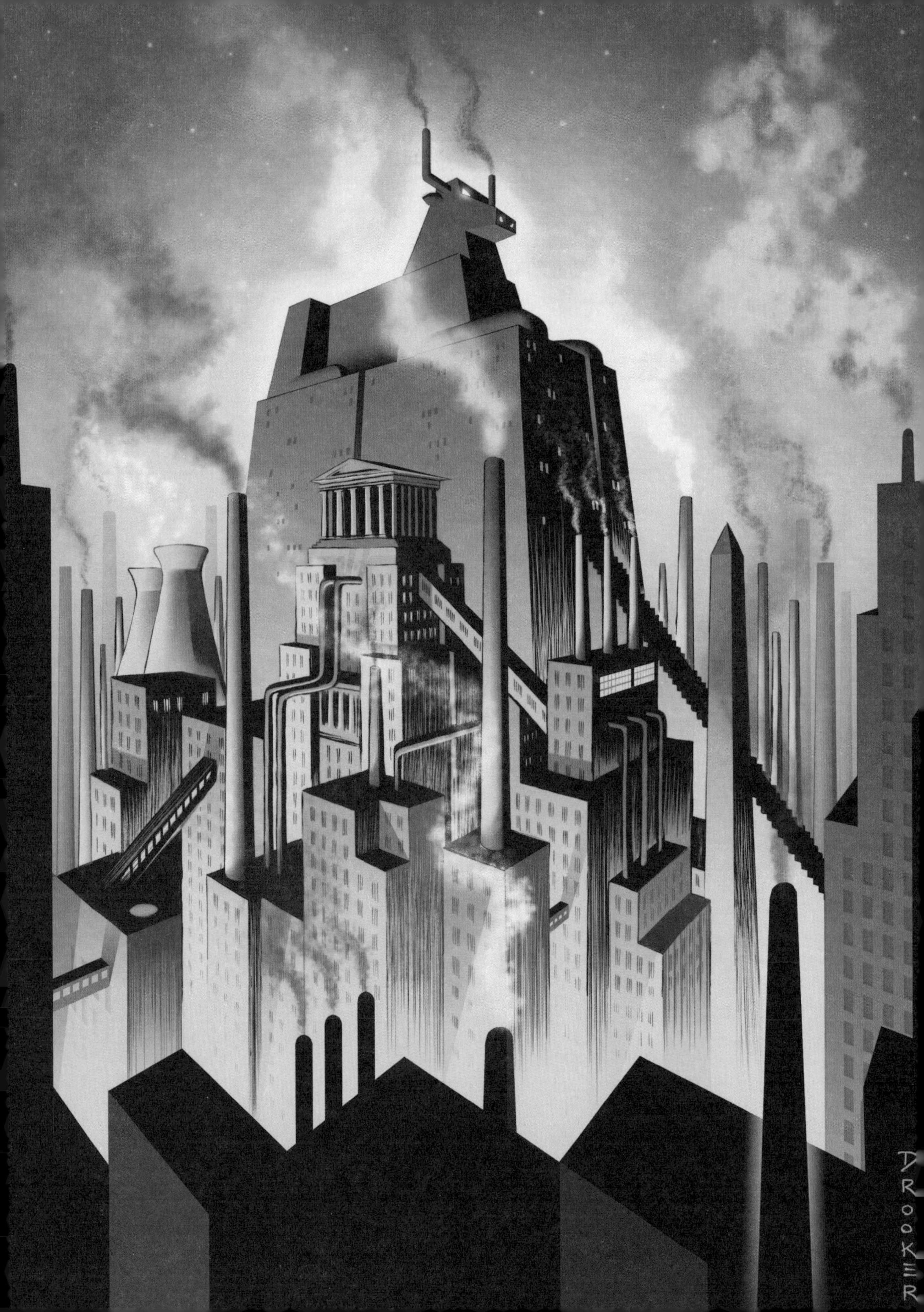
DROOKER

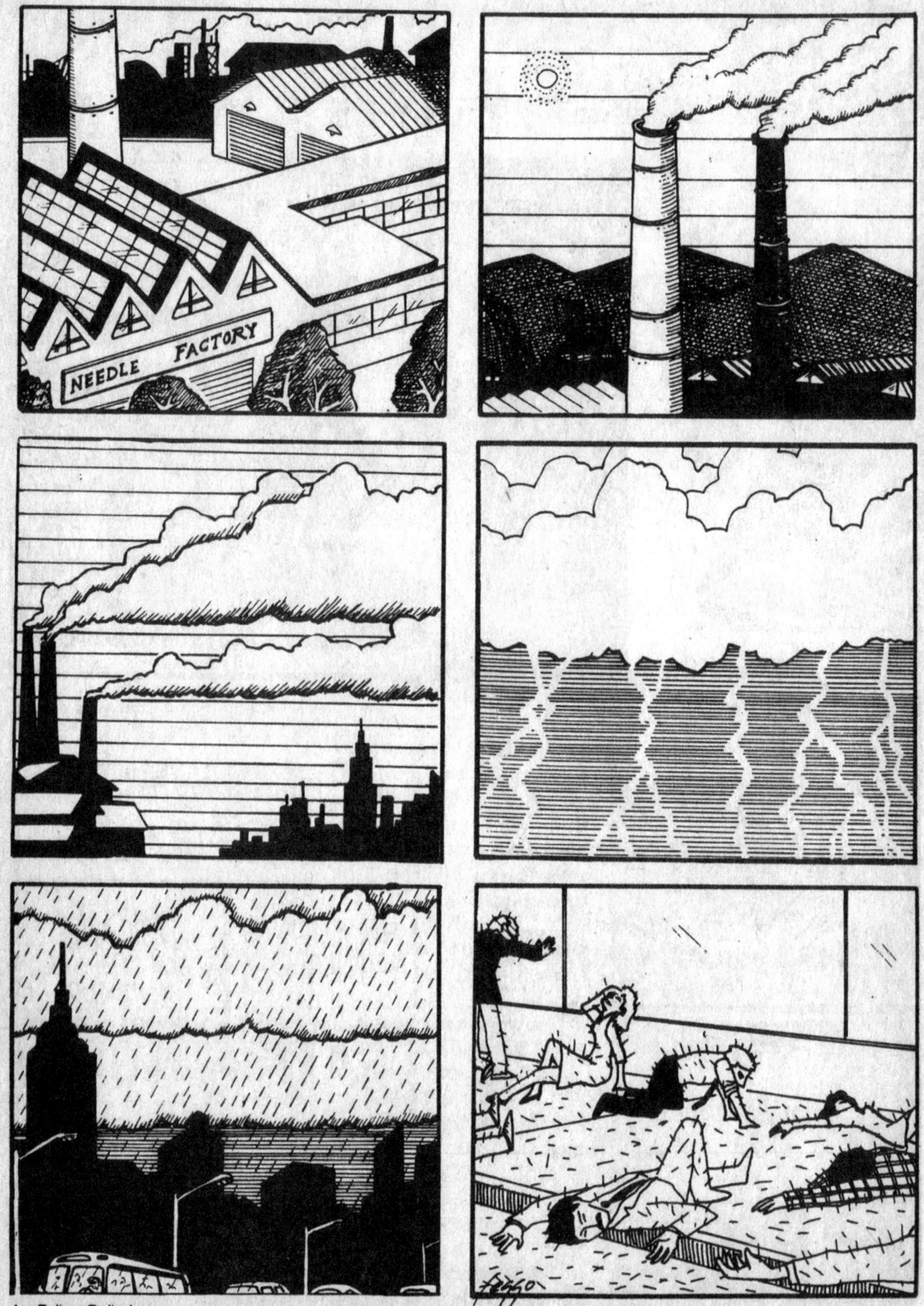
NEEDLE FACTORY

by Felipe Galindo

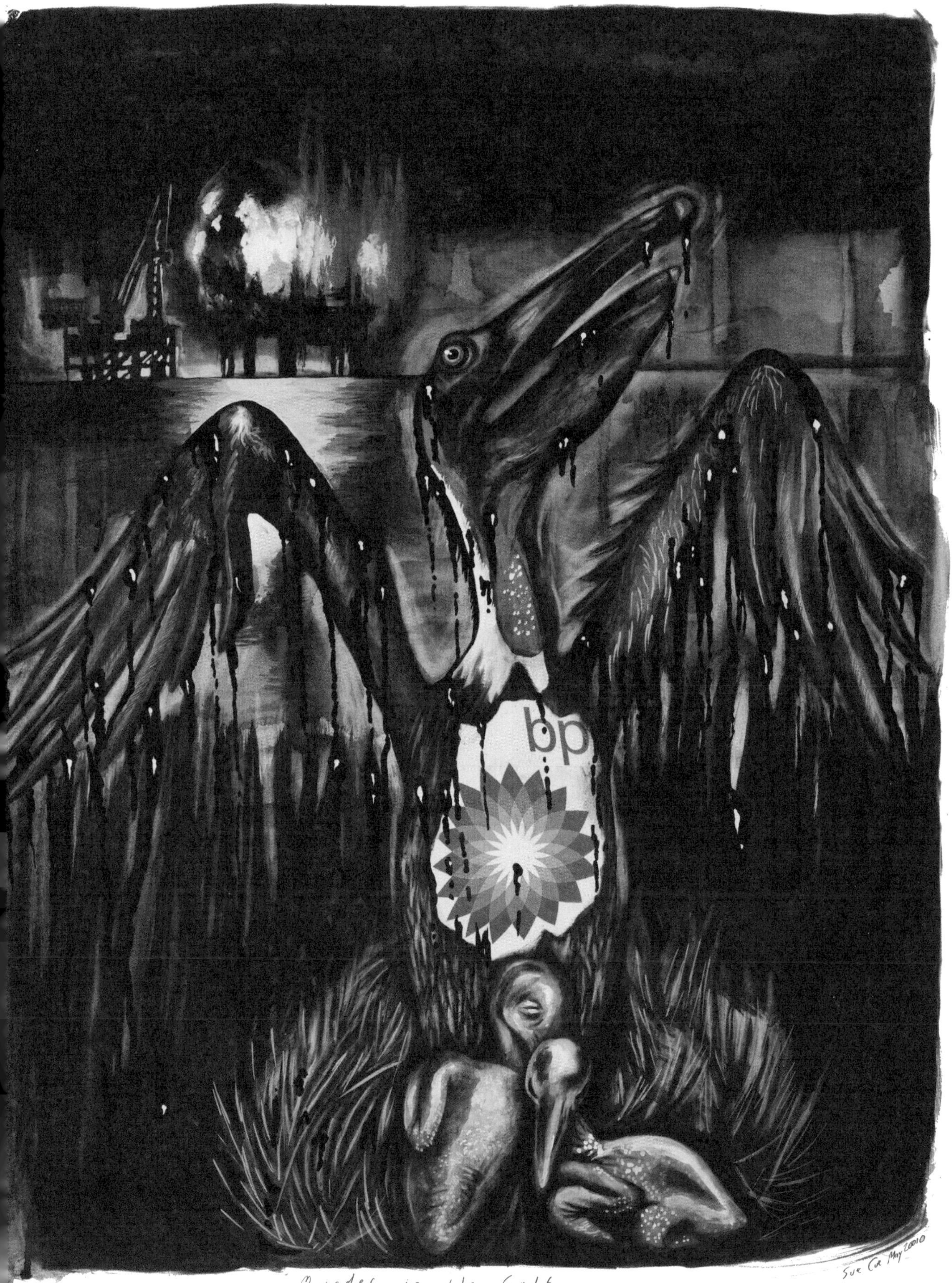
bp

Murder in the Gulf

Sue Coe May 2010

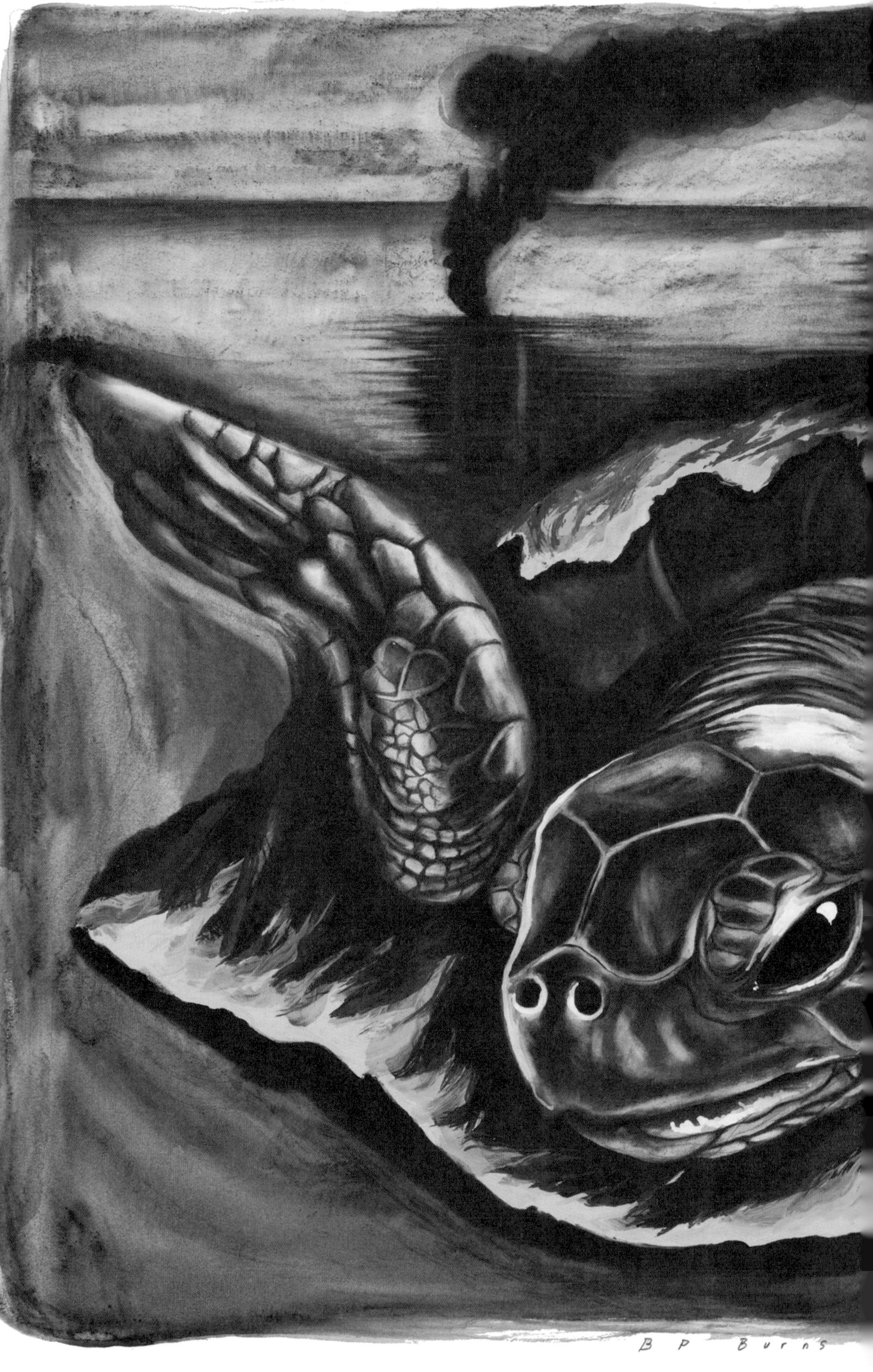
B P Burns

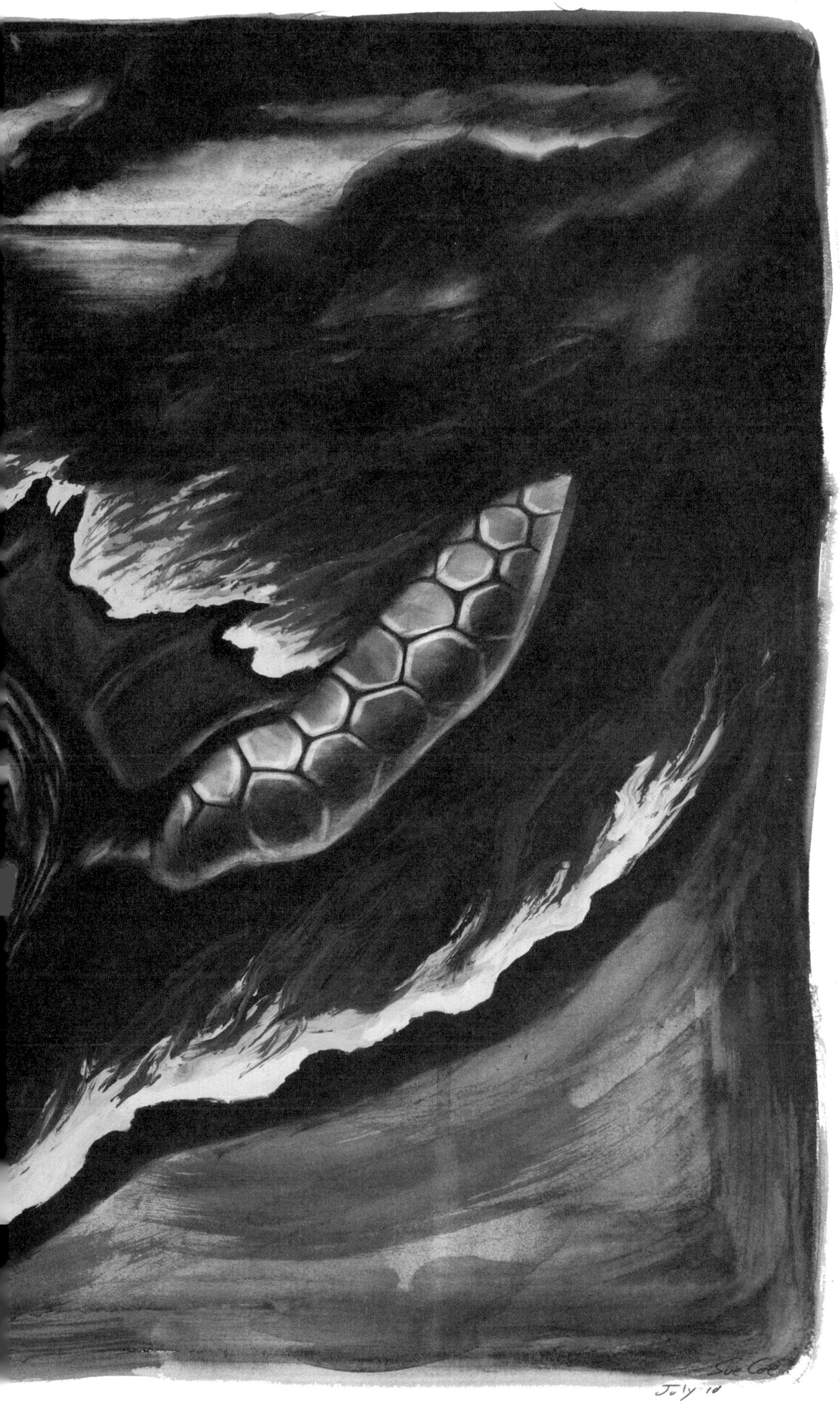
Sue Coe
July 10

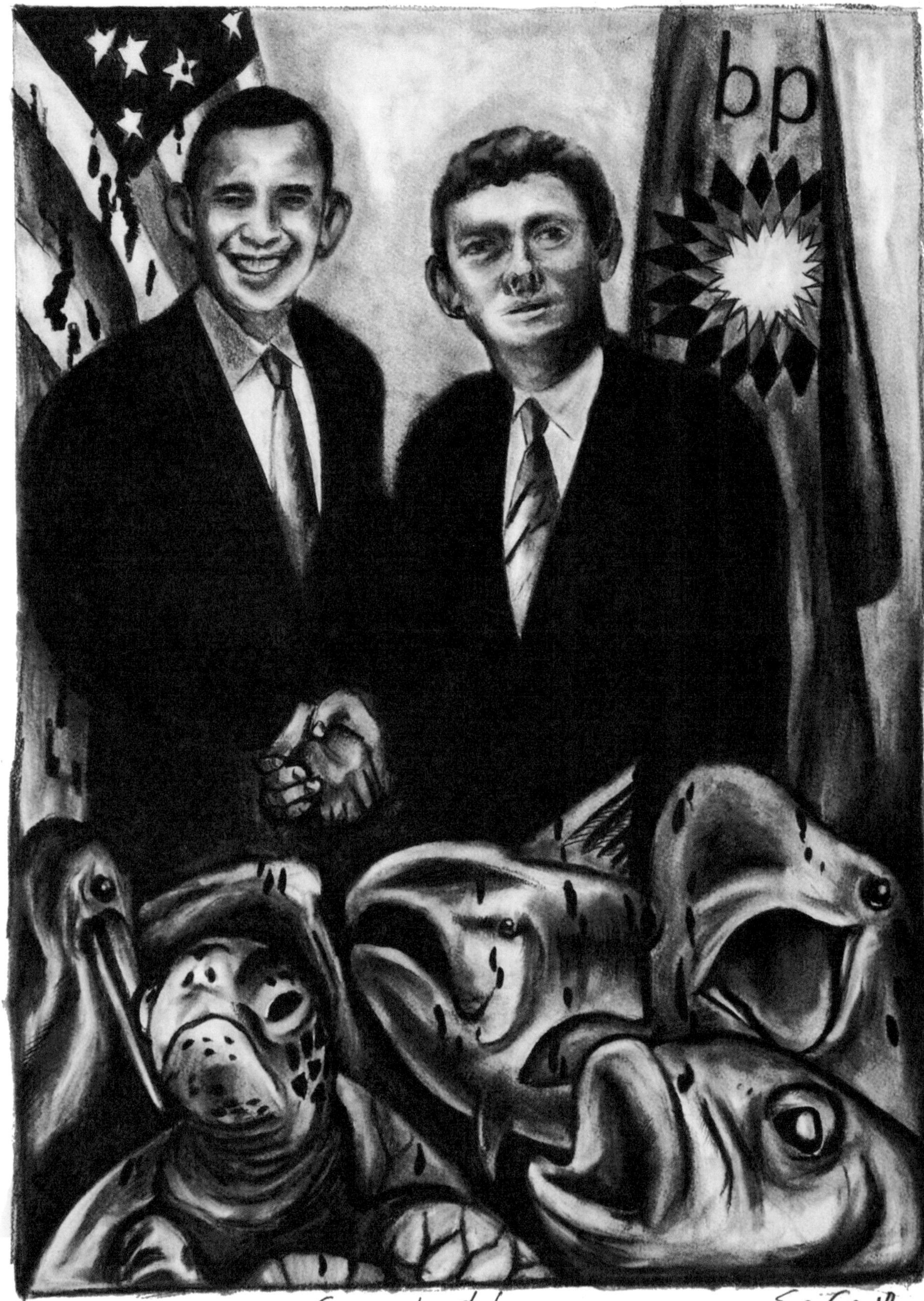
bp

S o l d! Sue Coe 10

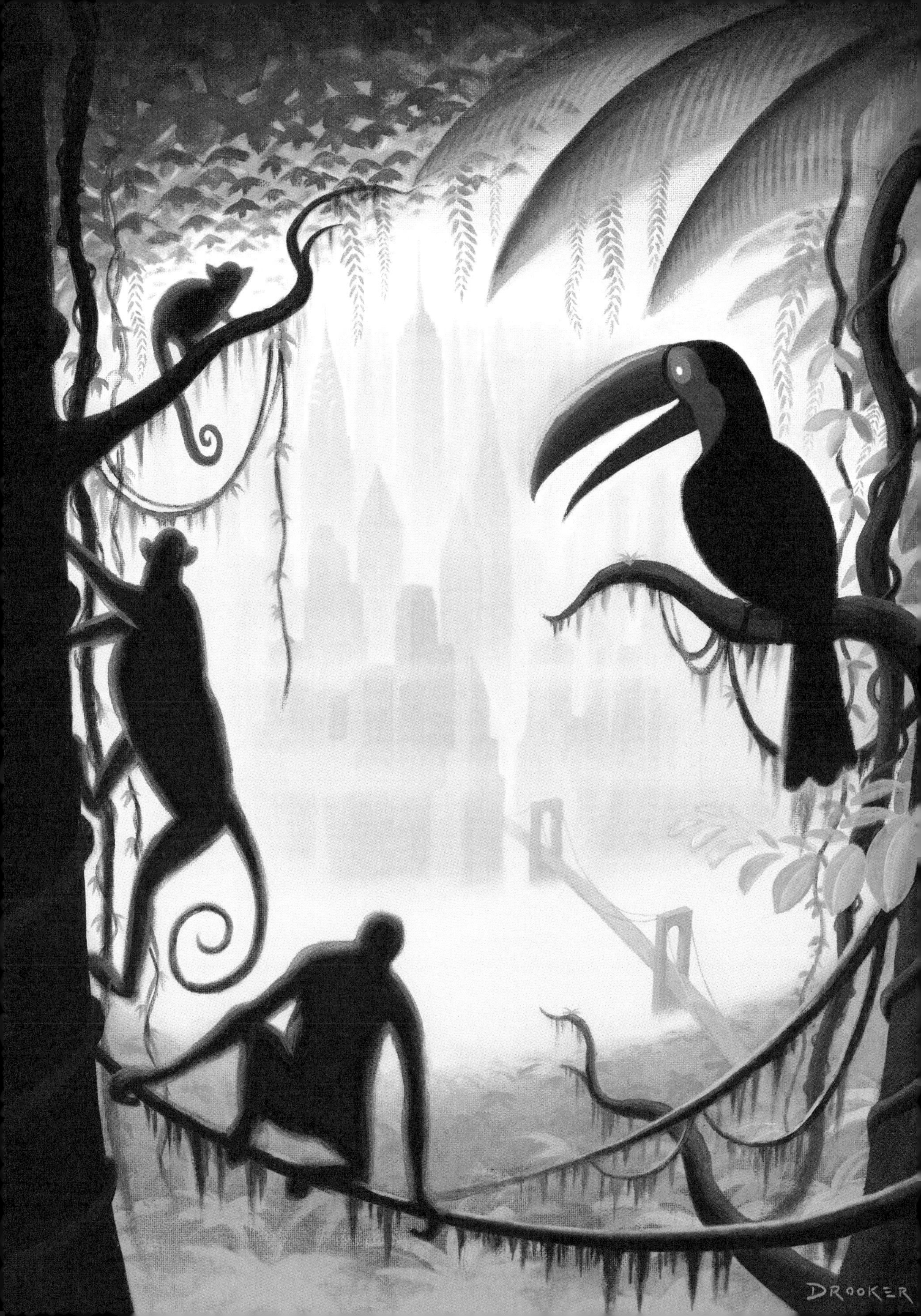
DROOKER

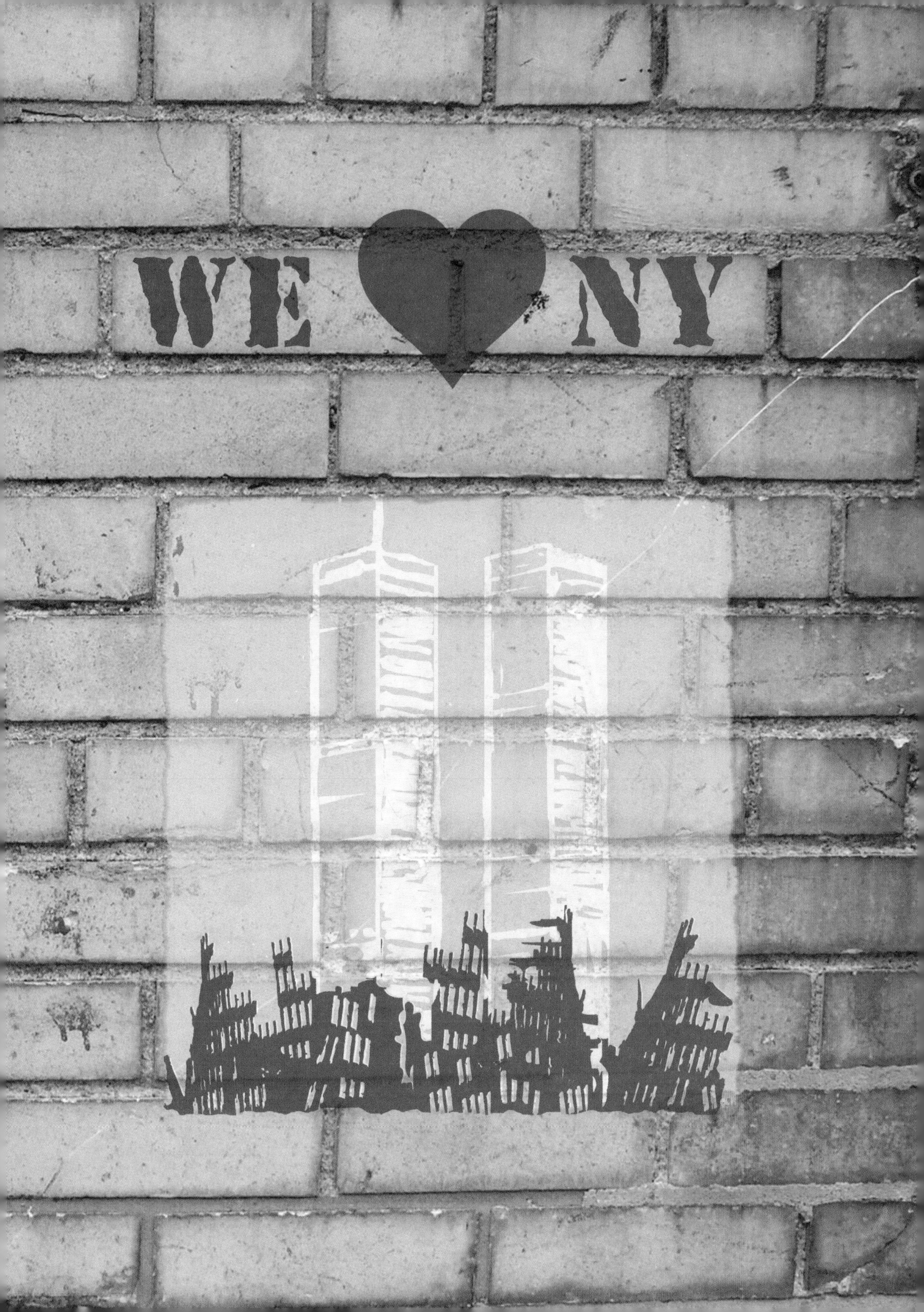
WE NY

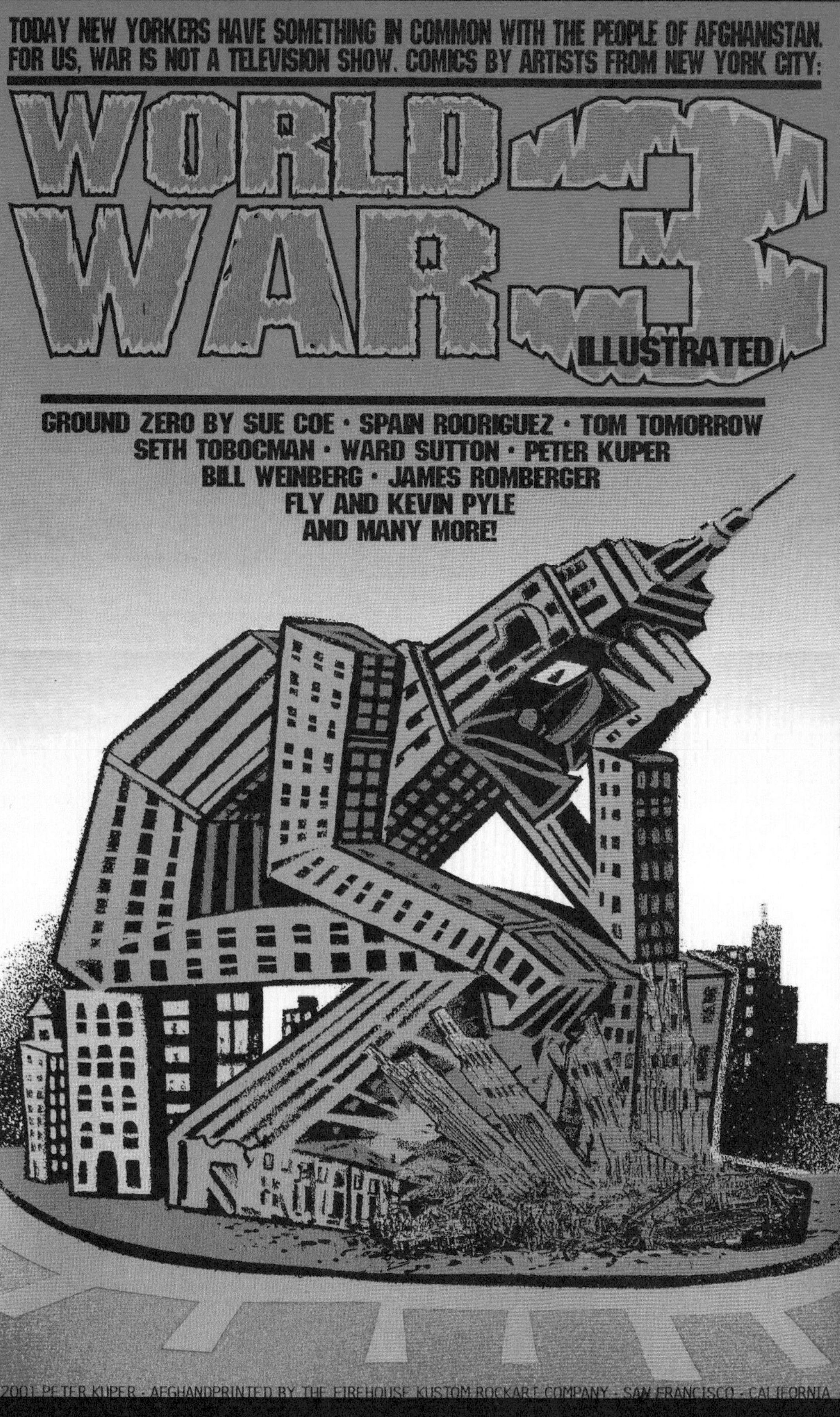
TODAY NEW YORKERS HAVE SOMETHING IN COMMON WITH THE PEOPLE OF AFGHANISTAN. FOR US, WAR IS NOT A TELEVISION SHOW. COMICS BY ARTISTS FROM NEW YORK CITY:
WORLD WAR 3 ILLUSTRATED
GROUND ZERO BY SUE COE · SPAIN RODRIGUEZ · TOM TOMORROW
SETH TOBOCMAN · WARD SUTTON · PETER KUPER
BILL WEINBERG · JAMES ROMBERGER
FLY AND KEVIN PYLE
AND MANY MORE!
©2001 PETER KUPER · AFGHANDPRINTED BY THE FIREHOUSE KUSTOM ROCKART COMPANY · SAN FRANCISCO · CALIFORNIA

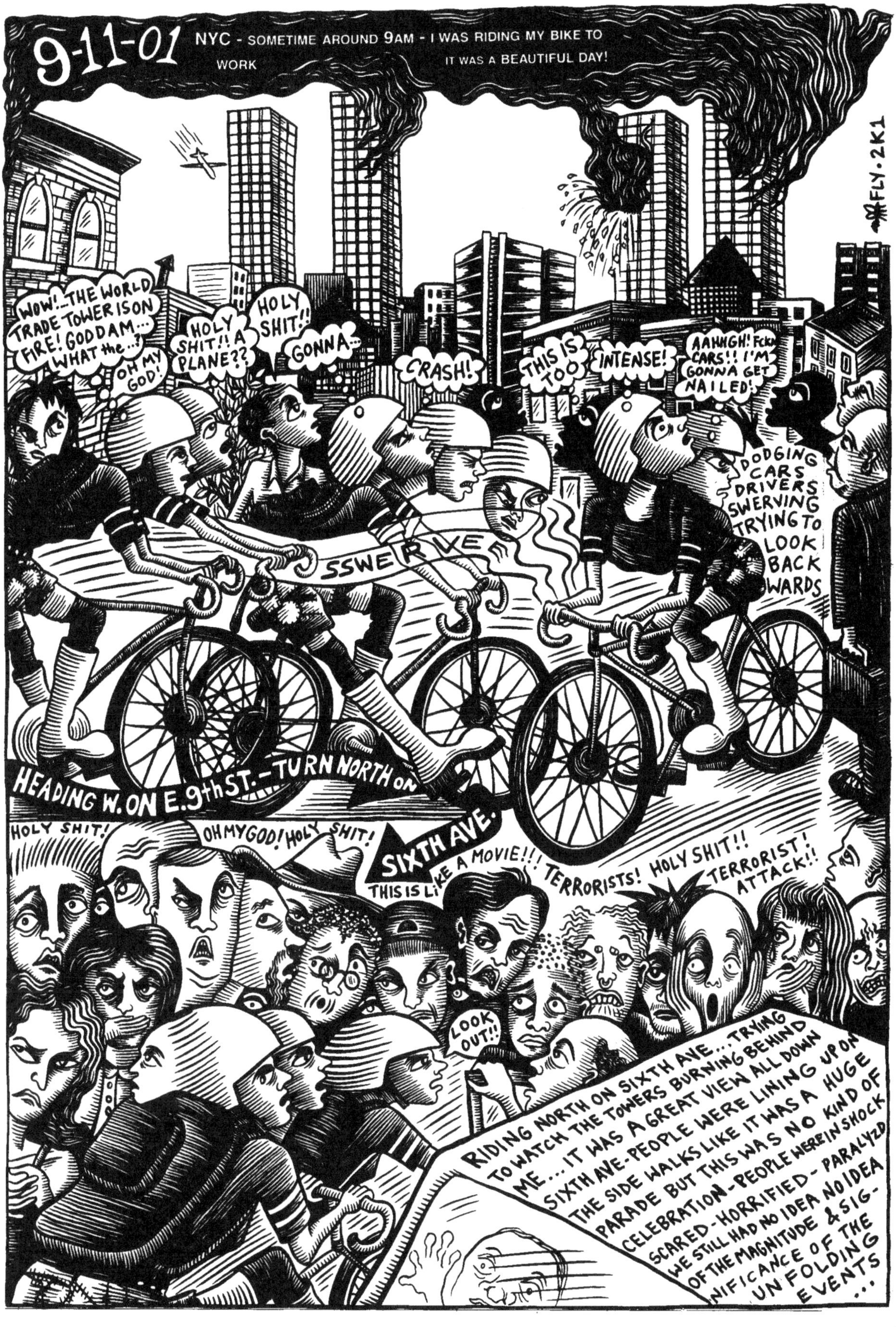
9-11-01
NYC - SOMETIME AROUND 9AM - I WAS RIDING MY BIKE TO WORK
IT WAS A BEAUTIFUL DAY!
WOW!...THE WORLD TRADE TOWER IS ON FIRE! GODDAM... WHAT the...?
OH MY GOD!
HOLY SHIT!! A PLANE??
HOLY SHIT!!
GONNA...
CRASH!
THIS IS TOO
INTENSE!
AAHNGH! FCKN CARS!! I'M GONNA GET NAILED!
DODGING CARS DRIVERS SWERVING TRYING TO LOOK BACK WARDS
SSWERVE
FLY·2K1
HEADING W. ON E. 9th ST. - TURN NORTH ON
SIXTH AVE.
HOLY SHIT!
OH MY GOD! HOLY SHIT!
THIS IS LIKE A MOVIE!!!
TERRORISTS! HOLY SHIT!!
TERRORIST! ATTACK!!
LOOK OUT!!
RIDING NORTH ON SIXTH AVE... TRYING TO WATCH THE TOWERS BURNING BEHIND ME... IT WAS A GREAT VIEW ALL DOWN SIXTH AVE - PEOPLE WERE LINING UP ON THE SIDE WALKS LIKE IT WAS A HUGE PARADE BUT THIS WAS NO KIND OF CELEBRATION - PEOPLE WERE IN SHOCK SCARED - HORRIFIED - PARALYZD WE STILL HAD NO IDEA NO IDEA OF THE MAGNITUDE & SIGNIFICANCE OF THE UNFOLDING EVENTS...

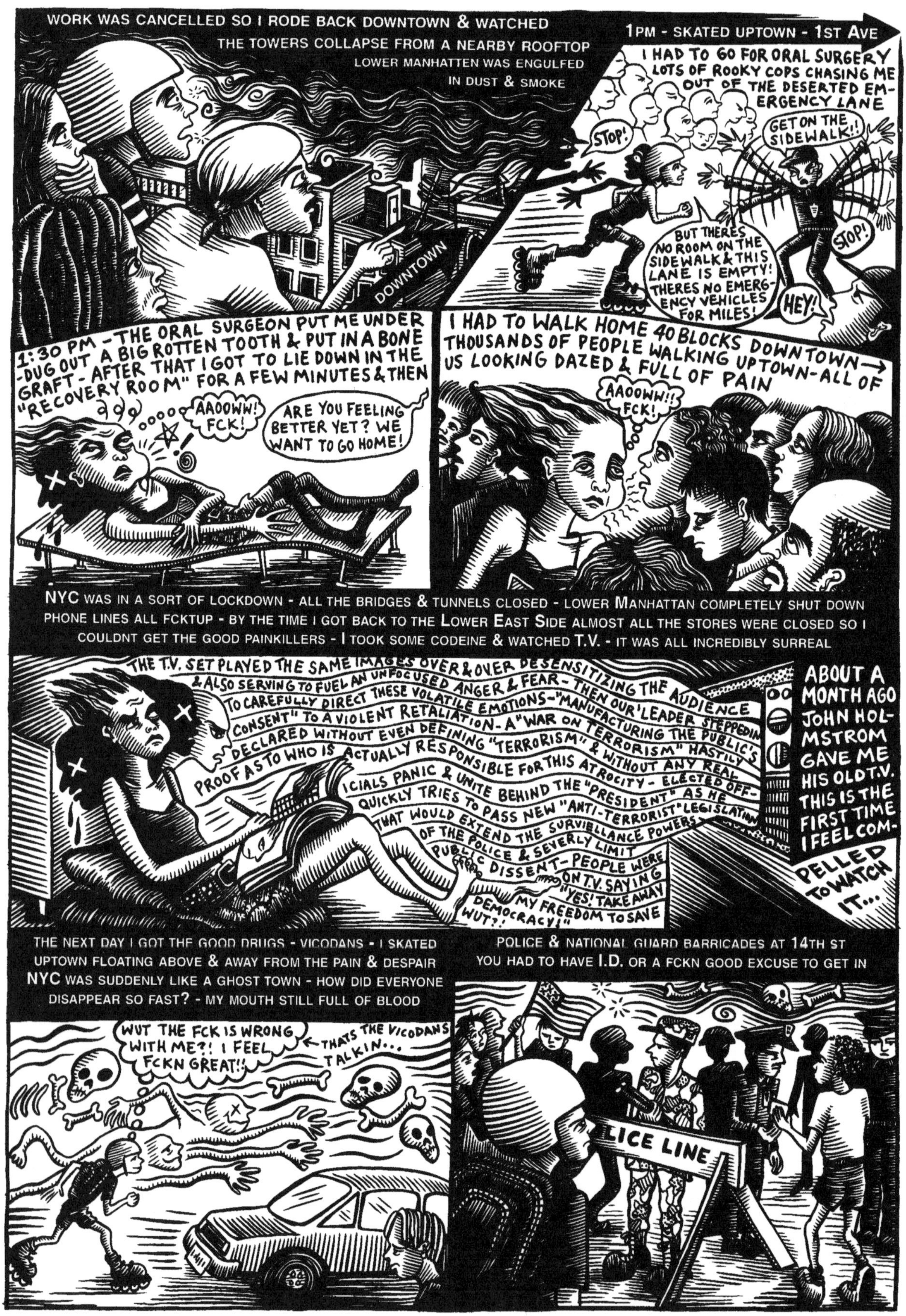
WORK WAS CANCELLED SO I RODE BACK DOWNTOWN & WATCHED THE TOWERS COLLAPSE FROM A NEARBY ROOFTOP LOWER MANHATTEN WAS ENGULFED IN DUST & SMOKE
DOWNTOWN
1PM - SKATED UPTOWN - 1ST AVE
I HAD TO GO FOR ORAL SURGERY LOTS OF ROOKY COPS CHASING ME OUT OF THE DESERTED EMERGENCY LANE
STOP!
GET ON THE SIDEWALK!!
BUT THERES NO ROOM ON THE SIDEWALK & THIS LANE IS EMPTY! THERES NO EMERGENCY VEHICLES FOR MILES!
STOP!
HEY!
1:30 PM - THE ORAL SURGEON PUT ME UNDER - DUG OUT A BIG ROTTEN TOOTH & PUT IN A BONE GRAFT - AFTER THAT I GOT TO LIE DOWN IN THE "RECOVERY ROOM" FOR A FEW MINUTES & THEN
AAOOWW! FCK!
ARE YOU FEELING BETTER YET? WE WANT TO GO HOME!
I HAD TO WALK HOME 40 BLOCKS DOWNTOWN → THOUSANDS OF PEOPLE WALKING UPTOWN - ALL OF US LOOKING DAZED & FULL OF PAIN
AAOOWW!! FCK!
NYC WAS IN A SORT OF LOCKDOWN - ALL THE BRIDGES & TUNNELS CLOSED - LOWER MANHATTAN COMPLETELY SHUT DOWN PHONE LINES ALL FCKTUP - BY THE TIME I GOT BACK TO THE LOWER EAST SIDE ALMOST ALL THE STORES WERE CLOSED SO I COULDNT GET THE GOOD PAINKILLERS - I TOOK SOME CODEINE & WATCHED T.V. - IT WAS ALL INCREDIBLY SURREAL
THE T.V. SET PLAYED THE SAME IMAGES OVER & OVER DESENSITIZING THE AUDIENCE & ALSO SERVING TO FUEL AN UNFOCUSED ANGER & FEAR - THEN OUR 'LEADER' STEPPED IN TO CAREFULLY DIRECT THESE VOLATILE EMOTIONS - "MANUFACTURING THE PUBLIC'S CONSENT" TO A VIOLENT RETALIATION - A "WAR ON TERRORISM" HASTILY DECLARED WITHOUT EVEN DEFINING "TERRORISM" & WITHOUT ANY REAL PROOF AS TO WHO IS ACTUALLY RESPONSIBLE FOR THIS ATROCITY - ELECTED OFFICIALS PANIC & UNITE BEHIND THE "PRESIDENT" AS HE QUICKLY TRIES TO PASS NEW "ANTI-TERRORIST" LEGISLATION THAT WOULD EXTEND THE SURVIELLANCE POWERS OF THE POLICE & SEVERLY LIMIT PUBLIC DISSENT - PEOPLE WERE ON T.V. SAYING "YES! TAKE AWAY MY FREEDOM TO SAVE DEMOCRACY!"
WUT?!
ABOUT A MONTH AGO JOHN HOLMSTROM GAVE ME HIS OLD T.V. THIS IS THE FIRST TIME I FEEL COMPELLED TO WATCH IT...
THE NEXT DAY I GOT THE GOOD DRUGS - VICODANS - I SKATED UPTOWN FLOATING ABOVE & AWAY FROM THE PAIN & DESPAIR NYC WAS SUDDENLY LIKE A GHOST TOWN - HOW DID EVERYONE DISAPPEAR SO FAST? - MY MOUTH STILL FULL OF BLOOD
WUT THE FCK IS WRONG WITH ME?! I FEEL FCKN GREAT!!
← THATS THE VICODANS TALKIN...
POLICE & NATIONAL GUARD BARRICADES AT 14TH ST YOU HAD TO HAVE I.D. OR A FCKN GOOD EXCUSE TO GET IN
LICE LINE

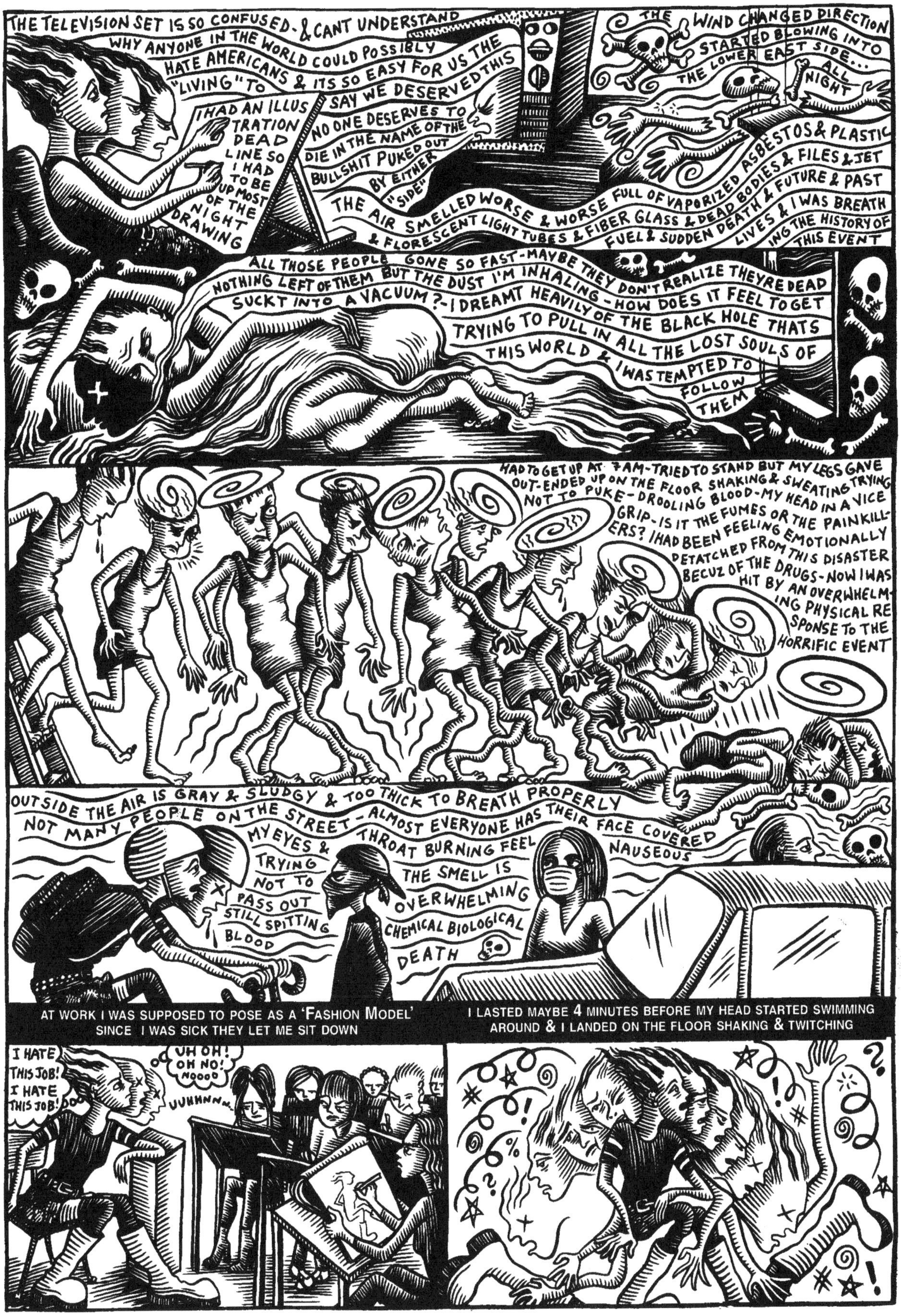
THE TELEVISION SET IS SO CONFUSED - & CANT UNDERSTAND WHY ANYONE IN THE WORLD COULD POSSIBLY HATE AMERICANS & ITS SO EASY FOR US THE "LIVING" TO SAY WE DESERVED THIS
I HAD AN ILLUSTRATION DEAD LINE SO I HAD TO BE UP MOST OF THE NIGHT DRAWING
NO ONE DESERVES TO DIE IN THE NAME OF THE BULLSHIT PUKED OUT BY EITHER "SIDE"
THE WIND CHANGED DIRECTION STARTED BLOWING INTO THE LOWER EAST SIDE... ALL NIGHT
THE AIR SMELLED WORSE & WORSE FULL OF VAPORIZED ASBESTOS & PLASTIC & FLORESCENT LIGHT TUBES & FIBER GLASS & DEAD BODIES & FILES & JET FUEL & SUDDEN DEATH & FUTURE & PAST LIVES & I WAS BREATHING THE HISTORY OF THIS EVENT
ALL THOSE PEOPLE GONE SO FAST - MAYBE THEY DON'T REALIZE THEYRE DEAD NOTHING LEFT OF THEM BUT THE DUST I'M INHALING - HOW DOES IT FEEL TO GET SUCKT INTO A VACUUM? - I DREAMT HEAVILY OF THE BLACK HOLE THATS TRYING TO PULL IN ALL THE LOST SOULS OF THIS WORLD & I WAS TEMPTED TO FOLLOW THEM
HAD TO GET UP AT 7AM - TRIED TO STAND BUT MY LEGS GAVE OUT - ENDED UP ON THE FLOOR SHAKING & SWEATING TRYING NOT TO PUKE - DROOLING BLOOD - MY HEAD IN A VICE GRIP - IS IT THE FUMES OR THE PAINKILLERS? I HAD BEEN FEELING EMOTIONALLY DETATCHED FROM THIS DISASTER BECUZ OF THE DRUGS - NOW I WAS HIT BY AN OVERWHELMING PHYSICAL RESPONSE TO THE HORRIFIC EVENT
OUTSIDE THE AIR IS GRAY & SLUDGY & TOO THICK TO BREATH PROPERLY
NOT MANY PEOPLE ON THE STREET - ALMOST EVERYONE HAS THEIR FACE COVERED
MY EYES & THROAT BURNING FEEL NAUSEOUS
TRYING NOT TO PASS OUT STILL SPITTING BLOOD
THE SMELL IS OVERWHELMING CHEMICAL BIOLOGICAL DEATH
AT WORK I WAS SUPPOSED TO POSE AS A 'FASHION MODEL' SINCE I WAS SICK THEY LET ME SIT DOWN
I LASTED MAYBE 4 MINUTES BEFORE MY HEAD STARTED SWIMMING AROUND & I LANDED ON THE FLOOR SHAKING & TWITCHING
I HATE THIS JOB! I HATE THIS JOB!
UH OH! OH NO! NOOOO
UUHHNN..

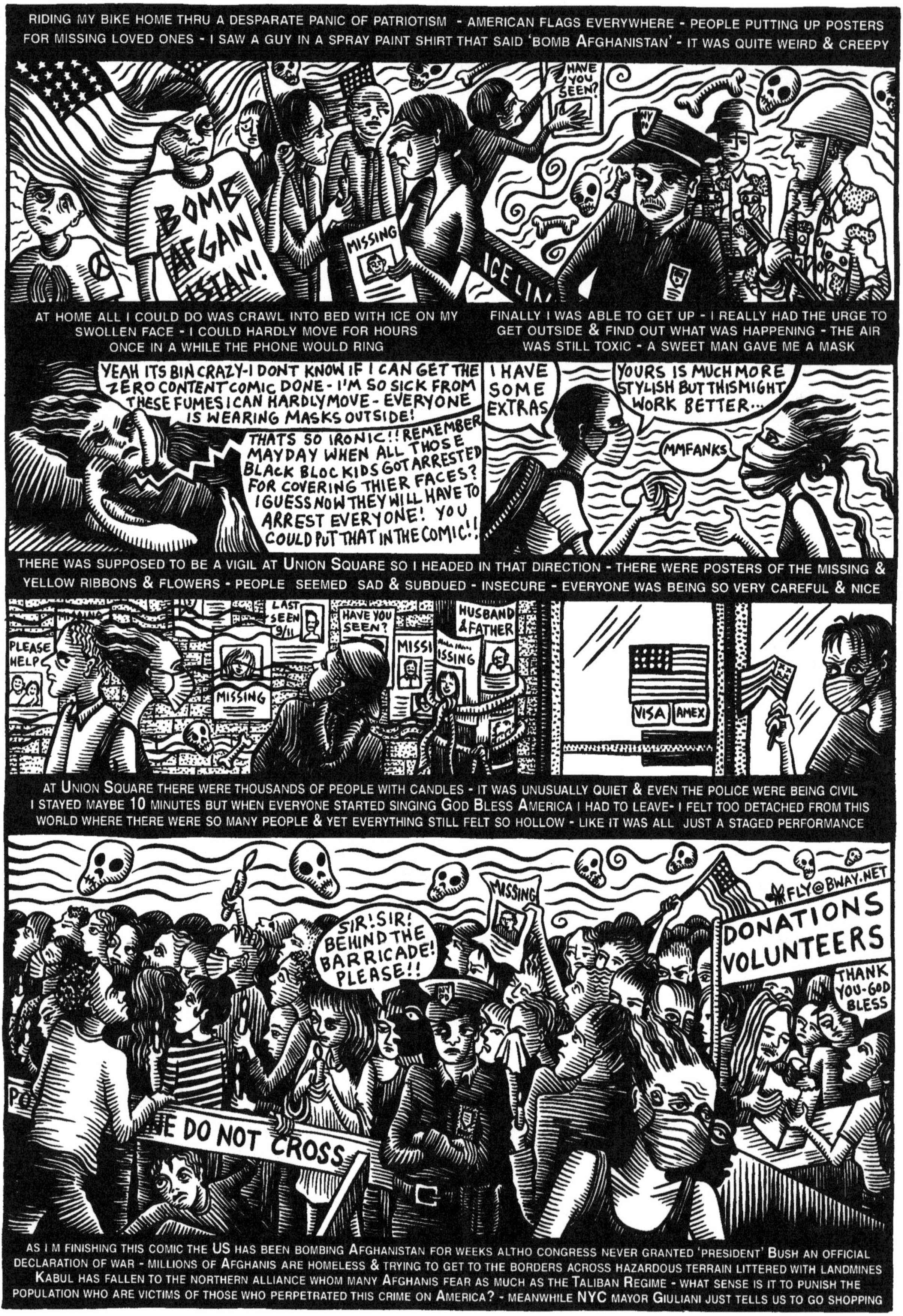
RIDING MY BIKE HOME THRU A DESPARATE PANIC OF PATRIOTISM - AMERICAN FLAGS EVERYWHERE - PEOPLE PUTTING UP POSTERS FOR MISSING LOVED ONES - I SAW A GUY IN A SPRAY PAINT SHIRT THAT SAID 'BOMB AFGHANISTAN' - IT WAS QUITE WEIRD & CREEPY
BOMB AFGAN ISTAN!
HAVE YOU SEEN?
MISSING
ICE LIN
AT HOME ALL I COULD DO WAS CRAWL INTO BED WITH ICE ON MY SWOLLEN FACE - I COULD HARDLY MOVE FOR HOURS ONCE IN A WHILE THE PHONE WOULD RING
YEAH ITS BIN CRAZY-I DONT KNOW IF I CAN GET THE ZERO CONTENT COMIC DONE - I'M SO SICK FROM THESE FUMES I CAN HARDLY MOVE - EVERYONE IS WEARING MASKS OUTSIDE!
THATS SO IRONIC!! REMEMBER MAYDAY WHEN ALL THOSE BLACK BLOC KIDS GOT ARRESTED FOR COVERING THIER FACES? I GUESS NOW THEY WILL HAVE TO ARREST EVERYONE! YOU COULD PUT THAT IN THE COMIC!!
FINALLY I WAS ABLE TO GET UP - I REALLY HAD THE URGE TO GET OUTSIDE & FIND OUT WHAT WAS HAPPENING - THE AIR WAS STILL TOXIC - A SWEET MAN GAVE ME A MASK
I HAVE SOME EXTRAS
YOURS IS MUCH MORE STYLISH BUT THIS MIGHT WORK BETTER...
MMFANKS
THERE WAS SUPPOSED TO BE A VIGIL AT UNION SQUARE SO I HEADED IN THAT DIRECTION - THERE WERE POSTERS OF THE MISSING & YELLOW RIBBONS & FLOWERS - PEOPLE SEEMED SAD & SUBDUED - INSECURE - EVERYONE WAS BEING SO VERY CAREFUL & NICE
PLEASE HELP
LAST SEEN 9/11
HAVE YOU SEEN?
MISSING
MISSI
ISSING
HUSBAND & FATHER
VISA
AMEX
AT UNION SQUARE THERE WERE THOUSANDS OF PEOPLE WITH CANDLES - IT WAS UNUSUALLY QUIET & EVEN THE POLICE WERE BEING CIVIL I STAYED MAYBE 10 MINUTES BUT WHEN EVERYONE STARTED SINGING GOD BLESS AMERICA I HAD TO LEAVE- I FELT TOO DETACHED FROM THIS WORLD WHERE THERE WERE SO MANY PEOPLE & YET EVERYTHING STILL FELT SO HOLLOW - LIKE IT WAS ALL JUST A STAGED PERFORMANCE
MISSING
FLY@BWAY.NET
SIR! SIR! BEHIND THE BARRICADE! PLEASE!!
DONATIONS VOLUNTEERS
THANK YOU-GOD BLESS
NE DO NOT CROSS
AS I M FINISHING THIS COMIC THE US HAS BEEN BOMBING AFGHANISTAN FOR WEEKS ALTHO CONGRESS NEVER GRANTED 'PRESIDENT' BUSH AN OFFICIAL DECLARATION OF WAR - MILLIONS OF AFGHANIS ARE HOMELESS & TRYING TO GET TO THE BORDERS ACROSS HAZARDOUS TERRAIN LITTERED WITH LANDMINES KABUL HAS FALLEN TO THE NORTHERN ALLIANCE WHOM MANY AFGHANIS FEAR AS MUCH AS THE TALIBAN REGIME - WHAT SENSE IS IT TO PUNISH THE POPULATION WHO ARE VICTIMS OF THOSE WHO PERPETRATED THIS CRIME ON AMERICA? - MEANWHILE NYC MAYOR GIULIANI JUST TELLS US TO GO SHOPPING

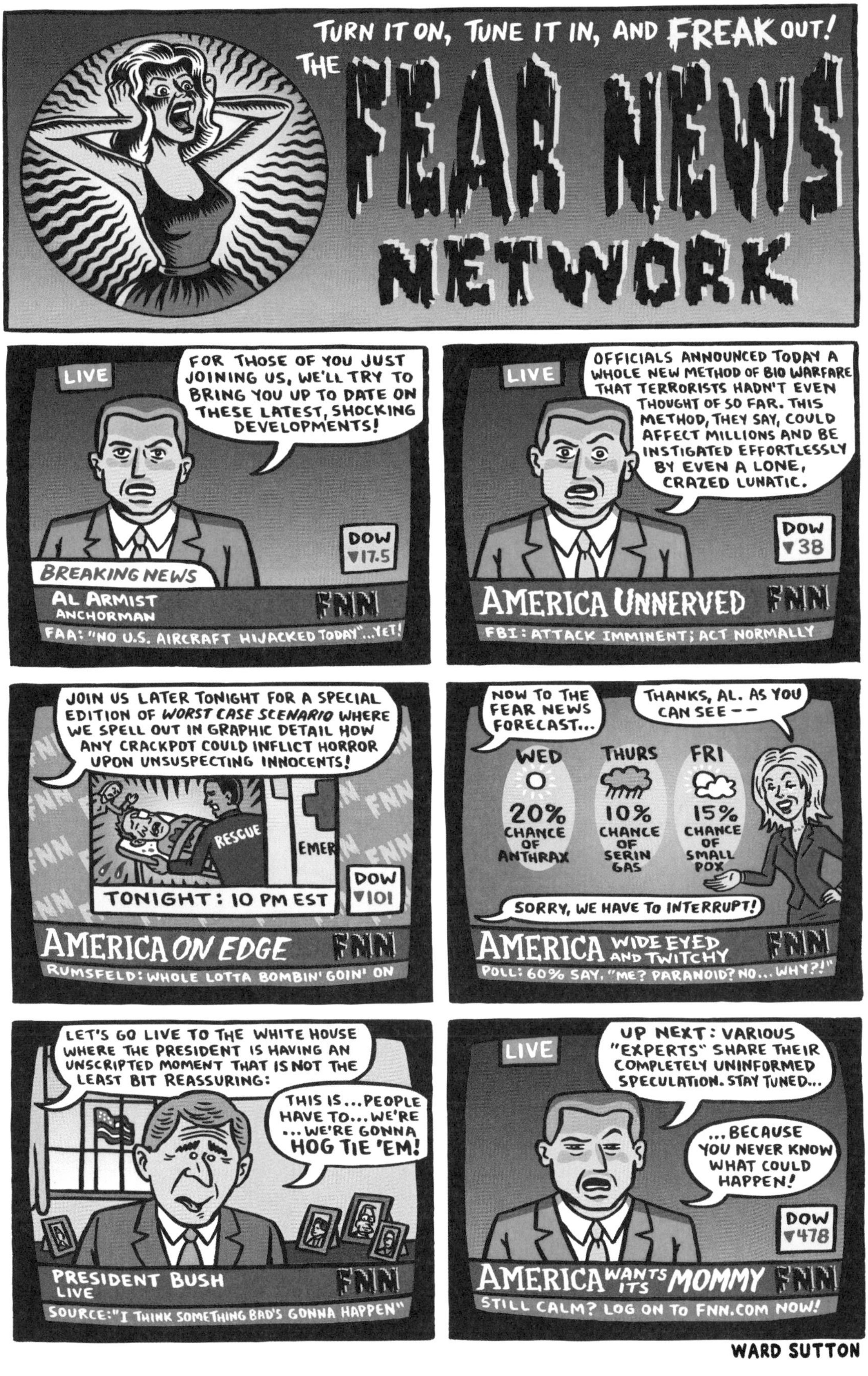
TURN IT ON, TUNE IT IN, AND FREAK OUT!
THE FEAR NEWS NETWORK
LIVE
FOR THOSE OF YOU JUST JOINING US, WE'LL TRY TO BRING YOU UP TO DATE ON THESE LATEST, SHOCKING DEVELOPMENTS!
DOW ▼17.5
BREAKING NEWS
AL ARMIST
ANCHORMAN
FNN
FAA: "NO U.S. AIRCRAFT HIJACKED TODAY"...YET!
LIVE
OFFICIALS ANNOUNCED TODAY A WHOLE NEW METHOD OF BIO WARFARE THAT TERRORISTS HADN'T EVEN THOUGHT OF SO FAR. THIS METHOD, THEY SAY, COULD AFFECT MILLIONS AND BE INSTIGATED EFFORTLESSLY BY EVEN A LONE, CRAZED LUNATIC.
DOW ▼38
AMERICA UNNERVED
FNN
FBI: ATTACK IMMINENT; ACT NORMALLY
JOIN US LATER TONIGHT FOR A SPECIAL EDITION OF WORST CASE SCENARIO WHERE WE SPELL OUT IN GRAPHIC DETAIL HOW ANY CRACKPOT COULD INFLICT HORROR UPON UNSUSPECTING INNOCENTS!
RESCUE
EMER
TONIGHT: 10 PM EST
DOW ▼101
AMERICA ON EDGE
FNN
RUMSFELD: WHOLE LOTTA BOMBIN' GOIN' ON
NOW TO THE FEAR NEWS FORECAST...
THANKS, AL. AS YOU CAN SEE --
WED
20% CHANCE OF ANTHRAX
THURS
10% CHANCE OF SERIN GAS
FRI
15% CHANCE OF SMALL POX
SORRY, WE HAVE TO INTERRUPT!
AMERICA WIDE EYED AND TWITCHY
FNN
POLL: 60% SAY, "ME? PARANOID? NO... WHY?!"
LET'S GO LIVE TO THE WHITE HOUSE WHERE THE PRESIDENT IS HAVING AN UNSCRIPTED MOMENT THAT IS NOT THE LEAST BIT REASSURING:
THIS IS...PEOPLE HAVE TO...WE'RE ...WE'RE GONNA HOG TIE 'EM!
PRESIDENT BUSH
LIVE
FNN
SOURCE: "I THINK SOMETHING BAD'S GONNA HAPPEN"
LIVE
UP NEXT: VARIOUS "EXPERTS" SHARE THEIR COMPLETELY UNINFORMED SPECULATION. STAY TUNED...
...BECAUSE YOU NEVER KNOW WHAT COULD HAPPEN!
DOW ▼478
AMERICA WANTS ITS MOMMY
FNN
STILL CALM? LOG ON TO FNN.COM NOW!

WARD SUTTON

Faith-Based Terrorism

"LET'S CALL IT WHAT IT REALLY IS"

TEXT AND ART BY SPAIN

© SPAIN RODRIGUEZ '01

WHEN ASKED ABOUT MOSLEMS KILLED IN THE WORLD TRADE CENTER OSAMA BIN LADEN RESPONDED...

I HAVE READ THE HOLY QUIR'AN AND IT IS PERMITTED.

THE EVENTS OF SEPTEMBER ELEVENTH WERE HORRIFYING BUT NOT SURPRISING.

I WONDER IF THE FAMILY'S OF MOSLEM VICTIMS RECIEVED ANY SOLACE FROM HIS INTERPRETATION OF ISLAM'S HOLY BOOK?

BUT AMERICA IS NO STRANGER TO FAITH BASED TERRORISM. THE MURDEROUS "PRO-LIFE" MOVEMENT HAS A FEW BLOODY NOTCHES ON ITS BELT.

AND OF COURSE, AMERICA'S WOULD BE AYATOLAH, THE REVEREND JERRY FALWELL WAS RIGHT THERE TO WAG HIS FINGER IN OUR FACE.

...THE PAGANS, THE ABORTIONISTS, THE ATHEISTS, THE FEMINISTS, THE TELETUBBIES SET THE TONE FOR ALL THIS TO HAPPEN

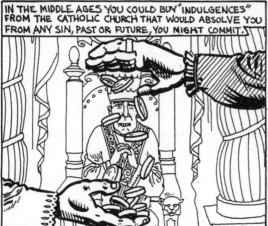

IN THE MIDDLE AGES YOU COULD BUY "INDULGENCES" FROM THE CATHOLIC CHURCH THAT WOULD ABSOLVE YOU FROM ANY SIN, PAST OR FUTURE, YOU MIGHT COMMIT.

EVEN BACK THEN, PEOPLE COULD SEE THIS FOR THE TRANSPARENT FRAUD THAT IT WAS. THOSE WHO SPOKE OUT WERE LABELED HERETICS AND BURNT AT THE STAKE.

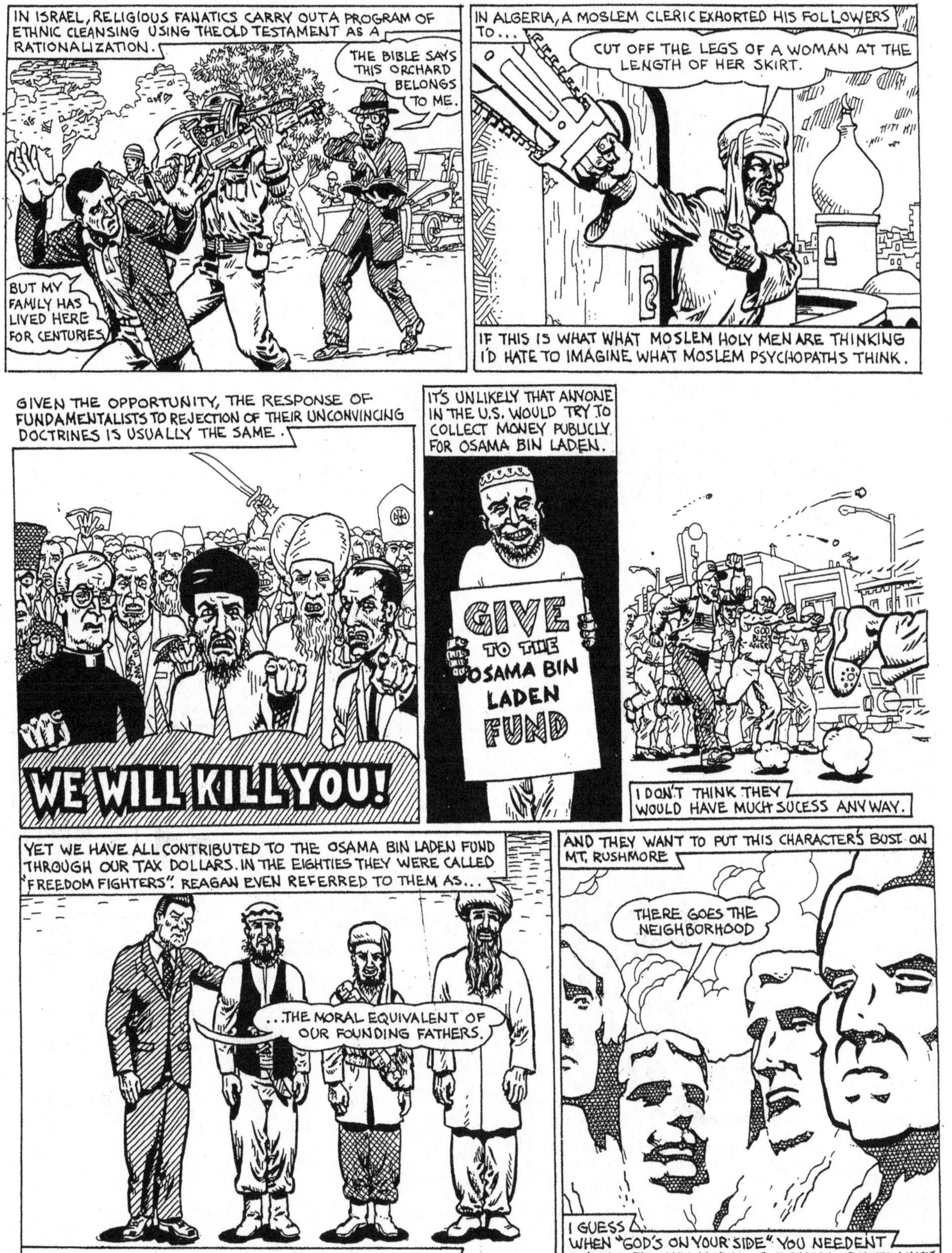
IN ISRAEL, RELIGIOUS FANATICS CARRY OUT A PROGRAM OF ETHNIC CLEANSING USING THE OLD TESTAMENT AS A RATIONALIZATION.
THE BIBLE SAYS THIS ORCHARD BELONGS TO ME.
BUT MY FAMILY HAS LIVED HERE FOR CENTURIES.
IN ALGERIA, A MOSLEM CLERIC EXHORTED HIS FOLLOWERS TO...
CUT OFF THE LEGS OF A WOMAN AT THE LENGTH OF HER SKIRT.
IF THIS IS WHAT WHAT MOSLEM HOLY MEN ARE THINKING I'D HATE TO IMAGINE WHAT MOSLEM PSYCHOPATHS THINK.
GIVEN THE OPPORTUNITY, THE RESPONSE OF FUNDAMENTALISTS TO REJECTION OF THEIR UNCONVINCING DOCTRINES IS USUALLY THE SAME.
WE WILL KILL YOU!
IT'S UNLIKELY THAT ANYONE IN THE U.S. WOULD TRY TO COLLECT MONEY PUBLICLY FOR OSAMA BIN LADEN.
GIVE TO THE OSAMA BIN LADEN FUND
I DON'T THINK THEY WOULD HAVE MUCH SUCESS ANYWAY.
YET WE HAVE ALL CONTRIBUTED TO THE OSAMA BIN LADEN FUND THROUGH OUR TAX DOLLARS. IN THE EIGHTIES THEY WERE CALLED "FREEDOM FIGHTERS". REAGAN EVEN REFERRED TO THEM AS...
...THE MORAL EQUIVALENT OF OUR FOUNDING FATHERS.
OF COURSE THEN THEY WERE BLOWING UP OTHER PEOPLE.
AND THEY WANT TO PUT THIS CHARACTER'S BUST ON MT. RUSHMORE
THERE GOES THE NEIGHBORHOOD
I GUESS WHEN "GOD'S ON YOUR SIDE" YOU NEEDENT ADHERE TO ANY MORAL OR ETHICAL RESTRAINTS

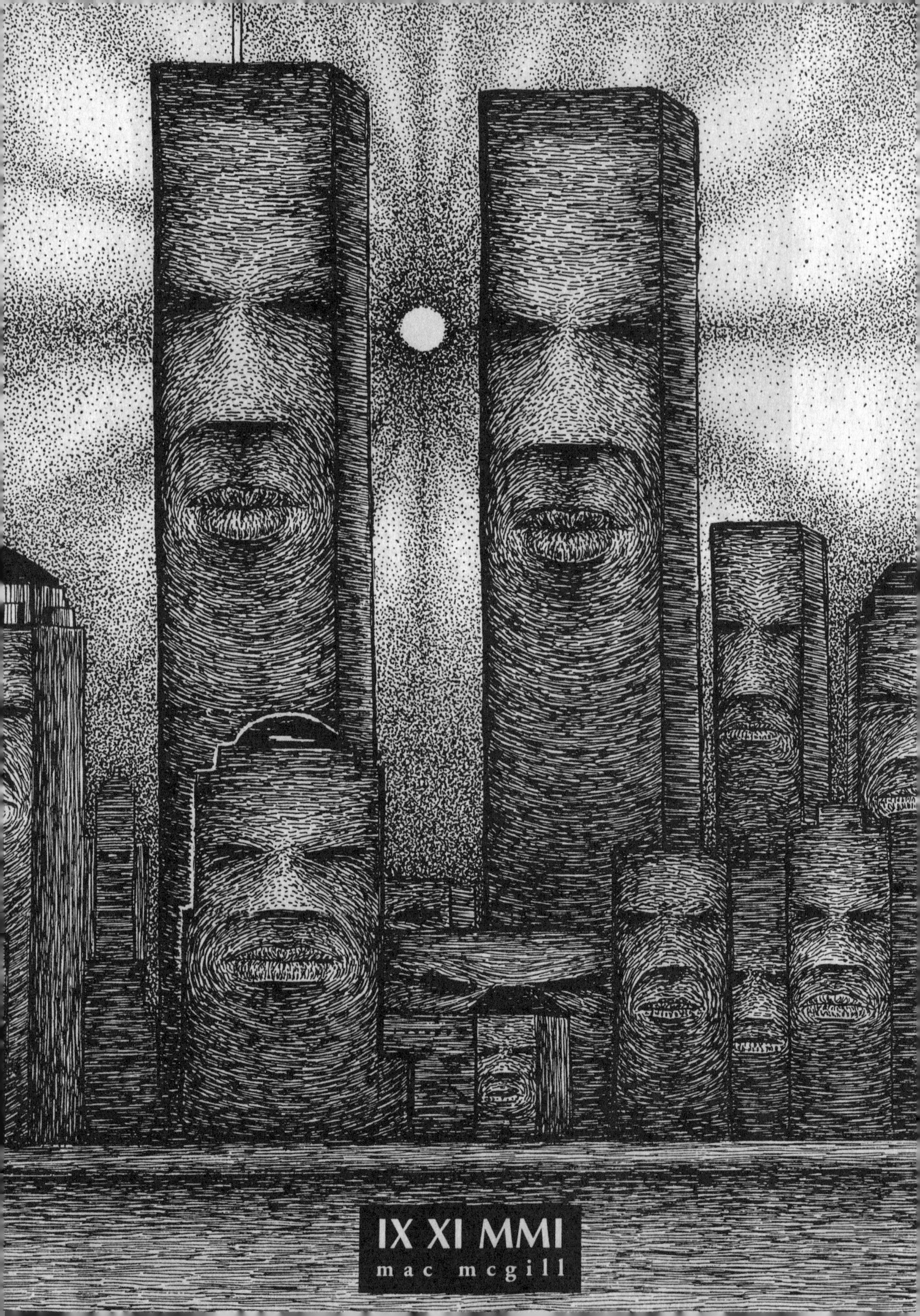
IX XI MMI
mac mcgill

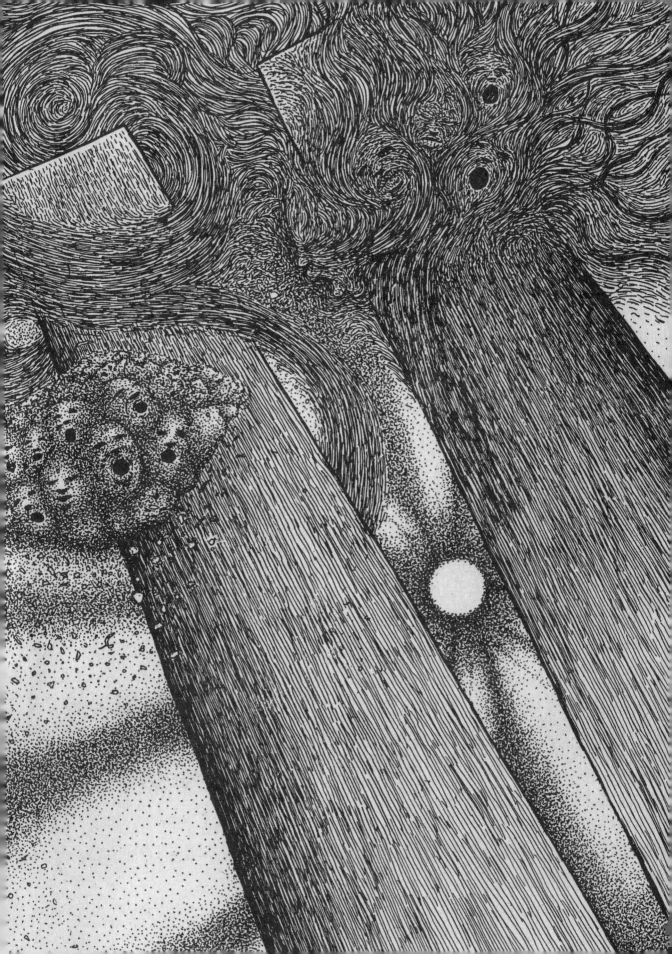

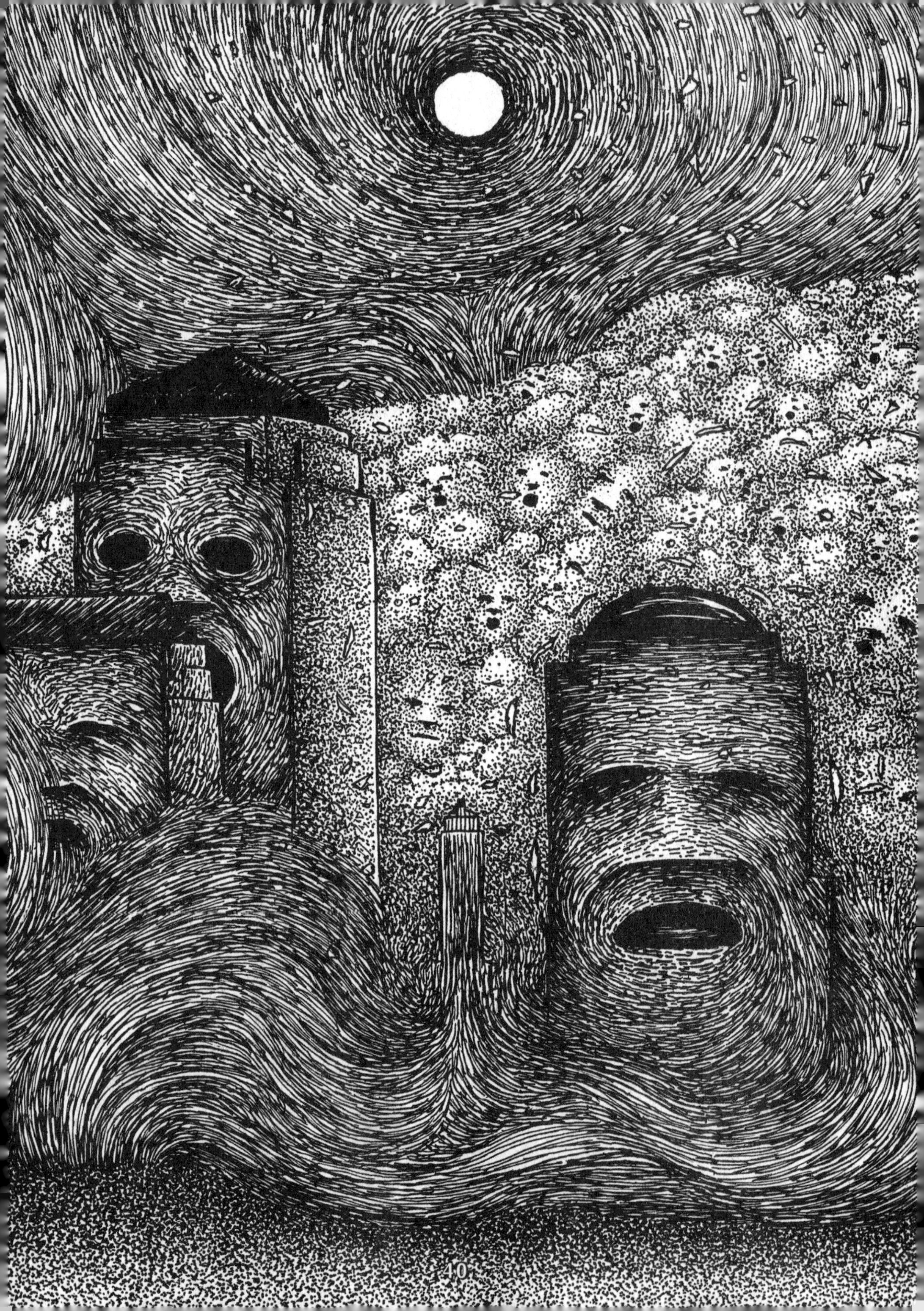

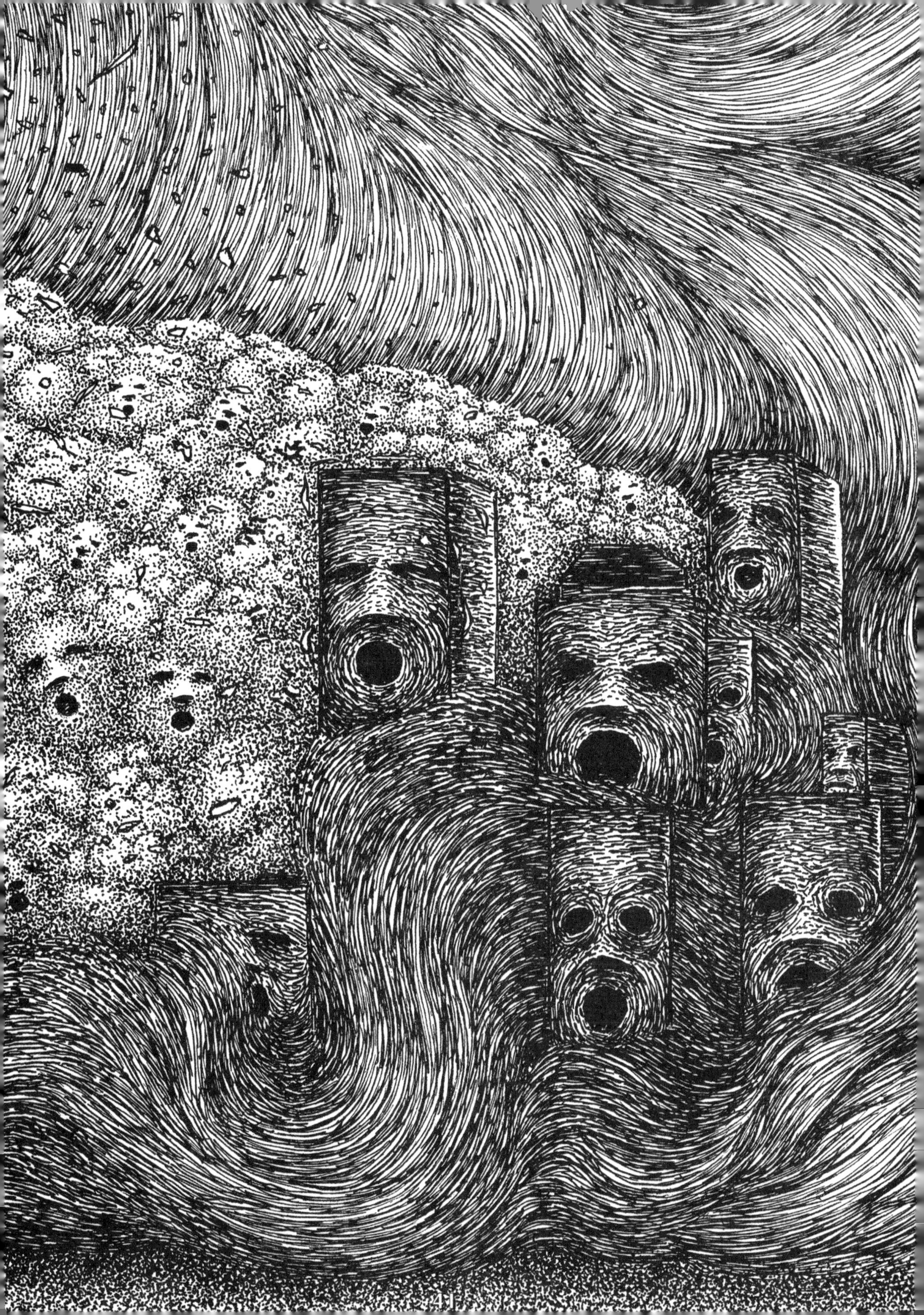

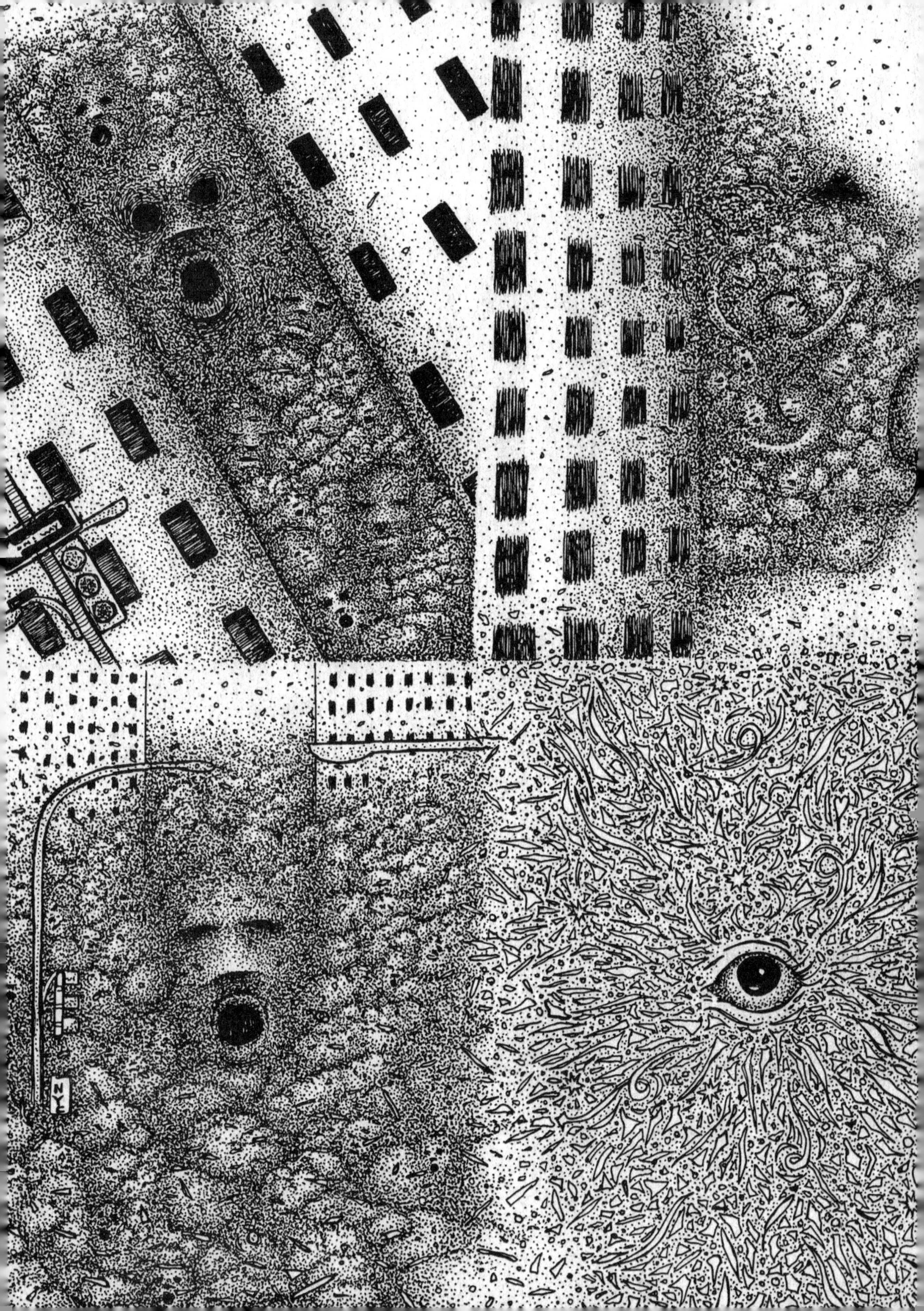
NYE

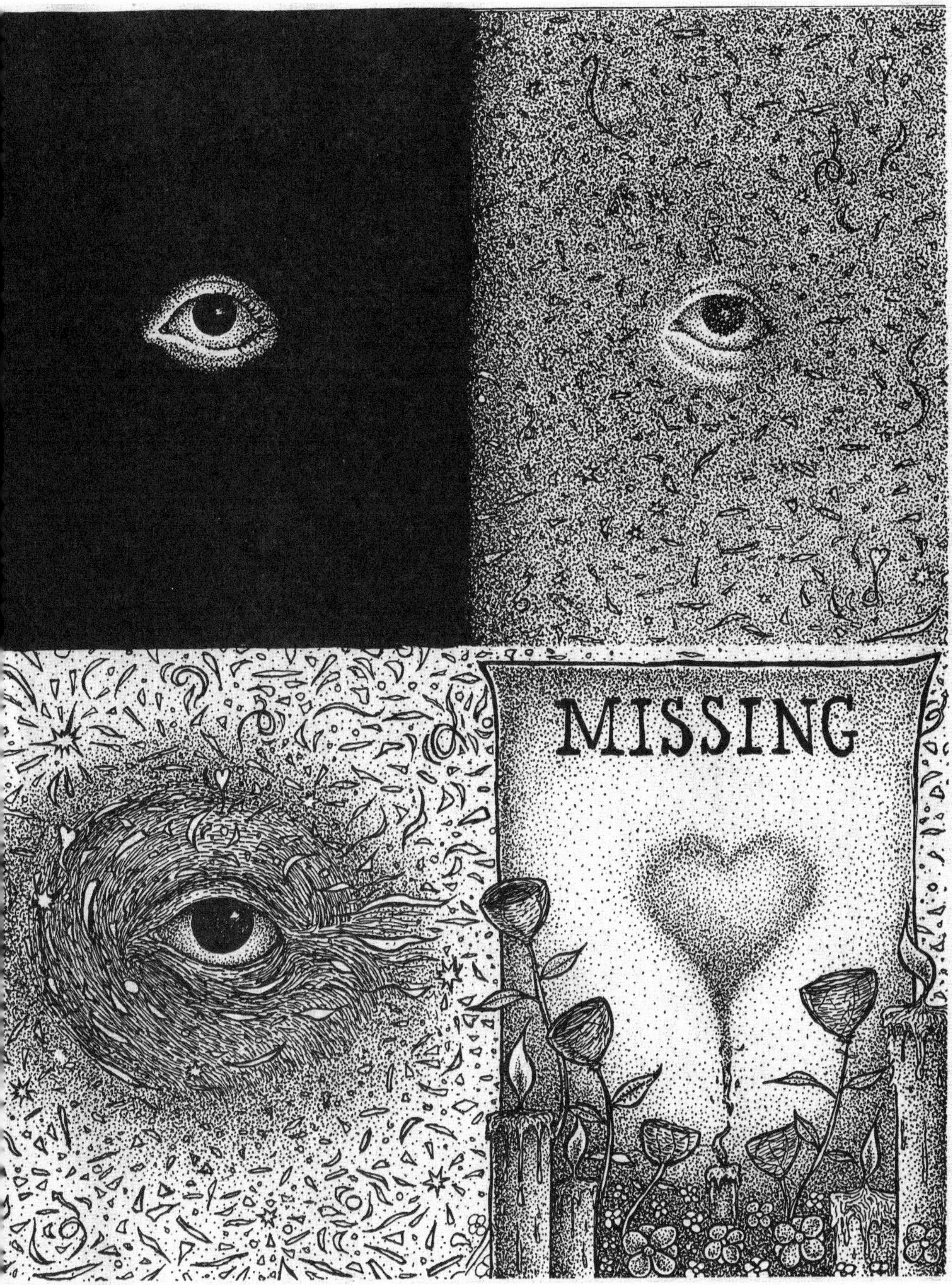
MISSING

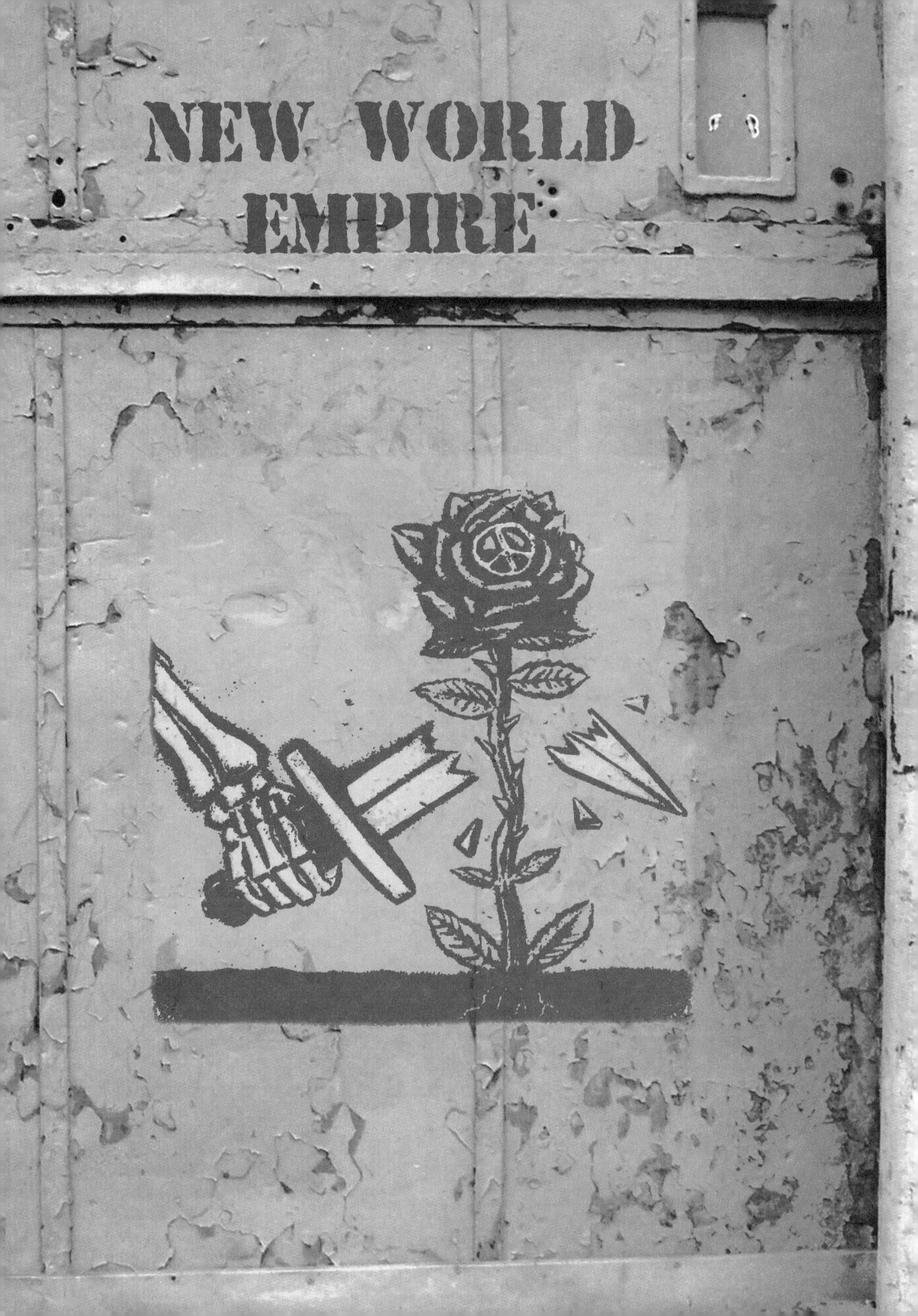
NEW WORLD
EMPIRE

FOSSIL FUEL

BY NICOLE SCHULMAN

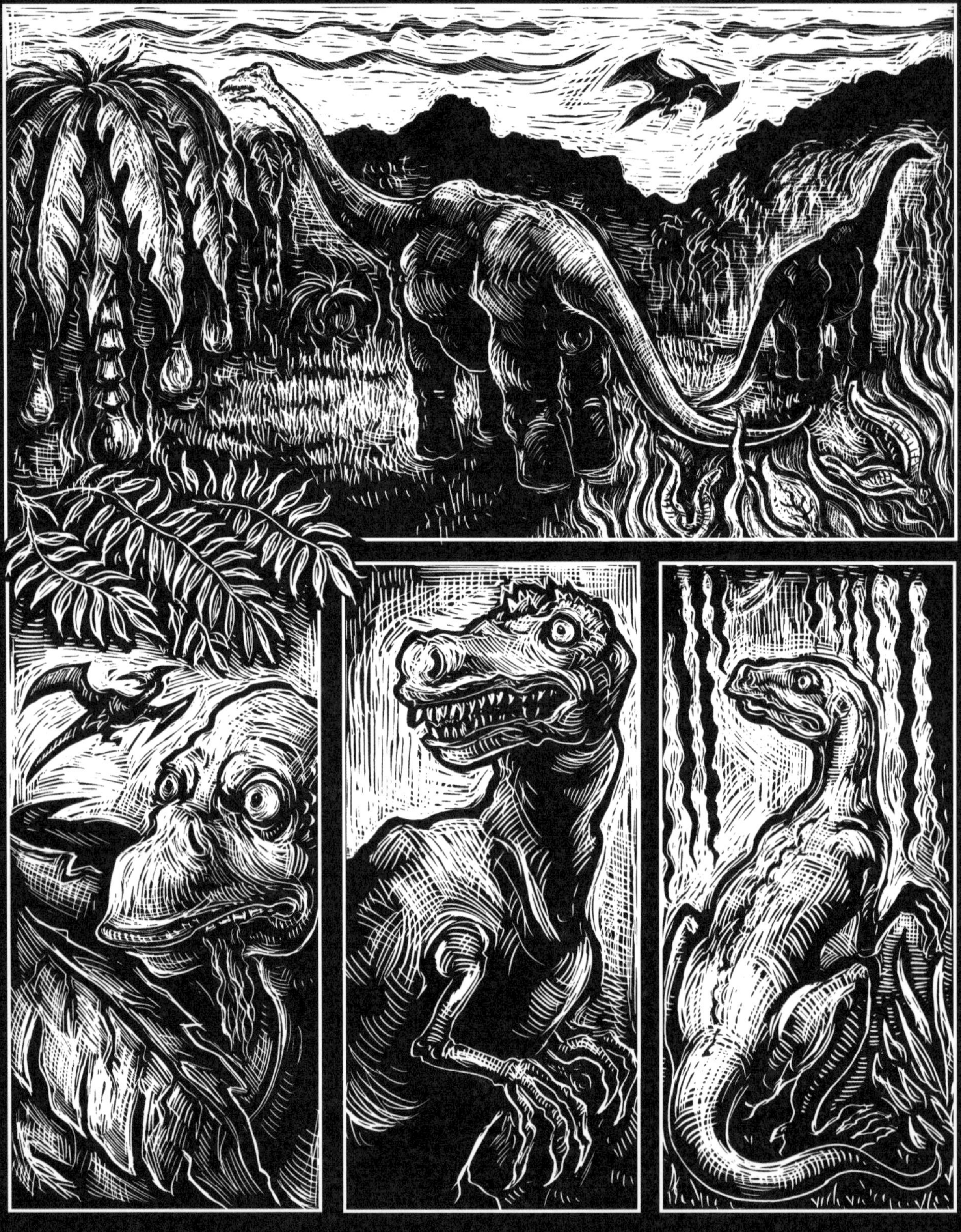

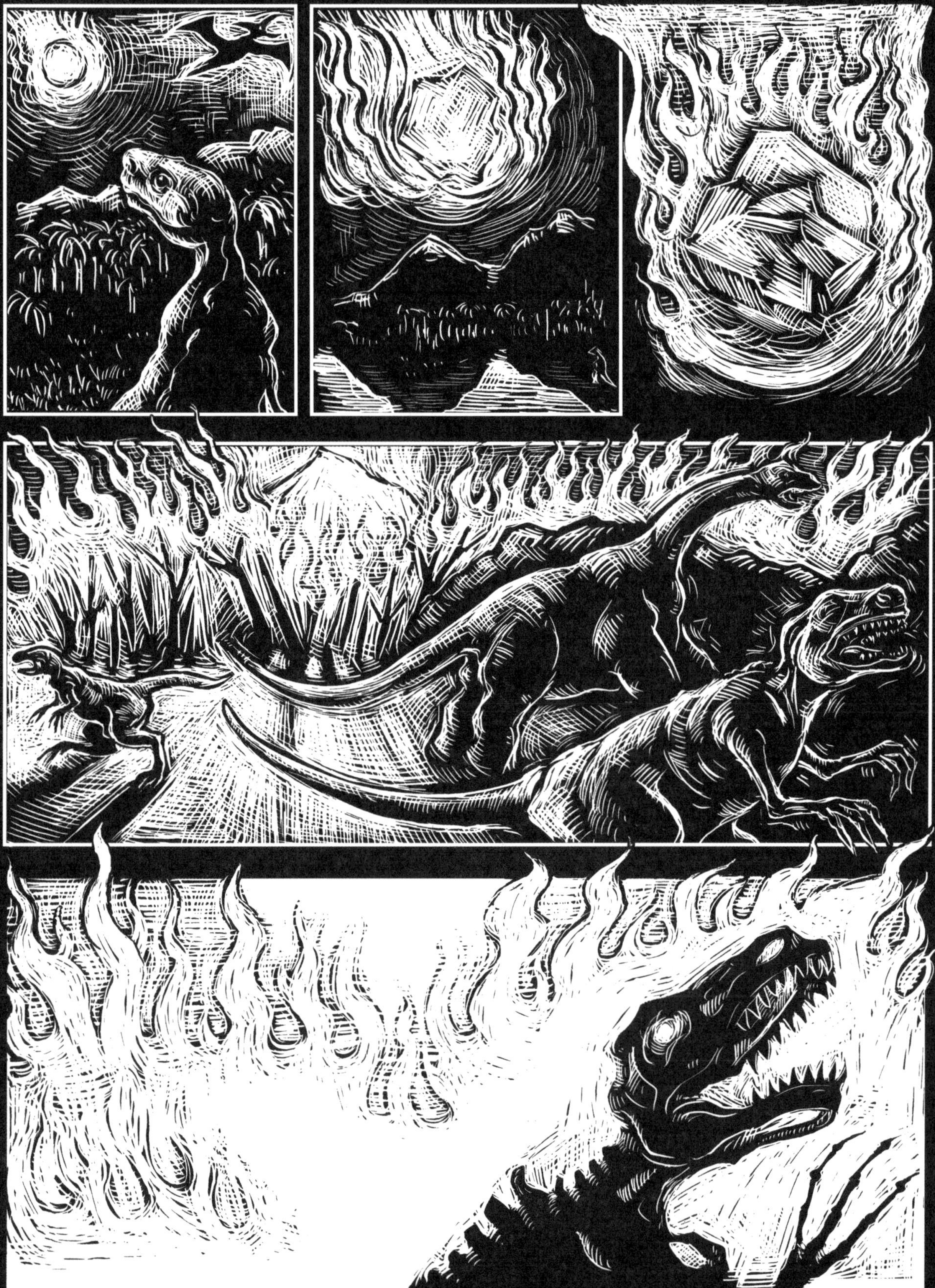

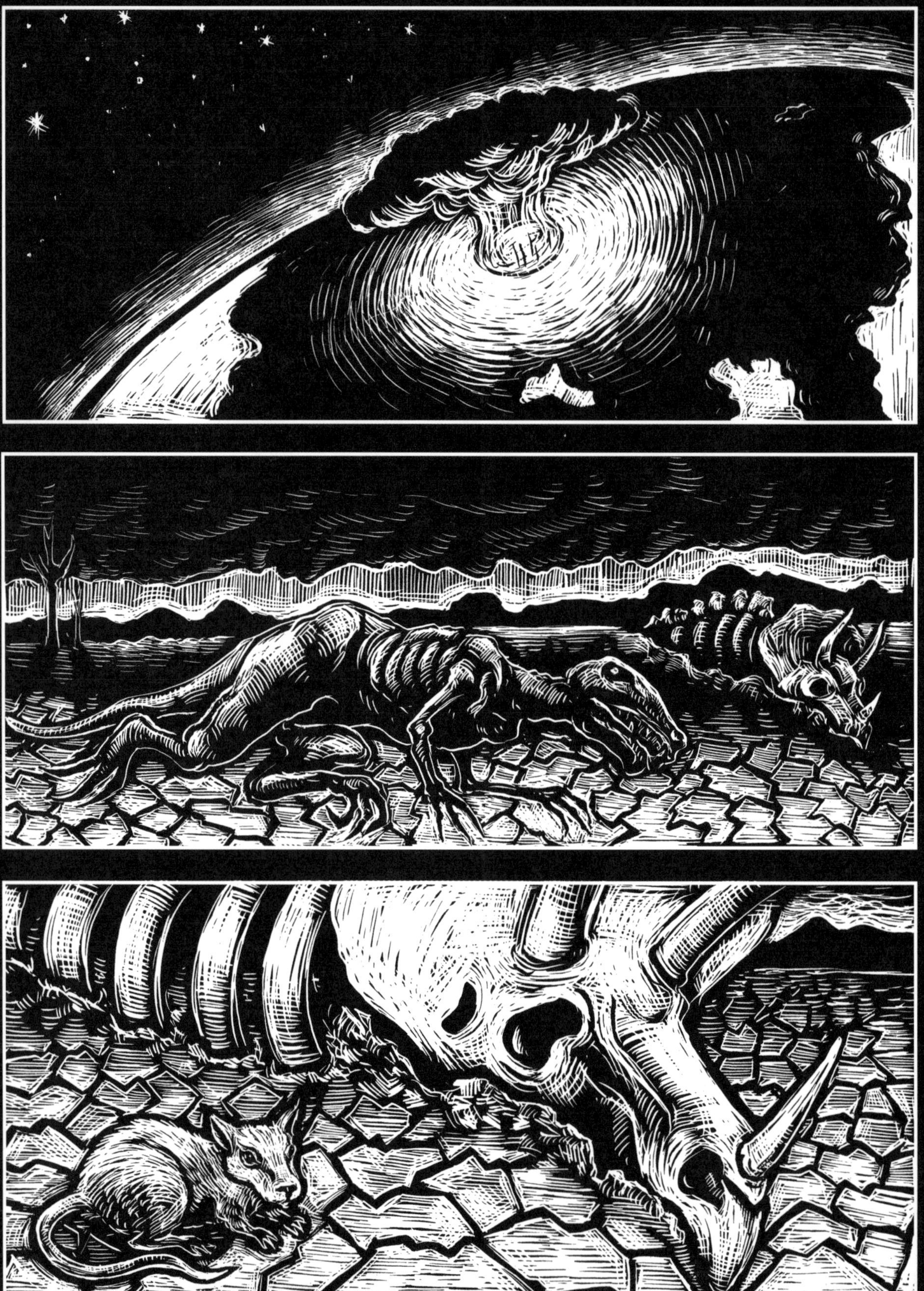

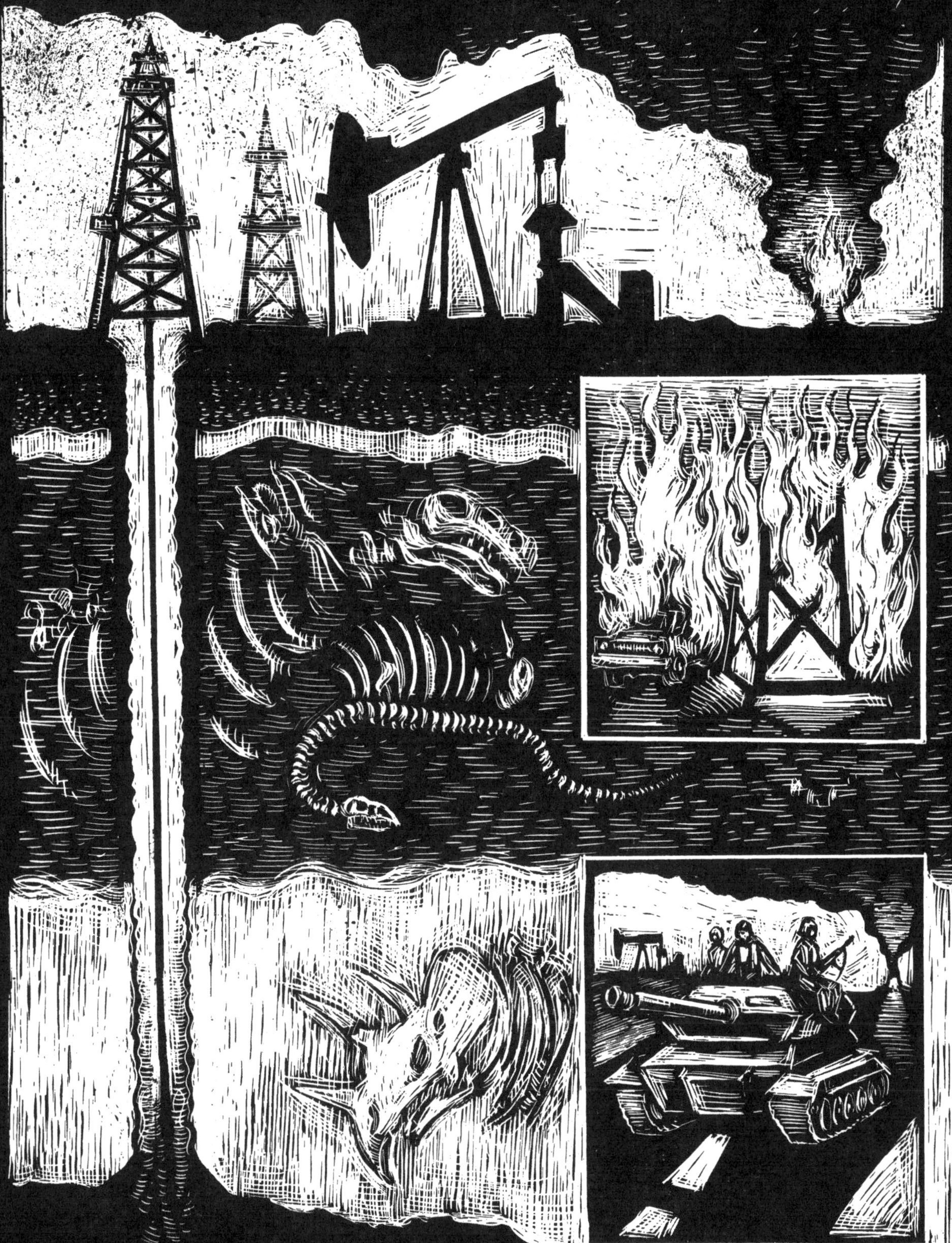

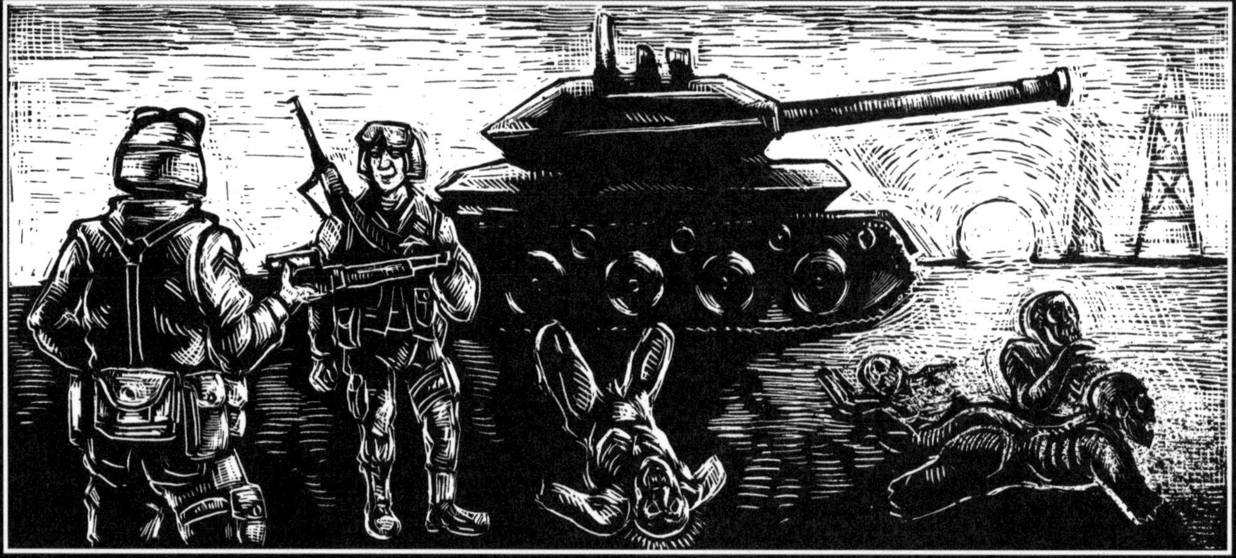
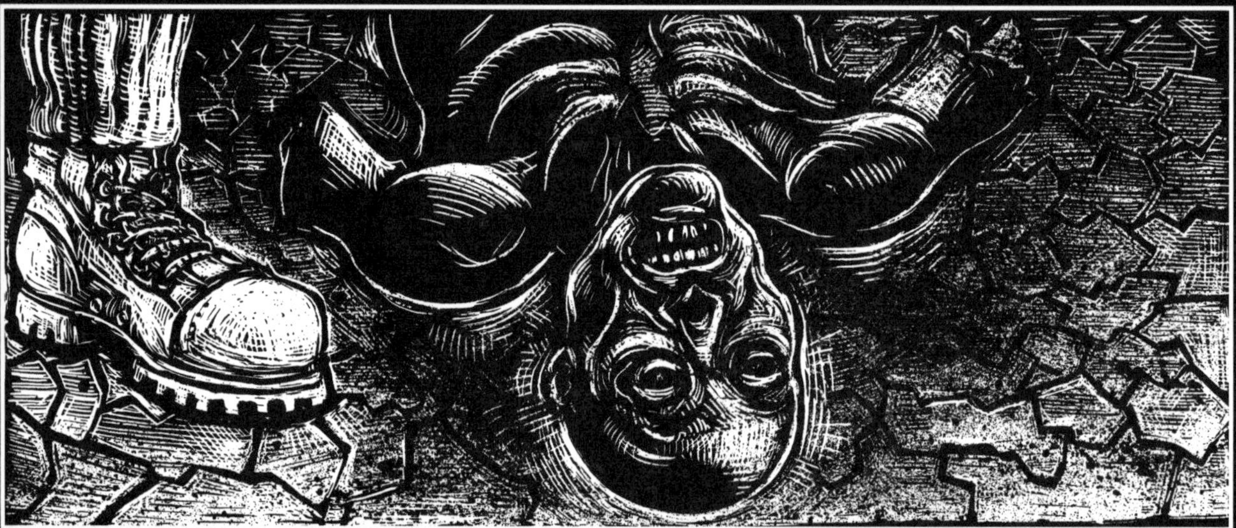
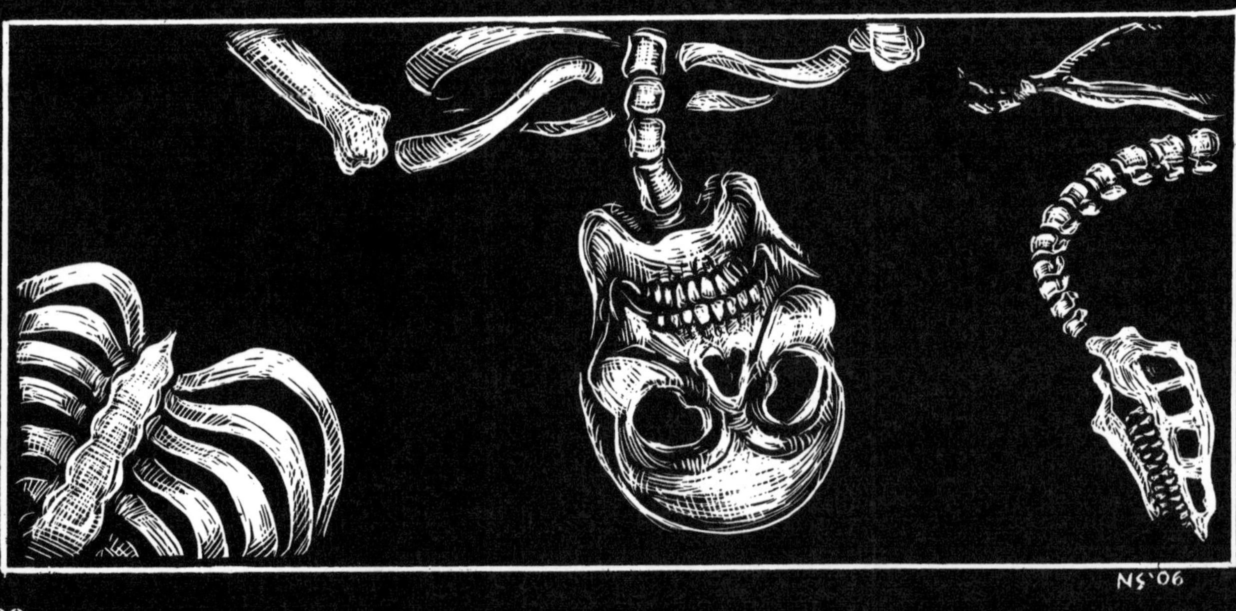
NS'06

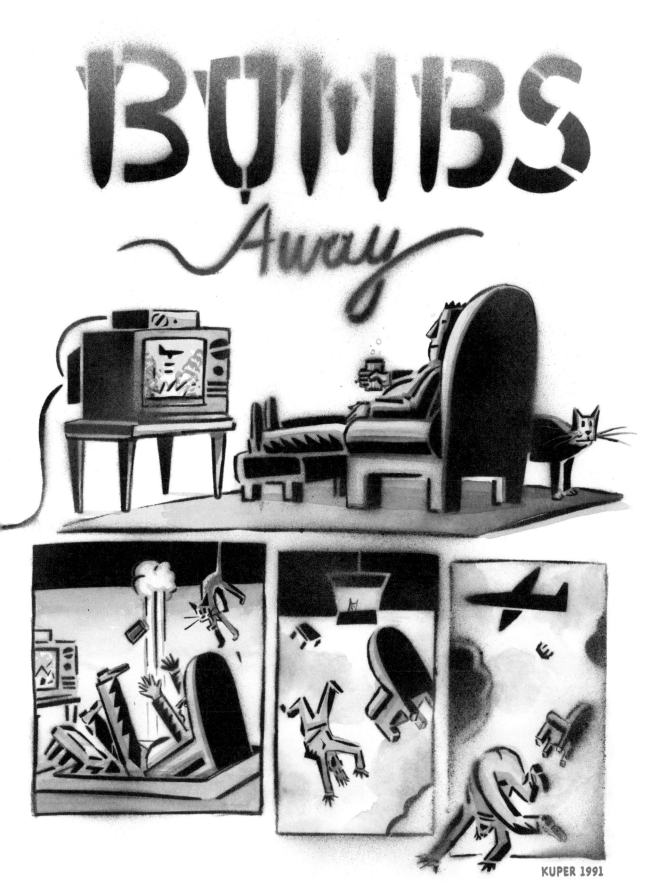

BOMBS

Away

KUPER 1991

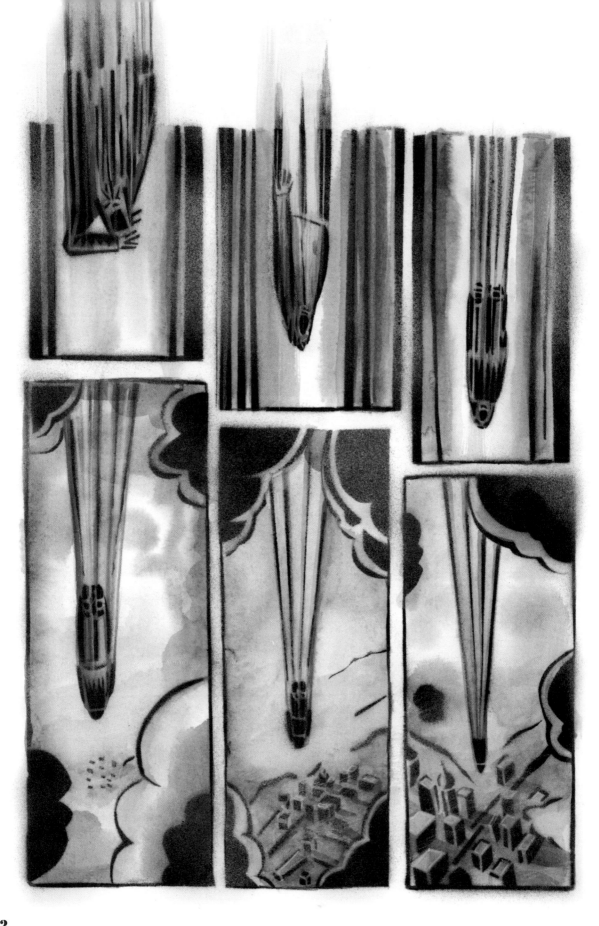

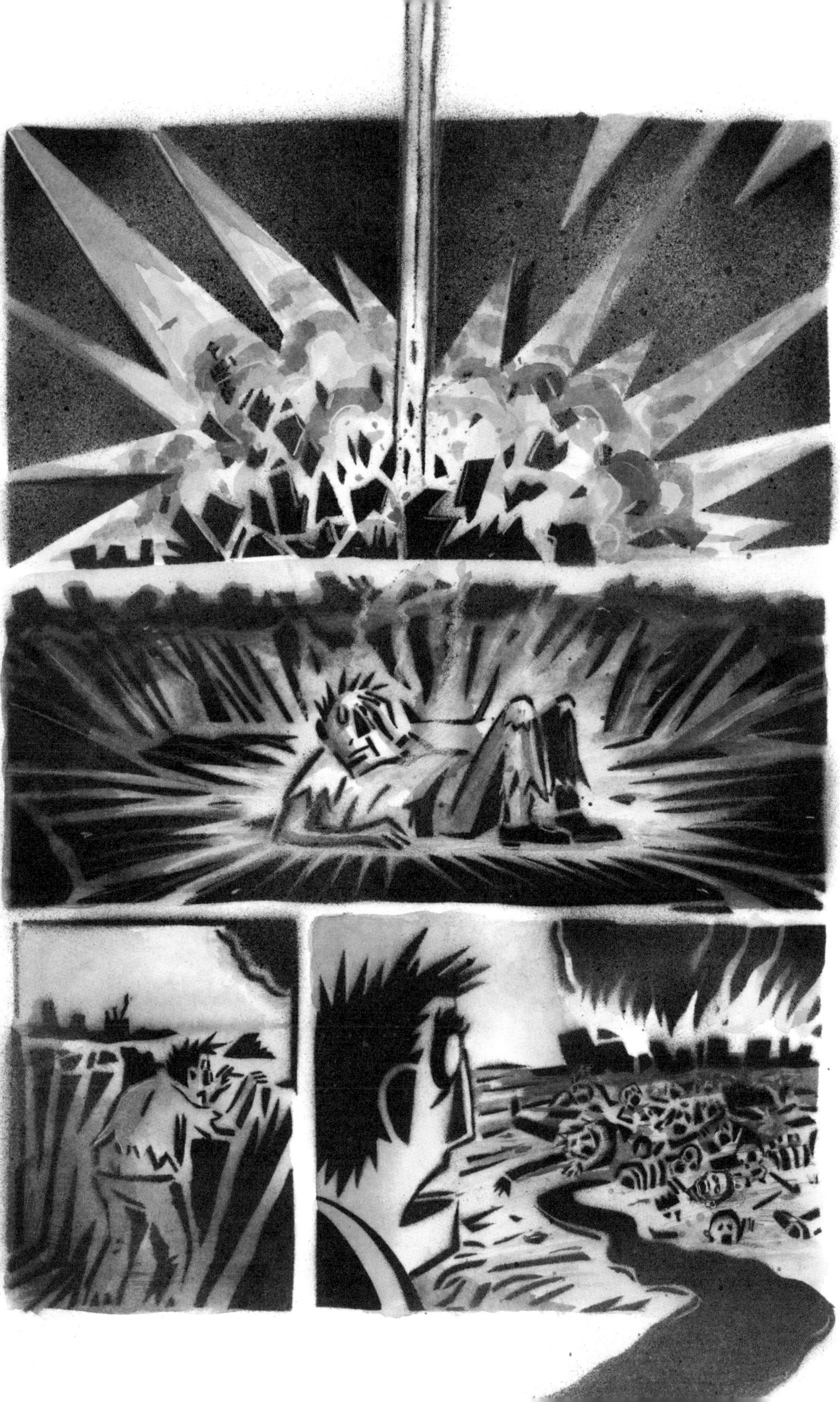

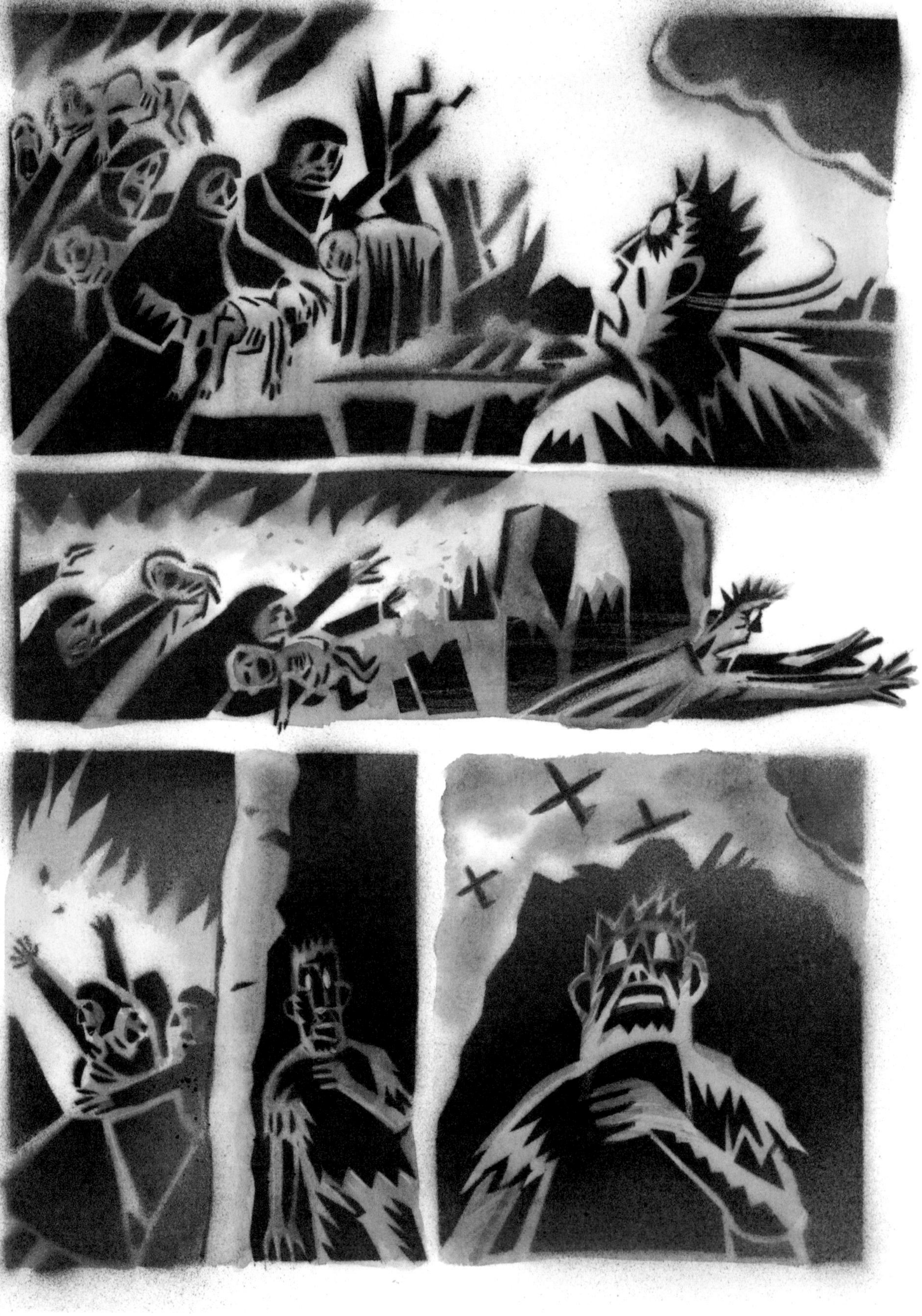

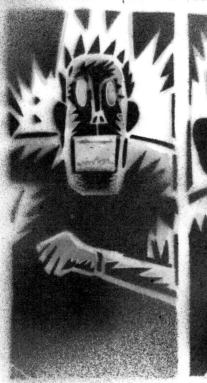

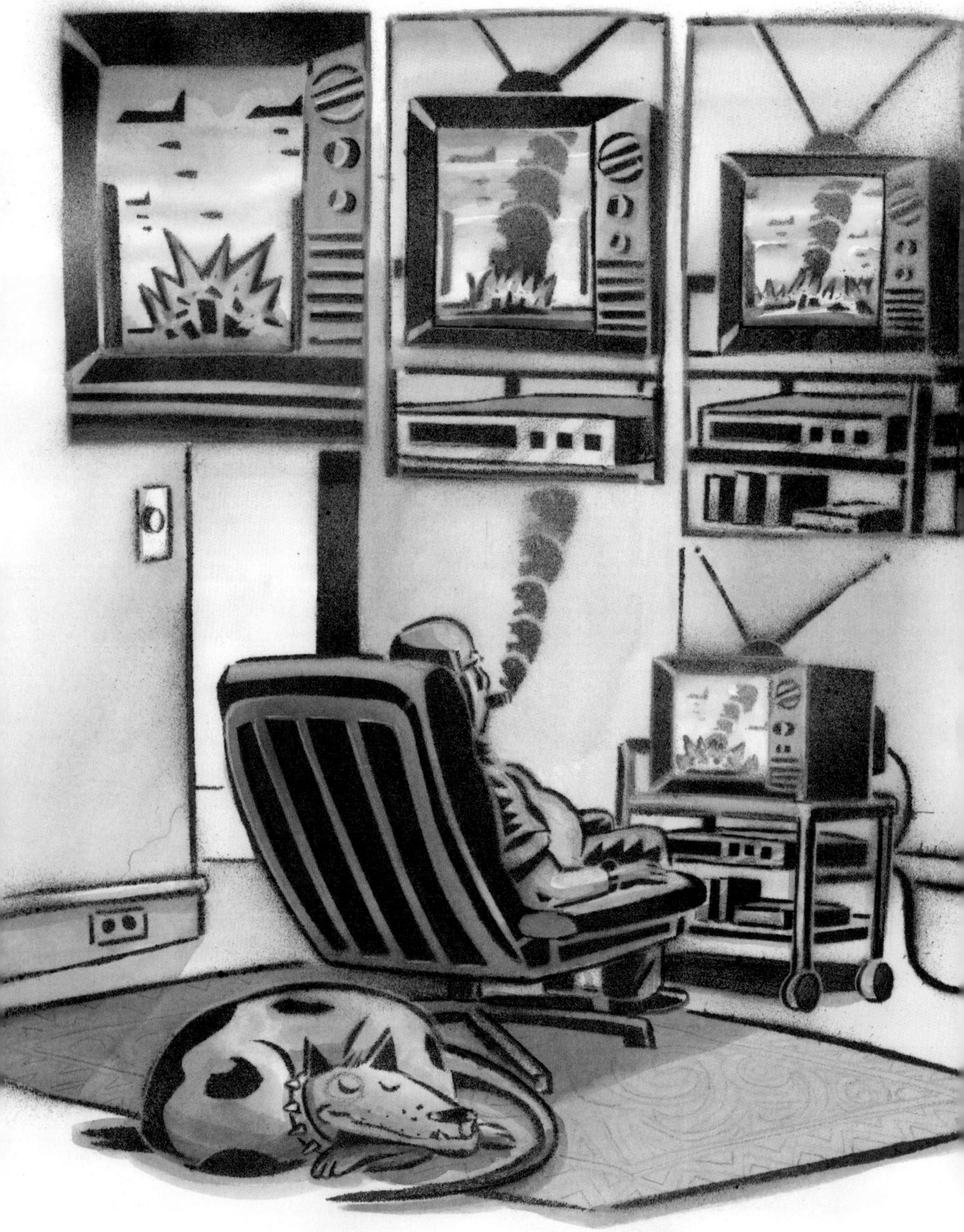

HEY, AMERICAN PROSPECT READER!
ARE YOU A REAL AMERICAN?
TAKE THIS QUIZ AND FIND OUT!

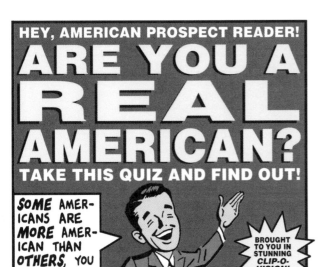

SOME AMERICANS ARE MORE AMERICAN THAN OTHERS, YOU KNOW!

BROUGHT TO YOU IN STUNNING CLIP-O-VISION!

ARE YOU **COMPLETELY UNINTERESTED** IN THE ROOTS AND/OR GEOPOLITICAL CONTEXT OF OUR CURRENT CONFLICT?

YES ☐ ← CHOOSE ONE → ☐ NO

DO YOU THINK IT WOULD BE **UNPATRIOTIC** OF THE DEMOCRATS TO OPPOSE CORPORATE TAX CUTS AND OIL DRILLING IN THE ALASKAN WILDERNESS AT A TIME LIKE THIS?

YES ☐ ← CHOOSE ONE → ☐ NO

ARE YOU **BLISSFULLY UNTROUBLED** BY SECRET SEARCHES, INDEFINITE DETENTIONS AND MILITARY TRIBUNALS--AS LONG AS THEY HAPPEN TO **SOMEONE ELSE**?

YES ☐ ← CHOOSE ONE → ☐ NO

AND FINALLY--DO YOU DRAW STRENGTH FROM YOUR **UNWAVERING FAITH** IN AN INVISIBLE, OMNISCIENT DIETY WHO LIVES IN A MAGICAL KINGDOM IN THE SKY SOMEWHERE?

YES ☐ ← CHOOSE ONE → ☐ NO

IF YOU ANSWERED "NO" TO ANY OF THESE QUESTIONS, IT'S INDISPUTABLE:
YOU ARE *NOT* A REAL AMERICAN!

WHY DON'T YOU JUST GO BACK TO YOUR **CAVE** IN **AFGHANISTAN**?

BUT--I LIVE IN **KANSAS**!

SORRY! BETTER LUCK NEXT TIME!

© 2001 TOM TOMORROW

207

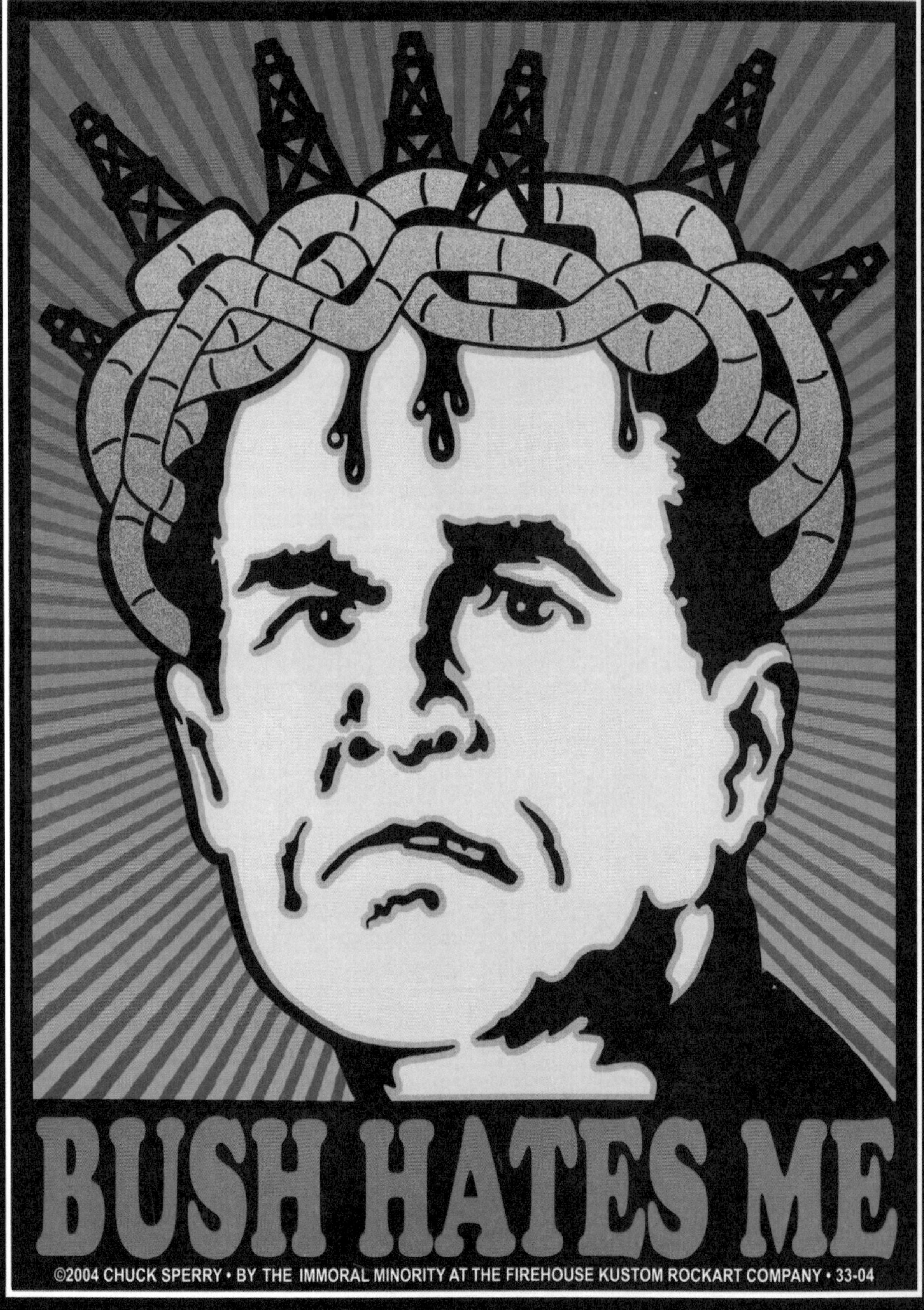
BUSH HATES ME
©2004 CHUCK SPERRY • BY THE IMMORAL MINORITY AT THE FIREHOUSE KUSTOM ROCKART COMPANY • 33-04

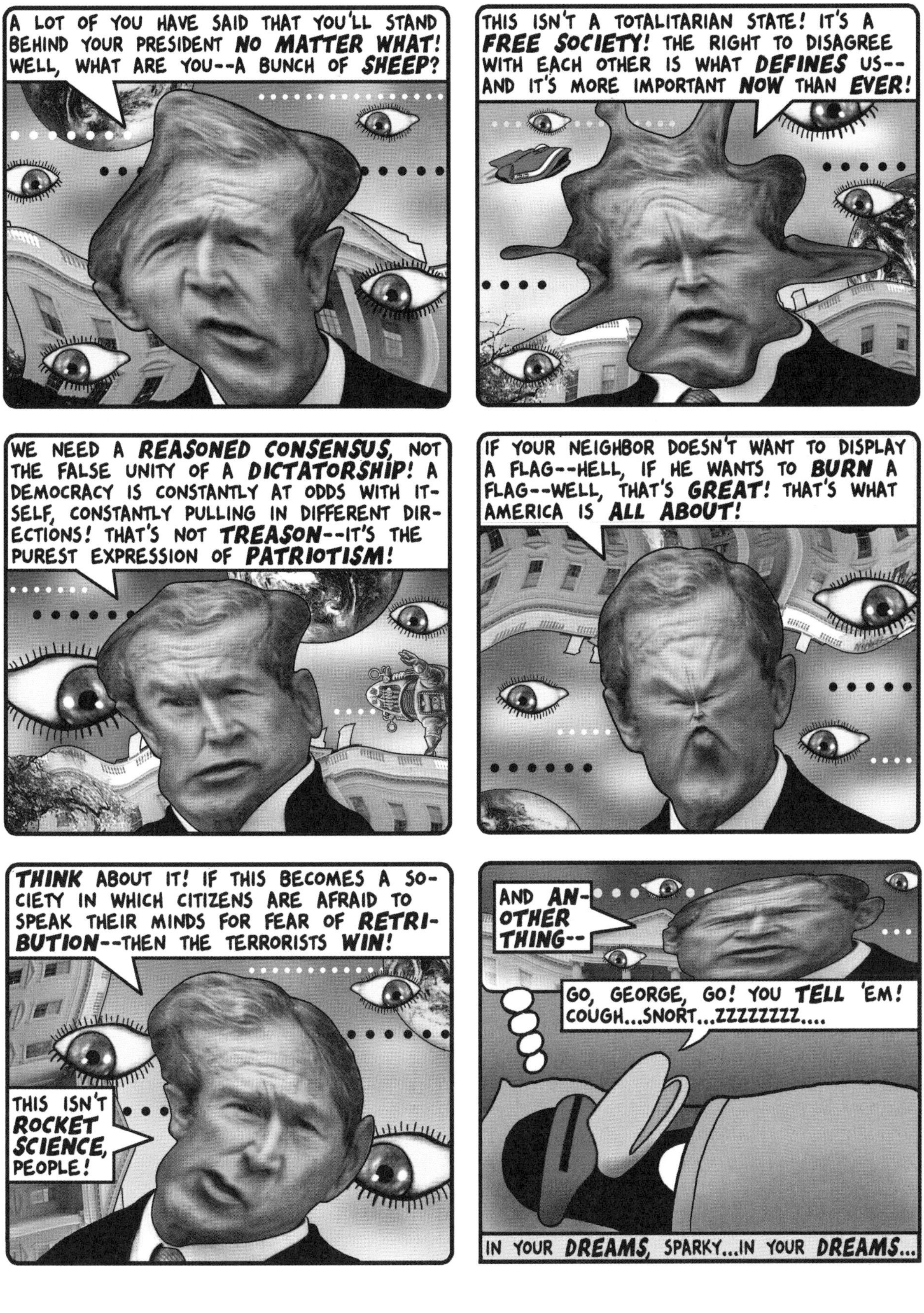

A LOT OF YOU HAVE SAID THAT YOU'LL STAND BEHIND YOUR PRESIDENT NO MATTER WHAT! WELL, WHAT ARE YOU--A BUNCH OF SHEEP?
THIS ISN'T A TOTALITARIAN STATE! IT'S A FREE SOCIETY! THE RIGHT TO DISAGREE WITH EACH OTHER IS WHAT DEFINES US--AND IT'S MORE IMPORTANT NOW THAN EVER!
WE NEED A REASONED CONSENSUS, NOT THE FALSE UNITY OF A DICTATORSHIP! A DEMOCRACY IS CONSTANTLY AT ODDS WITH IT-SELF, CONSTANTLY PULLING IN DIFFERENT DIR-ECTIONS! THAT'S NOT TREASON--IT'S THE PUREST EXPRESSION OF PATRIOTISM!
IF YOUR NEIGHBOR DOESN'T WANT TO DISPLAY A FLAG--HELL, IF HE WANTS TO BURN A FLAG--WELL, THAT'S GREAT! THAT'S WHAT AMERICA IS ALL ABOUT!
THINK ABOUT IT! IF THIS BECOMES A SO-CIETY IN WHICH CITIZENS ARE AFRAID TO SPEAK THEIR MINDS FOR FEAR OF RETRI-BUTION--THEN THE TERRORISTS WIN!
THIS ISN'T ROCKET SCIENCE, PEOPLE!
AND AN-OTHER THING--
GO, GEORGE, GO! YOU TELL 'EM! COUGH...SNORT...ZZZZZZZZ....
IN YOUR DREAMS, SPARKY...IN YOUR DREAMS...
©2001 TOM TOMORROW

Chronicle of the New Crusade

SABRINA JONES

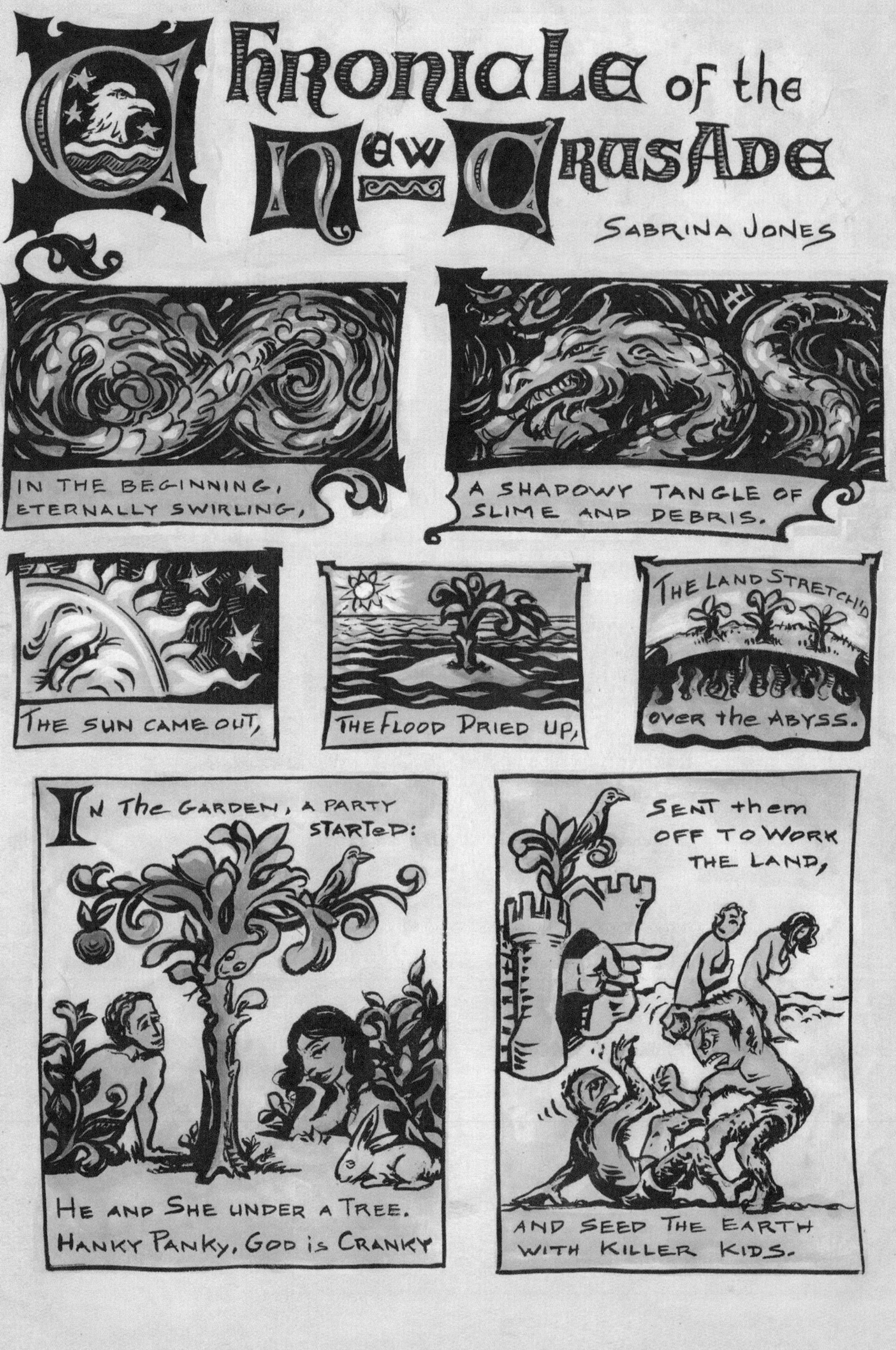
IN THE BEGINNING,
ETERNALLY SWIRLING,
A SHADOWY TANGLE OF
SLIME AND DEBRIS.
THE SUN CAME OUT,
THE FLOOD DRIED UP,
THE LAND STRETCH'D
OVER THE ABYSS.
IN THE GARDEN, A PARTY
STARTED:
HE AND SHE UNDER A TREE.
HANKY PANKY, GOD IS CRANKY
SENT THEM
OFF TO WORK
THE LAND,
AND SEED THE EARTH
WITH KILLER KIDS.

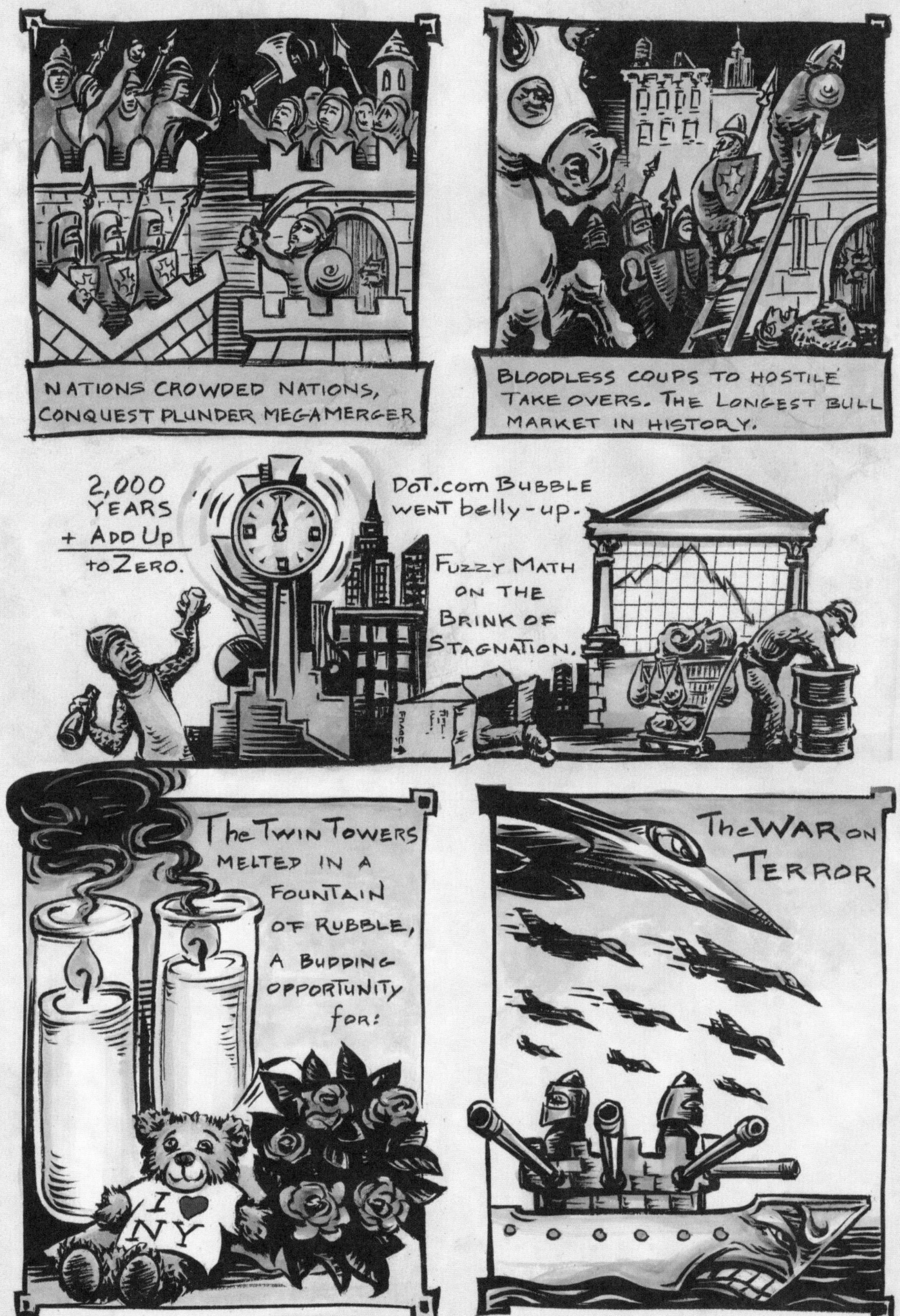

NATIONS CROWDED NATIONS, CONQUEST PLUNDER MEGAMERGER
BLOODLESS COUPS TO HOSTILE TAKE OVERS. THE LONGEST BULL MARKET IN HISTORY.
2,000 YEARS + ADD UP to ZERO.
DoT.com BUBBLE WENT belly-up.
FUZZY MATH ON THE BRINK OF STAGNATION.
The TWIN TOWERS MELTED IN A FOUNTAIN OF RUBBLE, A BUDDING OPPORTUNITY FOR:
I ♥ NY
The WAR ON TERROR

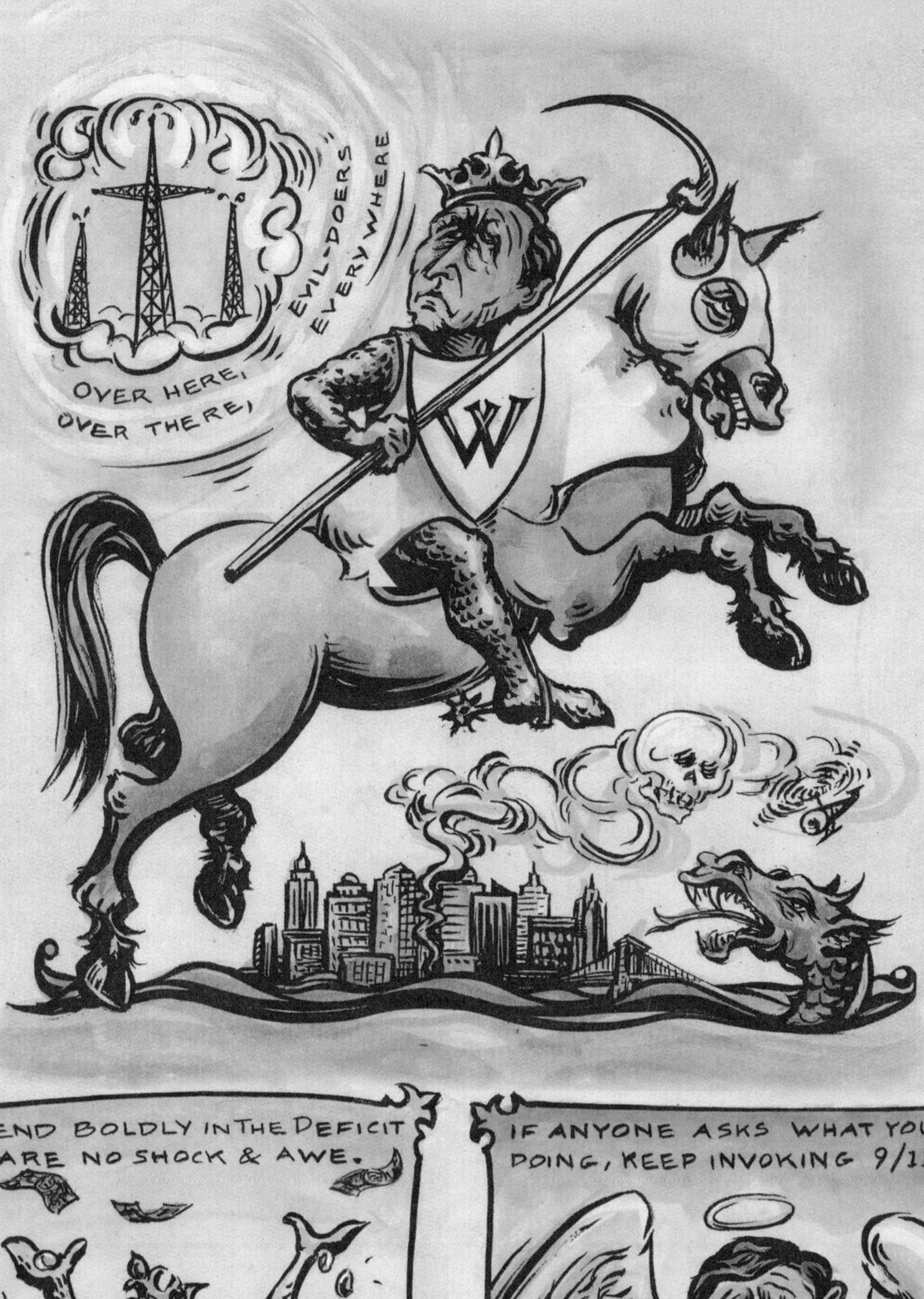
OVER HERE, OVER THERE, EVIL-DOERS EVERY WHERE

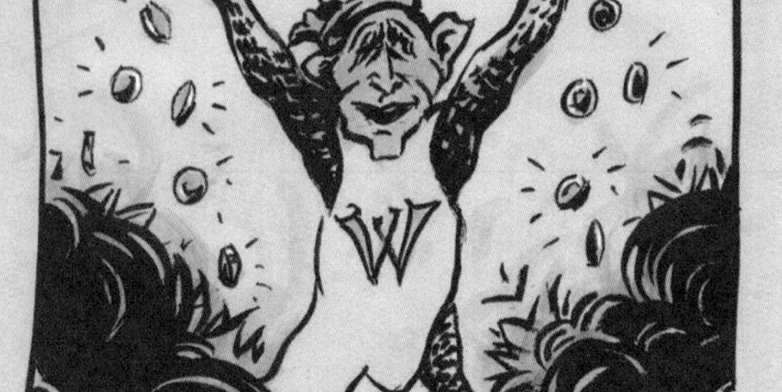
SPEND BOLDLY IN THE DEFICIT SPARE NO SHOCK & AWE.

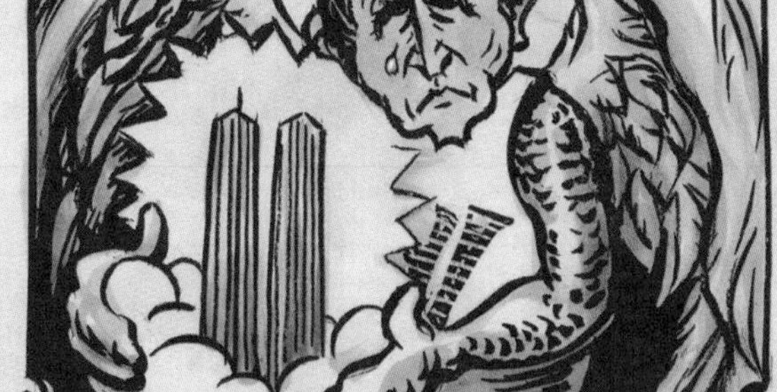
IF ANYONE ASKS WHAT YOU'RE DOING, KEEP INVOKING 9/11.

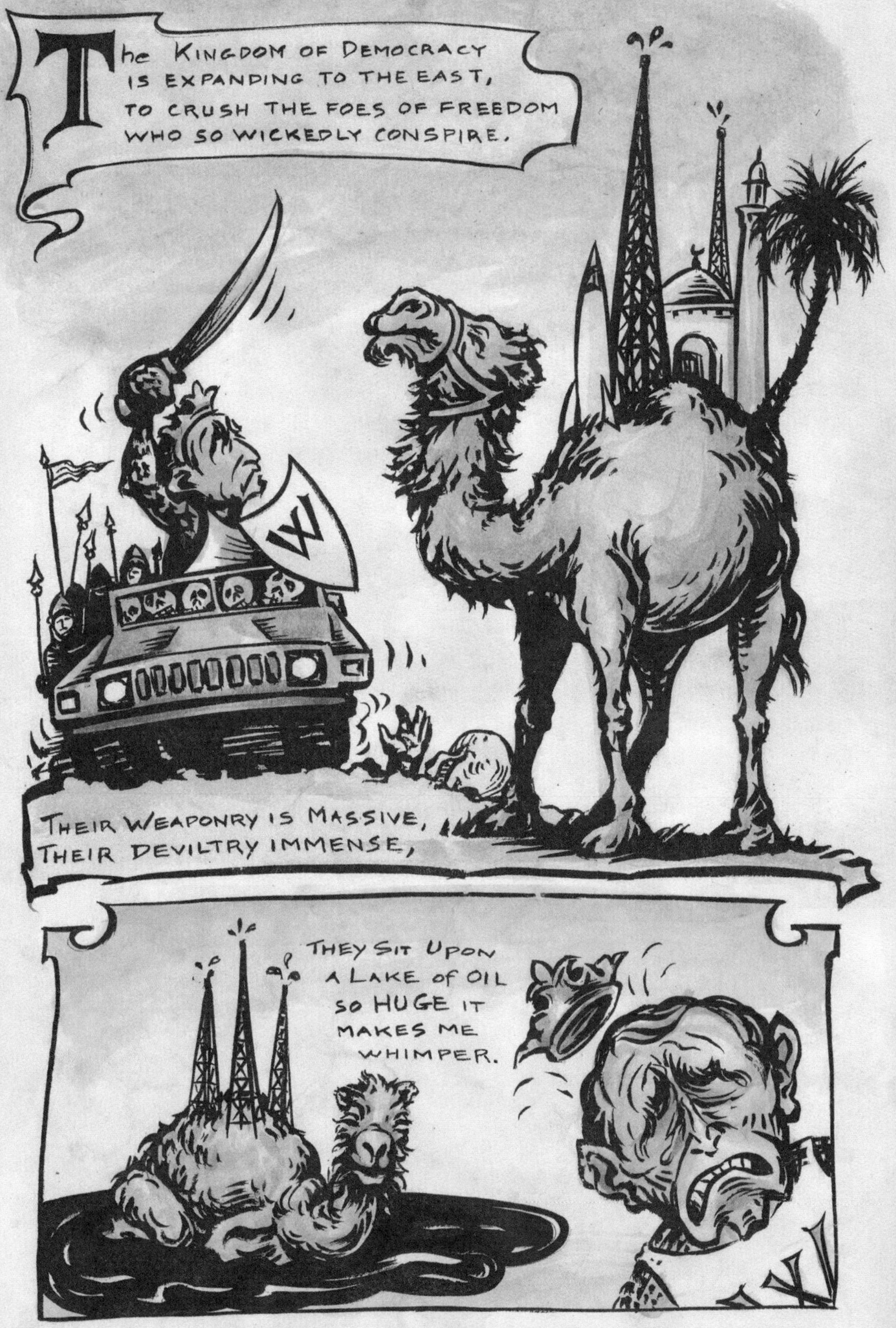
The Kingdom of Democracy
is expanding to the east,
to crush the foes of freedom
who so wickedly conspire.
Their weaponry is massive,
their deviltry immense,
They sit upon a lake of oil so HUGE it makes me whimper.

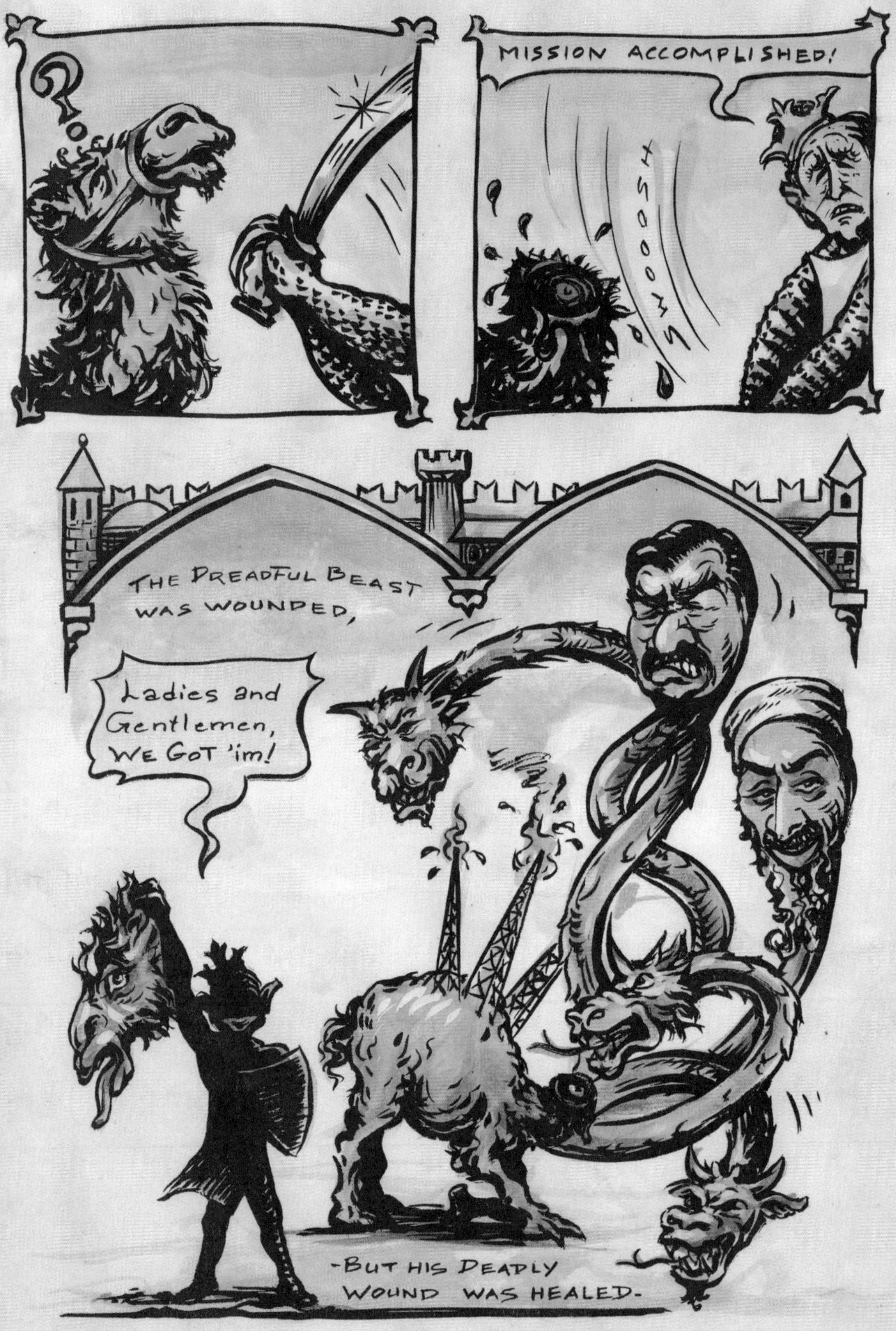
?
MISSION ACCOMPLISHED!
SWOOOOSH
THE DREADFUL BEAST WAS WOUNDED,
Ladies and Gentlemen, WE GOT 'im!
-BUT HIS DEADLY WOUND WAS HEALED-

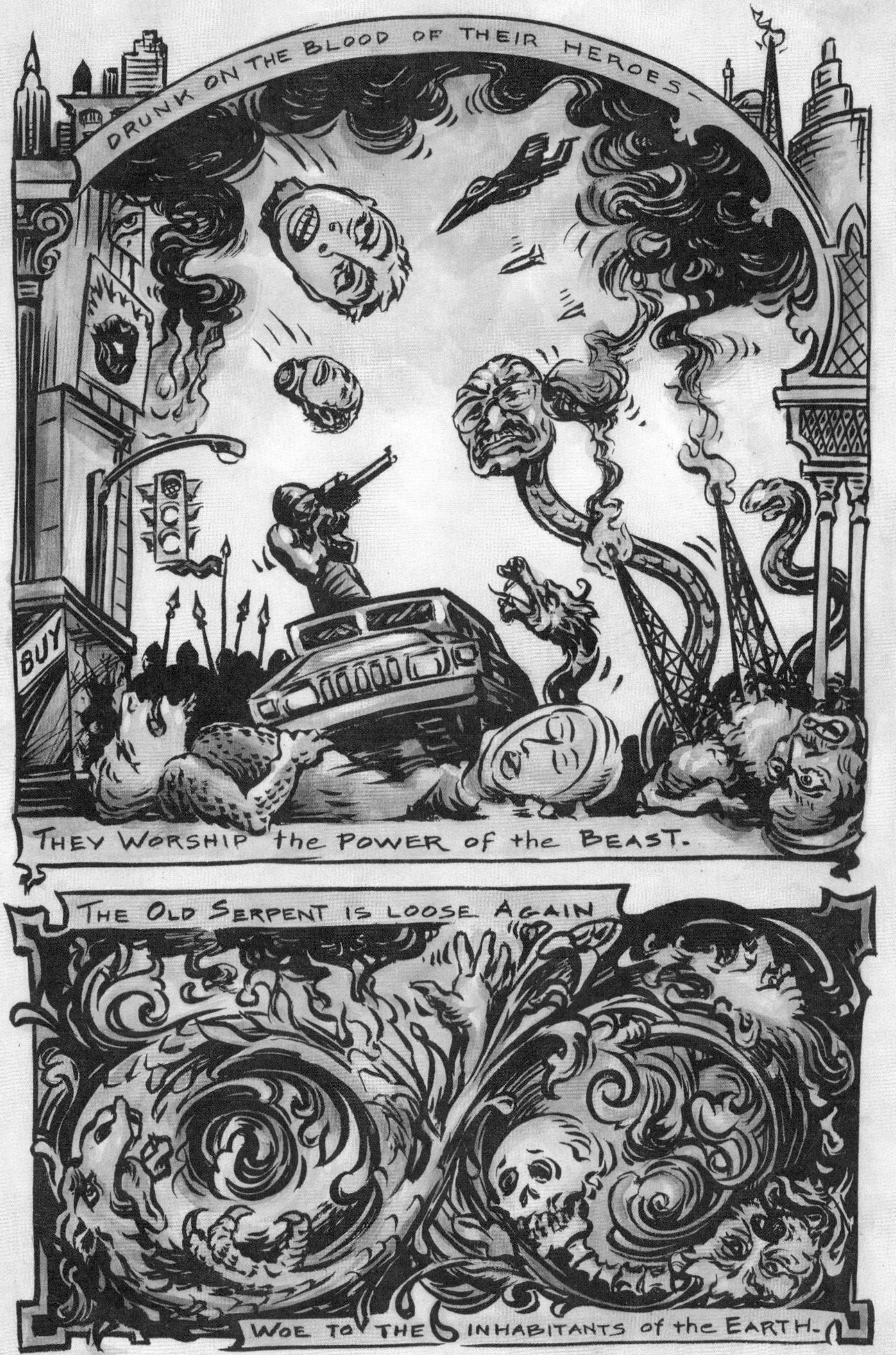
DRUNK ON THE BLOOD OF THEIR HEROES—
BUY
THEY WORSHIP the POWER of the BEAST.
THE OLD SERPENT IS LOOSE AGAIN
WOE TO THE INHABITANTS of the EARTH.

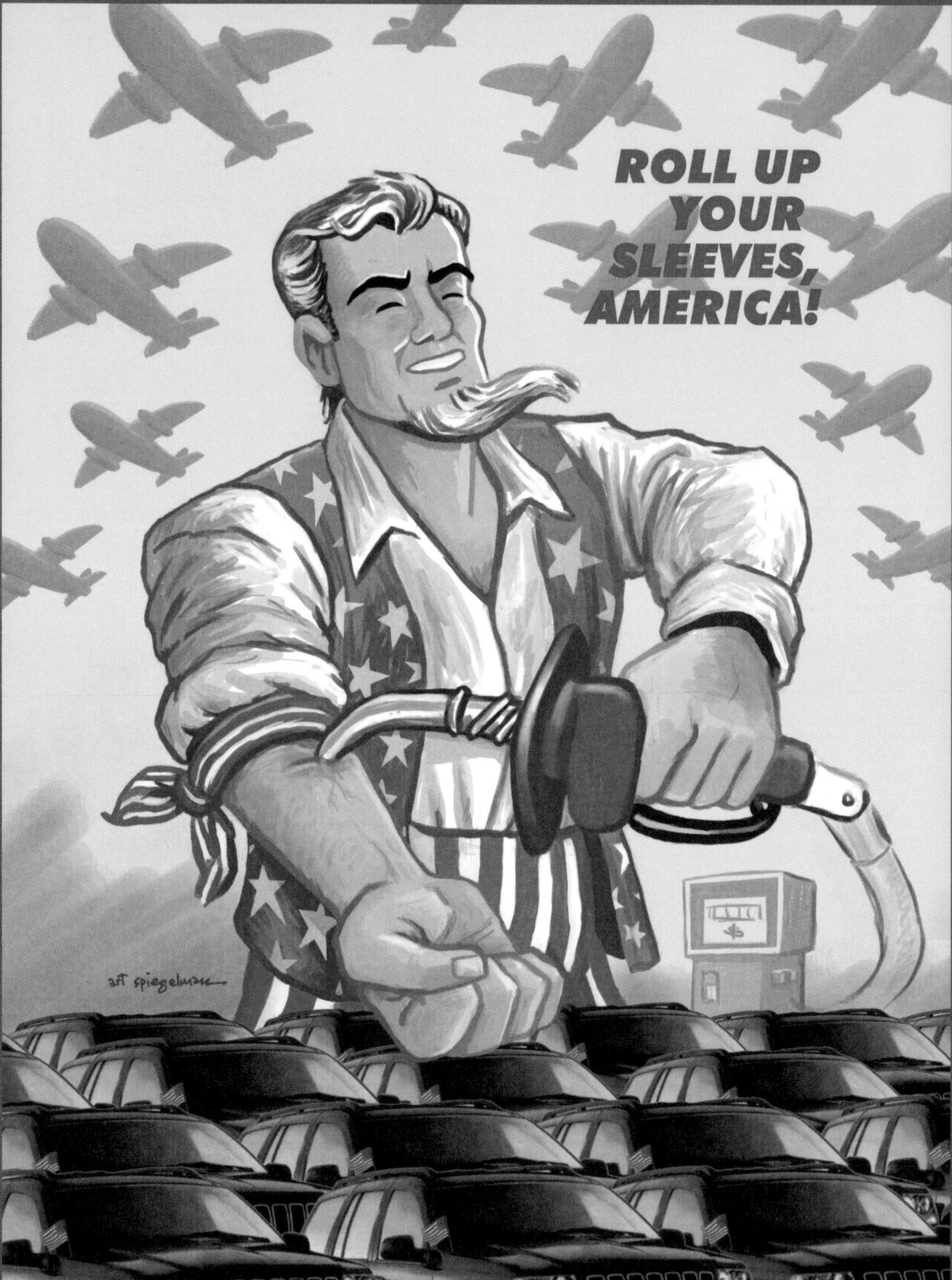
ROLL UP YOUR SLEEVES, AMERICA!
art spiegelman

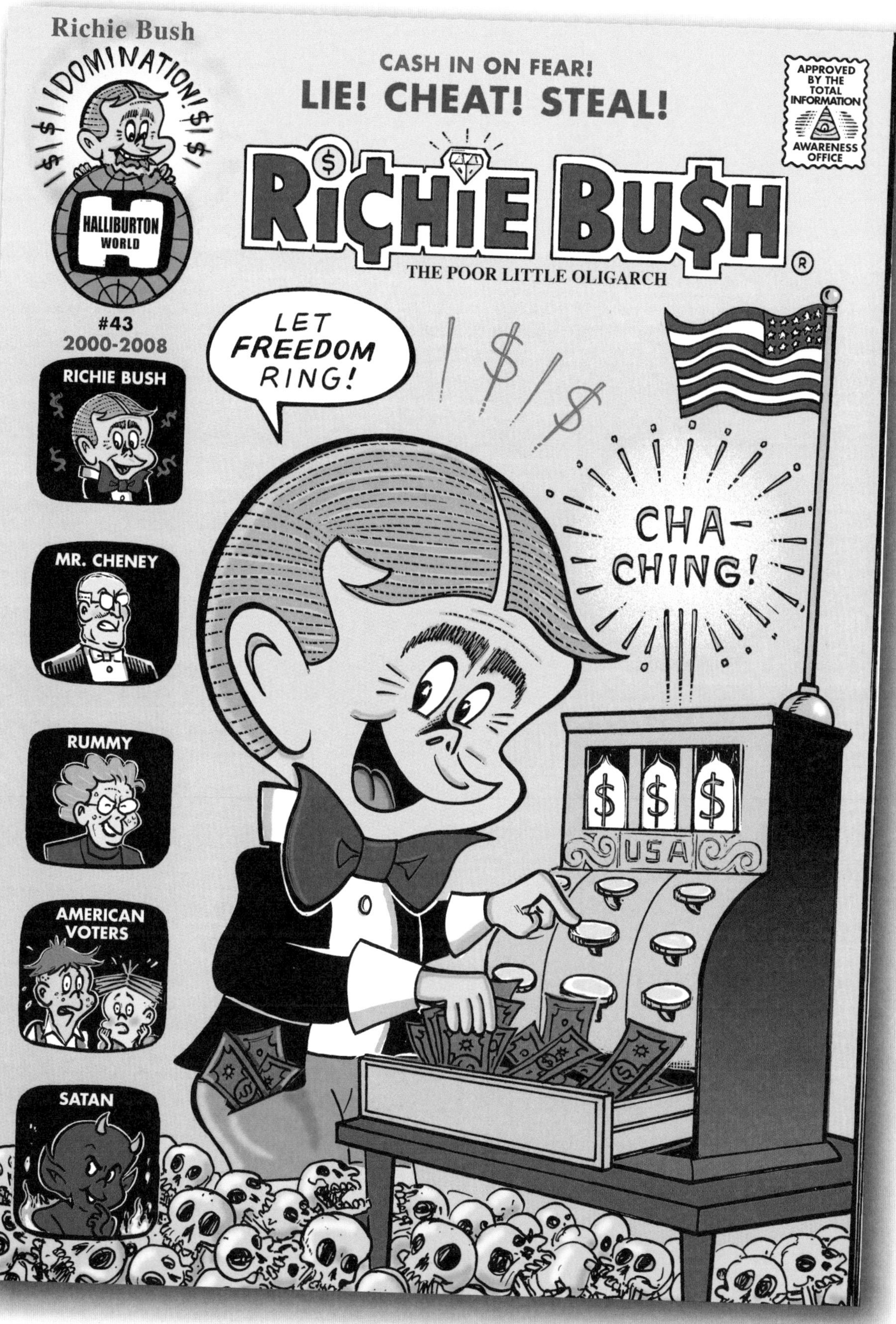
Richie Bush
$!$!!DOMINATION!!$!$
HALLIBURTON WORLD
#43
2000-2008
RICHIE BUSH
MR. CHENEY
RUMMY
AMERICAN VOTERS
SATAN
CASH IN ON FEAR!
LIE! CHEAT! STEAL!
APPROVED BY THE TOTAL INFORMATION AWARENESS OFFICE
RI¢HIE BU$H
THE POOR LITTLE OLIGARCH
LET FREEDOM RING!
CHA-CHING!
USA

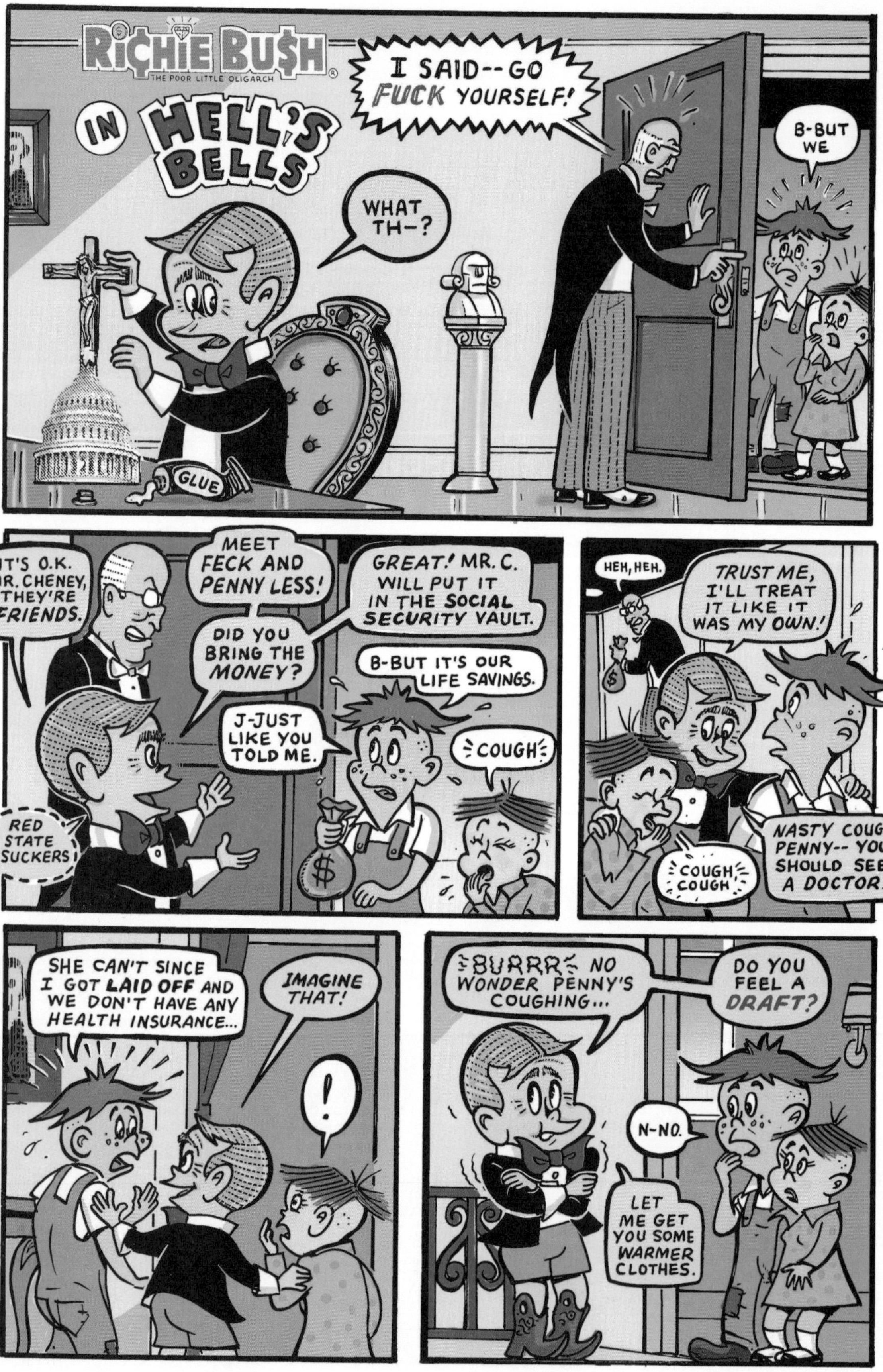
RICHIE BU$H
THE POOR LITTLE OLIGARCH
IN HELL'S BELLS
I SAID--GO FUCK YOURSELF!
B-BUT WE
WHAT TH-?
GLUE
IT'S O.K. MR. CHENEY, THEY'RE FRIENDS.
MEET FECK AND PENNY LESS!
DID YOU BRING THE MONEY?
GREAT! MR. C. WILL PUT IT IN THE SOCIAL SECURITY VAULT.
B-BUT IT'S OUR LIFE SAVINGS.
J-JUST LIKE YOU TOLD ME.
COUGH
RED STATE SUCKERS
HEH, HEH.
TRUST ME, I'LL TREAT IT LIKE IT WAS MY OWN!
COUGH COUGH
NASTY COUGH PENNY-- YOU SHOULD SEE A DOCTOR.
SHE CAN'T SINCE I GOT LAID OFF AND WE DON'T HAVE ANY HEALTH INSURANCE...
IMAGINE THAT!
!
BURRR NO WONDER PENNY'S COUGHING...
DO YOU FEEL A DRAFT?
N-NO.
LET ME GET YOU SOME WARMER CLOTHES.

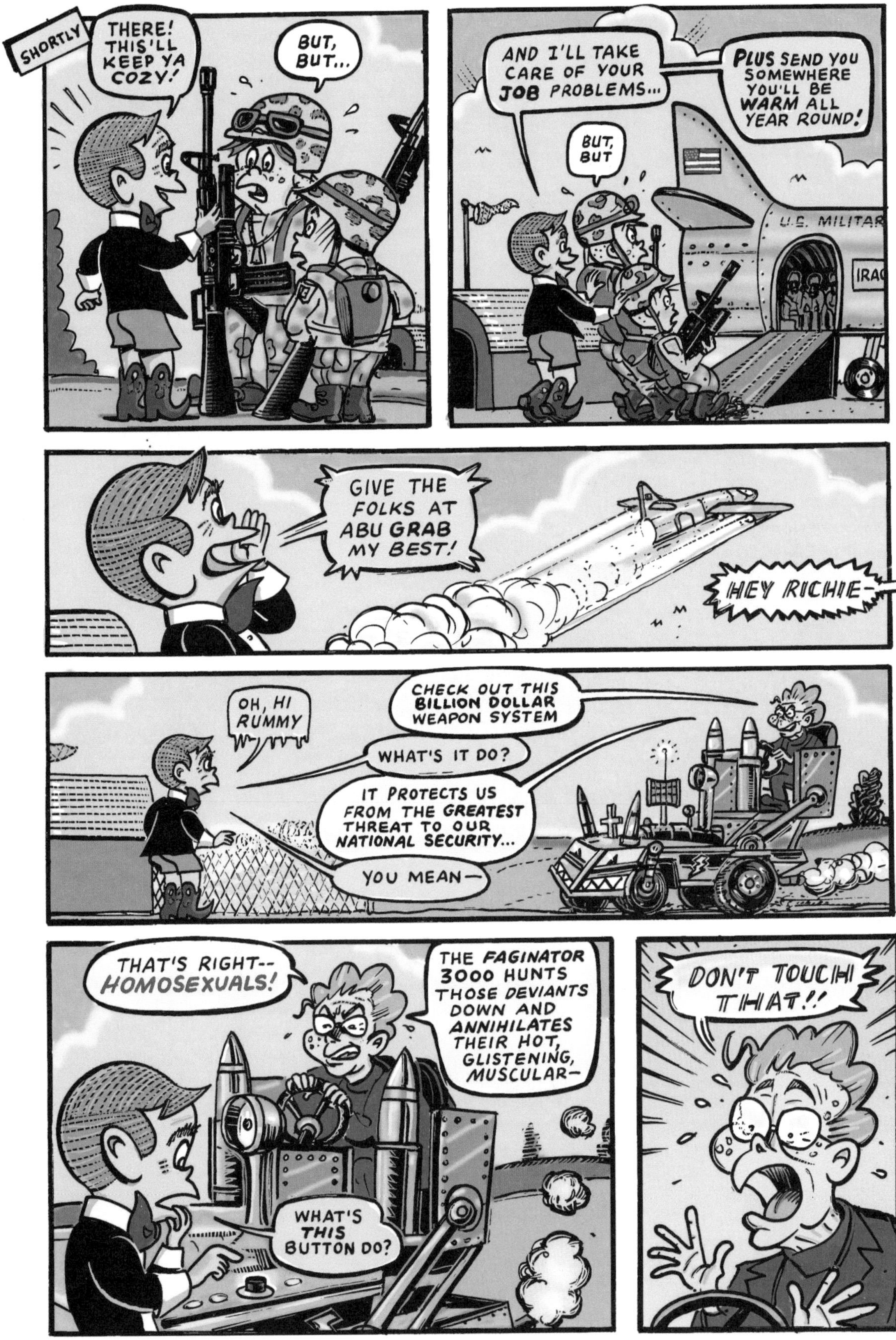
SHORTLY
THERE! THIS'LL KEEP YA COZY!
BUT, BUT...
AND I'LL TAKE CARE OF YOUR JOB PROBLEMS...
PLUS SEND YOU SOMEWHERE YOU'LL BE WARM ALL YEAR ROUND!
BUT, BUT
U.S. MILITAR
IRAQ
GIVE THE FOLKS AT ABU GRAB MY BEST!
HEY RICHIE-
OH, HI RUMMY
CHECK OUT THIS BILLION DOLLAR WEAPON SYSTEM
WHAT'S IT DO?
IT PROTECTS US FROM THE GREATEST THREAT TO OUR NATIONAL SECURITY...
YOU MEAN—
THAT'S RIGHT-- HOMOSEXUALS!
THE FAGINATOR 3000 HUNTS THOSE DEVIANTS DOWN AND ANNIHILATES THEIR HOT, GLISTENING, MUSCULAR—
WHAT'S THIS BUTTON DO?
DON'T TOUCH THAT!!

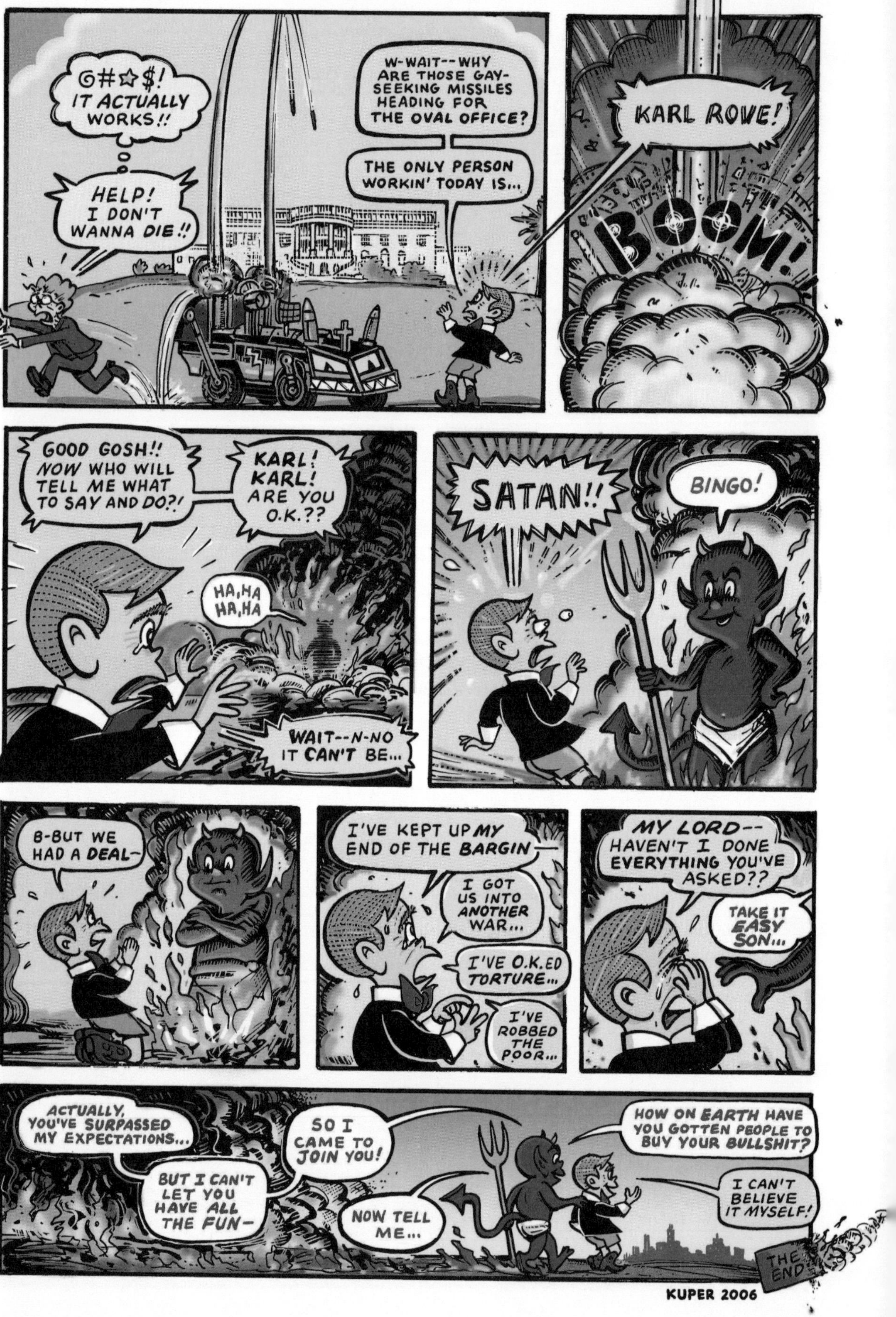

@#✩$! IT ACTUALLY WORKS!!
HELP! I DON'T WANNA DIE!!
W-WAIT--WHY ARE THOSE GAY-SEEKING MISSILES HEADING FOR THE OVAL OFFICE?
THE ONLY PERSON WORKIN' TODAY IS...
KARL ROVE!
BOOM!
GOOD GOSH!! NOW WHO WILL TELL ME WHAT TO SAY AND DO?!
KARL! KARL! ARE YOU O.K.??
HA,HA HA,HA
WAIT--N-NO IT CAN'T BE...
SATAN!!
BINGO!
B-BUT WE HAD A DEAL-
I'VE KEPT UP MY END OF THE BARGIN—
I GOT US INTO ANOTHER WAR...
I'VE O.K.ED TORTURE...
I'VE ROBBED THE POOR...
MY LORD-- HAVEN'T I DONE EVERYTHING YOU'VE ASKED??
TAKE IT EASY SON...
ACTUALLY, YOU'VE SURPASSED MY EXPECTATIONS...
BUT I CAN'T LET YOU HAVE ALL THE FUN-
SO I CAME TO JOIN YOU!
NOW TELL ME...
HOW ON EARTH HAVE YOU GOTTEN PEOPLE TO BUY YOUR BULLSHIT?
I CAN'T BELIEVE IT MYSELF!
THE END
KUPER 2006

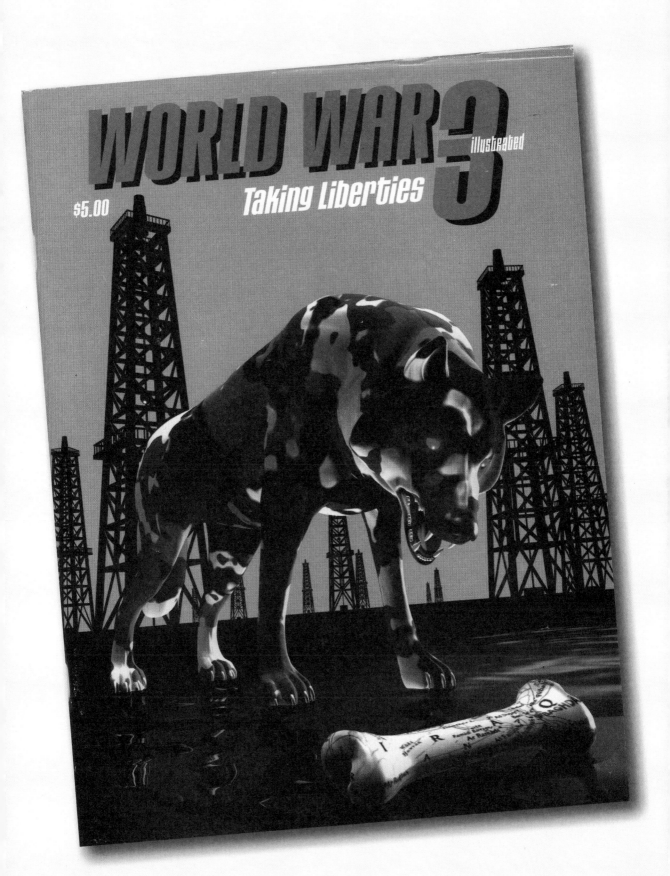

WORLD WAR 3

illustrated

Taking Liberties

$5.00

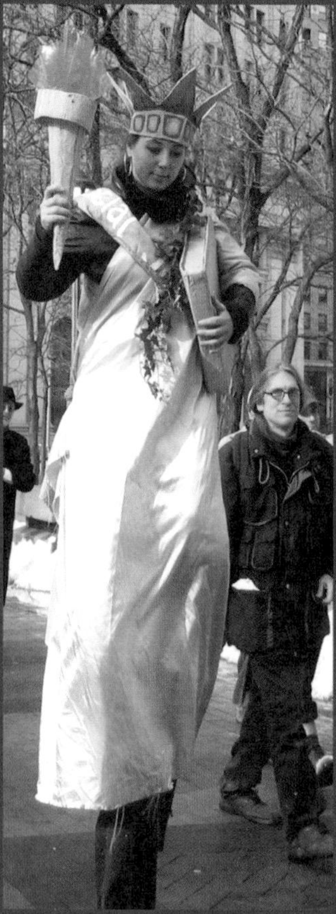

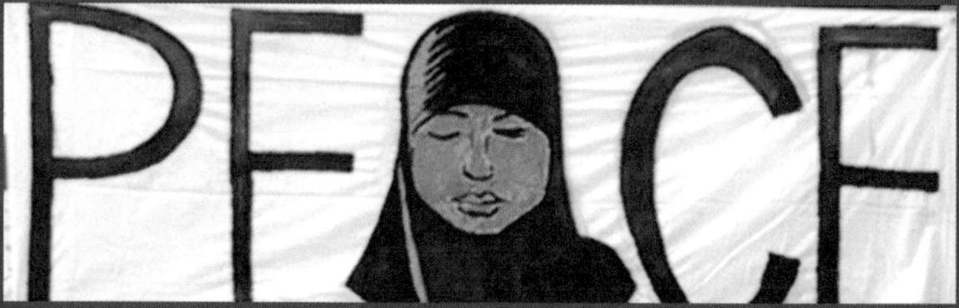
PEACE

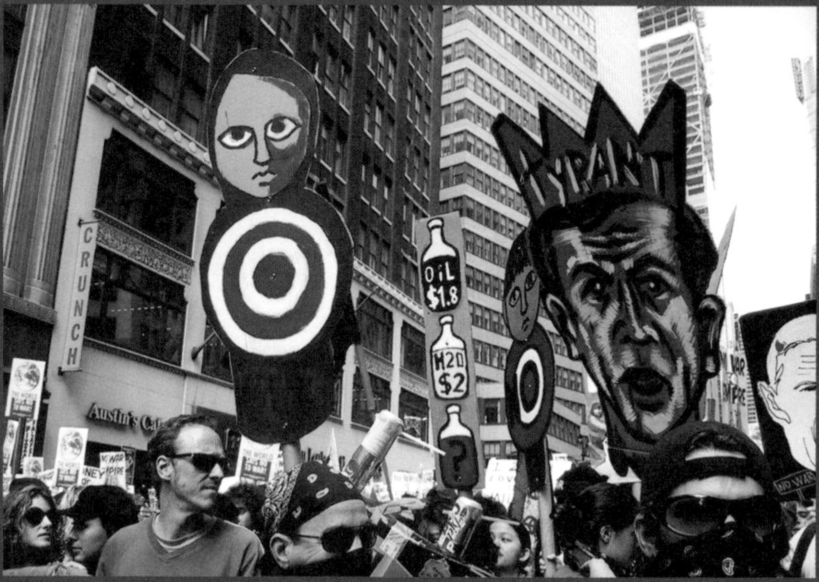
CRUNCH
OIL $1.8
H2O $2

AGAINST THE WAR IN IRAQ! Artists: Chris Cardinale, Samantha Wilson, Seth Tobocman, Paula Hewitt, Mary Frank, Kevin C. Pyle, Ketchup, Carlo Quispe, Nicole Schulman, Nancy Kogel, Sabrina Jones, others. Photos: Fred Askew, Chris Cardinale, others.

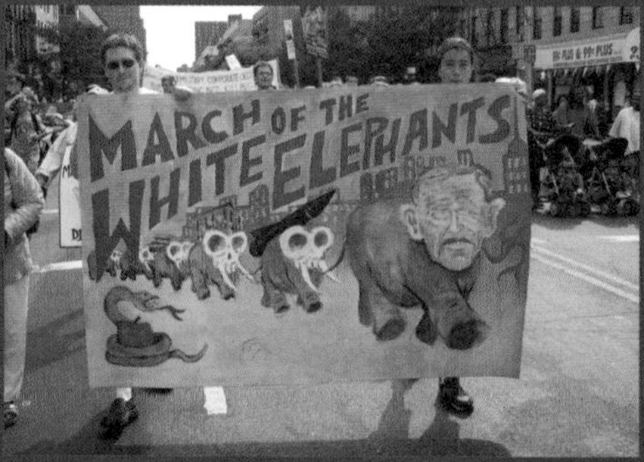
MARCH OF THE WHITE ELEPHANTS

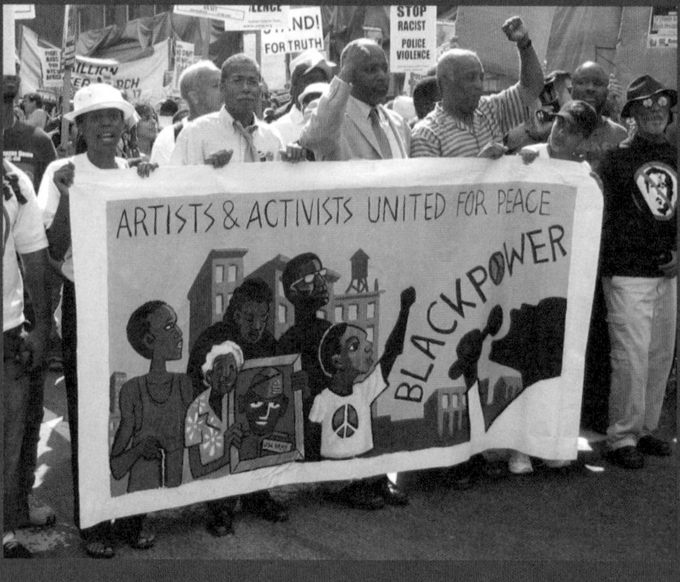
STOP RACIST POLICE VIOLENCE
FOR TRUTH
ARTISTS & ACTIVISTS UNITED FOR PEACE
BLACK POWER

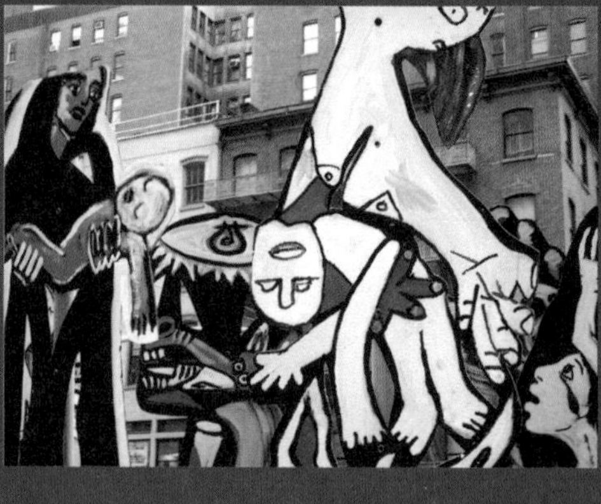

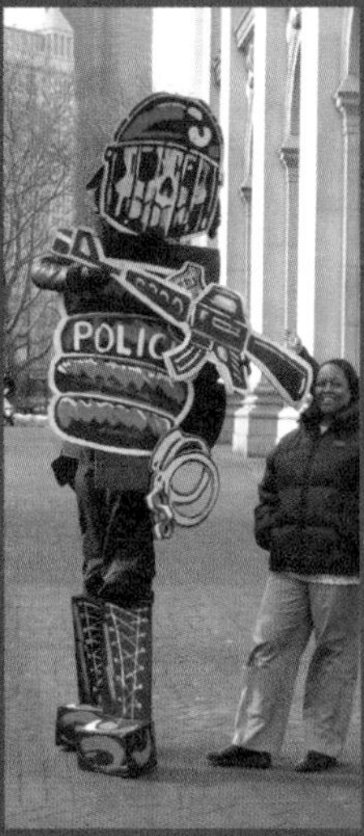
POLIC

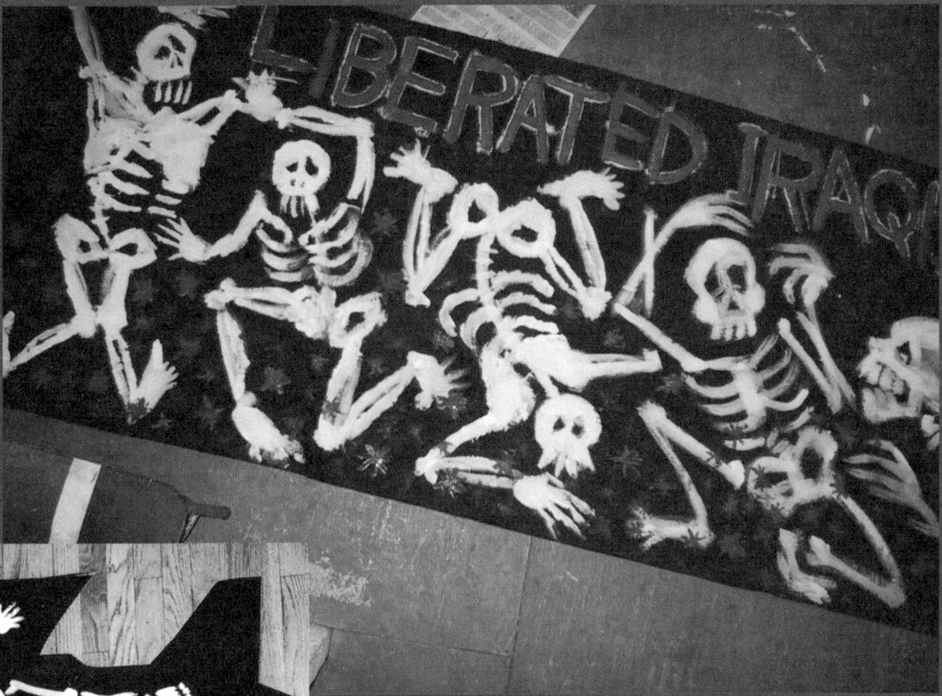
LIBERATED IRAQ

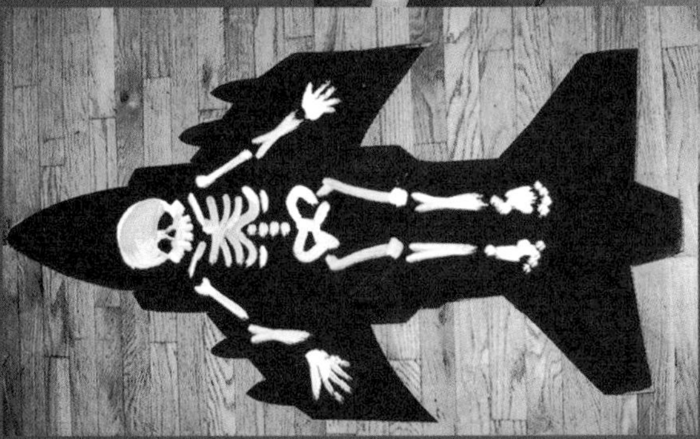

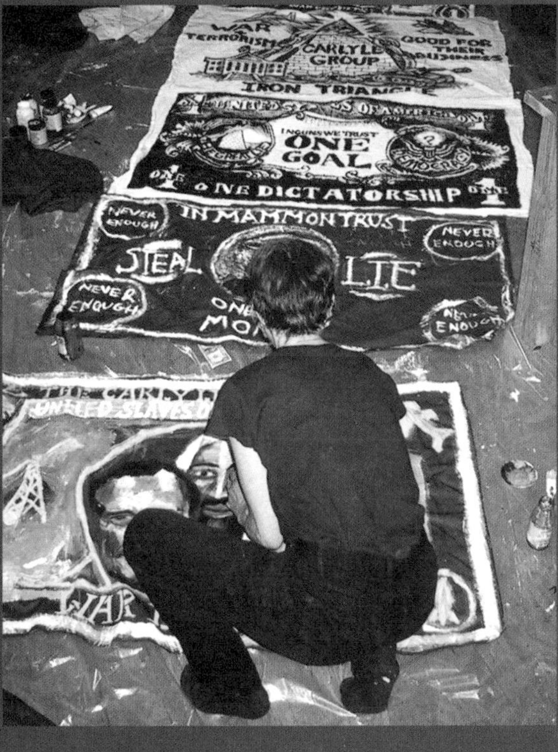
WAR
TERRORISM
CARLYLE GROUP
GOOD FOR THEIR BUSINESS
IRON TRIANGLE
ONE GOAL
ONE DICTATORSHIP
NEVER ENOUGH
IN MAMMON TRUST
NEVER ENOUGH
STEAL
LIE
NEVER ENOUGH
NEVER ENOUGH

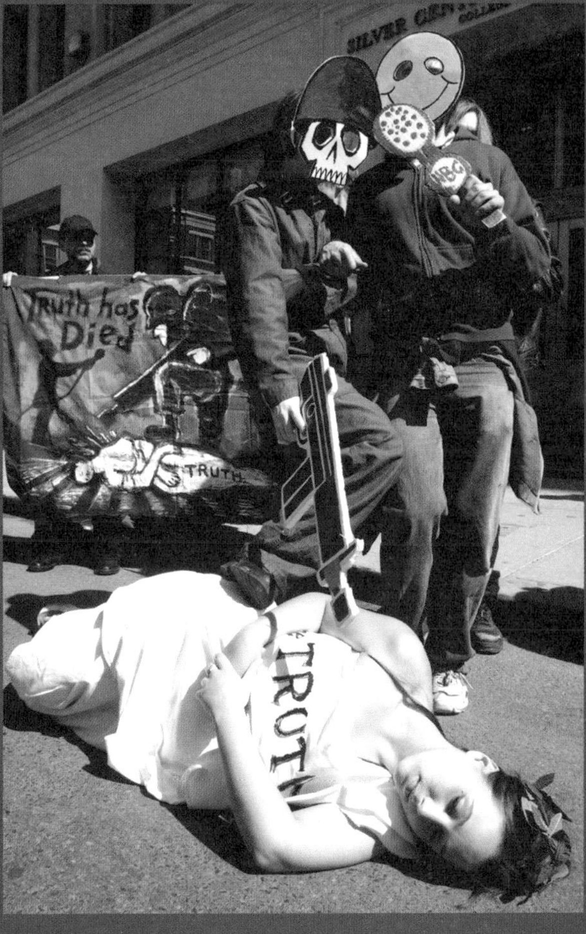
Truth has Died
TRUTH
TRUTH

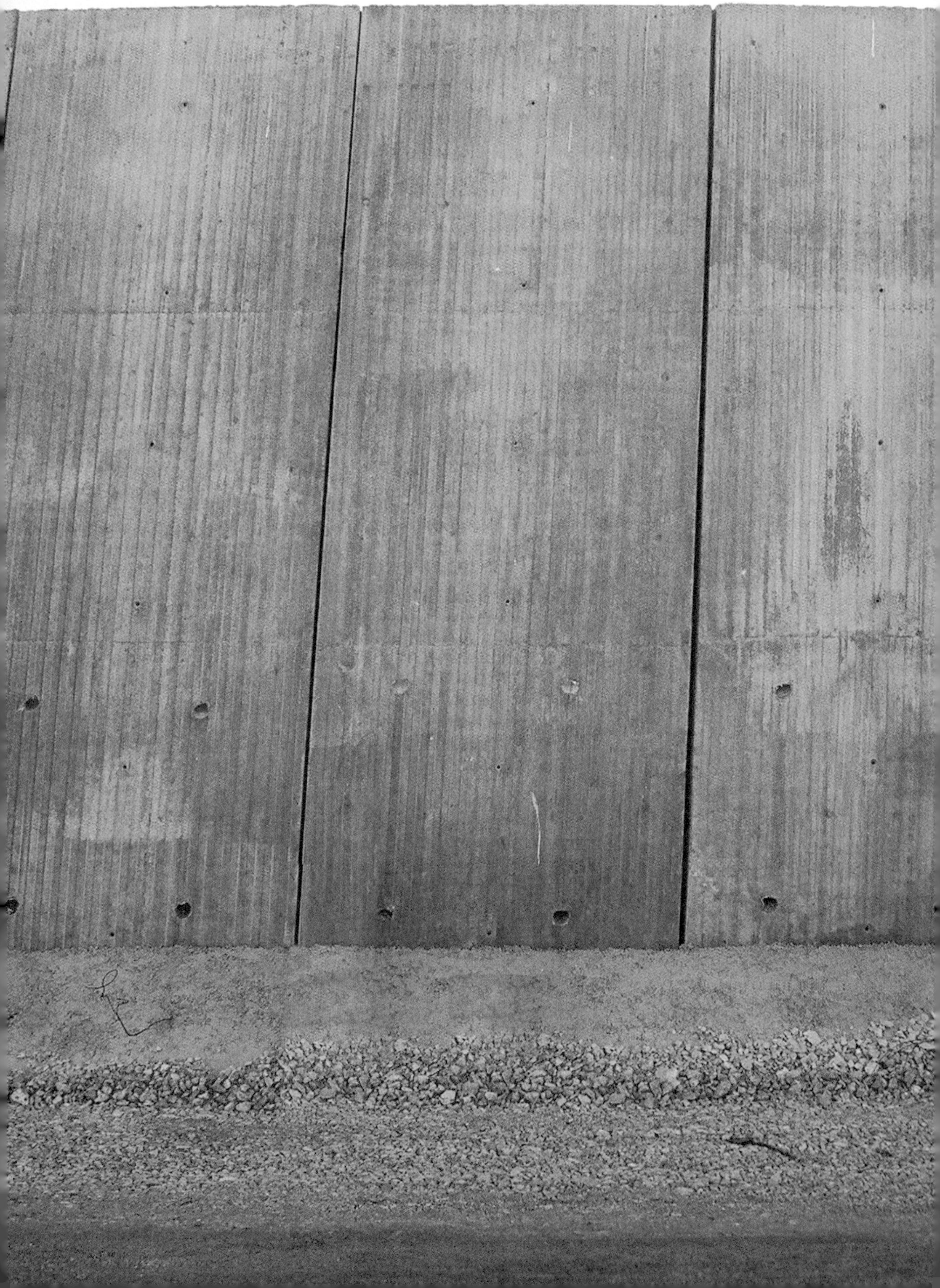

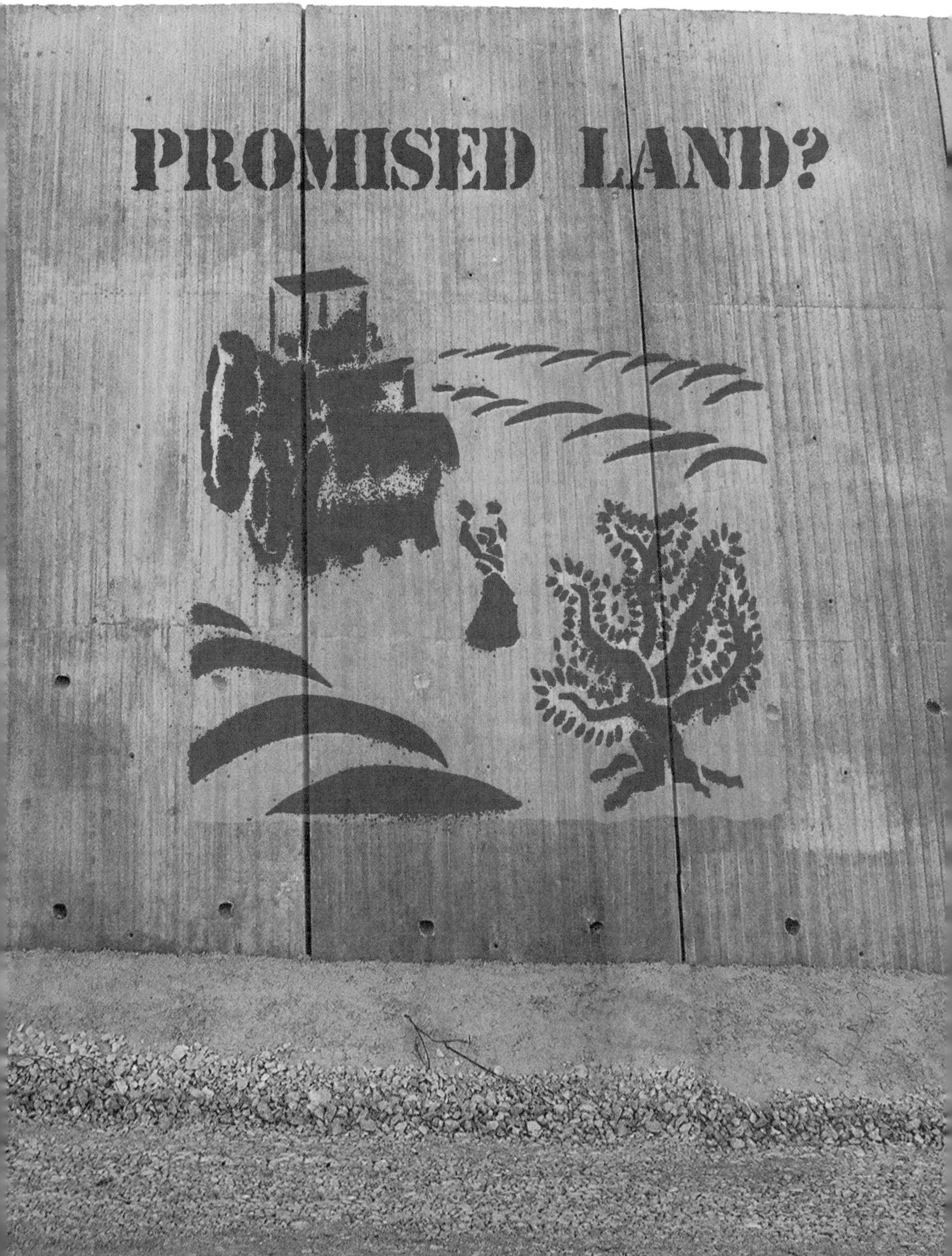
PROMISED LAND?

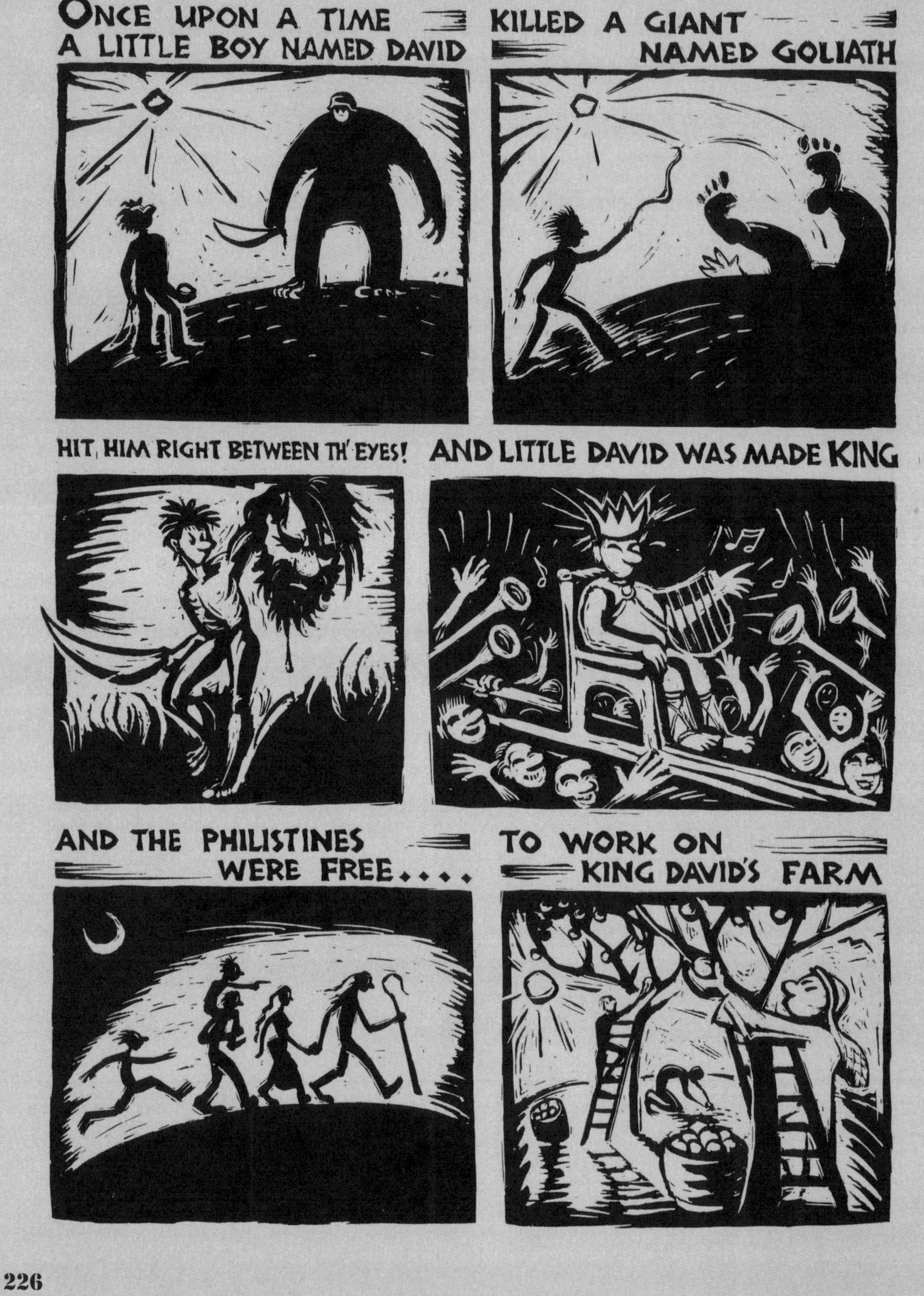
ONCE UPON A TIME
A LITTLE BOY NAMED DAVID
KILLED A GIANT
NAMED GOLIATH
HIT HIM RIGHT BETWEEN TH' EYES!
AND LITTLE DAVID WAS MADE KING
AND THE PHILISTINES
WERE FREE....
TO WORK ON
KING DAVID'S FARM

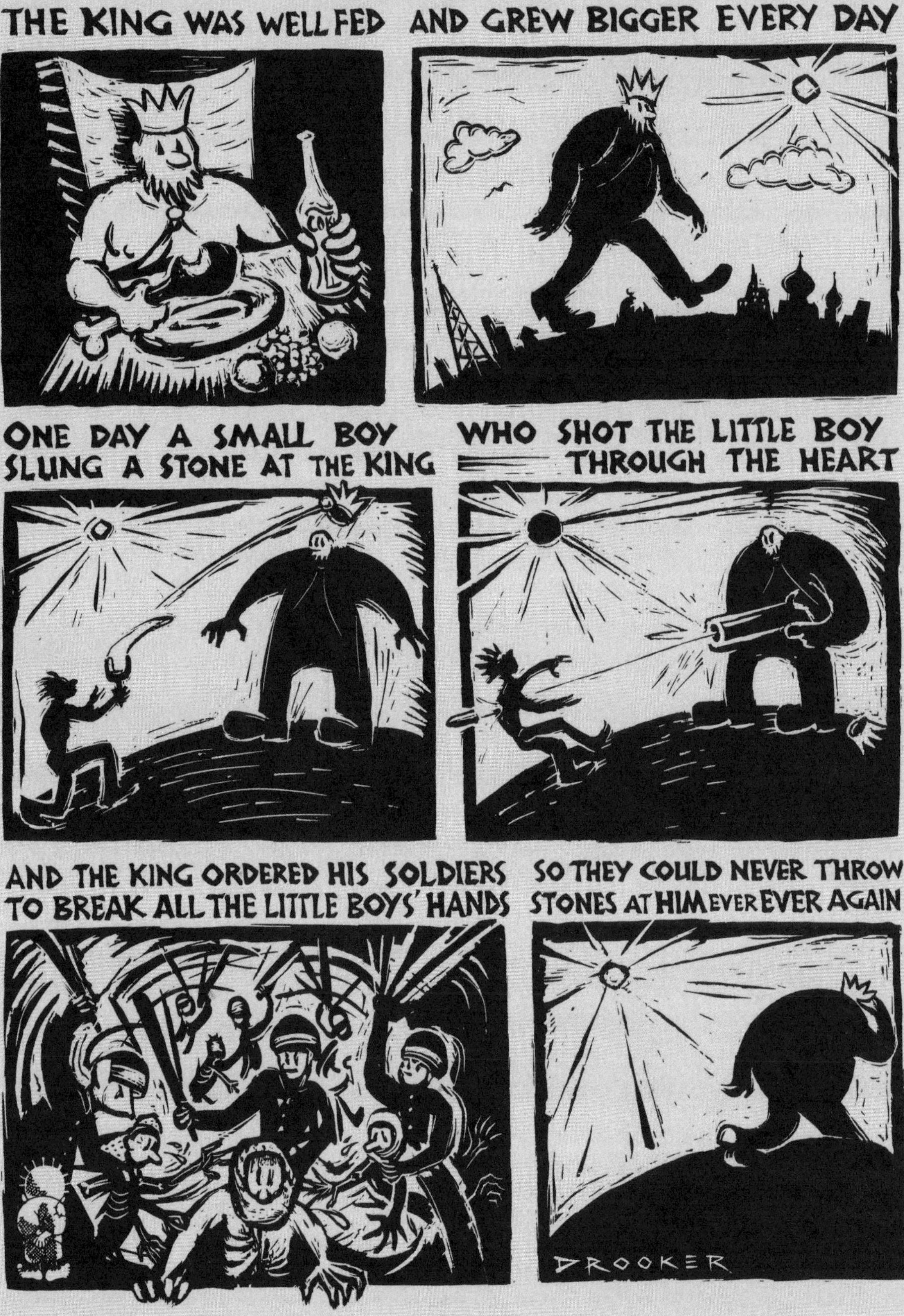
THE KING WAS WELL FED
AND GREW BIGGER EVERY DAY
ONE DAY A SMALL BOY
SLUNG A STONE AT THE KING
WHO SHOT THE LITTLE BOY
THROUGH THE HEART
AND THE KING ORDERED HIS SOLDIERS
TO BREAK ALL THE LITTLE BOYS' HANDS
SO THEY COULD NEVER THROW
STONES AT HIM EVER EVER AGAIN
DROOKER

PROMISED LAND

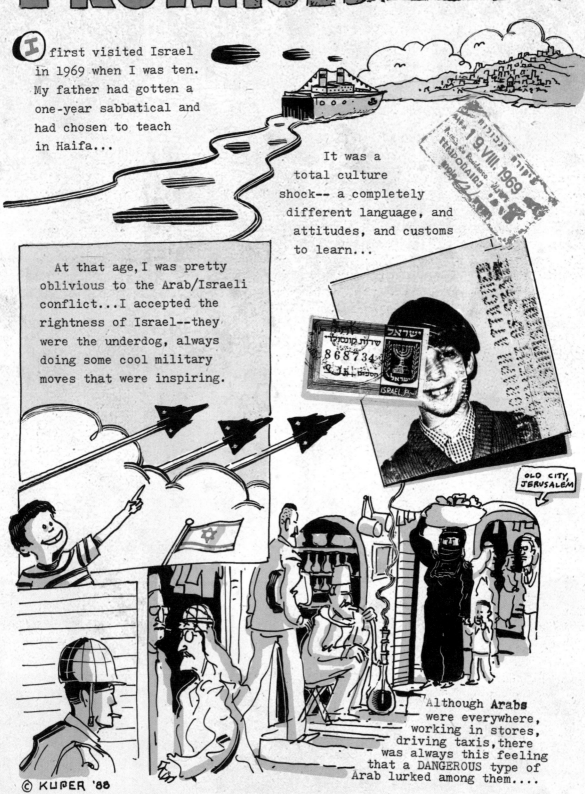

I first visited Israel in 1969 when I was ten. My father had gotten a one-year sabbatical and had chosen to teach in Haifa...

It was a total culture shock-- a completely different language, and attitudes, and customs to learn...

At that age, I was pretty oblivious to the Arab/Israeli conflict...I accepted the rightness of Israel--they were the underdog, always doing some cool military moves that were inspiring.

OLD CITY, JERUSALEM

Although **Arabs** were everywhere, working in stores, driving taxis, there was always this feeling that a DANGEROUS type of Arab lurked among them....

© KUPER '88

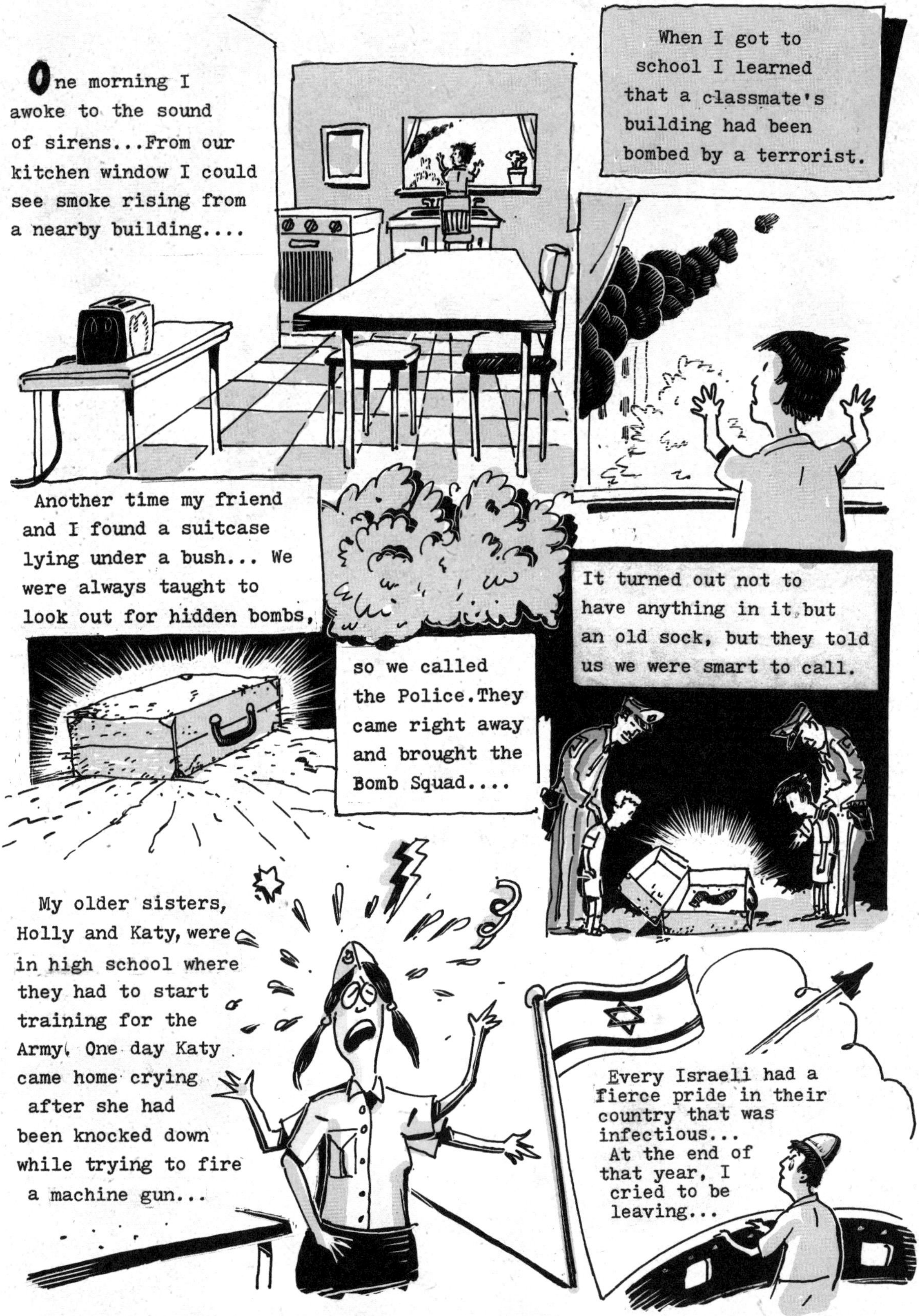
One morning I awoke to the sound of sirens...From our kitchen window I could see smoke rising from a nearby building....
When I got to school I learned that a classmate's building had been bombed by a terrorist.
Another time my friend and I found a suitcase lying under a bush... We were always taught to look out for hidden bombs,
so we called the Police.They came right away and brought the Bomb Squad....
It turned out not to have anything in it but an old sock, but they told us we were smart to call.
My older sisters, Holly and Katy, were in high school where they had to start training for the Army. One day Katy came home crying after she had been knocked down while trying to fire a machine gun...
Every Israeli had a fierce pride in their country that was infectious... At the end of that year, I cried to be leaving...

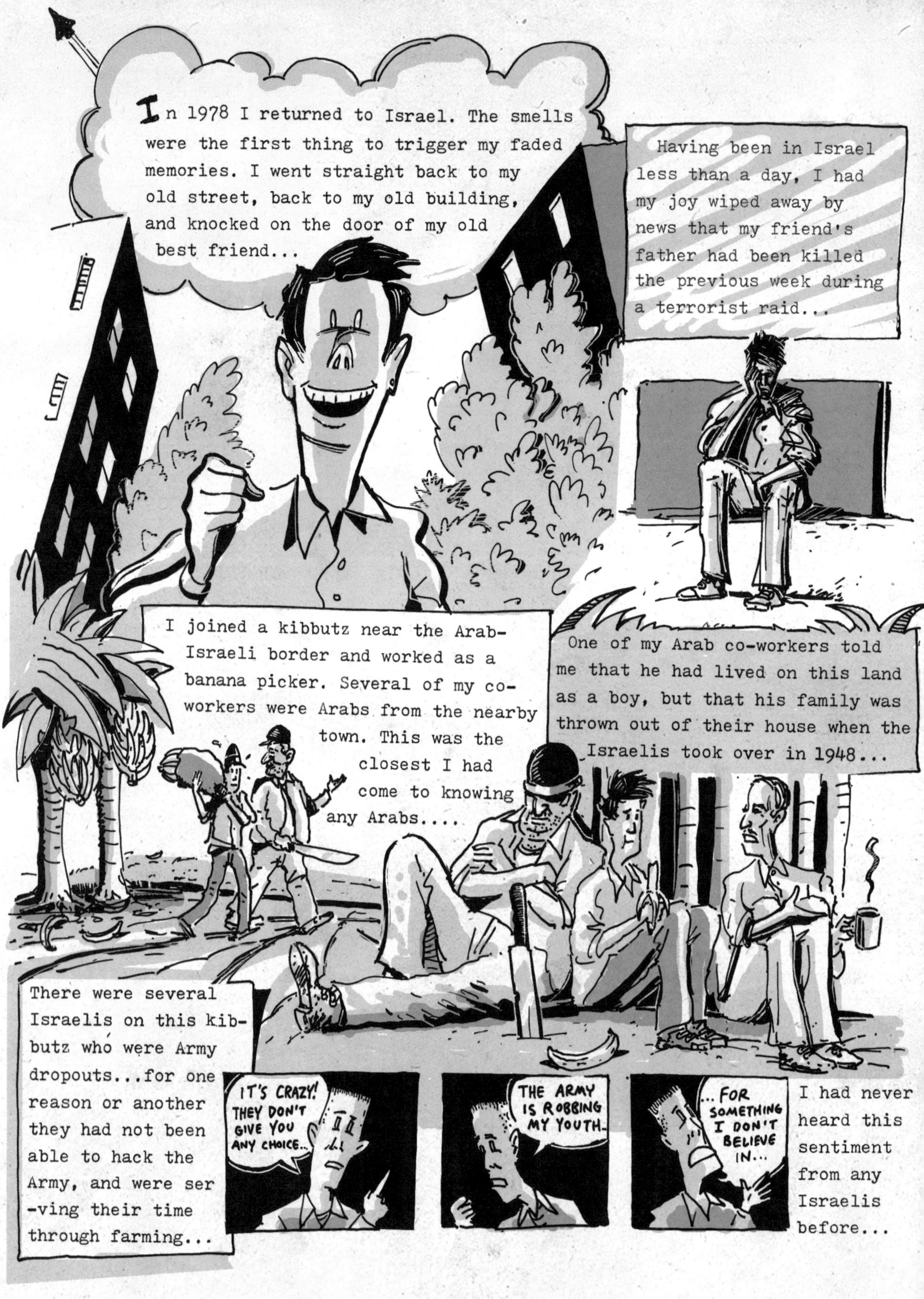
In 1978 I returned to Israel. The smells were the first thing to trigger my faded memories. I went straight back to my old street, back to my old building, and knocked on the door of my old best friend...
Having been in Israel less than a day, I had my joy wiped away by news that my friend's father had been killed the previous week during a terrorist raid...
I joined a kibbutz near the Arab-Israeli border and worked as a banana picker. Several of my co-workers were Arabs from the nearby town. This was the closest I had come to knowing any Arabs....
One of my Arab co-workers told me that he had lived on this land as a boy, but that his family was thrown out of their house when the Israelis took over in 1948...
There were several Israelis on this kibbutz who were Army dropouts...for one reason or another they had not been able to hack the Army, and were ser-ving their time through farming...
IT'S CRAZY! THEY DON'T GIVE YOU ANY CHOICE...
THE ARMY IS ROBBING MY YOUTH...
...FOR SOMETHING I DON'T BELIEVE IN...
I had never heard this sentiment from any Israelis before...

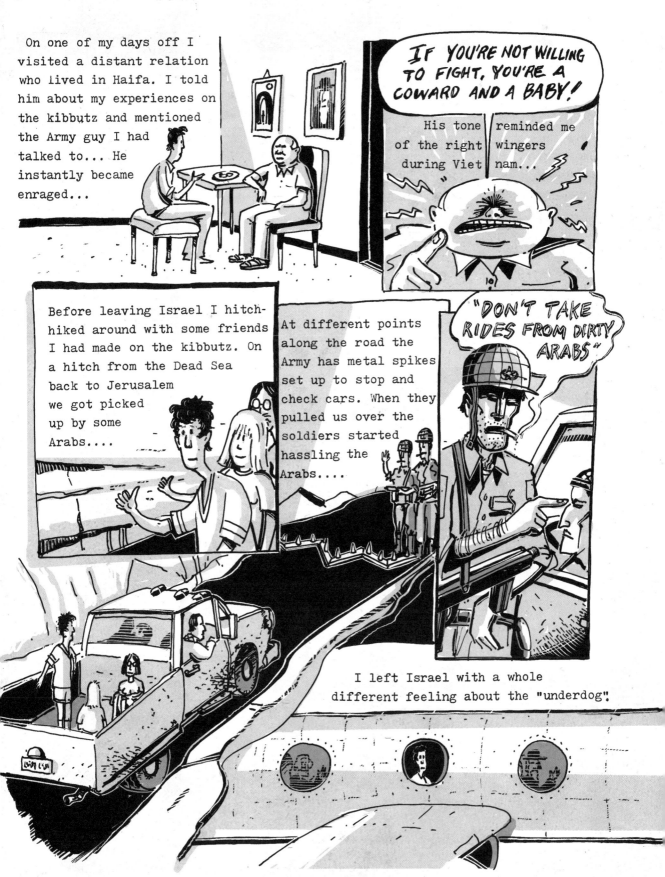

On one of my days off I visited a distant relation who lived in Haifa. I told him about my experiences on the kibbutz and mentioned the Army guy I had talked to... He instantly became enraged...

IF YOU'RE NOT WILLING TO FIGHT, YOU'RE A COWARD AND A BABY!

His tone reminded me of the right wingers during Viet nam...

Before leaving Israel I hitch-hiked around with some friends I had made on the kibbutz. On a hitch from the Dead Sea back to Jerusalem we got picked up by some Arabs....

At different points along the road the Army has metal spikes set up to stop and check cars. When they pulled us over the soldiers started hassling the Arabs....

"DON'T TAKE RIDES FROM DIRTY ARABS"

I left Israel with a whole different feeling about the "underdog".

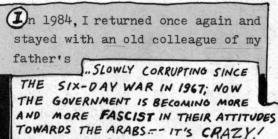

In 1984, I returned once again and stayed with an old colleague of my father's

"..SLOWLY CORRUPTING SINCE THE SIX-DAY WAR IN 1967; NOW THE GOVERNMENT IS BECOMING MORE AND MORE FASCIST IN THEIR ATTITUDES TOWARDS THE ARABS-- IT'S CRAZY!

In the Old City in Jerusalem (the part that has been occupied by Israel since 1967) I ordered coffee in Hebrew as I had done a hundred times before...

DON'T SPEAK THAT DIRTY LANGUAGE!!

OPEN YOUR BAG.

The tension was everywhere...

The day I left Israel a bomb exploded in the Old City market killing and maiming several people.

1988 To see news about Israel these days I don't feel as though I know the place...

It looks farther and farther away all the time...

More horror in some distant land.

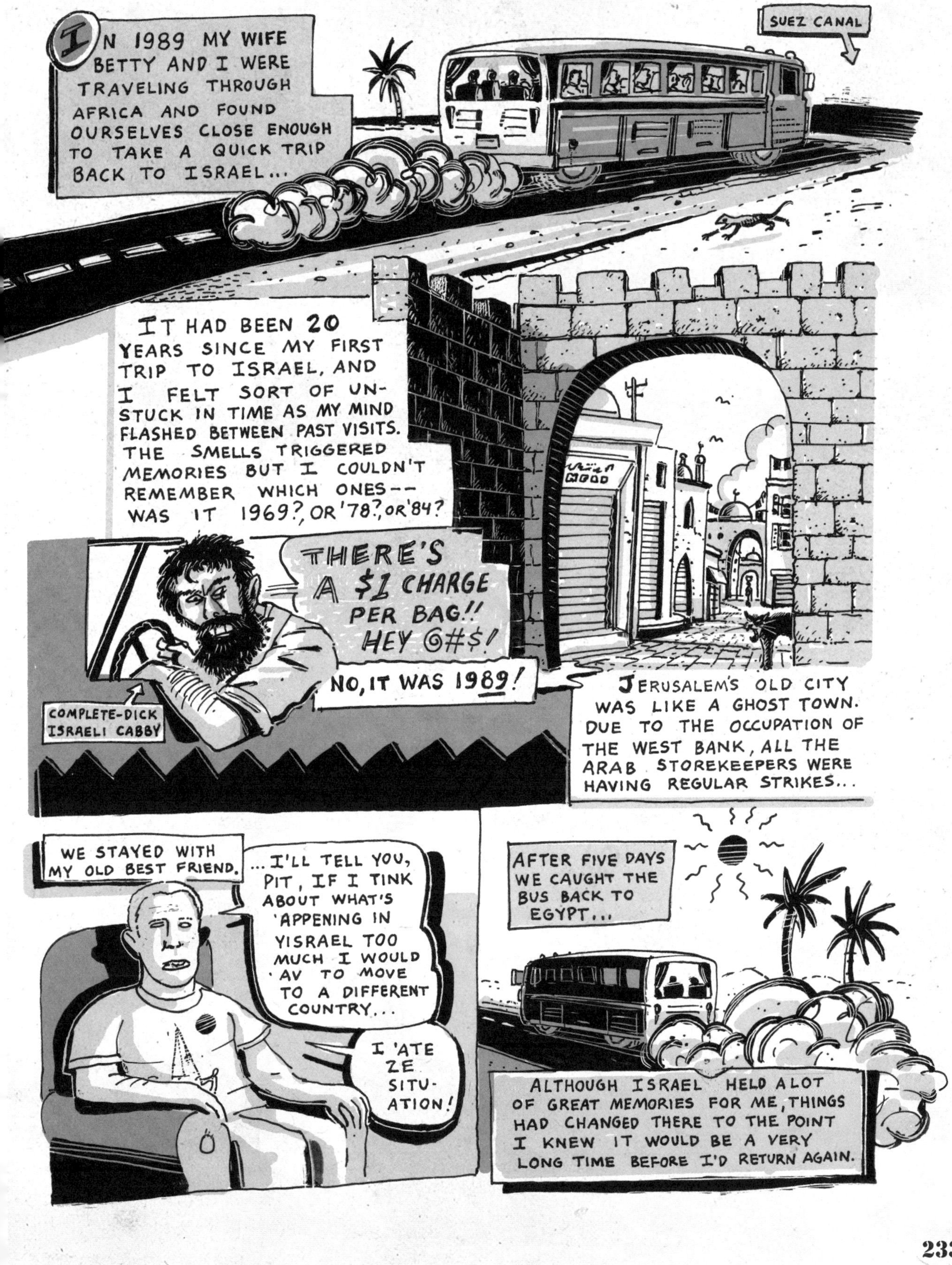

IN 1989 MY WIFE BETTY AND I WERE TRAVELING THROUGH AFRICA AND FOUND OURSELVES CLOSE ENOUGH TO TAKE A QUICK TRIP BACK TO ISRAEL...
SUEZ CANAL
IT HAD BEEN 20 YEARS SINCE MY FIRST TRIP TO ISRAEL, AND I FELT SORT OF UN-STUCK IN TIME AS MY MIND FLASHED BETWEEN PAST VISITS. THE SMELLS TRIGGERED MEMORIES BUT I COULDN'T REMEMBER WHICH ONES-- WAS IT 1969?, OR '78?, OR '84?
THERE'S A $1 CHARGE PER BAG!! HEY @#$!
NO, IT WAS 1989!
COMPLETE-DICK ISRAELI CABBY
JERUSALEM'S OLD CITY WAS LIKE A GHOST TOWN. DUE TO THE OCCUPATION OF THE WEST BANK, ALL THE ARAB STOREKEEPERS WERE HAVING REGULAR STRIKES...
WE STAYED WITH MY OLD BEST FRIEND.
...I'LL TELL YOU, PIT, IF I TINK ABOUT WHAT'S 'APPENING IN YISRAEL TOO MUCH I WOULD 'AV TO MOVE TO A DIFFERENT COUNTRY...
I 'ATE ZE SITU-ATION!
AFTER FIVE DAYS WE CAUGHT THE BUS BACK TO EGYPT...
ALTHOUGH ISRAEL HELD A LOT OF GREAT MEMORIES FOR ME, THINGS HAD CHANGED THERE TO THE POINT I KNEW IT WOULD BE A VERY LONG TIME BEFORE I'D RETURN AGAIN.

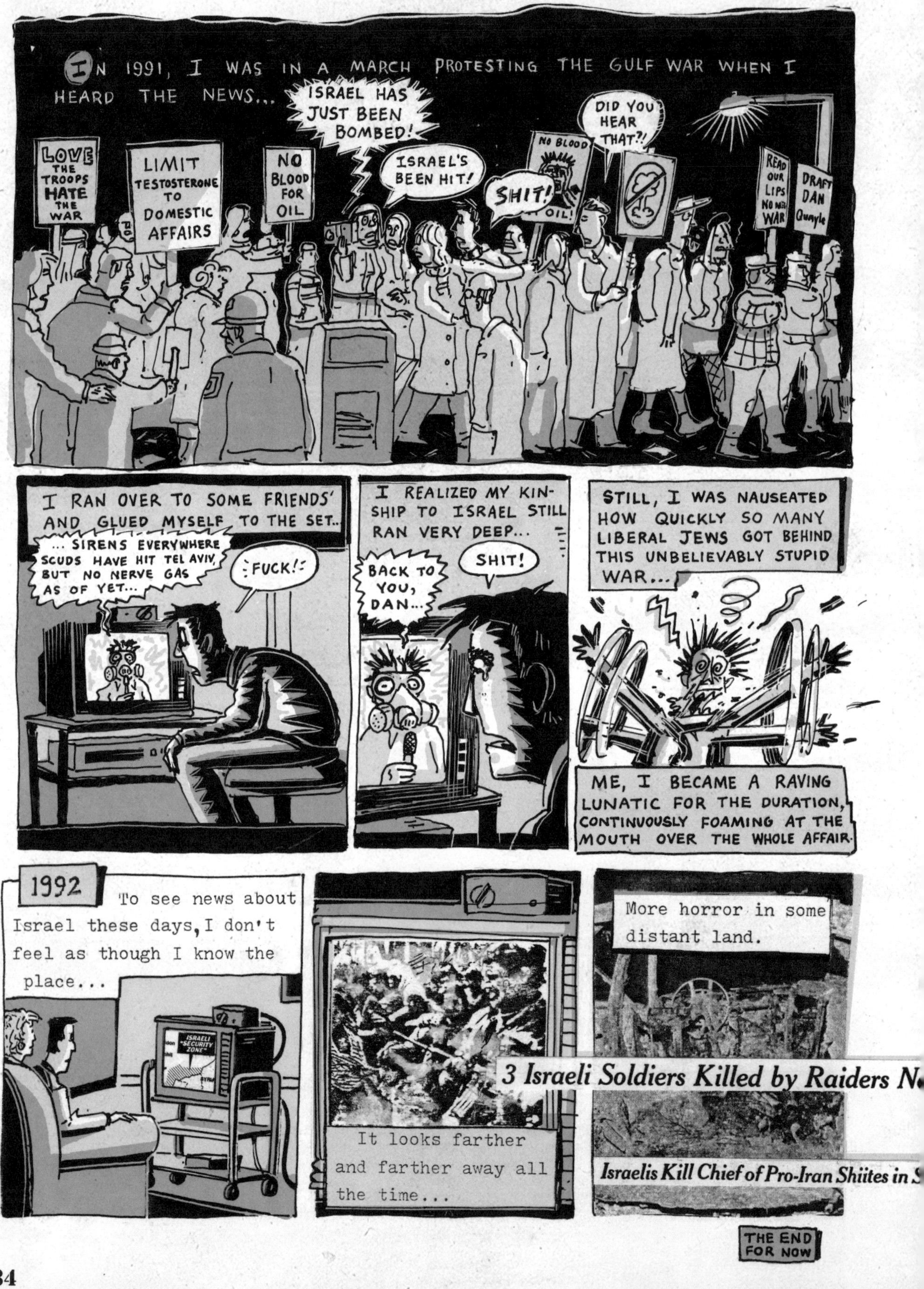

IN 1991, I WAS IN A MARCH PROTESTING THE GULF WAR WHEN I HEARD THE NEWS...
ISRAEL HAS JUST BEEN BOMBED!
LOVE THE TROOPS HATE THE WAR
LIMIT TESTOSTERONE TO DOMESTIC AFFAIRS
NO BLOOD FOR OIL
ISRAEL'S BEEN HIT!
DID YOU HEAR THAT?!
SHIT!
READ OUR LIPS
DRAFT DAN Quayle
I RAN OVER TO SOME FRIENDS' AND GLUED MYSELF TO THE SET...
... SIRENS EVERYWHERE SCUDS HAVE HIT TEL AVIV, BUT NO NERVE GAS AS OF YET...
FUCK!
I REALIZED MY KINSHIP TO ISRAEL STILL RAN VERY DEEP...
BACK TO YOU, DAN...
SHIT!
STILL, I WAS NAUSEATED HOW QUICKLY SO MANY LIBERAL JEWS GOT BEHIND THIS UNBELIEVABLY STUPID WAR...
ME, I BECAME A RAVING LUNATIC FOR THE DURATION, CONTINUOUSLY FOAMING AT THE MOUTH OVER THE WHOLE AFFAIR.
1992
To see news about Israel these days, I don't feel as though I know the place...
ISRAELI "SECURITY ZONE"
It looks farther and farther away all the time...
More horror in some distant land.
3 Israeli Soldiers Killed by Raiders N
Israelis Kill Chief of Pro-Iran Shiites in S
THE END FOR NOW

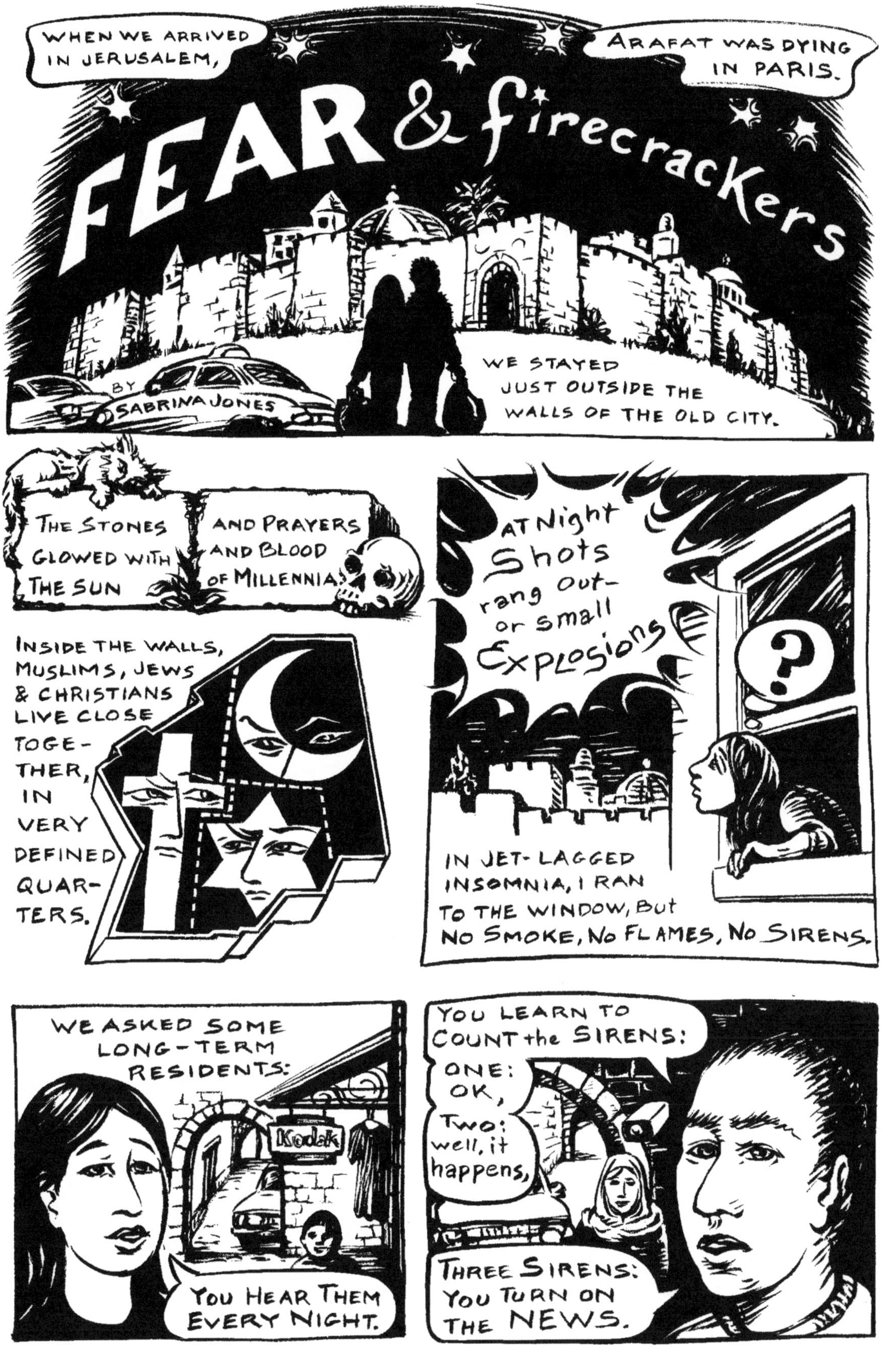

WHEN WE ARRIVED IN JERUSALEM,
ARAFAT WAS DYING IN PARIS.
FEAR & firecrackers
BY SABRINA JONES
WE STAYED JUST OUTSIDE THE WALLS OF THE OLD CITY.
THE STONES GLOWED WITH THE SUN
AND PRAYERS AND BLOOD OF MILLENNIA
INSIDE THE WALLS, MUSLIMS, JEWS & CHRISTIANS LIVE CLOSE TOGE-THER, IN VERY DEFINED QUAR-TERS.
AT Night Shots rang out- or small Explosions
?
IN JET-LAGGED INSOMNIA, I RAN TO THE WINDOW, But NO SMOKE, NO FLAMES, NO SIRENS.
WE ASKED SOME LONG-TERM RESIDENTS:
Kodak
YOU HEAR THEM EVERY NIGHT.
YOU LEARN TO COUNT the SIRENS:
ONE: OK,
TWO: well, it happens,
THREE SIRENS: YOU TURN ON THE NEWS.

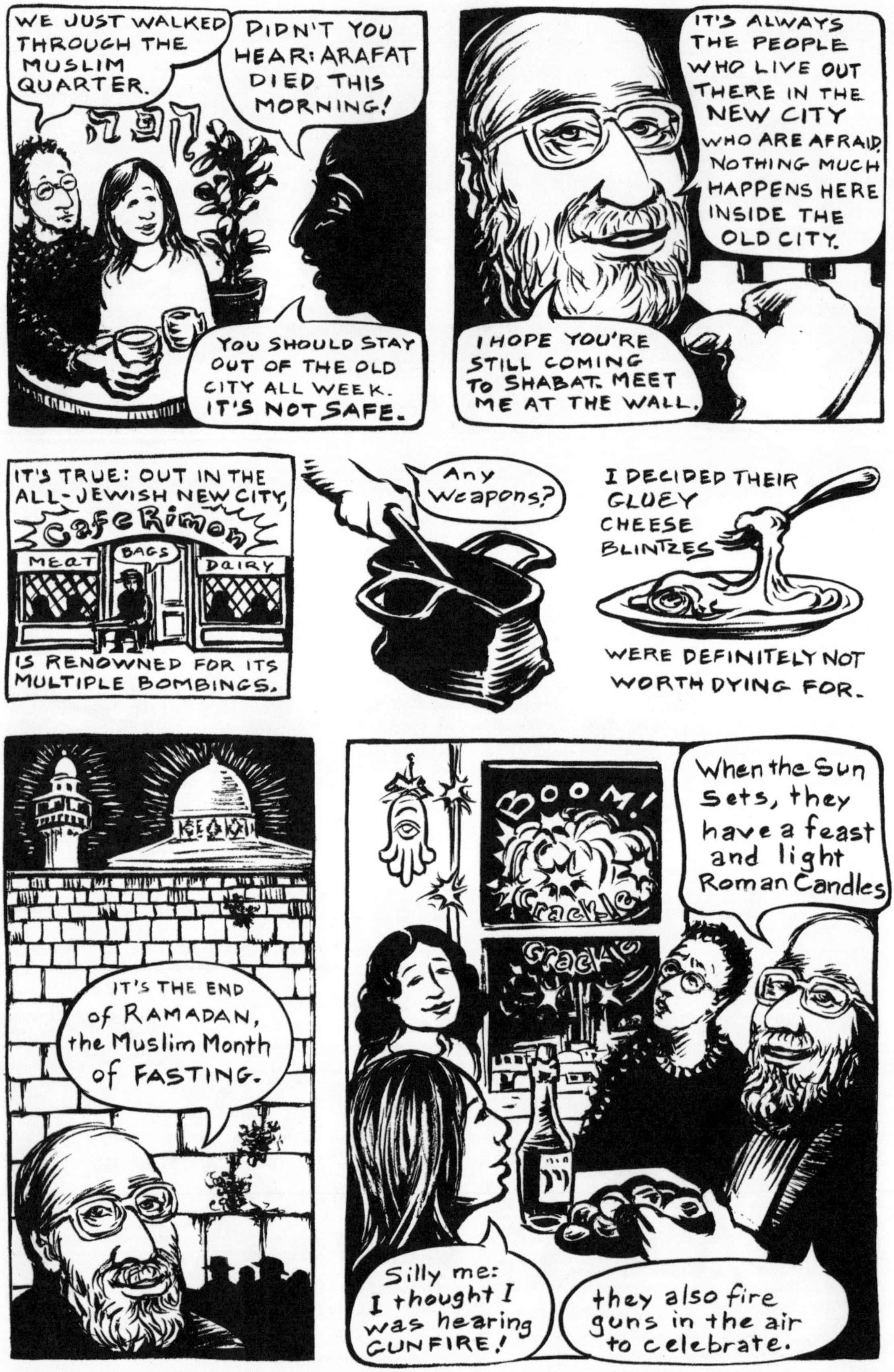
WE JUST WALKED THROUGH THE MUSLIM QUARTER.
DIDN'T YOU HEAR: ARAFAT DIED THIS MORNING!
YOU SHOULD STAY OUT OF THE OLD CITY ALL WEEK. IT'S NOT SAFE.
IT'S ALWAYS THE PEOPLE WHO LIVE OUT THERE IN THE NEW CITY WHO ARE AFRAID. NOTHING MUCH HAPPENS HERE INSIDE THE OLD CITY.
I HOPE YOU'RE STILL COMING TO SHABAT. MEET ME AT THE WALL.
IT'S TRUE: OUT IN THE ALL-JEWISH NEW CITY,
Cafe Rimon
MEAT
BAGS
DAIRY
IS RENOWNED FOR ITS MULTIPLE BOMBINGS.
Any Weapons?
I DECIDED THEIR GLUEY CHEESE BLINTZES
WERE DEFINITELY NOT WORTH DYING FOR.
IT'S THE END of RAMADAN, the Muslim Month of FASTING.
BOOM!
Crackle
Crackle
When the Sun Sets, they have a feast and light Roman Candles
Silly me: I thought I was hearing GUNFIRE!
they also fire guns in the air to celebrate.

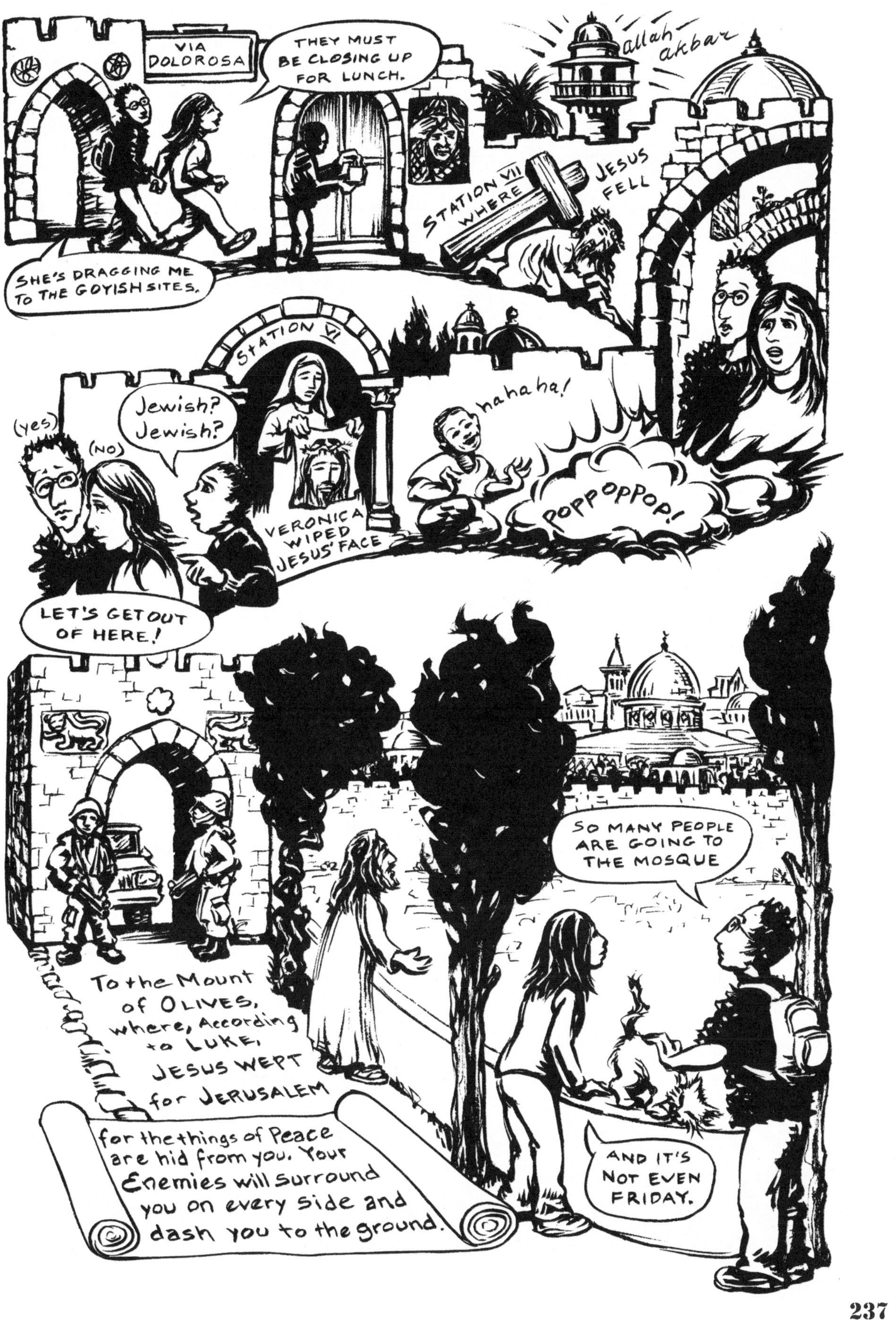
VIA DOLOROSA
SHE'S DRAGGING ME TO THE GOYISH SITES.
THEY MUST BE CLOSING UP FOR LUNCH.
allah-akbar
STATION VII WHERE JESUS FELL
STATION VI
(yes)
(NO)
Jewish? Jewish?
VERONICA WIPED JESUS' FACE
hahaha!
POPPOPPOP!
LET'S GET OUT OF HERE!
To the Mount of OLIVES, where, According to LUKE, JESUS WEPT for JERUSALEM
for the things of Peace are hid from you. Your Enemies will Surround you on every Side and dash you to the ground.
SO MANY PEOPLE ARE GOING TO THE MOSQUE
AND IT'S NOT EVEN FRIDAY.

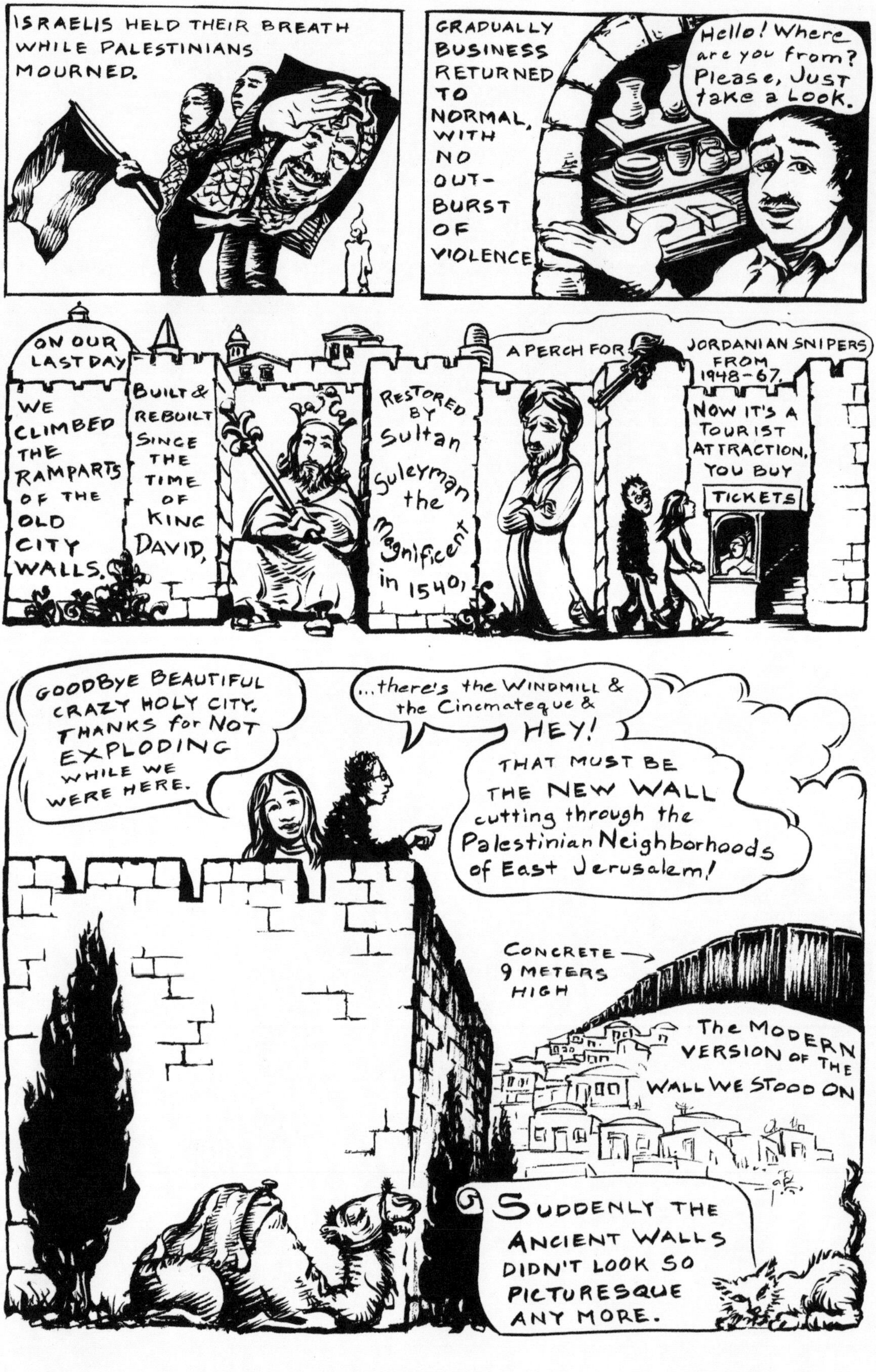

ISRAELIS HELD THEIR BREATH WHILE PALESTINIANS MOURNED.
GRADUALLY BUSINESS RETURNED TO NORMAL, WITH NO OUT-BURST OF VIOLENCE.
Hello! Where are you from? Please, Just take a Look.
ON OUR LAST DAY
WE CLIMBED THE RAMPARTS OF THE OLD CITY WALLS.
BUILT & REBUILT SINCE THE TIME OF KING DAVID,
RESTORED BY Sultan Suleyman the Magnificent in 1540,
A PERCH FOR JORDANIAN SNIPERS FROM 1948-67.
NOW IT'S A TOURIST ATTRACTION. YOU BUY TICKETS
TICKETS
GOODBYE BEAUTIFUL CRAZY HOLY CITY. THANKS for NOT EXPLODING WHILE WE WERE HERE.
...there's the WINDMILL & the Cinemateque &
HEY! THAT MUST BE THE NEW WALL cutting through the Palestinian Neighborhoods of East Jerusalem!
CONCRETE 9 METERS HIGH
The MODERN VERSION OF THE WALL WE STOOD ON
SUDDENLY THE ANCIENT WALLS DIDN'T LOOK SO PICTURESQUE ANY MORE.

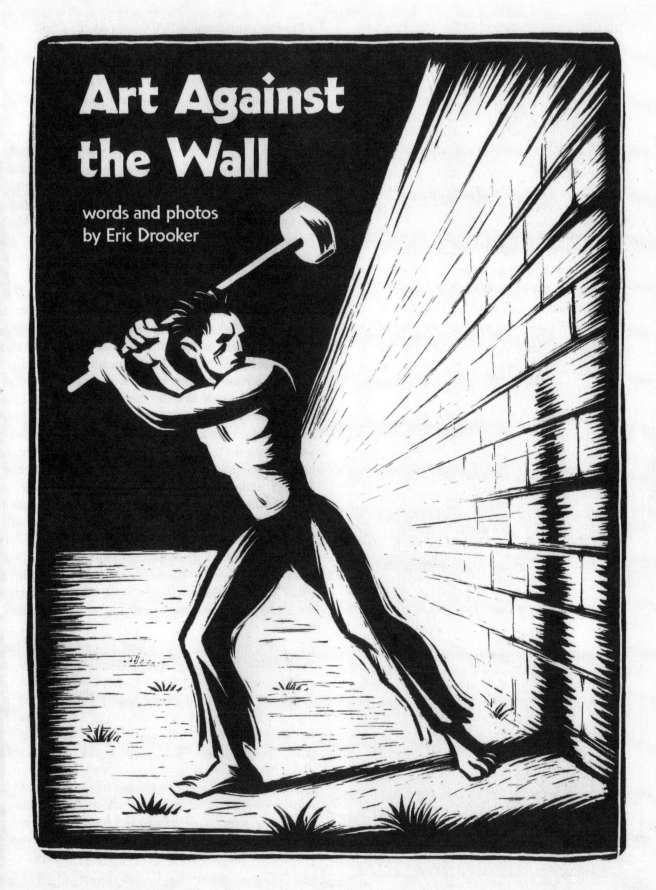

Art Against the Wall

words and photos
by Eric Drooker

The Israeli government calls it the "Security Fence." The Palestinians refer to it as the "Apartheid Wall." When I laid eyes on it this past summer, I called it "The Greatest Blank Canvas in the World."

Over twenty feet tall, with a projected span of five hundred miles, the wall is being built entirely on Palestinian land, snaking its way throughout the occupied West Bank. The massive concrete structure appeared to me a thinly veiled strategy to annex yet more land for the Israelis, under the pretext of stopping terrorism. In the dog days of July, I traveled through Palestine with fellow artist, Susan Green, of Break the Silence, painting colorful murals on the wall and neighborhood buildings.

I t was simultaneously a very good thing, and a very bad thing.

Neither Susan nor I expected to be allowed to enter Gaza in the first place. All of our Palestinian friends told us it was impossible and, at any rate, too dangerous these days....

But here we were, walking through the goddamn check point, with two hundred pounds of acrylic paint and two dozen brushes. Pleasantly surprised to be entering the Gaza Strip, on a hot mid-east morning, our euphoria proved to be as short lived as water on desert sand.

Oh shit...we're entering Gaza.

The Israeli government has, for months now, held the Gaza Strip under tight, military lockdown, with daily shelling, targeted assassinations, house demolitions, and generalized assault on the local population. Practically no one is allowed to enter or leave Gaza at this time. The checkpoint, which under "normal" circumstances is crowded with Palestinian laborers leaving for and returning from work, is all but deserted. Susan and I were among the last grains of sand to fall through this concrete hourglass. (The checkpoint resembles a New York City Subway turnstile, but with lots and lots of barbed wire...and a soldier pointing a machine gun at your head.)

The entire Strip is a sprawling, densely populated, outdoor prison—one of the most crowded zones on the planet—with Apache helicopters and F-16s (all made in the USA) buzzing through the air like insane, metallic hornets.

We spent the first night with a family who live in a sixteen-story high rise in Gaza City, with their four daughters. (Susan had become friends with them on a previous visit, years back.) The family's father, Nasser, arranged for us to stay with his seventy-year-old mother in the nearby village of Beit Hanoun, which has been under intense military siege for the past four weeks. A month ago, the military entered this lovely village of citrus groves and vineyards, and bulldozed every orange tree, lemon tree, grapefruit tree and grape vine in site. Every last fucking one.

Sharing the room with us, for our next three nights in Beit Hanoun, was a young orange tree planted in a large ceramic pot. Was it being hidden here in this second story room? Upon closer inspection, we noticed that it had a golden chain wrapped around its trunk, locking it, desperately, to the floor. For the next three nights, I slept with this young tree at my feet.

Earlier this month, the army also bombed and/or bulldozed over forty wells in the village. (The region of Beit Hanoun has the most plentiful underground sources of water in Gaza...which is what the current military incursion is really all about: Water for Israel.)

No one is permitted to enter or leave this village, this prison within a prison, encircled by soldiers with M-16s, tanks, bulldozers, and helicopters, around the clock.

At daybreak, we silently loaded our heavy-assed suitcase of paint and brushes onto a splintered wooden cart pulled by donkey, and quietly slipped, undetected, into town.

I immediately noticed that the landscape was littered with corpses of trees...a most horrifying site. A war atrocity. Fruit withered on the vine...bright oranges turned dusty brown, under the white-hot sun. This village, which for countless generations has been a prosperous farming community, is now, suddenly, a desert. Quite literally overnight, Beit Hanoun, legendary for its sweet abundance, has been stripped naked.

Everybody we met, and stayed with for the next three days, was visibly heartbroken, bewildered... traumatized. Too full of grief to feel anger. Too full of sorrow to feel rage.

Yet.

We met with the director of the local youth center, who was a cousin of the family we'd stayed with in Gaza City. He was a handsome man in his mid-40s, with lines of angst etched deep into his warm face. He was responsible, each day, for the hundreds of girls and boys who passed, barefoot, through the center.

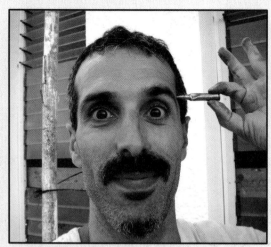

Portrait of the artist as a young *meshuggener*.

An 11-year-old boy handed me an M-16 bullet, a souvenir carried by many of the town's children. When I realized it was still unexploded, I warned him, "Careful, son! Someone might get hurt!"... the goddamn things were everywhere.

Of course, there was nothing much that he or anyone in the village could do but worry, and wait. What would the Israeli army do next? Start bulldozing homes? Poison the last remaining wells? Shell an unpaved village of sandy dirt roads, uprooted trees, donkeys, and scattered herds of goats? Chain-smoking, he agreed to let us organize a mural project for the youth center's front wall.

A makeshift scaffolding was quickly erected against the face of this stucco three story building. I immediately began to sketch, in charcoal, the outline of an enormous tree, branches reaching up to the roof, roots reaching into the ground.

With the regular RATATATATATATATATATAT!!! of machine gun fire in the distance, (heard every half hour or so, day and night) Susan and I poured out a large bucket of Viridian Green, always a good color for foliage, and handed out brushes to an energetic crew of teenage boys—brothers and friends of those recently killed—and got right to work. I mixed up a can of Raw Umber, with a splash of Sienna, and painted the tree's thick trunk around the front doorway. Whenever anyone entered the building, they were entering the body of a large and ancient tree. Above me, Taleb, Samir, Maḥmoud, and Susan were busy painting in the tree's leaves so furiously, that they quickly ran out of Viridian Green. Fuck...I knew I should have brought more Viridian!

I frantically mixed a quart of Cobalt Blue and Yellow Ochre together, yielding a curious Olive hue, and we were back in business, with enough green to finish painting all the leaves.

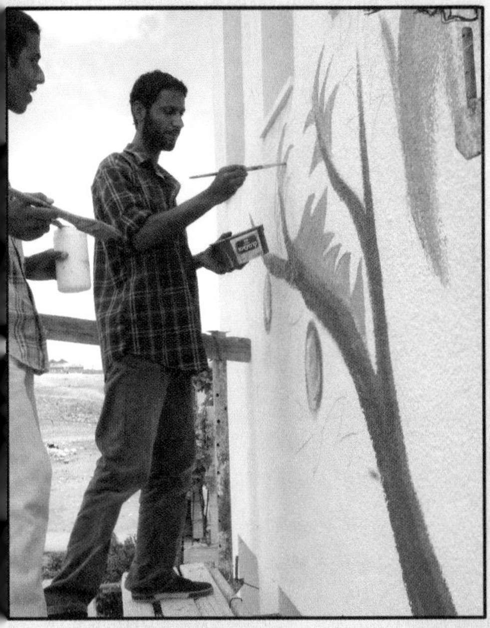

A bitter joke that never failed to produce wild laughter among the teenagers was that when the soldiers finally saw this giant tree, they would immediately uproot the entire building.

After we ate a brief meal on the floor, Mahmoud began thumping loudly on an hourglass-shaped hand drum, and suddenly we were all up and dancing, hysterically, to this odd, yet strangely familiar rhythm. And then it was back to work. Special care, and attention was given to painting the numerous, large, shiny oranges, which hung, plump and ripe, from every branch of the tree.

Eric Drooker
Occupied Palestine
August 5th, 2004

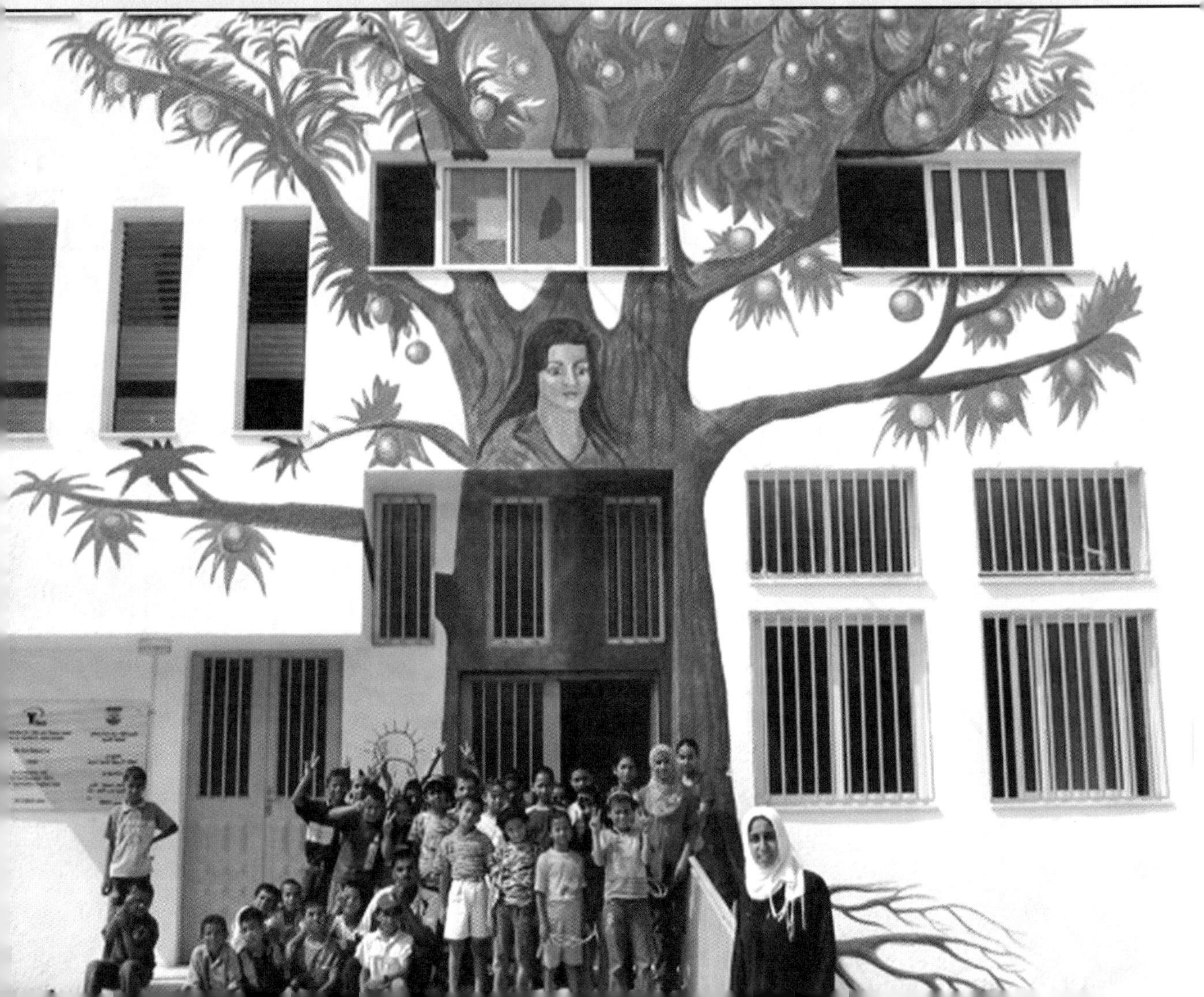

THE SERPENT OF STATE

BY SETH TOBOCMAN

OUT THE BULLET PROOF GLASS WINDOW OF THE SETTLER BUS, I SEE WHAT LOOKS LIKE AN AMERICAN SUBURB. THIS IS AN ISRAELI SETTLEMENT.

PAID FOR BY AMERICAN & ISRAELI TAX-E$

SIGNS POINT TO THE SETTLEMENT SIGNS POINT TO TEL-AVIV. BACK

NO SIGN POINTS TO THE END OF THE ROAD.

IT'S AS IF NOTHING LIES AT THE END OF THE ROAD.

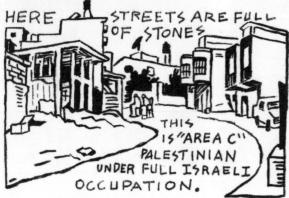

HERE STREETS ARE FULL OF STONES

THIS IS "AREA C" PALESTINIAN UNDER FULL ISRAELI OCCUPATION.

IT LOOKS NOTHING LIKE AN AMERICAN SUBURB.

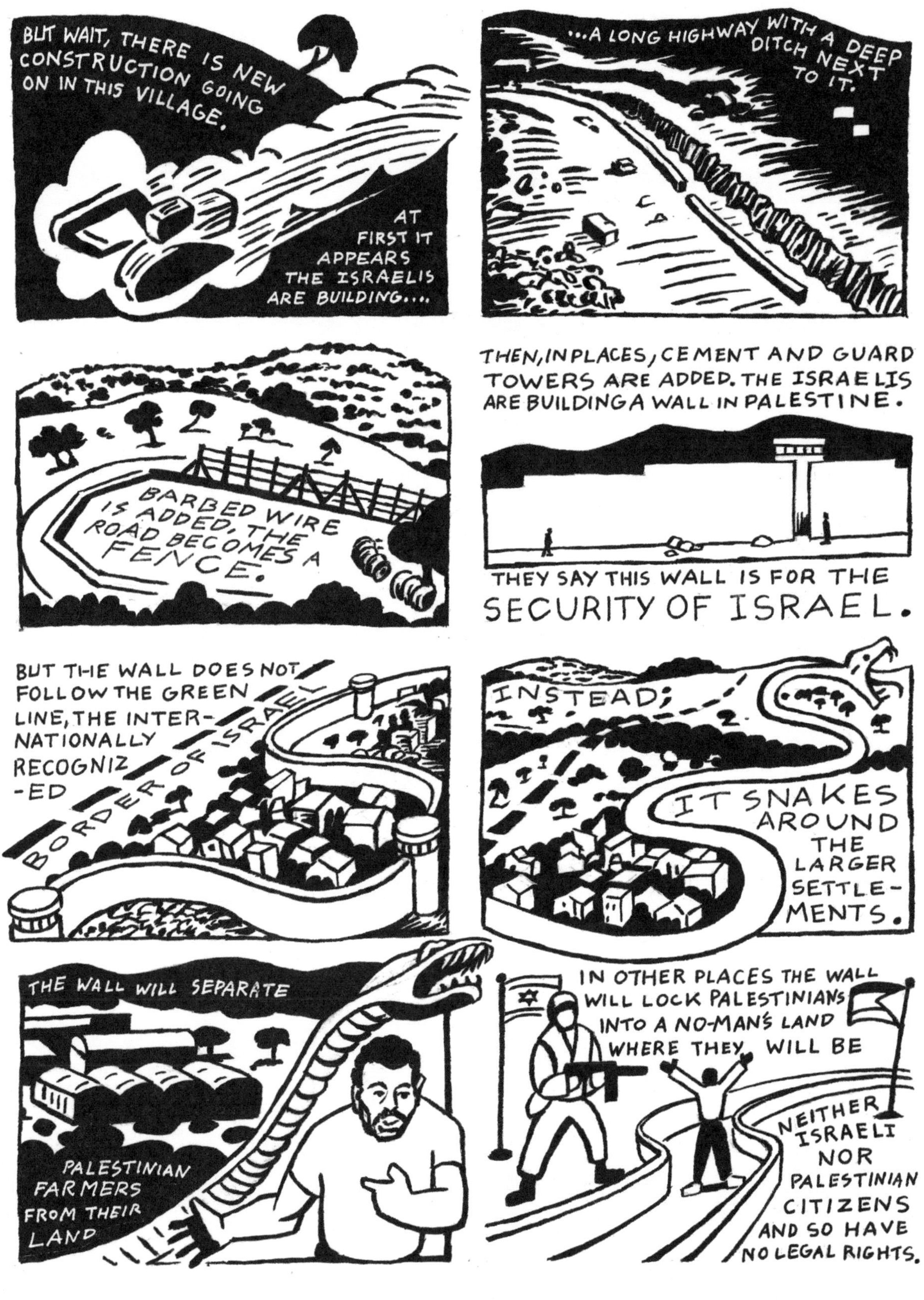
BUT WAIT, THERE IS NEW CONSTRUCTION GOING ON IN THIS VILLAGE.
AT FIRST IT APPEARS THE ISRAELIS ARE BUILDING....
...A LONG HIGHWAY WITH A DEEP DITCH NEXT TO IT.
BARBED WIRE IS ADDED, THE ROAD BECOMES A FENCE.
THEN, IN PLACES, CEMENT AND GUARD TOWERS ARE ADDED. THE ISRAELIS ARE BUILDING A WALL IN PALESTINE.
THEY SAY THIS WALL IS FOR THE SECURITY OF ISRAEL.
BUT THE WALL DOES NOT FOLLOW THE GREEN LINE, THE INTER-NATIONALLY RECOGNIZ-ED
BORDER OF ISRAEL
INSTEAD;
IT SNAKES AROUND THE LARGER SETTLE-MENTS.
THE WALL WILL SEPARATE
PALESTINIAN FARMERS FROM THEIR LAND
IN OTHER PLACES THE WALL WILL LOCK PALESTINIANS INTO A NO-MAN'S LAND WHERE THEY WILL BE
NEITHER ISRAELI NOR PALESTINIAN CITIZENS AND SO HAVE NO LEGAL RIGHTS.

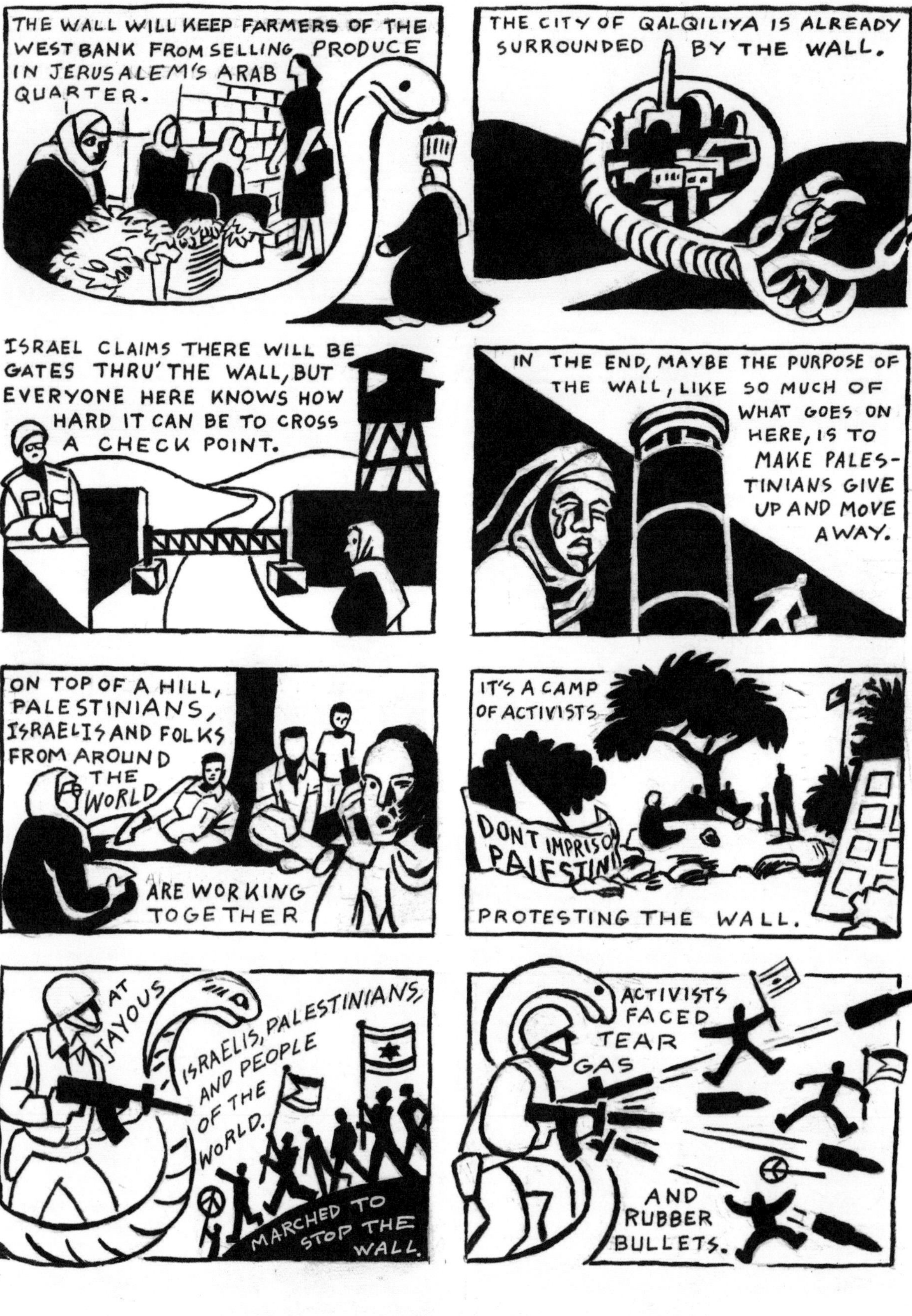

THE WALL WILL KEEP FARMERS OF THE WEST BANK FROM SELLING PRODUCE IN JERUSALEM'S ARAB QUARTER.
THE CITY OF QALQILIYA IS ALREADY SURROUNDED BY THE WALL.
ISRAEL CLAIMS THERE WILL BE GATES THRU' THE WALL, BUT EVERYONE HERE KNOWS HOW HARD IT CAN BE TO CROSS A CHECK POINT.
IN THE END, MAYBE THE PURPOSE OF THE WALL, LIKE SO MUCH OF WHAT GOES ON HERE, IS TO MAKE PALES-TINIANS GIVE UP AND MOVE AWAY.
ON TOP OF A HILL, PALESTINIANS, ISRAELIS AND FOLKS FROM AROUND THE WORLD
ARE WORKING TOGETHER
IT'S A CAMP OF ACTIVISTS
DONT IMPRISO
PALESTINI
PROTESTING THE WALL.
AT JAYOUS
ISRAELIS, PALESTINIANS, AND PEOPLE OF THE WORLD.
MARCHED TO STOP THE WALL.
ACTIVISTS FACED TEAR GAS
AND RUBBER BULLETS.

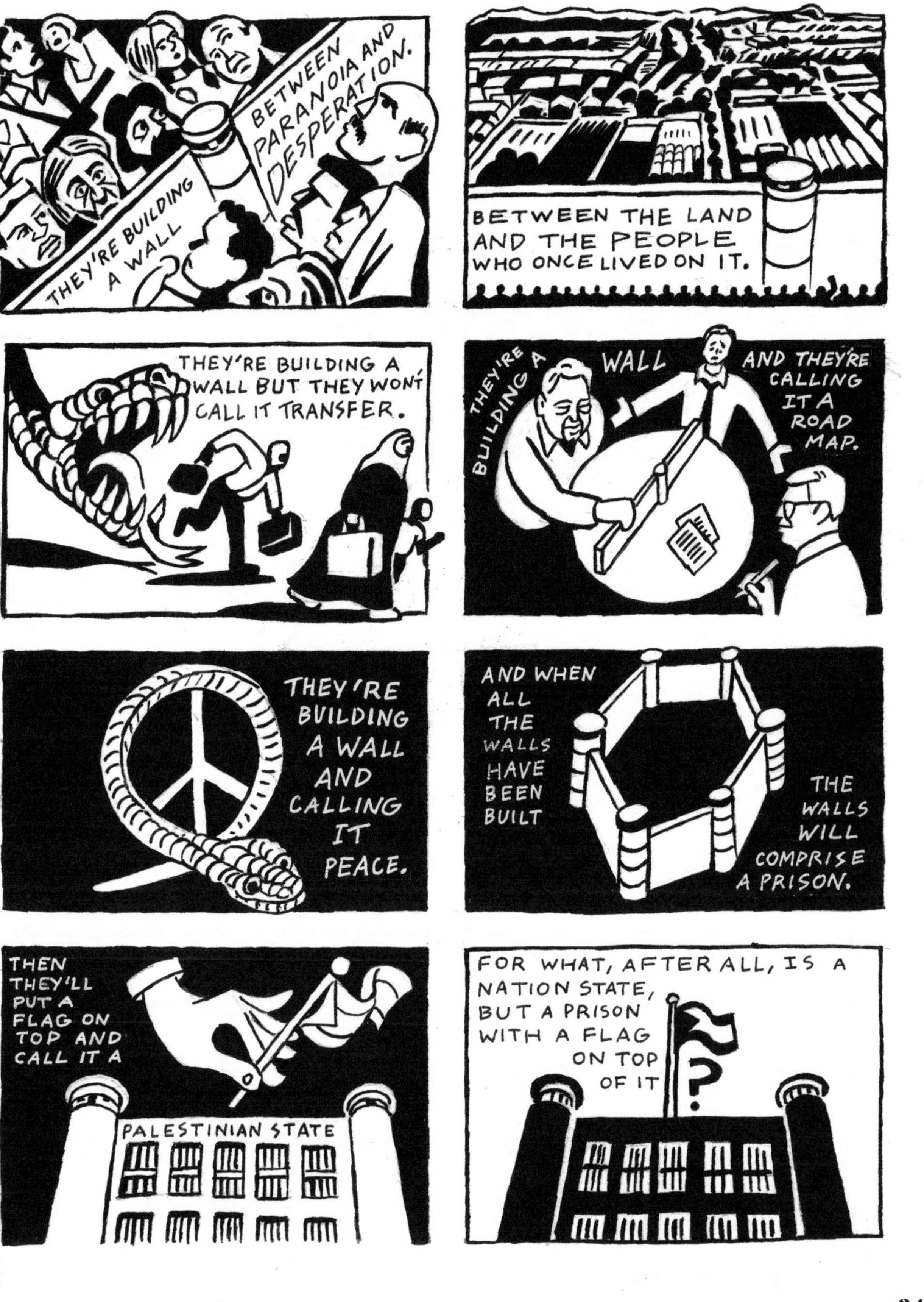
THEY'RE BUILDING A WALL
BETWEEN PARANOIA AND DESPERATION.
BETWEEN THE LAND AND THE PEOPLE WHO ONCE LIVED ON IT.
THEY'RE BUILDING A WALL BUT THEY WON'T CALL IT TRANSFER.
THEY'RE BUILDING A WALL
AND THEY'RE CALLING IT A ROAD MAP.
THEY'RE BUILDING A WALL AND CALLING IT PEACE.
AND WHEN ALL THE WALLS HAVE BEEN BUILT
THE WALLS WILL COMPRISE A PRISON.
THEN THEY'LL PUT A FLAG ON TOP AND CALL IT A
PALESTINIAN STATE
FOR WHAT, AFTER ALL, IS A NATION STATE, BUT A PRISON WITH A FLAG ON TOP OF IT
?

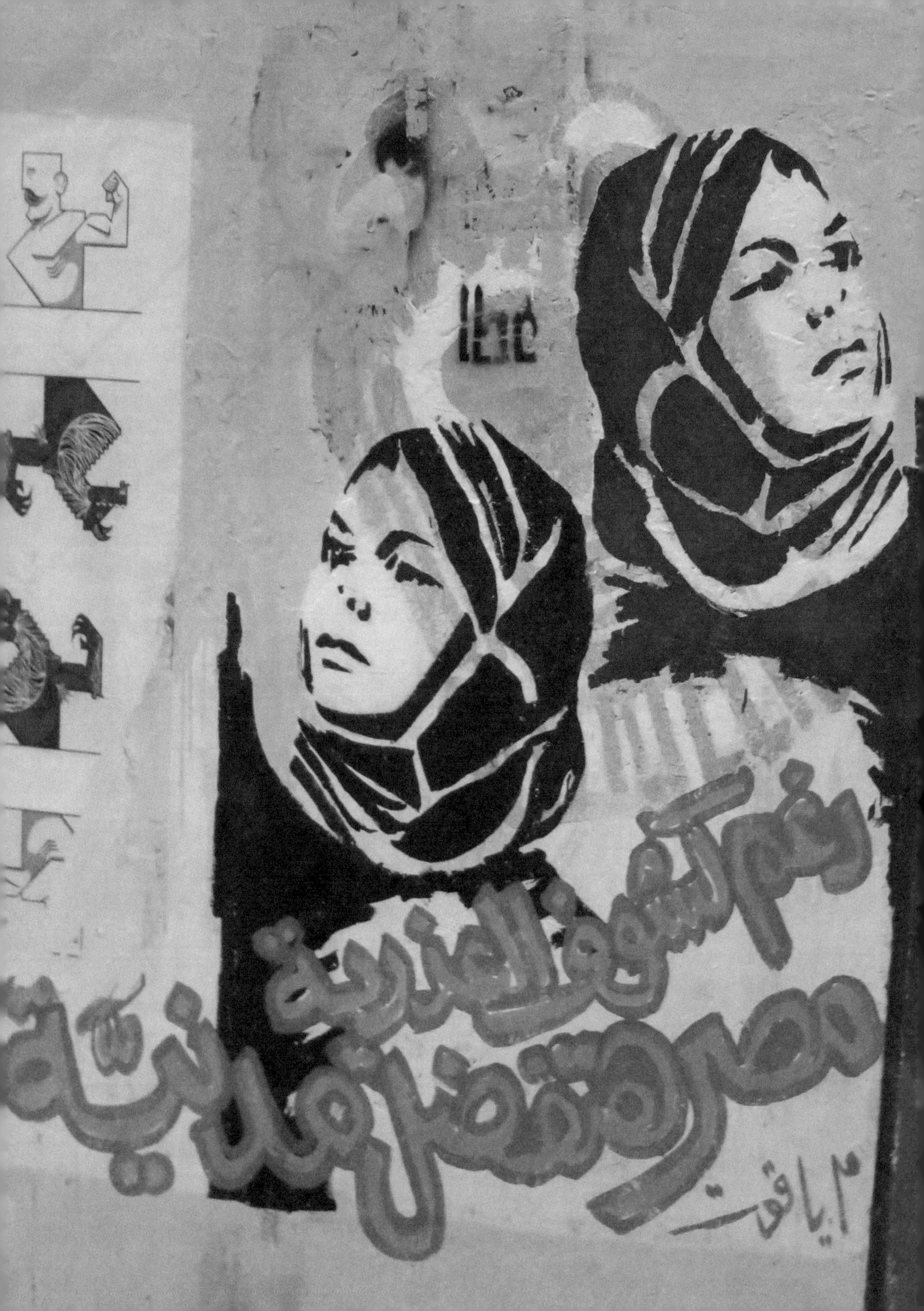

GOING GLOBAL

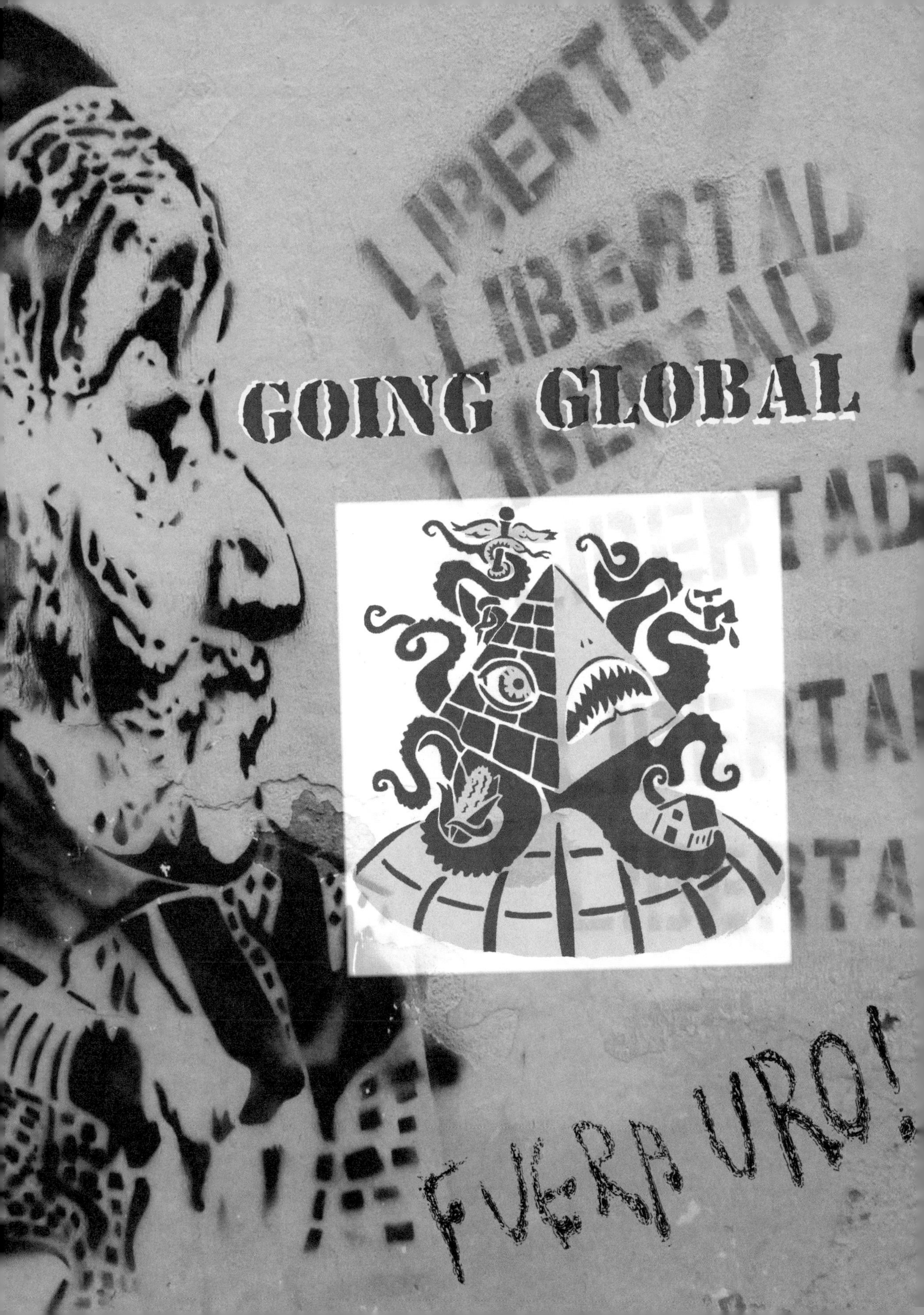
LIBERTAD
LIBERTAD
FUERA URO!

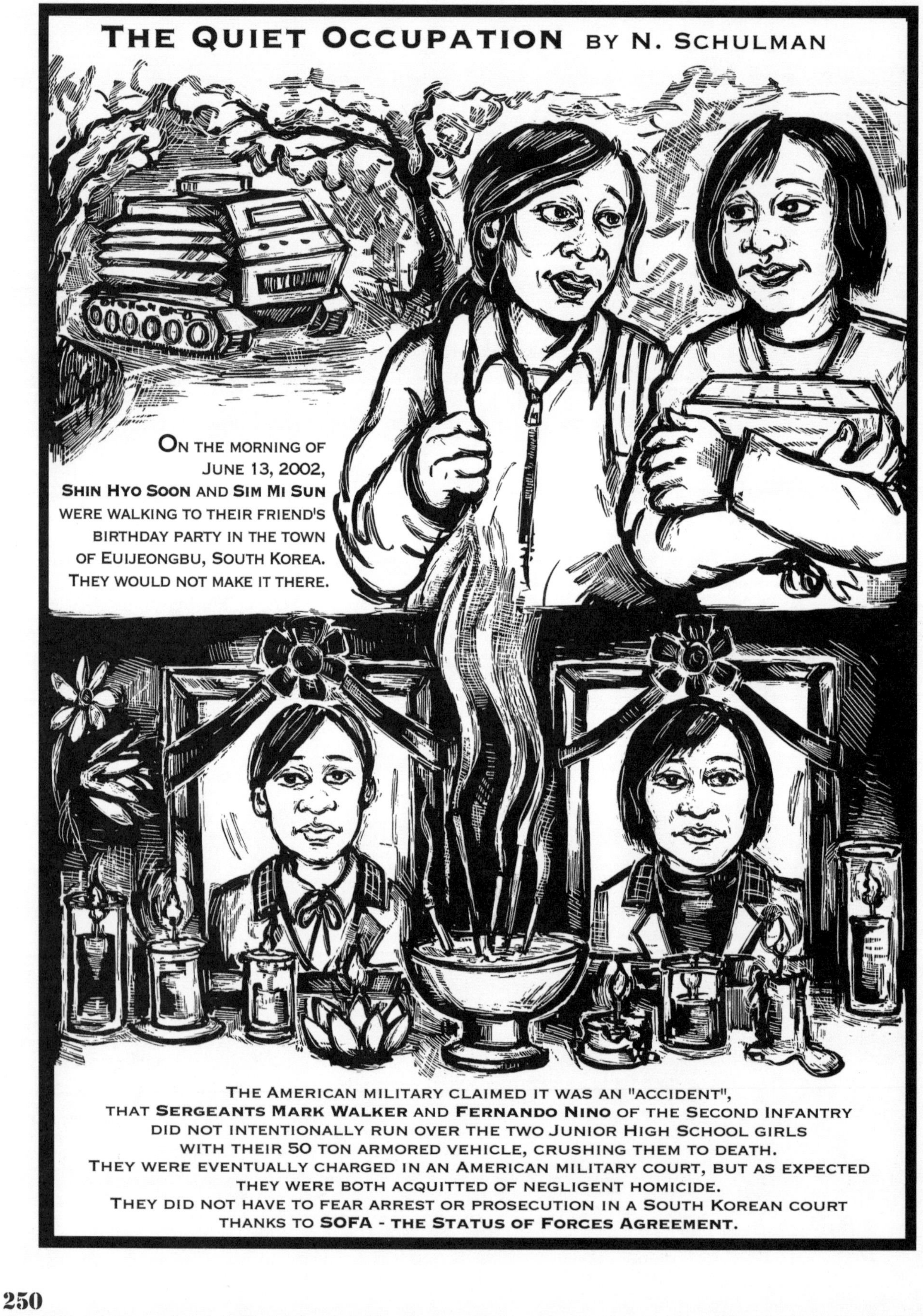
THE QUIET OCCUPATION BY N. SCHULMAN
ON THE MORNING OF JUNE 13, 2002, SHIN HYO SOON AND SIM MI SUN WERE WALKING TO THEIR FRIEND'S BIRTHDAY PARTY IN THE TOWN OF EUIJEONGBU, SOUTH KOREA. THEY WOULD NOT MAKE IT THERE.
THE AMERICAN MILITARY CLAIMED IT WAS AN "ACCIDENT", THAT SERGEANTS MARK WALKER AND FERNANDO NINO OF THE SECOND INFANTRY DID NOT INTENTIONALLY RUN OVER THE TWO JUNIOR HIGH SCHOOL GIRLS WITH THEIR 50 TON ARMORED VEHICLE, CRUSHING THEM TO DEATH. THEY WERE EVENTUALLY CHARGED IN AN AMERICAN MILITARY COURT, BUT AS EXPECTED THEY WERE BOTH ACQUITTED OF NEGLIGENT HOMICIDE. THEY DID NOT HAVE TO FEAR ARREST OR PROSECUTION IN A SOUTH KOREAN COURT THANKS TO SOFA - THE STATUS OF FORCES AGREEMENT.

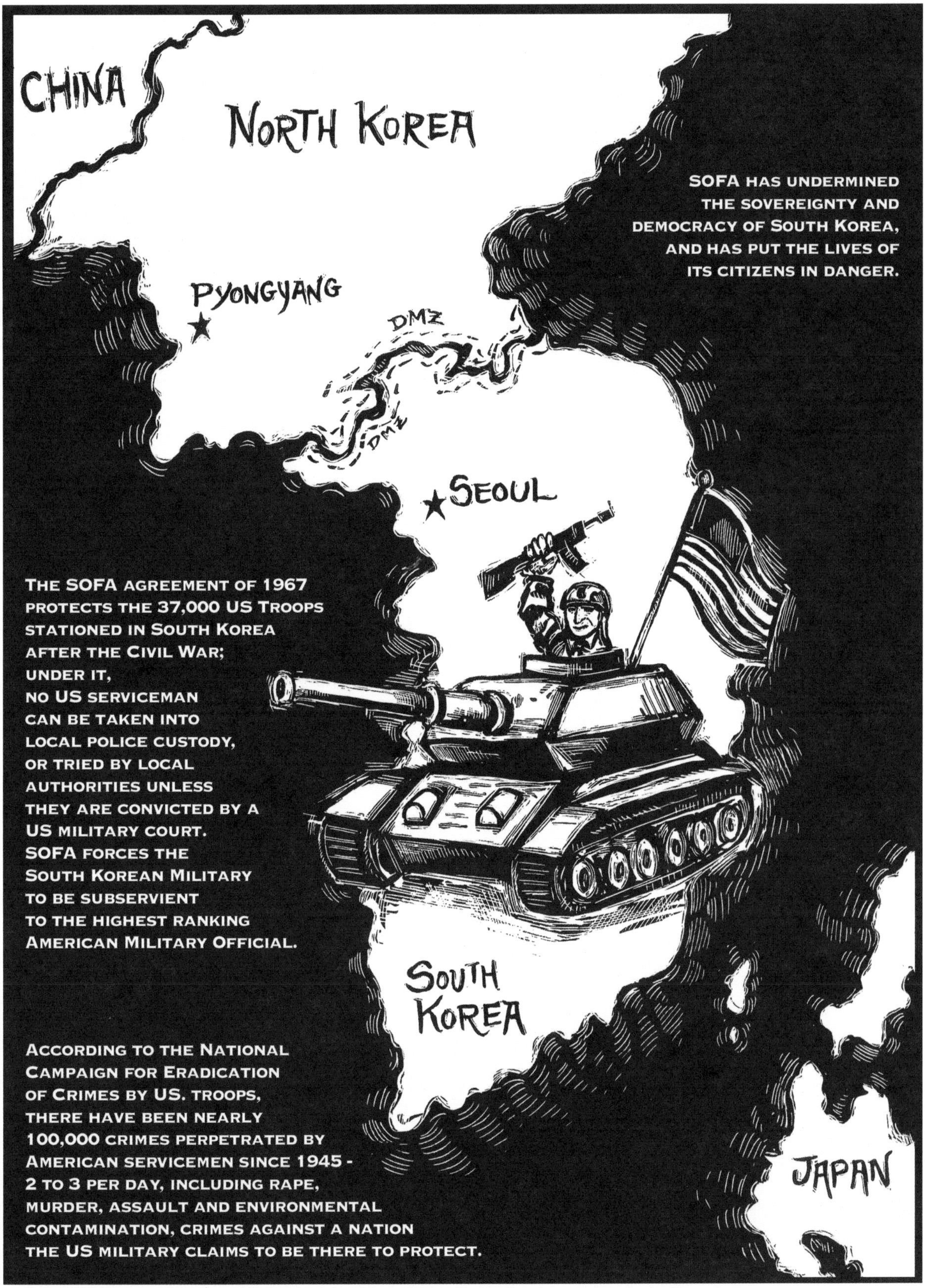
CHINA
NORTH KOREA
SOFA has undermined the sovereignty and democracy of South Korea, and has put the lives of its citizens in danger.
PYONGYANG
DMZ
DMZ
SEOUL
The SOFA agreement of 1967 protects the 37,000 US Troops stationed in South Korea after the Civil War; under it, no US serviceman can be taken into local police custody, or tried by local authorities unless they are convicted by a US military court. SOFA forces the South Korean Military to be subservient to the highest ranking American Military Official.
SOUTH KOREA
According to the National Campaign for Eradication of Crimes by US. troops, there have been nearly 100,000 crimes perpetrated by American servicemen since 1945 - 2 to 3 per day, including rape, murder, assault and environmental contamination, crimes against a nation the US military claims to be there to protect.
JAPAN

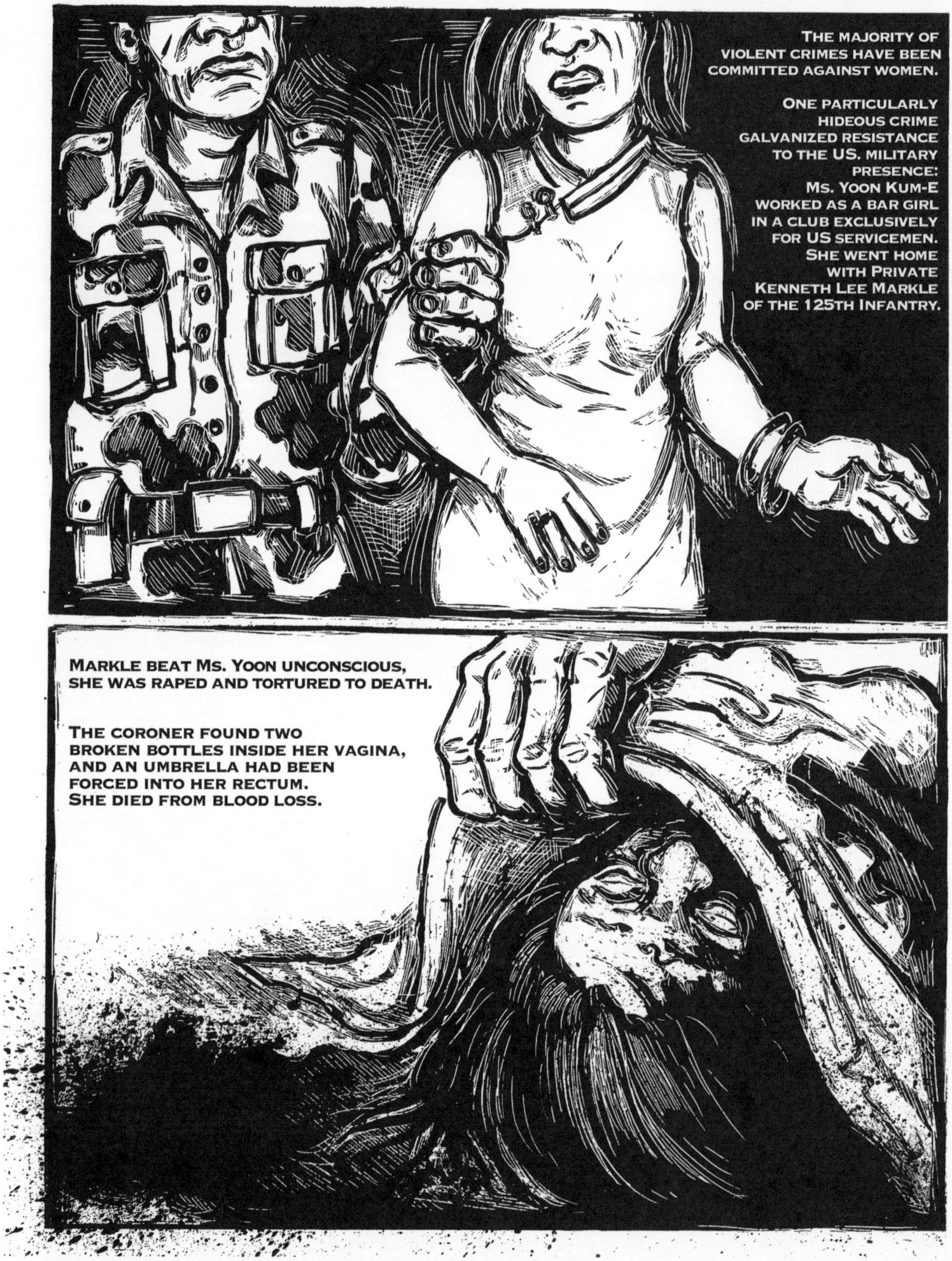
The majority of violent crimes have been committed against women.
One particularly hideous crime galvanized resistance to the US. military presence: Ms. Yoon Kum-E worked as a bar girl in a club exclusively for US servicemen. She went home with Private Kenneth Lee Markle of the 125th Infantry.
Markle beat Ms. Yoon unconscious, she was raped and tortured to death.
The coroner found two broken bottles inside her vagina, and an umbrella had been forced into her rectum. She died from blood loss.

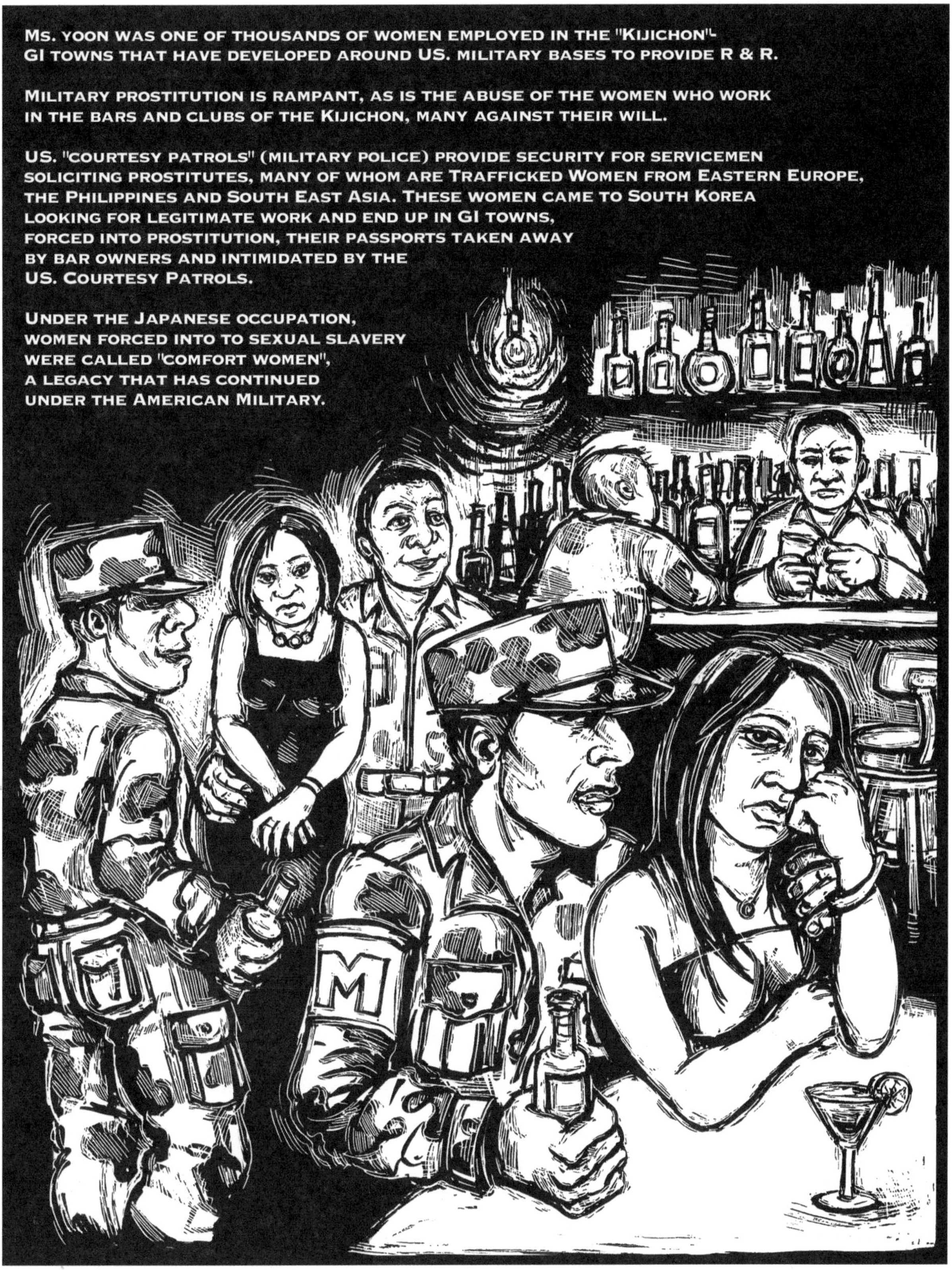
MS. YOON WAS ONE OF THOUSANDS OF WOMEN EMPLOYED IN THE "KIJICHON"-
GI TOWNS THAT HAVE DEVELOPED AROUND US. MILITARY BASES TO PROVIDE R & R.
MILITARY PROSTITUTION IS RAMPANT, AS IS THE ABUSE OF THE WOMEN WHO WORK
IN THE BARS AND CLUBS OF THE KIJICHON, MANY AGAINST THEIR WILL.
US. "COURTESY PATROLS" (MILITARY POLICE) PROVIDE SECURITY FOR SERVICEMEN
SOLICITING PROSTITUTES, MANY OF WHOM ARE TRAFFICKED WOMEN FROM EASTERN EUROPE,
THE PHILIPPINES AND SOUTH EAST ASIA. THESE WOMEN CAME TO SOUTH KOREA
LOOKING FOR LEGITIMATE WORK AND END UP IN GI TOWNS,
FORCED INTO PROSTITUTION, THEIR PASSPORTS TAKEN AWAY
BY BAR OWNERS AND INTIMIDATED BY THE
US. COURTESY PATROLS.
UNDER THE JAPANESE OCCUPATION,
WOMEN FORCED INTO TO SEXUAL SLAVERY
WERE CALLED "COMFORT WOMEN",
A LEGACY THAT HAS CONTINUED
UNDER THE AMERICAN MILITARY.
M

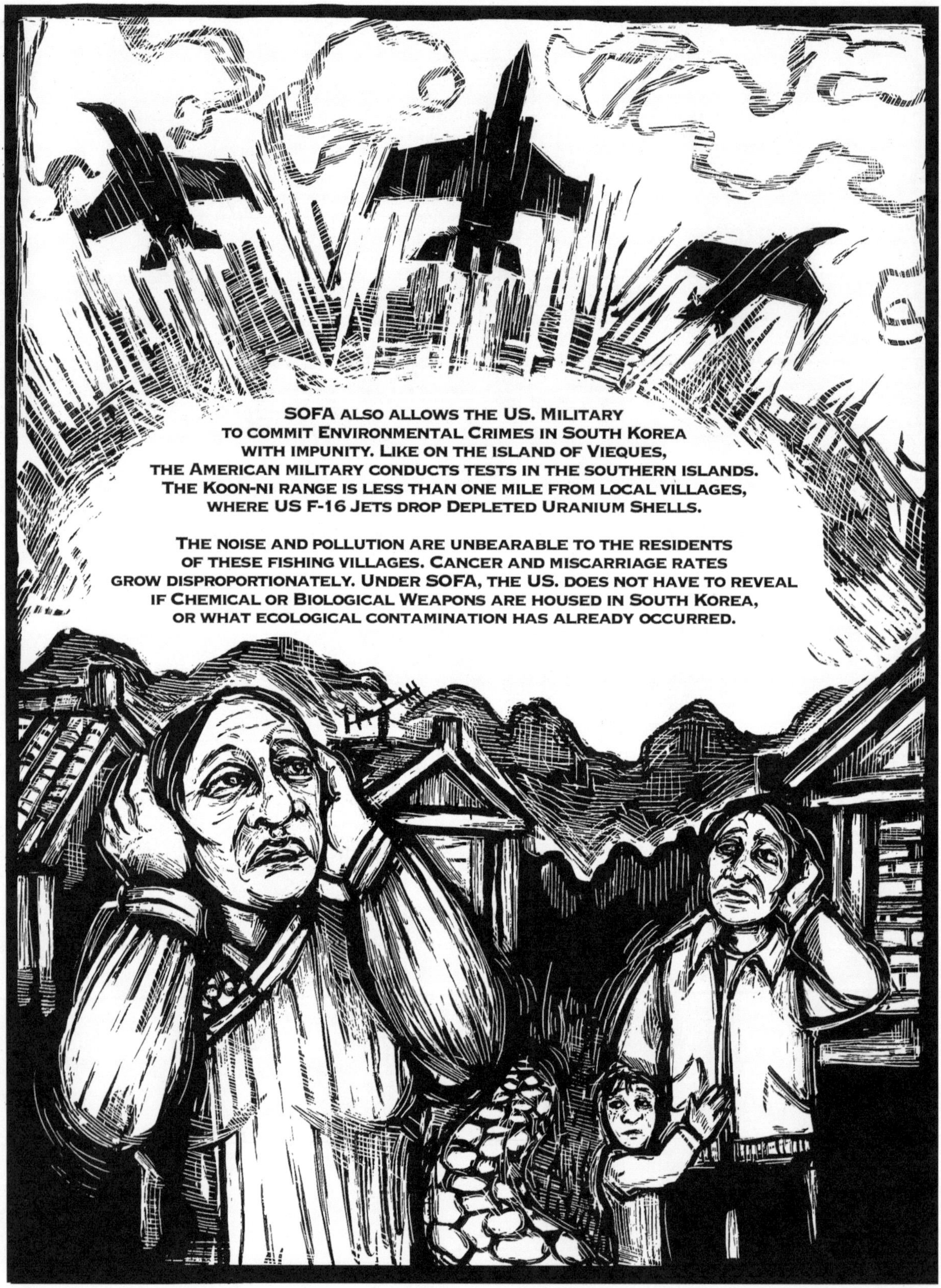
SOFA ALSO ALLOWS THE US. MILITARY
TO COMMIT ENVIRONMENTAL CRIMES IN SOUTH KOREA
WITH IMPUNITY. LIKE ON THE ISLAND OF VIEQUES,
THE AMERICAN MILITARY CONDUCTS TESTS IN THE SOUTHERN ISLANDS.
THE KOON-NI RANGE IS LESS THAN ONE MILE FROM LOCAL VILLAGES,
WHERE US F-16 JETS DROP DEPLETED URANIUM SHELLS.
THE NOISE AND POLLUTION ARE UNBEARABLE TO THE RESIDENTS
OF THESE FISHING VILLAGES. CANCER AND MISCARRIAGE RATES
GROW DISPROPORTIONATELY. UNDER SOFA, THE US. DOES NOT HAVE TO REVEAL
IF CHEMICAL OR BIOLOGICAL WEAPONS ARE HOUSED IN SOUTH KOREA,
OR WHAT ECOLOGICAL CONTAMINATION HAS ALREADY OCCURRED.

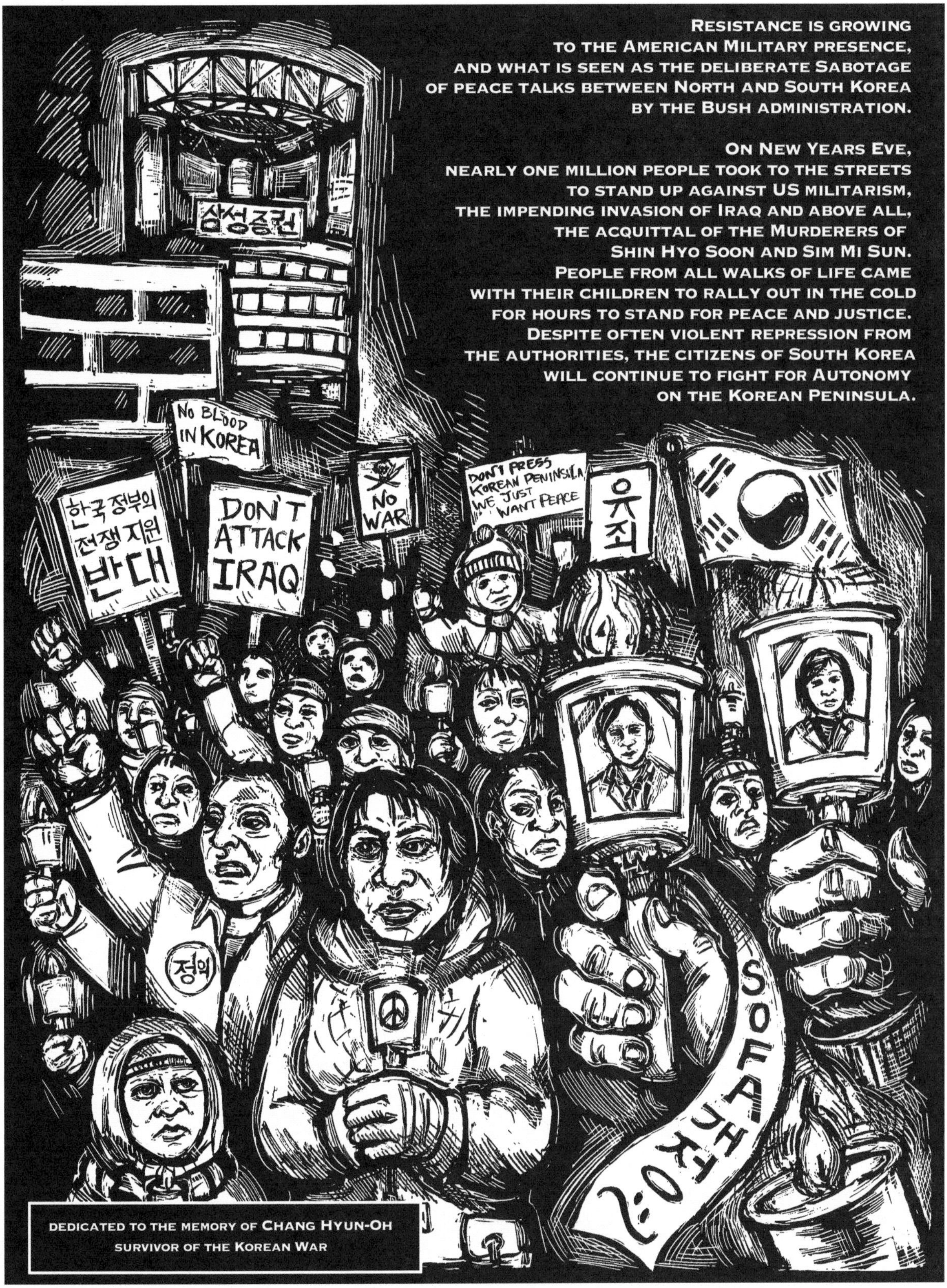
Resistance is growing
to the American Military presence,
and what is seen as the deliberate Sabotage
of peace talks between North and South Korea
by the Bush administration.

On New Years Eve,
nearly one million people took to the streets
to stand up against US militarism,
the impending invasion of Iraq and above all,
the acquittal of the Murderers of
Shin Hyo Soon and Sim Mi Sun.
People from all walks of life came
with their children to rally out in the cold
for hours to stand for peace and justice.
Despite often violent repression from
the authorities, the citizens of South Korea
will continue to fight for Autonomy
on the Korean Peninsula.
삼성증권
No BLOOD IN KOREA
한국정부의 전쟁지원 반대
DON'T ATTACK IRAQ
NO WAR
DON'T PRESS KOREAN PENINSULA WE JUST WANT PEACE
유죄
정의
SOFA 개정!
dedicated to the memory of Chang Hyun-Oh
survivor of the Korean War

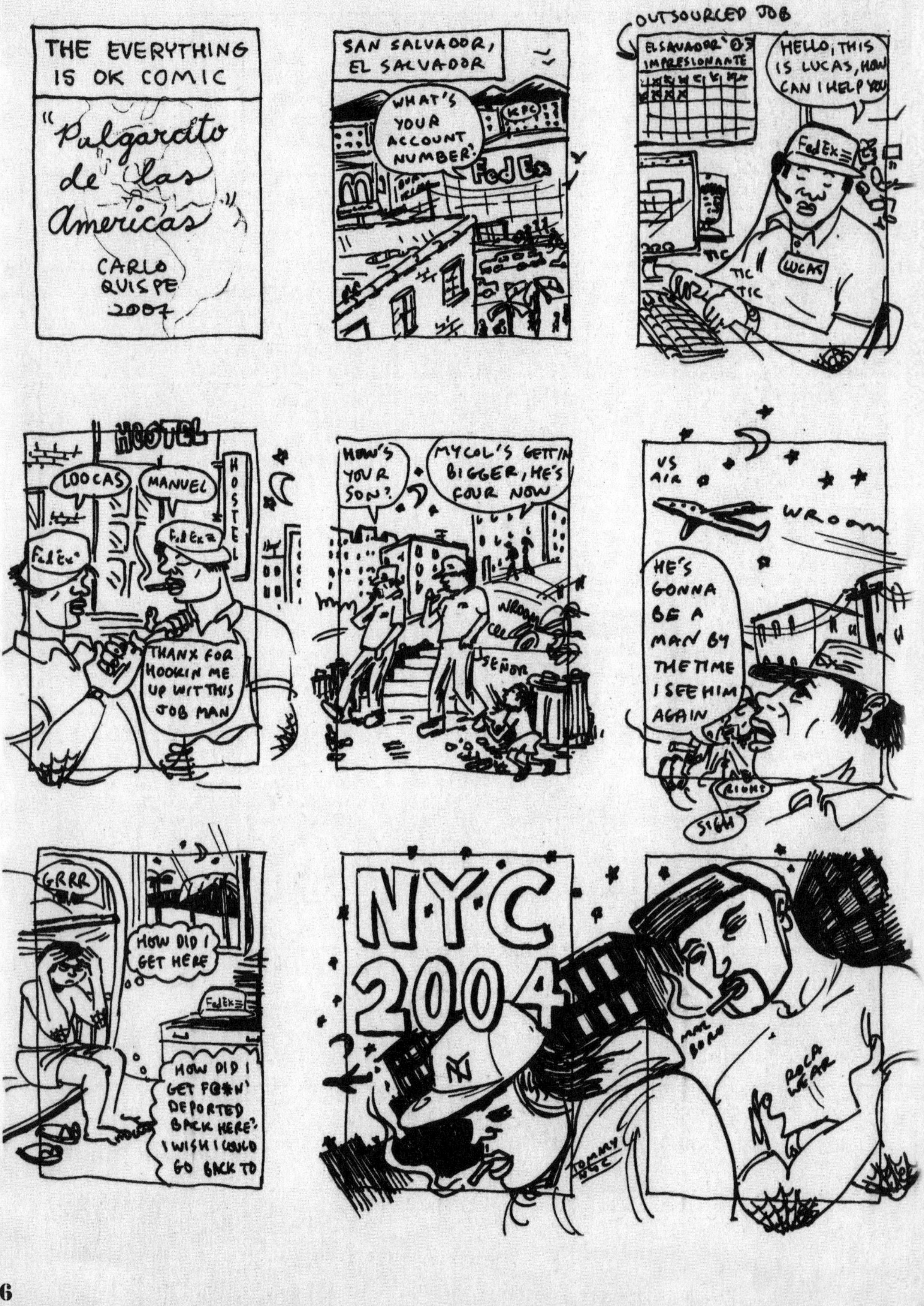

THE EVERYTHING IS OK COMIC
"Pulgarcito de las Americas"
CARLO QUISPE 2007
SAN SALVADOR, EL SALVADOR
WHAT'S YOUR ACCOUNT NUMBER?
FedEx
KFC
OUTSOURCED JOB
ELSAVADOR '07 IMPRESIONANTE
HELLO, THIS IS LUCAS, HOW CAN I HELP YOU
FedEx
LUCAS
TIC
TIC
TIC
HOSTEL
HOSTEL
LOOCAS
MANUEL
FedEx
FedEx
THANX FOR HOOKIN ME UP WIT THIS JOB MAN
HOW'S YOUR SON?
MYCOL'S GETTIN BIGGER, HE'S FOUR NOW
WROOM
SEÑOR
US AIR
WROOM
HE'S GONNA BE A MAN BY THE TIME I SEE HIM AGAIN
SIGH
GRRR
HOW DID I GET HERE
FedEx
HOW DID I GET F@#N' DEPORTED BACK HERE? I WISH I COULD GO BACK TO
NYC 2004
ROCA WEAR

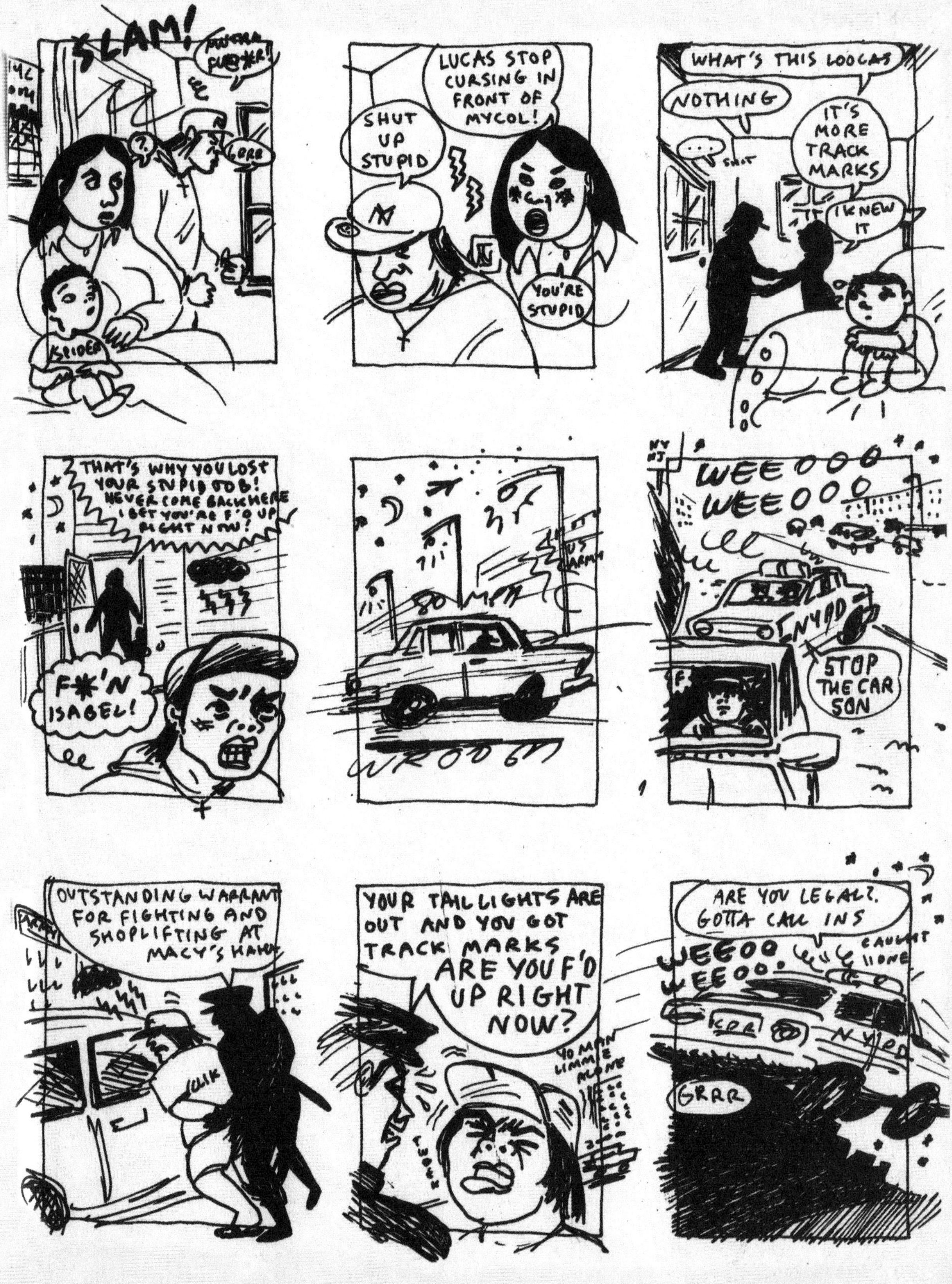
SLAM!
?
LUCAS STOP CURSING IN FRONT OF MYCOL!
SHUT UP STUPID
YOU'RE STUPID
WHAT'S THIS LOOCAS
NOTHING
IT'S MORE TRACK MARKS
I KNEW IT
THAT'S WHY YOU LOST YOUR STUPID JOB! NEVER COME BACK HERE I BET YOU'RE F'D UP RIGHT NOW!
F*'N ISABEL!
80 MPH
WEEOOO WEEOOO
NYPD
STOP THE CAR SON
OUTSTANDING WARRANT FOR FIGHTING AND SHOPLIFTING AT MACY'S
CLIK
YOUR TAILLIGHTS ARE OUT AND YOU GOT TRACK MARKS
ARE YOU F'D UP RIGHT NOW?
YO MAN LIMME ALONE
ARE YOU LEGAL?. GOTTA CALL INS
WEEOO WEEOO
NYPD
GRRR

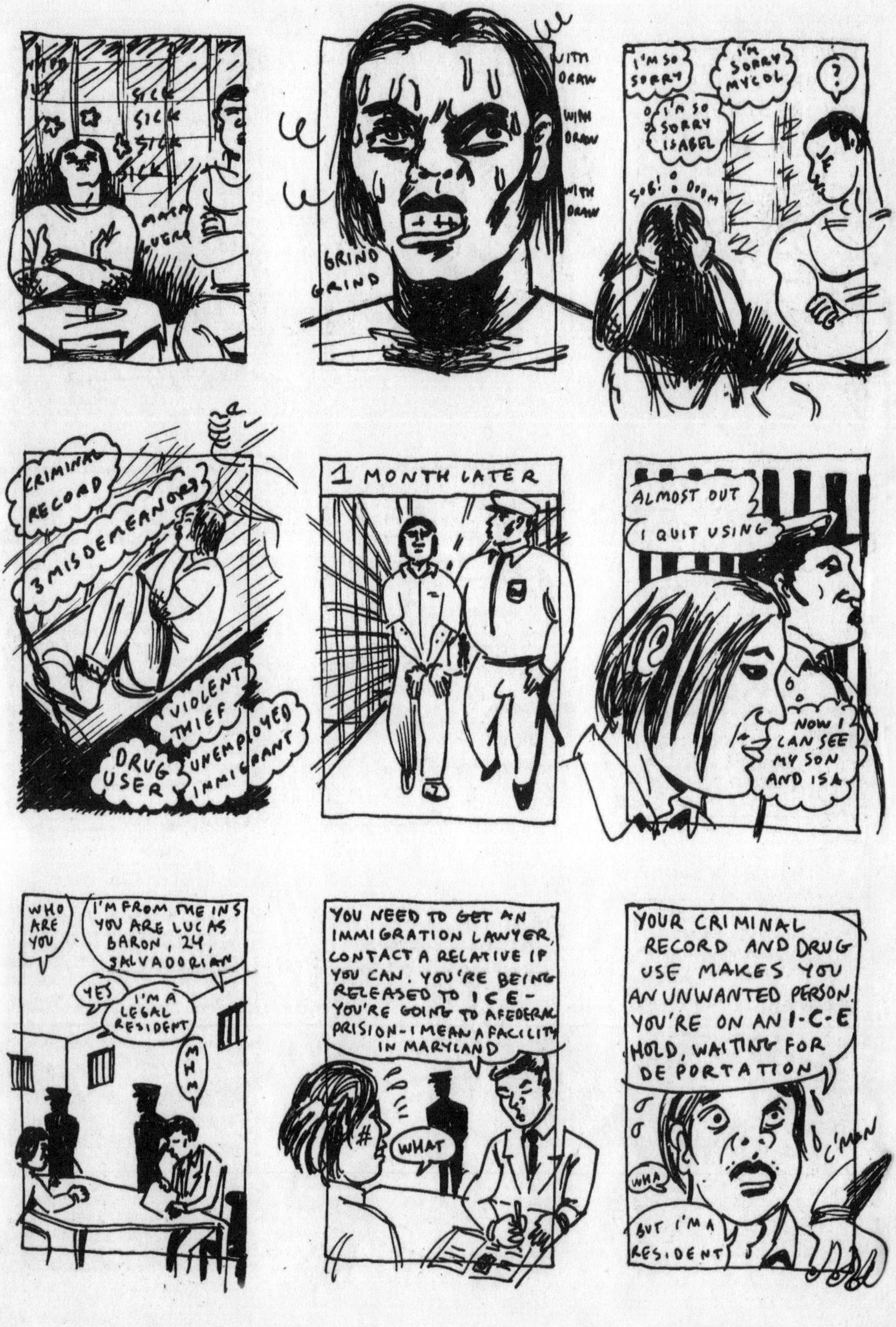
SICK
SICK
SICK
SICK
WITH
DRAW
WITH
DRAW
WITH
DRAW
GRIND
GRIND
I'M SO SORRY
I'M SORRY MYCOL
I'M SO SORRY ISABEL
?
SOB!
CRIMINAL RECORD
3 MISDEMEANORS
VIOLENT THIEF
UNEMPLOYED IMMIGRANT
DRUG USER
1 MONTH LATER
ALMOST OUT
I QUIT USING
NOW I CAN SEE MY SON AND ISA
WHO ARE YOU
I'M FROM THE INS YOU ARE LUCAS BARON, 24, SALVADORIAN
YES
I'M A LEGAL RESIDENT
MHM
YOU NEED TO GET AN IMMIGRATION LAWYER, CONTACT A RELATIVE IF YOU CAN. YOU'RE BEING RELEASED TO ICE - YOU'RE GOING TO A FEDERAL PRISION - I MEAN A FACILITY IN MARYLAND
WHAT
YOUR CRIMINAL RECORD AND DRUG USE MAKES YOU AN UNWANTED PERSON. YOU'RE ON AN I-C-E HOLD, WAITING FOR DEPORTATION
WHA
C'MON
BUT I'M A RESIDENT

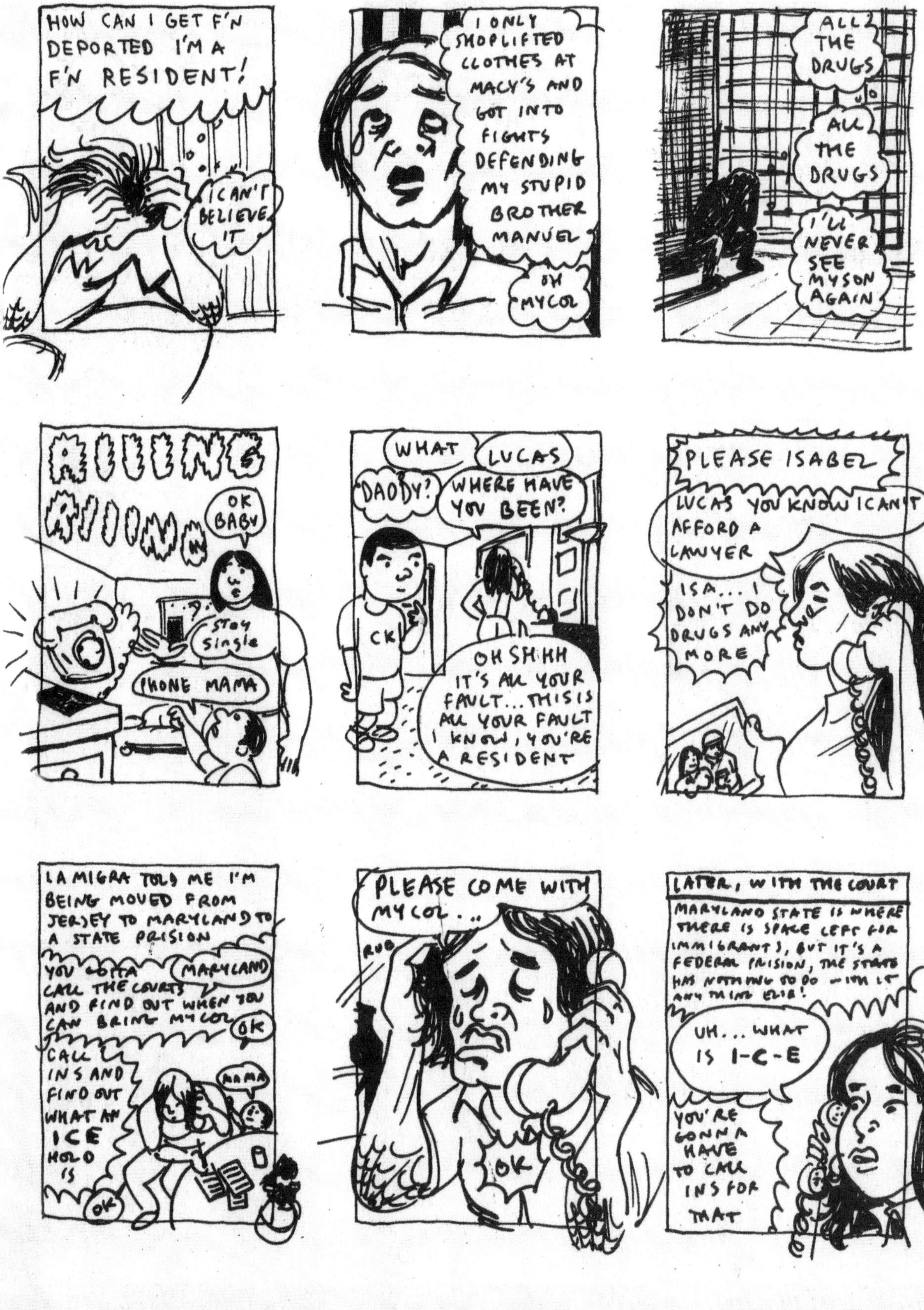
HOW CAN I GET F'N DEPORTED I'M A F'N RESIDENT!
I CAN'T BELIEVE IT
I ONLY SHOPLIFTED CLOTHES AT MACY'S AND GOT INTO FIGHTS DEFENDING MY STUPID BROTHER MANUEL
OH MYCOL
ALL THE DRUGS
ALL THE DRUGS
I'LL NEVER SEE MY SON AGAIN
RIIING RIING
OK BABY
STAY SINGLE
PHONE MAMA
WHAT
LUCAS
DADDY?
WHERE HAVE YOU BEEN?
OH SHHH IT'S ALL YOUR FAULT... THIS IS ALL YOUR FAULT I KNOW, YOU'RE A RESIDENT
PLEASE ISABEL
LUCAS YOU KNOW I CAN'T AFFORD A LAWYER
ISA... I DON'T DO DRUGS ANY MORE
LA MIGRA TOLD ME I'M BEING MOVED FROM JERSEY TO MARYLAND TO A STATE PRISION
YOU GOTTA CALL THE COURTS AND FIND OUT WHEN YOU CAN BRING MYCOL
MARYLAND
OK
CALL INS AND FIND OUT WHAT AN ICE HOLD IS
MAMA
OK
PLEASE COME WITH MYCOL...
OK
LATER, WITH THE COURT
MARYLAND STATE IS WHERE THERE IS SPACE LEFS FOR IMMIGRANTS, BUT IT'S A FEDERAL PRISION, THE STATE HAS NOTHING TO DO WITH IT ANY THING ELSE!
UH... WHAT IS I-C-E
YOU'RE GONNA HAVE TO CALL INS FOR THAT

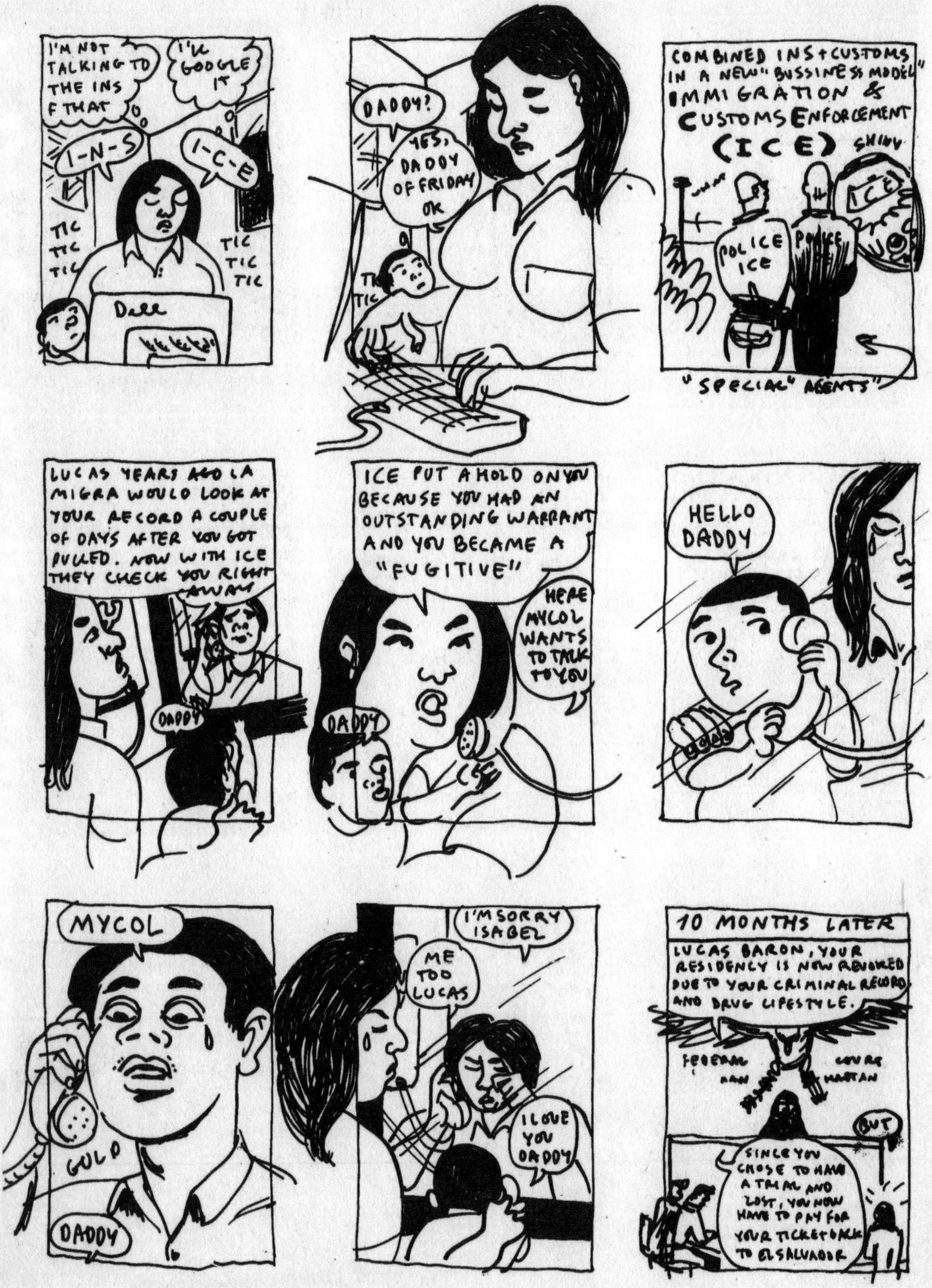
I'M NOT TALKING TO THE INS F THAT
I'LL GOOGLE IT
I-N-S
I-C-E
TIC TIC TIC
TIC TIC TIC
Dell
DADDY?
YES, DADDY OF FRIDAY OK
TIC TIC
COMBINED INS + CUSTOMS IN A NEW "BUSSINESS MODEL" IMMIGRATION & CUSTOMS ENFORCEMENT (ICE)
SHINY
ICE
POLICE ICE
POLICE
"SPECIAL" AGENTS
LUCAS YEARS AGO LA MIGRA WOULD LOOK AT YOUR RECORD A COUPLE OF DAYS AFTER YOU GOT PULLED. NOW WITH ICE THEY CHECK YOU RIGHT AWAY
DADDY
ICE PUT A HOLD ON YOU BECAUSE YOU HAD AN OUTSTANDING WARRANT AND YOU BECAME A "FUGITIVE"
HERE MYCOL WANTS TO TALK TO YOU
DADDY
HELLO DADDY
MYCOL
GULP
DADDY
I'M SORRY ISABEL
ME TOO LUCAS
I LOVE YOU DADDY
10 MONTHS LATER
LUCAS BARON, YOUR RESIDENCY IS NOW REVOKED DUE TO YOUR CRIMINAL RECORD AND DRUG LIFESTYLE.
BUT
SINCE YOU CHOSE TO HAVE A TRIAL AND LOST, YOU NOW HAVE TO PAY FOR YOUR TICKET BACK TO EL SALVADOR

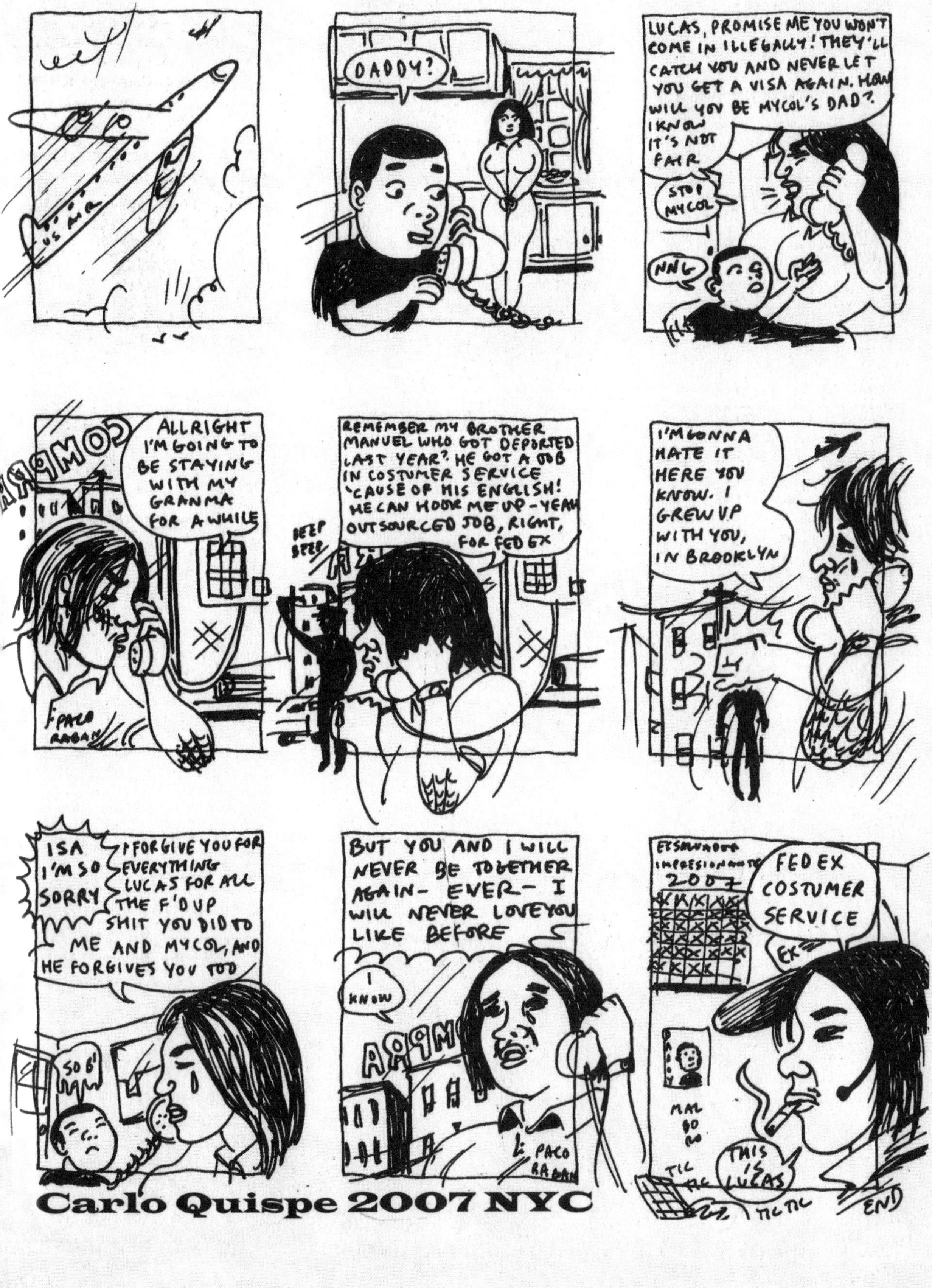
US AIR
DADDY?
LUCAS, PROMISE ME YOU WON'T COME IN ILLEGALLY! THEY'LL CATCH YOU AND NEVER LET YOU GET A VISA AGAIN. HOW WILL YOU BE MYCOL'S DAD?
I KNOW IT'S NOT FAIR
STOP MYCOL
NNG
COMPRA
ALLRIGHT I'M GOING TO BE STAYING WITH MY GRANMA FOR A WHILE
PACO RABAN
REMEMBER MY BROTHER MANUEL WHO GOT DEPORTED LAST YEAR? HE GOT A JOB IN COSTUMER SERVICE 'CAUSE OF HIS ENGLISH! HE CAN HOOK ME UP - YEAH OUTSOURCED JOB, RIGHT, FOR FEDEX
BEEP BEEP
I'M GONNA HATE IT HERE YOU KNOW. I GREW UP WITH YOU, IN BROOKLYN
ISA I'M SO SORRY
I FORGIVE YOU FOR EVERYTHING LUCAS FOR ALL THE F'D UP SHIT YOU DID TO ME AND MYCOL, AND HE FORGIVES YOU TOO
SOB
BUT YOU AND I WILL NEVER BE TOGETHER AGAIN - EVER - I WILL NEVER LOVE YOU LIKE BEFORE
I KNOW
PACO RABAN
2007
FEDEX COSTUMER SERVICE
EX
MAL BO RO
THIS IS LUCAS
TIC TIC
TIC TIC
END

Carlo Quispe 2007 NYC

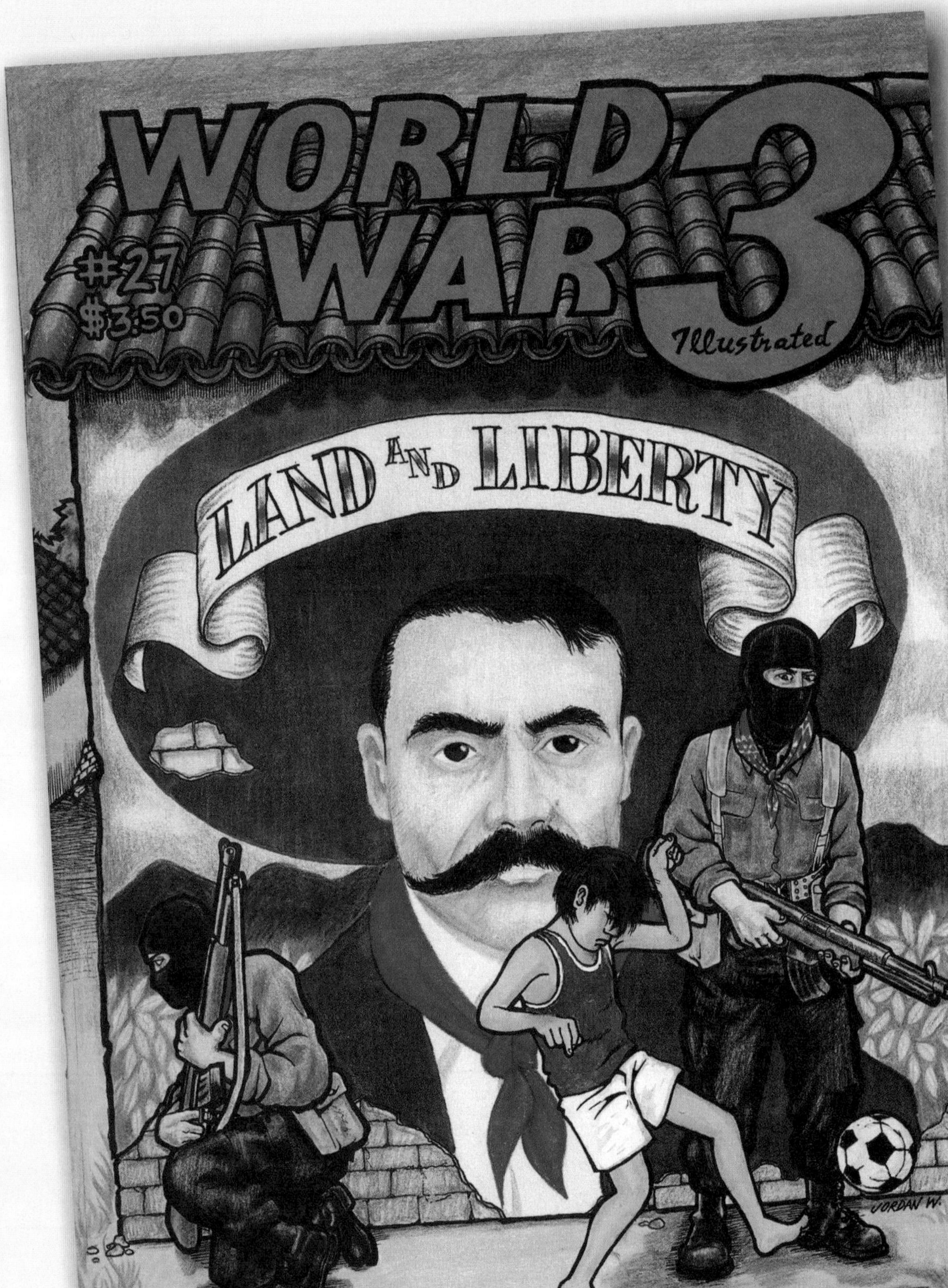
WORLD WAR 3
Illustrated
#27
$3.50
LAND AND LIBERTY
JORDAN W.

A journal of life and struggle in a Mexican town

OAXACA

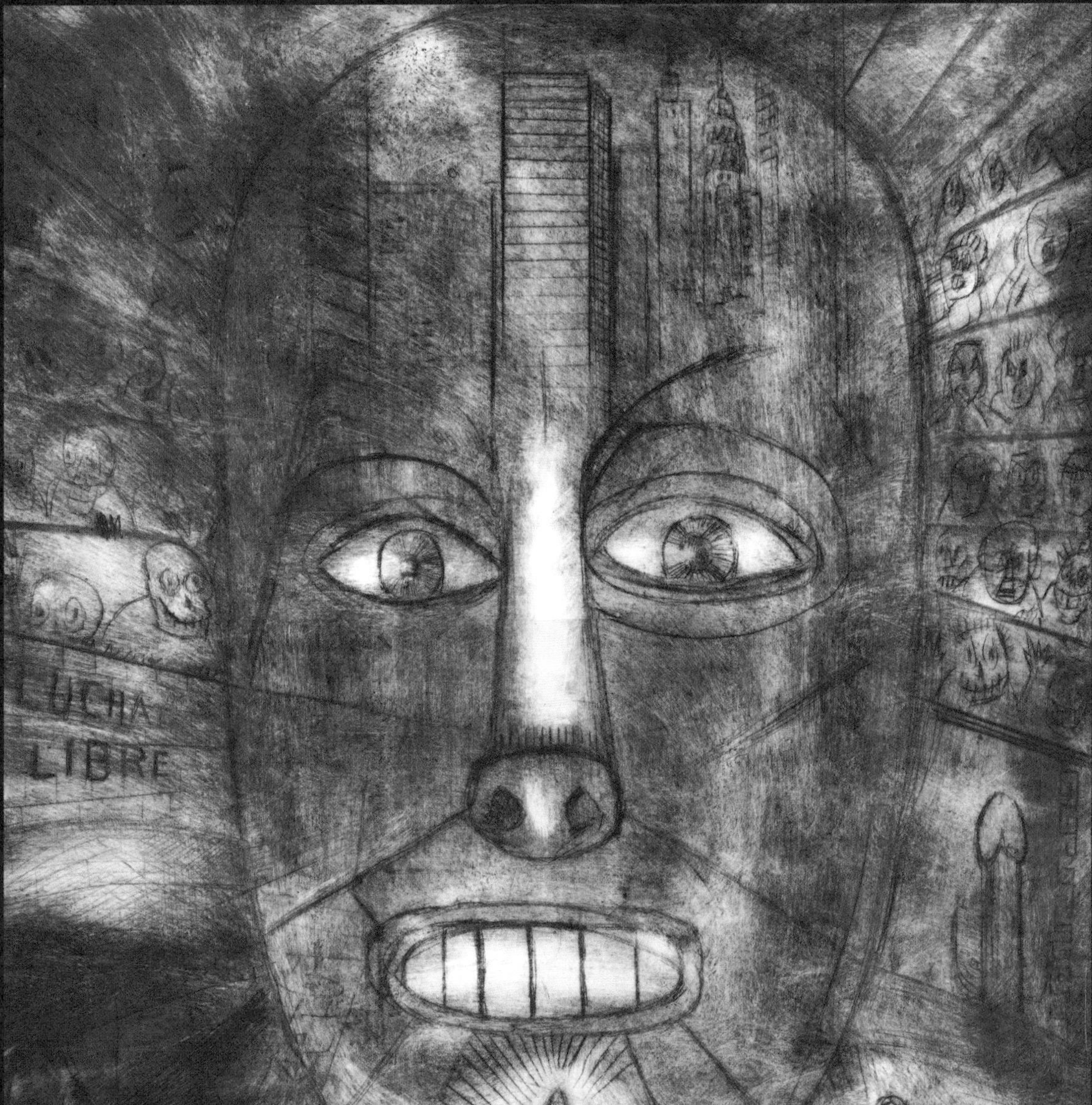
LUCHA
LIBRE

OAXACA

Peter Kuper

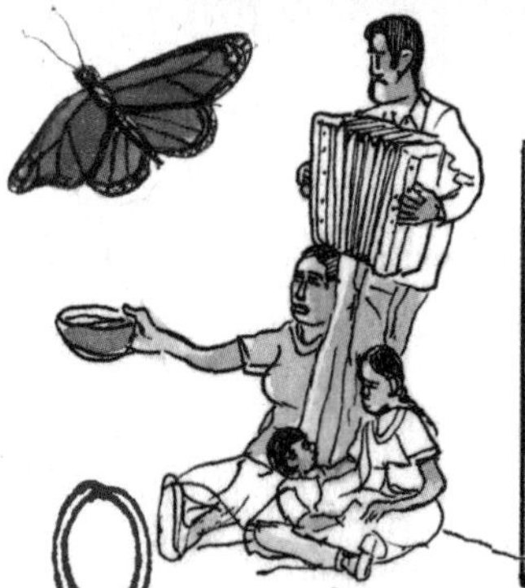

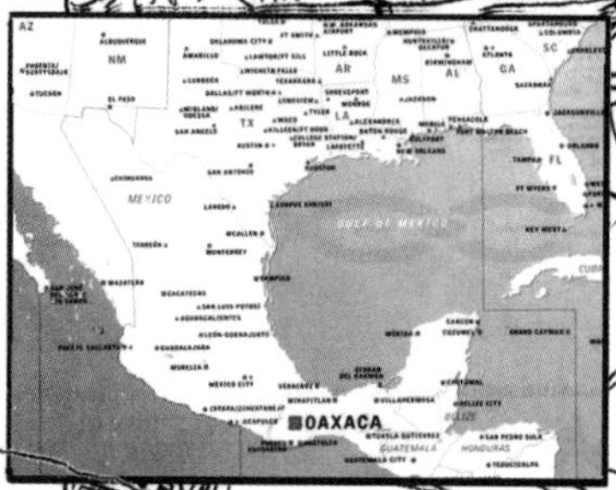

MEXICO
GULF OF MEXICO
OAXACA

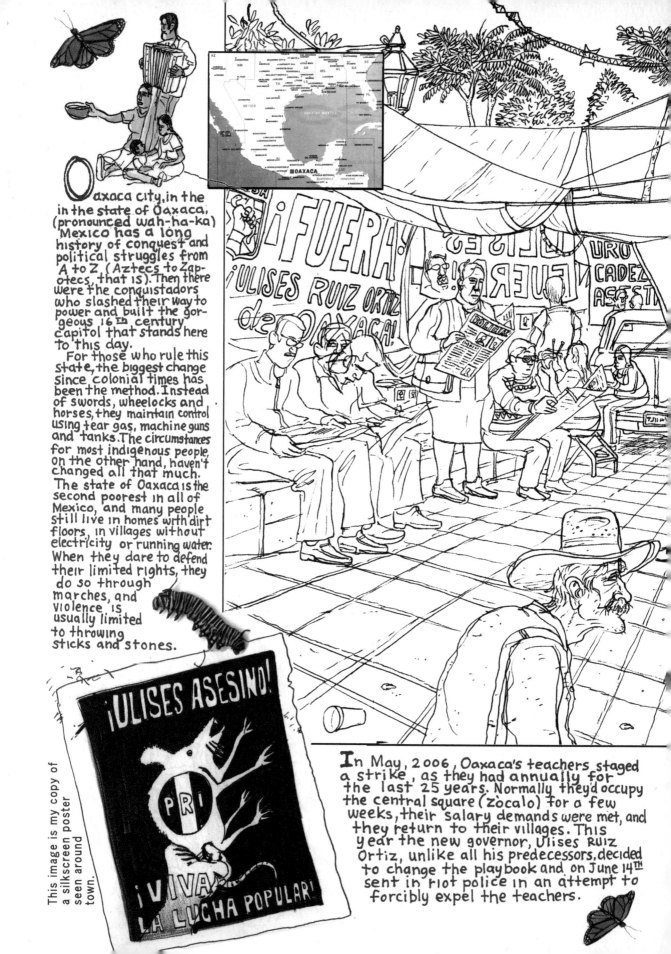

Oaxaca city, in the in the state of Oaxaca, (pronounced wah-ha-ka) Mexico has a long history of conquest and political struggles from A to Z (Aztecs to Zapotecs, that is). Then there were the conquistadors who slashed their way to power and built the gorgeous 16th century capitol that stands here to this day.

For those who rule this state, the biggest change since colonial times has been the method. Instead of swords, wheelocks and horses, they maintain control using tear gas, machine guns and tanks. The circumstances for most indigenous people, on the other hand, haven't changed all that much. The state of Oaxaca is the second poorest in all of Mexico, and many people still live in homes with dirt floors, in villages without electricity or running water. When they dare to defend their limited rights, they do so through marches, and violence is usually limited to throwing sticks and stones.

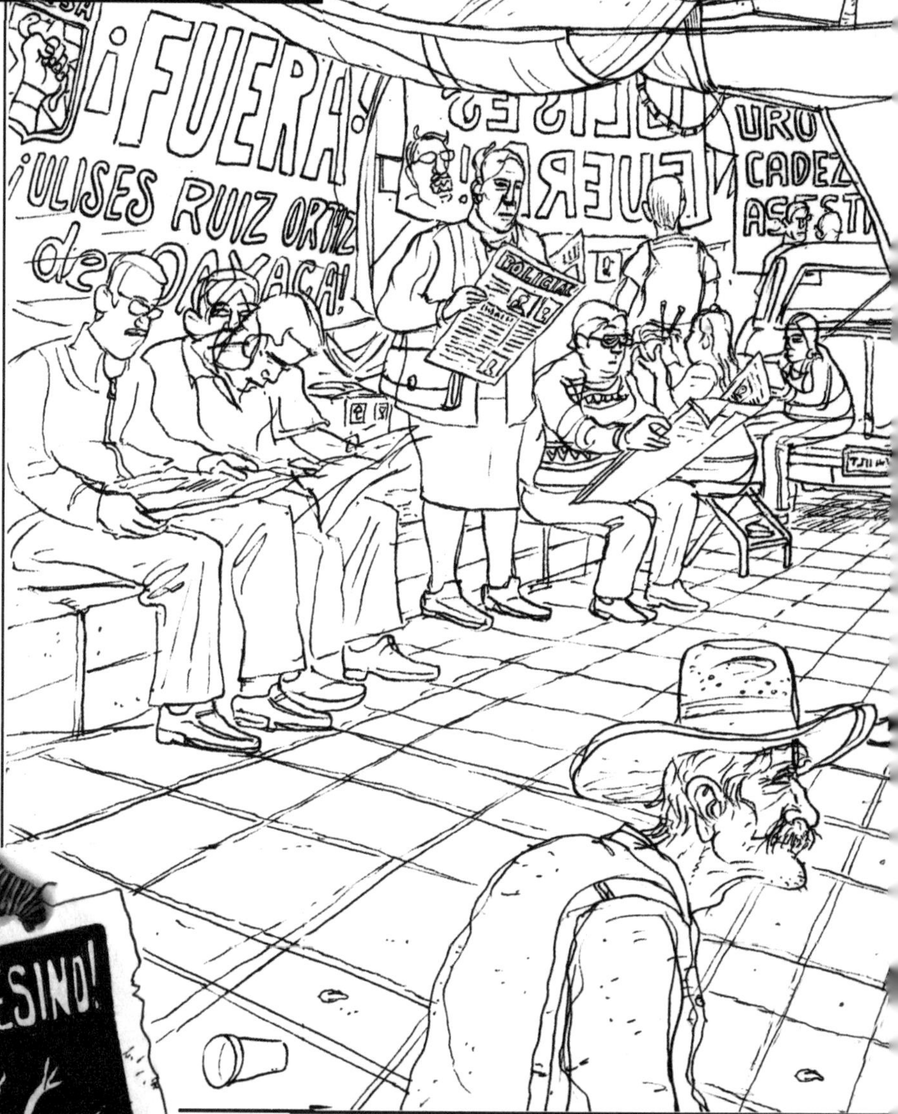

¡FUERA!
¡ULISES RUIZ ORTIZ de OAXACA!
ULISES FUERA!
URO CADEZ ASESTI
POLICIAL

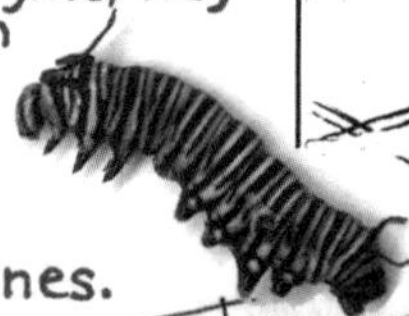

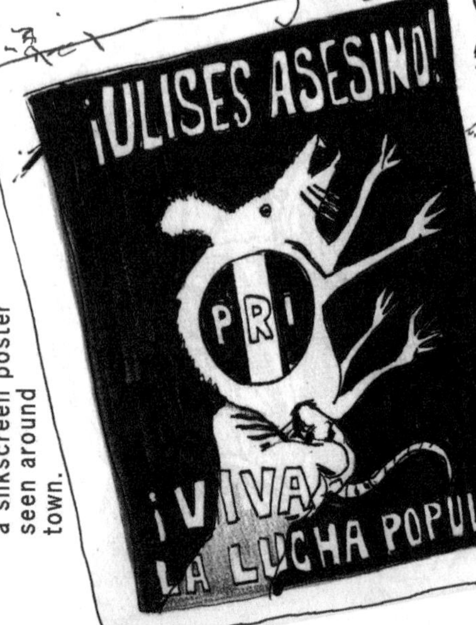

¡ULISES ASESINO!
PRI
¡VIVA LA LUCHA POPULAR!

This image is my copy of a silkscreen poster seen around town.

In May, 2006, Oaxaca's teachers staged a strike, as they had annually for the last 25 years. Normally they'd occupy the central square (zócalo) for a few weeks, their salary demands were met, and they return to their villages. This year the new governor, Ulises Ruiz Ortiz, unlike all his predecessors, decided to change the playbook and on June 14th sent in riot police in an attempt to forcibly expel the teachers.

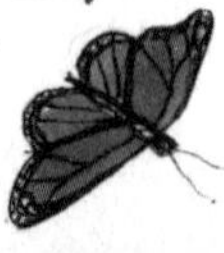

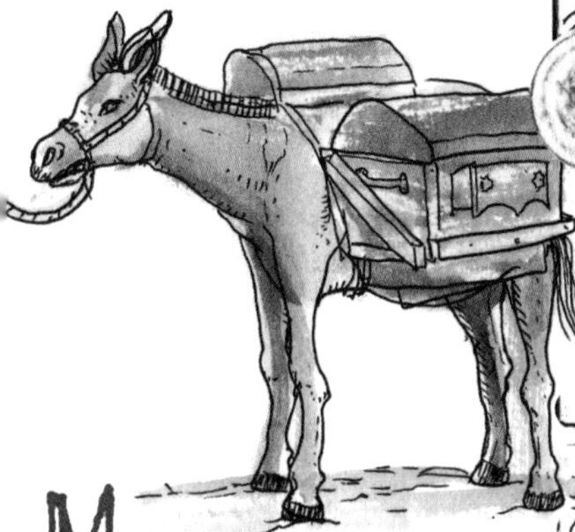

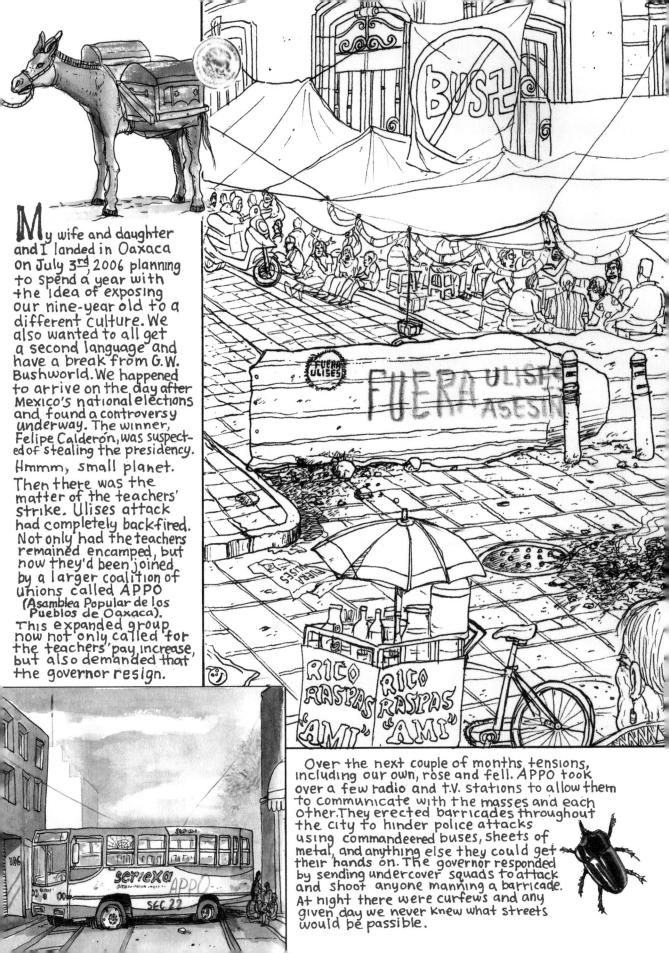

My wife and daughter and I landed in Oaxaca on July 3rd, 2006 planning to spend a year with the idea of exposing our nine-year old to a different culture. We also wanted to all get a second language and have a break from G.W. Bushworld. We happened to arrive on the day after Mexico's national elections and found a controversy underway. The winner, Felipe Calderón, was suspected of stealing the presidency. Hmmm, small planet.

Then there was the matter of the teachers' strike. Ulises attack had completely backfired. Not only had the teachers remained encamped, but now they'd been joined by a larger coalition of unions called APPO (Asamblea Popular de los Pueblos de Oaxaca). This expanded group now not only called for the teachers' pay increase, but also demanded that the governor resign.

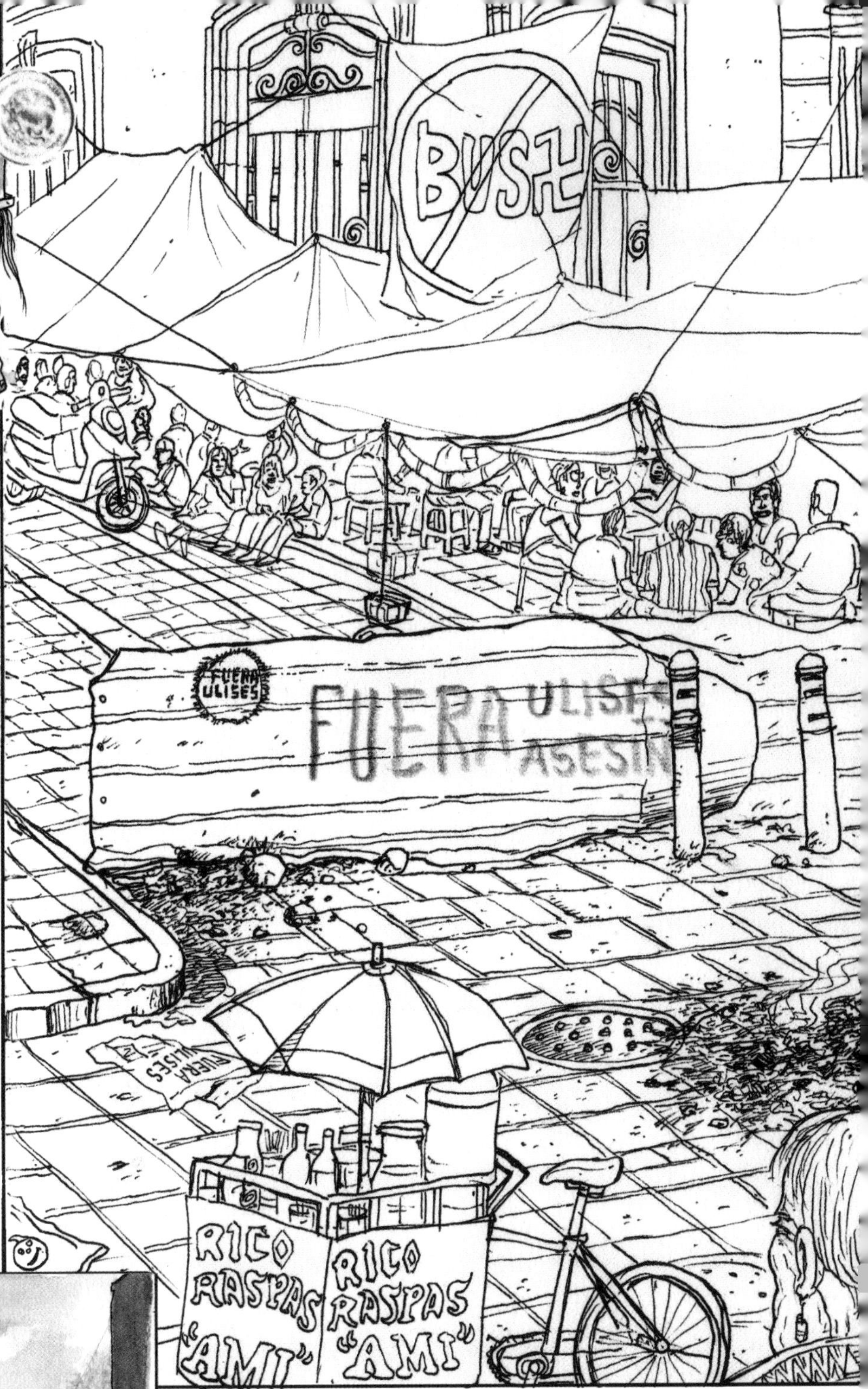
BUSH
FUERA ULISES
FUERA ULISES ASESIN
RICO RASPAS "AMI"
RICO RASPAS "AMI"

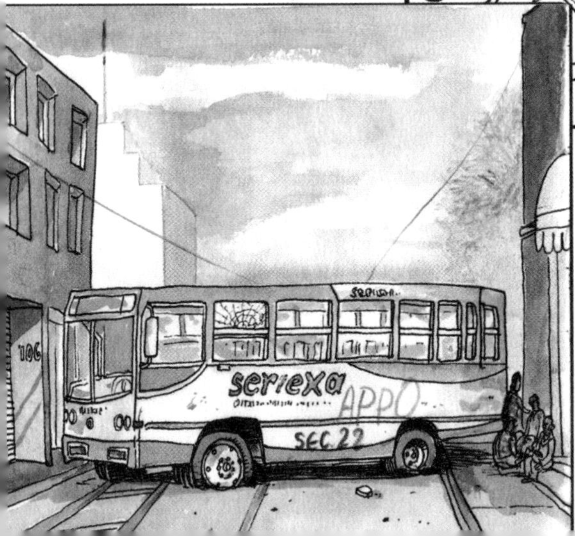
seriexa
APPO
SEC 22

Over the next couple of months tensions, including our own, rose and fell. APPO took over a few radio and t.v. stations to allow them to communicate with the masses and each other. They erected barricades throughout the city to hinder police attacks using commandeered buses, sheets of metal, and anything else they could get their hands on. The governor responded by sending undercover squads to attack and shoot anyone manning a barricade. At night there were curfews and any given day we never knew what streets would be passible.

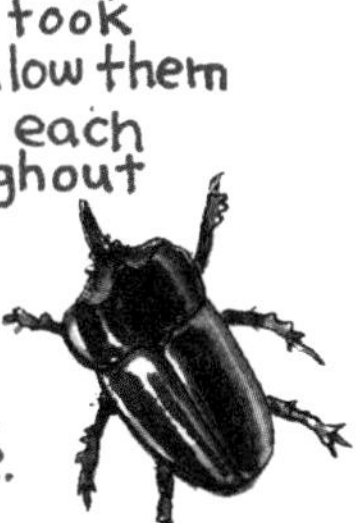

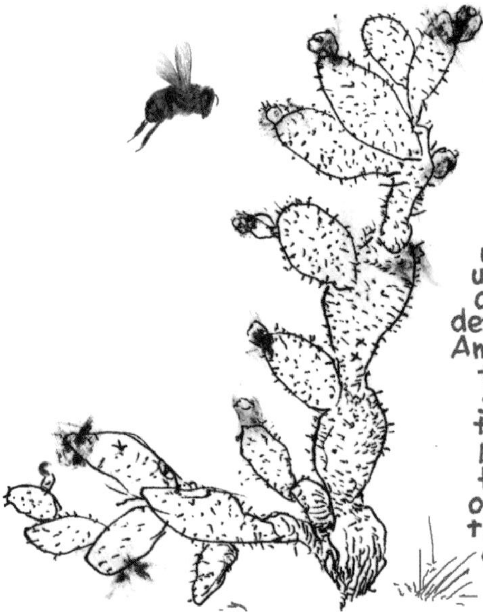

Even under assault the teachers remained peaceful. They sat around with their kids, reading newspapers, they organized marches and set up classes in the streets. In one action, women, armed only with pots and pans to bang, took over a t.v. station allowing them to broadcast stories the station had censored. Police stood down without arresting them, probably fearing the bad press! *In the zócalo,* walking past people who'd spent months living under tarps, cooking on sidewalks and sleeping on cold stone streets, I marvelled at their determination. I had trouble imagining too many Americans (myself included) willing to endure the kind of long-term discomfort they'd suffered for their cause; "Months sleeping on the Capitol steps? *No way, it would kill my back.*" Not only were the teachers willing to accept these hardships, the population as a whole overwhelmingly supported them even though this strike had translated into an economic downturn for the entire state.

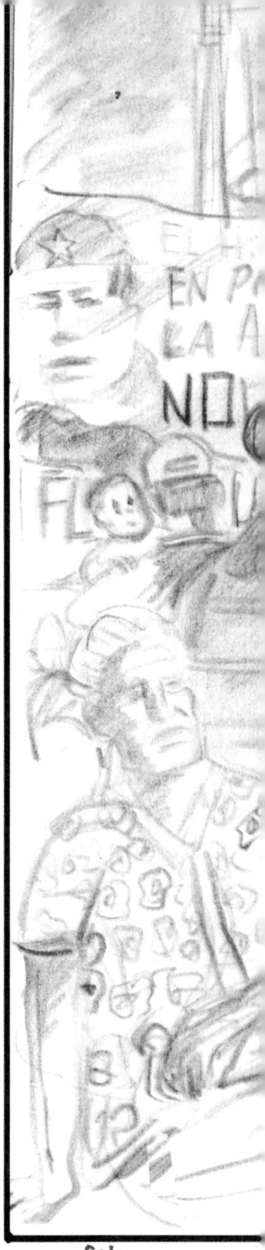

It was Friday, October 27th and the strike was now entering its 6th month when my friend, Antonio Turok, called to see if I wanted to join him for a behind the scenes tour of some of the barricades. Antonio is a photographer who has covered situations in Chiapas and El Salvador and had been documenting the teachers' strike for months. He said he'd call me when he reached the town center, where we'd rendezvous. I waited as the hours passed, but he didn't call. Toward the end of the day, it began to rain and I volunteered to pick up our daughter from a play date. As I drove along the cobblestone streets a mild drizzle suddenly became a torrential downpour. I'd never experienced a flash flood--that is, until that day! As I skirted yet another newly created blockade, I was confronted by a raging river where a street had been only moments before. After many twists and turns, I found a route through and managed to extract our (happily) drenched daughter from her friend's house and retrace my steps. Just as suddenly the rain subsided, but then the dam broke. A news report hit that while it was raining uptown, downtown a different kind of storm had struck. "*Porros*," the *paramilitary police working undercover for Ulises,* had attacked APPO members manning barricades. Two Oaxacaños and an American journalist had been shot and killed. Brad Will captured his own shooting on film then died on the way to the hospital. I didn't know Brad, but very quickly discovered that just about everyone I knew from the Lower East Side in NYC did, and it wasn't much of a stretch to imagine myself in his shoes.

Antonio called as night fell to say he was holed up in an office building with a group of journalists who had taken refuge there when the shooting had started. Needless to say, we wouldn't be meeting up.

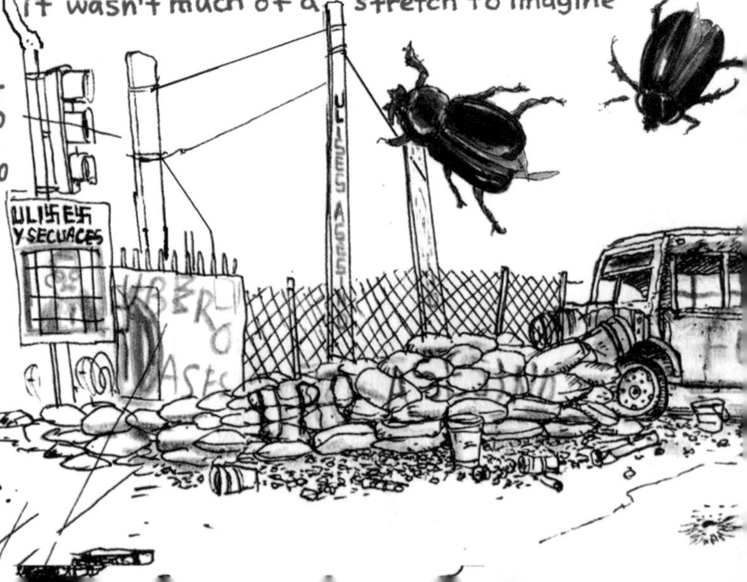
Y SECUACES

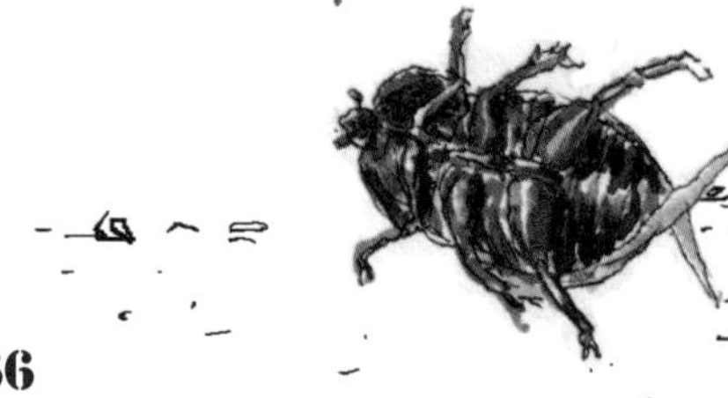

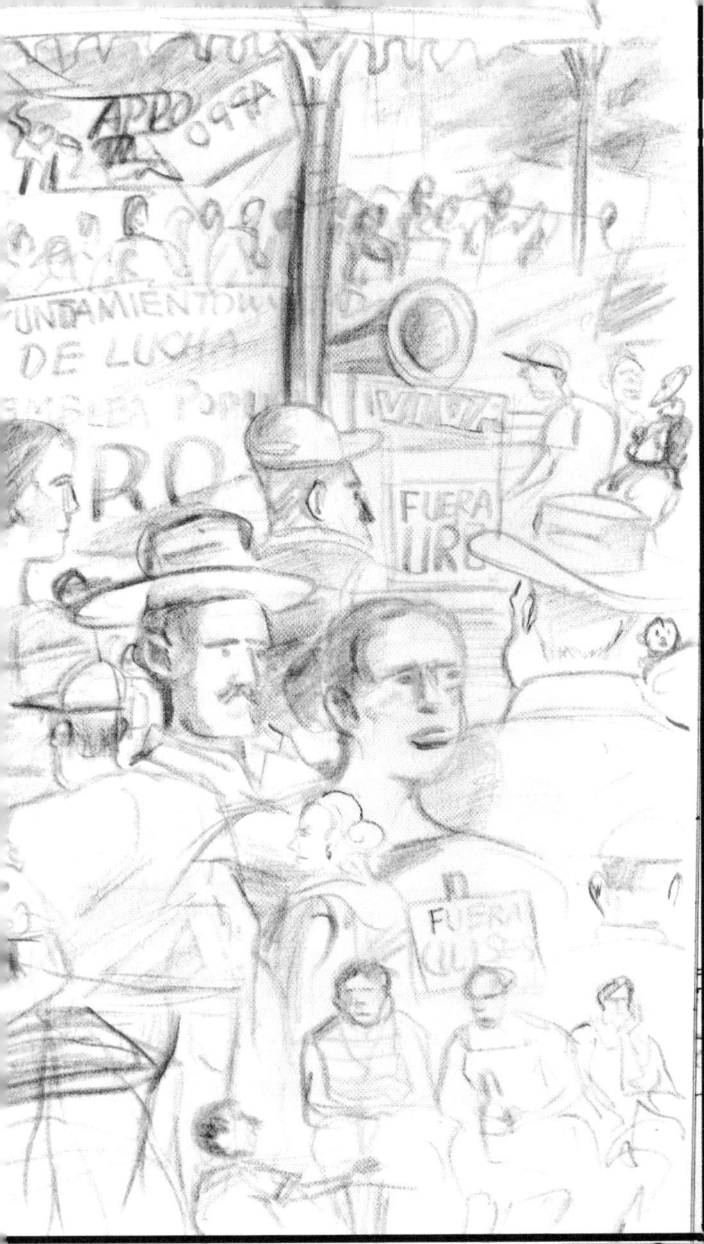

APPO
DE LUCHA
VIVA
FUERA URO
FUERA

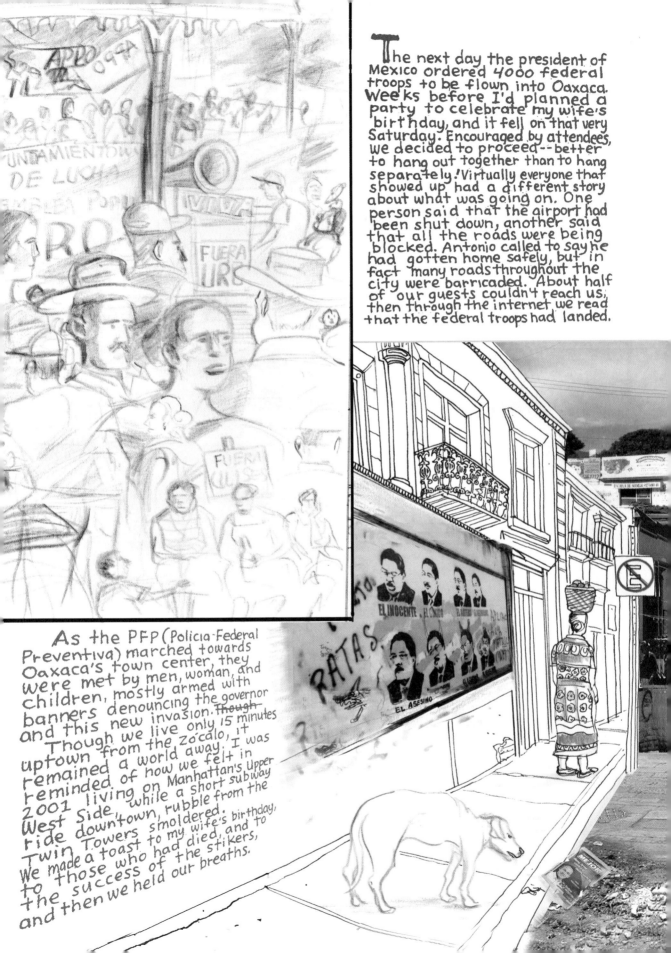

The next day the president of Mexico ordered 4000 federal troops to be flown into Oaxaca. Weeks before I'd planned a party to celebrate my wife's birthday, and it fell on that very Saturday. Encouraged by attendees, we decided to proceed -- better to hang out together than to hang separately! Virtually everyone that showed up had a different story about what was going on. One person said that the airport had been shut down, another said that all the roads were being blocked. Antonio called to say he had gotten home safely, but in fact many roads throughout the city were barricaded. About half of our guests couldn't reach us, then through the internet we read that the federal troops had landed.

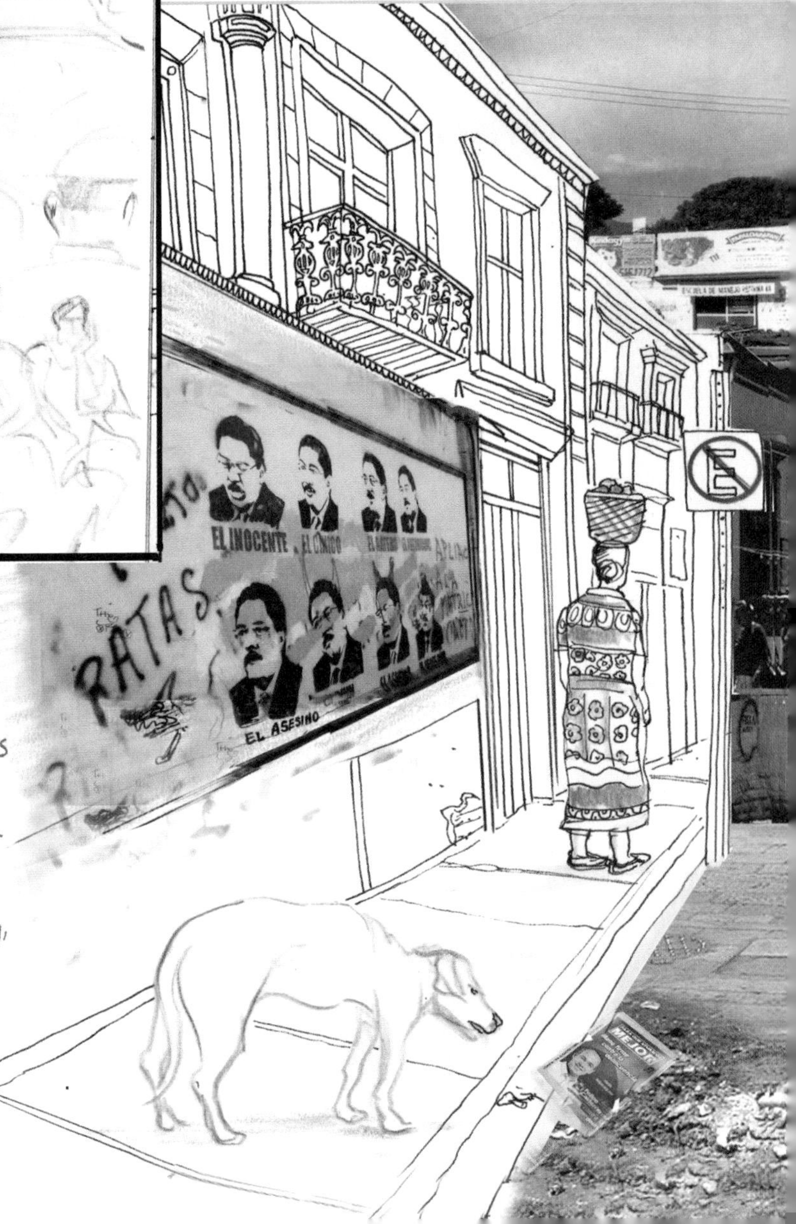

EL INOCENTE
EL ASESINO
RATAS

As the PFP (Policia Federal Preventiva) marched towards Oaxaca's town center, they were met by men, woman, and children, mostly armed with banners denouncing the governor and this new invasion. ~~Though~~

Though we live only 15 minutes uptown from the Zócalo, it remained a world away. I was reminded of how we felt in 2001 living on Manhattan's Upper West Side, while a short subway ride downtown, rubble from the Twin Towers smoldered.

We made a toast to my wife's birthday, to those who had died, and to the success of the stikers, and then we held our breaths.

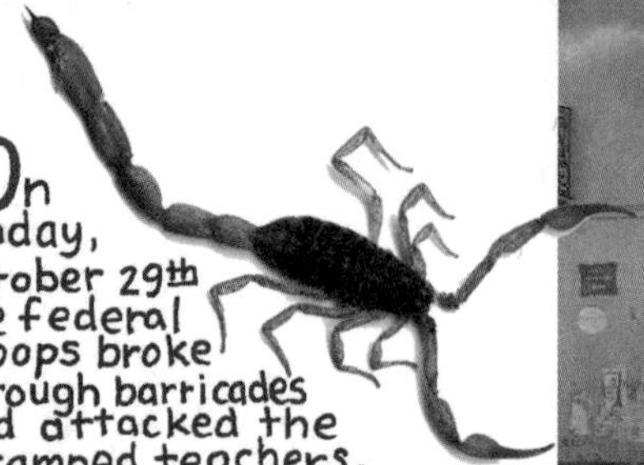

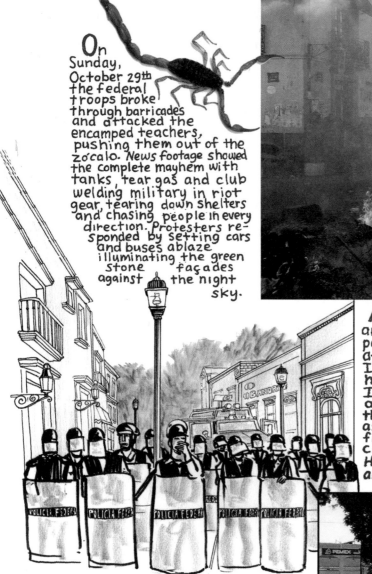

On Sunday, October 29th the federal troops broke through barricades and attacked the encamped teachers, pushing them out of the zócalo. *News footage* showed the complete mayhem with tanks, tear gas and club welding military in riot gear, tearing down shelters and chasing people in every direction. *Protesters* responded by setting cars and buses ablaze illuminating the green stone façades against the night sky.

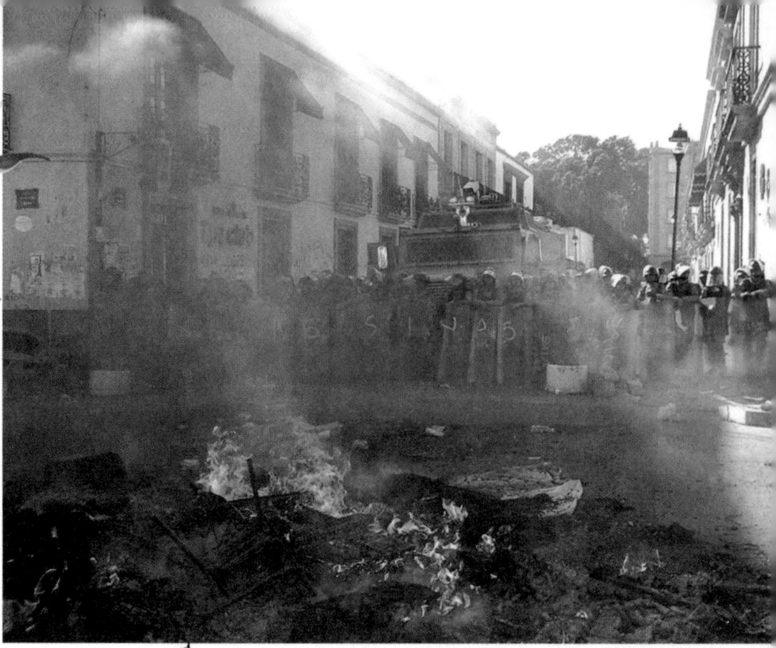

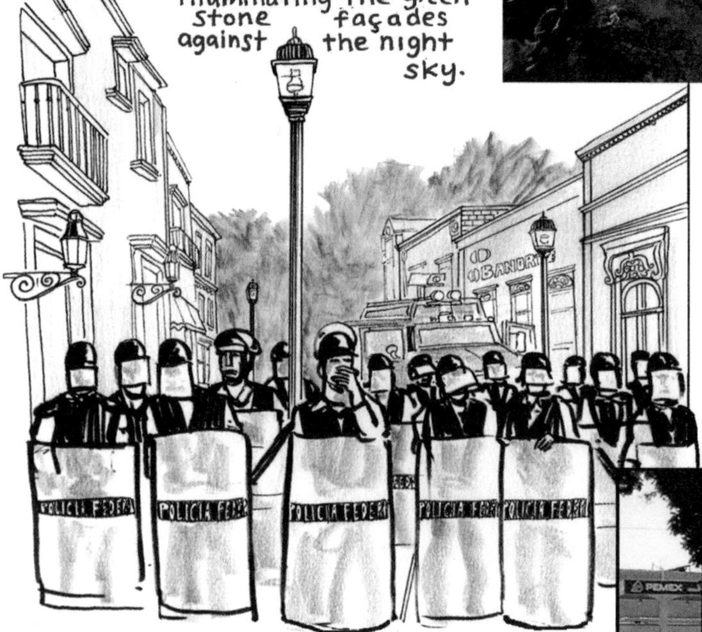
BANORTE
POLICIA FEDERAL
POLICIA FEDERAL
POLICIA FEDERAL
POLICIA FEDERAL
POLICIA FEDERAL

As foreigners, we can be arrested and deported just for attending any political rallies, but Monday morning, after reading about events downtown I was compelled to find out first hand what had actually taken place. I drove towards the town center and parked about five blocks from the zócalo. My heart rate jumped as I rounded a corner and saw smoke filling the streets. I got a half block closer before running into... *Antonio!* He had been up all night photographing. and looked as dazed as I was starting to feel.

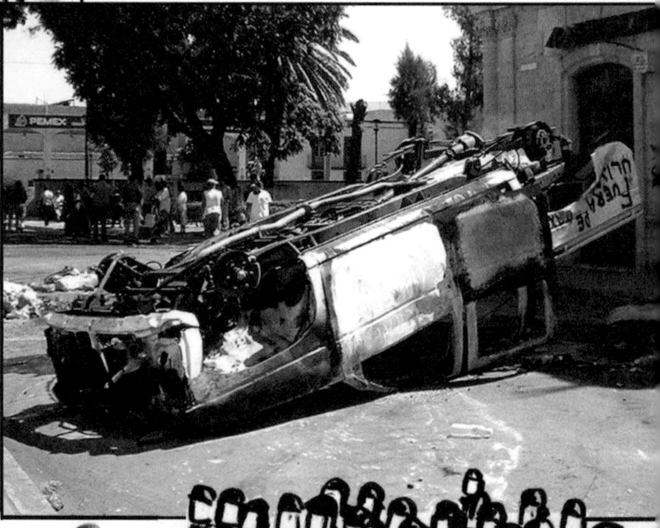
PEMEX

He told me I could get closer to the action without getting arrested; "YOU WON'T BELIEVE THE SHIT THAT WENT DOWN!" he said holding up his camera, then gave me a comradly hug before heading home to get some sleep. I made my way past a pile of burning tires and a few smoldering vehicles before reaching the zócalo–or as close as the menacing columns of riot police would allow. At each entrance to the square they stood shoulder to shoulder backed up by tanks. Though they were totally theatening, some *brave/crazy protesters* had discovered they weren't arresting people and had written "ASESINOS" (MURDERERS) along the line of riot shields! Various women also approached to scold soldiers **for** "participating in this shameful act against their own countrymen!"

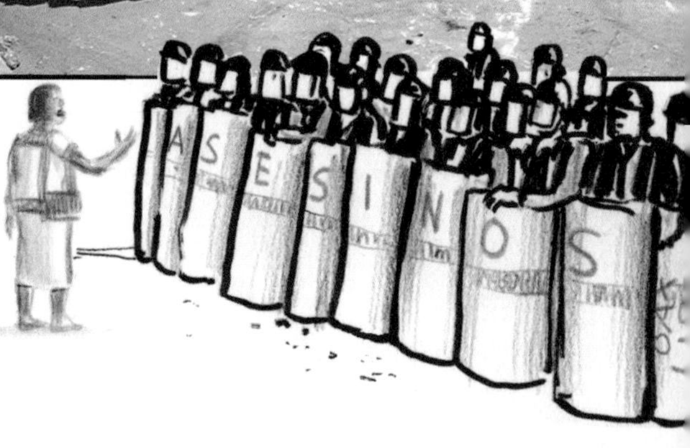
ASESINOS

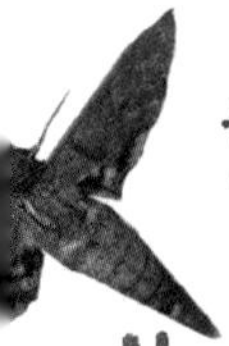

As for the striking teachers evicted from the zócalo? They simply moved four blocks up the street and re-encamped in front of Oaxaca's landmark church, Santo Domingo.

November 1st - 2nd is the famous Day of the Dead celebration time, and Oaxacaños gave it their all, creating amazing sand sculptures commemorating the teachers' battles and constructing effigies that honored the fallen (including Brad Will). They could have also mourned the death of their tourist based economy. The U.S. State Dept. had issued a travel warning, a kind of death sentence to the artisans and businesses whose lifeblood was now dried up.

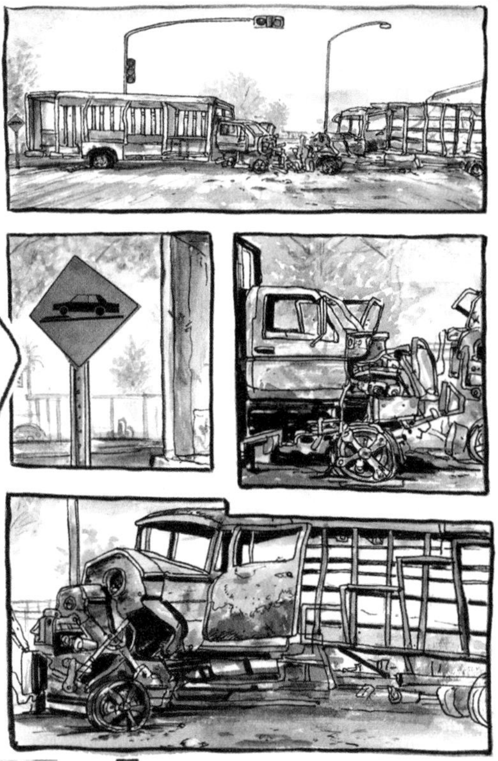

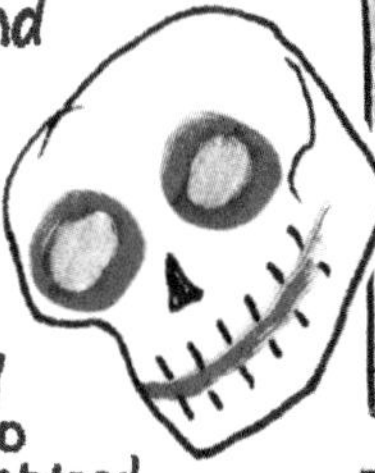

remnants of barricades in front of the university

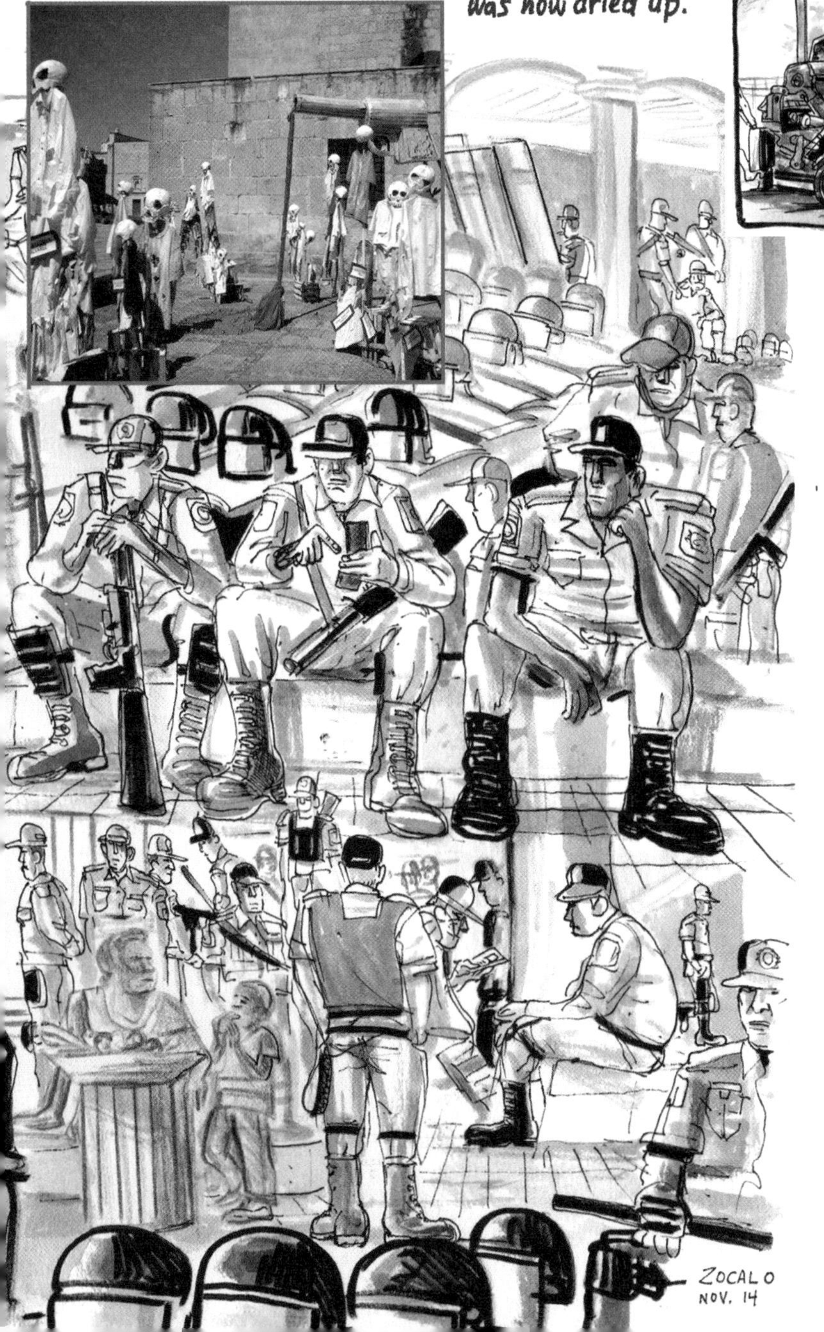
ZOCALO
NOV. 14

The zócalo, once filled with encamped teachers, was now filled with encamped soldiers. After a couple of days, civilians were allowed to walk through the square after submitting to a baggage search. It was remarkable how quickly we got accustomed to moving among storm troopers, but then again, the feeling that this was about as normal as life in 1930's *Berlin*, made me shudder.

On November 2nd, Ulises' police, along with the PFP attempted to take over the last remaining radio station held by APPO. The station broadcast from a university, and as troops moved in APPO rallied thousands of supporters to help defend it. Though the military pulled out all the stops, with helicopters, tanks with water cannons and teargas, amazingly the people repelled the attack by hurling rocks and bottles and erecting burning barricades.
The police relented when the university Dean stood his ground using a law that gave him the power to deny police entry to campus property.

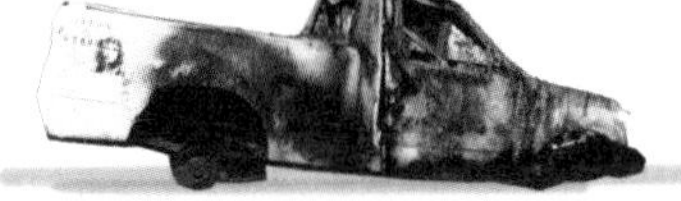

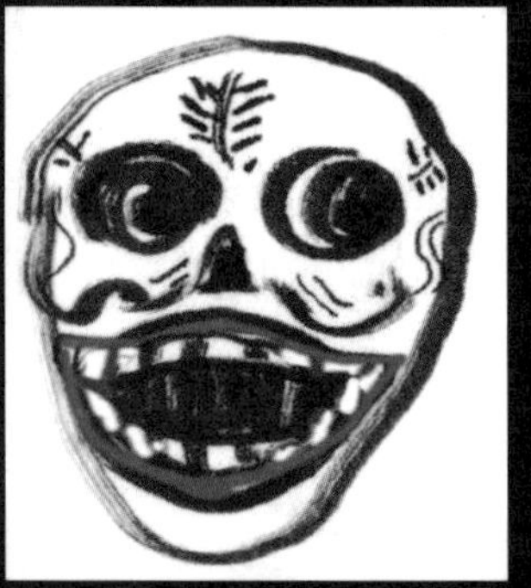

With the teachers' strike entering its seventh month, riot police filling the town square, Governor Ulises no closer to leaving office, and the economy of Oaxaca on its last leg, a cloud hung over the city. After Brad Will was killed, Oaxaca's crisis had become international news. Now though, reporters were scarce since the problems of this town were no longer juicy enough for headlines. That Ulises had been plundering the treasury from the moment he'd taken office just made it another business as usual tale. With this in mind, APPO leaders decided that they needed another action to bring attention to Oaxaca's continuing plight. It was decided that for 48 hours protesters would encircle the troops holding the zócalo to remind the government of the peoples' numbers and reinvigorate the press. The march was set for the last Saturday in November, which happened to coincide with our daughter having a sleepover. It was a rare weekend date for my wife and me and we decided it would be a good opportunity to walk around town and witness the protest.

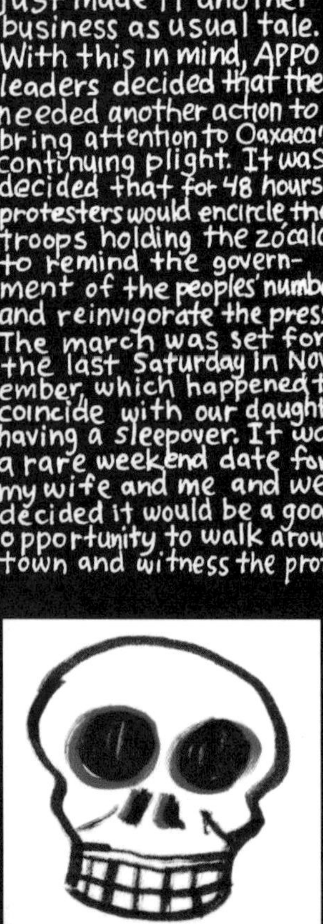

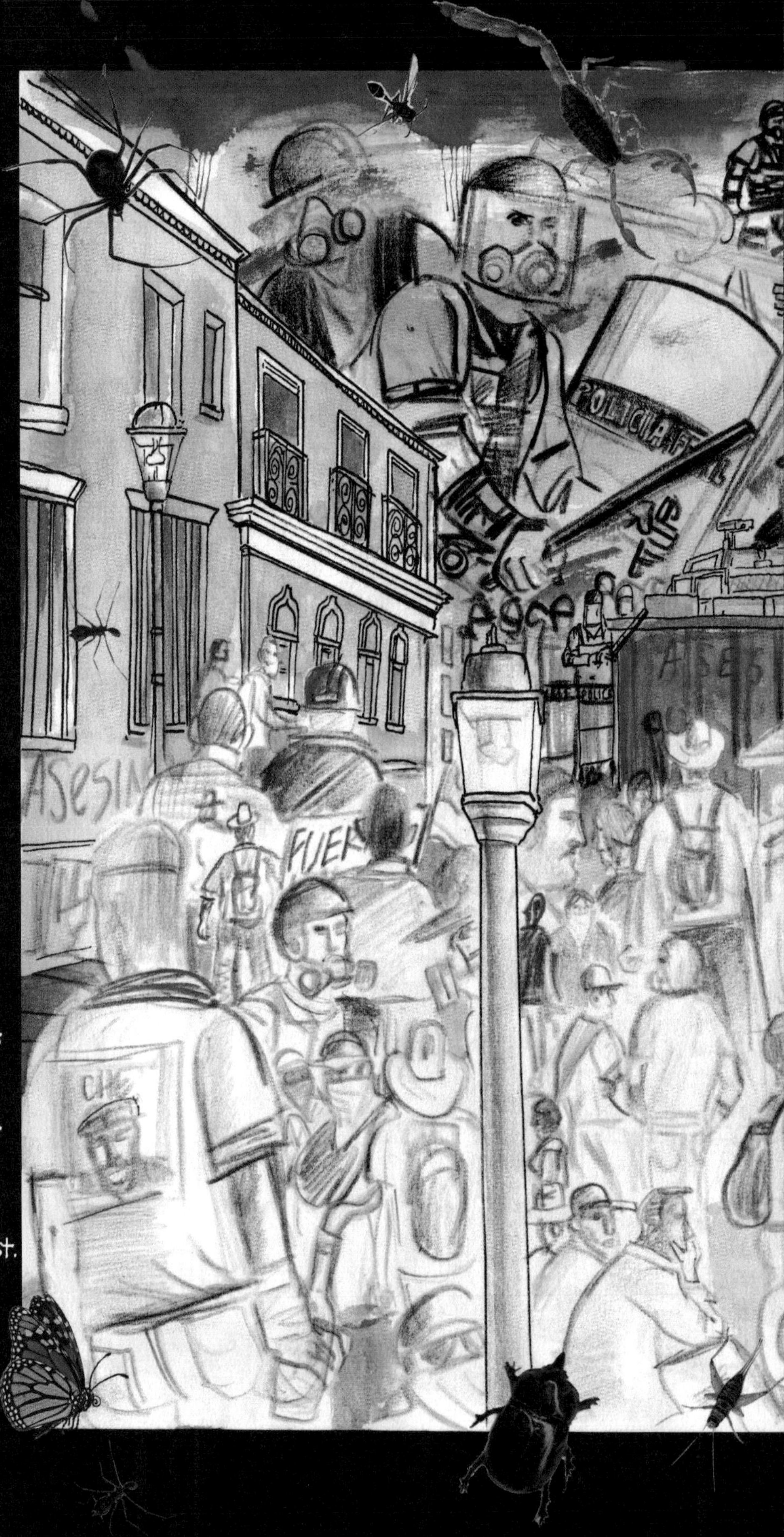
POLICIA F
ASESIN
FUER

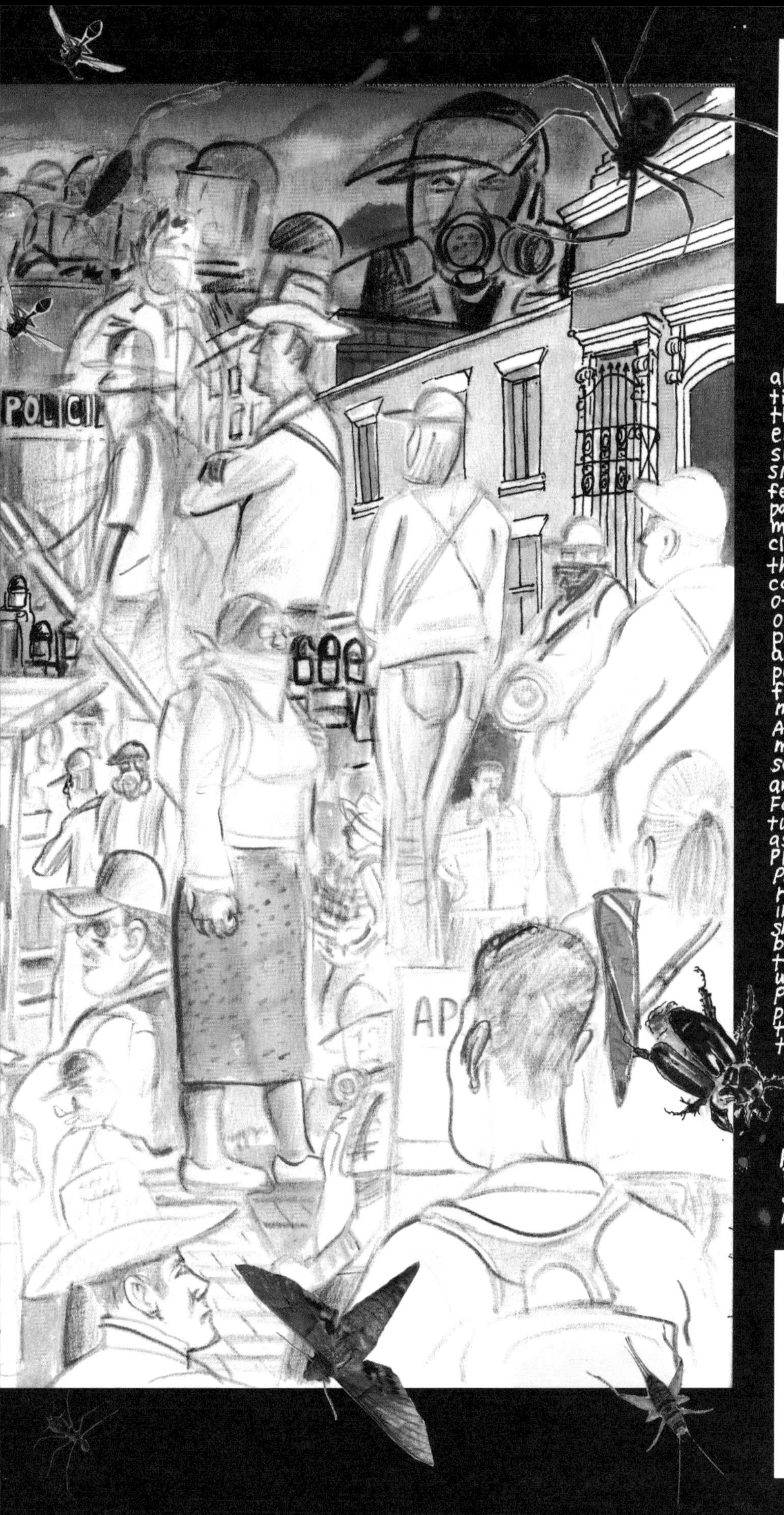
POLIC
AP

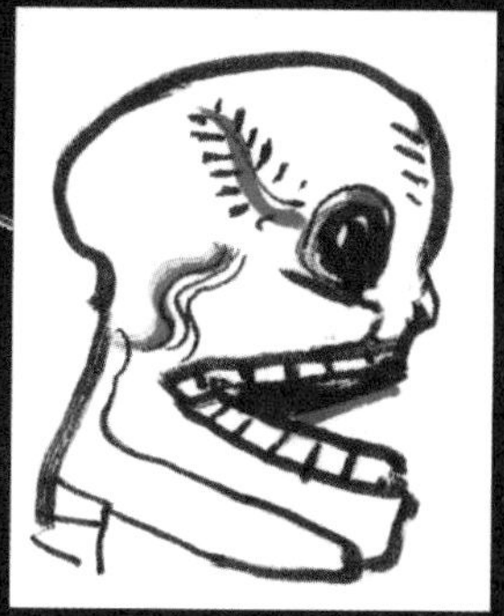

A large crowd had already formed by the time we arrived. As usual, the marchers included elderly folks as well as small children carrying signs and waving flags. It felt like a Day of the Dead parade with people wearing masks and colorful clothing, but even with this festive tone, you could see the weight of this long fight etched on peoples faces. Although planned as a non-violent action, I noticed some people carrying rocks, fireworks and a few molotov cocktails. After a few hours of milling around and doing some sketching my wife and I headed for our car. Fortuitous timing, as it turned out, since just as we drove uptown, the PFP suddenly attacked! Police hiding on the rooftops began shooting marbles with slingshots, while below they blasted the crowds with teargas. Instead of their usual slow march forward, PFP in gasmasks ran at protesters and herded them towards the teachers' encampment up the street. As night fell police began clubbing and arresting everyone in sight. By the evening, the police had torn through the encampment and jailed nearly 150 people.

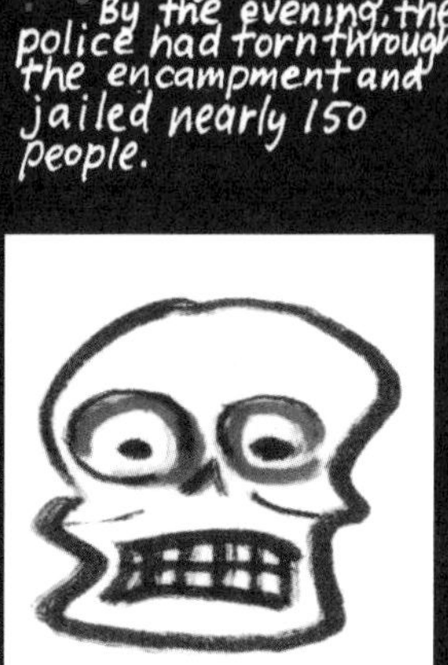

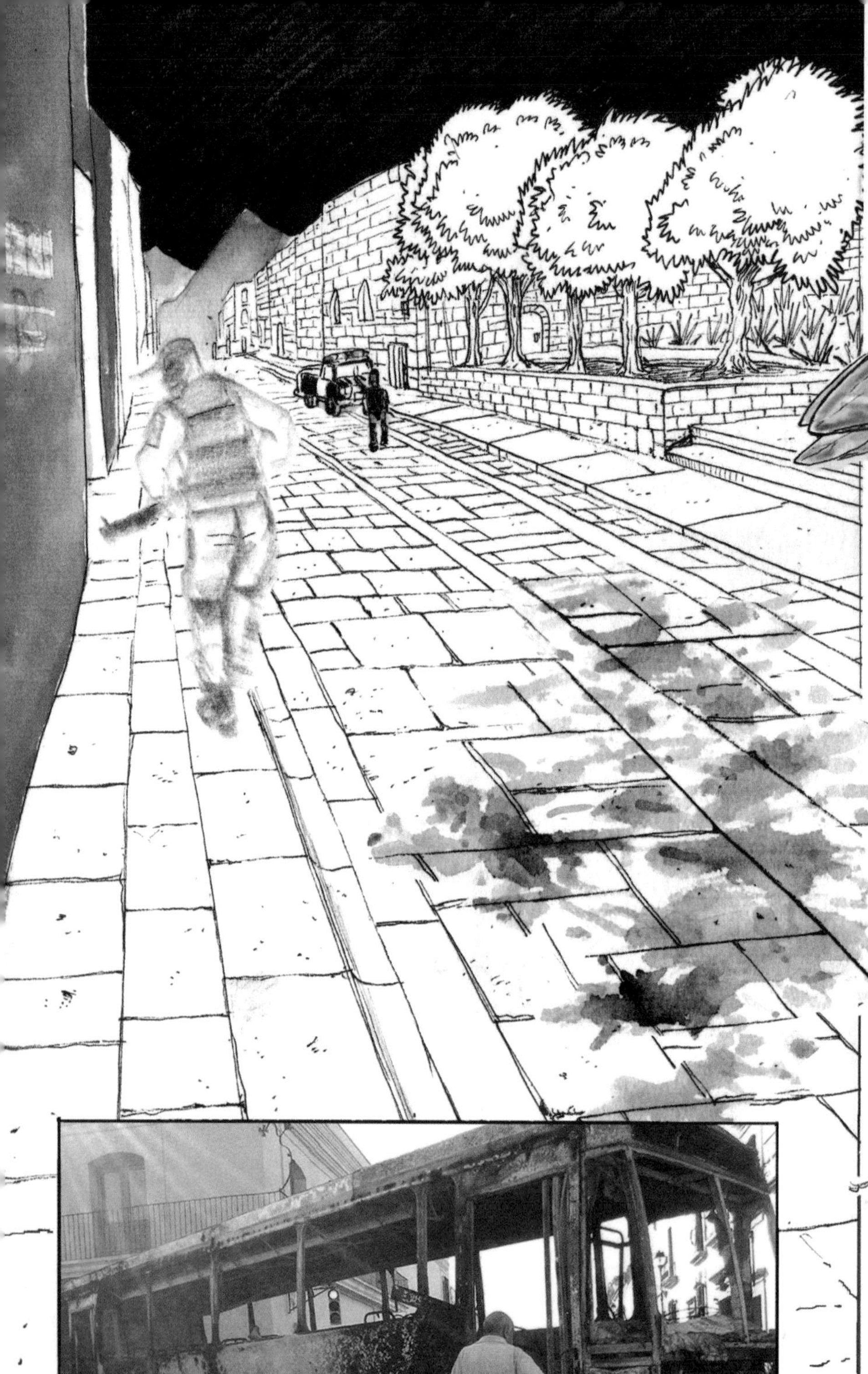

The following morning the world press reports sounded like they were dictated by the Governor's public relations office: *Everything had been the fault of violent protesters, but now,* **thank goodness**, *peace was restored!*

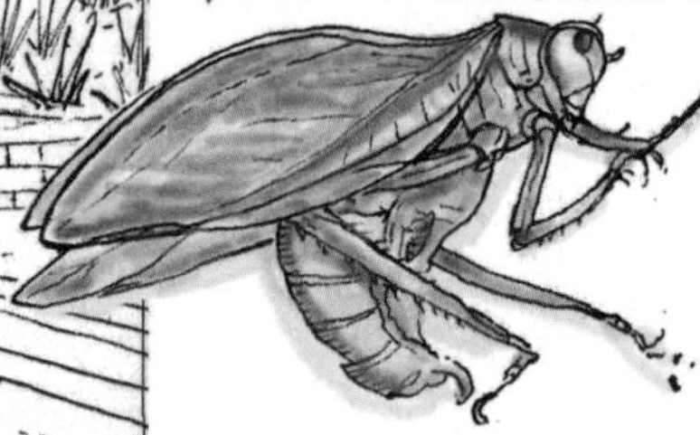

A few days passed before I ventured downtown again. It was eerily quiet with few people that weren't soldiers on the streets. All signs that there had ever been a huge encampment of teachers was gone. Even stranger, all the art and graffiti denouncing Ulises that had covered the city walls, had been completely **whitewashed**.

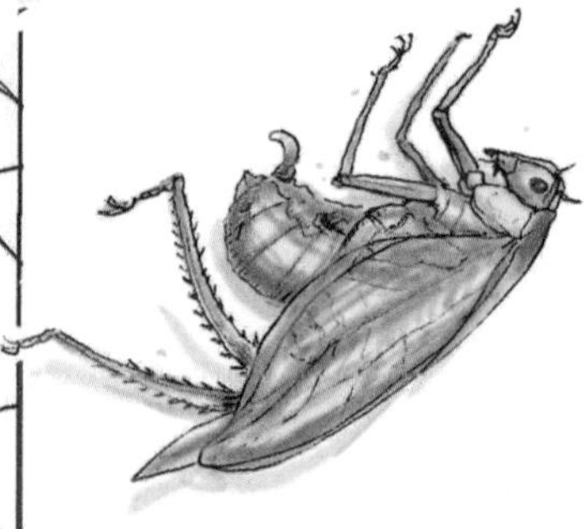

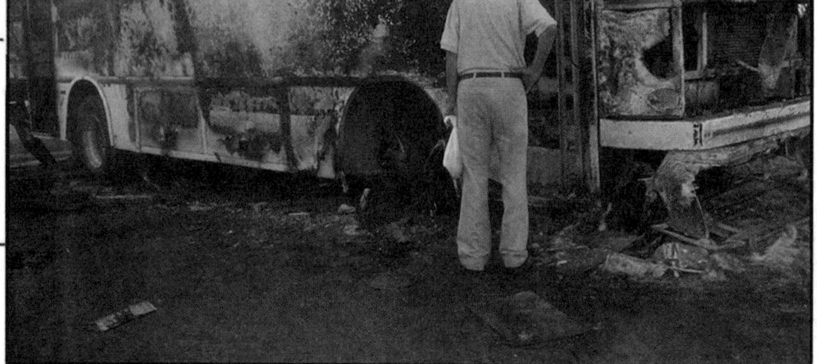

Though some buildings showed the scars of various confrontations, for me the most powerful evidence of the battles were the marks left on the cobblestones where vehicles had burned. No amount of scrubbing could make those indelible stains disappear.

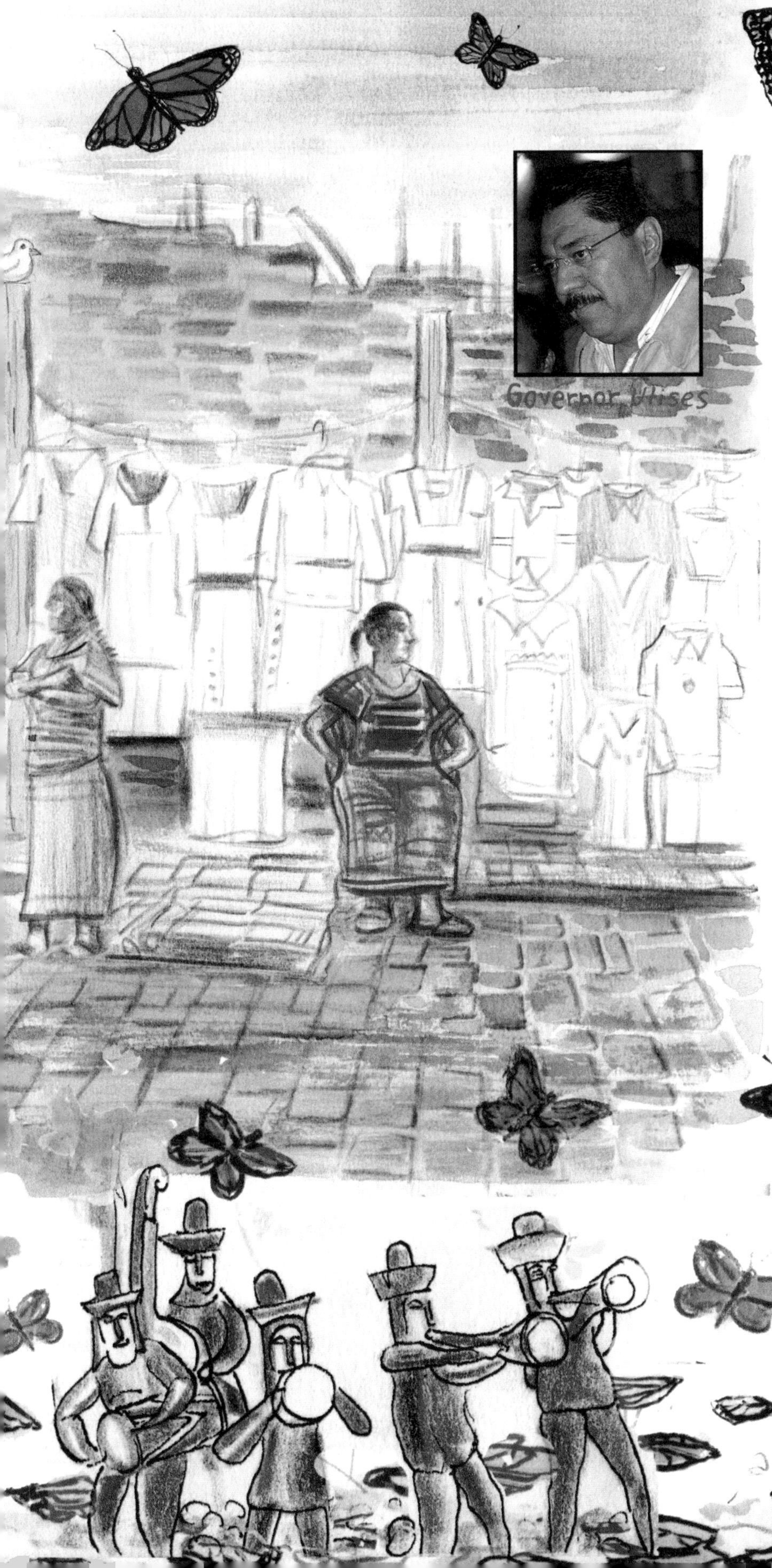
Governor Ulises

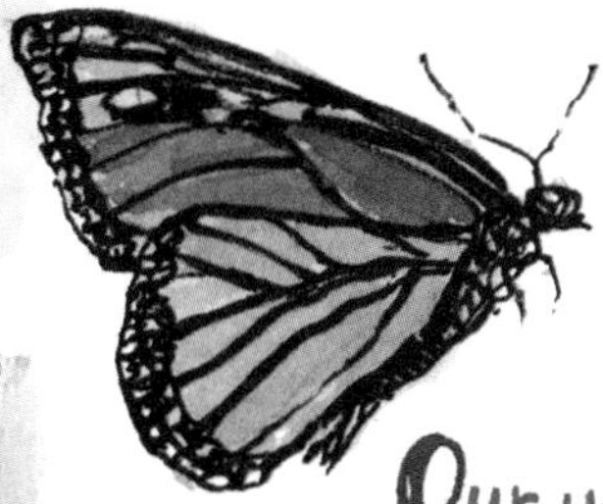

Our year in Mexico was not the retreat we'd anticipated. Our break from "Bushworld" has included riot police, burning buses, barricades and curfews. We were witness to major social upheavals that lasted nearly seven months involving hundreds of police, thousands of federal troops, tens of thousands of protesters and the loss of millions of dollars, all thanks to one corrupt governor.

Of course I wish none of this had ever happened, that no one came to harm, or was jailed, that the teachers had been payed what they deserved in the first place and that the economy of Oaxaca was booming. Nonetheless, being here during these historic events has felt like a privlege. Our encounters with the people living and struggling through this difficult period, have been an inspiration and the beauty of this town remains a traveler's dream.

All of these various factors have brought us to one final conclusion;

we're staying a second year.

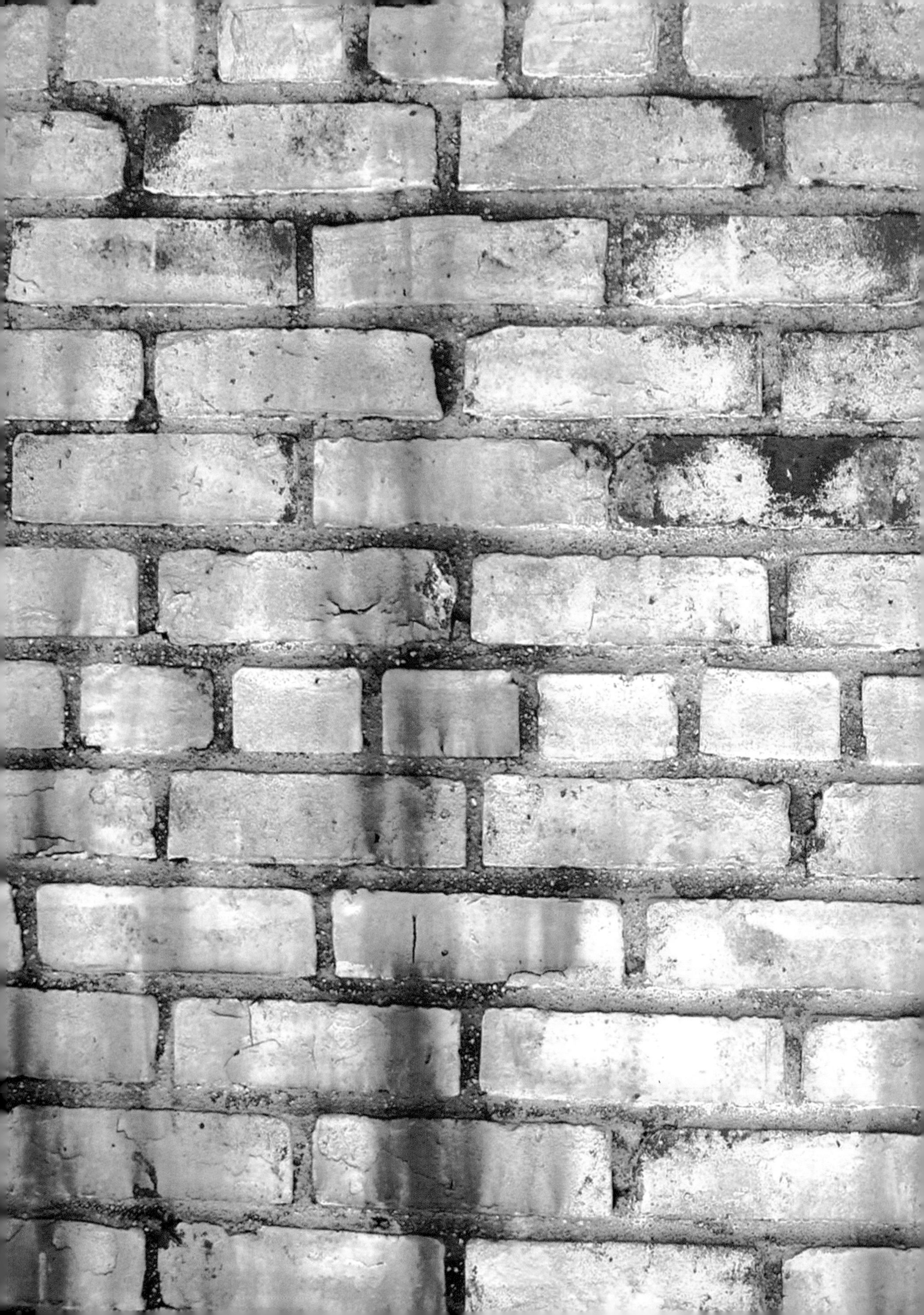

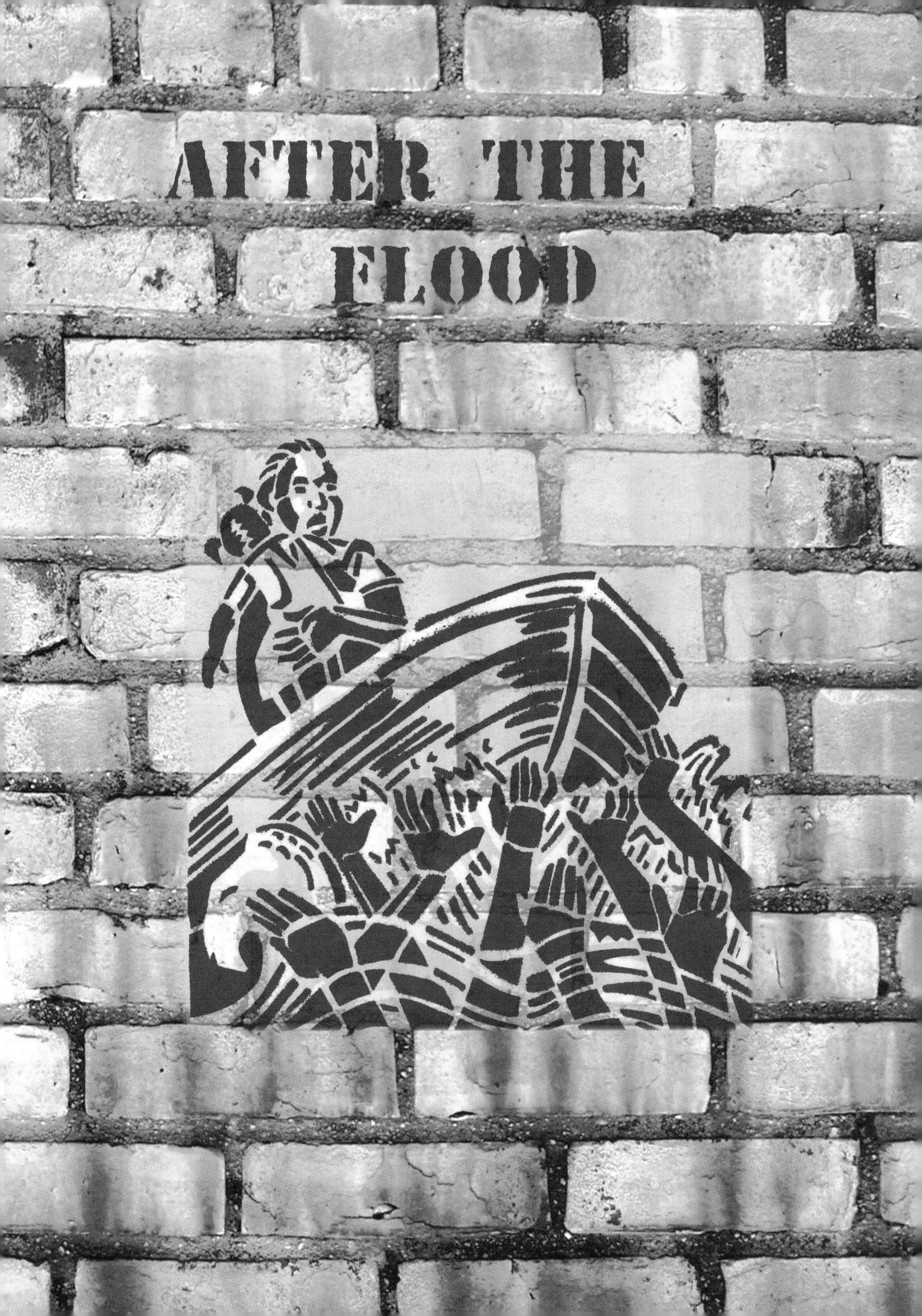
AFTER THE
FLOOD

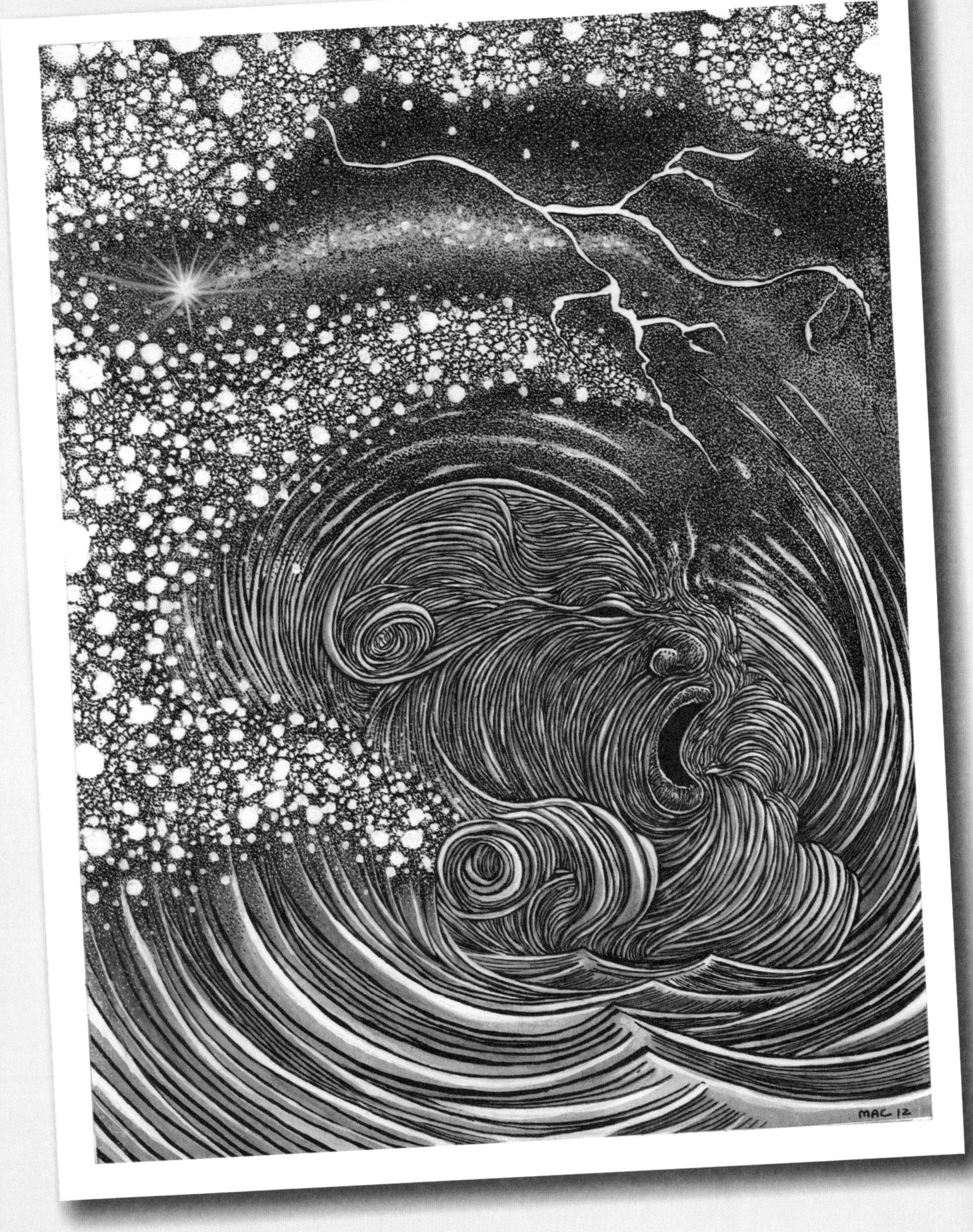
MAC 12

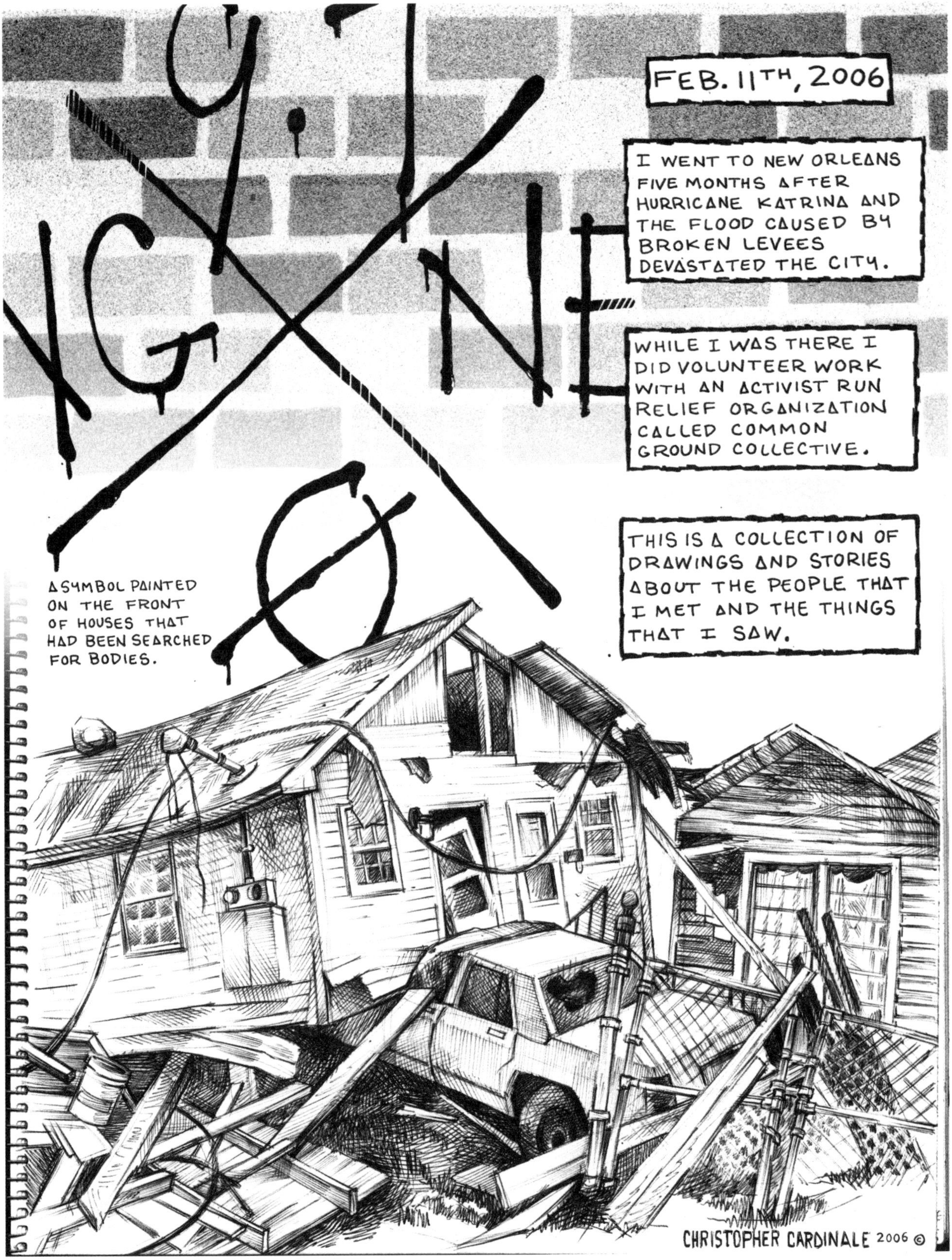
FEB. 11TH, 2006
I WENT TO NEW ORLEANS FIVE MONTHS AFTER HURRICANE KATRINA AND THE FLOOD CAUSED BY BROKEN LEVEES DEVASTATED THE CITY.
WHILE I WAS THERE I DID VOLUNTEER WORK WITH AN ACTIVIST RUN RELIEF ORGANIZATION CALLED COMMON GROUND COLLECTIVE.
THIS IS A COLLECTION OF DRAWINGS AND STORIES ABOUT THE PEOPLE THAT I MET AND THE THINGS THAT I SAW.
A SYMBOL PAINTED ON THE FRONT OF HOUSES THAT HAD BEEN SEARCHED FOR BODIES.
CHRISTOPHER CARDINALE 2006 ©

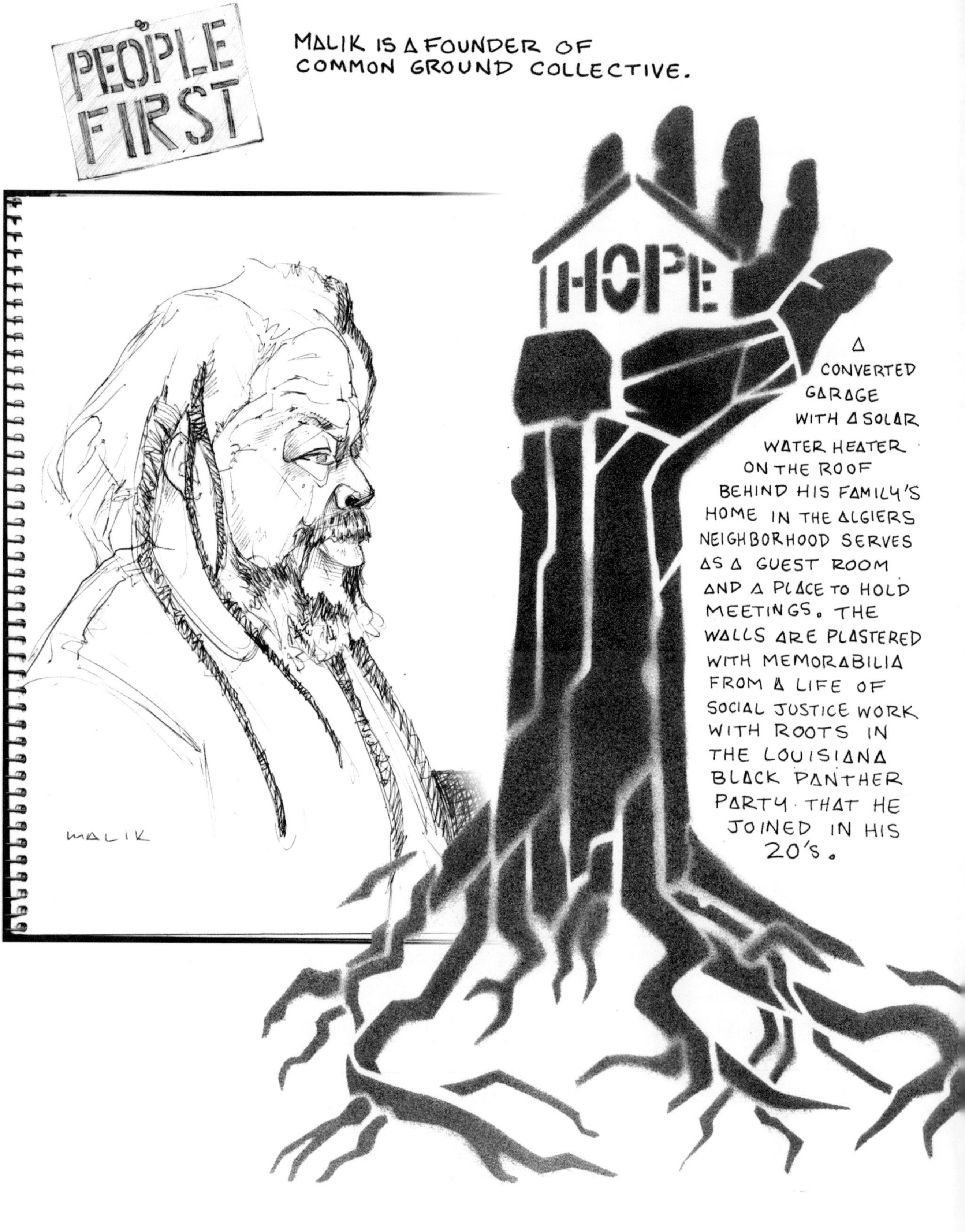
PEOPLE FIRST
MALIK IS A FOUNDER OF COMMON GROUND COLLECTIVE.
HOPE
A CONVERTED GARAGE WITH A SOLAR WATER HEATER ON THE ROOF BEHIND HIS FAMILY'S HOME IN THE ALGIERS NEIGHBORHOOD SERVES AS A GUEST ROOM AND A PLACE TO HOLD MEETINGS. THE WALLS ARE PLASTERED WITH MEMORABILIA FROM A LIFE OF SOCIAL JUSTICE WORK WITH ROOTS IN THE LOUISIANA BLACK PANTHER PARTY THAT HE JOINED IN HIS 20'S.
MALIK

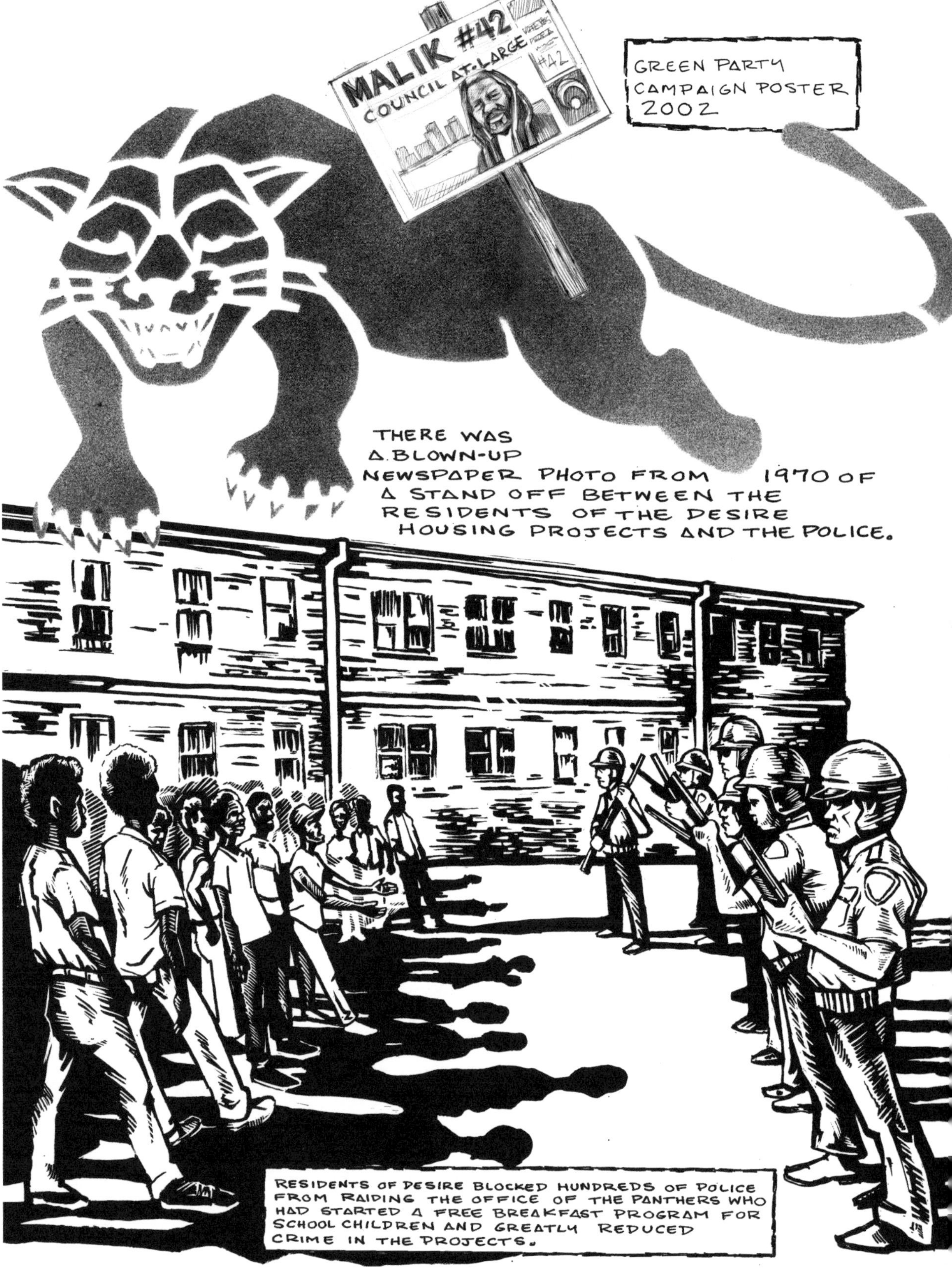
MALIK #42
COUNCIL AT-LARGE
#42
GREEN PARTY
CAMPAIGN POSTER
2002
THERE WAS
A BLOWN-UP
NEWSPAPER PHOTO FROM 1970 OF
A STAND OFF BETWEEN THE
RESIDENTS OF THE DESIRE
HOUSING PROJECTS AND THE POLICE.
RESIDENTS OF DESIRE BLOCKED HUNDREDS OF POLICE FROM RAIDING THE OFFICE OF THE PANTHERS WHO HAD STARTED A FREE BREAKFAST PROGRAM FOR SCHOOL CHILDREN AND GREATLY REDUCED CRIME IN THE PROJECTS.

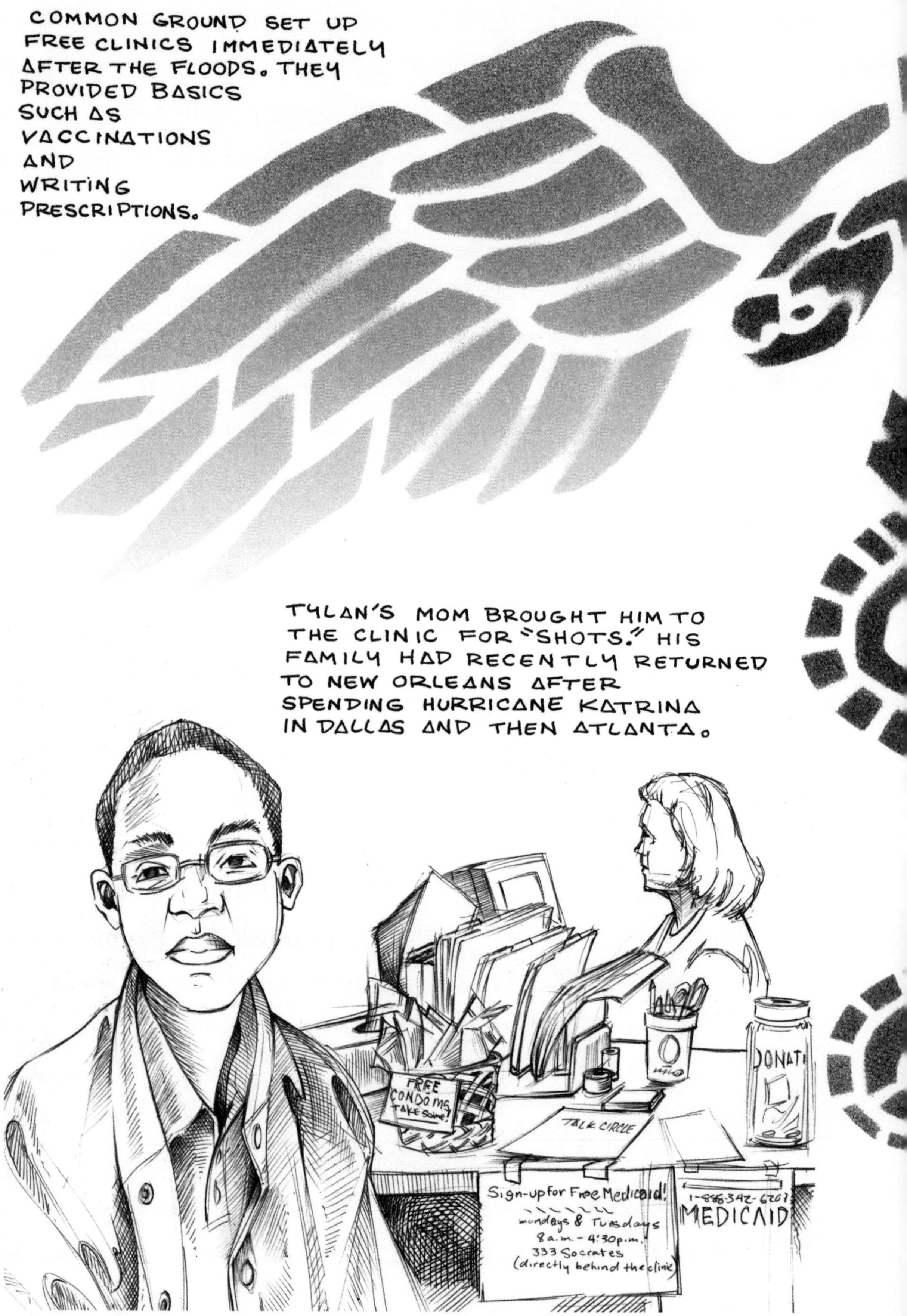
COMMON GROUND SET UP FREE CLINICS IMMEDIATELY AFTER THE FLOODS. THEY PROVIDED BASICS SUCH AS VACCINATIONS AND WRITING PRESCRIPTIONS.
TYLAN'S MOM BROUGHT HIM TO THE CLINIC FOR "SHOTS." HIS FAMILY HAD RECENTLY RETURNED TO NEW ORLEANS AFTER SPENDING HURRICANE KATRINA IN DALLAS AND THEN ATLANTA.
FREE CONDOMS TAKE SOME!
TALK CIRCLE
DONATI
Sign-up for Free Medicaid!
Mondays & Tuesdays
8 a.m. - 4:30 p.m.
333 Socrates
(directly behind the clinic)
1-888-342-6207
MEDICAID

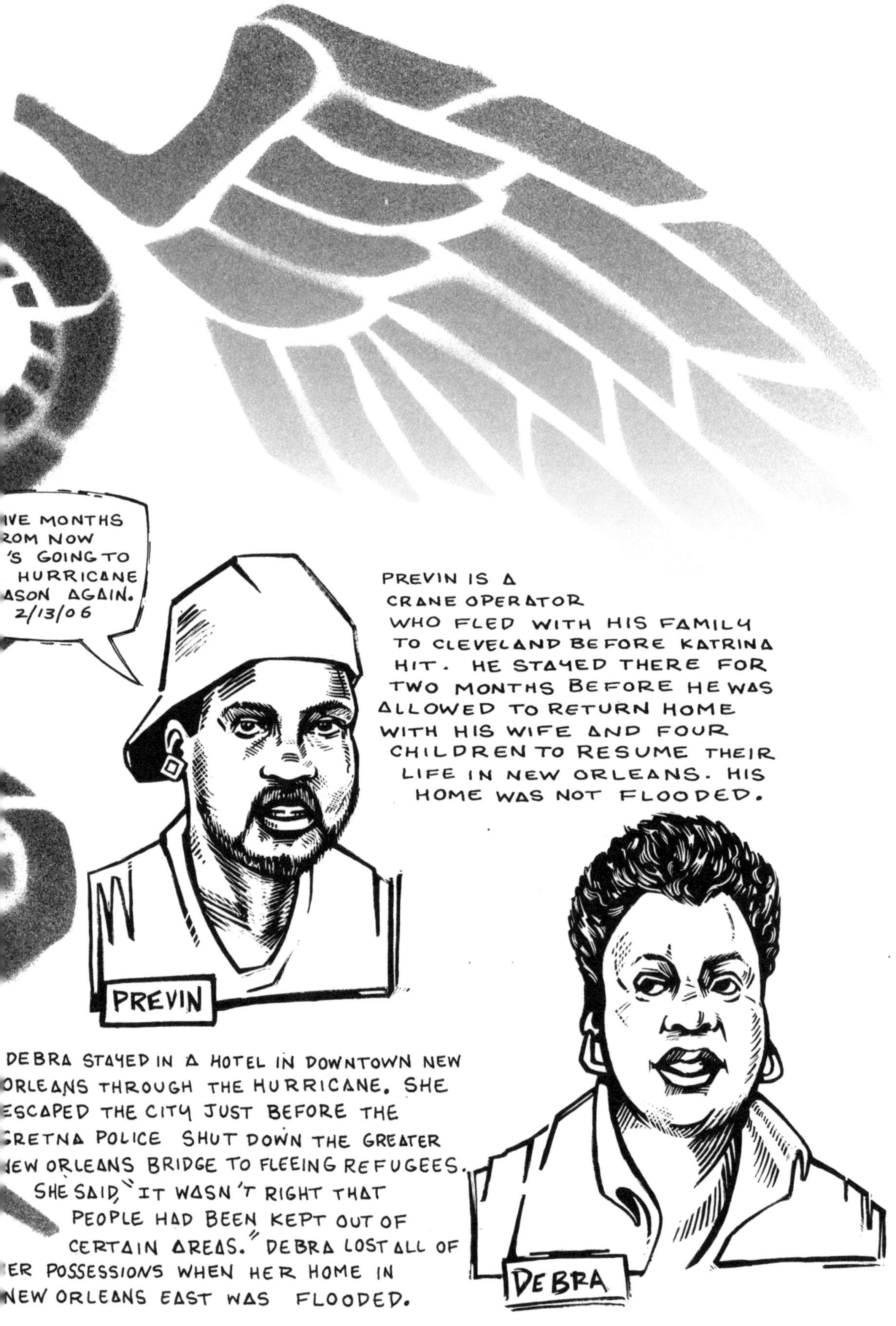

IVE MONTHS ROM NOW 'S GOING TO HURRICANE ASON AGAIN. 2/13/06
PREVIN IS A CRANE OPERATOR WHO FLED WITH HIS FAMILY TO CLEVELAND BEFORE KATRINA HIT. HE STAYED THERE FOR TWO MONTHS BEFORE HE WAS ALLOWED TO RETURN HOME WITH HIS WIFE AND FOUR CHILDREN TO RESUME THEIR LIFE IN NEW ORLEANS. HIS HOME WAS NOT FLOODED.
PREVIN
DEBRA STAYED IN A HOTEL IN DOWNTOWN NEW ORLEANS THROUGH THE HURRICANE. SHE ESCAPED THE CITY JUST BEFORE THE RETNA POLICE SHUT DOWN THE GREATER EW ORLEANS BRIDGE TO FLEEING REFUGEES. SHE SAID, "IT WASN'T RIGHT THAT PEOPLE HAD BEEN KEPT OUT OF CERTAIN AREAS." DEBRA LOST ALL OF ER POSSESSIONS WHEN HER HOME IN NEW ORLEANS EAST WAS FLOODED.
DEBRA

HUNDREDS OF VOLUNTEERS WERE STAYING AT A COMMUNITY CENTER IN THE NINTH WARD THAT COMMON GROUND HAD EMPTIED AND DECONTAMINATED. EVERY MORNING THEY BROKE INTO WORK TEAMS THAT WENT TO HOMES AND CHURCHES IN THE LOWER NINTH WARD AND OTHER NEIGHBORHOODS THAT HAD BEEN FLOODED.

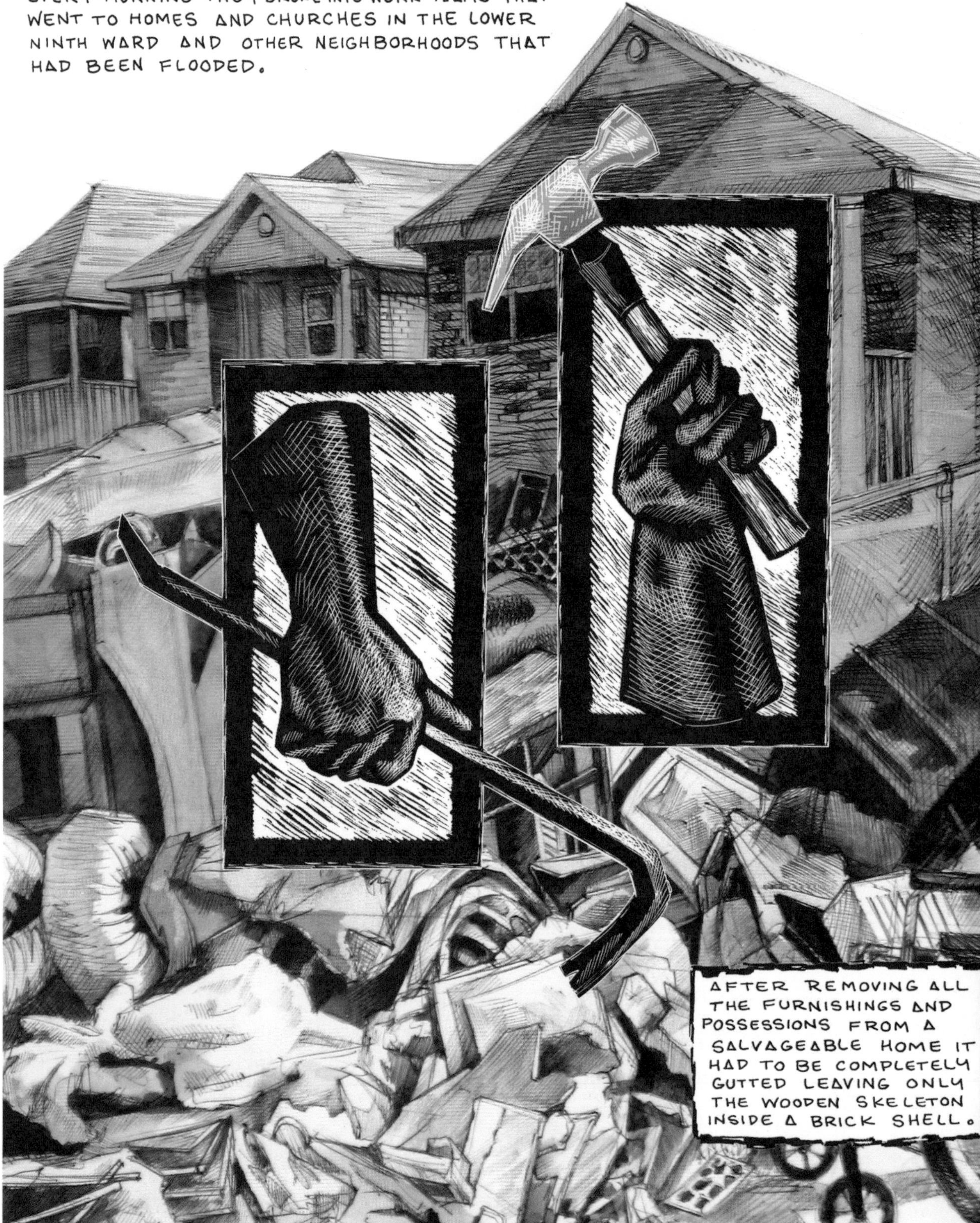
AFTER REMOVING ALL THE FURNISHINGS AND POSSESSIONS FROM A SALVAGEABLE HOME IT HAD TO BE COMPLETELY GUTTED LEAVING ONLY THE WOODEN SKELETON INSIDE A BRICK SHELL.

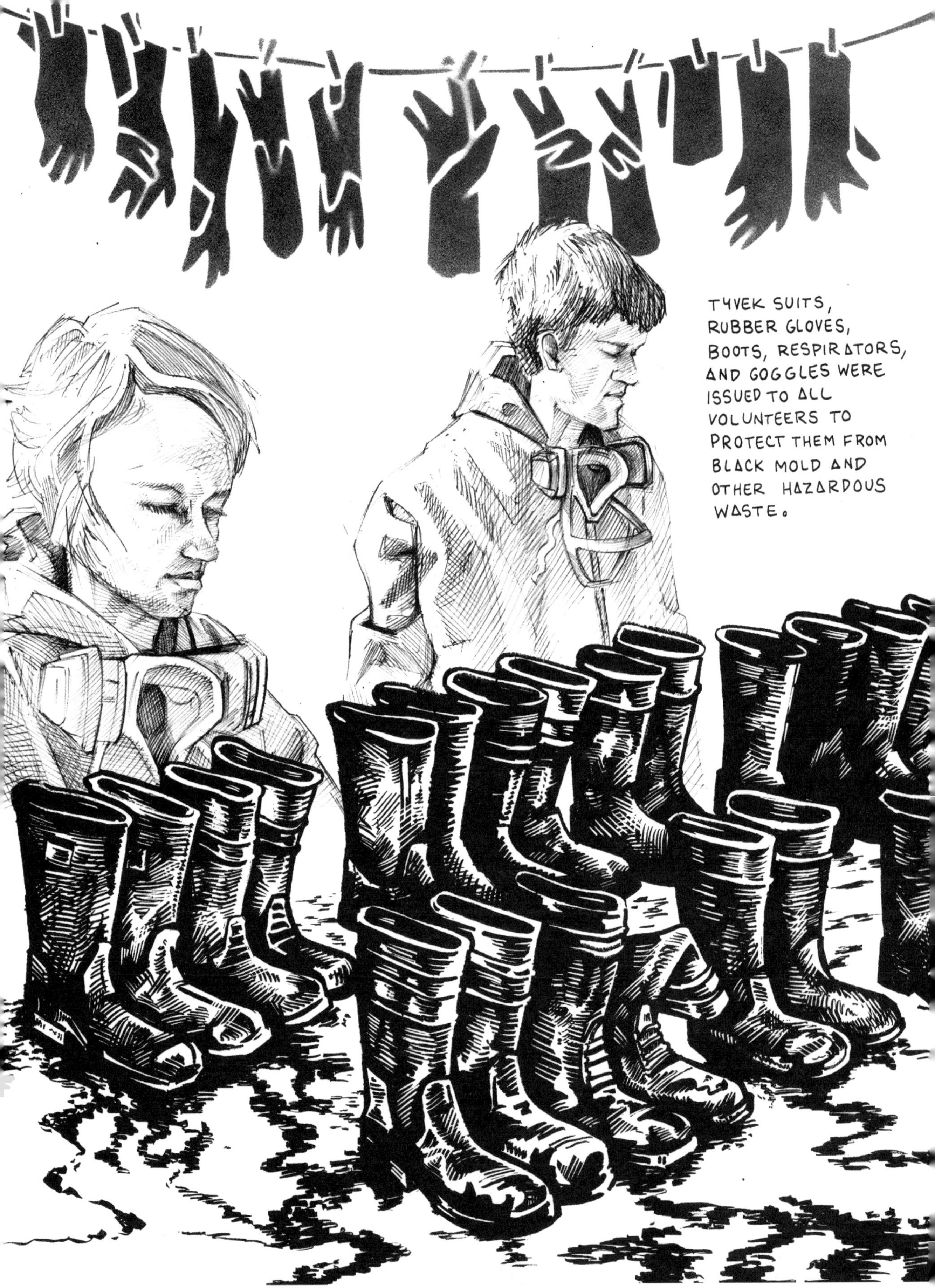
TYVEK SUITS, RUBBER GLOVES, BOOTS, RESPIRATORS, AND GOGGLES WERE ISSUED TO ALL VOLUNTEERS TO PROTECT THEM FROM BLACK MOLD AND OTHER HAZARDOUS WASTE.

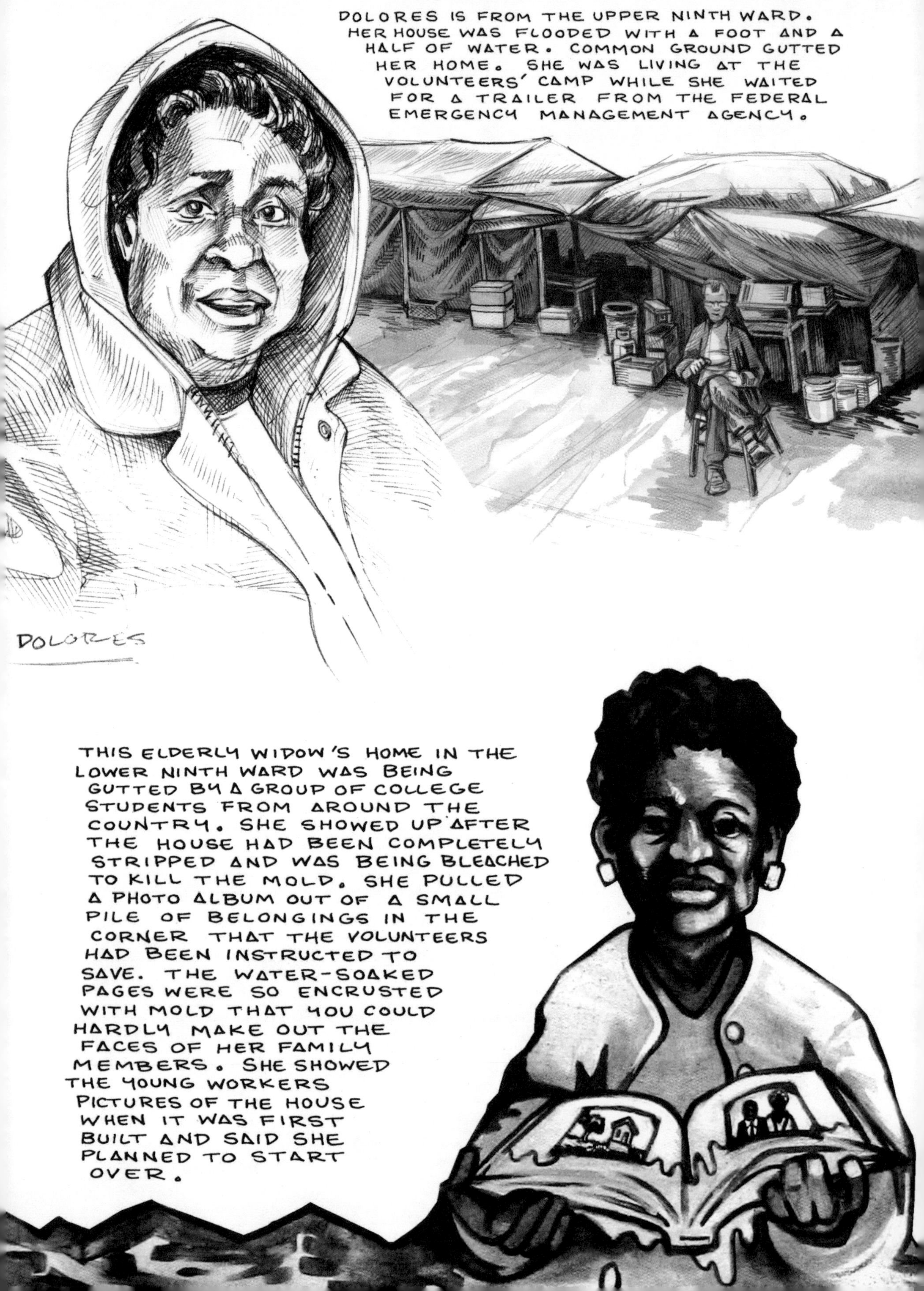
DOLORES IS FROM THE UPPER NINTH WARD. HER HOUSE WAS FLOODED WITH A FOOT AND A HALF OF WATER. COMMON GROUND GUTTED HER HOME. SHE WAS LIVING AT THE VOLUNTEERS' CAMP WHILE SHE WAITED FOR A TRAILER FROM THE FEDERAL EMERGENCY MANAGEMENT AGENCY.
DOLORES
THIS ELDERLY WIDOW'S HOME IN THE LOWER NINTH WARD WAS BEING GUTTED BY A GROUP OF COLLEGE STUDENTS FROM AROUND THE COUNTRY. SHE SHOWED UP AFTER THE HOUSE HAD BEEN COMPLETELY STRIPPED AND WAS BEING BLEACHED TO KILL THE MOLD. SHE PULLED A PHOTO ALBUM OUT OF A SMALL PILE OF BELONGINGS IN THE CORNER THAT THE VOLUNTEERS HAD BEEN INSTRUCTED TO SAVE. THE WATER-SOAKED PAGES WERE SO ENCRUSTED WITH MOLD THAT YOU COULD HARDLY MAKE OUT THE FACES OF HER FAMILY MEMBERS. SHE SHOWED THE YOUNG WORKERS PICTURES OF THE HOUSE WHEN IT WAS FIRST BUILT AND SAID SHE PLANNED TO START OVER.

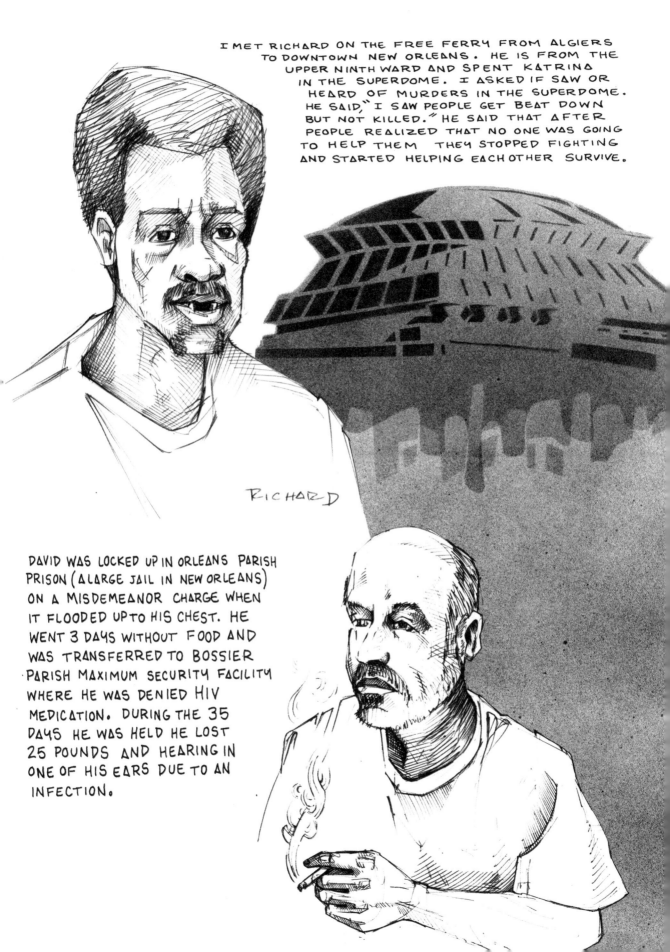

I MET RICHARD ON THE FREE FERRY FROM ALGIERS TO DOWNTOWN NEW ORLEANS. HE IS FROM THE UPPER NINTH WARD AND SPENT KATRINA IN THE SUPERDOME. I ASKED IF SAW OR HEARD OF MURDERS IN THE SUPERDOME. HE SAID, "I SAW PEOPLE GET BEAT DOWN BUT NOT KILLED." HE SAID THAT AFTER PEOPLE REALIZED THAT NO ONE WAS GOING TO HELP THEM THEY STOPPED FIGHTING AND STARTED HELPING EACH OTHER SURVIVE.

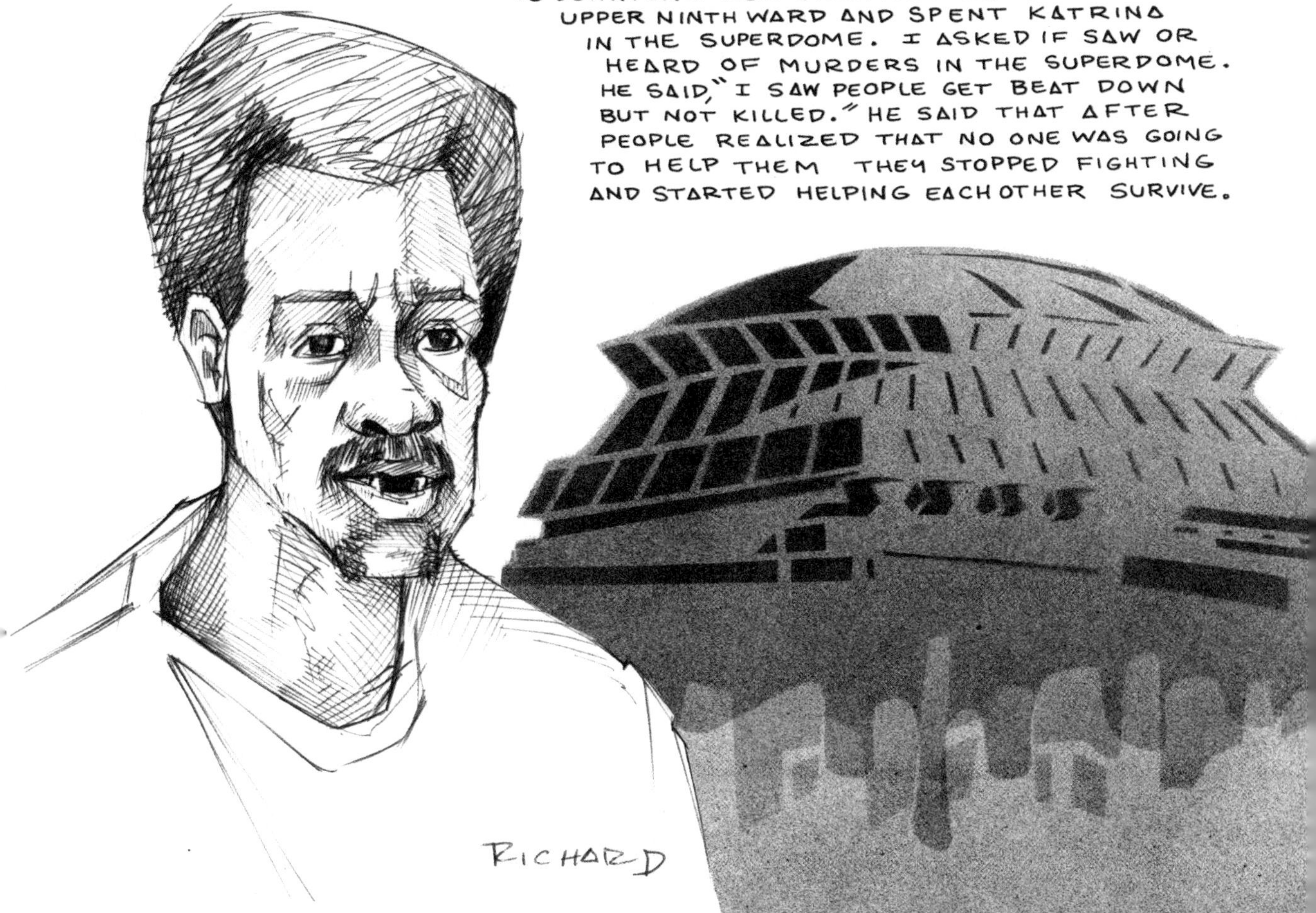
RICHARD

DAVID WAS LOCKED UP IN ORLEANS PARISH PRISON (A LARGE JAIL IN NEW ORLEANS) ON A MISDEMEANOR CHARGE WHEN IT FLOODED UP TO HIS CHEST. HE WENT 3 DAYS WITHOUT FOOD AND WAS TRANSFERRED TO BOSSIER PARISH MAXIMUM SECURITY FACILITY WHERE HE WAS DENIED HIV MEDICATION. DURING THE 35 DAYS HE WAS HELD HE LOST 25 POUNDS AND HEARING IN ONE OF HIS EARS DUE TO AN INFECTION.

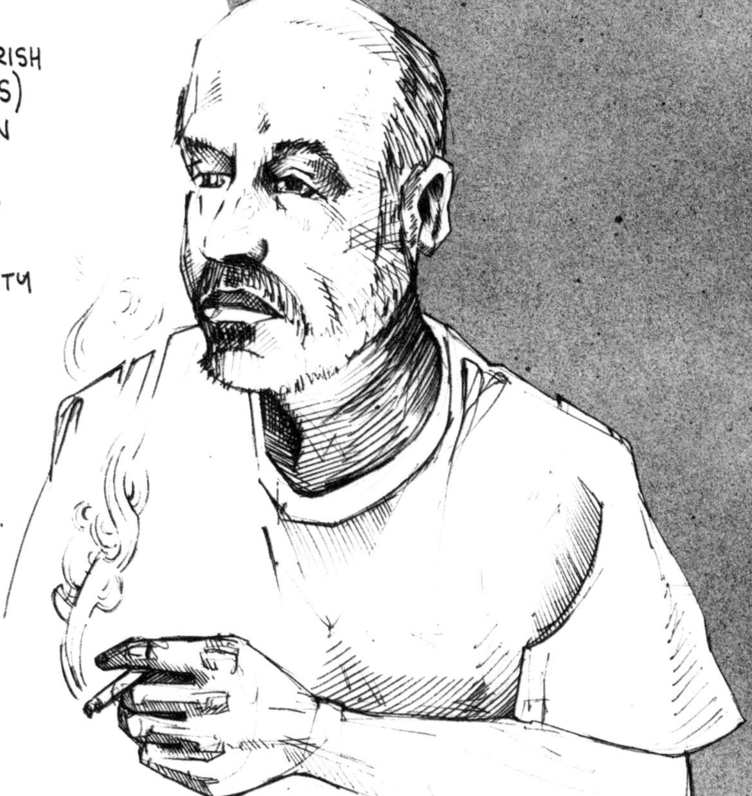

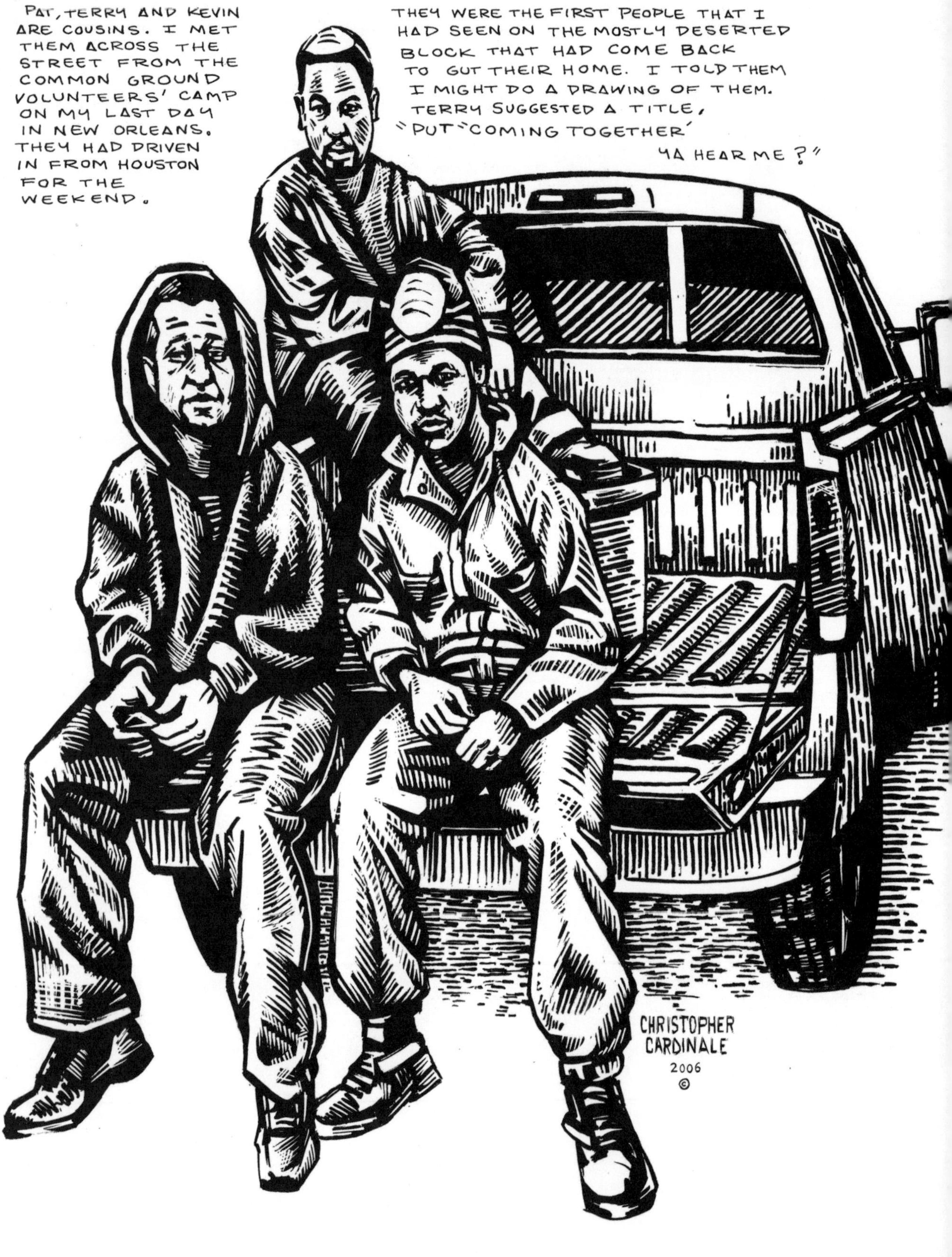
PAT, TERRY AND KEVIN ARE COUSINS. I MET THEM ACROSS THE STREET FROM THE COMMON GROUND VOLUNTEERS' CAMP ON MY LAST DAY IN NEW ORLEANS. THEY HAD DRIVEN IN FROM HOUSTON FOR THE WEEKEND.
THEY WERE THE FIRST PEOPLE THAT I HAD SEEN ON THE MOSTLY DESERTED BLOCK THAT HAD COME BACK TO GUT THEIR HOME. I TOLD THEM I MIGHT DO A DRAWING OF THEM. TERRY SUGGESTED A TITLE, "PUT 'COMING TOGETHER' YA HEAR ME?"
CHRISTOPHER CARDINALE 2006 ©

I lived here a long time....since 1952.

I raised my children here in this house...
...and my grandchildren.

I don't want to live anywhere else...
...New Orleans is my home...

I want to come back...

...and die here.

Mrs. Spencers' home..........................May 4, 2006

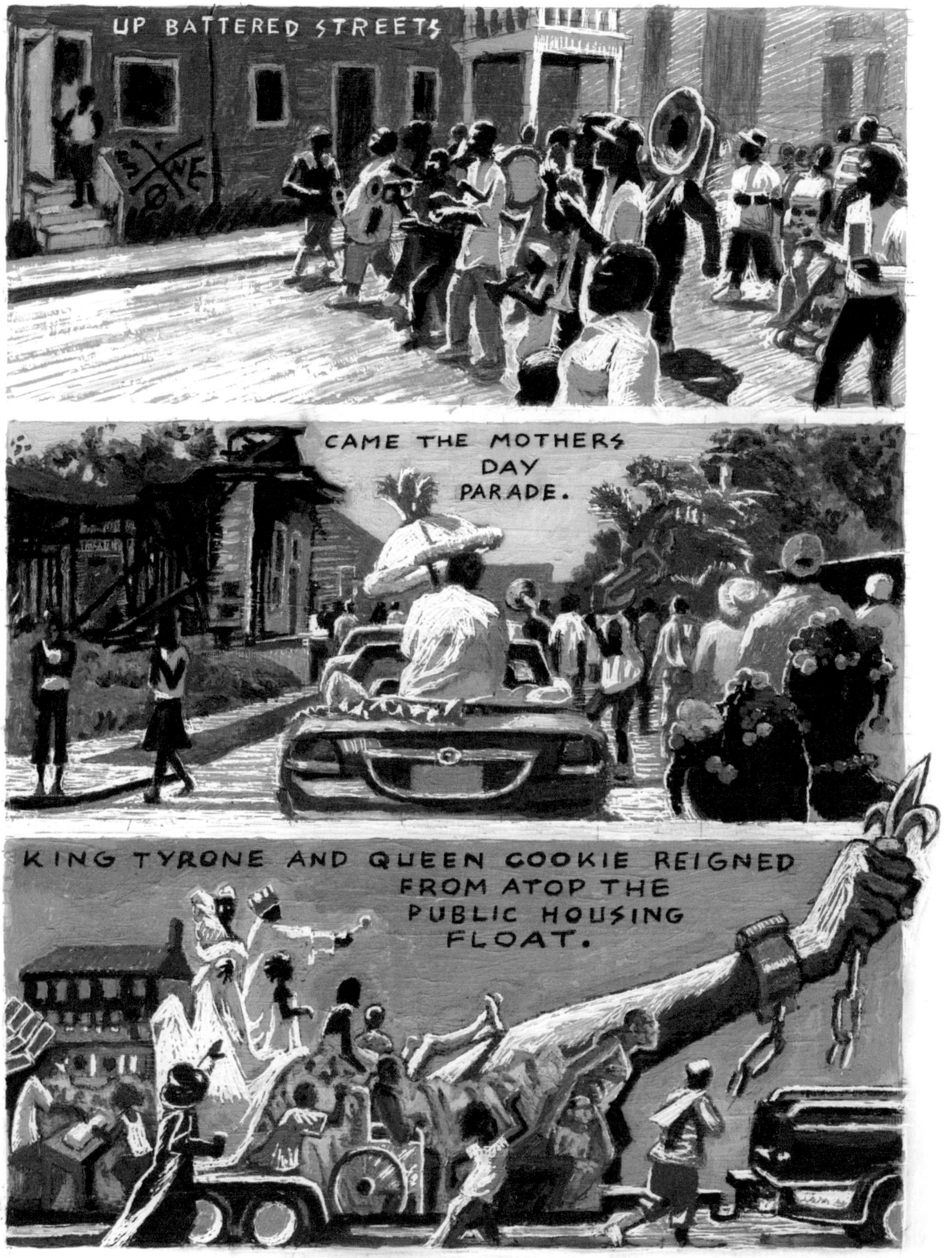
UP BATTERED STREETS
CAME THE MOTHERS DAY PARADE.
KING TYRONE AND QUEEN COOKIE REIGNED FROM ATOP THE PUBLIC HOUSING FLOAT.

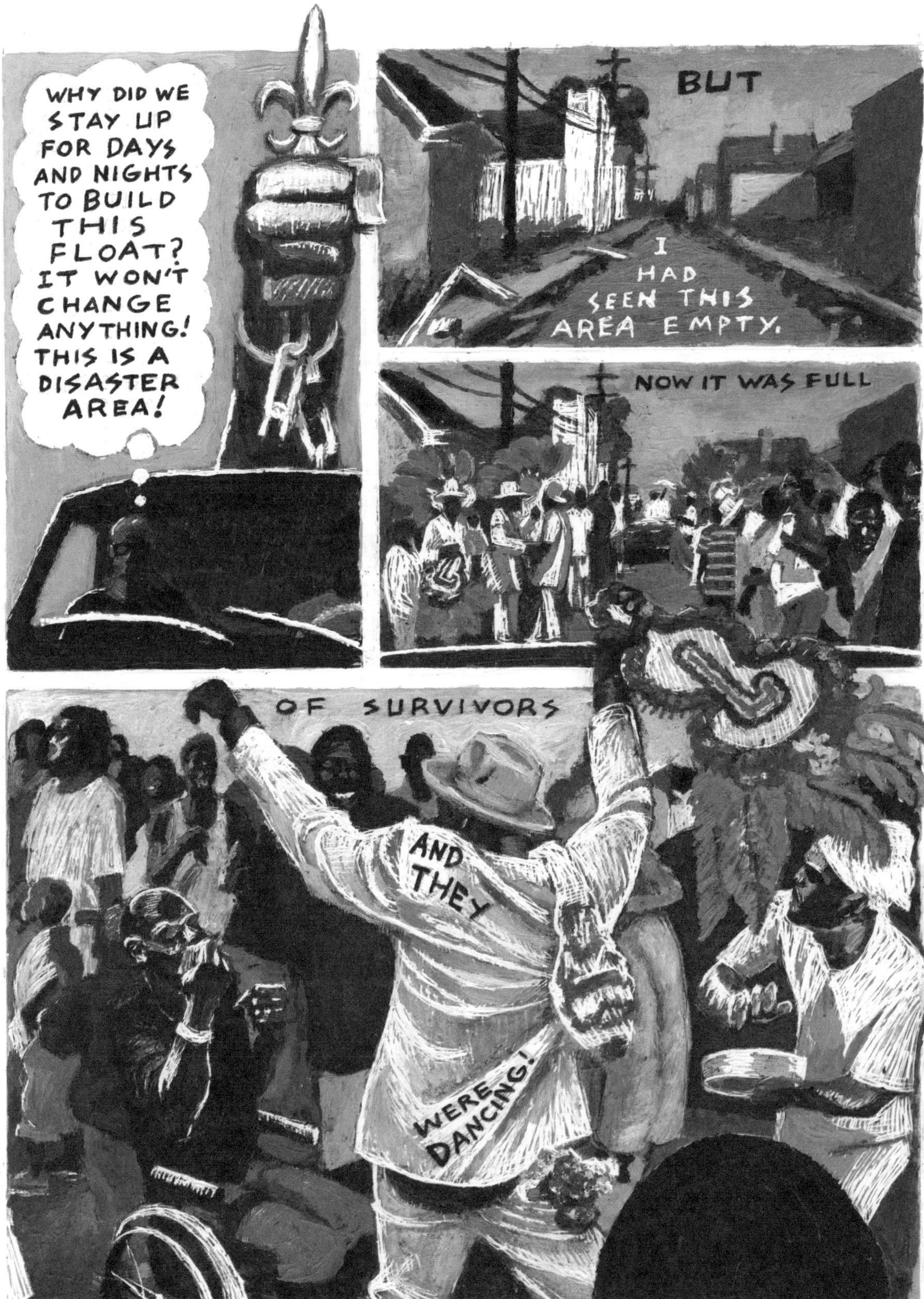
WHY DID WE STAY UP FOR DAYS AND NIGHTS TO BUILD THIS FLOAT? IT WON'T CHANGE ANYTHING! THIS IS A DISASTER AREA!
BUT
I HAD SEEN THIS AREA EMPTY.
NOW IT WAS FULL
OF SURVIVORS
AND THEY
WERE DANCING!

SETH TOBOCMAN

THE PEOPLE
WILL HAVE JUSTIC
IN THIS LIFE OR
THE NEXT
citi®
CROOK
ous Pizza
is, is
t all
DBE
Delici
18
OHIO
in
Solidarity
FE
TH
D
YOU
THE LOG

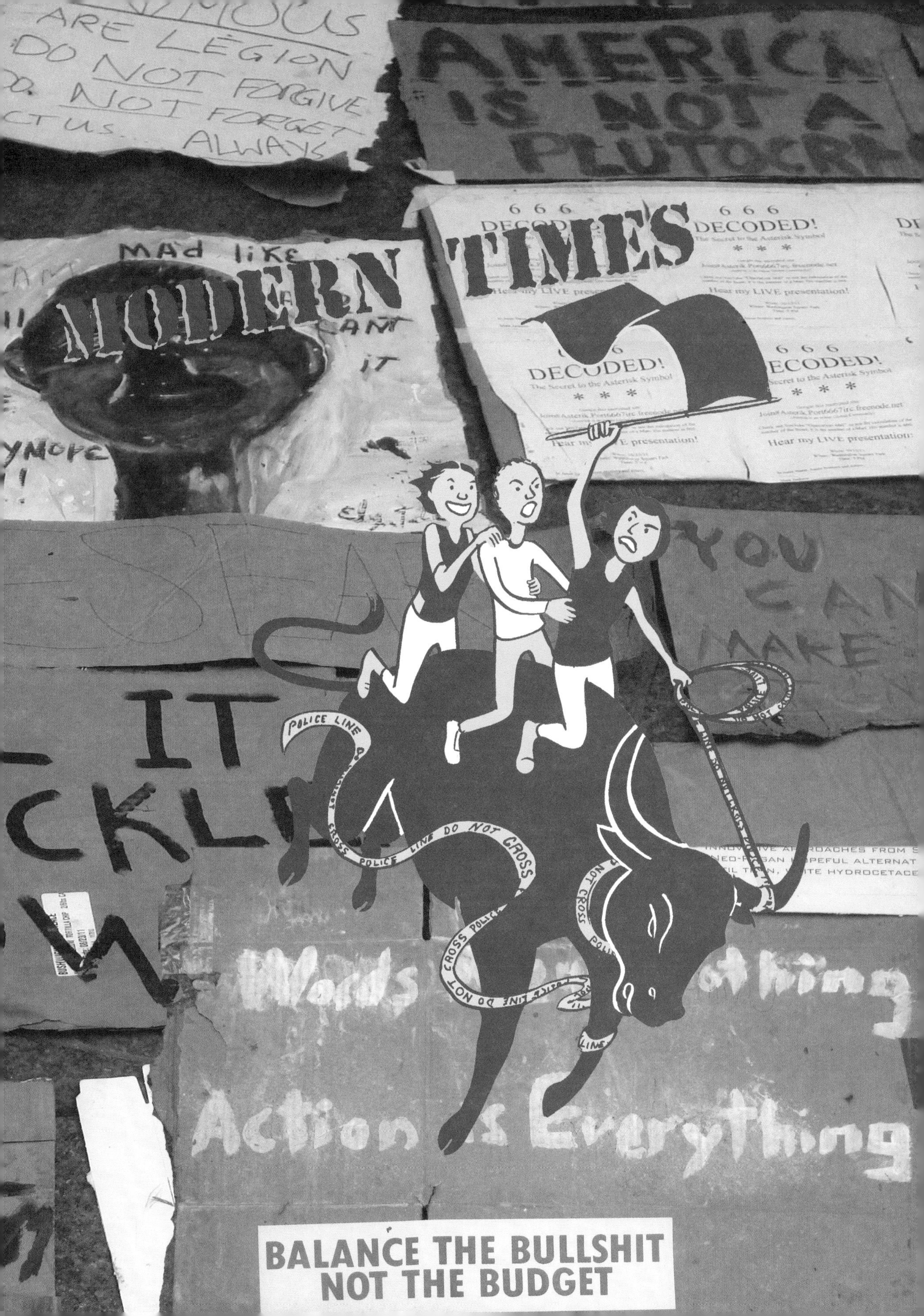

ARE LEGION
DO NOT FORGIVE
NOT FORGET
ALWAYS
MODERN TIMES
666 DECODED!
The Secret to the Asterisk Symbol
Hear my LIVE presentation!
MAD LIKE
POLICE LINE DO NOT CROSS
Action is Everything
BALANCE THE BULLSHIT NOT THE BUDGET

ON THE TEA PARTY TRAIL

WITH WW3 NEWS REPORTER: PETER KUPER

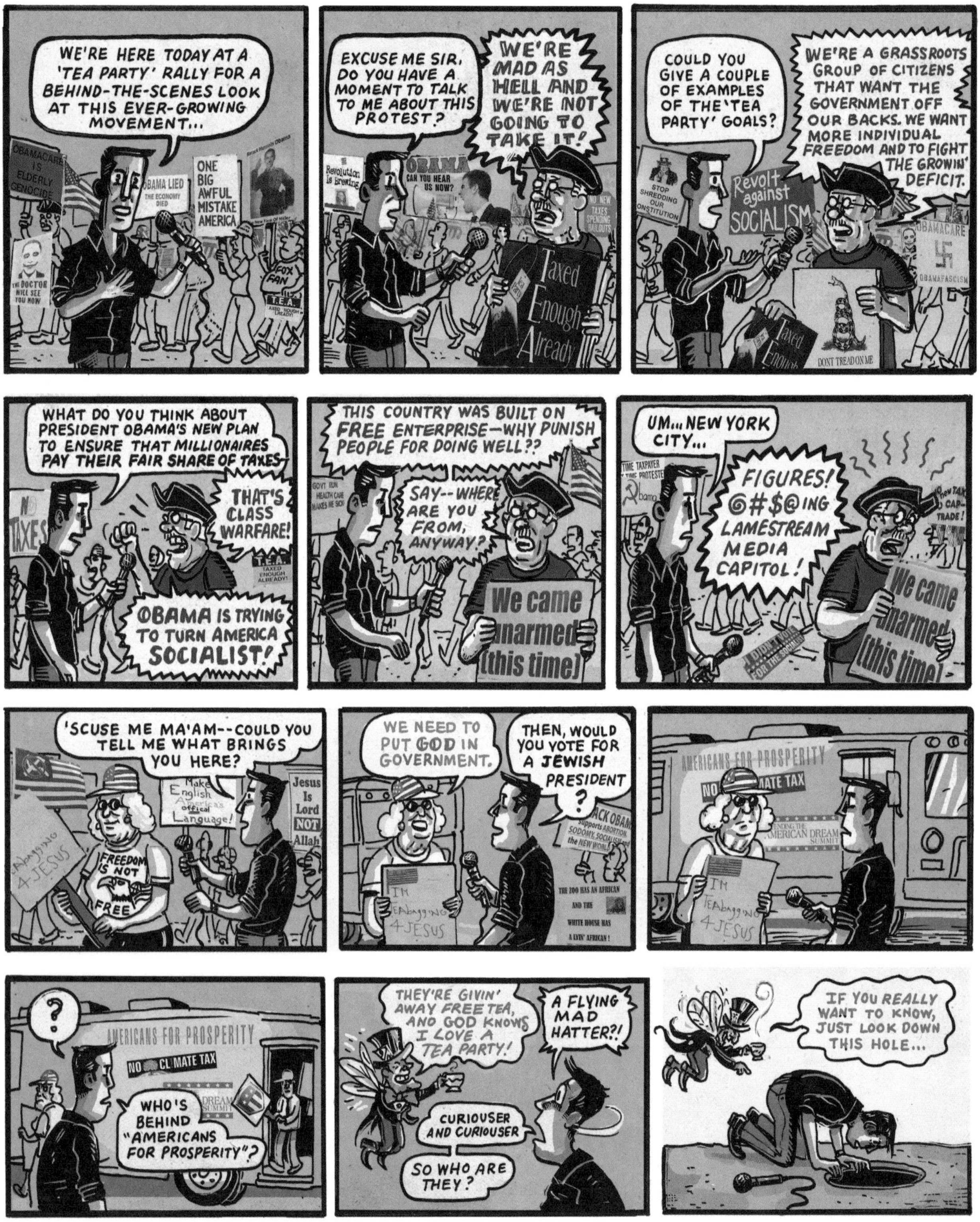

WE'RE HERE TODAY AT A 'TEA PARTY' RALLY FOR A BEHIND-THE-SCENES LOOK AT THIS EVER-GROWING MOVEMENT...
OBAMACARE IS ELDERLY GENOCIDE
OBAMA LIED THE ECONOMY DIED
ONE BIG AWFUL MISTAKE AMERICA
THE DOCTOR WILL SEE YOU NOW
FOX FAN
T.E.A.
EXCUSE ME SIR, DO YOU HAVE A MOMENT TO TALK TO ME ABOUT THIS PROTEST?
WE'RE MAD AS HELL AND WE'RE NOT GOING TO TAKE IT!
Revolution is Brewing
OBAMA CAN YOU HEAR US NOW?
NO NEW TAXES SPENDING BAILOUTS
Taxed Enough Already
COULD YOU GIVE A COUPLE OF EXAMPLES OF THE 'TEA PARTY' GOALS?
WE'RE A GRASSROOTS GROUP OF CITIZENS THAT WANT THE GOVERNMENT OFF OUR BACKS. WE WANT MORE INDIVIDUAL FREEDOM AND TO FIGHT THE GROWIN' DEFICIT.
STOP SHREDDING OUR CONSTITUTION
Revolt against SOCIALISM
OBAMACARE
OBAMAFASCISM
DONT TREAD ON ME
WHAT DO YOU THINK ABOUT PRESIDENT OBAMA'S NEW PLAN TO ENSURE THAT MILLIONAIRES PAY THEIR FAIR SHARE OF TAXES-
THAT'S CLASS WARFARE!
OBAMA IS TRYING TO TURN AMERICA SOCIALIST!
NO TAXES
T.E.A. TAXED ENOUGH ALREADY!
THIS COUNTRY WAS BUILT ON FREE ENTERPRISE—WHY PUNISH PEOPLE FOR DOING WELL??
SAY--WHERE ARE YOU FROM, ANYWAY?
GOV'T RUN HEALTH CARE MAKES ME SICK
We came unarmed (this time)
UM... NEW YORK CITY...
FIGURES! @#$@ING LAMESTREAM MEDIA CAPITOL!
NO NEW TAX CAP-TRADE!
I DIDN'T VOTE FOR THE SOCIALIST
We came unarmed (this time)
'SCUSE ME MA'AM--COULD YOU TELL ME WHAT BRINGS YOU HERE?
Make English America's offical Language!
Jesus Is Lord NOT Allah
FREEDOM IS NOT FREE
TEAbagging 4 JESUS
WE NEED TO PUT GOD IN GOVERNMENT.
THEN, WOULD YOU VOTE FOR A JEWISH PRESIDENT?
IM TEAbagging 4 JESUS
THE ZOO HAS AN AFRICAN AND THE WHITE HOUSE HAS A LYIN' AFRICAN!
AMERICANS FOR PROSPERITY
NO CLIMATE TAX
AMERICAN DREAM SUMMIT
IM TEAbagging 4 JESUS
?
AMERICANS FOR PROSPERITY
NO CLIMATE TAX
WHO'S BEHIND "AMERICANS FOR PROSPERITY"?
THEY'RE GIVIN' AWAY FREE TEA, AND GOD KNOWS I LOVE A TEA PARTY!
A FLYING MAD HATTER?!
CURIOUSER AND CURIOUSER
SO WHO ARE THEY?
IF YOU REALLY WANT TO KNOW, JUST LOOK DOWN THIS HOLE...

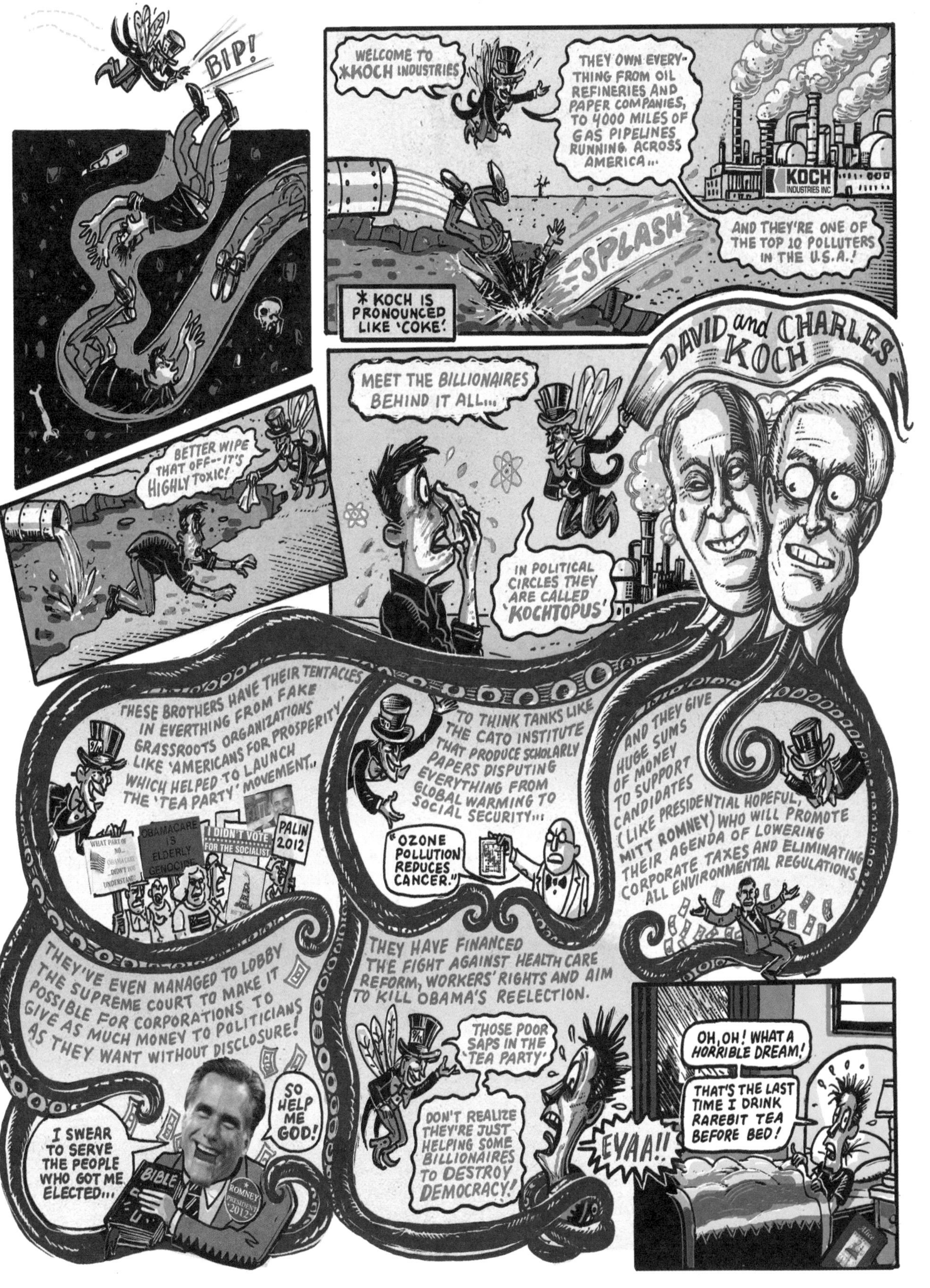
BIP!
WELCOME TO *KOCH INDUSTRIES
THEY OWN EVERY-THING FROM OIL REFINERIES AND PAPER COMPANIES, TO 4000 MILES OF GAS PIPELINES RUNNING ACROSS AMERICA...
KOCH INDUSTRIES INC
AND THEY'RE ONE OF THE TOP 10 POLLUTERS IN THE U.S.A.!
SPLASH
* KOCH IS PRONOUNCED LIKE 'COKE'.
BETTER WIPE THAT OFF--IT'S HIGHLY TOXIC!
MEET THE BILLIONAIRES BEHIND IT ALL...
DAVID and CHARLES KOCH
IN POLITICAL CIRCLES THEY ARE CALLED 'KOCHTOPUS'
THESE BROTHERS HAVE THEIR TENTACLES IN EVERTHING FROM FAKE GRASSROOTS ORGANIZATIONS LIKE 'AMERICANS FOR PROSPERITY' WHICH HELPED TO LAUNCH THE 'TEA PARTY' MOVEMENT...
WHAT PART OF NO... OBAMACARE ...DIDN'T YOU UNDERSTAND?
OBAMACARE IS ELDERLY GENOCIDE
I DIDN'T VOTE FOR THE SOCIALIST
PALIN 2012
TO THINK TANKS LIKE THE CATO INSTITUTE THAT PRODUCE SCHOLARLY PAPERS DISPUTING EVERYTHING FROM GLOBAL WARMING TO SOCIAL SECURITY...
"OZONE POLLUTION REDUCES CANCER."
AND THEY GIVE HUGE SUMS OF MONEY TO SUPPORT CANDIDATES (LIKE PRESIDENTIAL HOPEFUL, MITT ROMNEY) WHO WILL PROMOTE THEIR AGENDA OF LOWERING CORPORATE TAXES AND ELIMINATING ALL ENVIRONMENTAL REGULATIONS.
THEY'VE EVEN MANAGED TO LOBBY THE SUPREME COURT TO MAKE IT POSSIBLE FOR CORPORATIONS TO GIVE AS MUCH MONEY TO POLITICIANS AS THEY WANT WITHOUT DISCLOSURE!
THEY HAVE FINANCED THE FIGHT AGAINST HEALTH CARE REFORM, WORKERS' RIGHTS AND AIM TO KILL OBAMA'S REELECTION.
I SWEAR TO SERVE THE PEOPLE WHO GOT ME ELECTED...
SO HELP ME GOD!
BIBLE
ROMNEY PRESIDENT 2012
THOSE POOR SAPS IN THE 'TEA PARTY'
DON'T REALIZE THEY'RE JUST HELPING SOME BILLIONAIRES TO DESTROY DEMOCRACY!
EYAA!!
OH, OH! WHAT A HORRIBLE DREAM!
THAT'S THE LAST TIME I DRINK RAREBIT TEA BEFORE BED!

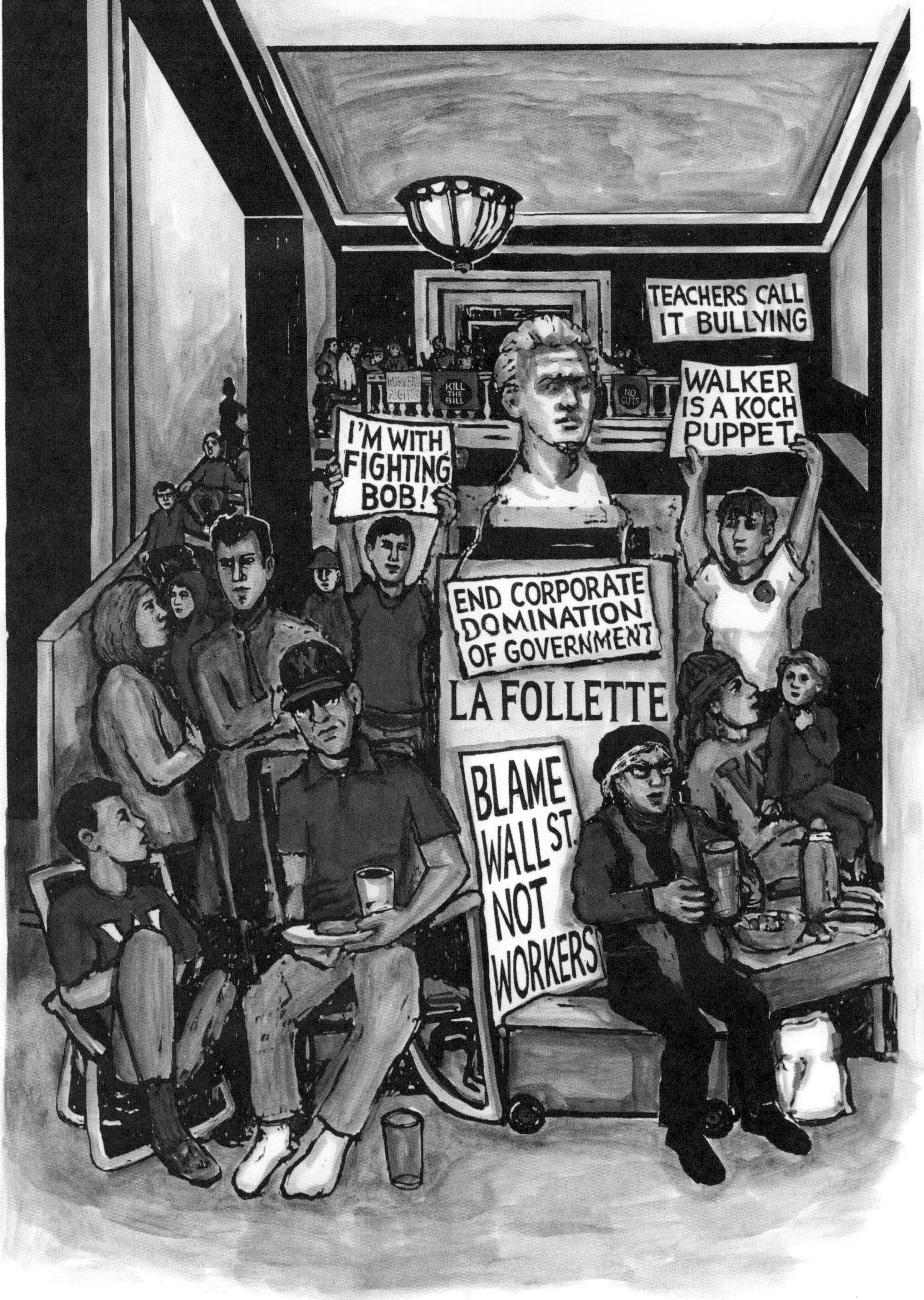

TEACHERS CALL IT BULLYING
WORKERS RIGHTS
KILL THE BILL
NO CUTS
WALKER IS A KOCH PUPPET
I'M WITH FIGHTING BOB!
END CORPORATE DOMINATION OF GOVERNMENT
LA FOLLETTE
BLAME WALL ST. NOT WORKERS

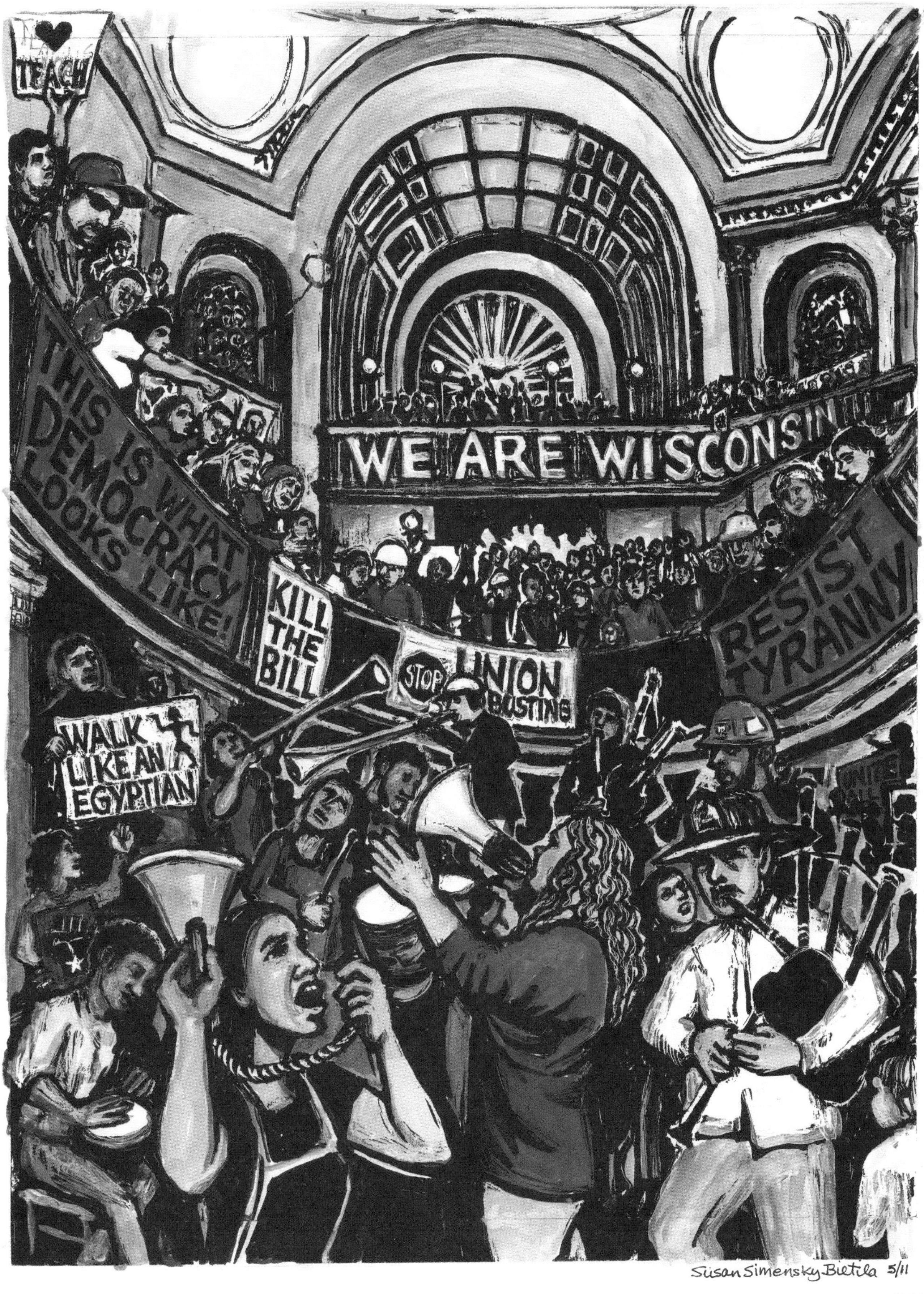
TEACH
THIS IS WHAT DEMOCRACY LOOKS LIKE!
WE ARE WISCONSIN
KILL THE BILL
STOP
UNION BUSTING
RESIST TYRANNY
WALK LIKE AN EGYPTIAN
Susan Simensky Bietila 5/11

OCCUPY THE CITY

BY SETH TOBOCMAN AND JESSICA WEHRLE

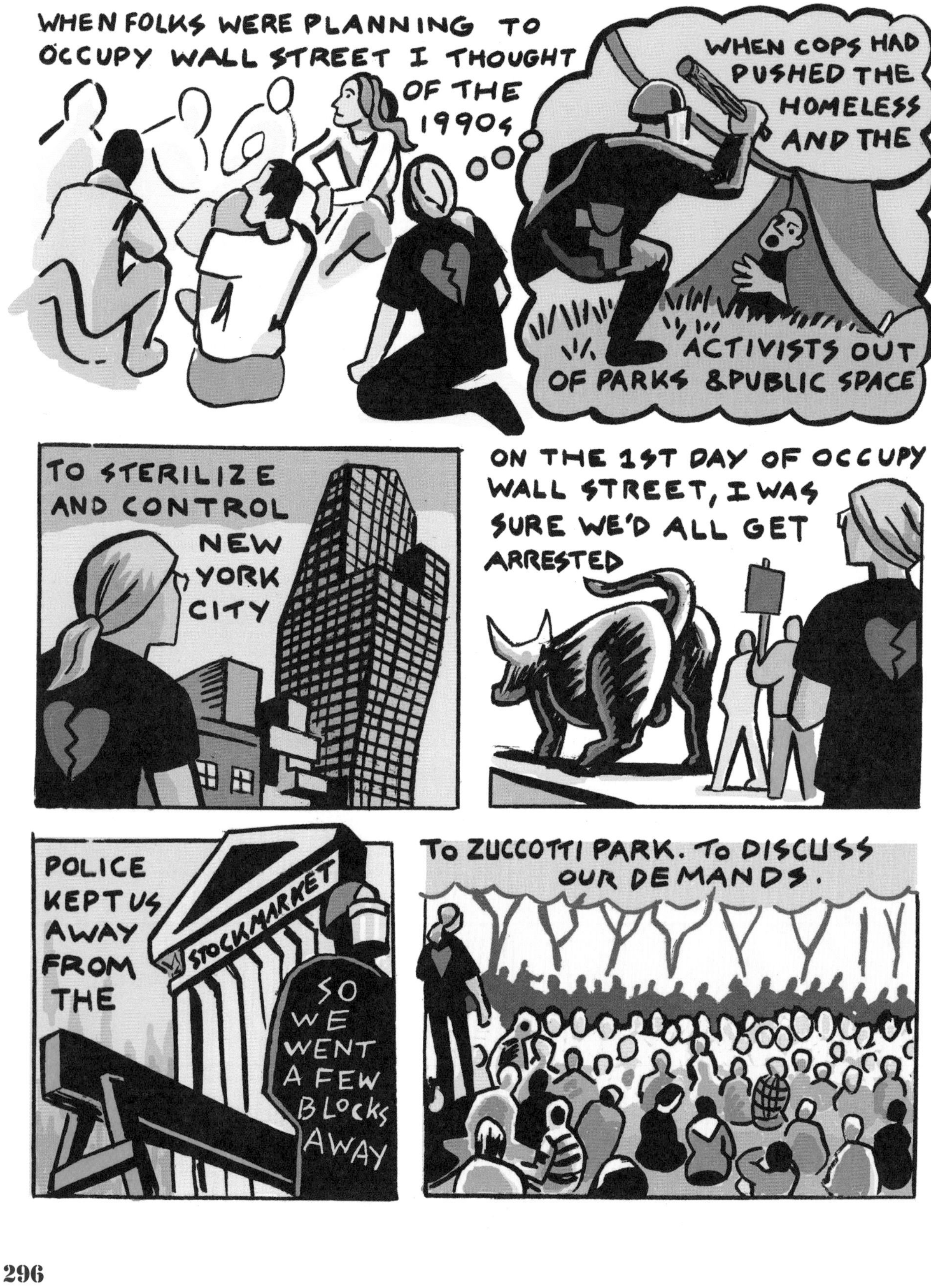

WHEN FOLKS WERE PLANNING TO OCCUPY WALL STREET I THOUGHT OF THE 1990s
WHEN COPS HAD PUSHED THE HOMELESS AND THE ACTIVISTS OUT OF PARKS &PUBLIC SPACE
TO STERILIZE AND CONTROL NEW YORK CITY
ON THE 1ST DAY OF OCCUPY WALL STREET, I WAS SURE WE'D ALL GET ARRESTED
POLICE KEPT US AWAY FROM THE
STOCKMARKET
SO WE WENT A FEW BLOCKS AWAY
To ZUCCOTTI PARK. To DISCUSS OUR DEMANDS.

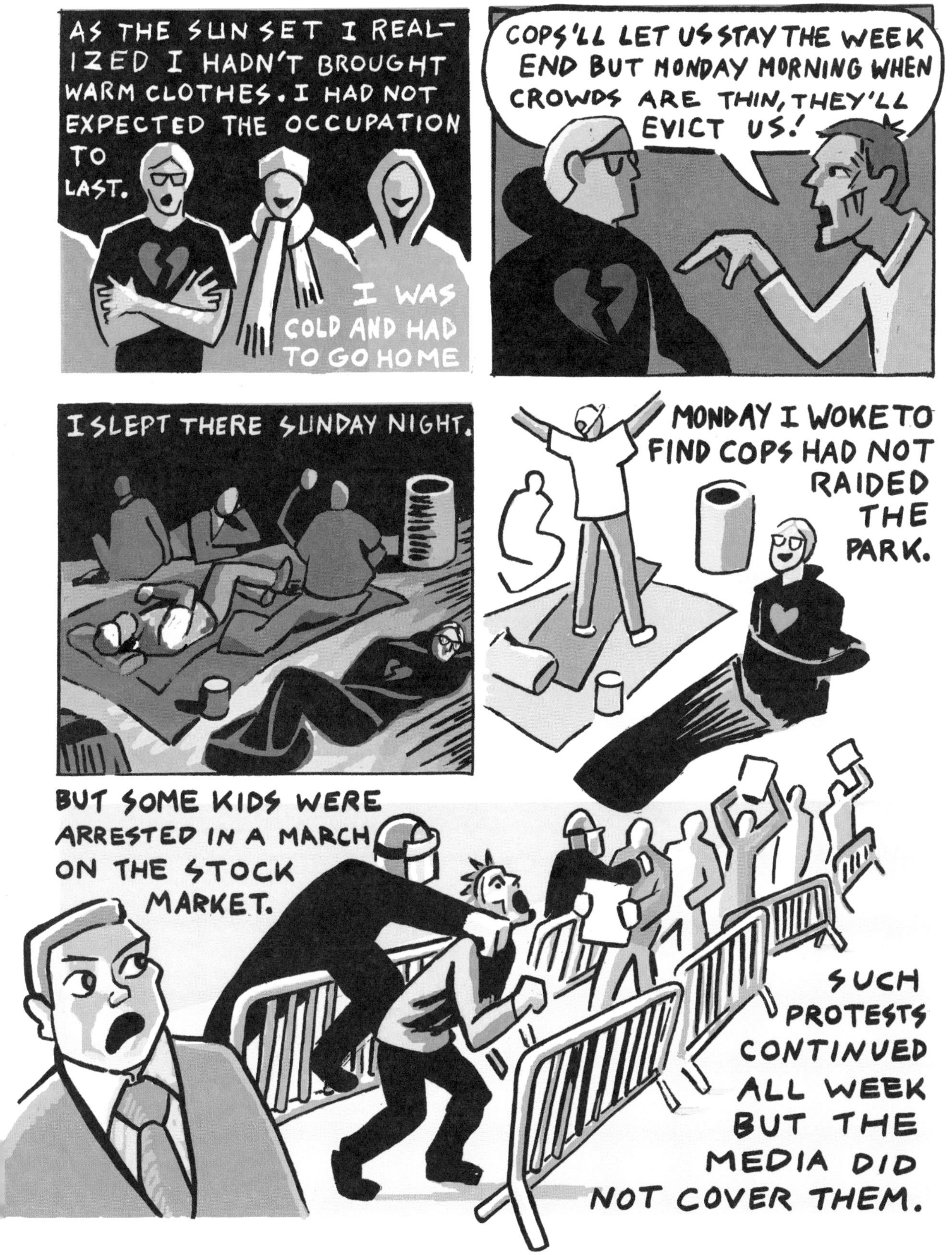
AS THE SUN SET I REALIZED I HADN'T BROUGHT WARM CLOTHES. I HAD NOT EXPECTED THE OCCUPATION TO LAST.
I WAS COLD AND HAD TO GO HOME
COPS'LL LET US STAY THE WEEK END BUT MONDAY MORNING WHEN CROWDS ARE THIN, THEY'LL EVICT US!
I SLEPT THERE SUNDAY NIGHT.
MONDAY I WOKE TO FIND COPS HAD NOT RAIDED THE PARK.
BUT SOME KIDS WERE ARRESTED IN A MARCH ON THE STOCK MARKET.
SUCH PROTESTS CONTINUED ALL WEEK BUT THE MEDIA DID NOT COVER THEM.

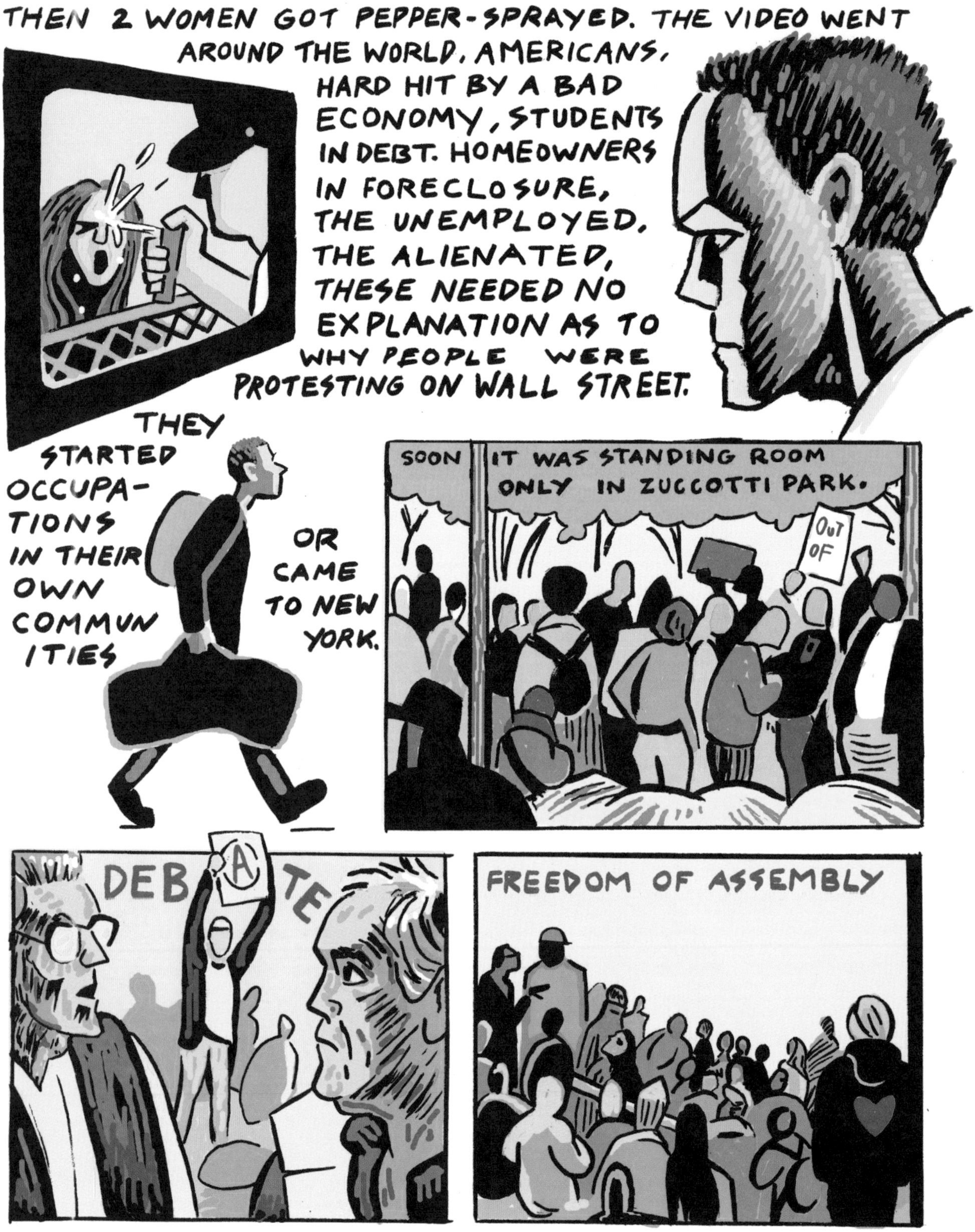
THEN 2 WOMEN GOT PEPPER-SPRAYED. THE VIDEO WENT AROUND THE WORLD. AMERICANS, HARD HIT BY A BAD ECONOMY, STUDENTS IN DEBT. HOMEOWNERS IN FORECLOSURE, THE UNEMPLOYED. THE ALIENATED, THESE NEEDED NO EXPLANATION AS TO WHY PEOPLE WERE PROTESTING ON WALL STREET.
THEY STARTED OCCUPATIONS IN THEIR OWN COMMUNITIES
OR CAME TO NEW YORK.
SOON IT WAS STANDING ROOM ONLY IN ZUCCOTTI PARK.
OUT OF
DEB A TE
FREEDOM OF ASSEMBLY

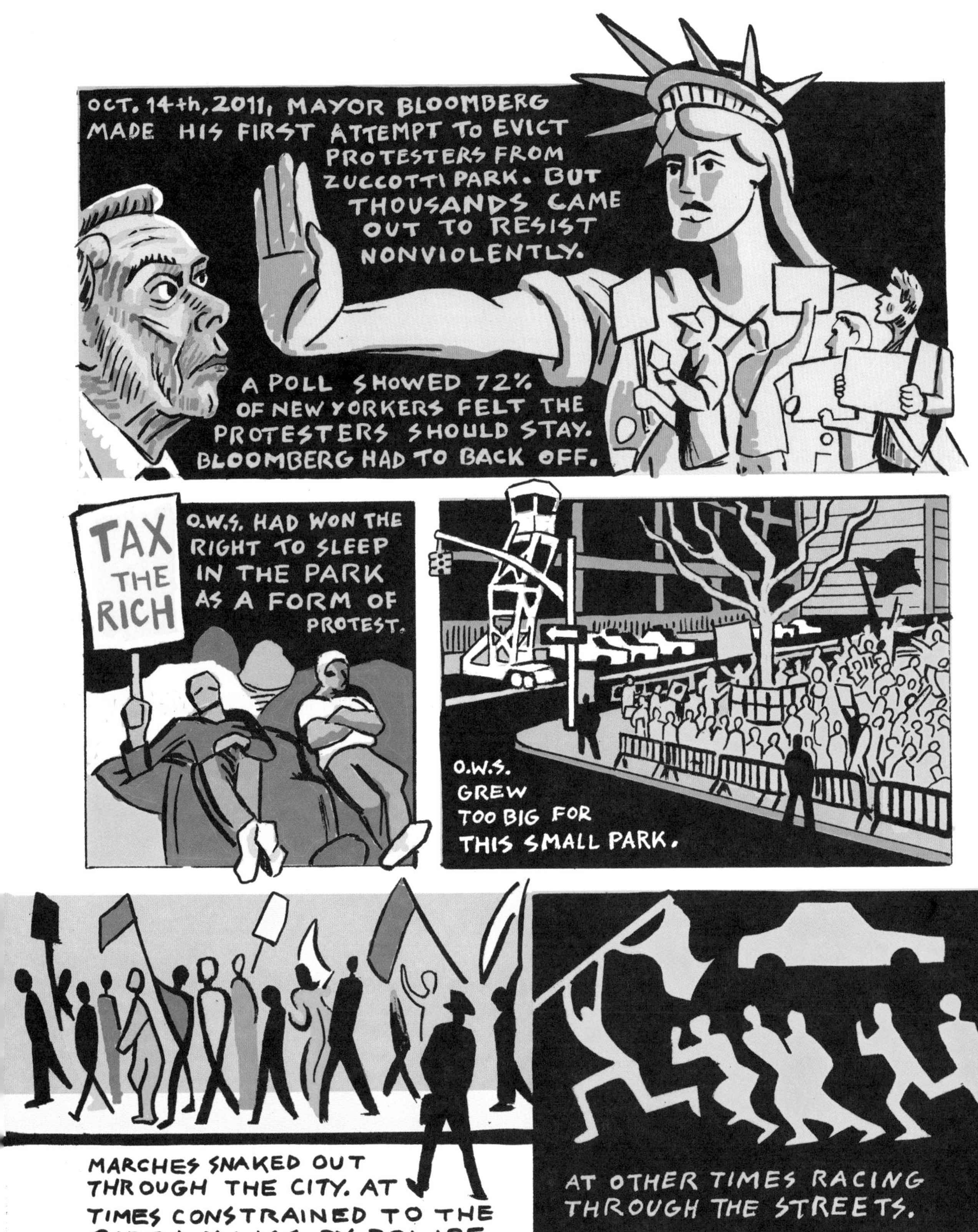
OCT. 14th, 2011, MAYOR BLOOMBERG MADE HIS FIRST ATTEMPT TO EVICT PROTESTERS FROM ZUCCOTTI PARK. BUT THOUSANDS CAME OUT TO RESIST NONVIOLENTLY.
A POLL SHOWED 72% OF NEW YORKERS FELT THE PROTESTERS SHOULD STAY. BLOOMBERG HAD TO BACK OFF.
TAX THE RICH
O.W.S. HAD WON THE RIGHT TO SLEEP IN THE PARK AS A FORM OF PROTEST.
O.W.S. GREW TOO BIG FOR THIS SMALL PARK.
MARCHES SNAKED OUT THROUGH THE CITY. AT TIMES CONSTRAINED TO THE SIDE WALKS BY POLICE.
AT OTHER TIMES RACING THROUGH THE STREETS.

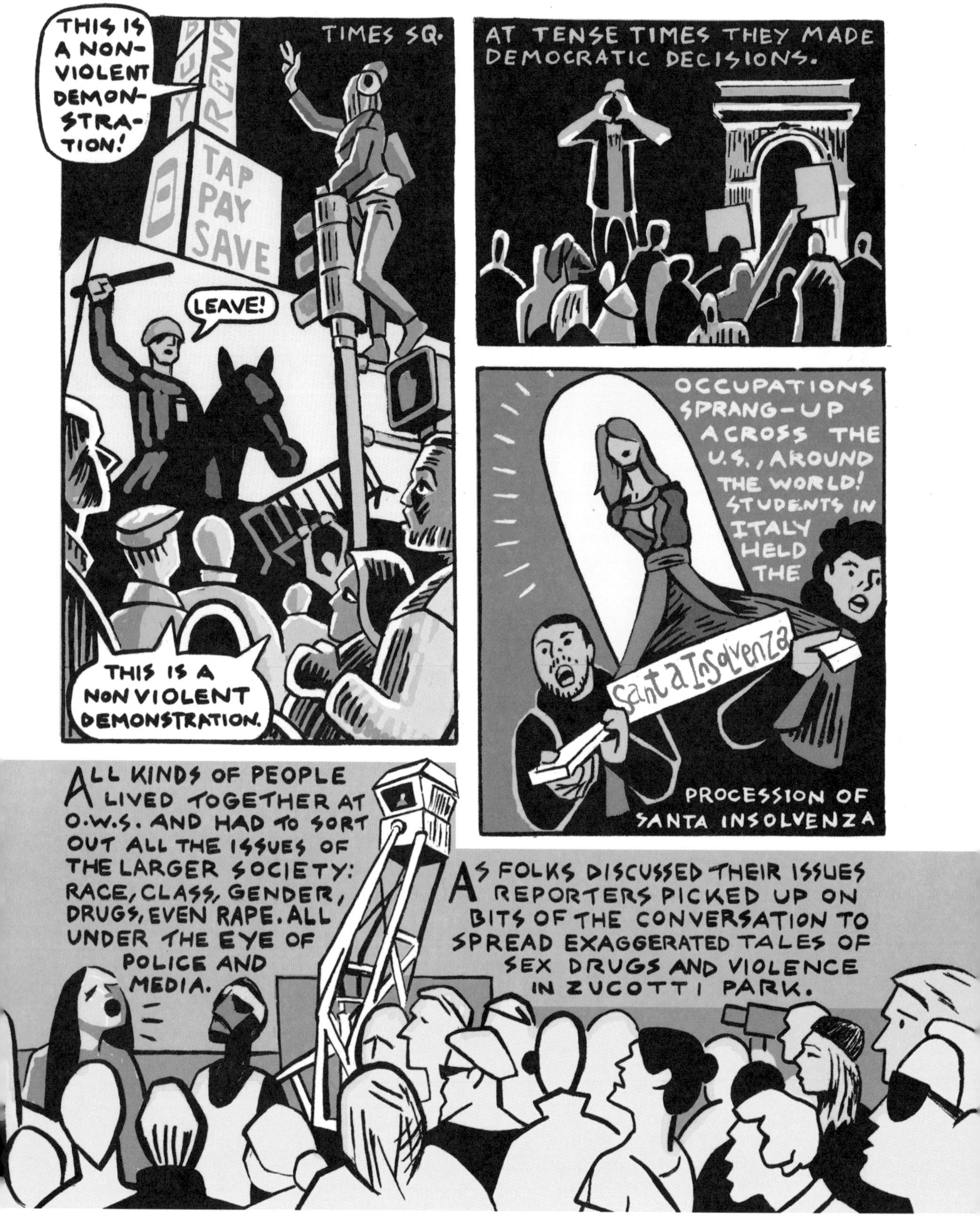
TIMES SQ.
THIS IS A NON-VIOLENT DEMON-STRA-TION!
TAP PAY SAVE
LEAVE!
THIS IS A NON VIOLENT DEMONSTRATION.
AT TENSE TIMES THEY MADE DEMOCRATIC DECISIONS.
OCCUPATIONS SPRANG-UP ACROSS THE U.S., AROUND THE WORLD! STUDENTS IN ITALY HELD THE
Santa Insolvenza
PROCESSION OF SANTA INSOLVENZA
ALL KINDS OF PEOPLE LIVED TOGETHER AT O.W.S. AND HAD TO SORT OUT ALL THE ISSUES OF THE LARGER SOCIETY: RACE, CLASS, GENDER, DRUGS, EVEN RAPE. ALL UNDER THE EYE OF POLICE AND MEDIA.
AS FOLKS DISCUSSED THEIR ISSUES REPORTERS PICKED UP ON BITS OF THE CONVERSATION TO SPREAD EXAGGERATED TALES OF SEX DRUGS AND VIOLENCE IN ZUCOTTI PARK.

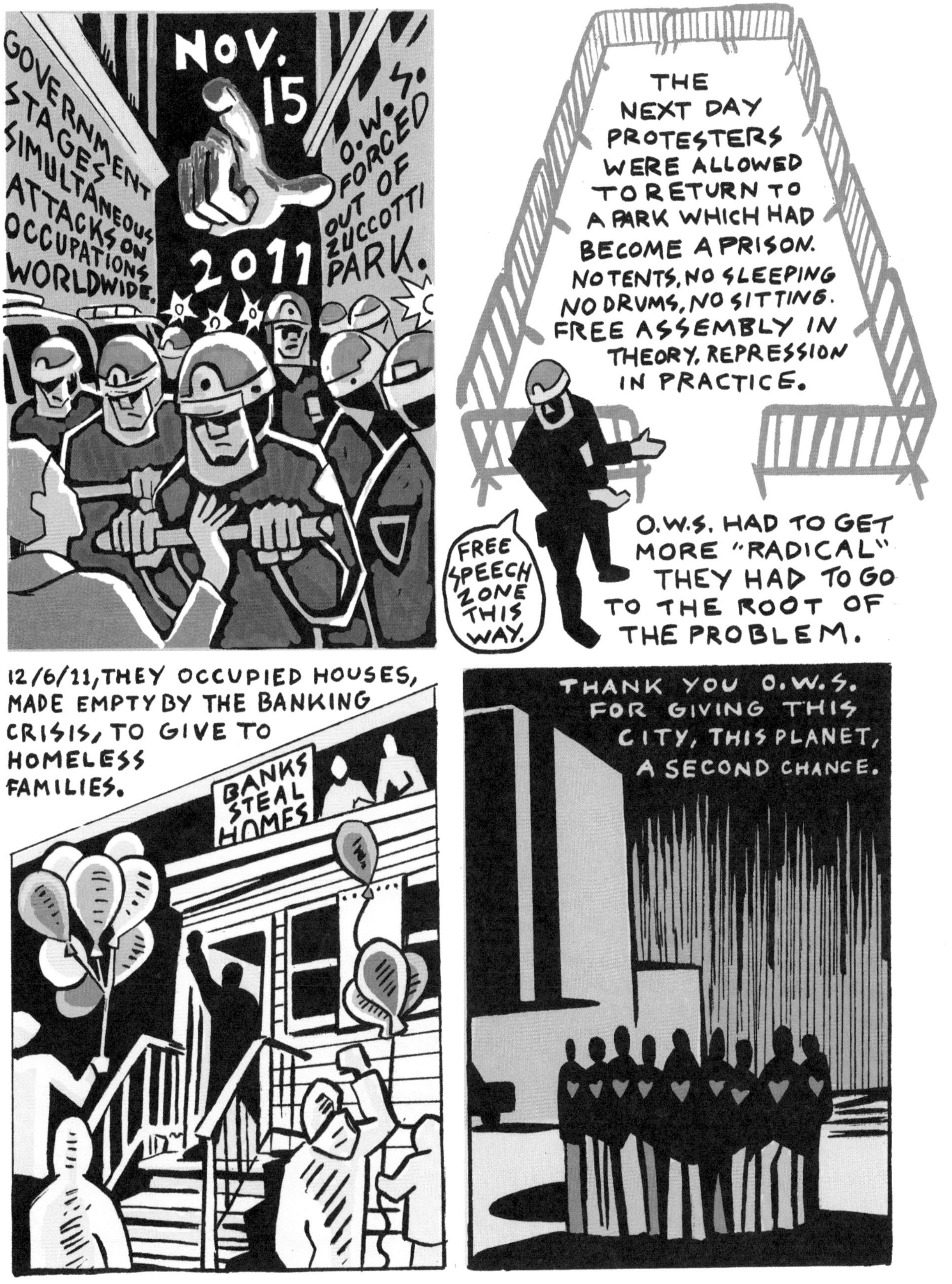
NOV. 15 2011
GOVERNMENT STAGES SIMULTANEOUS ATTACKS ON OCCUPATIONS WORLDWIDE.
O.W.S. FORCED OUT OF ZUCCOTTI PARK.
THE NEXT DAY PROTESTERS WERE ALLOWED TO RETURN TO A PARK WHICH HAD BECOME A PRISON. NO TENTS, NO SLEEPING NO DRUMS, NO SITTING. FREE ASSEMBLY IN THEORY, REPRESSION IN PRACTICE.
FREE SPEECH ZONE THIS WAY.
O.W.S. HAD TO GET MORE "RADICAL" THEY HAD TO GO TO THE ROOT OF THE PROBLEM.
12/6/11, THEY OCCUPIED HOUSES, MADE EMPTY BY THE BANKING CRISIS, TO GIVE TO HOMELESS FAMILIES.
BANKS STEAL HOMES
THANK YOU O.W.S. FOR GIVING THIS CITY, THIS PLANET, A SECOND CHANCE.

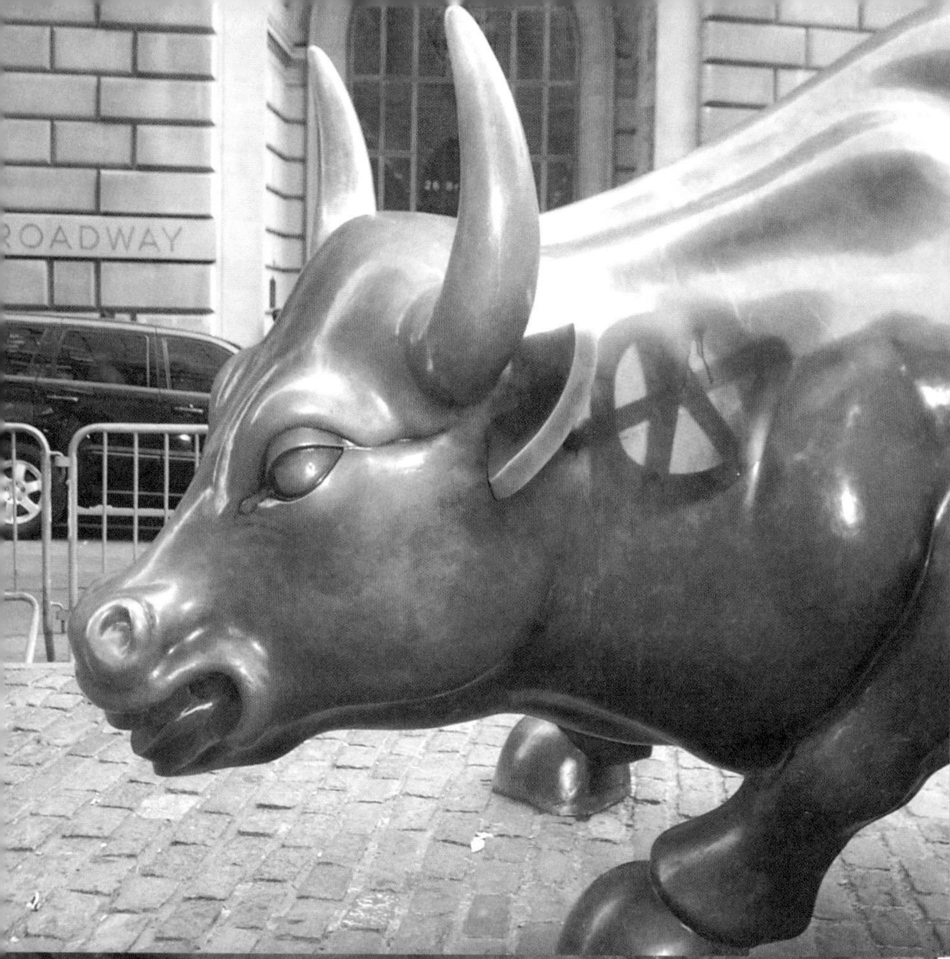
ROADWAY

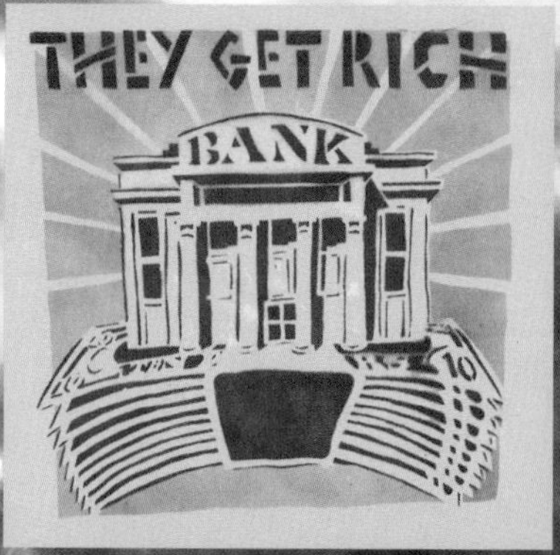
THEY GET RICH
BANK

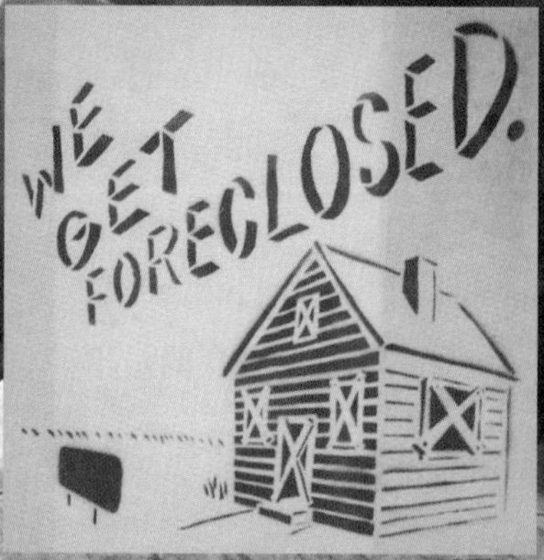
WE GET FORECLOSED.

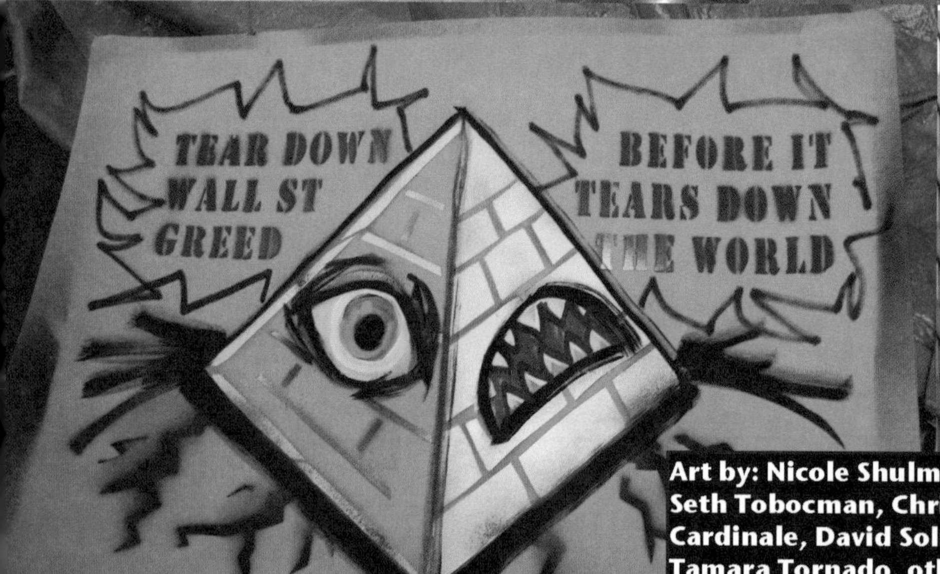
TEAR DOWN
WALL ST
GREED
BEFORE IT
TEARS DOWN
THE WORLD

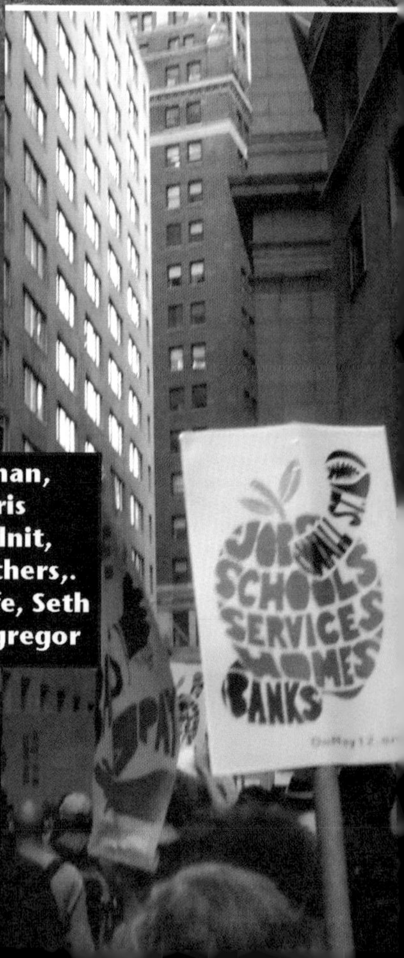
SCHOOLS
SERVICES
HOMES
BANKS

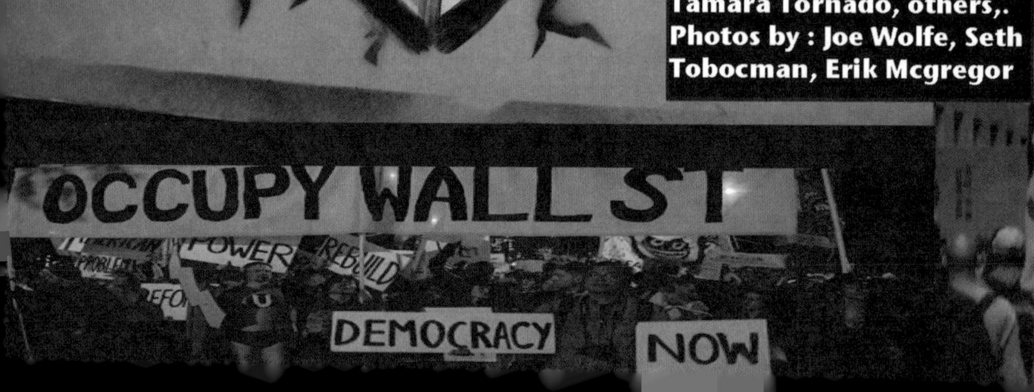
OCCUPY WALL ST
POWER
REBUILD
DEMOCRACY
NOW

Art by: Nicole Shulman, Seth Tobocman, Chris Cardinale, David Solnit, Tamara Tornado, others,. Photos by : Joe Wolfe, Seth Tobocman, Erik Mcgregor

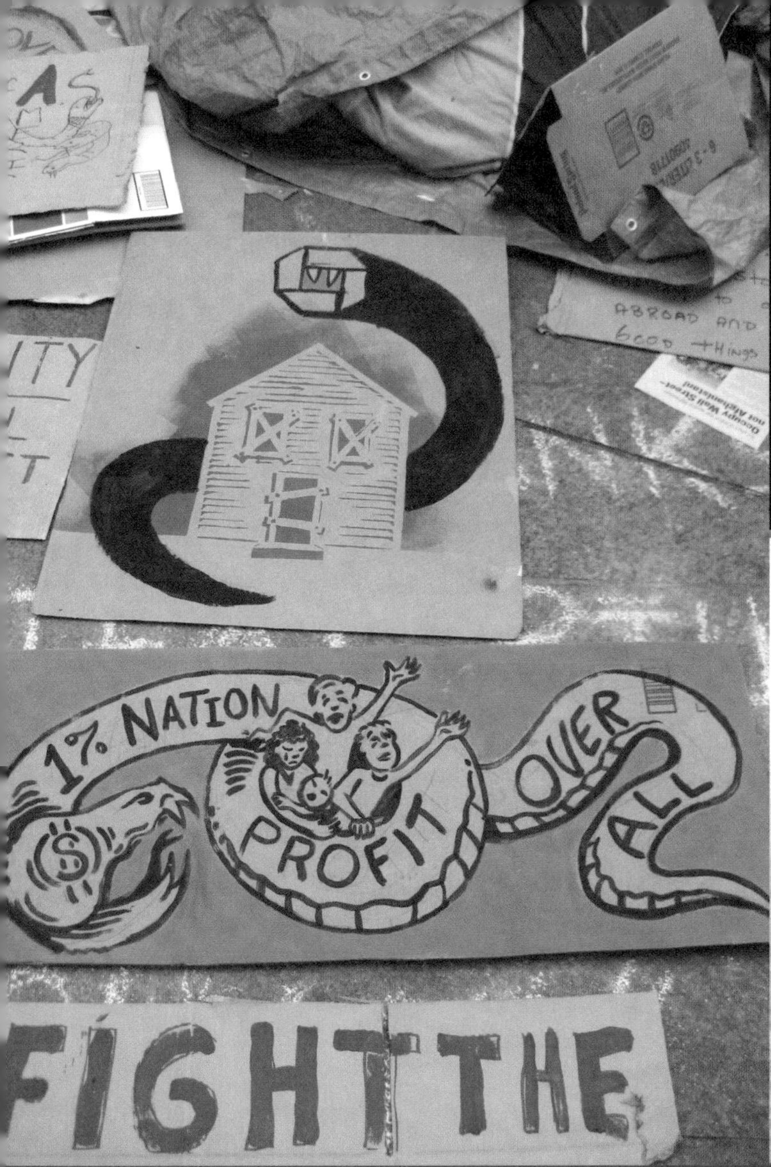
ABROAD AND
GOOD THINGS
1% NATION
PROFIT OVER ALL
FIGHT THE
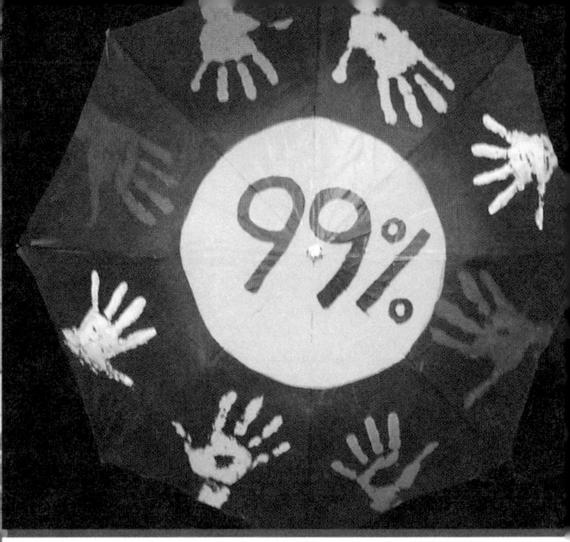
99%
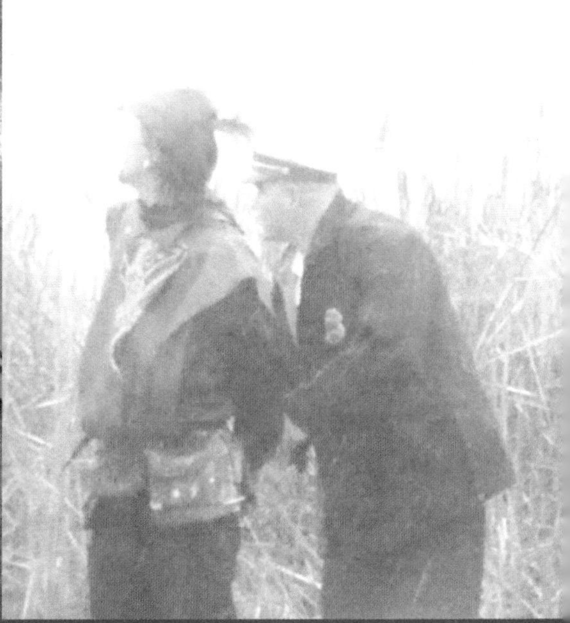
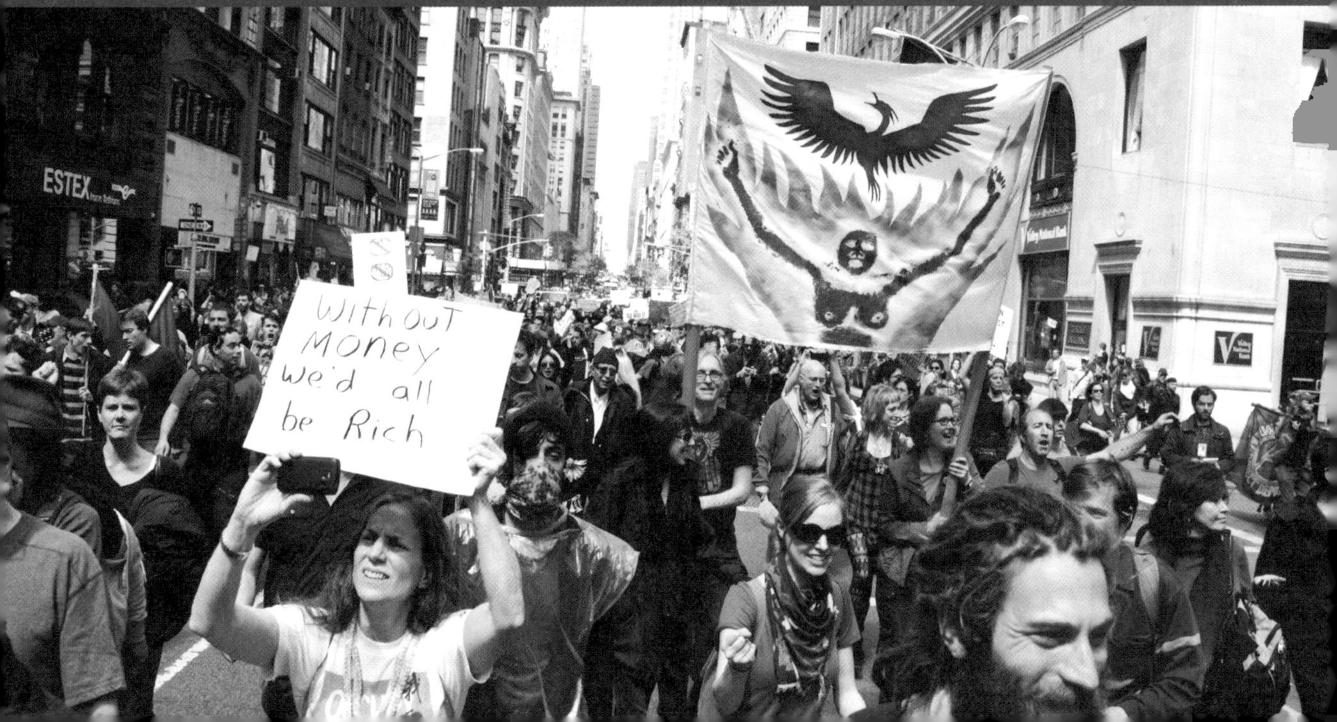
ESTEX
Without Money we'd all be Rich

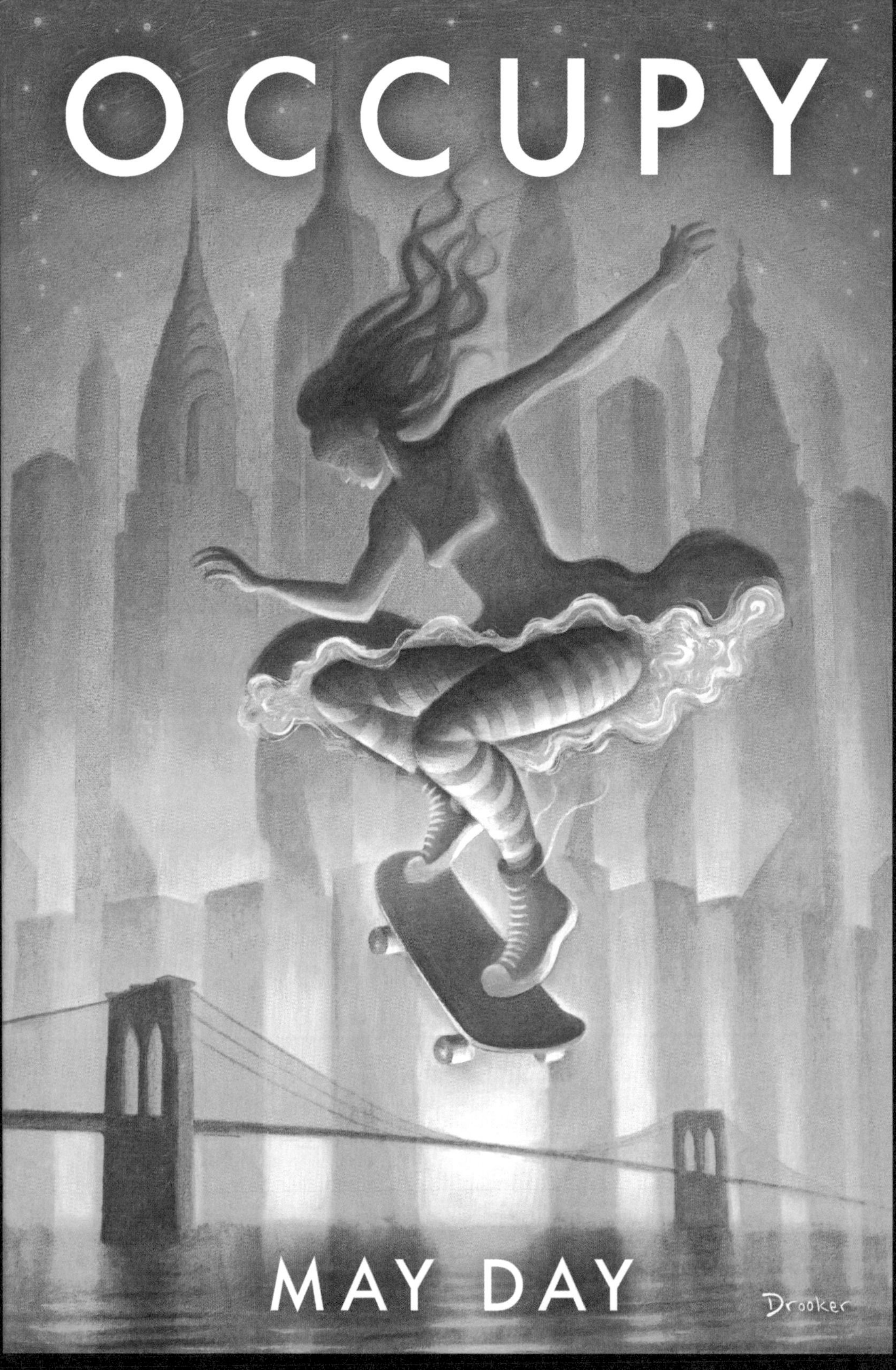
OCCUPY
MAY DAY
Drooker

TIME LINE

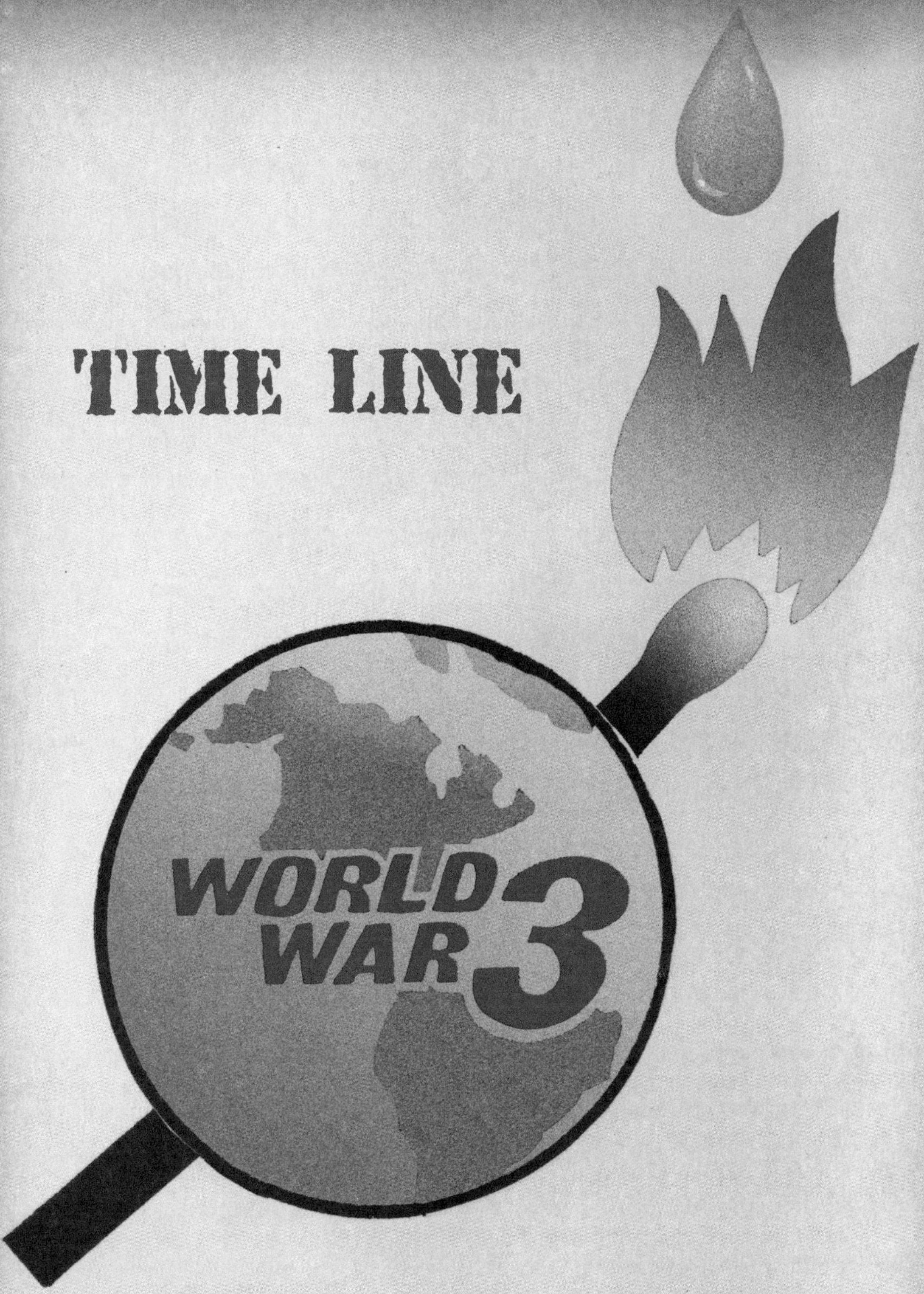
WORLD
WAR
3

1970–74

Nationwide protests against the Vietnam War.

National Guard kills four students at Kent State University.

President Richard Nixon resigns over Watergate scandal.

In Cleveland, Ohio, childhood friends Seth Tobocman and Peter Kuper, involved in comic book fandom, collaborated on a fanzine titled *Phanzine* and *G.A.S. Lite* (the official magazine of the Cleveland Graphic Arts Society). Kuper also publishes two collections of R. Crumb sketches called *Melotoons*. Kuper and Tobocman are introduced to Crumb by Harvey Pekar.

Phanzine 1970 art by Jack Kirby and Dan Adkins

1975–76

South Vietnam surrenders to North Vietnam; Vietnam War ends.

Harvey Pekar publishes the first issue of *American Splendor.*

John Holmstrom publishes the first issue of *PUNK* magazine.

G.A.S. Lite 1972 art by Gary Dumm

1979

Ben Katchor publishes *Picture Story.*

A meltdown at the Three Mile Island nuclear plant in Pennsylvania releases radiation and alerts the public to the dangers of nuclear energy.

Future *WW3* artists Tom Keough and Ben Hillman work with the SHAAD alliance (Sound Hudson Against Atomic Development).

"White Nights" San Francisco riots break out in response to the murder of gay politician Harvey Milk. Author Peter Plate (who will later write for *WW3*) is prosecuted for allegedly burning police cars. He is eventually found not guilty.

Jerry Falwell founds the "Moral Majority," a conservative, Christian lobbying group for anti-gay, anti-abortion, anti-equal rights political organizations.

NATO stations Pershing II and Cruise nuclear missiles in Europe.

The Iranian monarch is overthrown. Rebels seize the U.S. Embassy in Tehran and take hostages.

Peter Kuper and Seth Tobocman, who are both attending Pratt Institute in Brooklyn, decide it is the right time for an anti-war comic book.

Melotoons
Truckin' Along With R. Crumb.

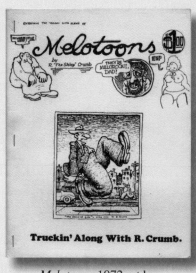

Melotoons 1972 art by R. Crumb

World War 3 Illustrated #1, edited by Seth Tobocman, Peter Kuper, and Christof Kohlhofer, with production help from Ben Katchor.

1980

The Real Estate Show: Artists seize a City-owned building to hold an illegal art show. After they are thrown out, the Koch administration agrees to give them space for a gallery to be called ABC No Rio.

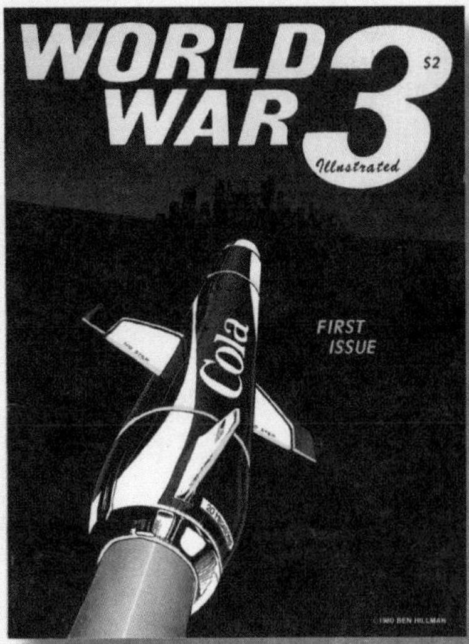
WORLD WAR 3
$2
Illustrated
Cola
FIRST ISSUE
#1 art by Ben Hillman

Ronald Reagan is elected president with the support of the "Moral Majority." He advocates a military build-up and confrontation with the Soviet Union. Domestically, he advocates for "free-market" economics, lifting restrictions on foreign imports, smashing unions, cutting welfare, and eliminating affirmative action. Culturally, he advocates a return to "family values"—code for a crackdown on drugs, persecution of gays, discrimination against women, and media censorship.

INX, a syndicated, political illustration collective, is founded by John Macleod, Randy Jones, Frances Jetter, Robert Neubecker, Bob Gale, Charles Waller, and Oliver Williams.

John Lennon is murdered in New York City.

Art Spiegelman and Françoise Mouly publish *Raw* #1.

1981

WW3 #2: "Twin Titans Threaten Earth!" edited by Seth Tobocman.

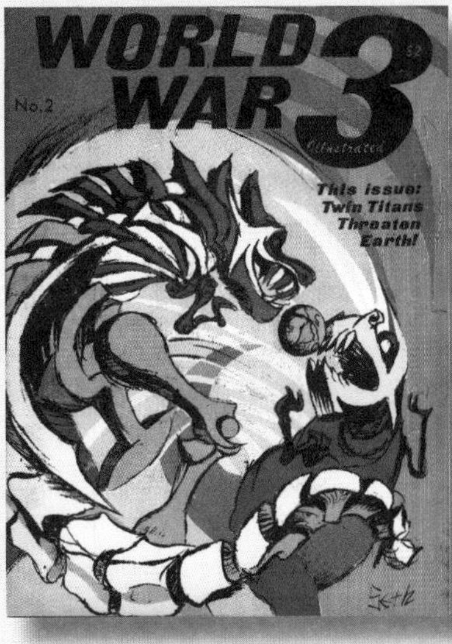
WORLD WAR 3
$2
No. 2
Illustrated
This issue: Twin Titans Threaten Earth!
#2 art by Seth Tobocman

Sabrina Jones and Anton Van Dalen join Carnival Knowledge, a feminist art collective.

Robert Crumb publishes *Weirdo* #1.

Journalist Mumia Abu-Jamal is charged with shooting police officer Daniel Faulkner. Mumia will spend the next three decades on death row, writing books and articles, performing radio commentaries, and later contributing text and graphics to *WW3*.

1982

WW3 artists participate in huge anti-nuclear demonstration in Central Park.

Israel invades Lebanon.

Severe recession begins in the United States.

1983

Reagan proposes space-based missile defense and increases military funding.

WW3 artists participate in Artists Call against U.S. Intervention in Central America and in community organizing on the Lower East Side.

WW3 artists teach art classes for local kids at the Charas Community Center.

Lower East Side artist Michael Stewart is killed by NYPD.

WW3 artists begin contributing to syndicated political illustration group INX.

The U.S. invades Grenada.

WW3 artists protest the invasion of Grenada with street art.

WORLD WAR 3
#3
$1.50
Illustrated
CAPTIVE CITY

#3 art by Michael Roman

1984

WW3 #3: "Captive City," edited by Seth Tobocman with production assistance from Peter Kuper.

New York City Police respond to community complaints with a massive drug raid called Operation Pressure Point. Residents are dismayed that the primary targets are local youth and not big-time drug dealers or bridge-and-tunnel buyers.

WW3 artists James Romberger and Marguerite Van Cook start the Ground Zero Gallery.

Federal agents surround the homes and meeting places of eight black community organizers, arrest them, and prosecute them on false conspiracy charges. They come to be known as the New York 8. Their successful defense rests on the proposition that fascism is being consolidated in the United States. They go on to organize the "Days of Outrage" against police brutality.

Hit and Run, an art show popularizing the use of spray paint stencils, opens at Edward Brezinski's Magic Gallery, curated by Michael Roman, Marguerite Van Cook, James Romberger, and Seth Tobocman.

WORLD WAR 3
#4
$2.00
Illustrated

#4 art by Seth Tobocman

Grandmother Eleanor Bumpurs is shot and killed by one of the NYPD officers the City had called in to evict her from her apartment.

WW3 artists do street art against Reagan, police brutality, and gentrification.

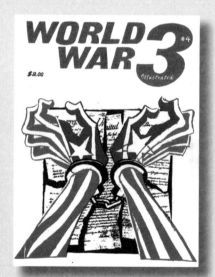

1985

WW3 artists participate in Artists United Against Apartheid.

Police bomb the headquarters of MOVE, a black liberation group in Philadelphia, setting fire to surrounding houses.

WW3 #4: "Police State America," edited by Seth Tobocman, Eric Drooker, Paula Hewitt Amram, and Joshua Whalen.

Reagan goes to Bitburg cemetery in Germany to honor fallen SS soldiers.

WW3 artists participate in "No Business As Usual" national anti-nuclear mobilization.

WORLD WAR 3
#5
Illustrated
God thinks you're worth
#5 art by Peter Kuper

1986

WW3 #5: "Religion Issue," edited by Peter Kuper and Paula Hewitt Amram.

WW3 collective produces "The Art of Demonstration" for *Cultural Correspondence*, a manual for protest art edited by Jim Murray.

Joshua Whalen introduces *WW3* to Mordam Records, a national punk music distributor that would go on to distribute the magazine.

A neighborhood march puts signs on abandoned buildings that say "Property of the People of the Lower East Side." Whalen introduces *WW3* artists to Lower East Side squatters. Lower East Side landmark Adam Purple's Garden is bulldozed.

WORLD WAR 3
#6
$2.00
Illustrated
#6 art by Seth Tobocman

WW3 #6: "Keep Your Tired, Keep Your Poor," edited by Seth Tobocman and Joshua Whalen.

WW3 artists Seth Tobocman and Eric Drooker provide posters for a Valentine's Day protest at the New York City Department of Housing, Preservation and Development to demand squatter rights.

WW3 #7: "Pissed-Off Peace Dove," edited by Peter Kuper, Joshua Whalen, and Seth Tobocman.

WW3 artists participate in civil disobedience against South African Airways.

Iran-Contra Scandal: Lebanese press reveal that the CIA has traded arms for hostages with Iran and used the funds generated by the deal to fund the anti-communist contra rebels in Nicaragua.

WORLD WAR 3
#7
$2
Illustrated
KUPER
#7 art by Peter Kuper

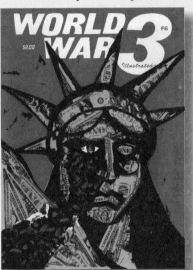

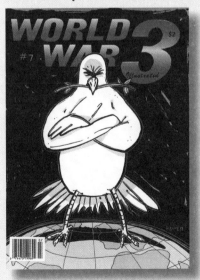

1987

WW3 #8: "Long Last Look at Reagan," edited by Peter Kuper, Seth Tobocman, Josh Whalen, and Chuck Sperry.

Palestinian cartoonist Naji al-Ali is assassinated in London.

The First Intifada: a Palestinian uprising against the Israeli occupation in the Palestinian Territories that lasts until 1993.

Stock market crashes.

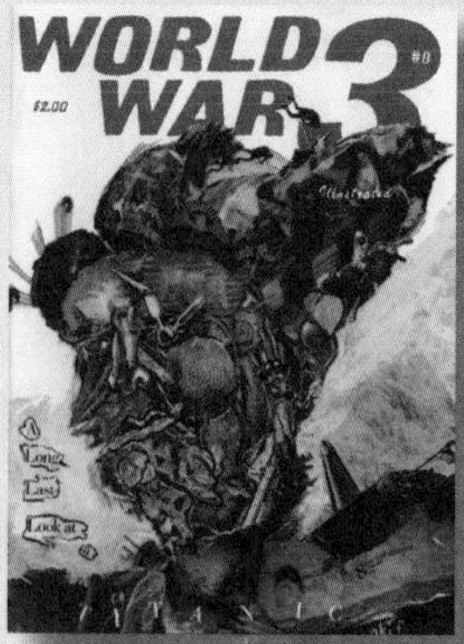
WORLD WAR 3
#8
$2.00
#8 art by Aki Fujiyoshi

1988

WW3 #9: "The Buck Stops," edited by Seth Tobocman, Peter Kuper, Aki Fujiyoshi, and Eric Drooker.

WW3 editor Peter Kuper becomes co–art director of INX.

WW3 #10: "Fascism Issue," edited by Peter Kuper, Eric Drooker, and Seth Tobocman.

Cartoons by *WW3* artists are used in posters that call people to a protest against a midnight curfew. This protest becomes the 1988 Tompkins Square Park Riot, which starts with police beating hundreds of protesters and ends with rioters smashing the doors of a condominium, stealing a tree from the lobby, and planting it in the park. Scott Cunningham draws the riot in progress from a fire escape. His drawings are later made into posters and pasted around the neighborhood. While police officers are never prosecuted, the protest results in the curfew being lifted for the next few years.

Steve Brodner attends the Republican National Convention and illustrates it for *WW3*.

George Bush Sr. becomes president.

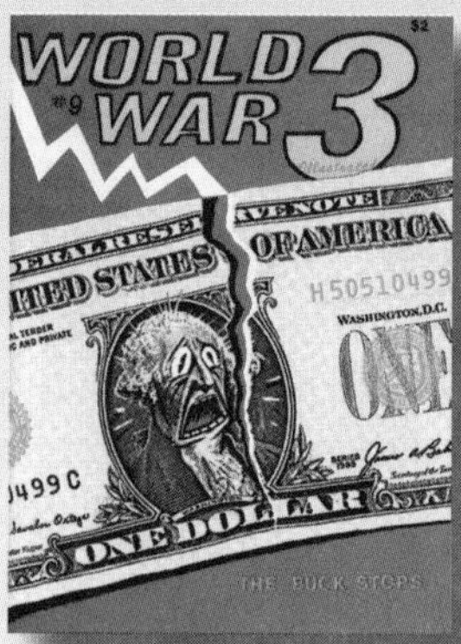
$2
WORLD WAR 3
#9
THE BUCK STOPS
#9 art by Peter Kuper

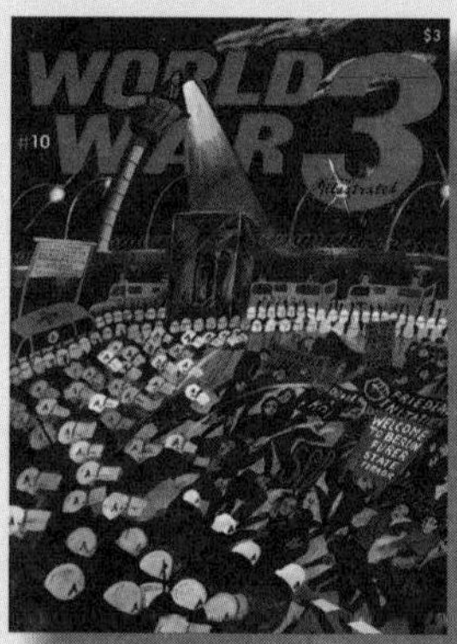
$3
WORLD WAR 3
#10
#10 art by Sue Coe

1989

World War 3 Illustrated: 1980–1988, an anthology edited by Peter Kuper and Seth Tobocman, is published by Fantagraphics Books.

WW3 #11: "Riot Issue," edited by Eric Drooker, Seth Tobocman, and Peter Kuper.

WW3 artists participate in ACT-UP's massive civil disobedience action at City Hall to protest lack of funding for AIDS patients.

Squats on East 8th Street are evicted and demolished. *WW3* artists participate in anti-eviction protests.

WW3 #12: "Biohazard," edited by Seth Tobocman and Sabrina Jones.

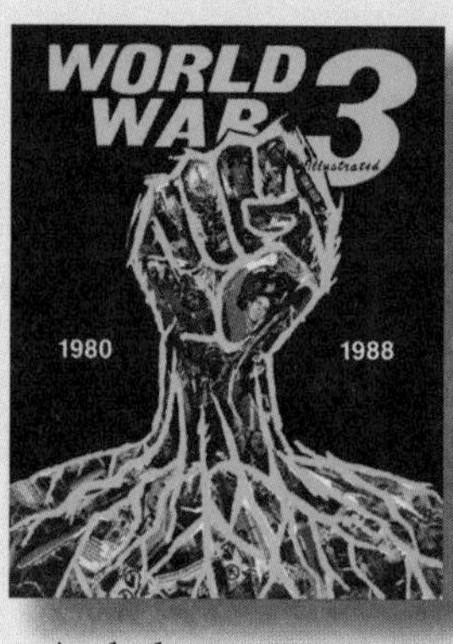
WORLD WAR 3
1980
1988
Anthology cover art by Aki Fujiyoshi

Tent city is set up by the homeless in Tompkins Square Park.

WW3 editor Seth Tobocman and *WW3* contributors Lawrence Van Abbema and Siobhan participate in the successful defense of the Umbrella House squat against eviction and prevent the demolition of the building.

David Dinkins becomes mayor of New York City.

Work by *WW3* contributor James Romberger is purchased by the Metropolitan Museum of Art.

Homeless are evicted from Tompkins Square Park. They burn their tents in protest. Activists respond by occupying an abandoned school building (the ABC Community Center) as a place for the homeless. The occupation goes on for three weeks and includes an art show with work by *WW3* artists James Romberger, Ron English, Sue Coe, Sabrina Jones, and Seth Tobocman.

Iran's Ayatollah Khomeini dies.

Reunification of Germany. Fall of the Berlin Wall.

WORLD WAR 3
THE RIOT ISSUE

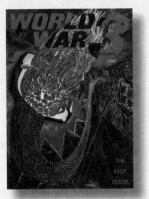

#11 art by
Helena Munninghoff

WORLD WAR 3
ECOLOGY HEALTH CRISIS

#12 art by James Romberger
and Marguerite Van Cook

1990

Nelson Mandela released from South African prison, signaling the end of apartheid.

Kuper and Tobocman travel to Eastern Europe, where they recruit dissident writers and cartoonists to contribute to *WW3*.

WW3 artist Brian Damage dies of AIDS.

WW3 #13: "Ripped Witness," edited by Peter Kuper, Seth Tobocman, and Sabrina Jones.

WW3 has a retrospective show in San Francisco's Mission District.

WORLD WAR 3

#13 art by James Romberger

1991

The U.S. and other countries declare war on Iraq. *WW3* artists join protests against the war.

WW3 #14: "New World Empire," edited by Peter Kuper, Seth Tobocman, Sabrina Jones, and Scott Cunningham.

Local artist Grady Alexis is killed by police. People riot in Tompkins Square area in protest. The Dinkins administration responds by closing the park for a year and surrounding it with a two-story fence and a continuous police presence.

WORLD WAR 3
Illustrated
NEW WORLD EMPIRE

#14 art by Peter Kuper

WW3 artists participate in protests and mount an illegal art show on the fence. James Romberger, Marguerite Van Cook, and Leonard Abrams form the Park Rights Council demanding that the park be reopened.

WW3 editor Scott Cunningham designs sets and an accompanying publication for *Collateral Damage*, a stage performance protesting the Gulf War at La MaMa Experimental Theatre Club in NYC.

WW3 #15: "Park Issue," edited by Scott Cunningham, Sabrina Jones, Peter Kuper, Seth Tobocman, and Villa Piazza.

Show of *WW3* art at La Flora squat in Hamburg, Germany, is vandalized by feminists offended by nudity in some pieces.

Breakup of Yugoslavia leads to a series of genocidal wars.

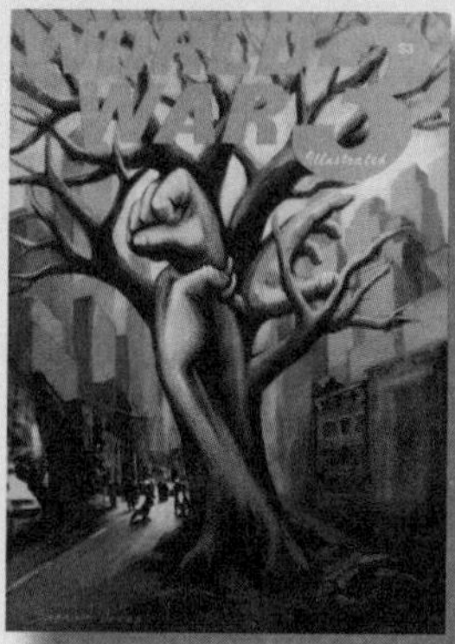

#15 art by Sabrina Jones

1992

WW3 #16: "Herstories," edited by Isabella Bannerman, Scott Cunningham, Sabrina Jones, Sandy Jimenez, Villa Piazza, and Peter Kuper. This issue contains a radical article by Trina Robbins that catalyzed controversy among feminists.

The police beating of Rodney King in Los Angeles sparks riots across the United States.

WW3 #17: "L.A. Riots," edited by Seth Tobocman, Peter Kuper, and Scott Cunningham.

Bill Clinton is elected president.

WW3 contributor and *Boiled Angel* zine publisher Mike Diana is arrested for obscenity in Florida.

WW3 contributor Stephen Kroninger has solo exhibition at Muscum of Modcrn Art, NY.

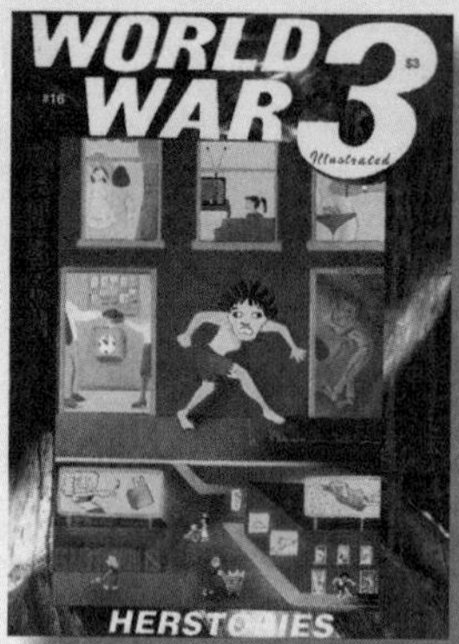
WORLD WAR 3
Illustrated
HERSTORIES

#16 art by Isabella Bannerman

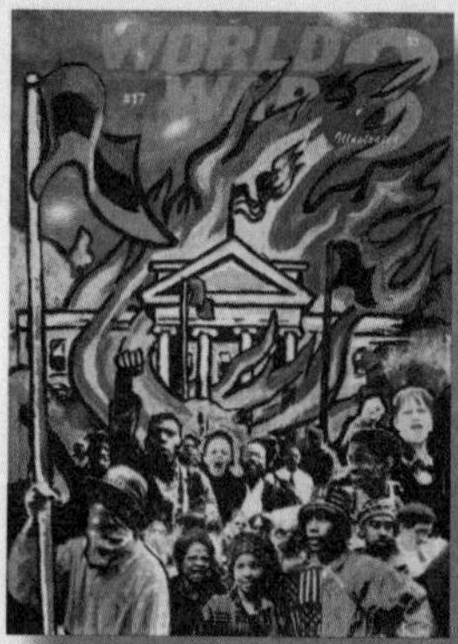

#17 art by Seth Tobocman

1993

WW3 #18: "Conquest," edited by Sandy Jimenez, Seth Tobocman, and Sabrina Jones.

Rudy Giuliani becomes mayor of New York City.

WW3 artists join protests to stop the execution of Mumia Abu-Jamal.

Exit Art organizes the first major exhibition of comic art, called *Comic Power.*

WW3 #19: "Child Abuse," edited by Sandy Jimenez, Seth Tobocman, and Sabrina Jones.

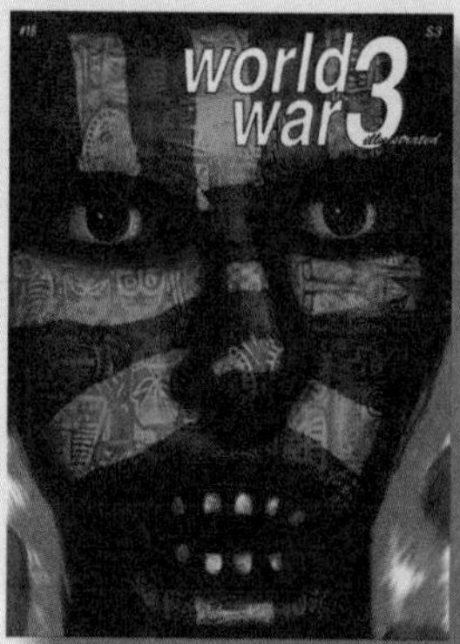
world war 3

#18 art by Jose Ortega

Community Board 3 meets to discuss the eviction of Glass House, a Lower East Side squat. *WW3* contributor Fly participates in a protest during the meeting, where other squatters and community board members are arrested for talking out of turn.

In Waco, Texas, American federal and Texas state law enforcement and military attack the compound of the Branch Davidians, a Christian sect, killing 76 people.

WW3 #20: "Television," edited by Scott Cunningham, Peter Kuper, and Kevin C. Pyle.

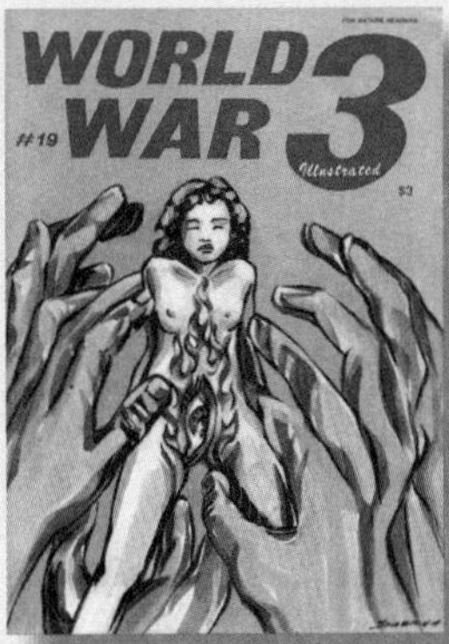
WORLD WAR 3
#19
Illustrated
$3

#19 art by Sabrina Jones

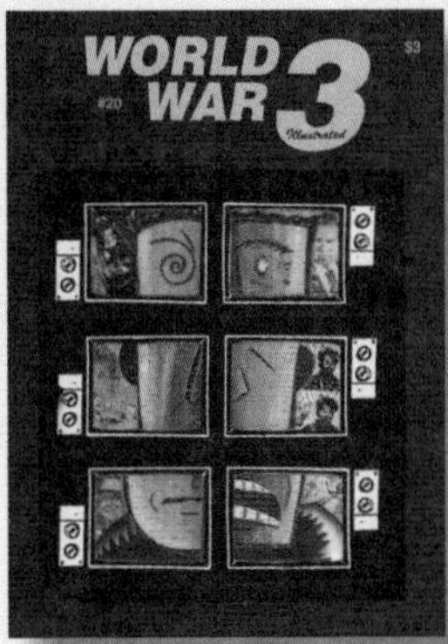
WORLD WAR 3
#20
$3
Illustrated

#20 art by Peter Kuper

1994

Zapatista uprising in Mexico.

Mumia Abu-Jamal joins *WW3* as writer and cartoonist.

Genocide in Rwanda.

WW3 #21: "The Threat," edited by Sandy Jimenez, Mac McGill, Seth Tobocman, and Kevin C. Pyle.

WW3 editor Peter Kuper is flown to Florida by the Comic Book Legal Defense Fund to be an expert witness in the obscenity trial of cartoonist Mike Diana. Diana is convicted. The court orders Diana to stop drawing for three years.

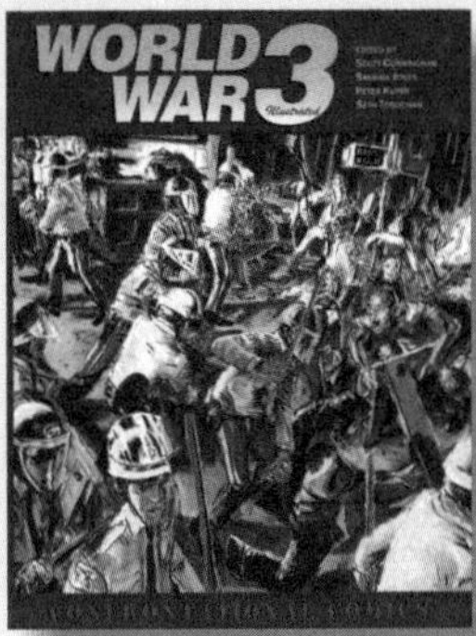
WORLD WAR 3
Illustrated

Anthology cover art by James Romberger

1995

O.J. Simpson goes on trial for murder in California.

World War 3 Illustrated: Confrontational Comics, an anthology edited by Scott Cunningham, Sabrina Jones, Peter Kuper, and Seth Tobocman, is published by Four Walls Eight Windows.

Sabrina Jones, Isabella Bannerman, and Anne Decker form *Girltalk*, a comic book featuring women's stories for Fantagraphics Books.

WW3 #22: "Deception," edited by Gregory Benton and Kevin C. Pyle.

Illustrations by *WW3* contributor Eric Drooker begin appearing regularly on the cover of the *New Yorker.*

The NYPD use a tank to evict squats on 13th Street.

Oklahoma City Bombing: U.S. Army veteran Timothy McVeigh detonates a truck bomb in front of a federal building, killing 168 people.

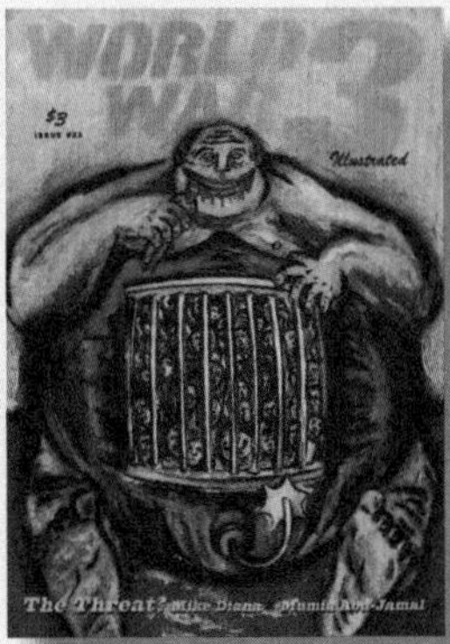
$3
Illustrated
The Threat!
Mike Diana
Mumia Abu-Jamal

#21 art by Scott Cunningham

1996

WW3 #23: “Miseducation,” edited by Sabrina Jones and Sandy Jimenez.

ABC No Rio cultural center is threatened with eviction.

WW3 contributor Susan Simensky Bietila is active in a community struggle against the construction of a shopping center along the Milwaukee River at the Humboldt Yards, later depicted in her work for *WW3*.

IMPORTANT!
AMERICA'S
LOVE AFFAIR
WITH
DECEPTION

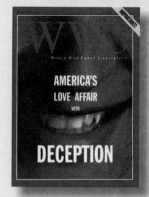

#22 art by Kevin C. Pyle and Gregory Benton

War on the Poor—written by Randy Albelda, Nancy Folbre, and the Center for Popular Economics, designed by *WW3* contributor Nicholas Blechman and Leah Lococo, and featuring illustrations by many *WW3* artists—is published by The New Press.

WW3 #24: “Prison Issue,” edited by Gregory Benton, Scott Cunningham, Sabrina Jones, Sandy Jimenez, and Kevin C. Pyle.

WORLD WAR 3
#23
MISEDUCATION
$3.50

#23 art by Sabrina Jones

1997

WW3 artists participate in the struggle to save ABC No Rio from eviction. After a series of protests and civil disobedience actions, the City agrees to sell the building to the ABC No Rio collective for one dollar plus the cost of renovations.

Peter Kuper takes over writing and drawing Antonio Prohías’s *Spy vs. Spy* for *Mad* magazine.

WW3 has a retrospective show at Parsons School of Design, NY.

Susan Simensky Bietila creates artwork in support of the movement against the Crandon Mine, also depicted in her work for *WW3*.

Heaven’s Gate cult members commit mass suicide in California.

WORLD WAR 3

#24 art by Eric Drooker

1998

Summer temperatures are highest on record.

President Clinton has sexual relations with intern Monica Lewinsky, leading to impeachment proceedings.

WW3 #25: “Freaks, Cults, Saints, and Revelations,” edited by Ebon Dodd, Laird Ogden, and Susan Willmarth.

WW3 contributor Sue Coe sells prints to benefit animal rights organizations.

WW3 #26: “Female Complaints,” edited by Samantha Berger and Sabrina Jones.

Justseeds Artists’ Cooperative is founded.

WORLD WAR 3

#25 art by Ebon Dodd

1999

WW3 artists included in *Urban Encounters* exhibition at the New Museum of Contemporary Art, NY.

Amadou Diallo is shot 41 times by the NYPD, who claim that they mistook his wallet for a gun. Art Spiegelman draws a satirical cover for the *New Yorker*, titled "41 Shots, Ten Cents." The Fraternal Order of Police pickets the *New Yorker*.

Seth Tobocman, Lawrence Van Abbema, Becky Minnich, Cosmo, Sandy Jimenez, and others work on *Killer Kop Komix* for Shadow Press.

More Gardens Coalition prevents the Giuliani administration from auctioning off New York's community gardens. *WW3* artists participate.

Armando Perez, director of the Charas Community Center, is murdered. At the time, Perez was involved in a struggle with the Center's landlord, Greg Singer, who had attempted to evict the organization.

The first Reclaim the Streets action in New York City. *WW3* contributor Brad Will is a key organizer.

WW3 #27: "Land and Liberty," edited by Gregory Benton, Jordan Worley, and Seth Tobocman.

NATO intervenes in the conflict in Yugoslavia by bombing Serbia.

WW3 #28: "War and Genocide," edited by Seth Tobocman and Jordan Worley.

Massive anti-globalization protest disrupts World Trade Organization meeting in Seattle.

2000

Reflections on Seattle, a zine collaboration between *WW3* and the New York Direct Action Network, is published. Brad Will writes an article.

WW3 artists participate in A16 anti–World Bank protests in Washington, DC.

WW3 #29: "Land Pt. 2," edited by Seth Tobocman and Jordan Worley.

Bill Clinton repeals the Glass-Steagall Act, eliminating regulations on banking and achieving Ronald Reagan's vision of a "free-market" economy.

WORLD WAR 3
#26
$3.50
Illustrated
female Complaints

#26 art by Sabrina Jones

WORLD WAR 3
#27
$3.50
Illustrated
LAND AND LIBERTY

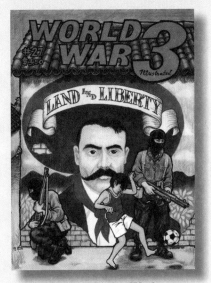

#27 art by Jordan Worley

WORLD WAR 3
28
$ 3.50
Illustrated
WAR
and
GENOCIDE

#28 art by Miro Stefanovic

George W. Bush is declared the winner of the presidential election.

Drawing Resistance, a traveling political art show that includes many *WW3* artists, is curated by Susan Simensky Bietila and Nicolas Lampert.

WW3 #30: "Bitchcraft," edited by Sabrina Jones, Denise Ozker, and Isabella Bannerman.

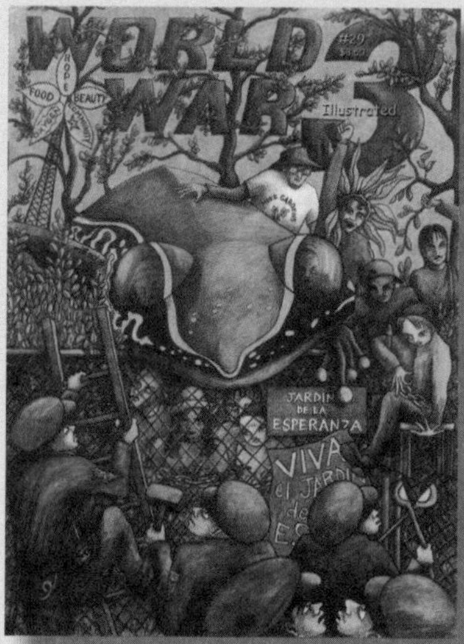
WORLD WAR 3
#29
Illustrated
JARDIN DE LA ESPERANZA

#29 art by Fly

2001

WW3 artists participate in New York Direct Action Network's contested attempt to travel to Quebec City to protest the FTAA summit.

WW3 #31: "Against Global Capital," edited by Seth Tobocman and Jordan Worley.

Carlo Giuliani is killed by police during an anti-globalization protest in Italy.

World Trade Center and Pentagon attacked on September 11.

WW3 #32: "9/11 Issue," edited by Seth Tobocman, Peter Kuper, and Jordan Worley.

WW3 artists participate in Exit Art's post-9/11 show, *Reactions*.

WW3 9/11 art donated to the Library of Congress appears in an exhibition in Washington, DC.

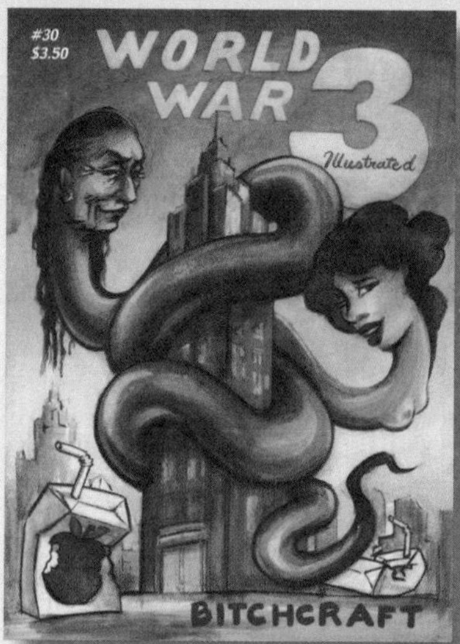
#30
$3.50
WORLD WAR 3
Illustrated
BITCHCRAFT

#30 art by Sabrina Jones

2002

Department of Homeland Security is founded.

Charas Community Center is evicted.

After more than a decade of evictions and riots, and several years of closed-door meetings, New York City finally decides to legalize the remaining 11 squats on the Lower East Side.

The U.S. invades Afghanistan. Operation "Enduring Freedom" begins. Israel invades the West Bank.

WW3 artists participate in the International Solidarity Movement, which goes to the West Bank to defend the human rights of Palestinians through nonviolent civil disobedience.

Bush announces his intention to invade Iraq.

WW3 artists participate in No Blood For Oil, a group staging anti-war protests in front of the UN. They form an affinity group called World War 3 Arts in Action, which provides

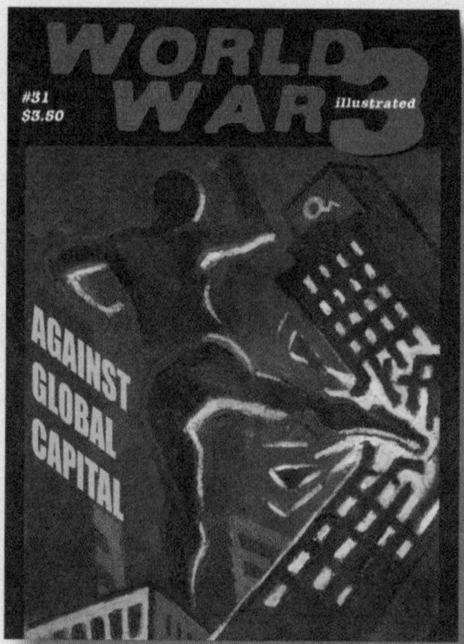
WORLD WAR 3
#31
$3.50
illustrated
AGAINST
GLOBAL
CAPITAL

#31 art by Seth Tobocman

banners and performs street theater for the peace movement. The group includes Seth Tobocman, Christopher Cardinale, Carlo Quispe, Rebecca Migdal, Nicole Schulman, Sharon Qwik, Samantha Wilson, and many others.

WW3 #33: “The Situation,” edited by Seth Tobocman and Nicole Schulman.

WORLD WAR 3
KUPER

#32 art by Peter Kuper

2003

The U.S. invades Iraq.

WW3 artists Mac McGill, Christopher Cardinale, Seth Tobocman, and Peter Kuper are invited to participate in exhibitions in Milan, Italy, and to create wall murals during shows at COX18, a squatted community center.

Rachel Corrie is killed by Israeli Defense Forces while nonviolently blocking the path of a bulldozer set to destroy a Palestinian home in Gaza.

Several *WW3* artists travel to the Middle East to participate in protests against the building of the wall, which imprisons the Palestinian communities of the West Bank.

WW3 #34: “Taking Liberties,” edited by Peter Kuper, Kevin C. Pyle, and Susan Willmarth.

WW3 editor Seth Tobocman and other *WW3* contributors work with artists in Israel and Palestine to plan *Three Cities Against the Wall*, a series of exhibitions in Ramallah, Palestine, Tel-Aviv, Israel, and New York City in opposition to the wall Israel is building in the Occupied Palestinian Territories.

WORLD WAR 3
#33
$4.00

#33 art by Mac McGill

2004

WW3 #35: “Life During Wartime,” edited by Seth Tobocman, Sabrina Jones, and Christopher Cardinale.

Saddam Hussein is captured in Iraq and executed.

Former president Reagan dies from complications of Alzheimer’s disease and lies in state at the Capitol.

WW3 artists participate in protests against the Republican National Convention in New York.

George W. Bush wins a second presidential term.

The International Court of Justice issues an advisory opinion that Israel’s “security barrier” and its territory settlements conquered in 1967 are illegal.

WORLD WAR 3
$5.00
Taking Liberties

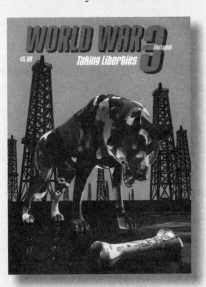

#34 art by Mirko Ilic

U.S. Customs confiscates copies of the Slovenian zine *Stripburger*, containing a reprint of Peter Kuper's *Richie Bush* story. Customs claims that it constitutes piracy. The Comic Book Legal Defense Fund steps in and makes the case that it's parody. Customs relents.

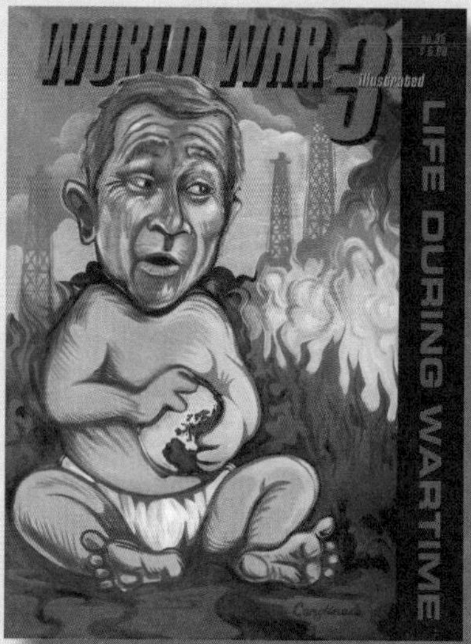
WORLD WAR 3
illustrated
LIFE DURING WARTIME
#35 art by
Christopher Cardinale

2005

WW3 #36: "Neo-Cons," edited by Peter Kuper and Ryan Inzana.

WW3 retrospective at Exit Art.

Three Cities Against the Wall opens at ABC No Rio in New York and in Tel-Aviv. The show in Ramallah does not open because of problems with Israeli customs and political issues. It opens instead at the Palestinian Institute in Hebron.

WOBBLIES! a graphic non-fiction anthology about the Industrial Workers of the World, edited by Nicole Schulman and Paul Buhle, and drawn primarily by *WW3* artists, is published by Verso.

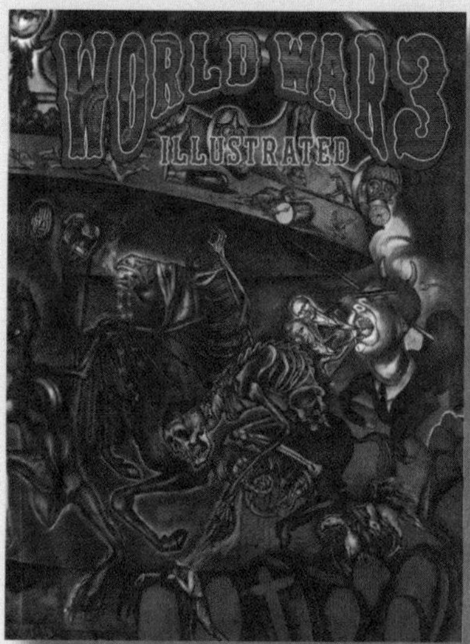
WORLD WAR 3
ILLUSTRATED
#36 art by Sue Coe

Hurricane Katrina hits New Orleans.

WW3 editors Kevin C. Pyle, Susan Willmarth, and Sabrina Jones author a series of informational comics critiquing the prison industrial complex titled *The Real Cost of Prisons*.

A coalition of Palestinian civil society groups, unions, NGOs, and organizations issue the Unified Palestinian Call for Boycott, Divestment and Sanctions against Israel until it complies with international law and ceases violating human rights.

WW3 launches website worldwar3illustrated.org.

The Design of Dissent edited by Milton Glaser and Mirko Ilic features protest art by many *WW3* artists, published by Rockport Press.

2006

Seth Tobocman, Mac McGill, Christopher Cardinale, Carlo Quispe, Zeph Fishlyn, and other *WW3* artists go to New Orleans to help Common Ground in reconstruction efforts.

WW3 #37: "Unnatural Disasters," edited by Seth Tobocman, Nicole Schulman, Tom Keough, and Rebecca Migdal.

WW3 produces *After the Flood*, a benefit book for Common Ground.

A teachers' strike in Oaxaca, Mexico, escalates into an occupation of the public square and a general uprising.

WW3 editor Peter Kuper is in Oaxaca and covers the strike.

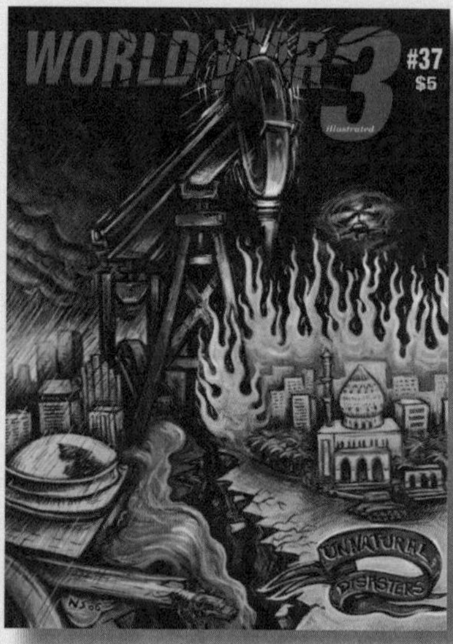
#37
$5
illustrated
UNNATURAL
DISASTERS
#37 art by Nicole Schulman

WW3 contributor Brad Will is shot and killed while filming undercover police who are firing into the crowd.

2007

Seth Tobocman and Zeph Fishlyn work with float-builder Jules Stack to design a second-line float in support of public housing residents trying to return to New Orleans.

WW3 #38: "Facts on the Ground," edited by Christopher Cardinale, Seth Tobocman, Nicole Schulman, and Rebecca Migdal.

WW3 contributor Ethan Hietner draws leaflet comics for Adalah-NY, advocating a boycott of Israel.

#38
WORLD WAR 3
$5
Facts on the ground
KUPER
#38 art by Peter Kuper

WW3 editors Christopher Cardinale, Nicole Schulman, and later Edwin Vazquez become involved with the Groundswell Community Mural Project in New York City.

2008

A wave of home foreclosures sets off an economic crash. The "free-market" economic model advocated by Reagan is discredited by this development. In response, President Bush signs the Emergency Economic Stabilization Act into law, creating a $700 billion treasury fund to purchase toxic bank assets, bailing out Wall Street but leaving homeowners to face eviction.

Barack Obama is elected the first African-American president of the United States.

WORLD WAR 3
ILLUSTRATED
$5
#39 art by Eric Drooker

In Egypt, Magdy El Shafee authors what many consider the first Arab-language graphic novel, *Metro*. This crime story criticizes government corruption and accurately describes how Cairo police recruit unemployed young men to beat up and rape protesters. The government soon bans the book. Magdy and his publisher face a night in jail and are forced to pay a fine. All copies are confiscated.

2009

WW3 #39: "Wordless Worlds," edited by Peter Kuper and Kevin C. Pyle.

Studs Terkel's *Working*, edited by Paul Buhle, is adapted by Harvey Pekar and many *WW3* contributors into comics, published by The New Press.

Military analyst Bradley Manning leaks a video of American troops in Iraq gunning down journalists to the website WikiLeaks.

WORLD WAR 3
#40
Illustrated
$5
WHAT
WE WANT
#40 art by Seth Tobocman

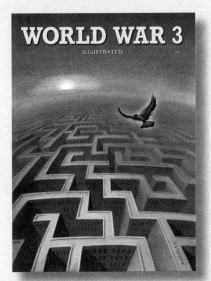

WW3 editor Carlo Quispe becomes project manager at the Bronx Academy of Art and Dance.

COX18, a squatted community center in Milan, Italy, is evicted. Banners by Seth Tobocman and Peter Kuper are used in the successful struggle to reopen the building.

2010

WW3 #40: "What We Want," edited by Seth Tobocman, Susan Simensky Bietila, Rebecca Migdal, Carlo Quispe, and Sandy Jimenez.

The Smithsonian removes a video by the late David Wojnarowicz, a *WW3* contributor, from *Hide/Seek*, a show of portraits by gay artists at the Smithsonian, following complaints from some Christian groups.

Graphic Radicals: 30 Years of World War 3 Illustrated opens at Exit Art gallery in New York.

An anti-war mural by European graffiti artist Blu is sandblasted off the wall of the Los Angeles Museum of Contemporary Art because it is deemed offensive to veterans.

WW3 #41: "The Food Chain," edited by Ame Gilbert, Ethan Heitner, Sandy Jimenez, Rebecca Migdal, and Edwin Vazquez.

A Tunisian street vendor, Mohamed Bouazizi, sets himself on fire in protest against mistreatment by police. This incites demonstrations and riots for political and economic rights throughout the Arab world.

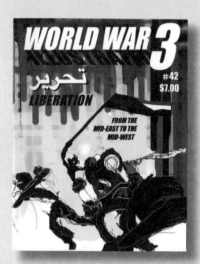

30TH ANNIVERSARY ISSUE
3
$7.00
Pfizer
#41 art by Rebecca Migdal

WORLD WAR 3
تحرير
#42
$7.00
LIBERATION
FROM THE
MID-EAST TO THE
MID-WEST
#42 art by Magdy El Shafee

2011

Egyptians occupy Tahrir Square forcing the president (and effective dictator) Hosni Mubarak to resign.

As a representative of the public school nurses' union, *World War 3* editor Susan Simensky Bietila participates in the occupation of the capitol rotunda in Madison, Wisconsin.

WW3 artists work with David Solnit on "Make Banks Pay" protests on Wall Street and in Columbus, Ohio.

People occupy Zucotti Park, a few blocks from Wall Street, to protest economic inequality and the role of the Banks in the financial crises. This stretches out for several months and comes to be known as Occupy Wall Street.

WORLD WAR 3
Illustrated
#43
$7
Expression
Repression
Revolution
MANNING
U.S.ARMY
#43 art by Sue Coe

Graphic Radicals: 30 Years of World War 3 Illustrated travels to University of North Dakota.

WW3 artists provide visuals to Occupy Wall Street publications and street art.

WW3 #42: "Liberation from the Mid-East to the Mid-West," edited by Ethan Heitner, Jordan Worley, and Seth Tobocman.

WW3 magazines and art included in New York Museum of Modern Art contemporary gallery show *1980–Now*.

Launch of Egyptian comics magazine *Tok Tok*.

WORLD WAR 3
#44 the other issue

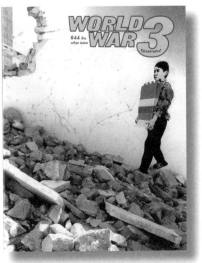

#44 art by ICY and SOT

2012

Bradley Manning goes on trial for leaking the Collateral Murder video and other military documents to WikiLeaks.

WW3 #43: "Expression/Repression/Revolution," edited by Seth Tobocman, Carlo Quispe, Rebecca Migdal, and Hilary Allison.

Hurricane Sandy hits New York City.

WW3 artists involved in disaster relief.

Barack Obama is reelected president of the United States.

WW3 #44: "The Other Issue," edited by Hilary Allison and Ethan Heitner.

WORLD WAR 3
BEFORE AND AFTER

#45 art by Peter Kuper (after Roland Topor)

2013

WW3 contributor Magdy El Shafee is arrested in Tahrir Square for protests against the Morsi regime. He is freed after an international campaign puts pressure on the Egyptian government.

Military coup in Egypt overthrows Morsi and for the moment ends Egyptian democracy.

Former National Security Agency contractor, Edward Snowden, leaks classified documents outlining mass surveillance of U.S. citizens by NSA.

WW3 #45: "Before and After," edited by Peter Kuper and Scott Cunningham.

2014

World War 3 Illustrated: 1979–2014 anthology published by PM Press.

WW3 contributors, old and new, begin work on another issue…

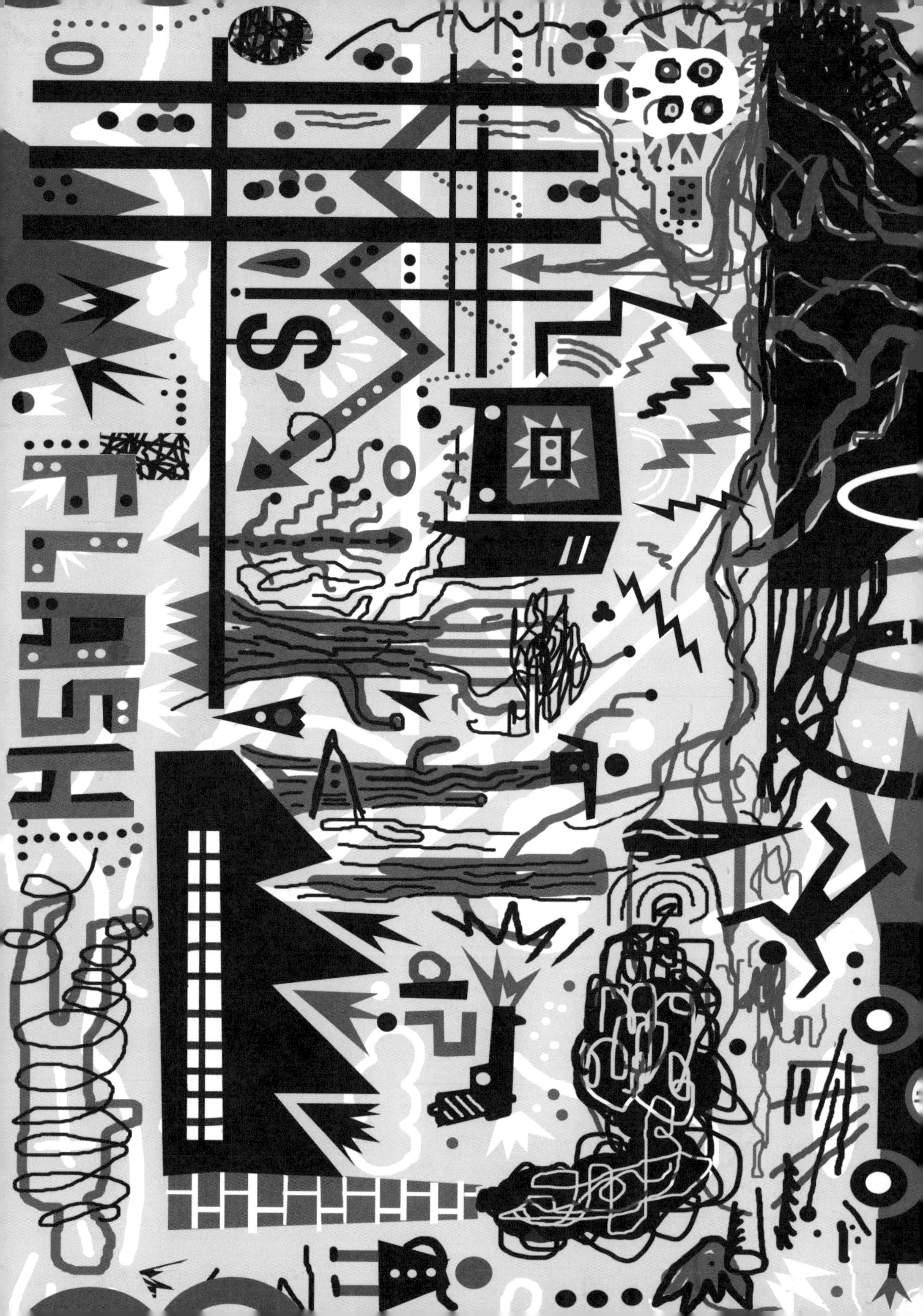
FLASH